AF539601

ABANDONED LONDON

ABANDONED LONDON

Discover the hidden secrets of the city in photographs

KATIE WIGNALL

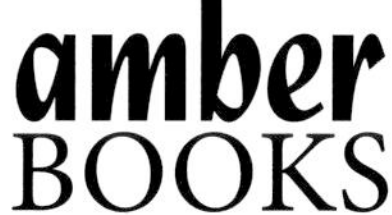

Published by
Amber Books Ltd
United House
North Road
London N7 9DP
United Kingdom
www.amberbooks.co.uk
Instagram: amberbooksltd
Facebook: amberbooks
Twitter: @amberbooks
Pinterest: amberbooksltd

Project Editor: Michael Spilling
Designer: Mark Batley
Picture Research: Terry Forshaw

ISBN: 978-1-83886-020-2

Printed in China

Contents

Introduction 6

Industry, Factories and Offices 8

Transport 48

Public Spaces 78

Shops and Retail 126

Pubs, Cafes and Restaurants 152

Residential Property 176

Sport and Leisure 202

Picture Credits 224

Introduction

It seems bizarre that in a place as crowded, noisy and expensive as London there are still wasted, unused spaces. The relentless drive for regeneration across Britain's capital fools us into thinking that every inch is under development. It is true that London is in a state of constant renewal, buildings torn down and replaced so suddenly you think you imagined their presence. But some structures are quite easily left behind, pushed to one side and forgotten.

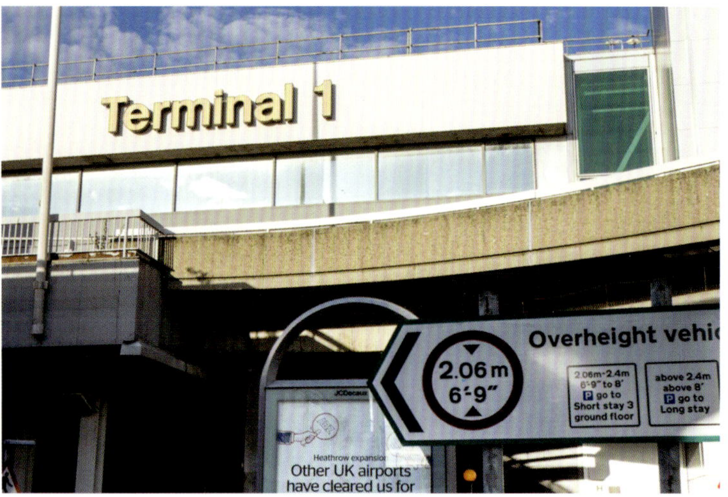

These photographs of abandoned places capture a moment in time. Some of the buildings have since been demolished or refurbished, but many are still there, derelict and uncared for. We can choose whether to view them as eyesores, or as windows into past worlds with a rich significance and history. One thing is certain: in an ancient city like London, there is much these places can share with us. Each empty hospital, derelict football stadium or run-down cinema is part of a particular time and place in London's story, waiting to reveal its secrets.

ABOVE:
Old Terminal 1, Heathrow Airport
When it opened in 1969, this was the largest new airport terminal in Western Europe. The final flight departed in 2015.

OPPOSITE:
Princelet Street, Spitalfields
Built in 1723 for wealthy East London merchants, this house is kept looking intentionally derelict for filming and events.

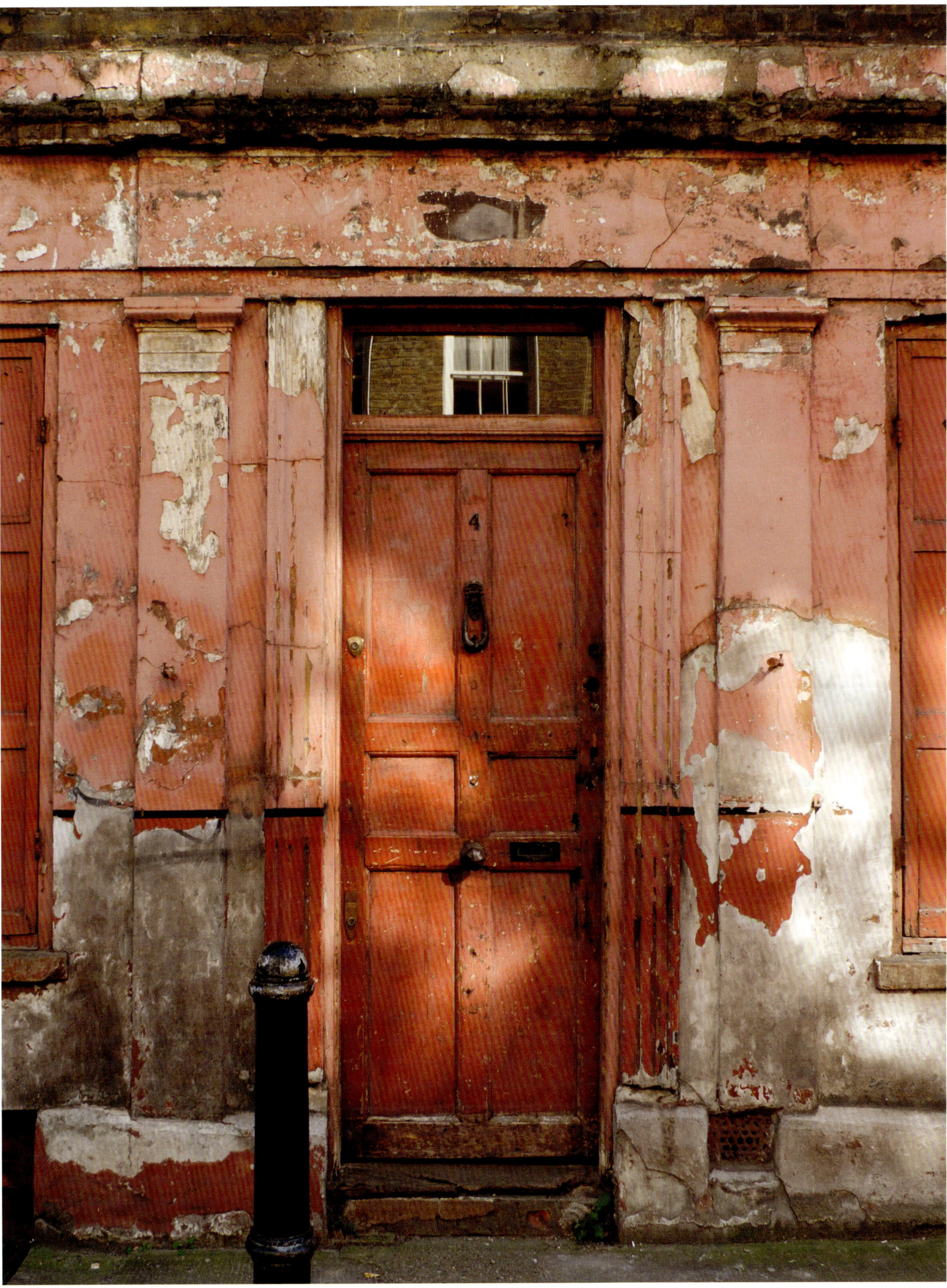
4

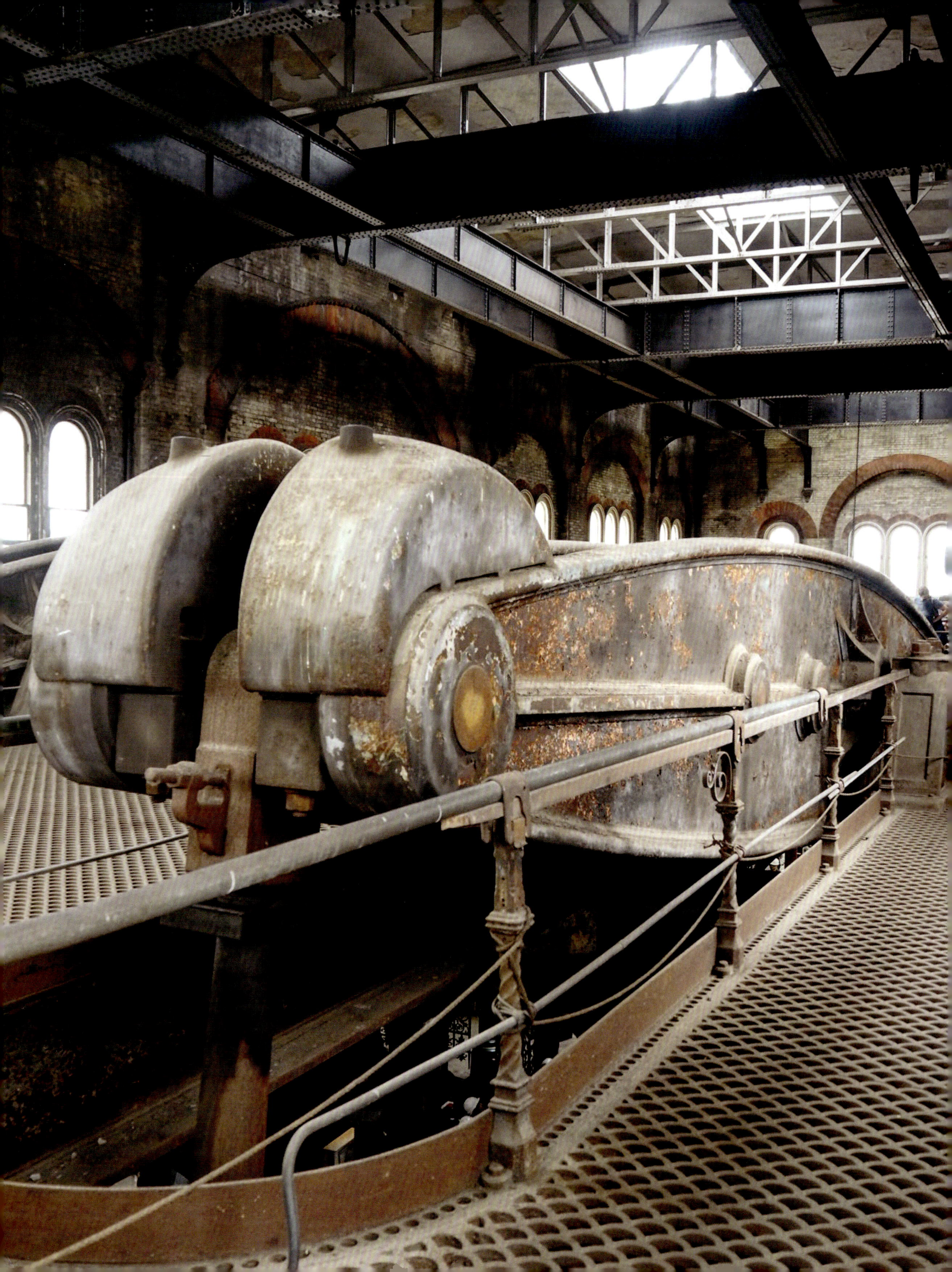

Industry, Factories and Offices

What did the Victorian ever do for us? This chapter looks at the relentless push for expansion and progress across London. During the 19th century, London's population jumped from around one million to almost 6.6 million. Developments in machinery and technology drove dramatic change, with huge infrastructure projects overhauling London's landscape. Sewage plants, power stations and reservoirs were built to improve the lives of millions of inhabitants; brick warehouses multiplied along London's streets to aid industry; and the docks of East London were the largest of their kind in the world.

Most of the buildings in this chapter were built to last and to impress. From the 1800s into the mid-1900s, this chapter shows the development from awe-inspiring factories to handsome brick warehouses and finally hastily built office blocks. Once-mighty industrial spaces across London have been transformed, the large windows and exposed brick of factories converted into attractive modern homes.

It is an irony that the newest buildings designed for London are now not built to survive in perpetuity. They have a lifespan of perhaps 40 years. The shiny new blocks of today's London may be outlived by many of the structures included in this chapter.

OPPOSITE:
Crossness Pumping Station, Crossness Sewage Treatment Works
Designed by Joseph Bazalgette and completed in 1865, the pumping station was decommissioned in the 1950s. This is one of four engines in the former Abbey Wood sewage treatment works. Each engine was named after a Royal family member: Victoria, Albert, Edward, Prince Consort and Alexandra.

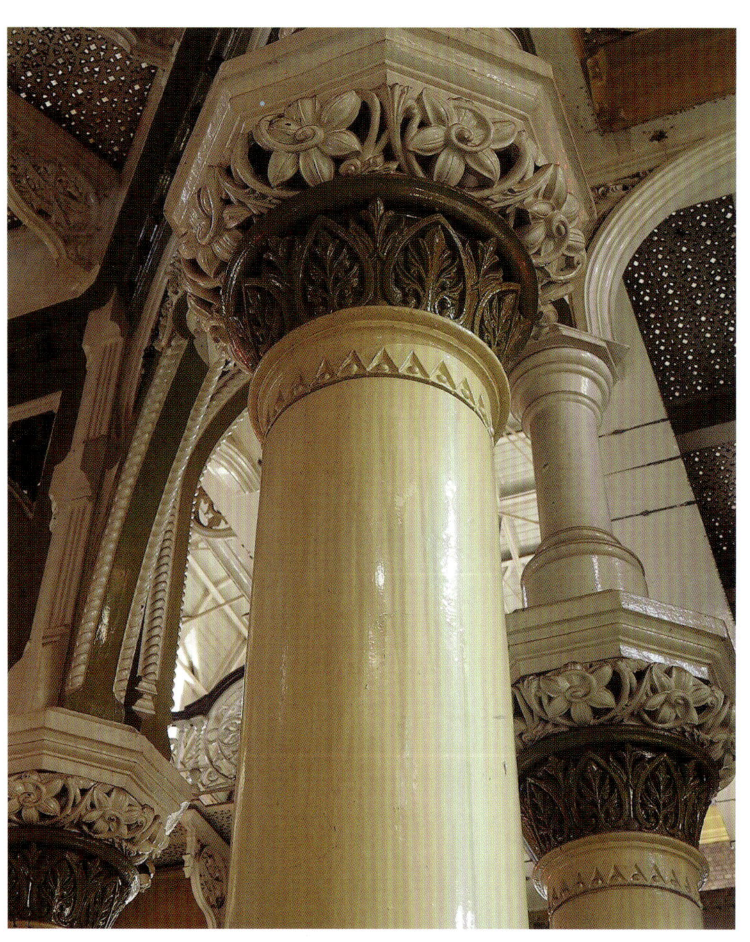

ALL PHOTOGRAPHS ON THESE PAGES:

Abbey Mills Pumping Station, Mill Meades, West Ham

In the summer of 1858 London experienced a period that would become known as 'The Great Stink'. The poor sanitation across the city was solved thanks to Joseph Bazalgette, a civil engineer who overhauled London's sewerage system. Finished in 1875, the majority of the construction is – naturally – underground. However, when there were opportunities to showcase his design above ground, Bazalgette didn't shy away.

Referred to as the 'Cathedral of Sewage', Abbey Mills is a striking mix of Italian Gothic and Byzantine flourishes. Column capitals and ironwork are covered with floral motifs, while in the centre a Russian Orthodox-style octagonal lantern rises above the fine brickwork.

The architecture disguises a dirtier function. The sewer system was designed to flow downhill, but in Chelsea, Stratford and Thamesmead, it needs an extra lift for gravity to do its work. Still operational today, Abbey Mills pumps London's sewage to the treatment works in Beckton.

OVERLEAF:

Finsbury Park Underground Reservoir

Beneath the green space of Finsbury Park is a place that can hold five million gallons of water. Only accessible through a manhole inside the park, the reservoir was built in the 1860s by the East London Water Works Company. Worried it could collapse, in 2012 Thames Water decommissioned the reservoir, but the space is still occasionally used for films, including *Sherlock Holmes* (2009) and *Paddington* (2014).

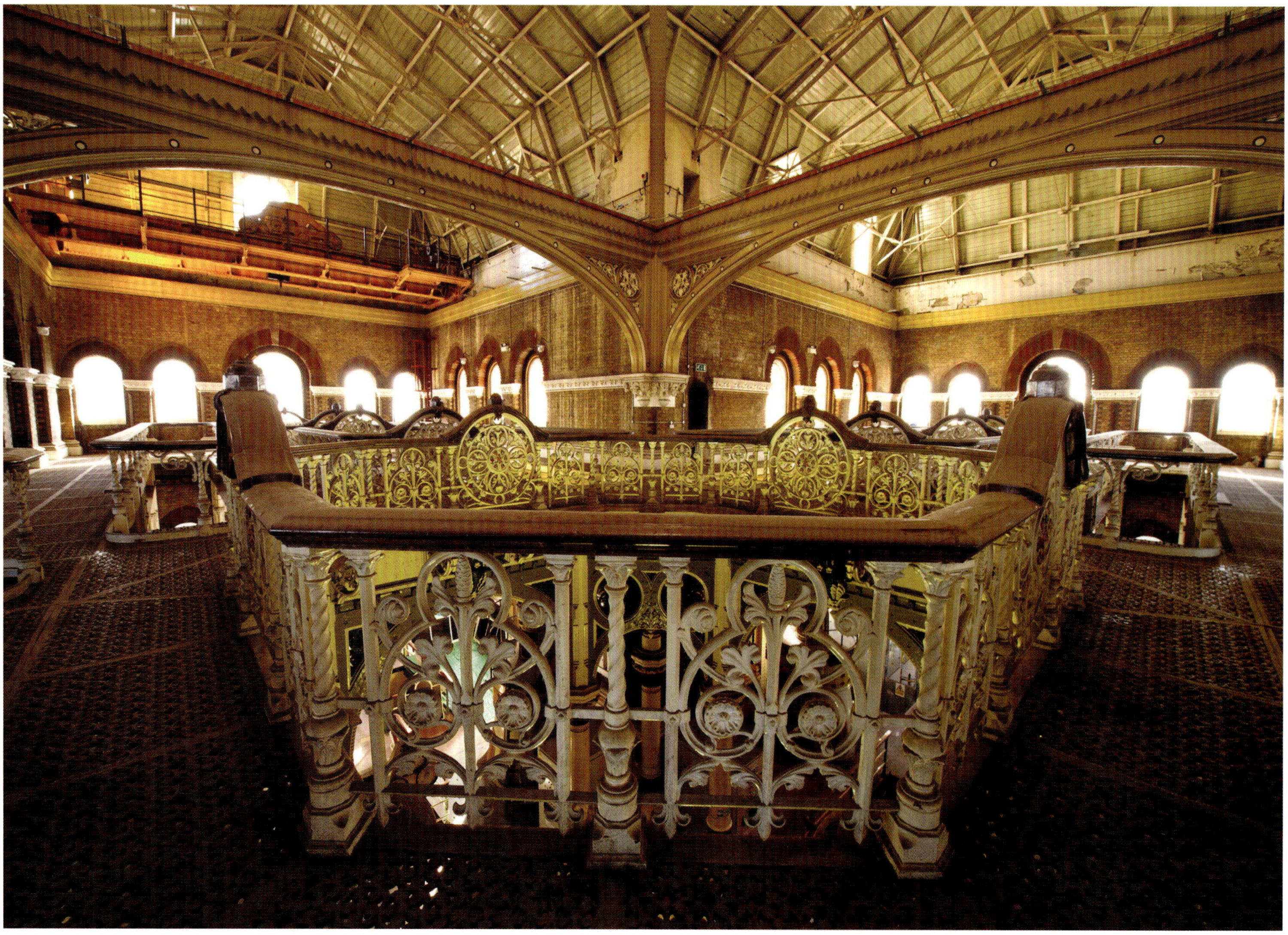

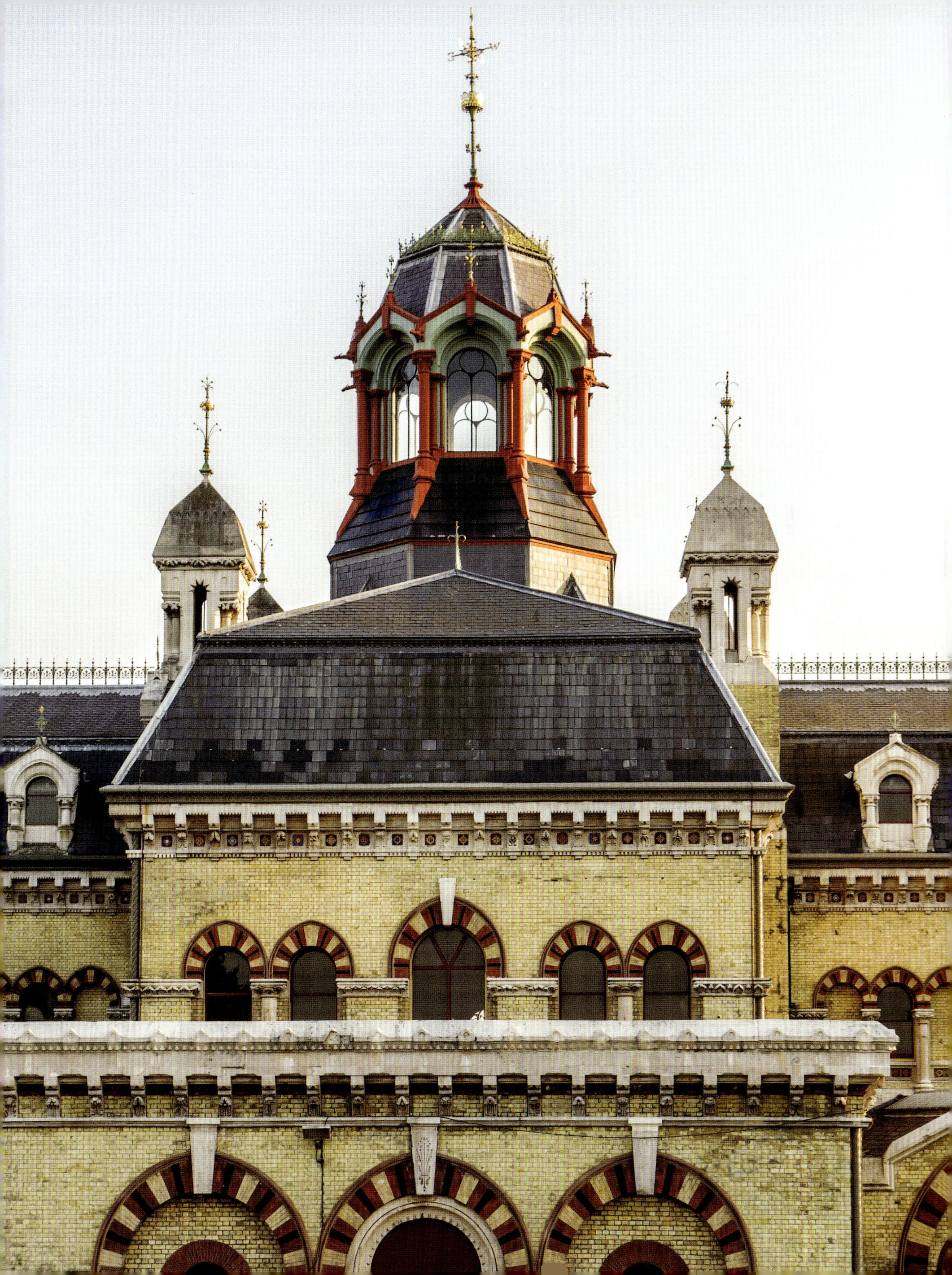

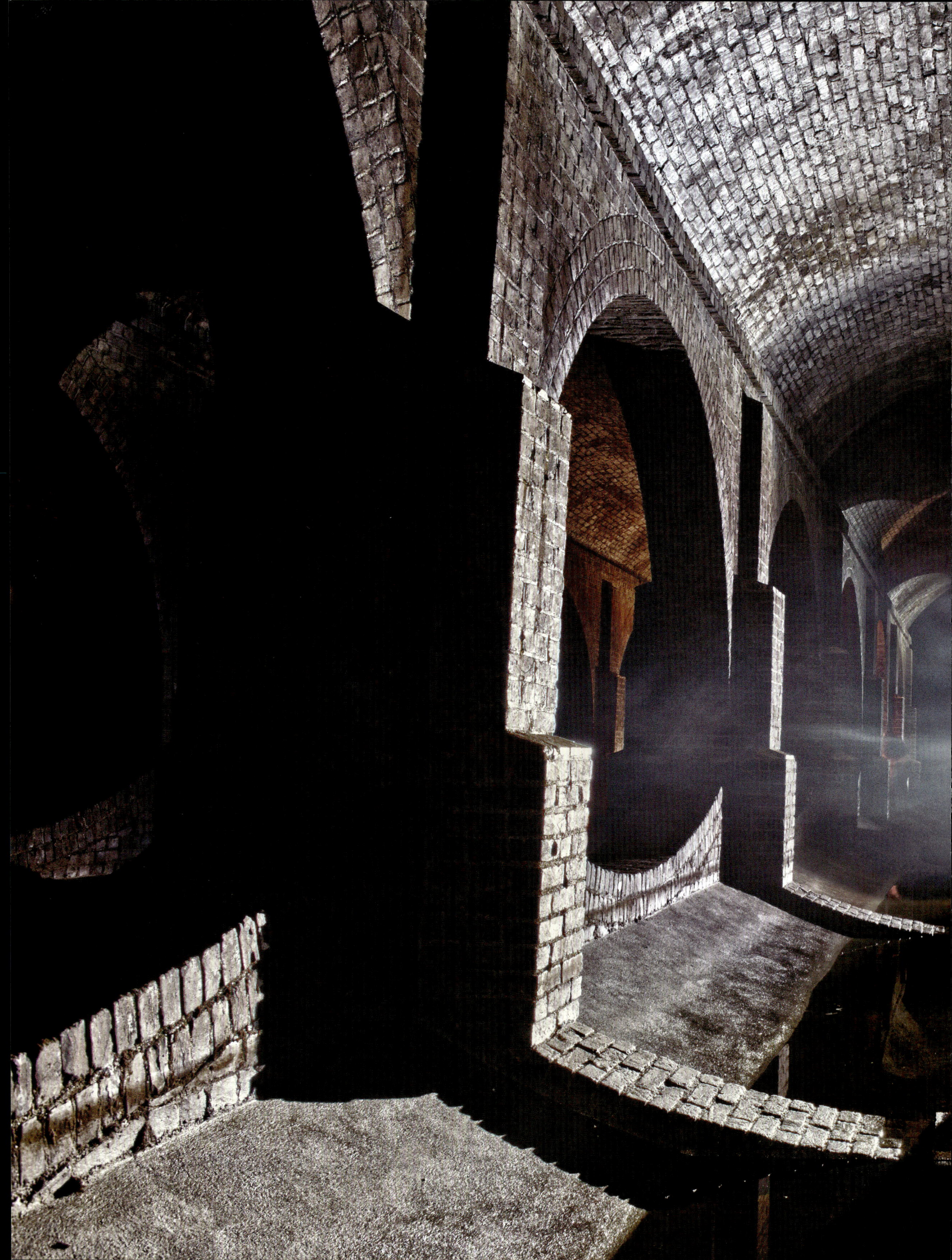

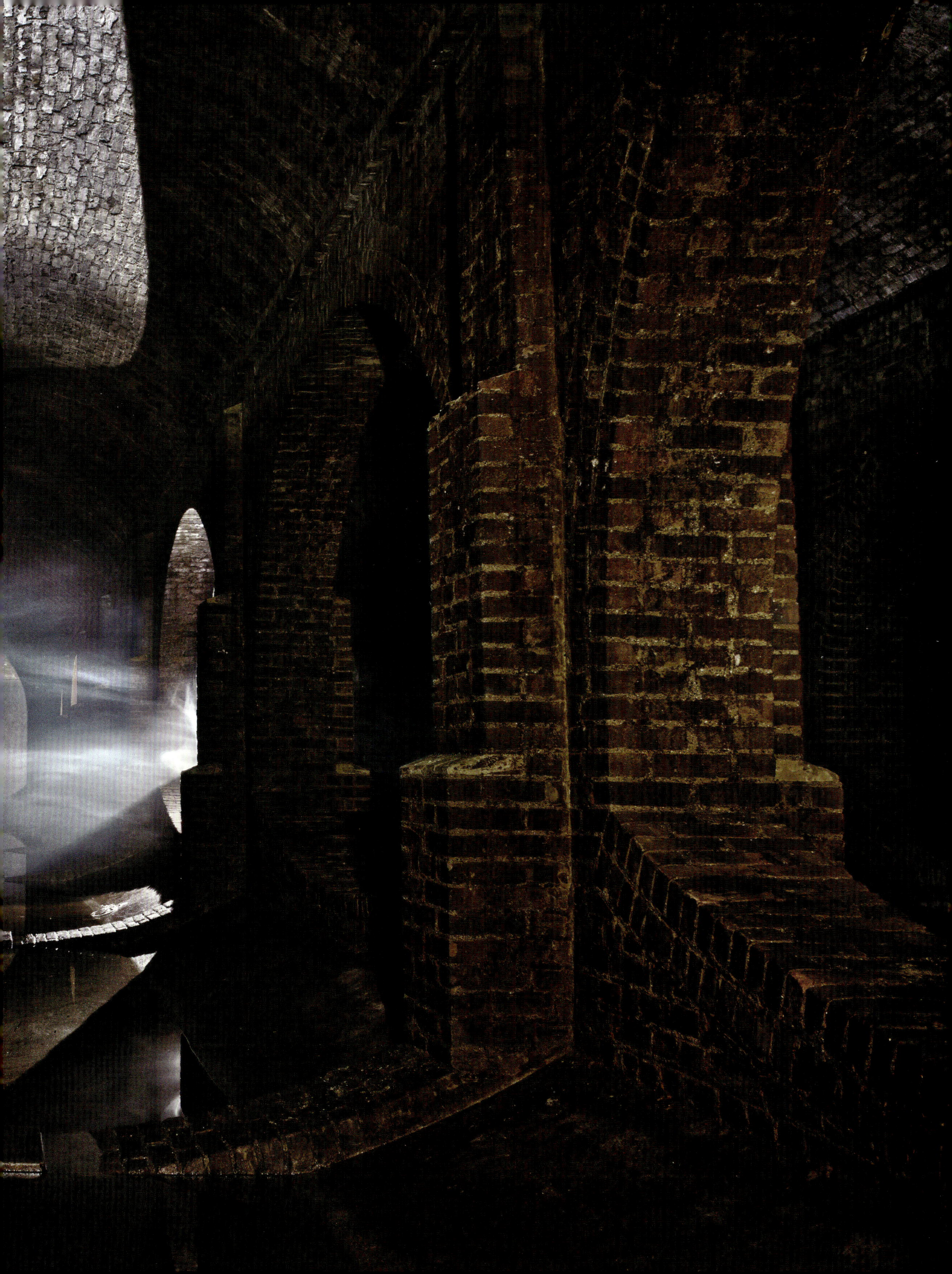

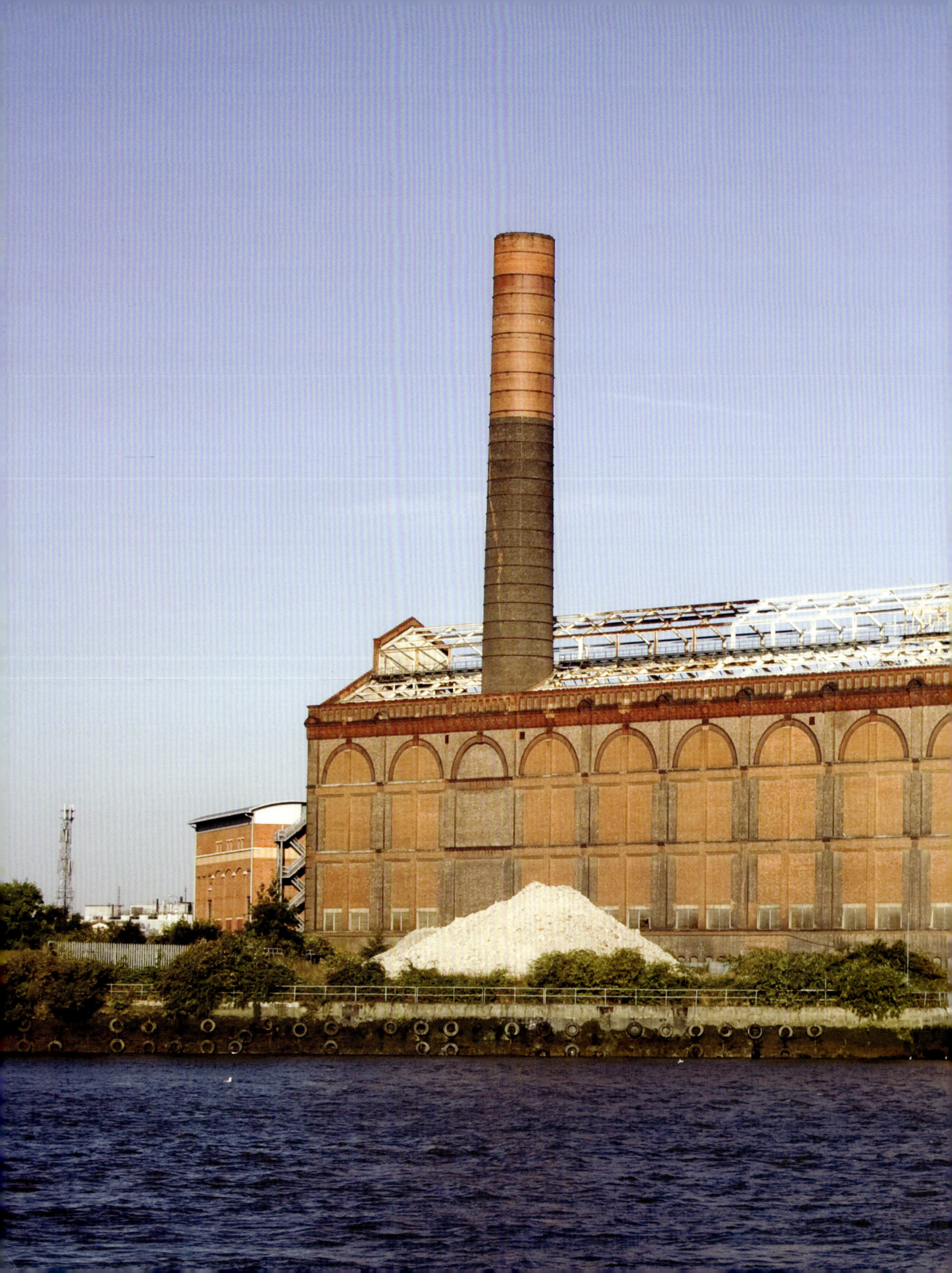

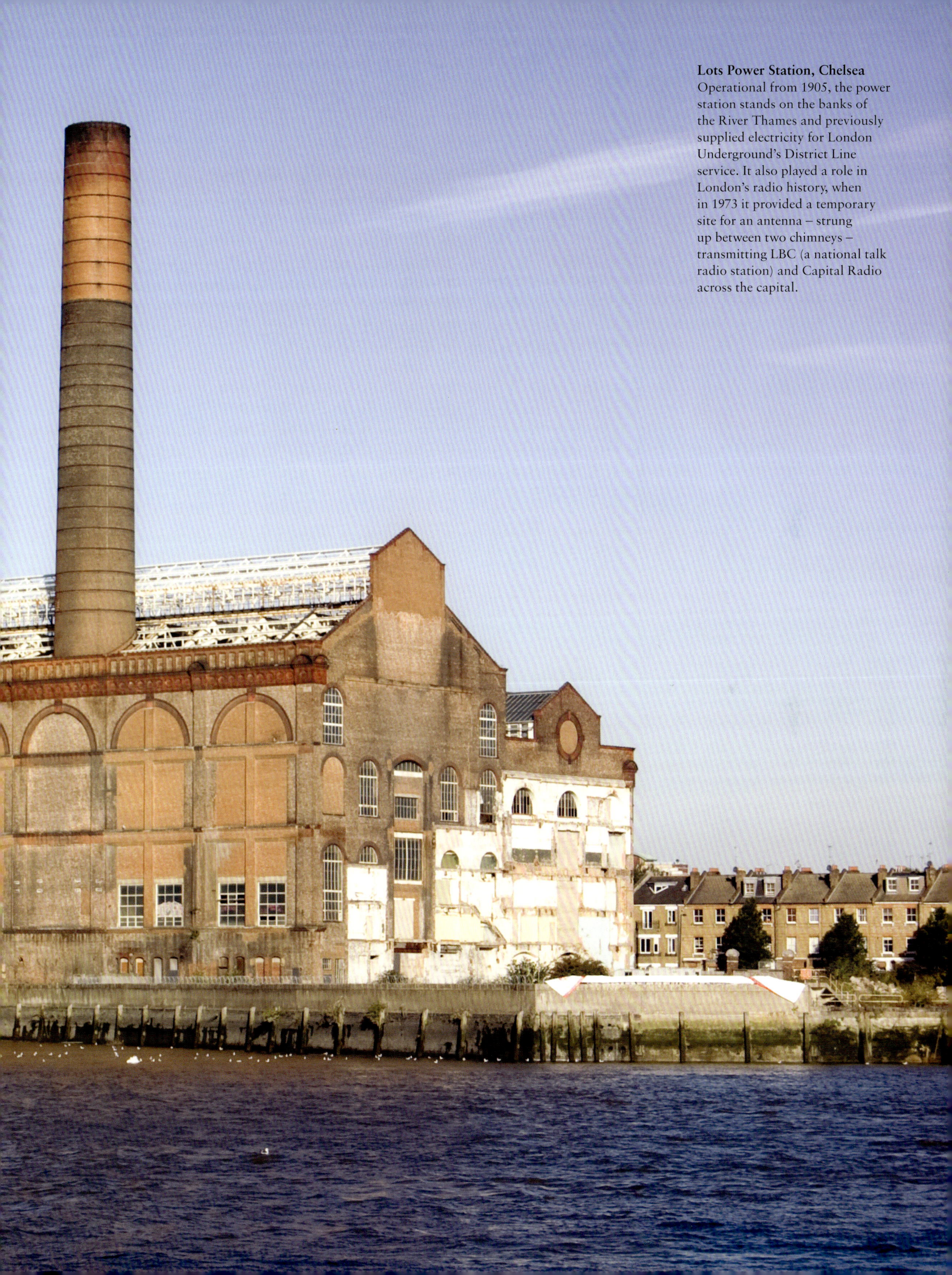

Lots Power Station, Chelsea
Operational from 1905, the power station stands on the banks of the River Thames and previously supplied electricity for London Underground's District Line service. It also played a role in London's radio history, when in 1973 it provided a temporary site for an antenna – strung up between two chimneys – transmitting LBC (a national talk radio station) and Capital Radio across the capital.

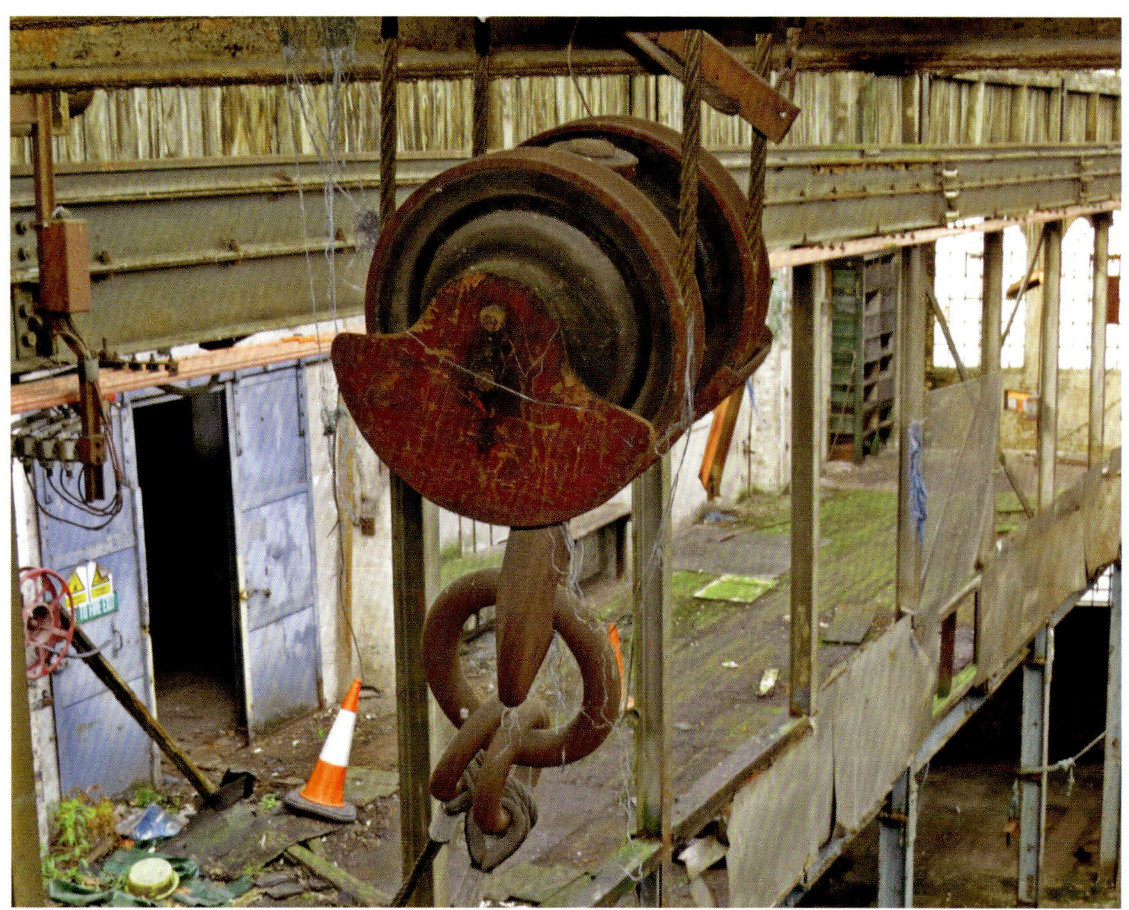

ALL PHOTOGRAPHS ON THESE PAGES:

Caird and Rayner Workshop, 777–778 Commercial Road, Tower Hamlets

By 1800, London needed a route connecting the expanding West and East India Docks and the City of London. The Commercial Road Company cut a direct road, just under three kilometres (two miles) long, by Act of Parliament in 1802. This former sail maker and warehouse for ship supplies is the last of its kind; built in 1869, today it is a Grade II listed building. Planning permission for an office conversion has been approved.

OVERLEAF:

EU Linco, Fish Island, Bow

Developed as a factory town in the late 19th century, Fish Island still has a concentration of industrial spaces as well as many artists' studios. Previously known just as 'The Island', many of the surrounding streets are named after freshwater fish – Bream Street, Dace Road and Roach Road.

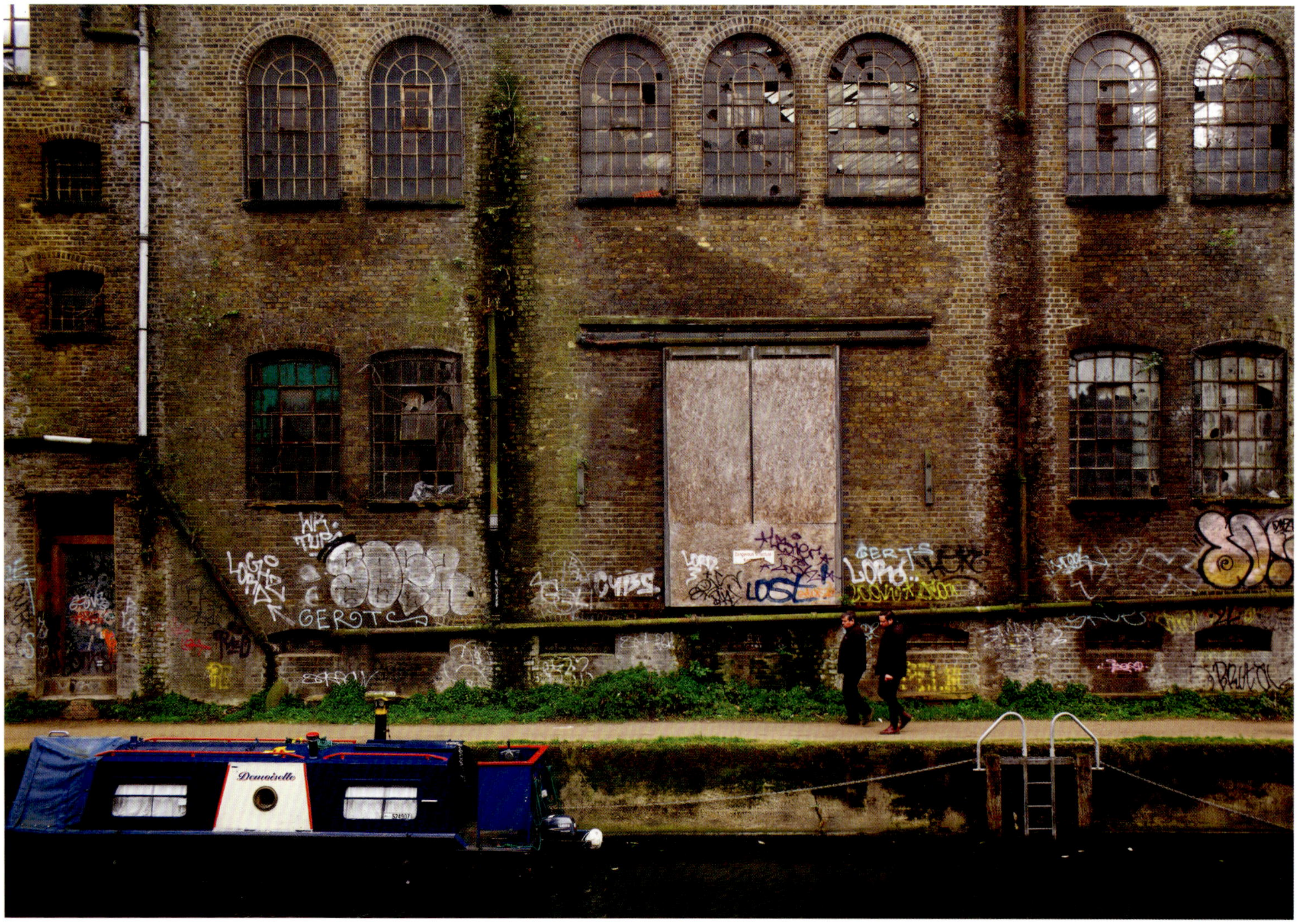

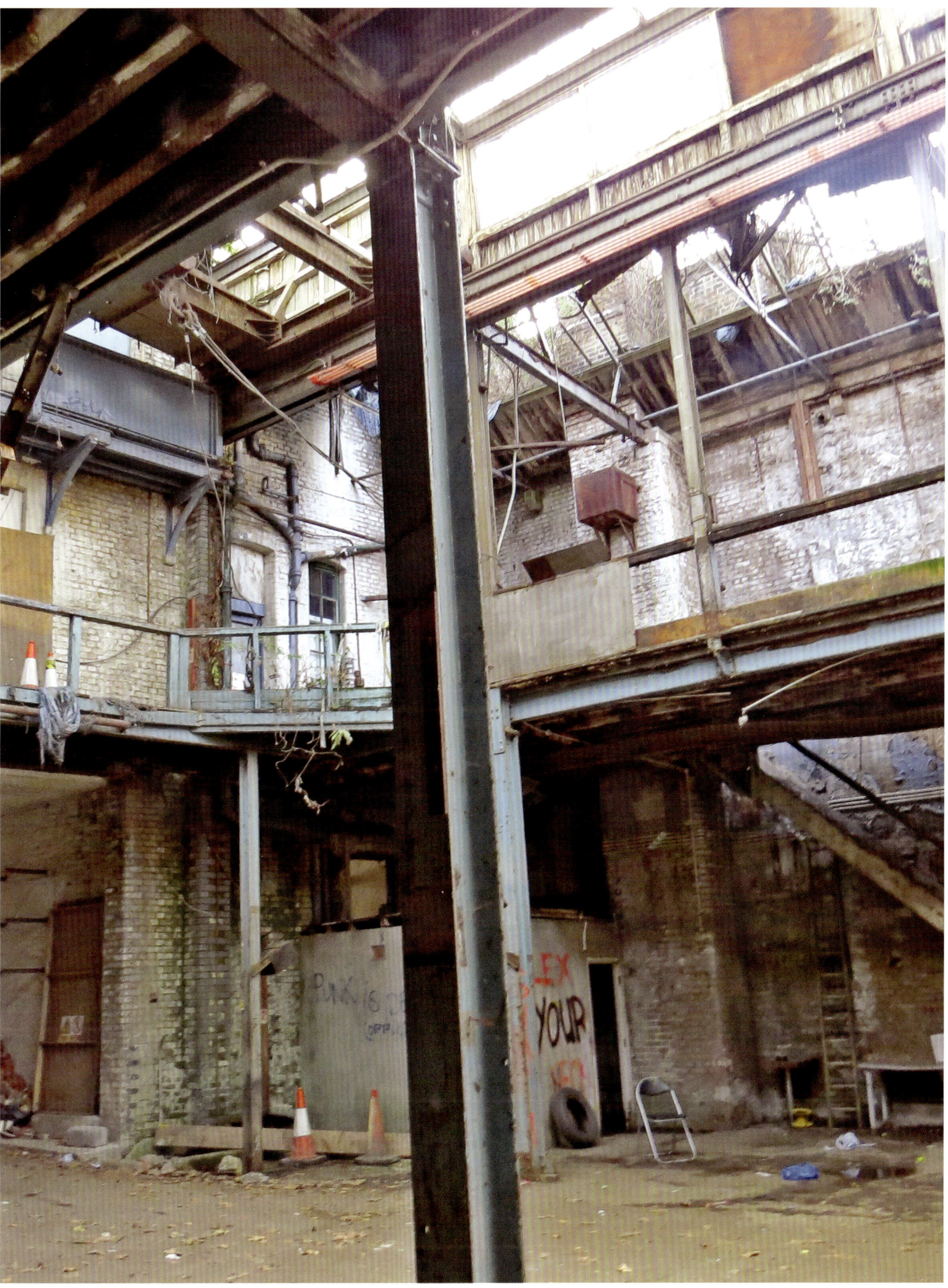
YOUR

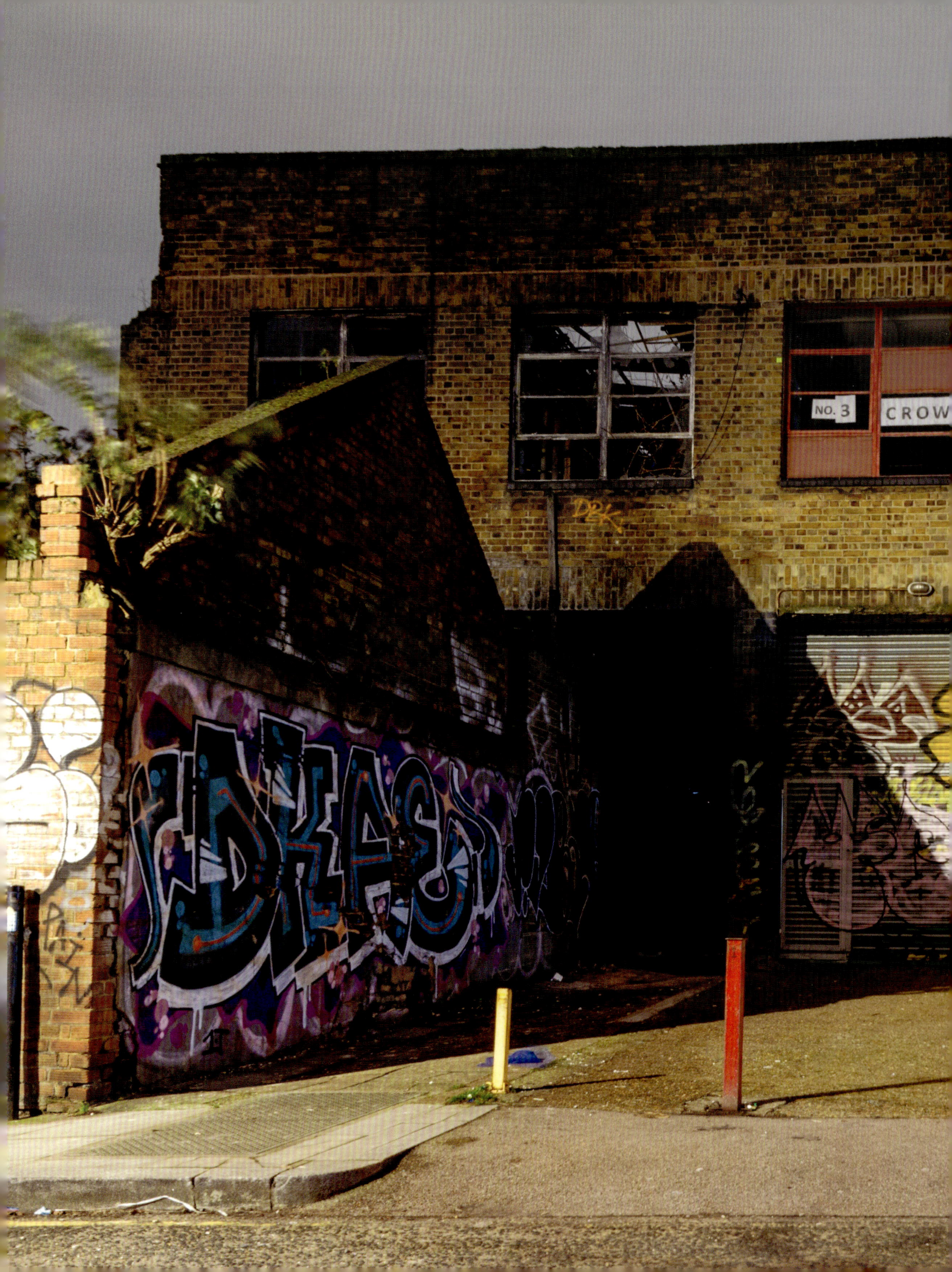
NO. 3
CROW

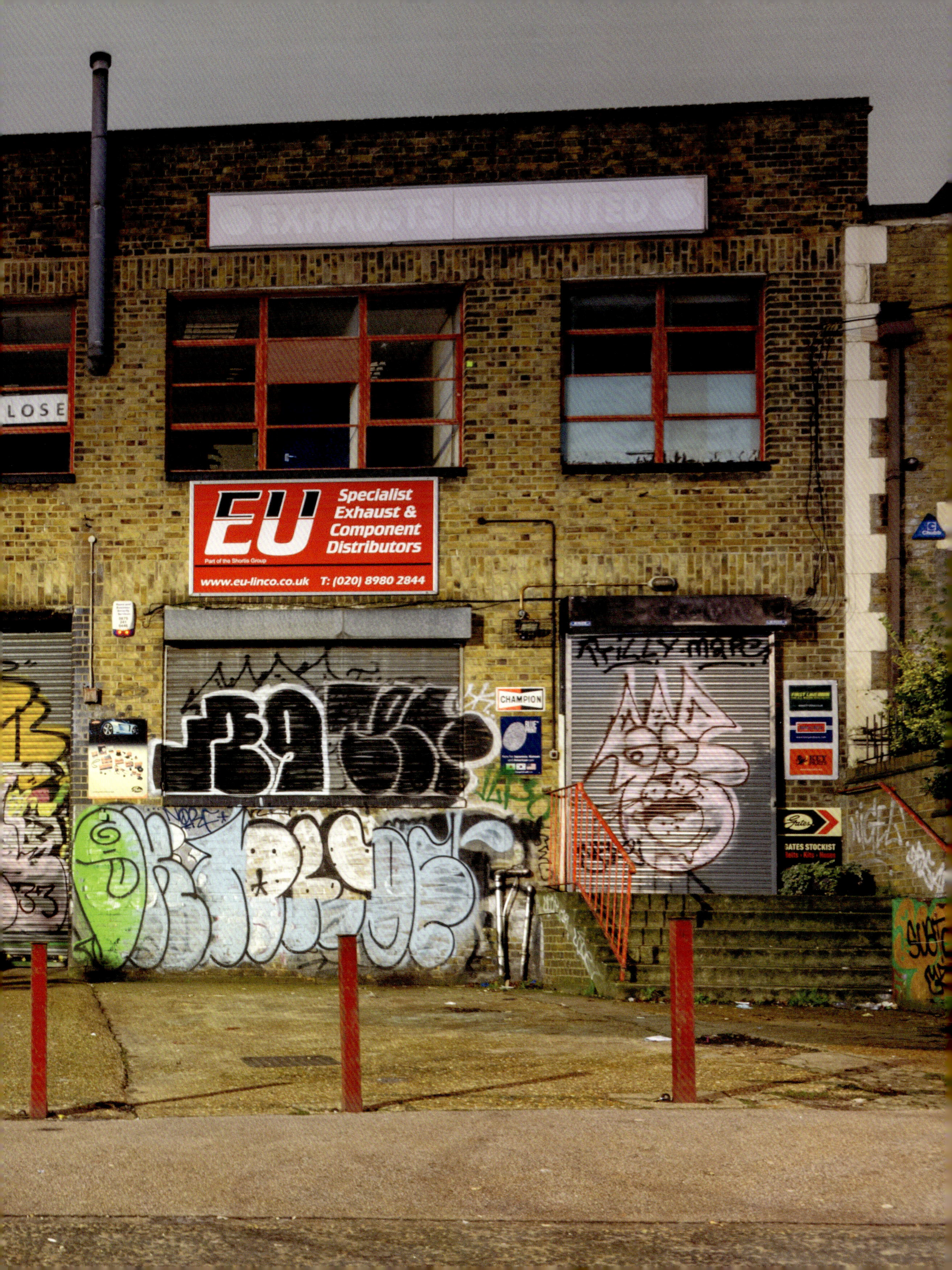
EXHAUSTS UNLIMITED
LOSE
EU
Specialist
Exhaust &
Component
Distributors
www.eu-linco.co.uk T: (020) 8980 2844
CHAMPION
GATES STOCKIST

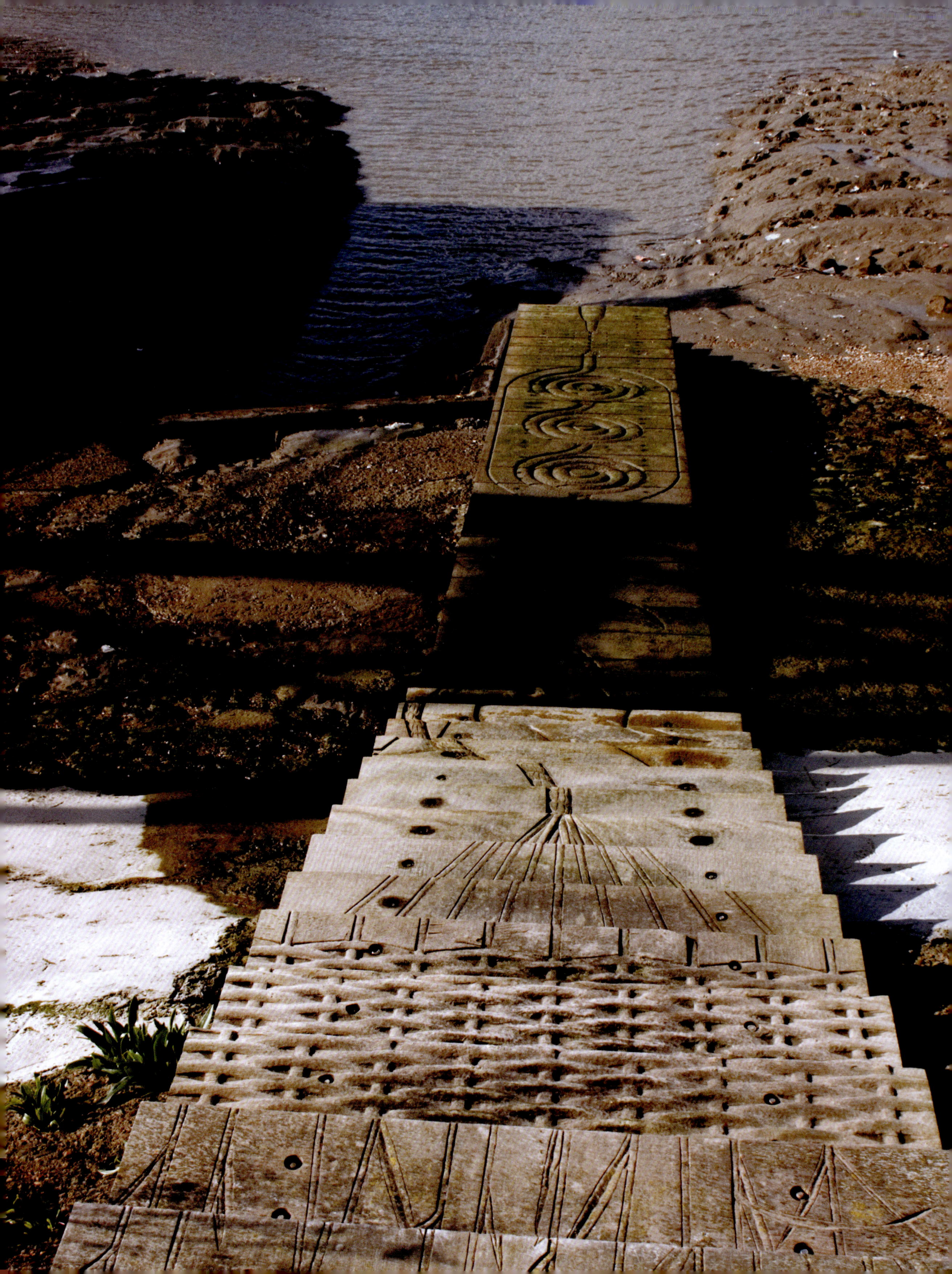

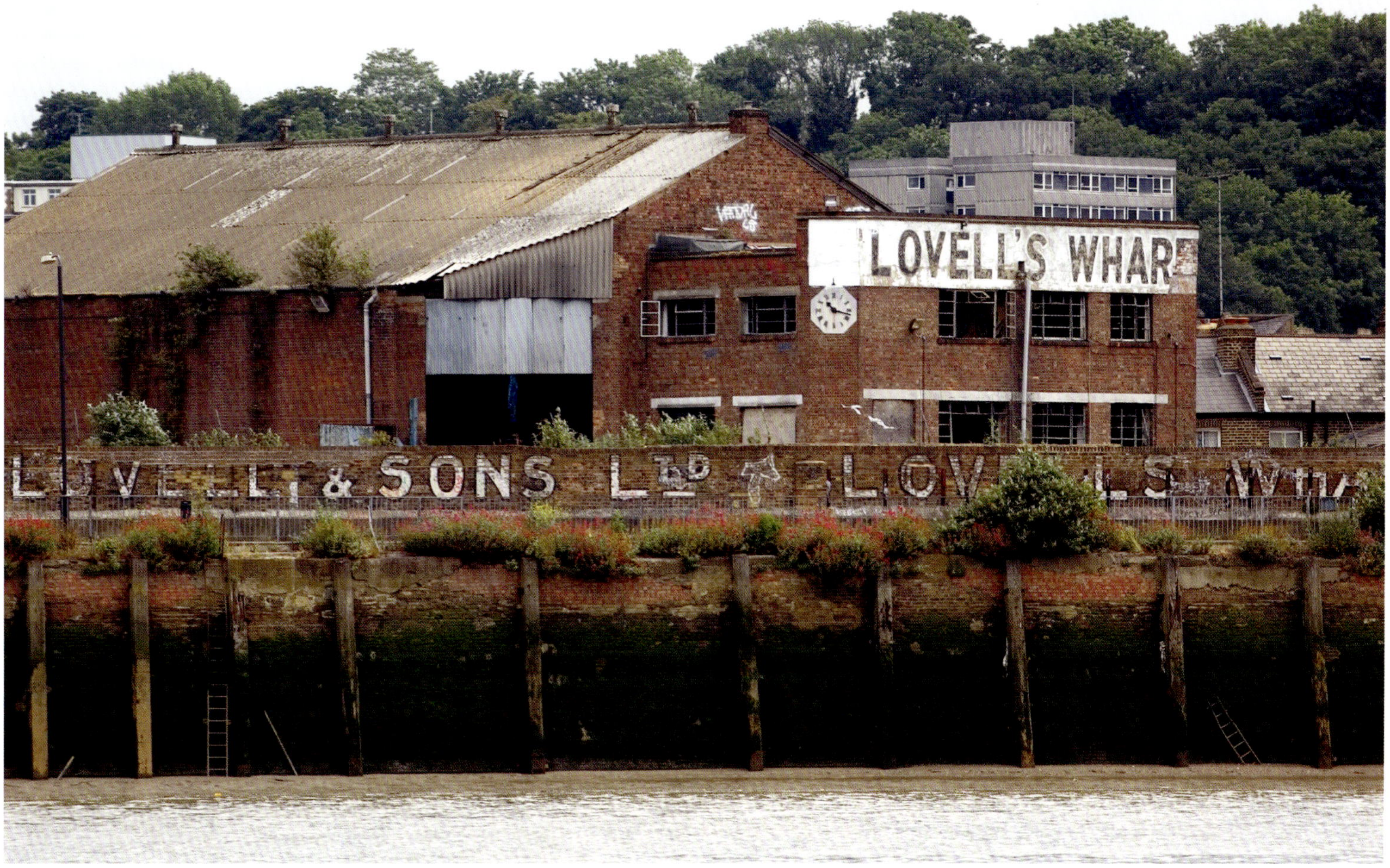

OPPOSITE AND ABOVE:

Lovell's Wharf, Greenwich

In 1911 the Bristol-based family business Lovell's took over this site in Greenwich, largely dealing in scrap metal. By the 1980s the wharf was still handling large amounts of steel, aluminium and gas pipes, but the rise in container cargo saw trade decline in the 1990s and eventually Lovell's surrendered the lease. The site is currently being developed into housing.

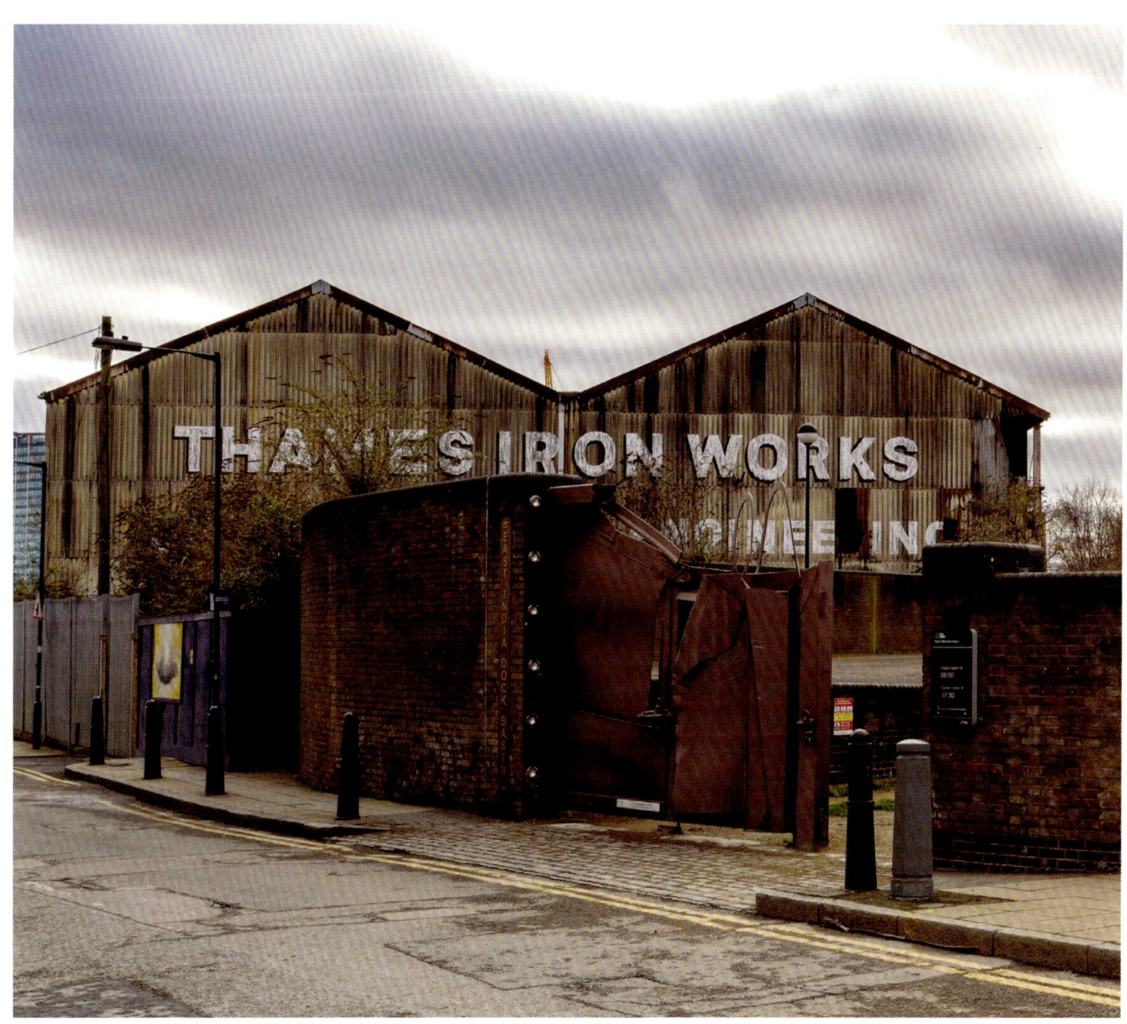

RIGHT:

The Thames Ironworks and Shipbuilding Company, Leamouth Wharf

Established in 1837, the company was among the first to build iron ships. However, they have a more famous legacy in football: founded in 1895, the Thames Ironworks Football Club became known as West Ham United in 1900 – hence the club's nicknames of 'The Irons' and 'The Hammers'.

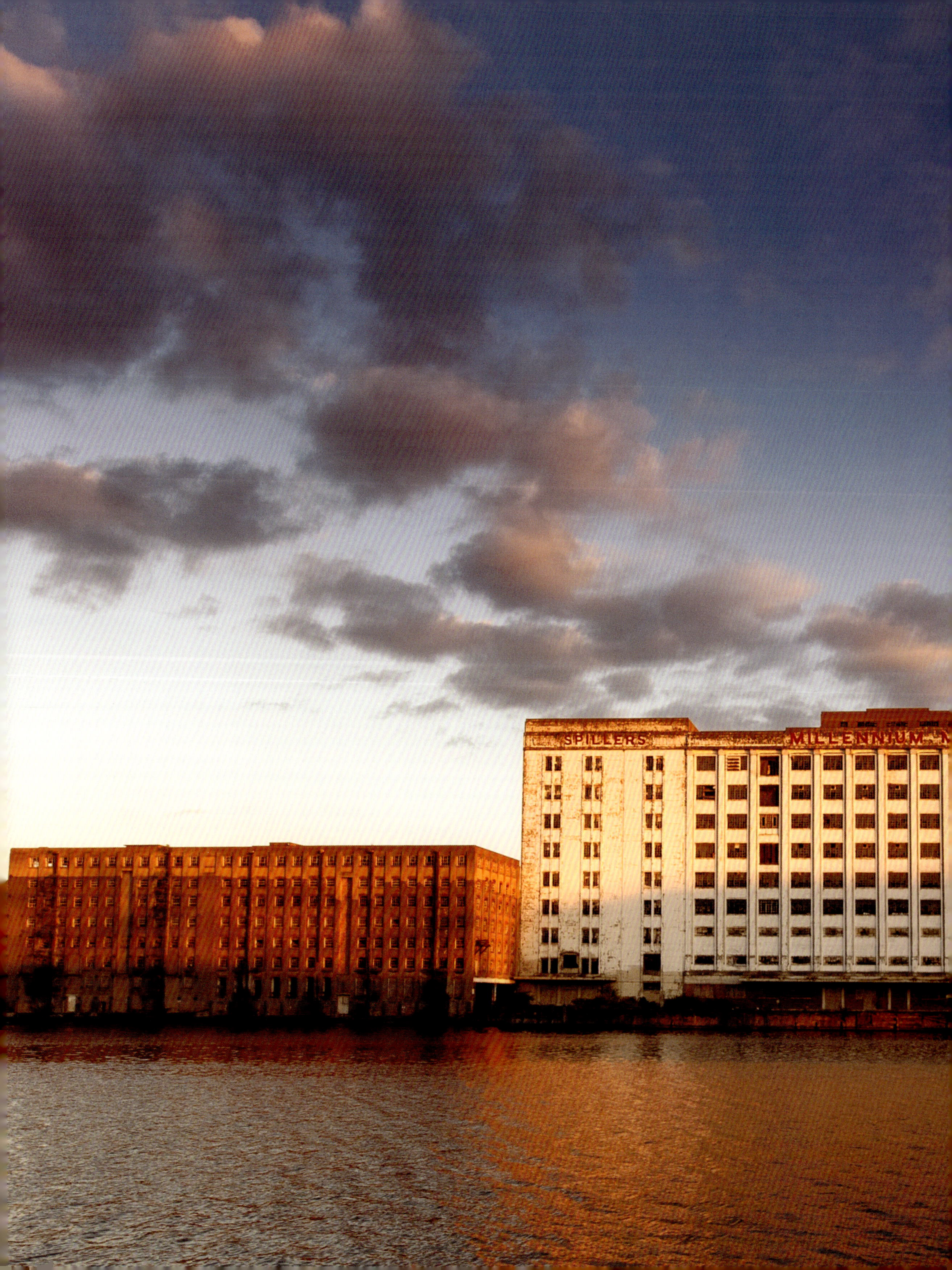
SPILLERS
MILLENNIUM

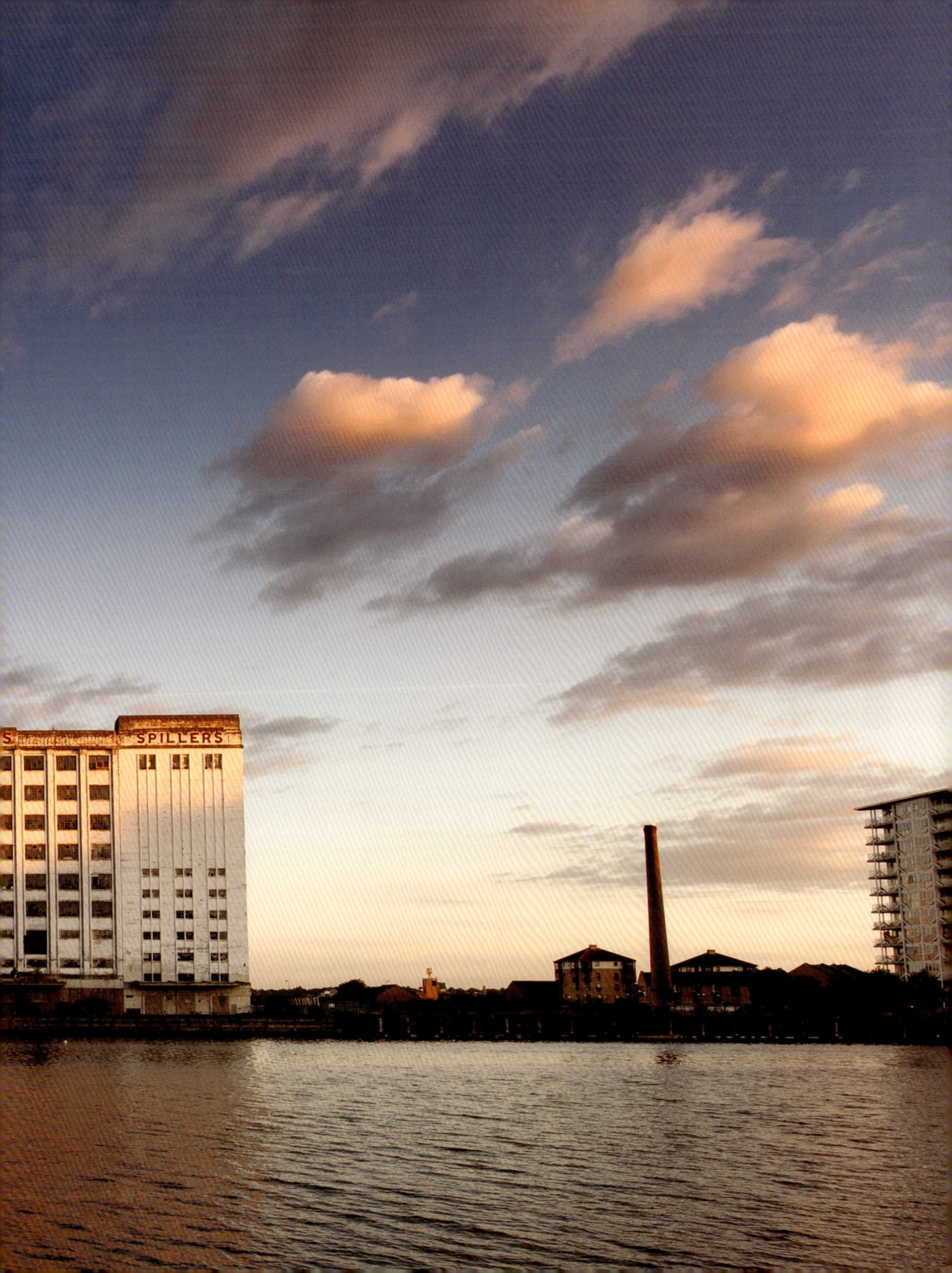
SPILLERS

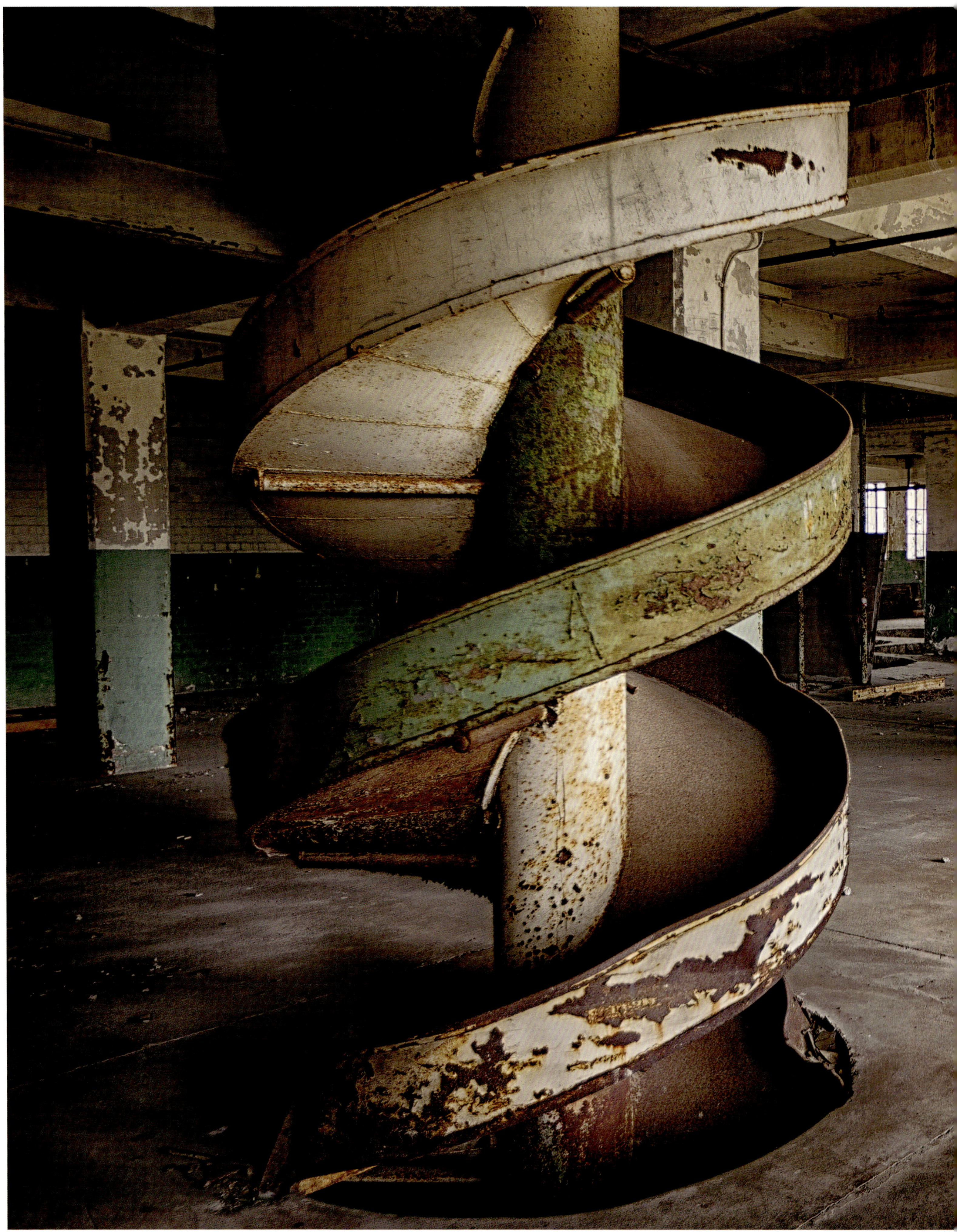

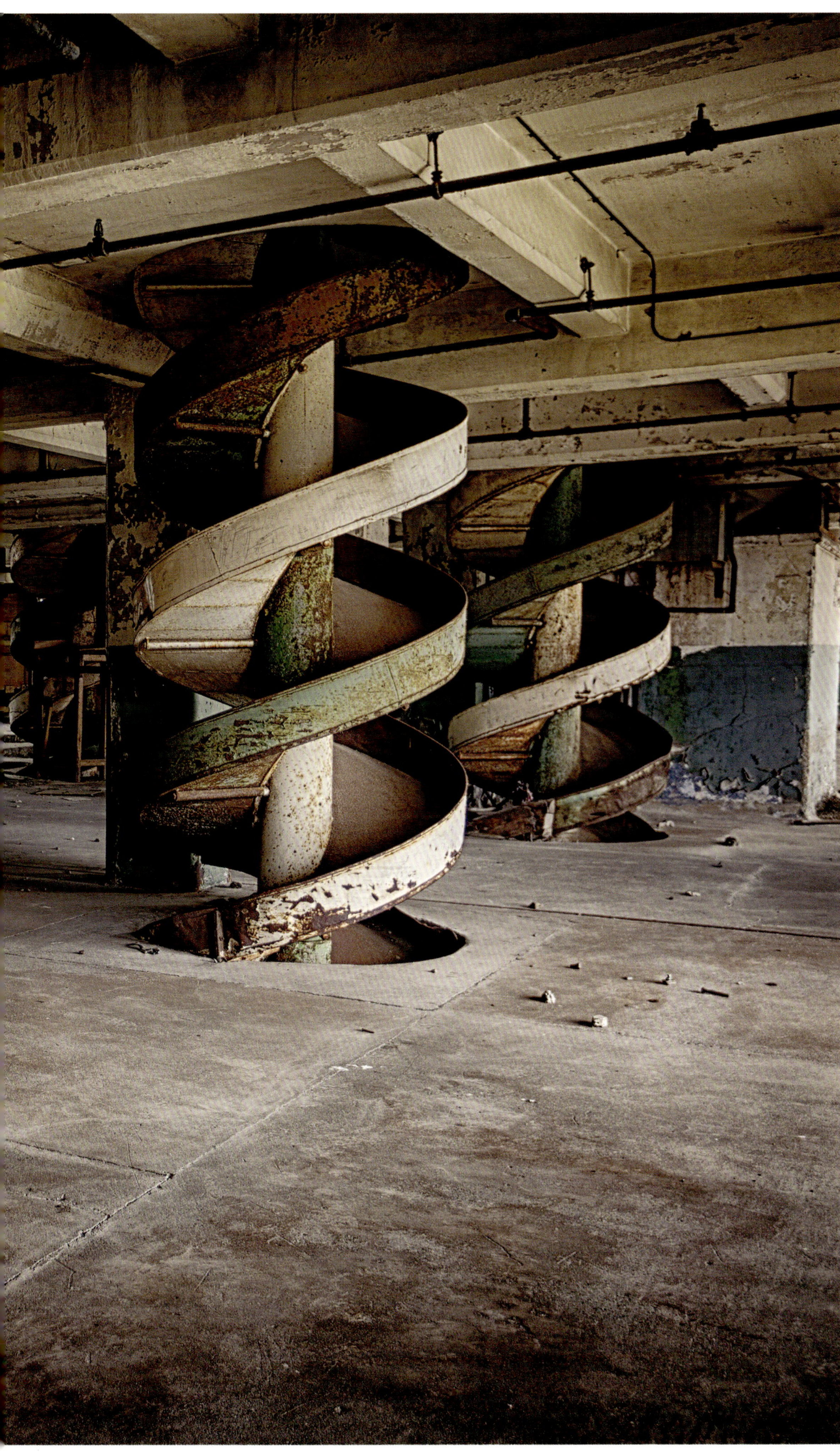

PREVIOUS PAGES AND LEFT:

Millennium Mills, Silvertown

Silvertown, part of the Port of London to the East of the City, was a hub of industry in the 19th century. It gets its name from Samuel Winkworth Silver, who owned a rubber factory here in the 1850s, but is most famous now for the Tate & Lyle sugar refinery.

The area was also the centre of flour milling in London and in 1905 a huge flour factory was built, producing 100 sacks of flour an hour. Featured left are the spiral slides used for moving sacks of flour from one floor to another.

On 19 January 1917 there was an explosion in a munitions factory in Silvertown, just 100 metres from Millennium Mills, where 73 people lost their lives and a further 400 were injured.

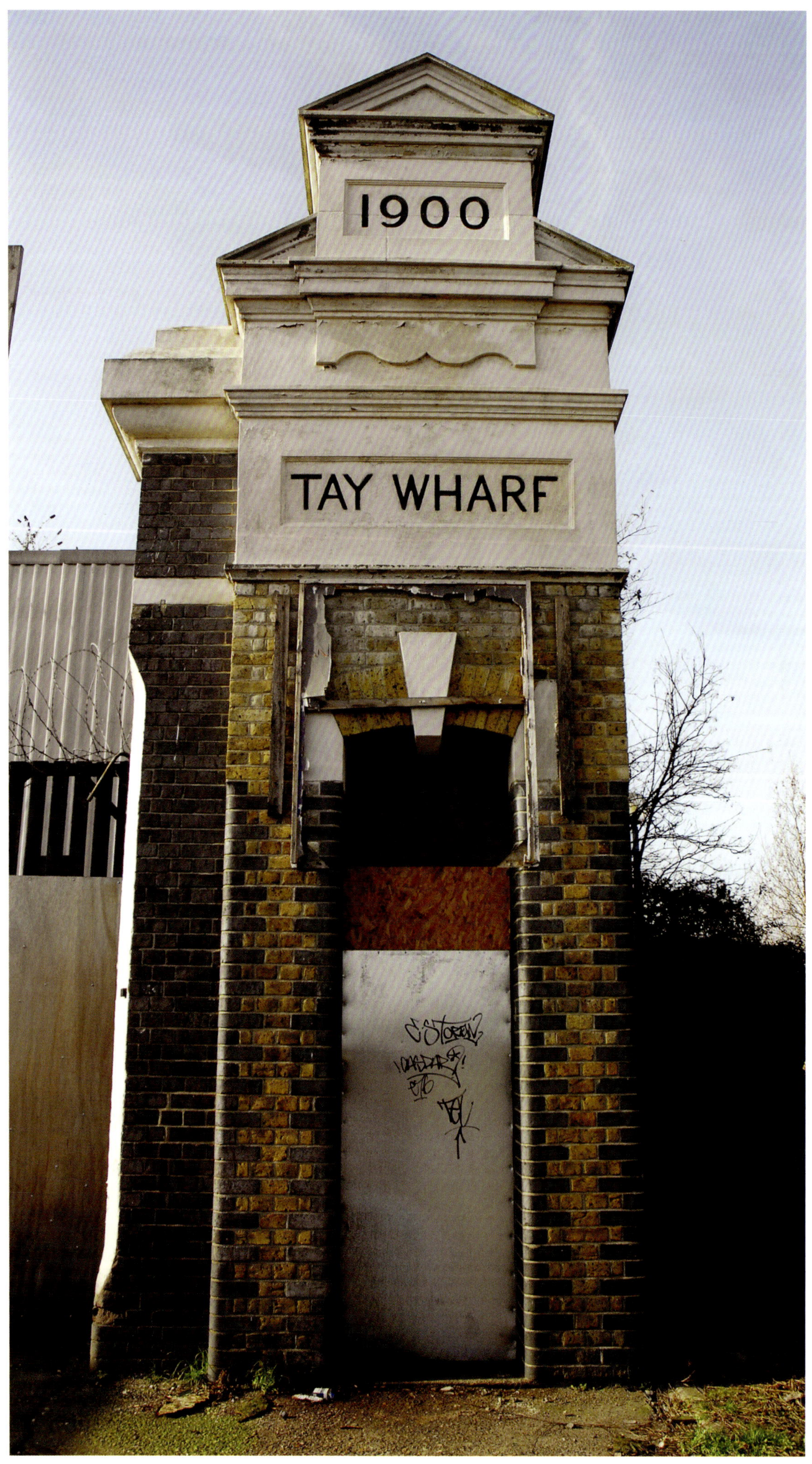

LEFT:

Tay Wharf, Silvertown

The former entrance gate of a jam factory, Tay Wharf was established here in 1878. James Keiller & Sons ran a successful marmalade company in Scotland before acquiring this site in Silvertown. It was close to the river for importing fruit and the Tate & Lyle sugar factory, so an ideal location. In 1920 the firm was bought and is now a subsidiary of Nestlé.

OPPOSITE:

Millennium Mills, Silvertown

Despite surviving multiple bombing raids during World War II, the mills closed in 1981. The buildings have since appeared as the backdrop for films such as Derek Jarman's *The Last of England*, the TV series *Ashes to Ashes* and music videos by the Arctic Monkeys, Snow Patrol and Coldplay.

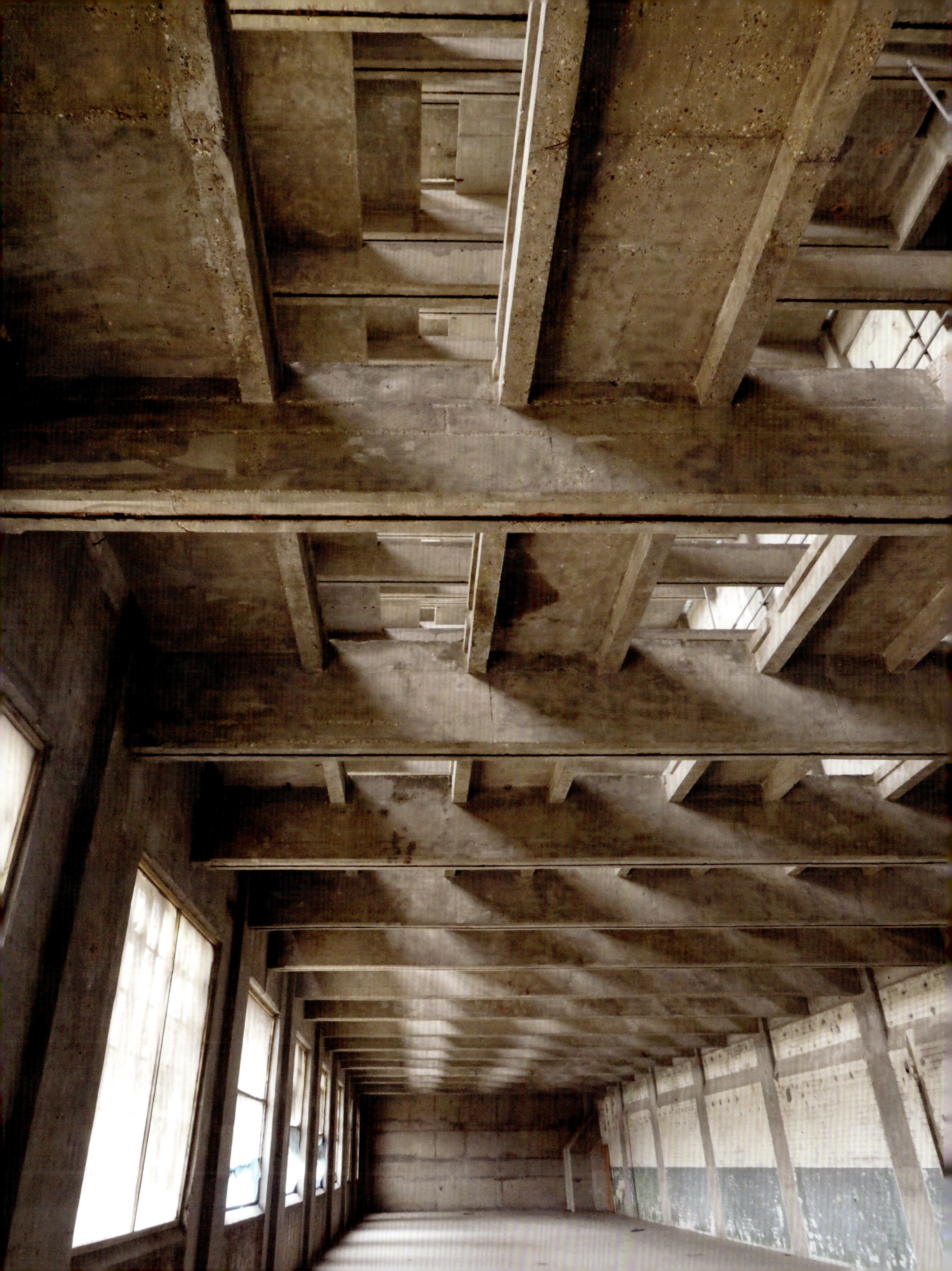

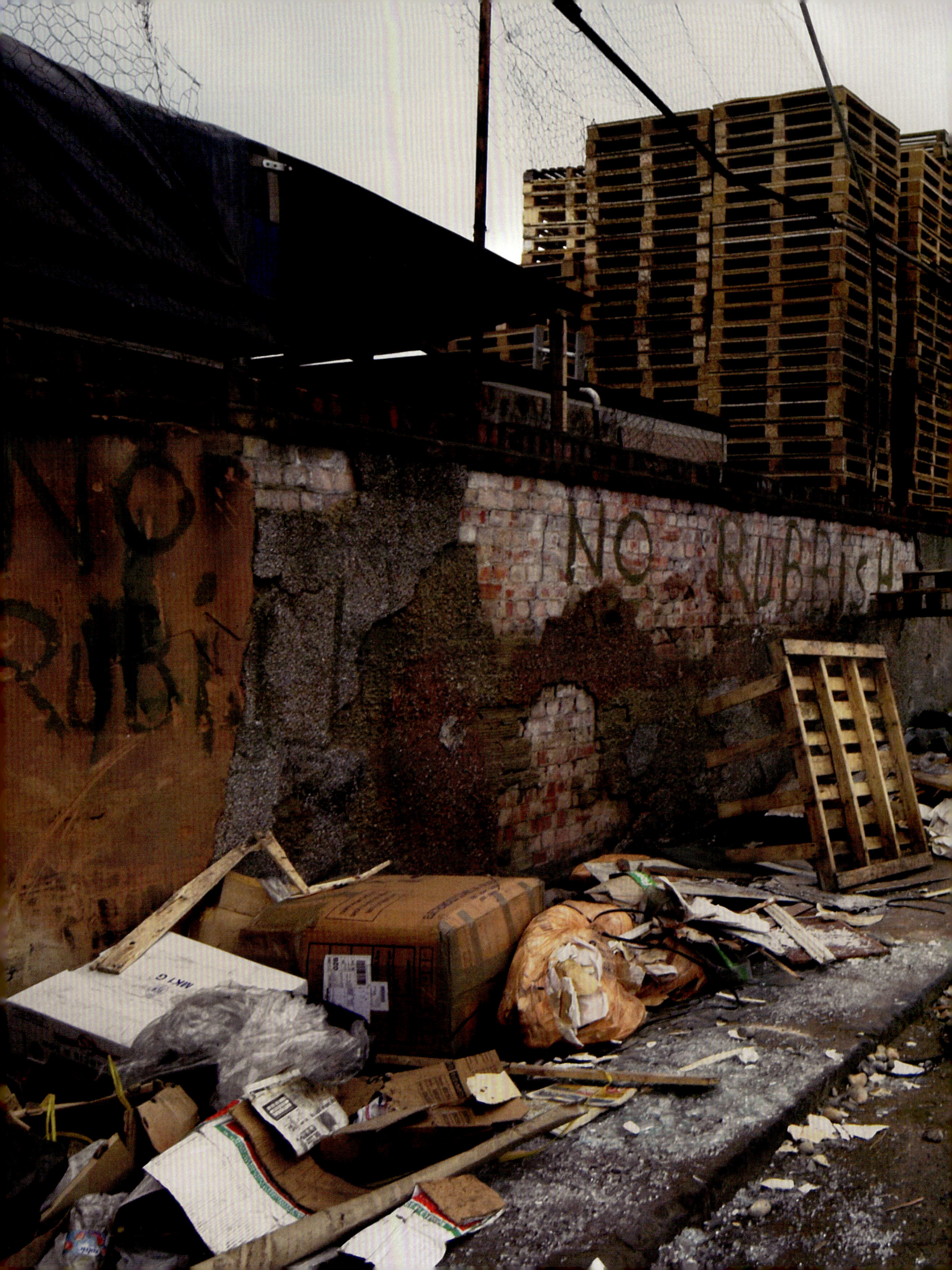
NO RUBBISH

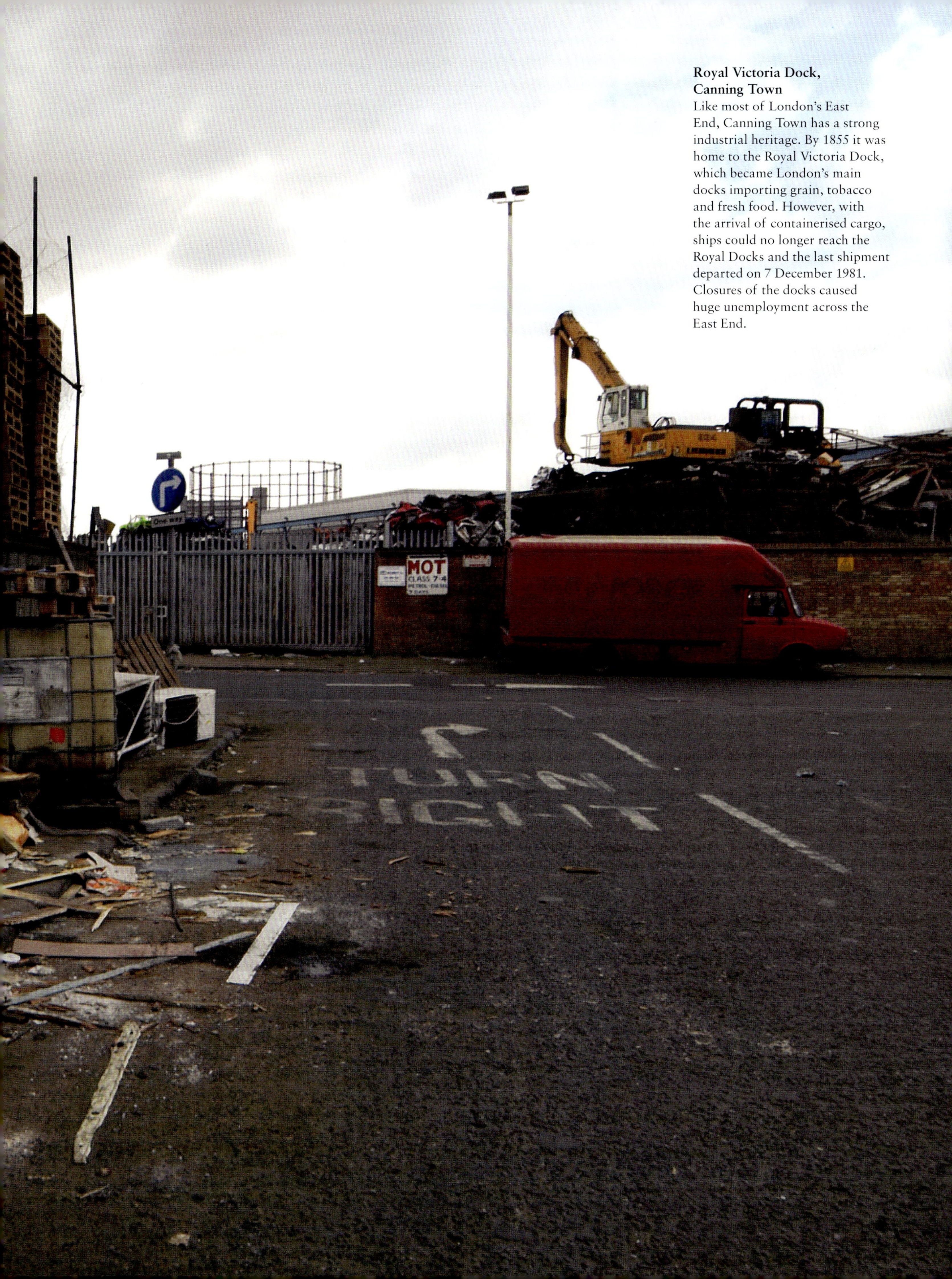

Royal Victoria Dock, Canning Town

Like most of London's East End, Canning Town has a strong industrial heritage. By 1855 it was home to the Royal Victoria Dock, which became London's main docks importing grain, tobacco and fresh food. However, with the arrival of containerised cargo, ships could no longer reach the Royal Docks and the last shipment departed on 7 December 1981. Closures of the docks caused huge unemployment across the East End.

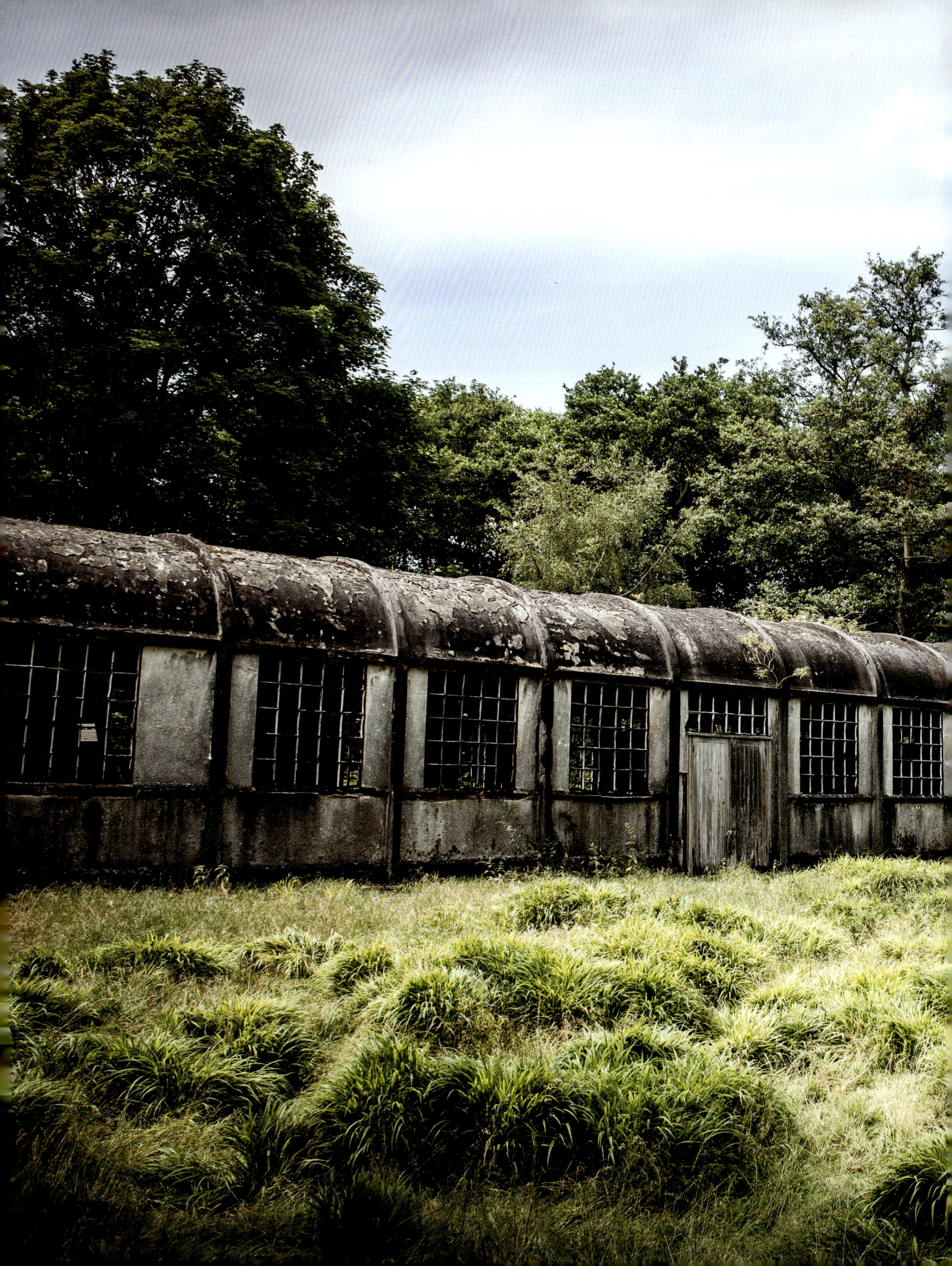

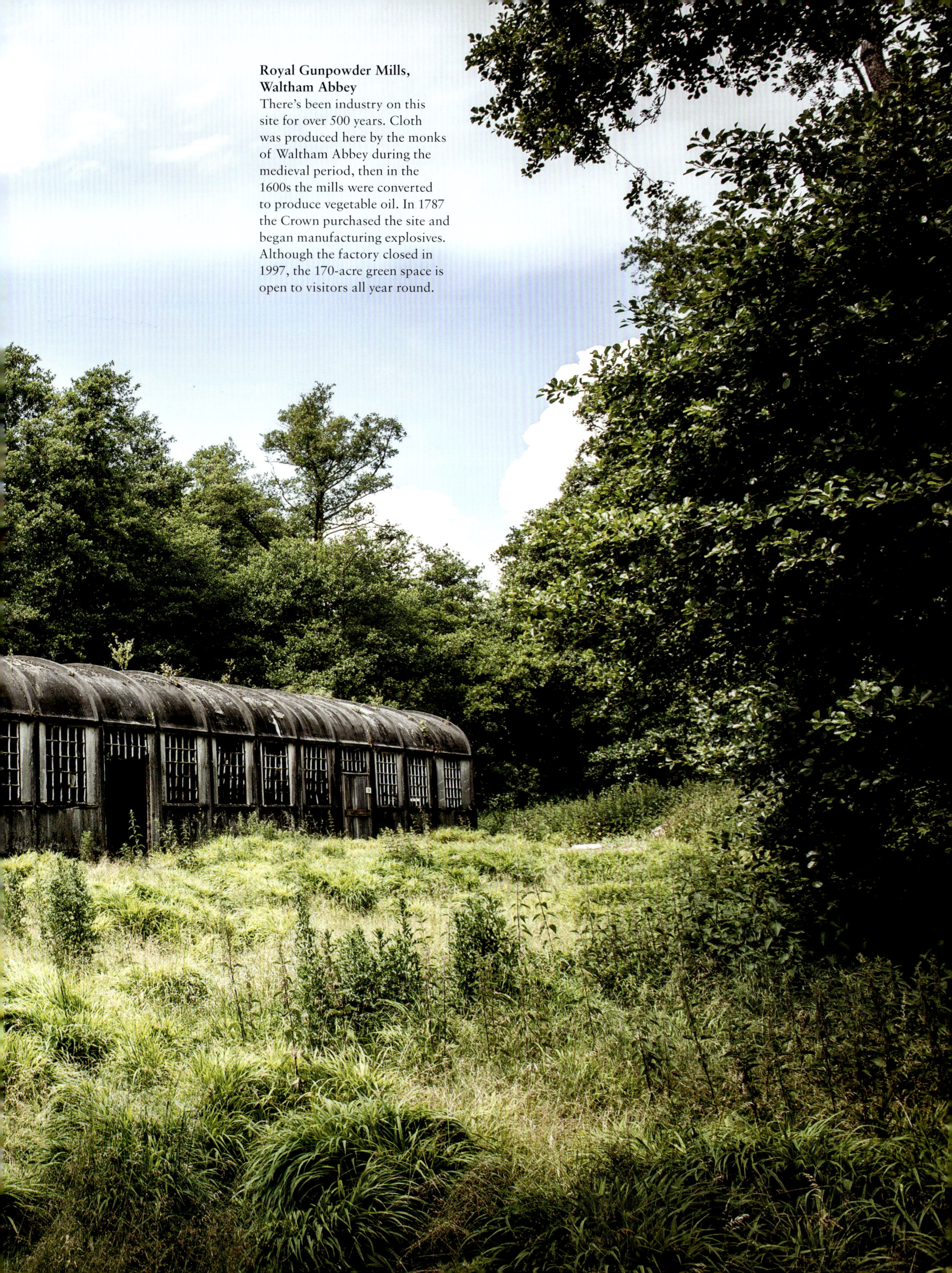

Royal Gunpowder Mills, Waltham Abbey
There's been industry on this site for over 500 years. Cloth was produced here by the monks of Waltham Abbey during the medieval period, then in the 1600s the mills were converted to produce vegetable oil. In 1787 the Crown purchased the site and began manufacturing explosives. Although the factory closed in 1997, the 170-acre green space is open to visitors all year round.

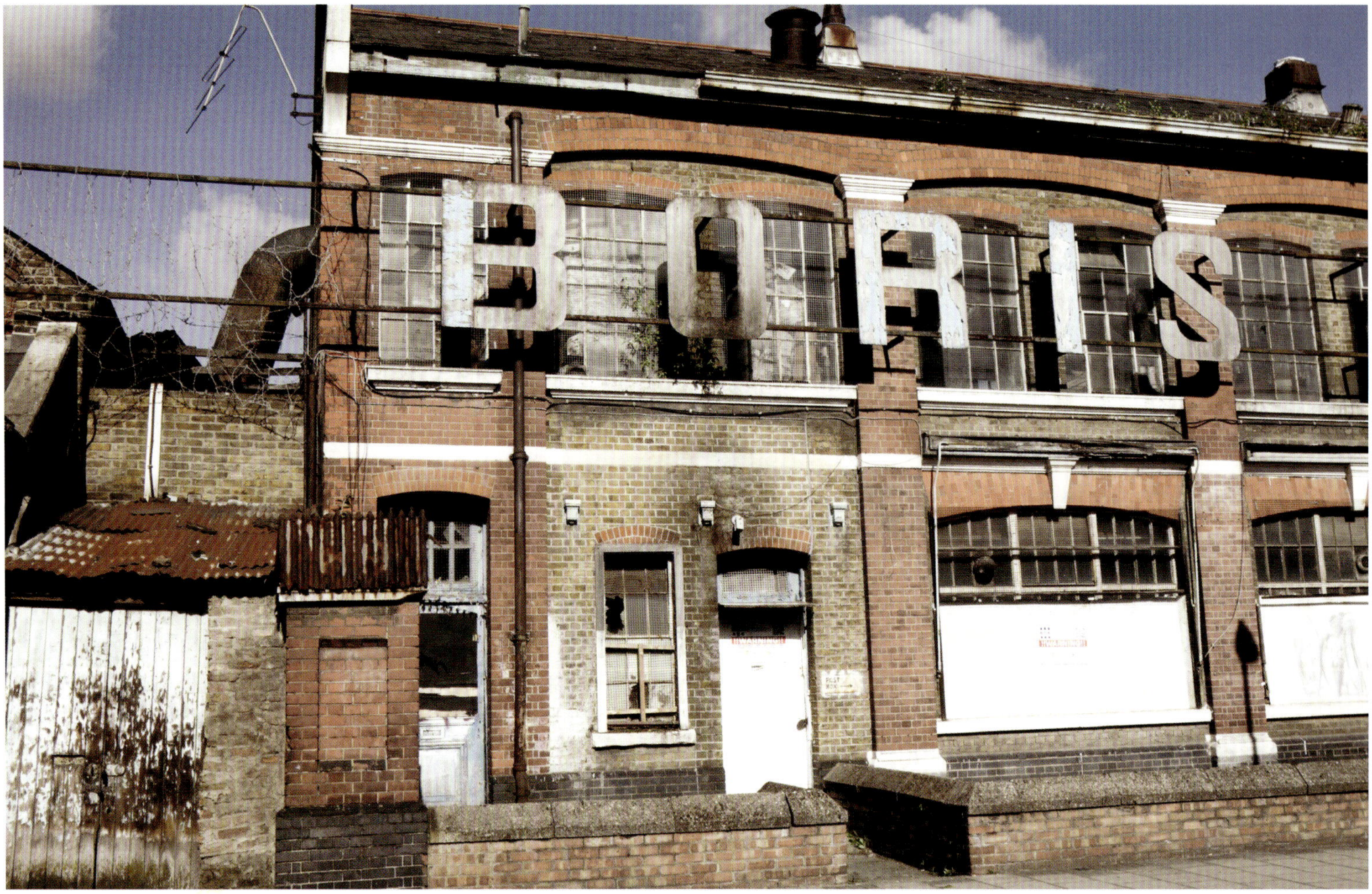
BORIS

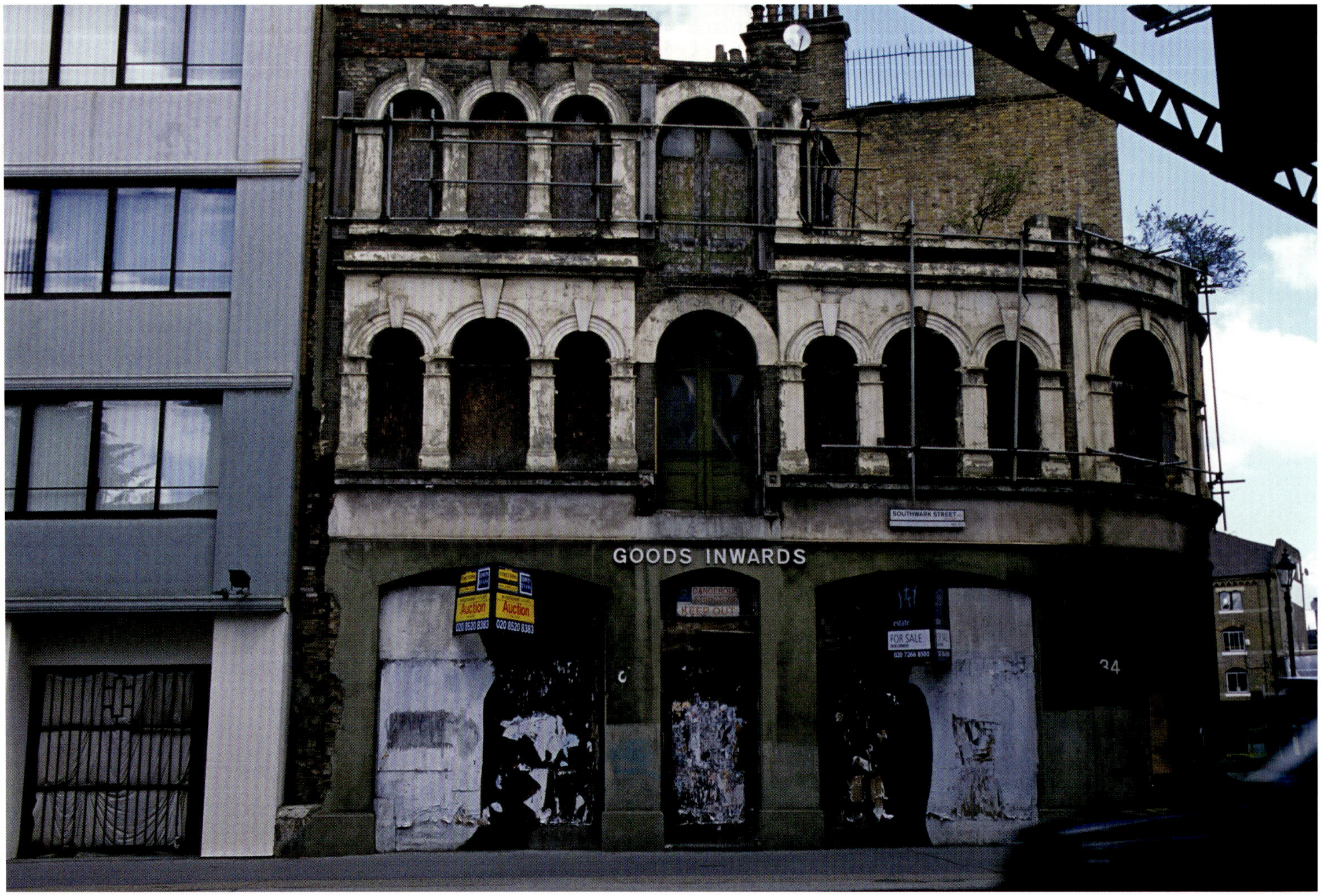
SOUTHWARK STREET
GOODS INWARDS
Auction
Auction
KEEP OUT
FOR SALE
34

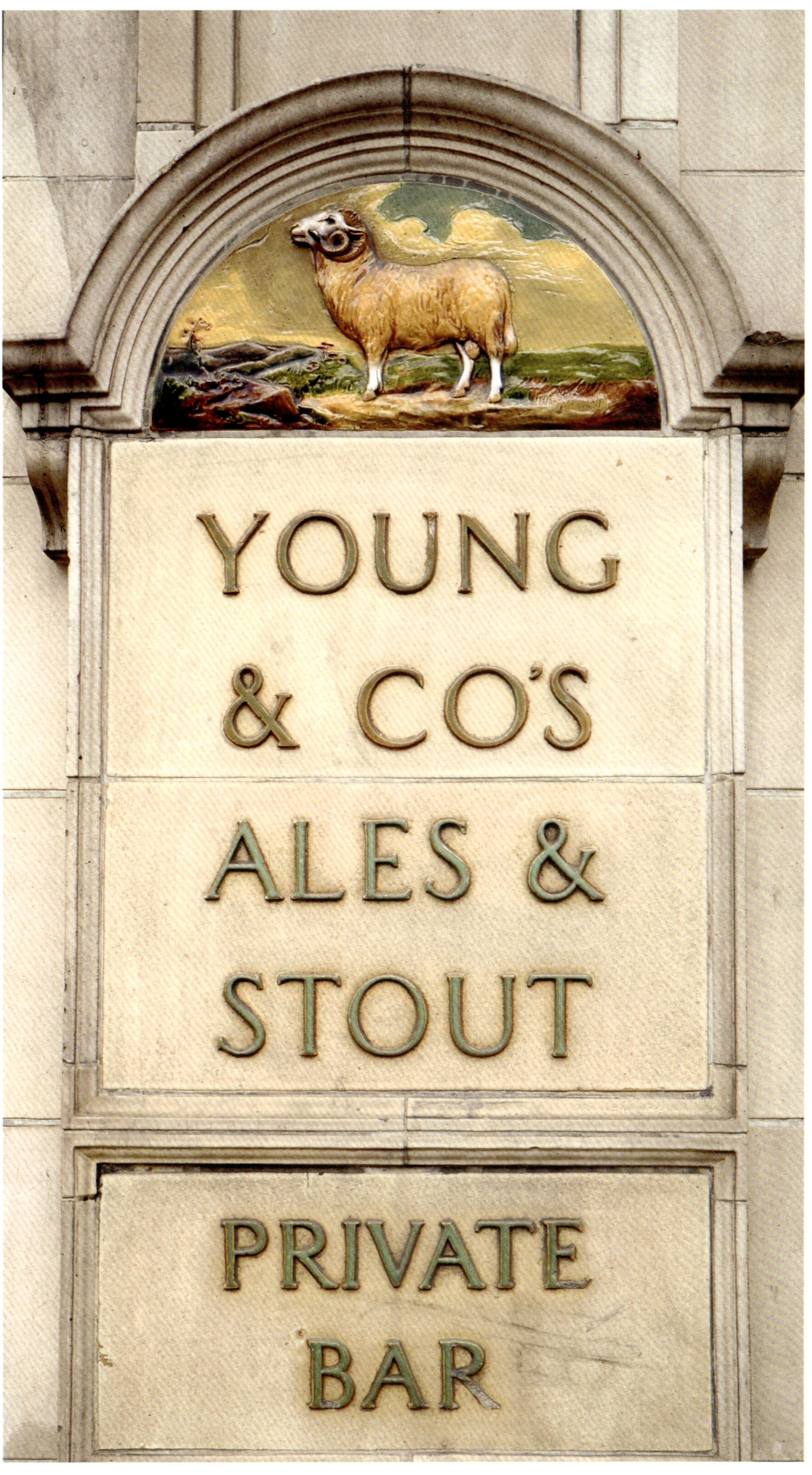

OPPOSITE TOP:

Boris Ltd, Hackney

Although the building dates from 1913, Boris Ltd has only been here since the 1980s, manufacturing bags and storing imported luggage. Since 2009, Hackney Council has been in talks to develop the building into artists' studios.

OPPOSITE BOTTOM:

Goods Inwards, Southwark Street

In 1856 the Metropolitan Board of Works was petitioned to create a new street that connected the relatively new rail terminus station at London Bridge with the fashionable West End. Southwark Street was the result. The road was lined with large commercial buildings in an Italian Gothic style. This site, on 34–35 Southwark Street, has since reopened as a Chinese restaurant.

LEFT:

Young & Co Brewery, Wandsworth

Founded in 1831 by Charles Young and Anthony Bainbridge, Youngs was based at the Ram Brewery in Wandsworth until it closed in 2006. The chain runs 220 pubs across Britain and the new development – Ram Quarter – hired a Young's brewer to continue the production of beer on-site in a nanobrewery.

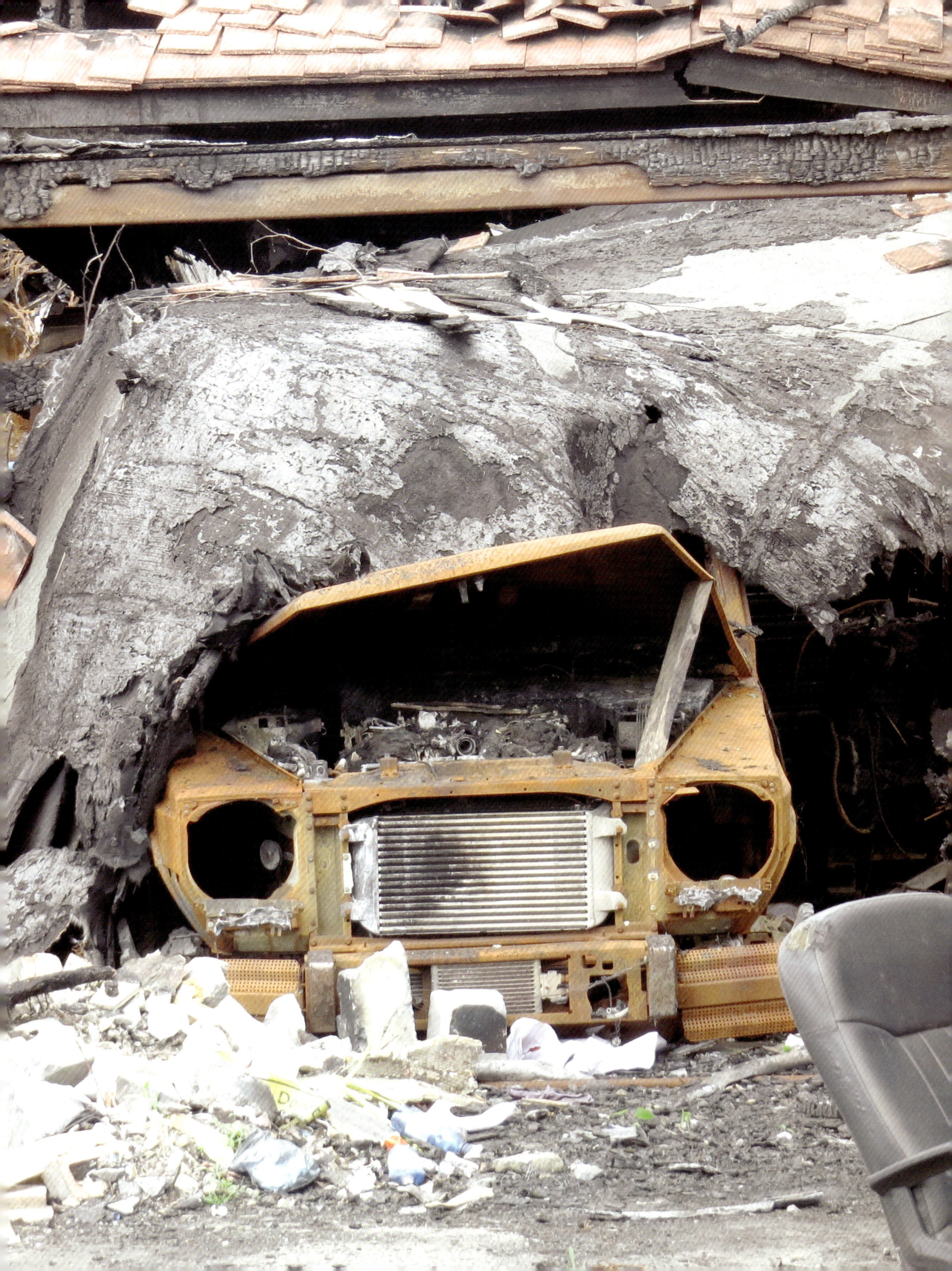

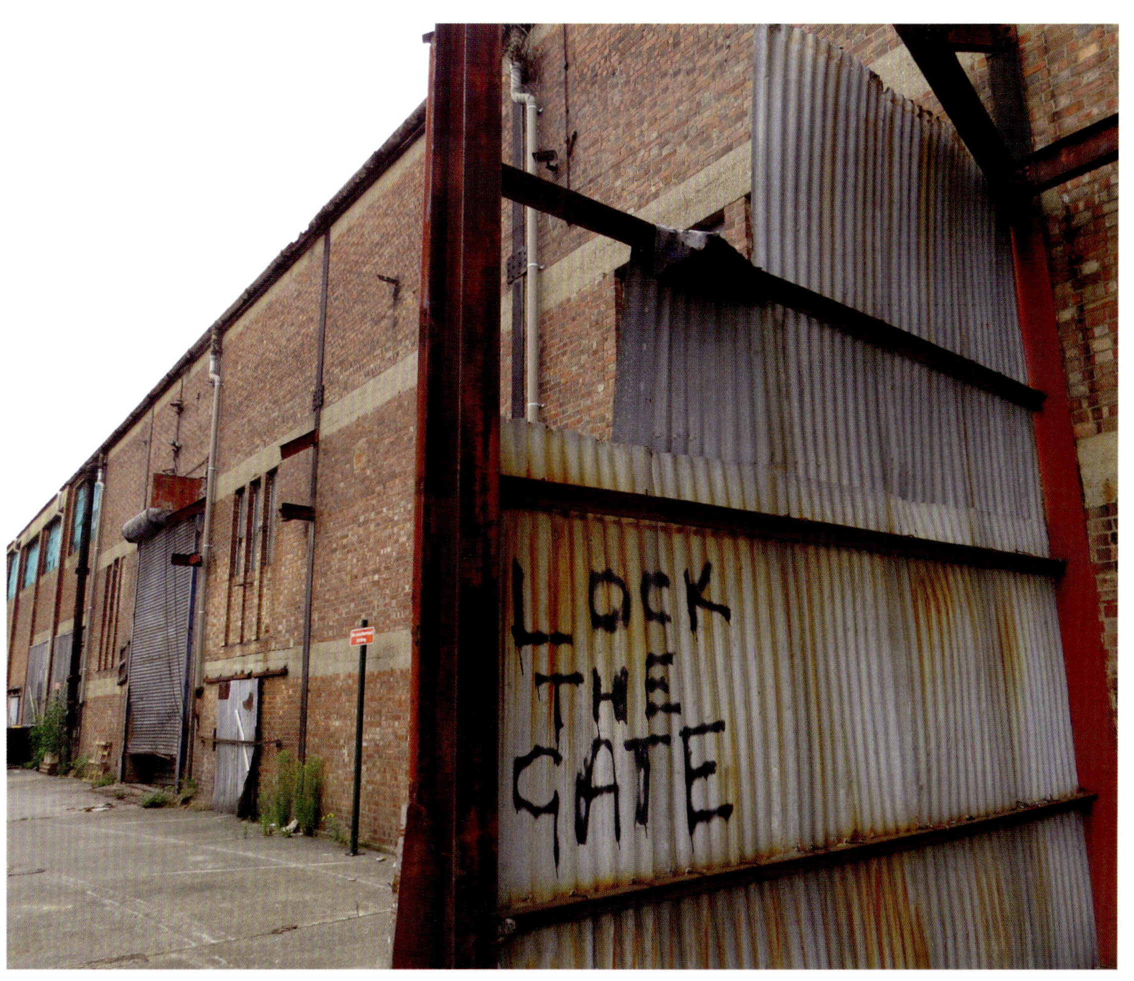

OPPOSITE:

Imperials Prestige Used Cars, Romford

Although the Imperials company still operates, selling luxury sports cars from its headquarters in Essex, the Chadwell Heath site in Romford closed in 2018.

LEFT:

Derelict Export Packers, Brickfield Road, Bromley-by-Bow

Acquired by John Stevenson & Sons in 1953 and then sold in 1967, the derelict warehouse in East London is beside the Limehouse Cut, London's oldest canal, which first opened on 17 September 1770.

BELOW:

Derelict Cold Storage Warehouse, Seven Sisters, Tottenham

The first British cold store opened in 1877, built under Cannon Street Railway. Today this office space of a former cold storage warehouse stands derelict.

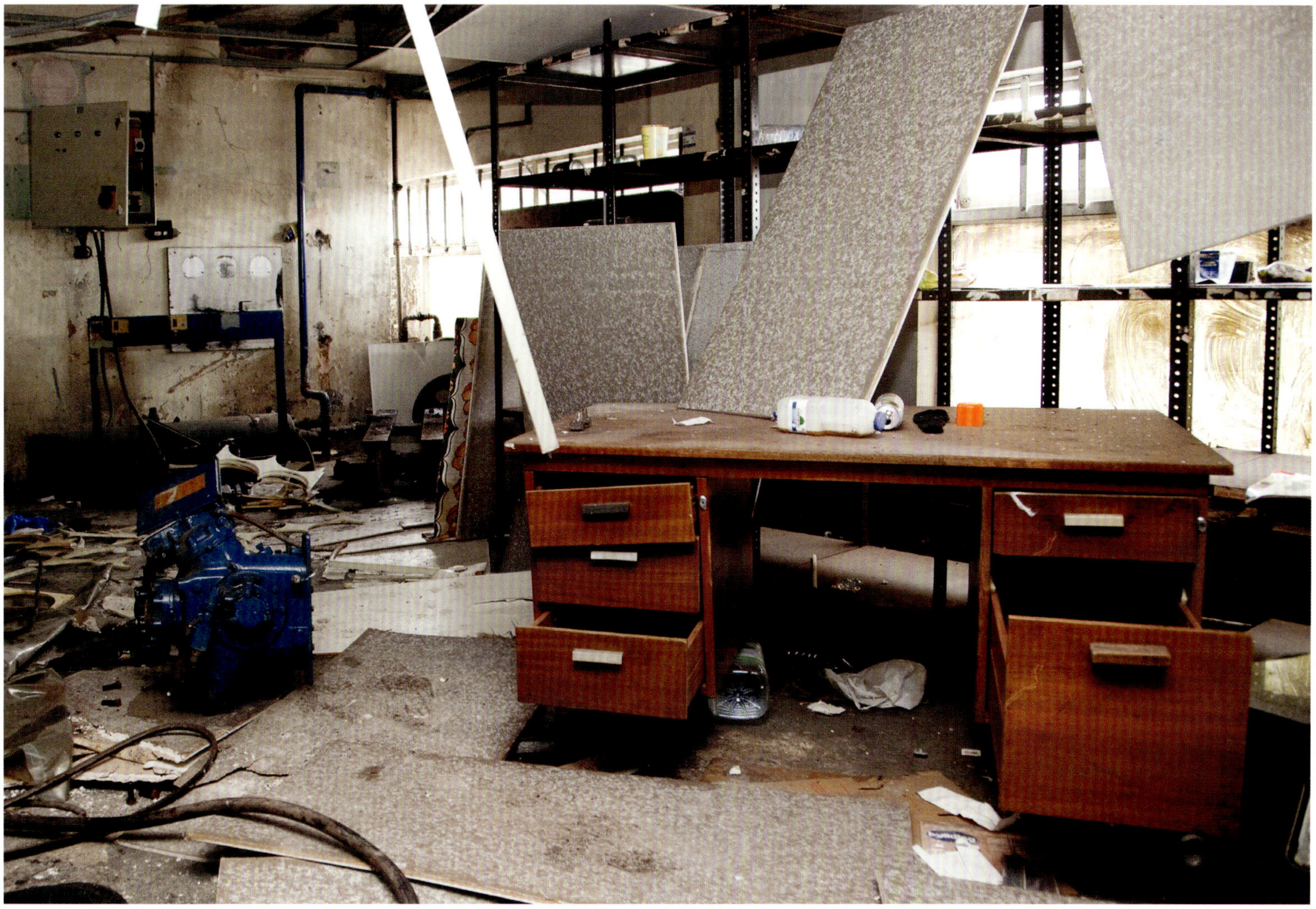

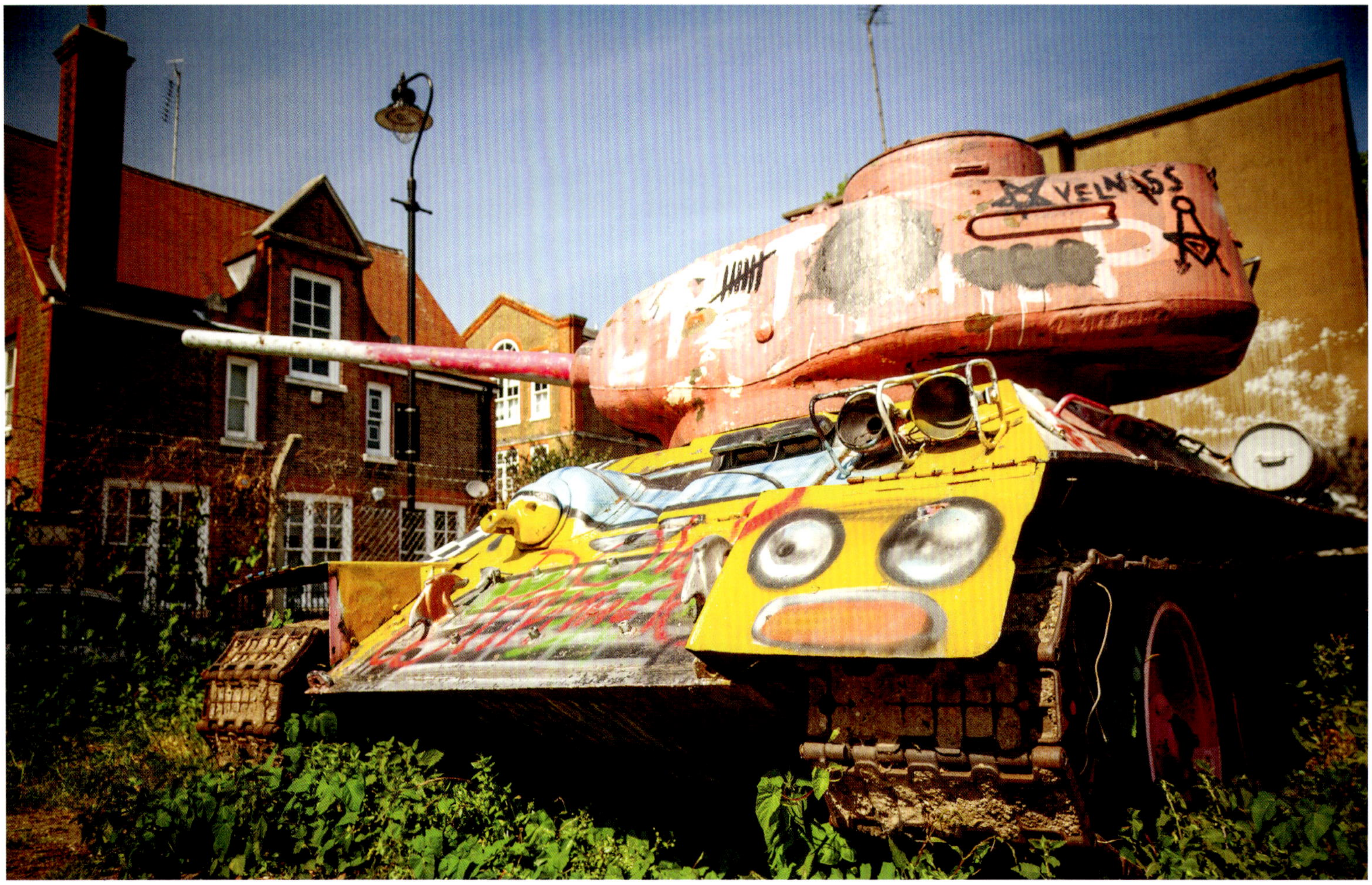

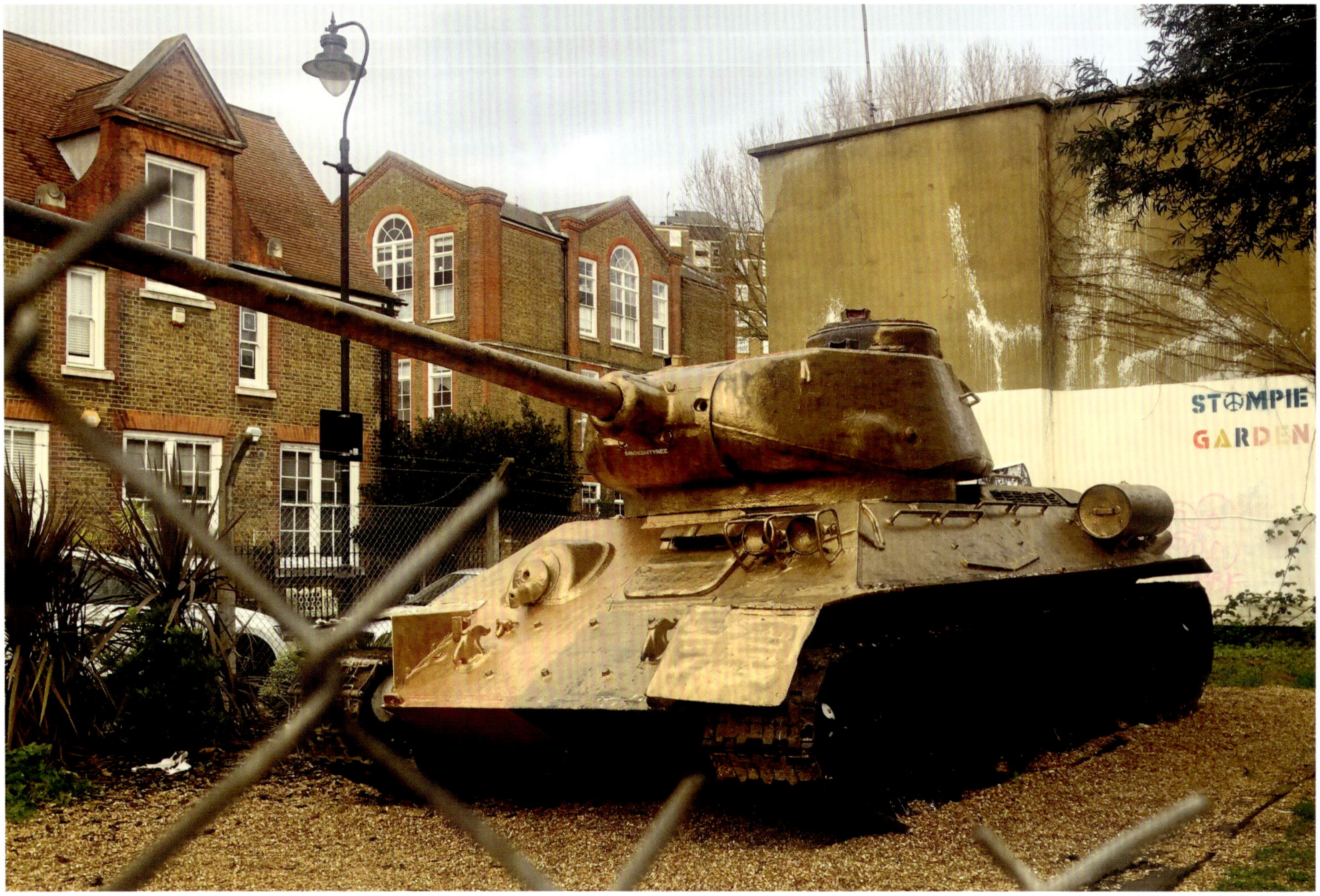

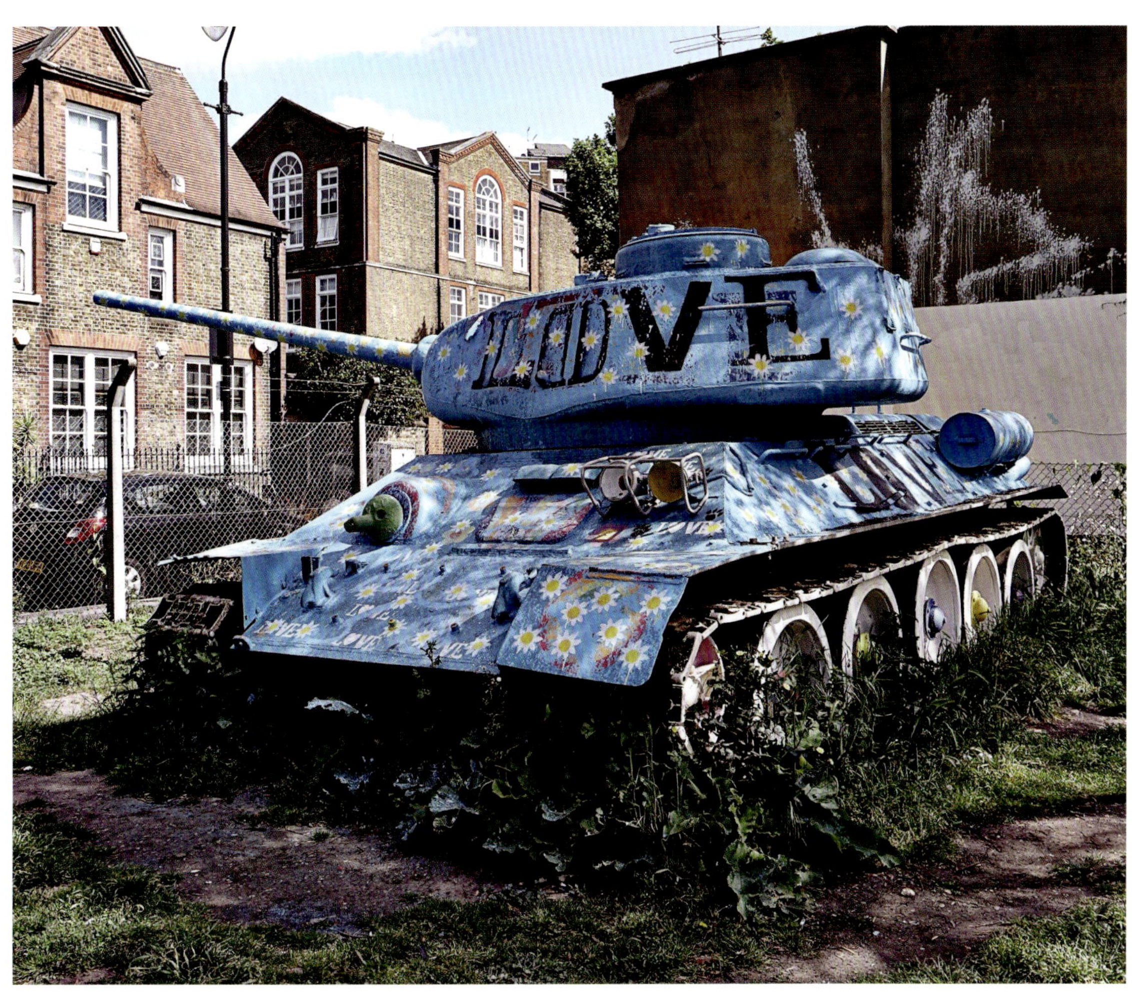

ALL PHOTOGRAPHS:

'Stompie' (former Soviet T-34/85 Medium Tank)

A 32-ton Russian tank is an incongruous site anywhere, but even more so beside a row of pretty 19th century houses in London's Bermondsey. Nicknamed 'Stompie' the tank arrived in London in the 1990s and was used for the 1995 film adaptation of *Richard III* staring Ian McKellen. It was bought by local resident Russell Gray and stands at the end of his road, following a planning misunderstanding about installing a 'tank'. Presumably Southwark Council assumed it would be the water or septic variety when they approved the application.

The photographs reflect the different paint schemes applied over the years.

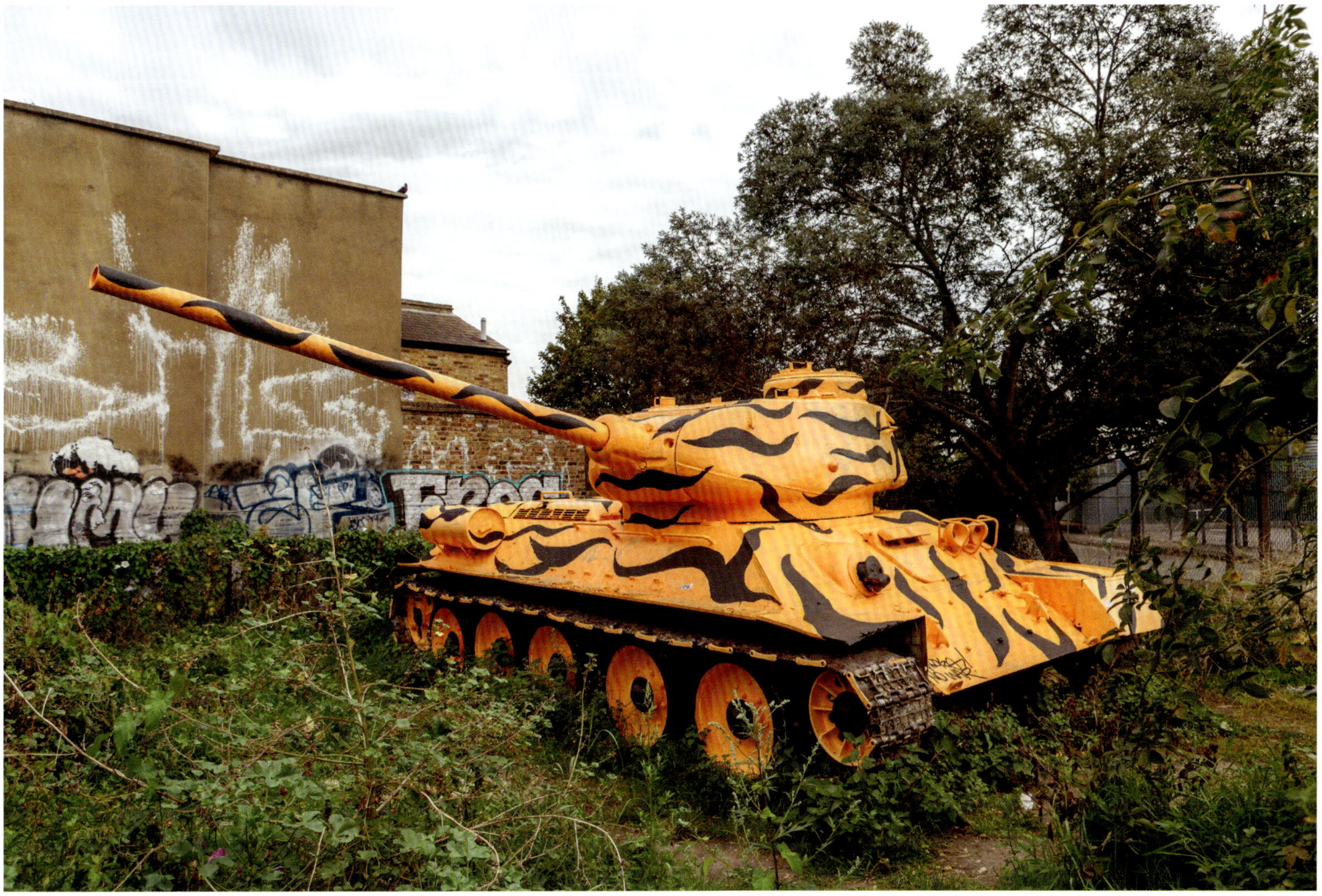

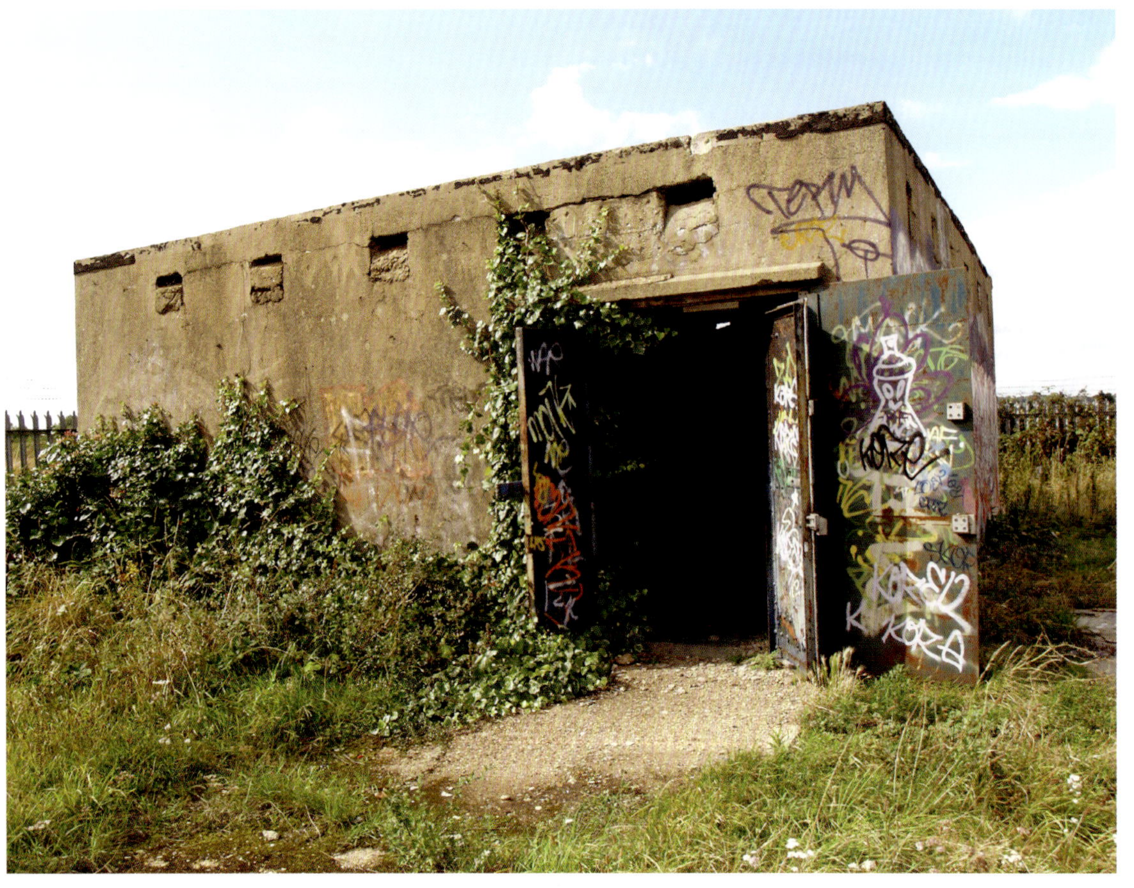

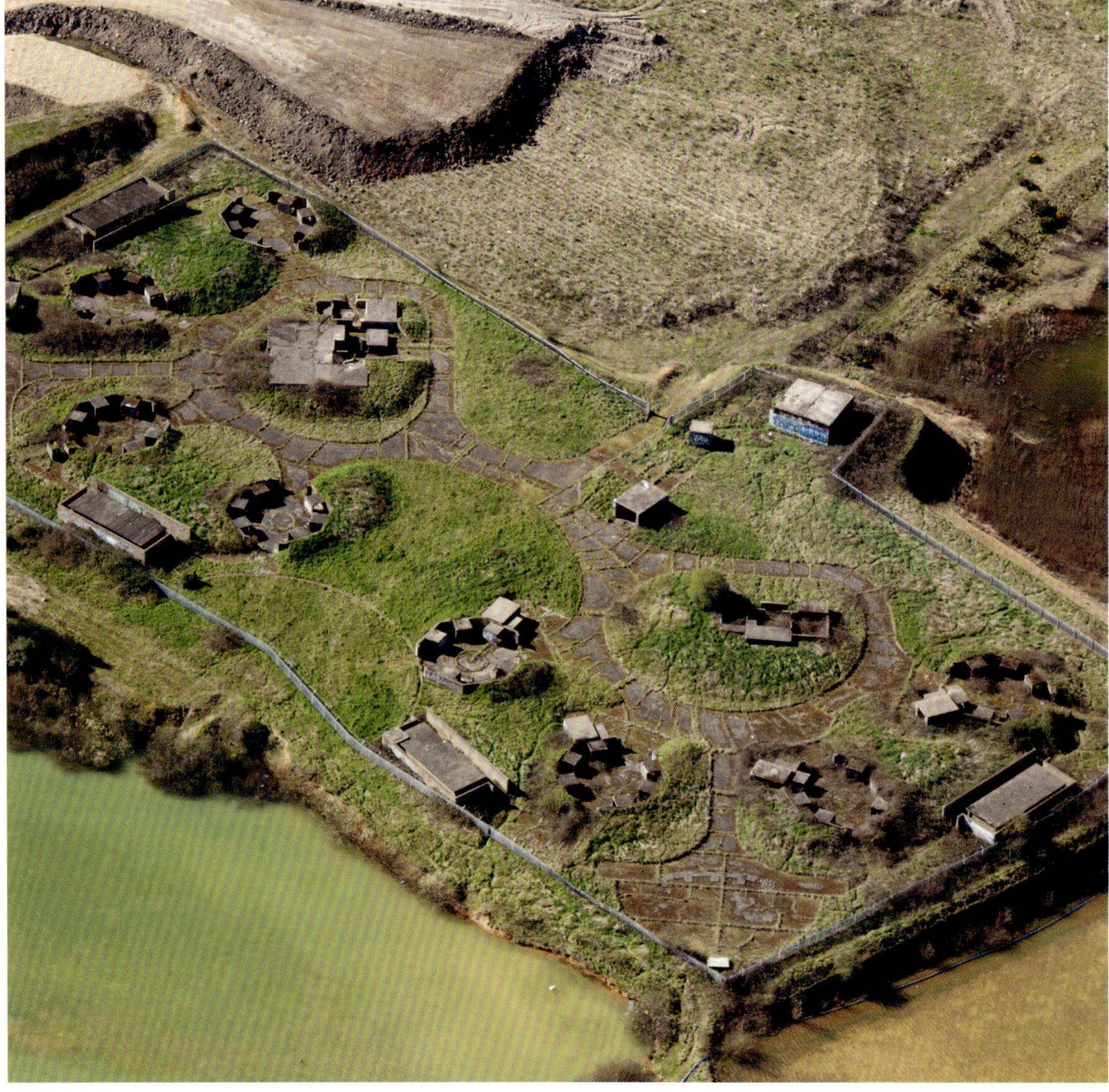

LEFT:

Slade Green, Dartford

In the peaceful, green expanse of Crayford Marshes one doesn't expect to stumble across a well-preserved chunk of World War II defences. This Grade II-listed anti-aircraft battery was built in the late 1930s and comprised a four-gun command post, pillboxes and an air raid shelter. With the emergence of strategic bombing in World War II, these batteries had heavy guns to defend against enemy bombers and were placed on the periphery of possible targets, such as large cities and industrial or military bases.

BELOW:

Anti-aircraft Battery, Chadwell Heath

Now part of a conservation area, the Chadwell Heath gun site was established in 1935 and had eight pits constructed for anti-aircraft guns. By 1942 the site was manned by over 280 personnel.

OPPOSITE:

Hammersmith Police Station

Built in 1939 and closed since late 2016, the station at 226 Shepherd's Bush Road is undergoing a £59 million renovation. The coat of arms seen here was carved by George Kruger Gray CBE, who is best-known for his designs of British and Commonwealth coins.

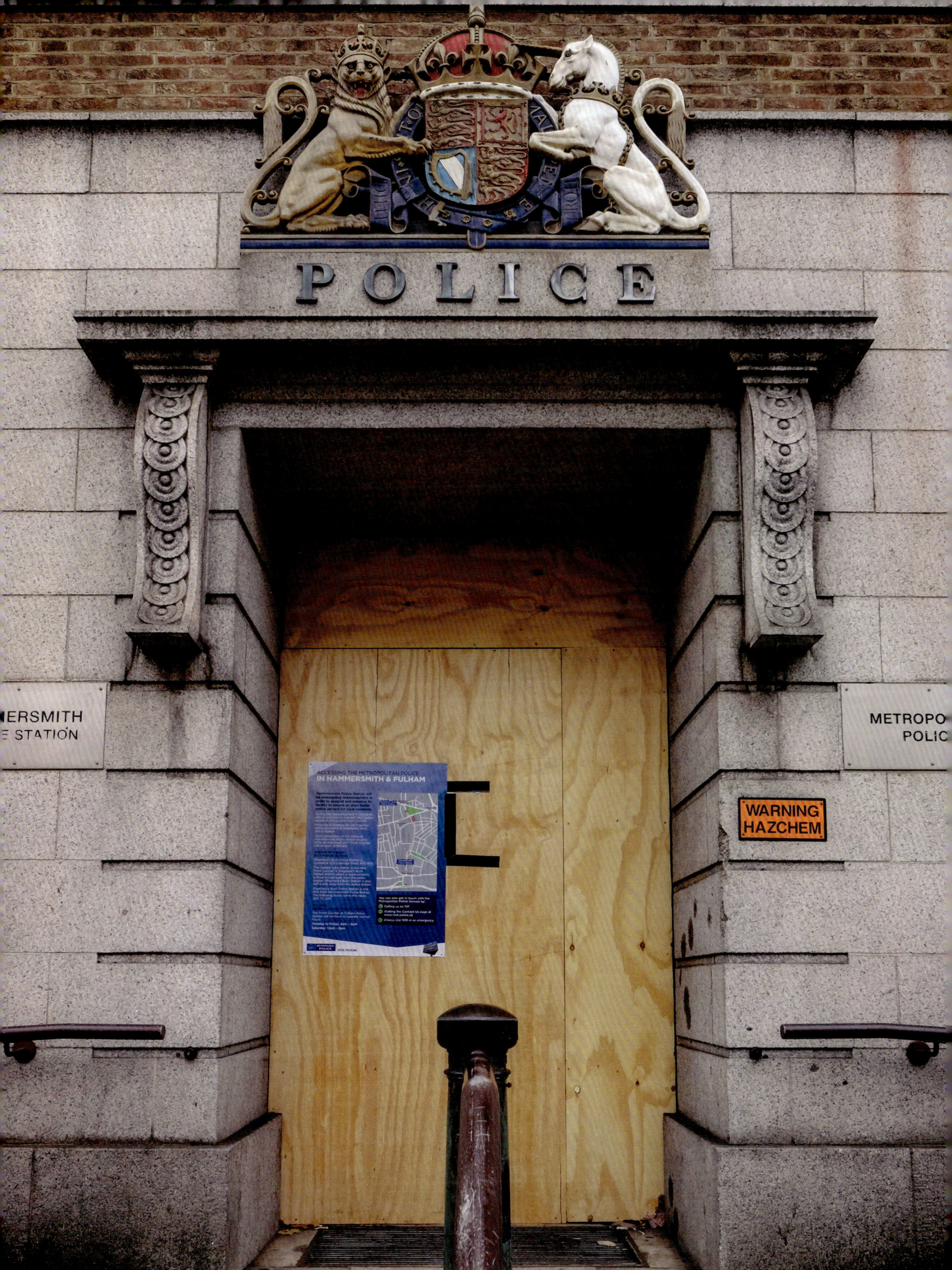
POLICE
ACCESSING THE METROPOLITAN POLICE
IN HAMMERSMITH & FULHAM
WARNING
HAZCHEM

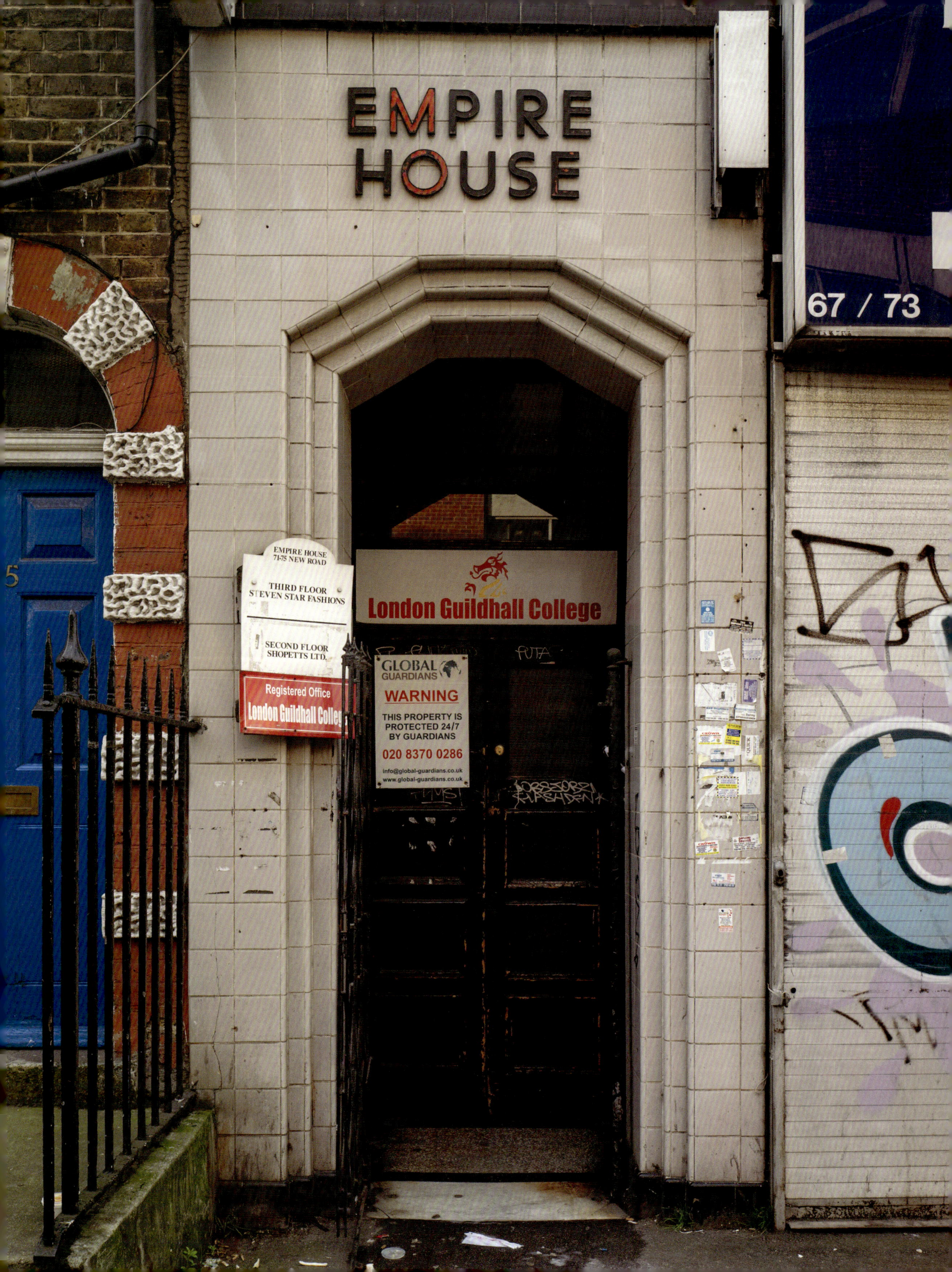

EMPIRE HOUSE
67 / 73
EMPIRE HOUSE
71-75 NEW ROAD
THIRD FLOOR
STEVEN STAR FASHIONS
SECOND FLOOR
SHOPETTS LTD.
Registered Office
London Guildhall College
London Guildhall College
GLOBAL GUARDIANS
WARNING
THIS PROPERTY IS PROTECTED 24/7 BY GUARDIANS
020 8370 0286
info@global-guardians.co.uk
www.global-guardians.co.uk

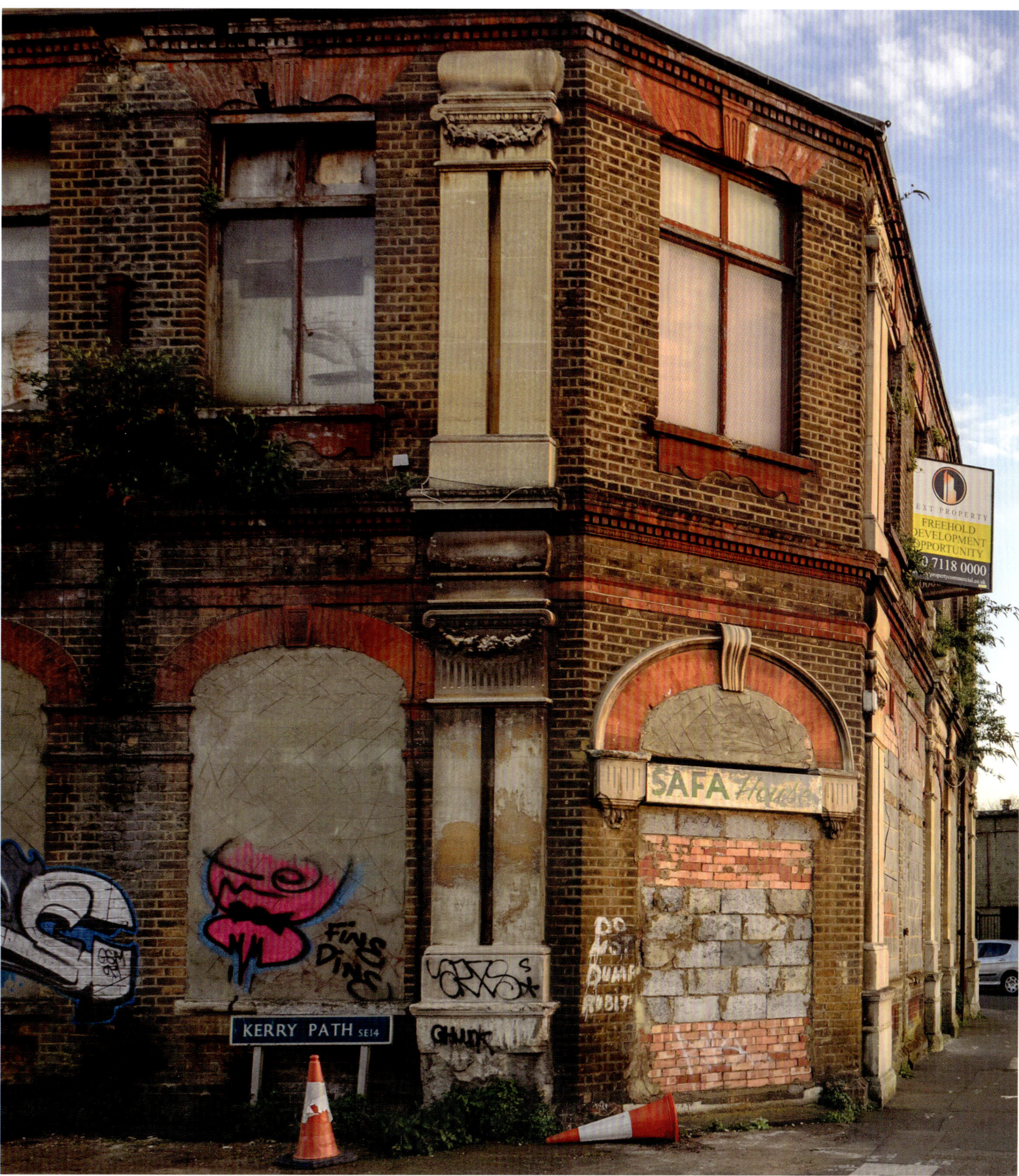

OPPOSITE:

Empire House,
67–73 New Road, Whitechapel

Clues like the typography, recessed geometric doorway and tiles hint at Empire House's Art Deco design. This entrance is part of a large clothing factory built in 1934, which is currently being converted into offices and workshops.

ABOVE:

Safa House, Deptford

Built in 1890 as a leisure and entertainment space, Safa House previously catered to local workers. These were mainly from J. Stone & Co Ltd, which produced nails for shipbuilding in Greenwich and later established a foundry on Arklow Road in 1881.

As the company expanded to over 700 employees, the working men's club included a concert room, gymnasium, reading room, library, coffee bar and dining rooms.

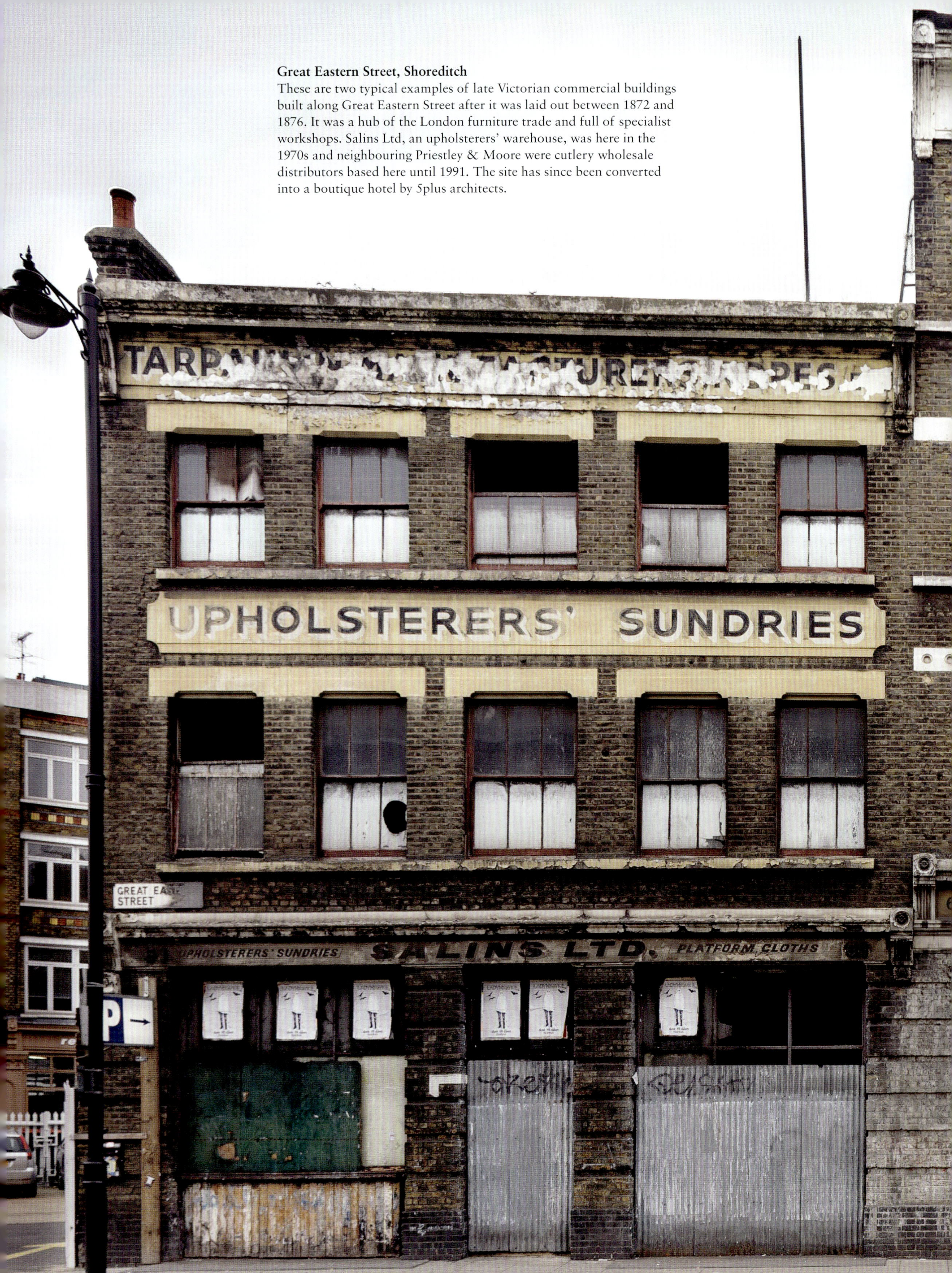

Great Eastern Street, Shoreditch

These are two typical examples of late Victorian commercial buildings built along Great Eastern Street after it was laid out between 1872 and 1876. It was a hub of the London furniture trade and full of specialist workshops. Salins Ltd, an upholsterers' warehouse, was here in the 1970s and neighbouring Priestley & Moore were cutlery wholesale distributors based here until 1991. The site has since been converted into a boutique hotel by 5plus architects.

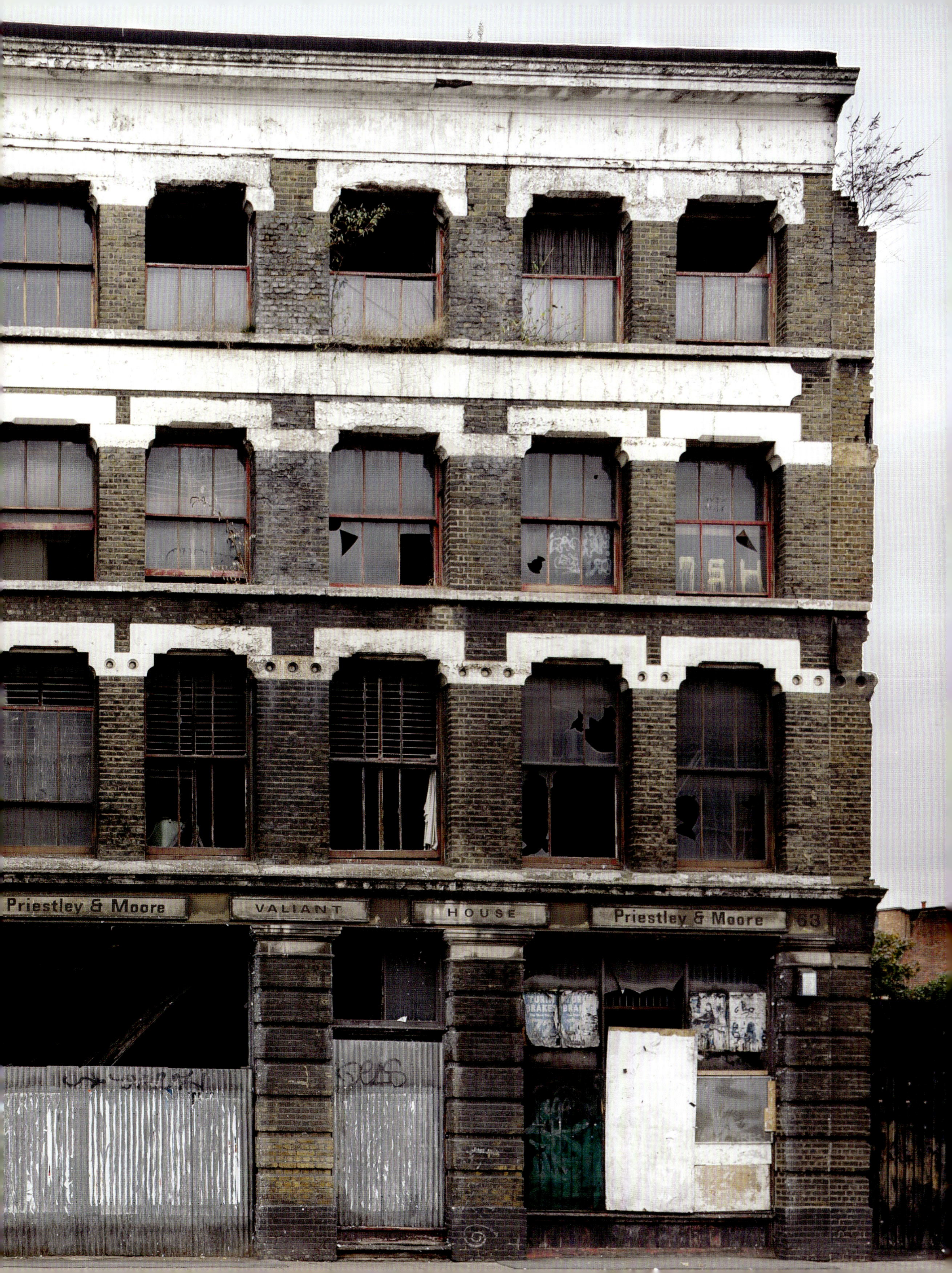
Priestley & Moore
VALIANT
HOUSE
Priestley & Moore
63

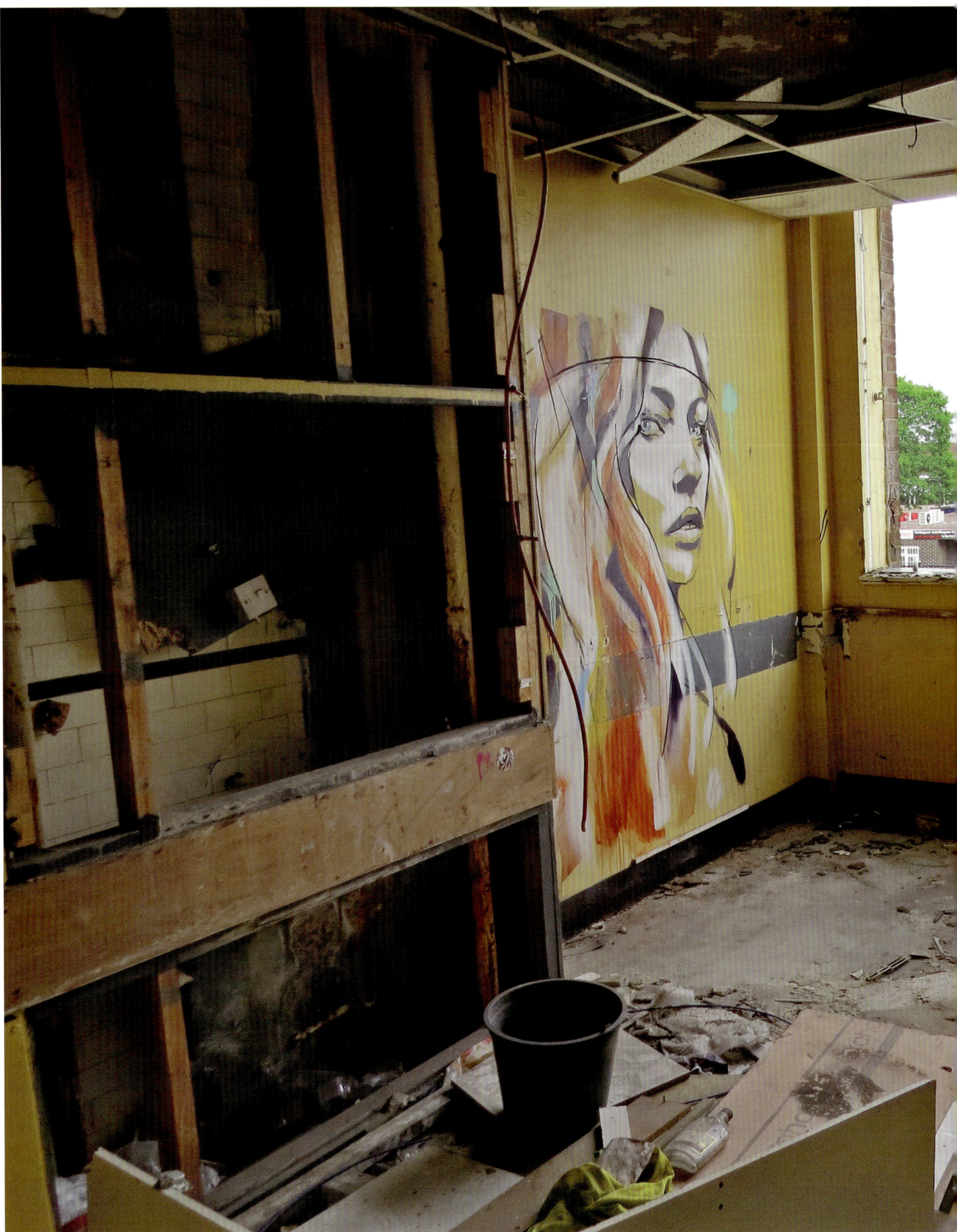

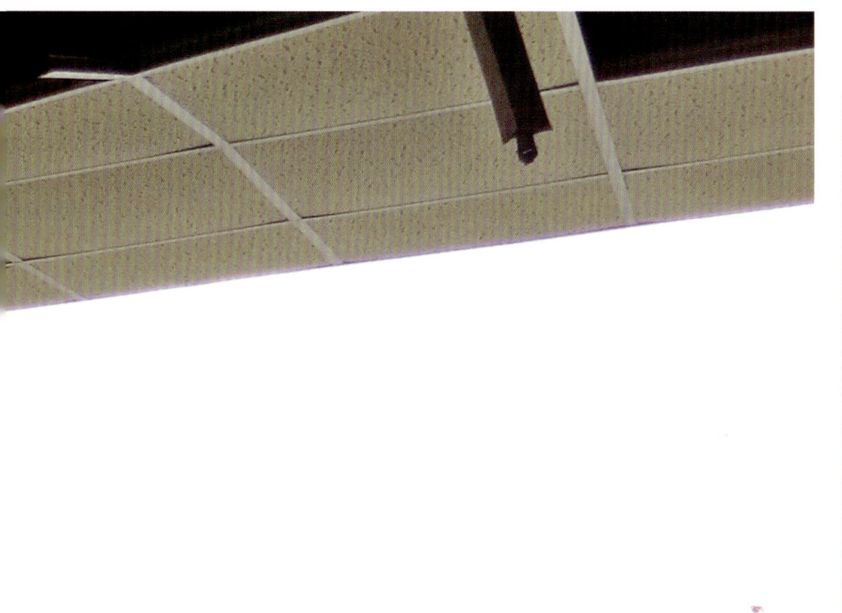

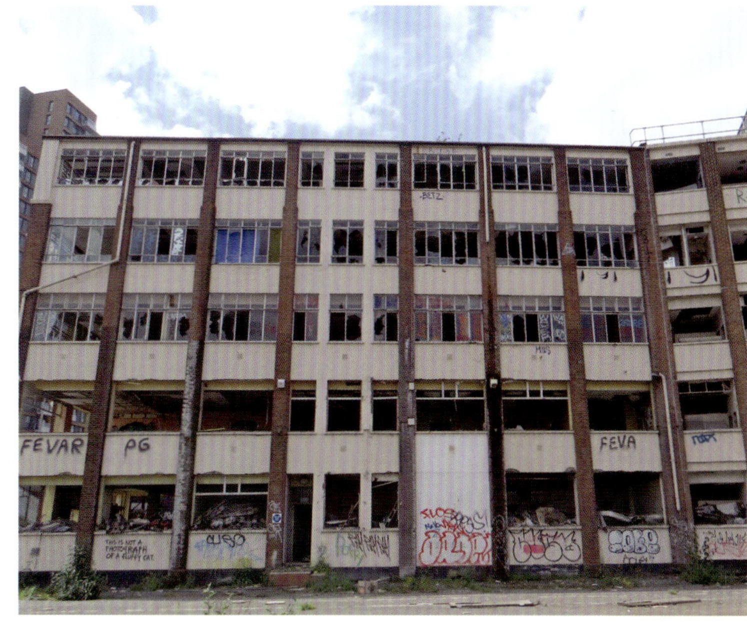

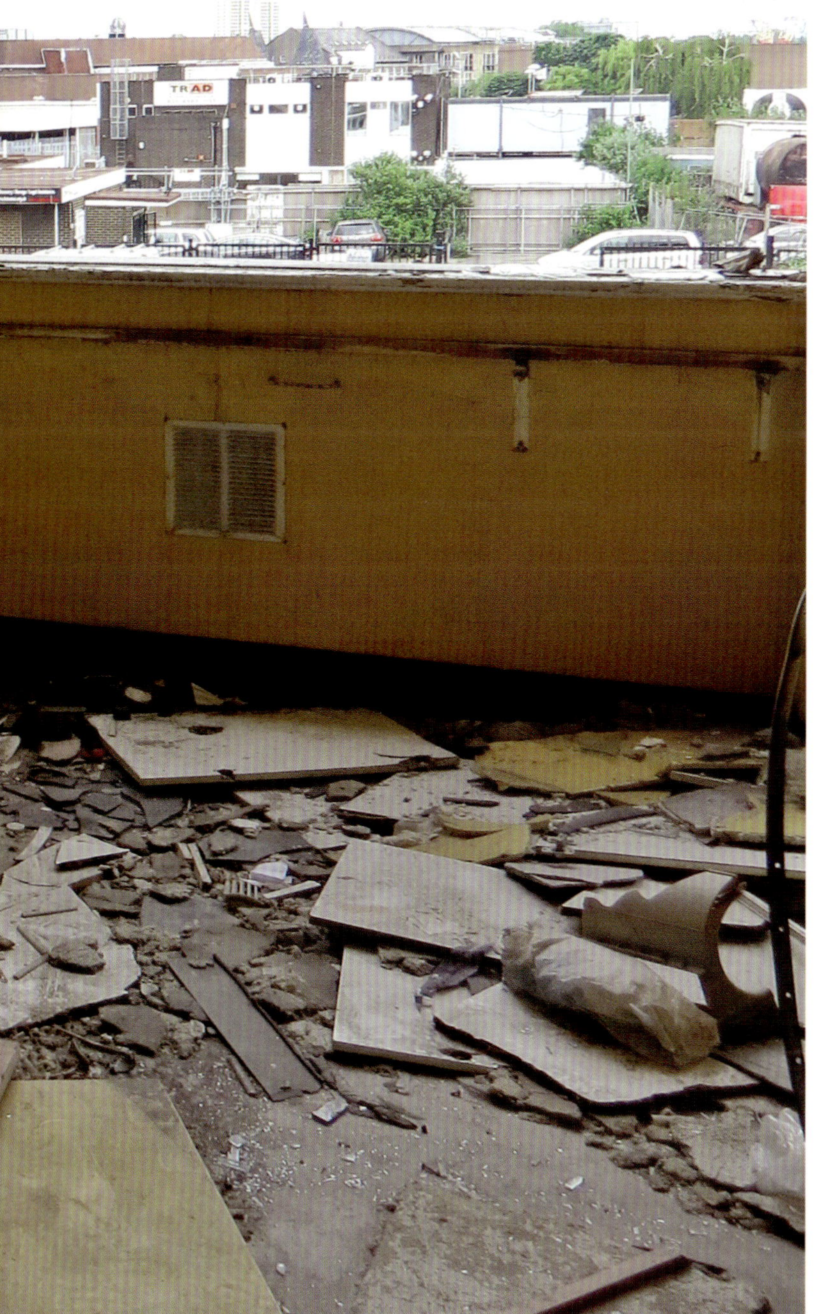

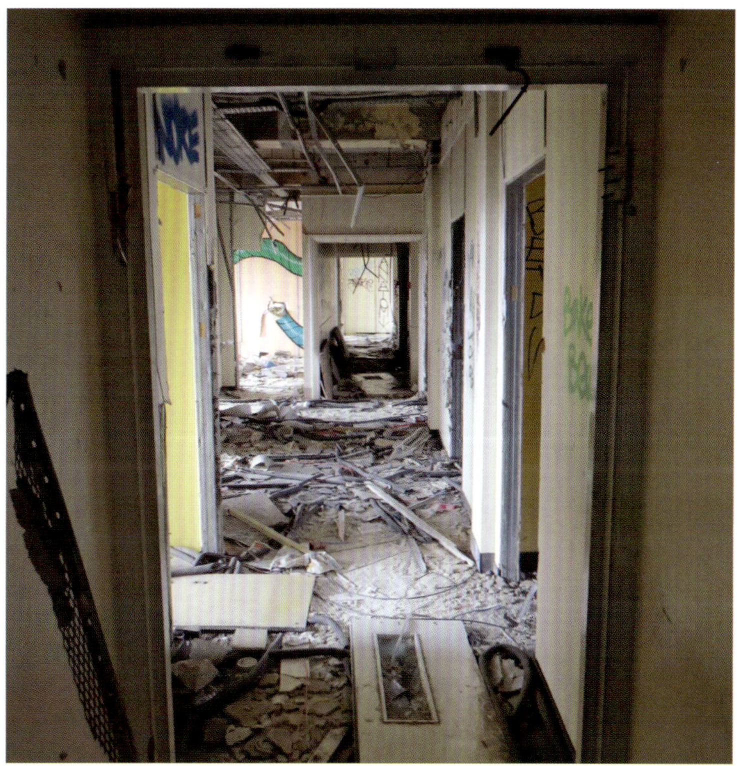

ALL PHOTOGRAPHS:

Tawse Offices, Bromley-by-Bow

Opposite Bromley-By-Bow Station stood a gutted office block that was once owned by Brown & Tawse, a Scottish iron merchants founded in 1881. In 1897 the company bought two of its largest customers in London, one of which was based in Bromley-By-Bow. Although the building has since been demolished the company is still in business. Today, the site is being developed to provide 900 homes.

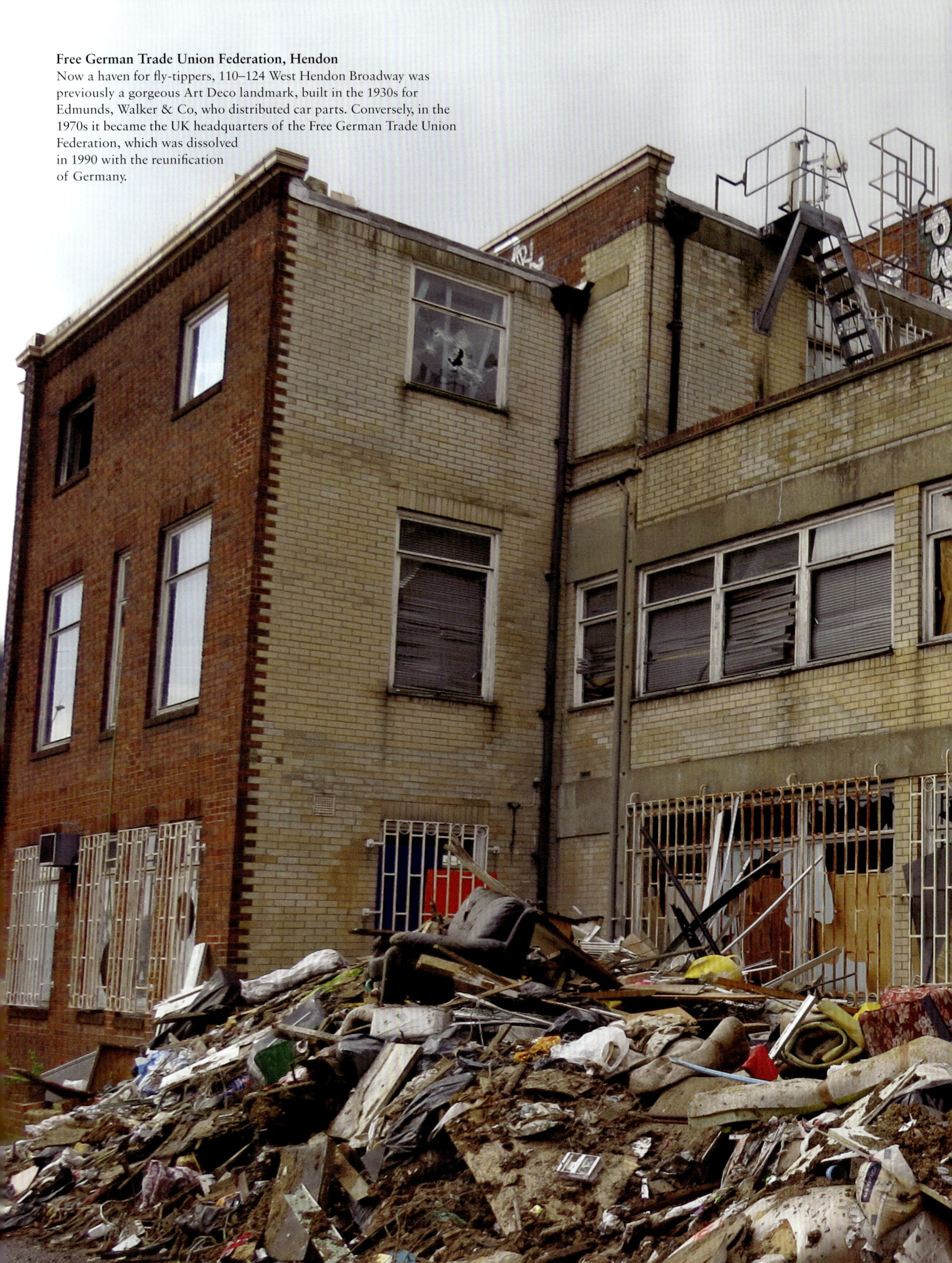

Free German Trade Union Federation, Hendon
Now a haven for fly-tippers, 110–124 West Hendon Broadway was previously a gorgeous Art Deco landmark, built in the 1930s for Edmunds, Walker & Co, who distributed car parts. Conversely, in the 1970s it became the UK headquarters of the Free German Trade Union Federation, which was dissolved in 1990 with the reunification of Germany.

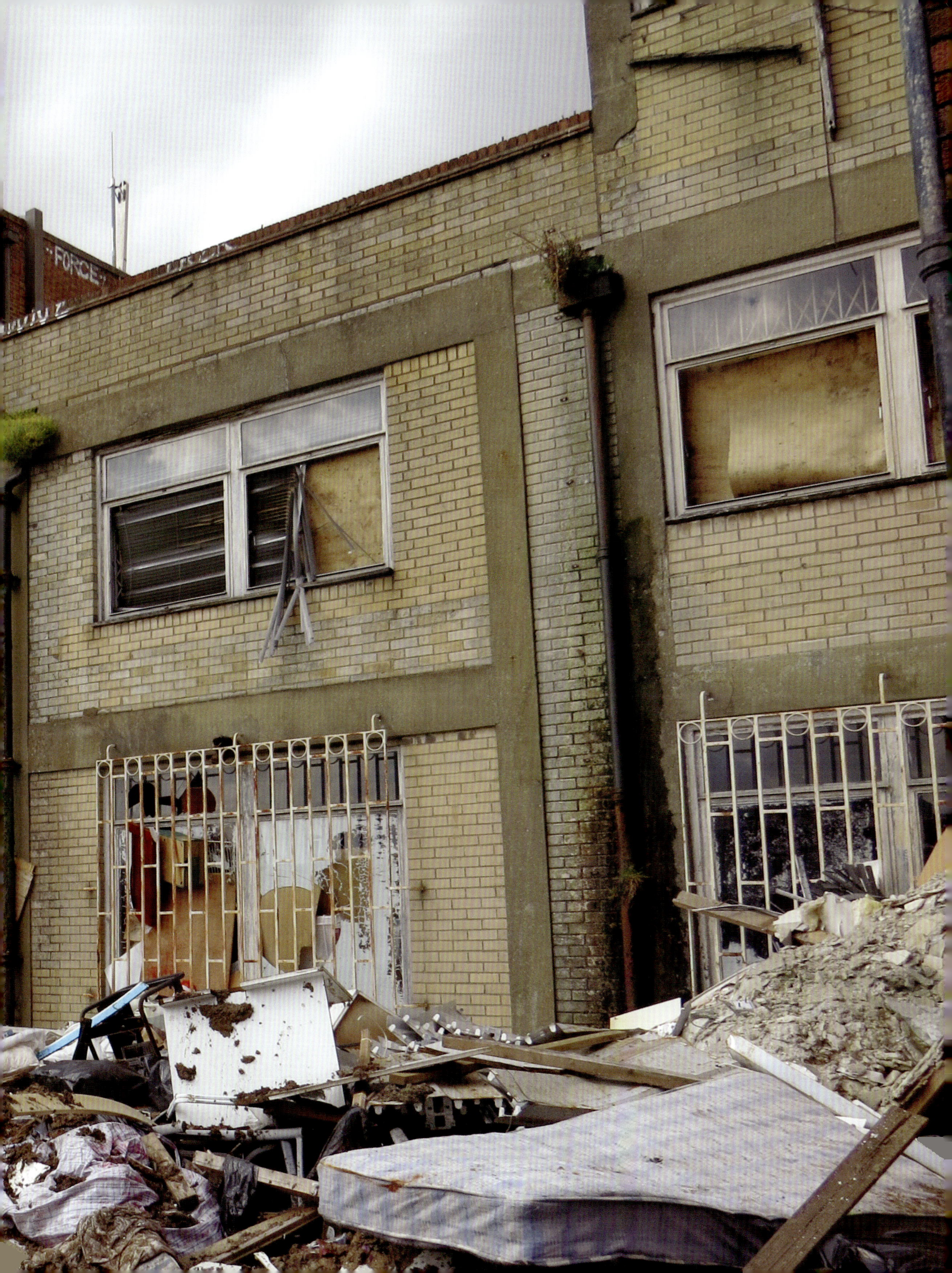
FORCE

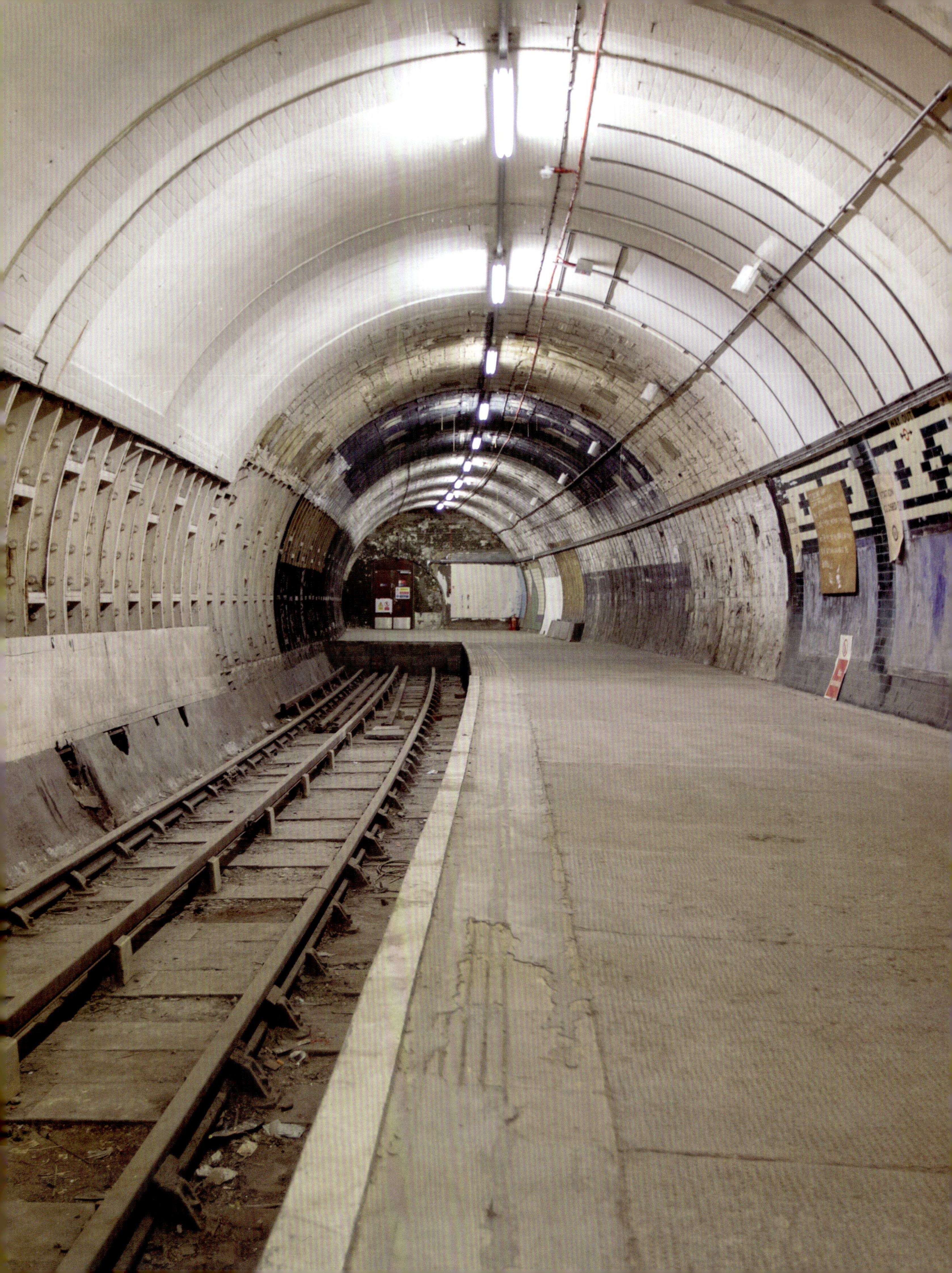

Transport

London has been a pioneer in transportation throughout history, most famously with the world's first underground railway, which was established in 1863. Over a century and a half later, the methods for travelling across London have been upgraded and some aspects have been pushed to one side. In this chapter we explore abandoned tube stations, referred to as 'ghost stations', which – though redundant for commuters – are far too valuable to lie in ruin and have been used for many unusual purposes. Happily many of them are also now accessible through guided tours run by the London Transport Museum.

Those tours are very popular, because if there's one thing that gets a London history geek fired up, it's the prospect of 'secret' tunnels and passageways under the regular city thoroughfares. London has never existed as a sensible, grid-like design, carefully imagined by urban planners. Its streets are not straight, they wiggle all over the place, and the growth beyond the City walls was no less haphazard. During its 2,000-year lifespan, London has developed many layers of architecture – what remains of the Roman city is on average seven metres (22 ft) below the current street level. It is to some of these subterranean spaces that we now turn.

OPPOSITE:
Aldwych Station
Aldwych tube station opened to the public in 1907 but never got enough footfall to warrant its existence. It did, however, prove useful, acting as a bomb shelter for Londoners during both World Wars and providing a safe place to store artefacts from London's museums. Today it's mainly used for filming purposes.

OVERLEAF:
Kingsway Tram Subway, Holborn
In 1898 the London County Council wanted to clear the Holborn slums. The new, wide street was named Kingsway after King Edward VII and provided an opportunity to install a tramway tunnel beneath. The last tram journey was in 1952 and the south section of the Tunnel has since been converted for road vehicles.

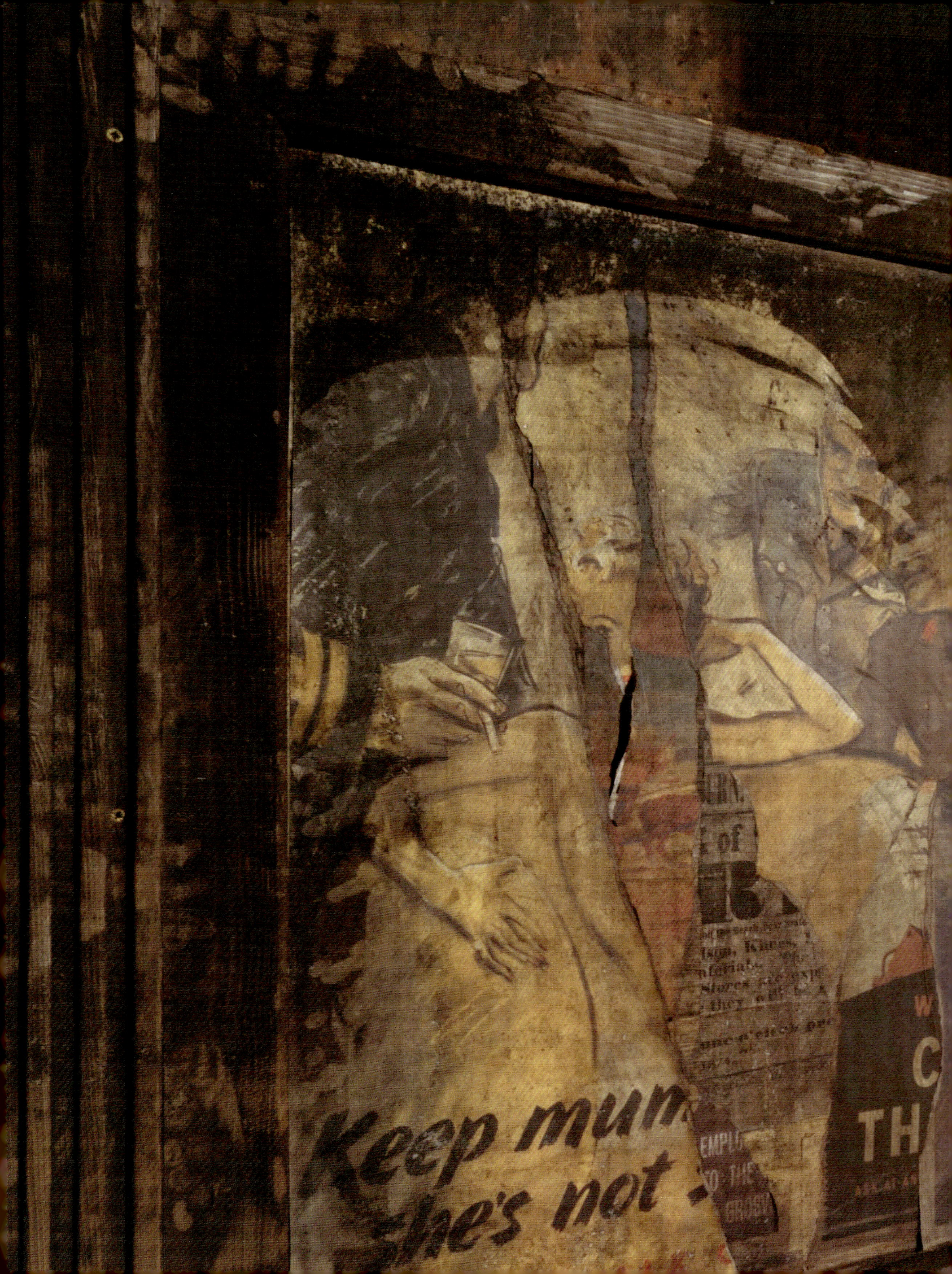
Keep mum
she's not

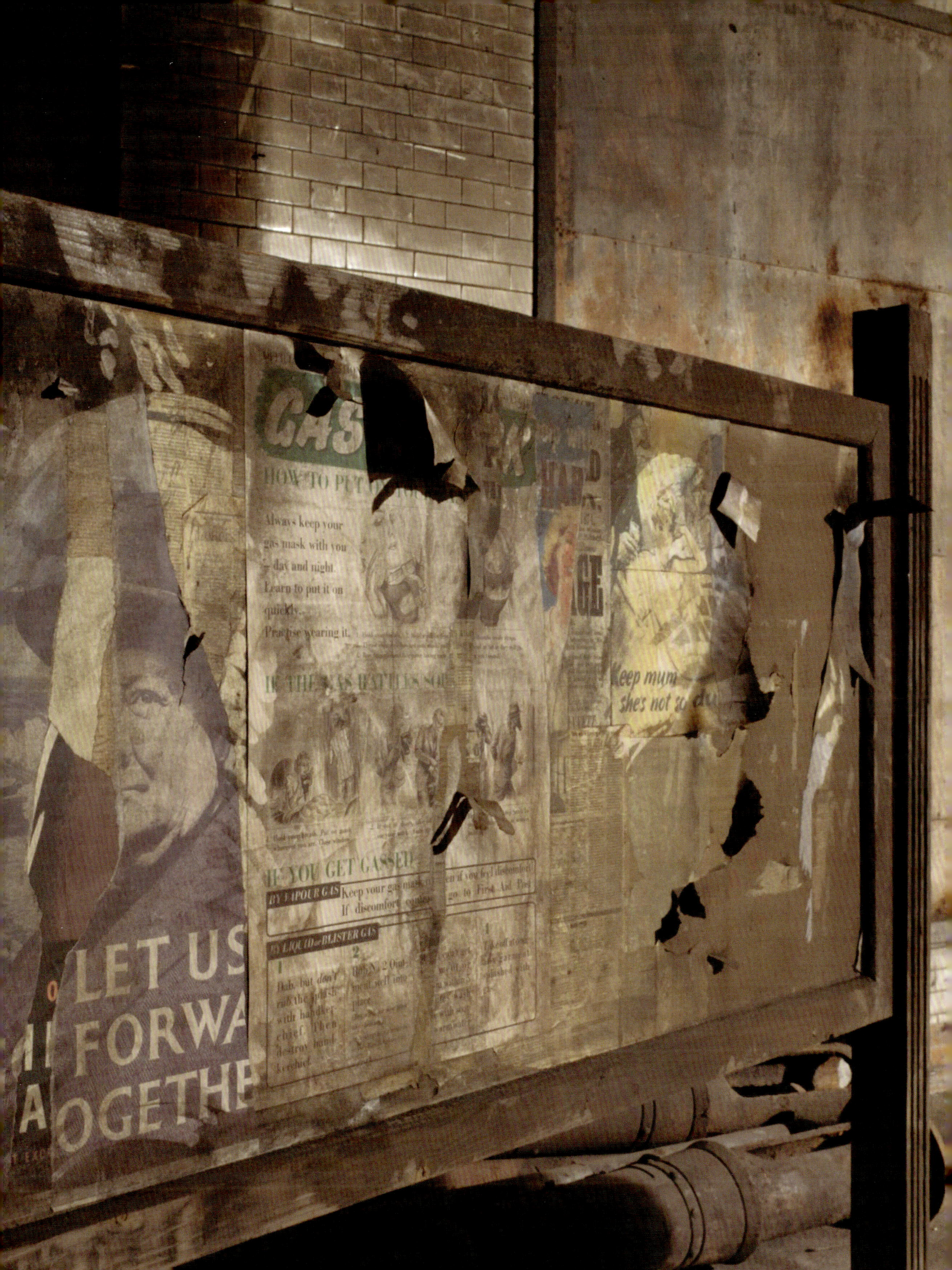

GAS
Always keep your
gas mask with you
day and night.
Learn to put it on
quickly.
Practise wearing it.
IF YOU GET GASSED
BY VAPOUR GAS
BY LIQUID or BLISTER GAS
LET US
FORWA
OGETHE
Keep mum
she's not so

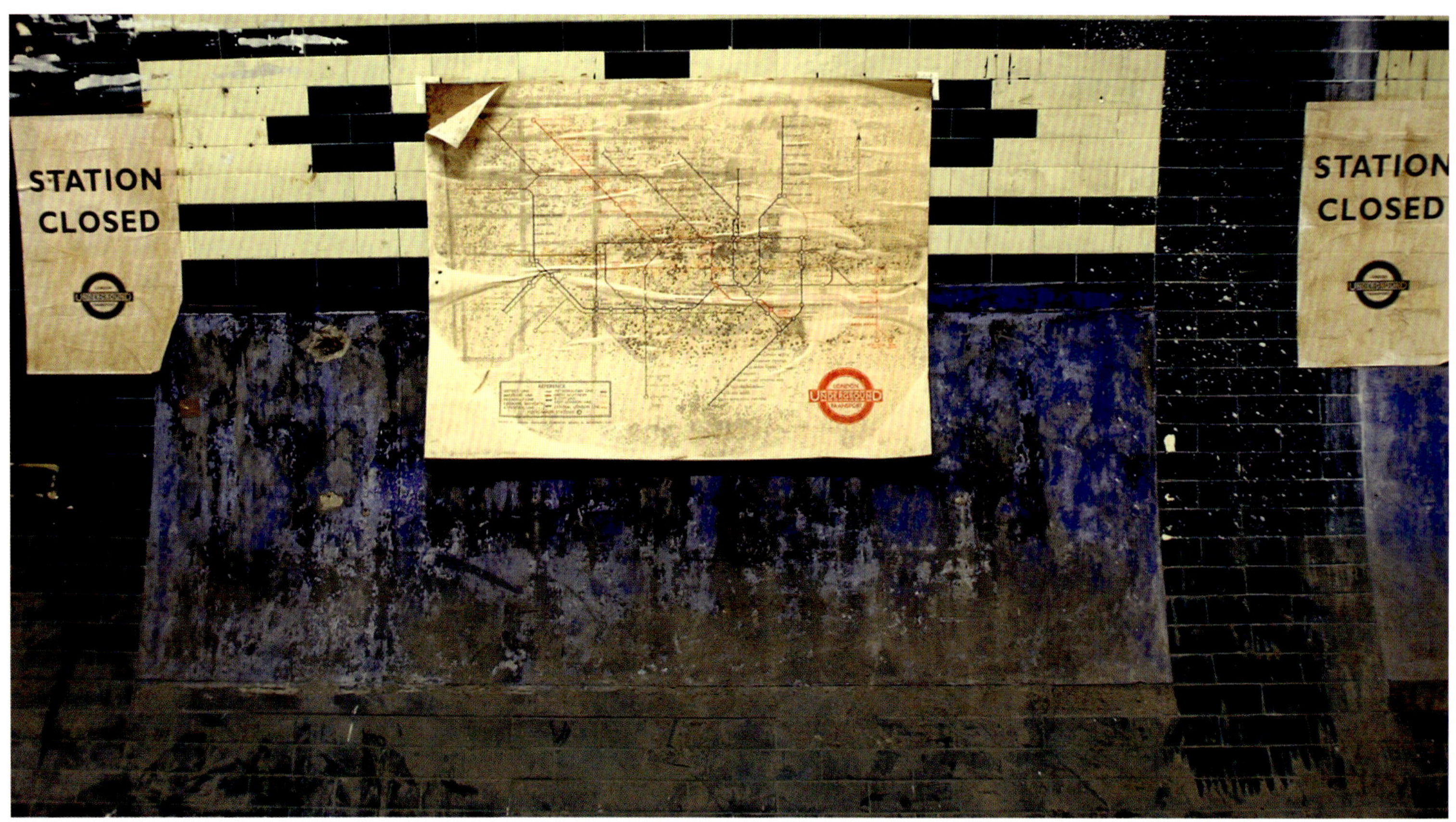
STATION
CLOSED
STATION
CLOSED

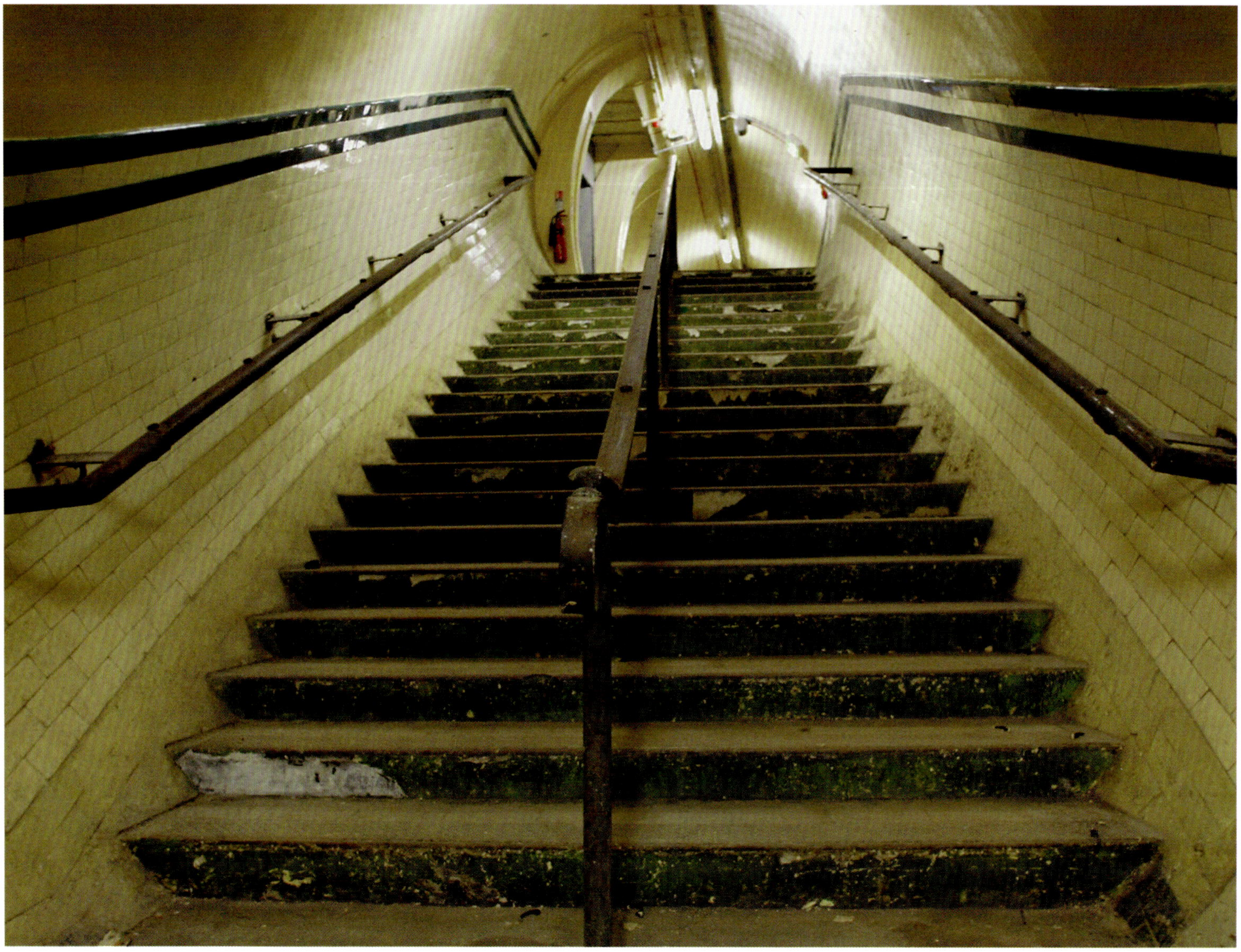

ALL PHOTOGRAPHS ON THESE PAGES:

Aldwych Station

'Aldwych' is an Anglo-Saxon word meaning 'old market' or 'trading' place. When they arrived in London after the Romans had departed in around 410 CE, the Saxons chose not settle in the old City of London, instead establishing a settlement outside the walls near today's Covent Garden. Confusingly, when this station first opened it was known as Strand Station, changing its name to Aldwych in 1915.

OVERLEAF:

Down Street Station, Mayfair

Another defunct tube station, Down Street was built close to Green Park Station and its entrance can still be seen. It was unpopular as a station because of its design and closed after only 25 years. The rich oxblood glazed tiles of the former tube station are easy to spot along Down Street in Mayfair today.

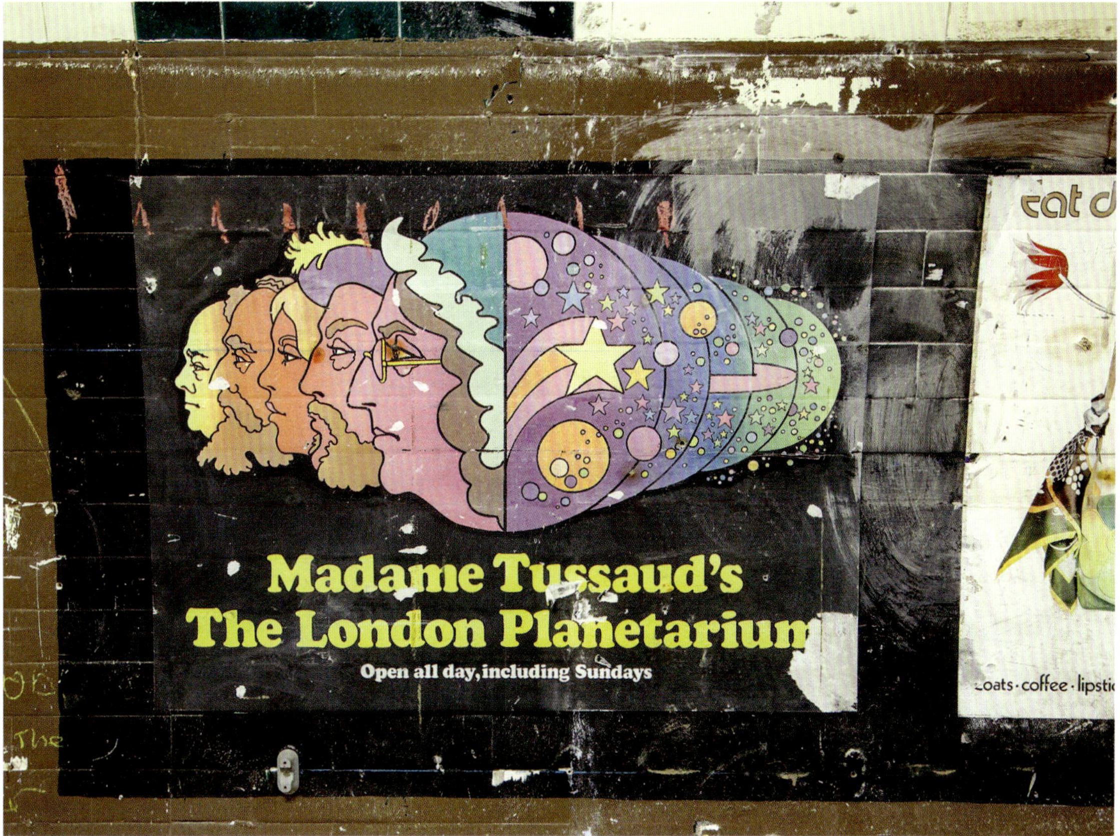

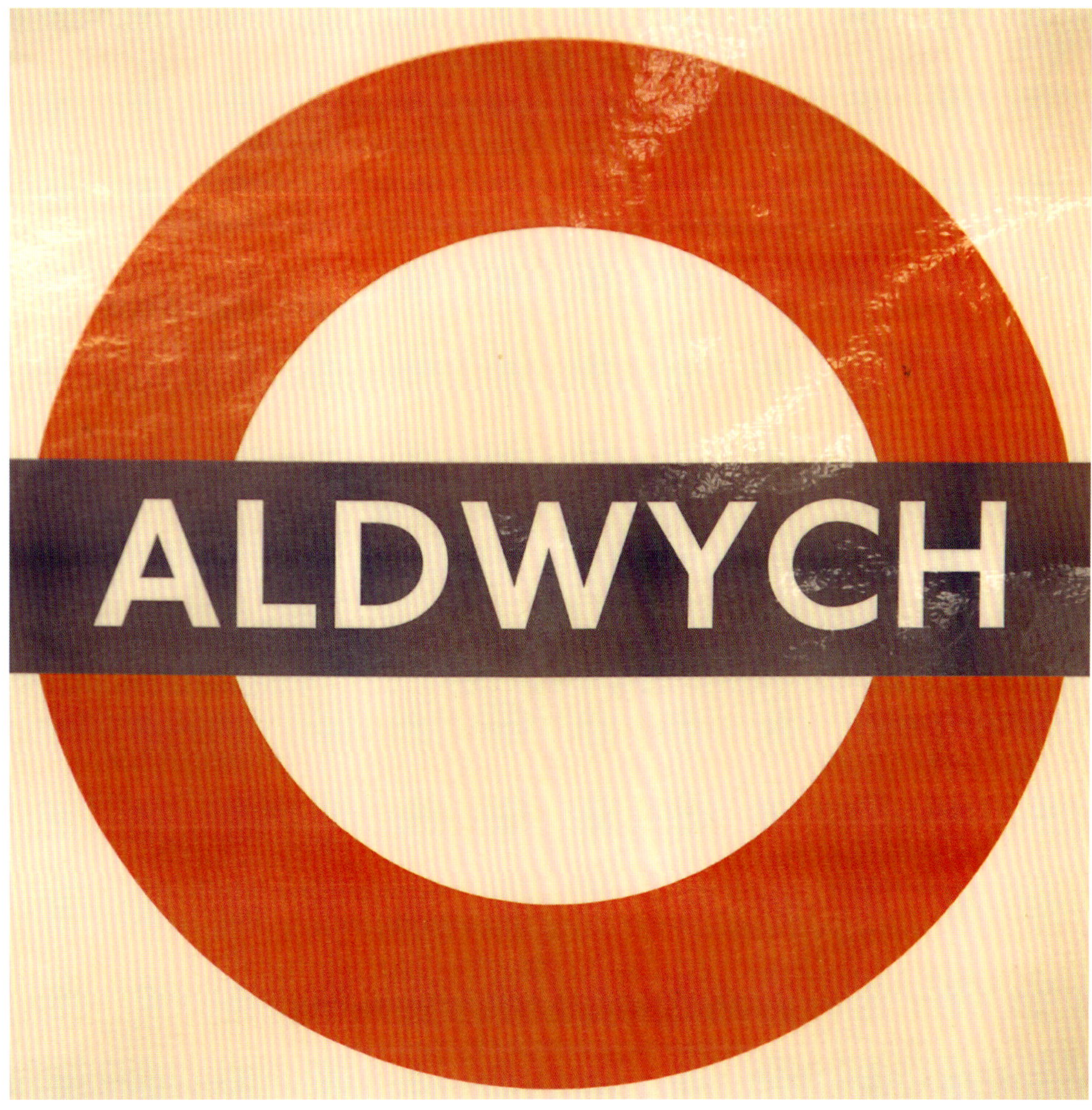

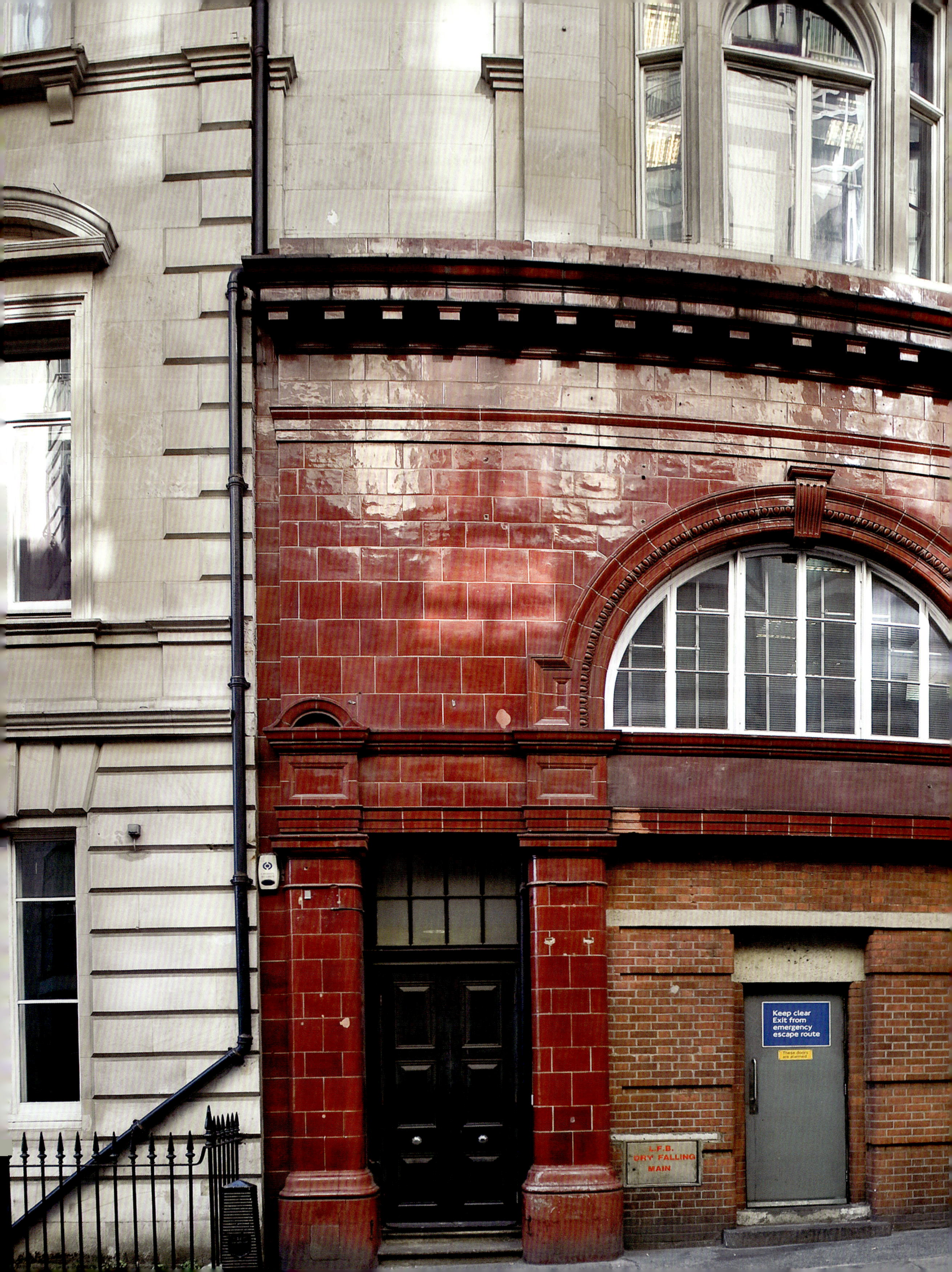
Keep clear
Exit from
emergency
escape route
L.F.B.
DRY FALLING
MAIN

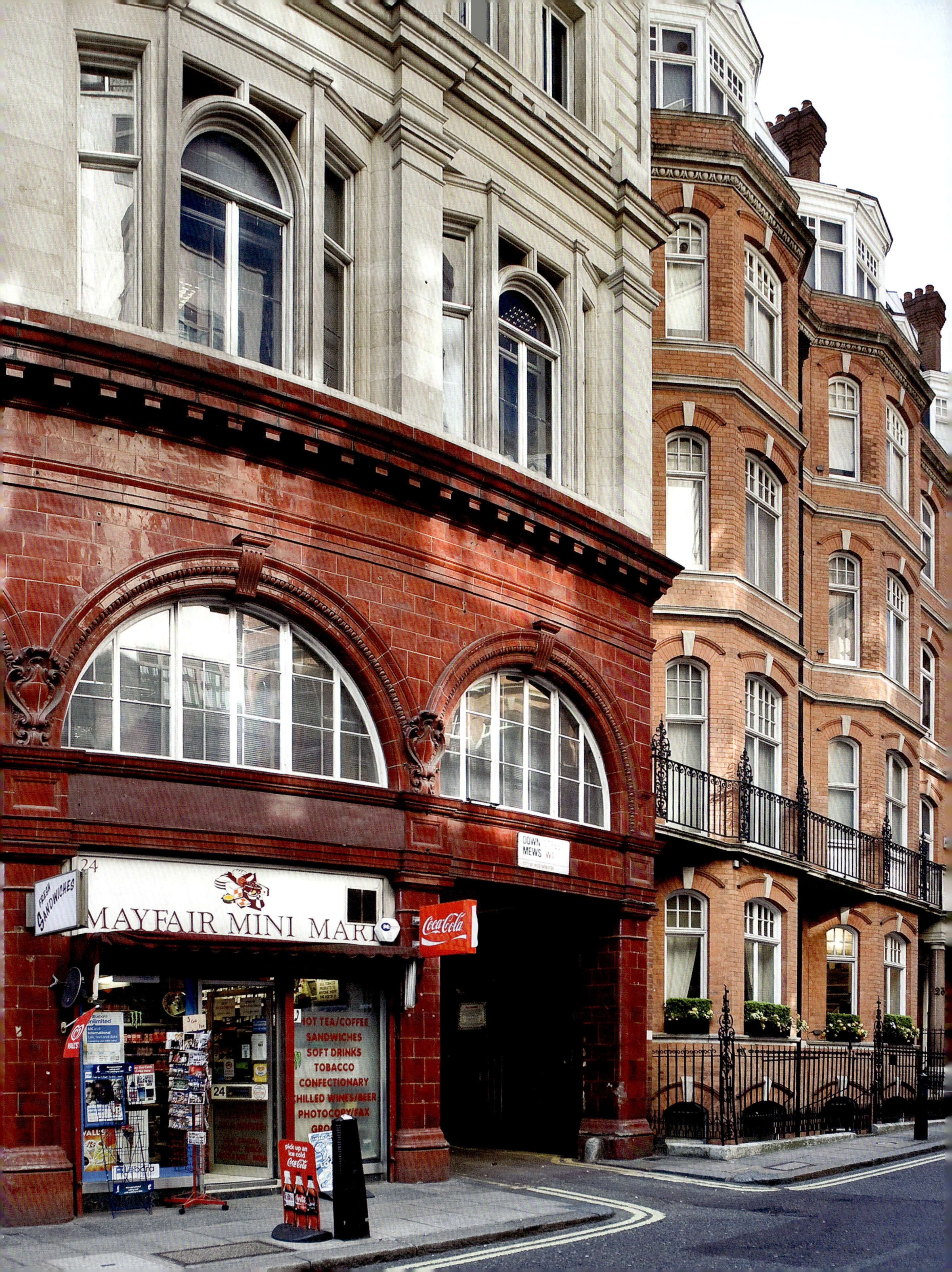
SANDWICHES
Coca-Cola
SANDWICHES
SOFT DRINKS
TOBACCO
CONFECTIONARY
24

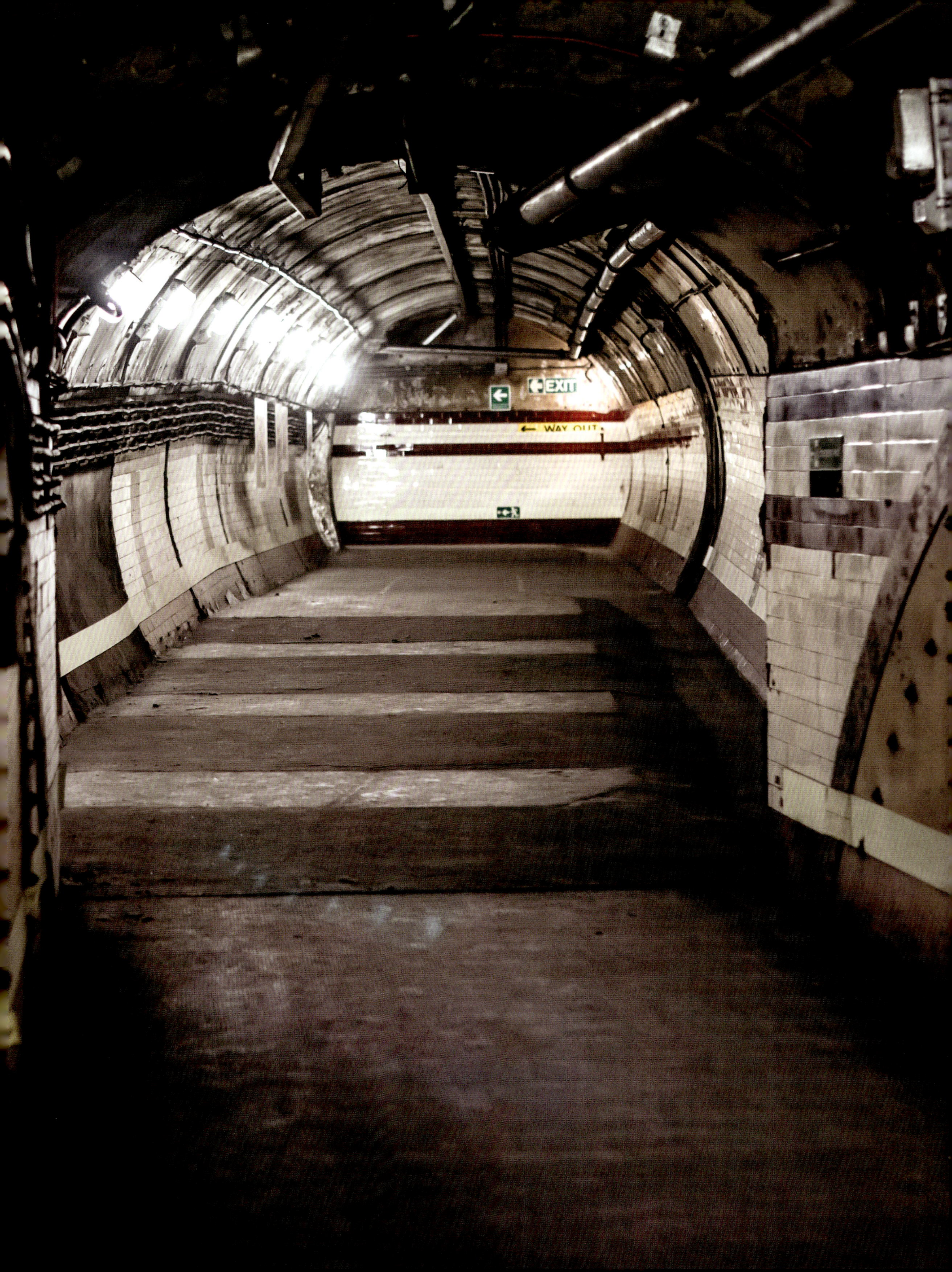
EXIT
WAY OUT

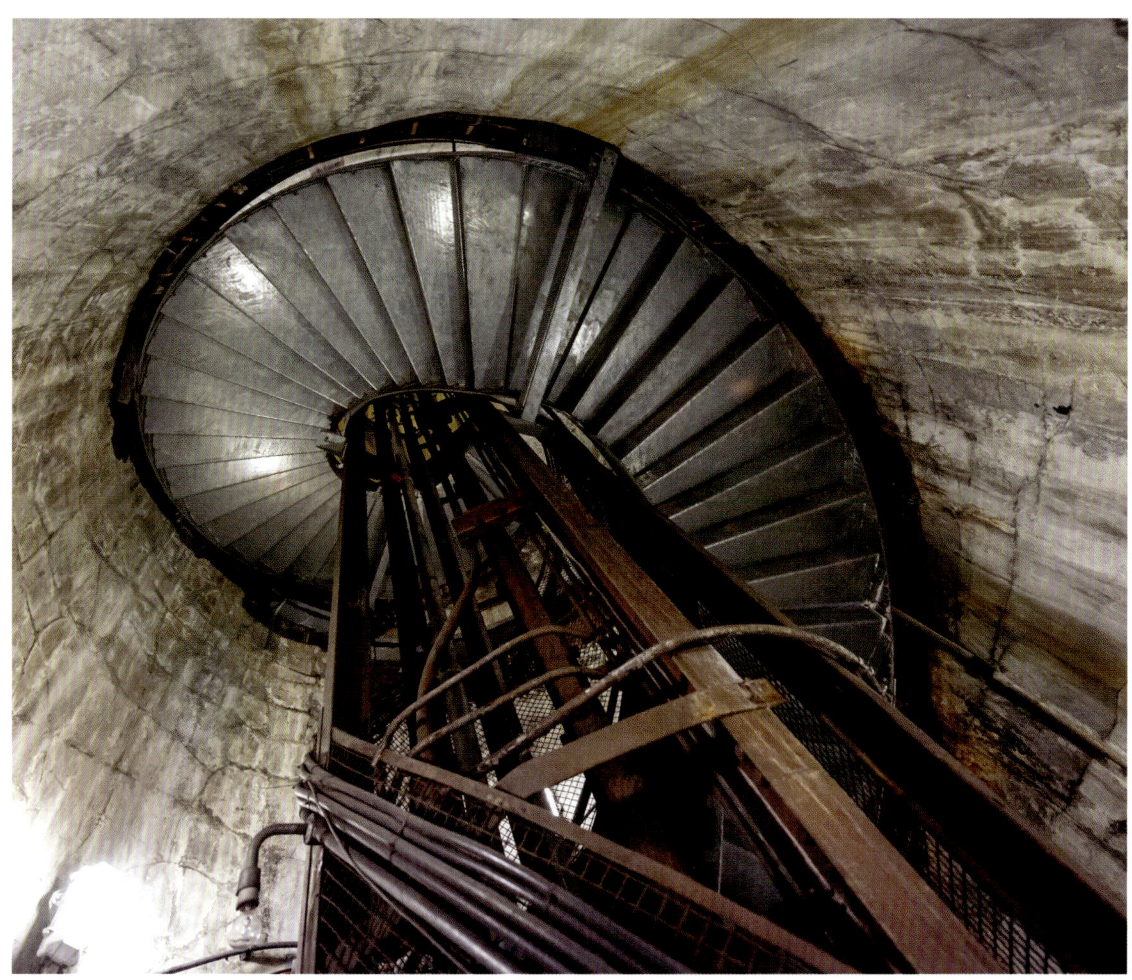

ALL PHOTOGRAPHS:

Down Street Station, Mayfair

To reach the former Down Street platforms, commuters had to descend 22 metres (72 ft) down a spiral staircase and then walk along long tunnels below the rumbling traffic of Piccadilly above. Although this was a nuisance for commuters, the tunnels found new tenants during World War II, when they were transformed into an office space for the Railway Executive Committee (REC). The REC worked to keep trains running throughout the country – vital for the transport of people, supplies and war material – and these tunnels housed around 40 members of staff, spending up to two weeks continually underground. The REC even persuaded Prime Minister Winston Churchill to use Down Street as an air raid shelter, something he did on occasion.

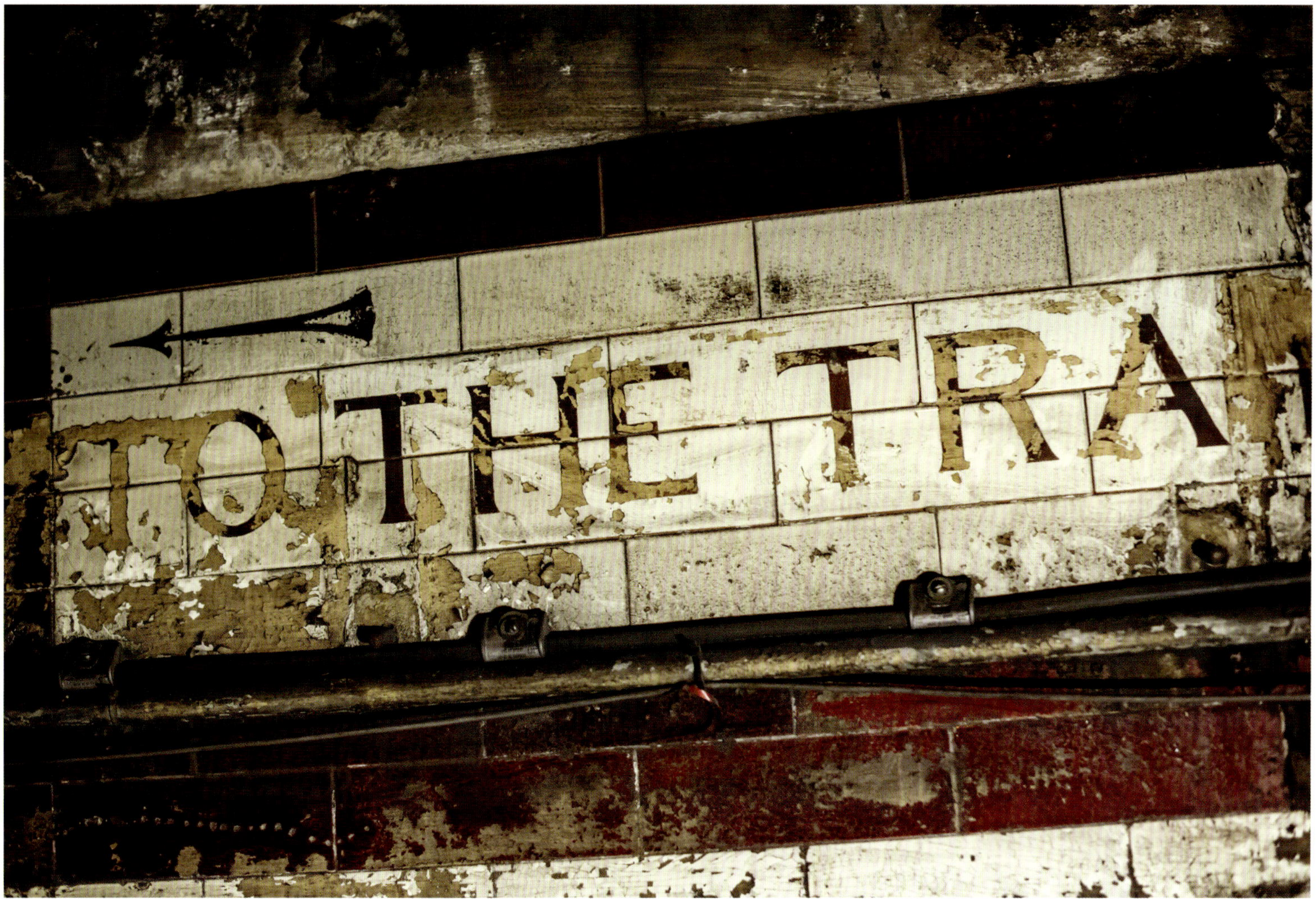

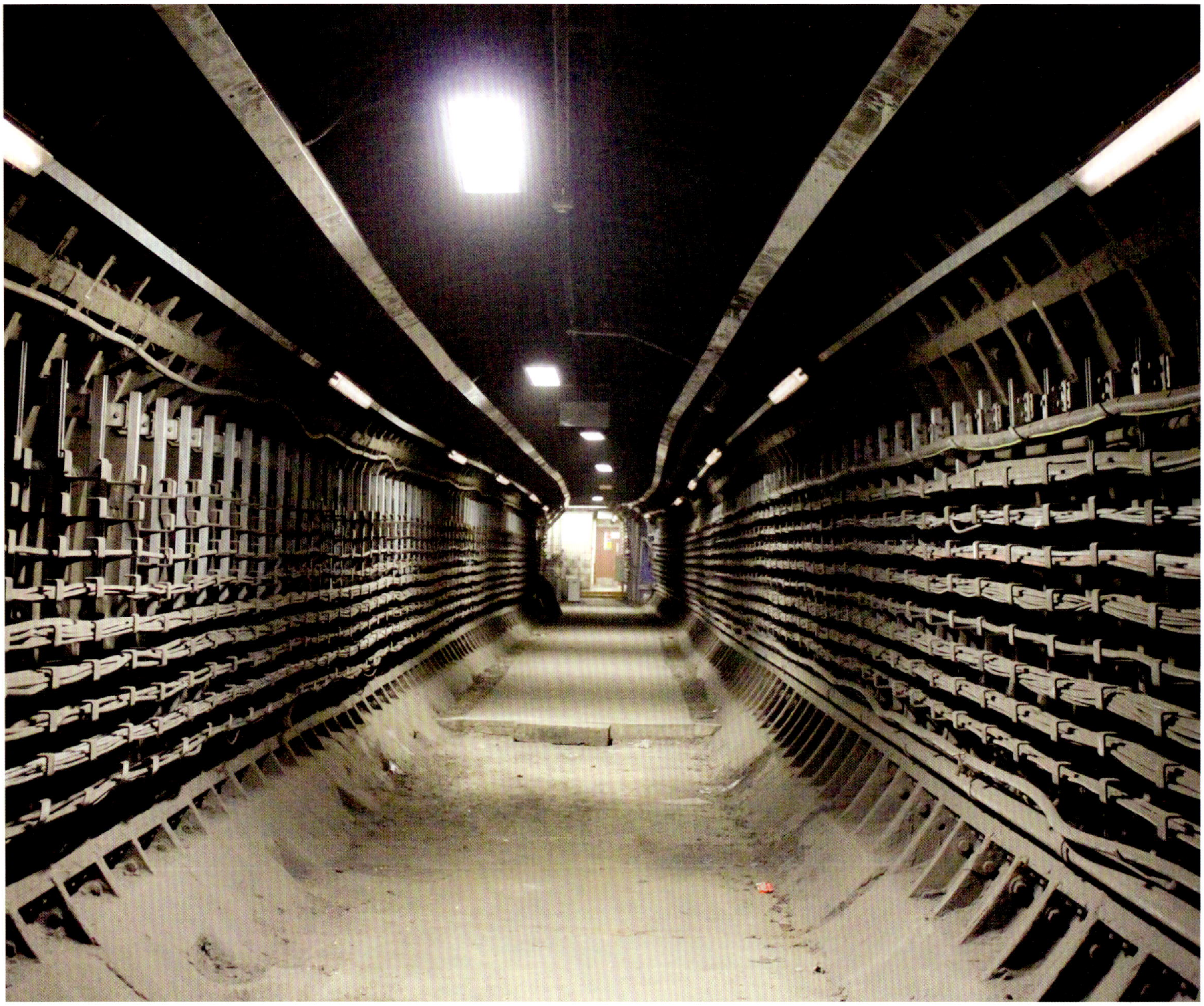

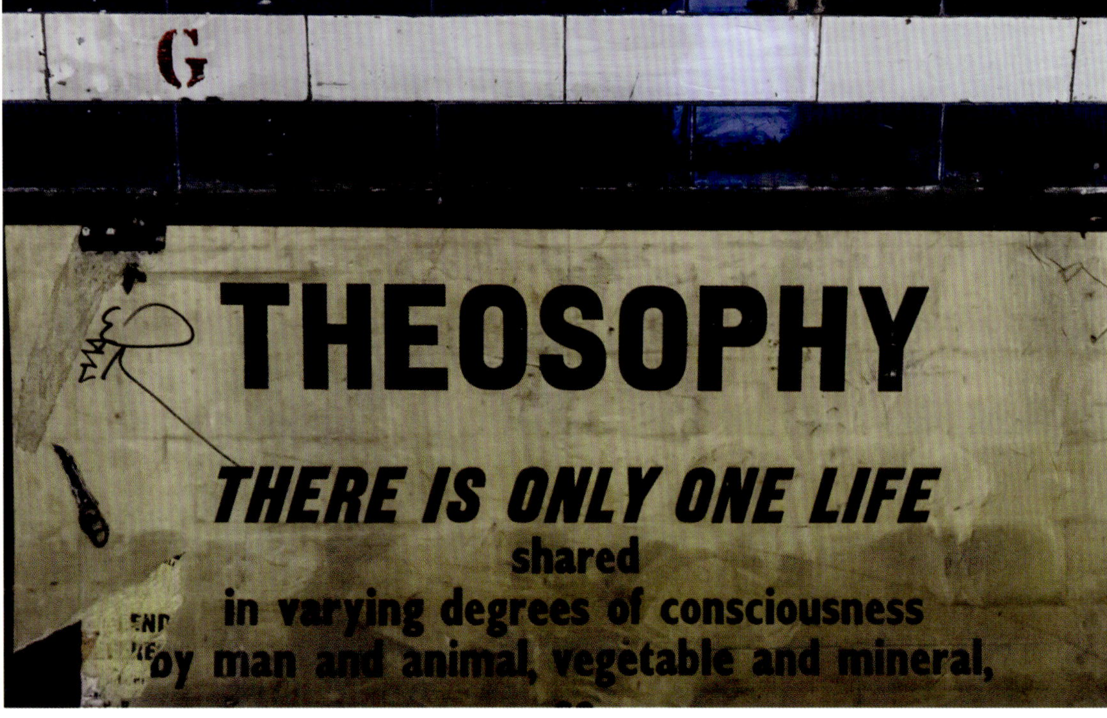

ALL PHOTOGRAPHS:

Euston Station

When Euston station was rebuilt in the 1960s, the earlier underground passageways used by tube travellers were closed. The tunnels today are a time capsule sealed on 29 April 1962, with original advertising posters. A well-preserved ticket collection window can also be seen, a reminder that before the amalgamation of most underground railway companies in 1933, separate tickets had to be purchased when changing lines.

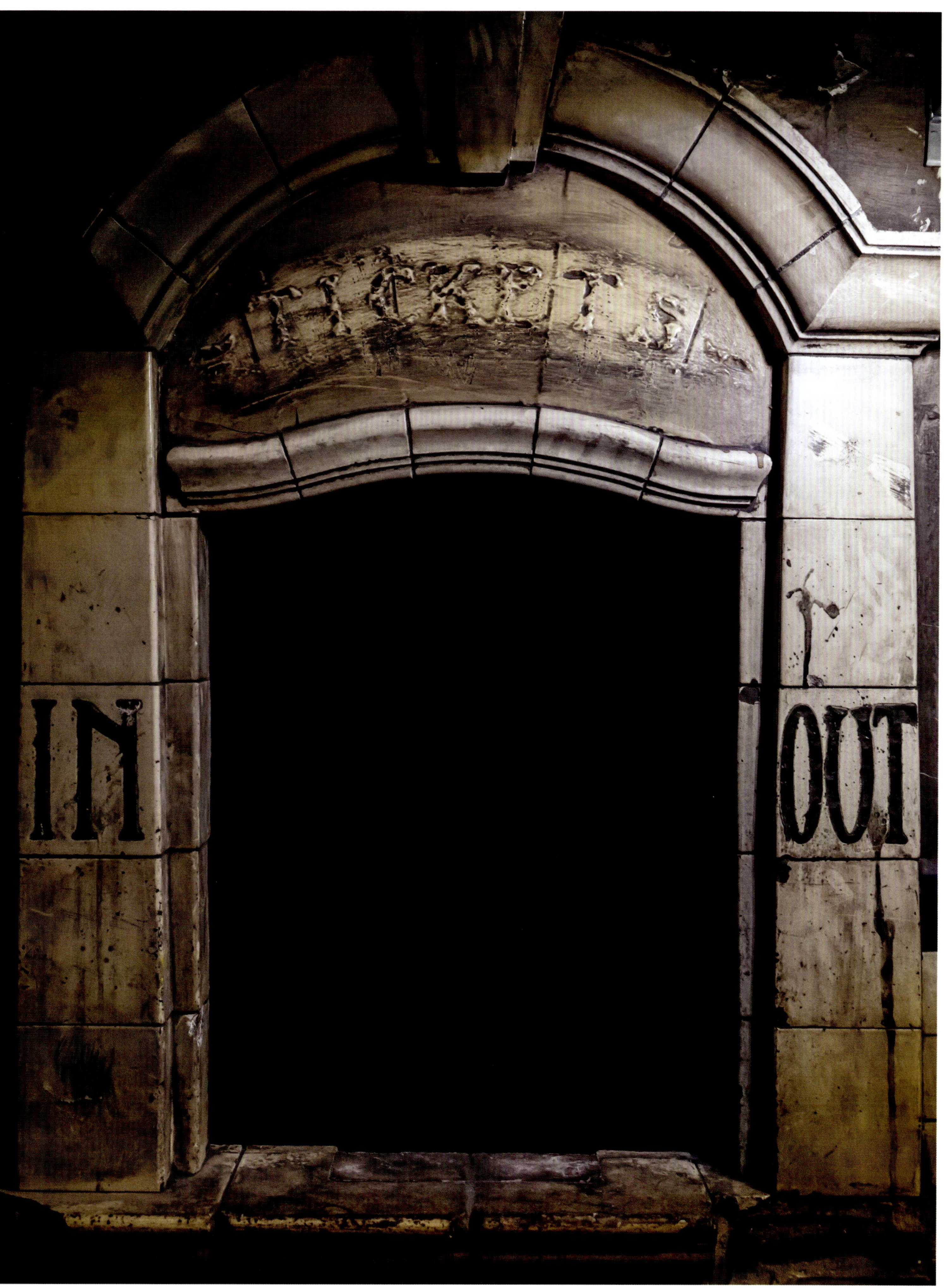
TICKETS
IN
OUT

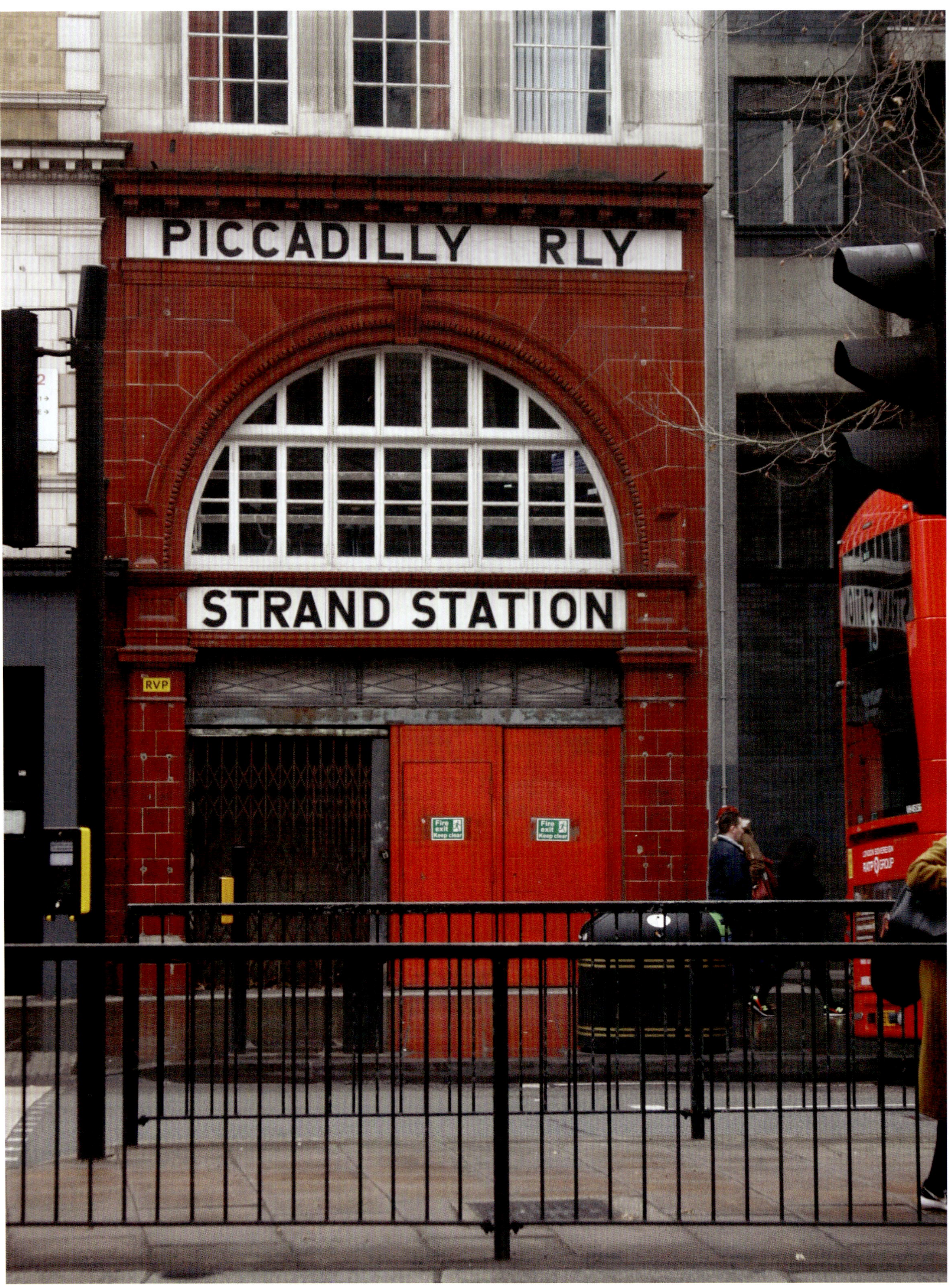
PICCADILLY RLY
STRAND STATION
RVP
Fire exit Keep clear
Fire exit Keep clear

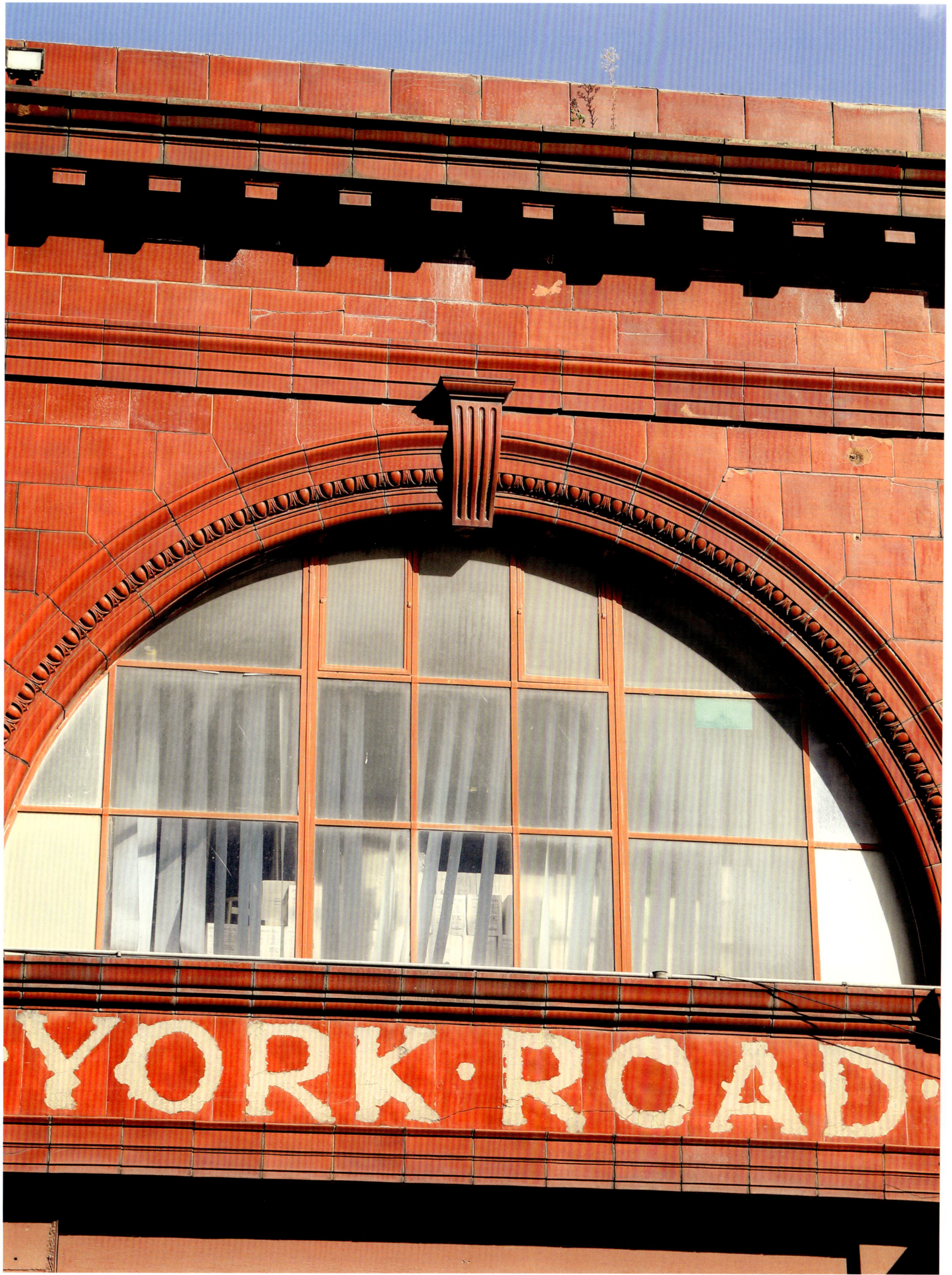
YORK · ROAD ·

PREVIOUS PAGES:

Strand Station and York Road

The eye-catching tiles make spotting a former tube station easy. These are the work of Leslie Green, appointed architect for the Underground Electric Railways Company of London Ltd (UERL) in 1903. Over just four years Green was responsible for the design and completion of over 50 stations on three tube lines. The brief was to make the stations bold and distinctive, constructed as two-storey, steel-framed buildings. The sturdy structure was intended to support further buildings on top, allowing the company to rent office space above.

RIGHT AND OVERLEAF:

Highgate Station

Long before Highgate had an underground station, an overground steam railway station was opened in 1867, and later there were big plans to extend lines further into North London, known as the Northern Heights project. Unfortunately World War II interrupted plans and by the 1950s the scheme was abandoned. The former railway tunnels (seen overleaf) are now closed off, but these spaces have become a protected bat habitat, London's very own Bat Cave!

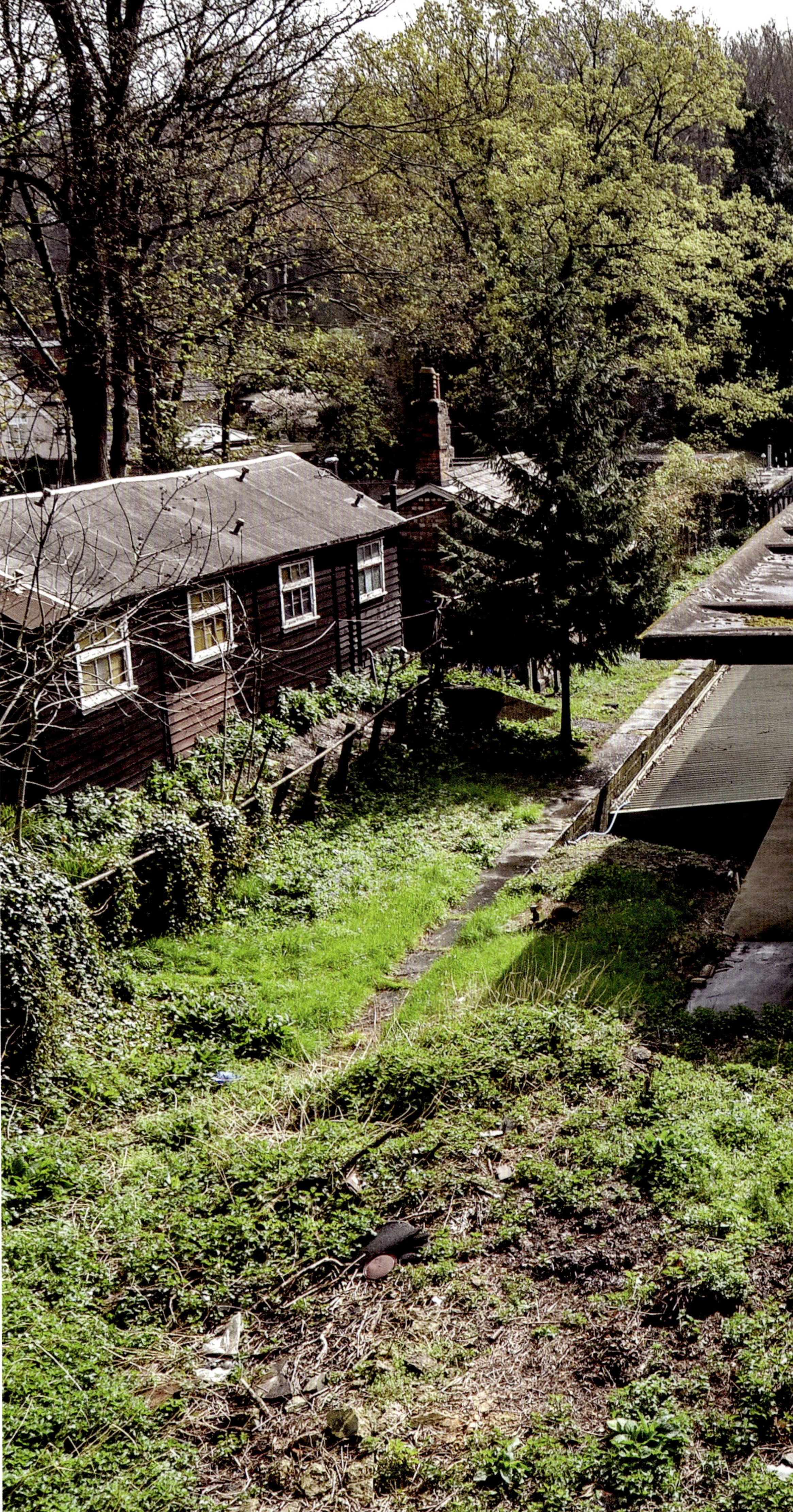

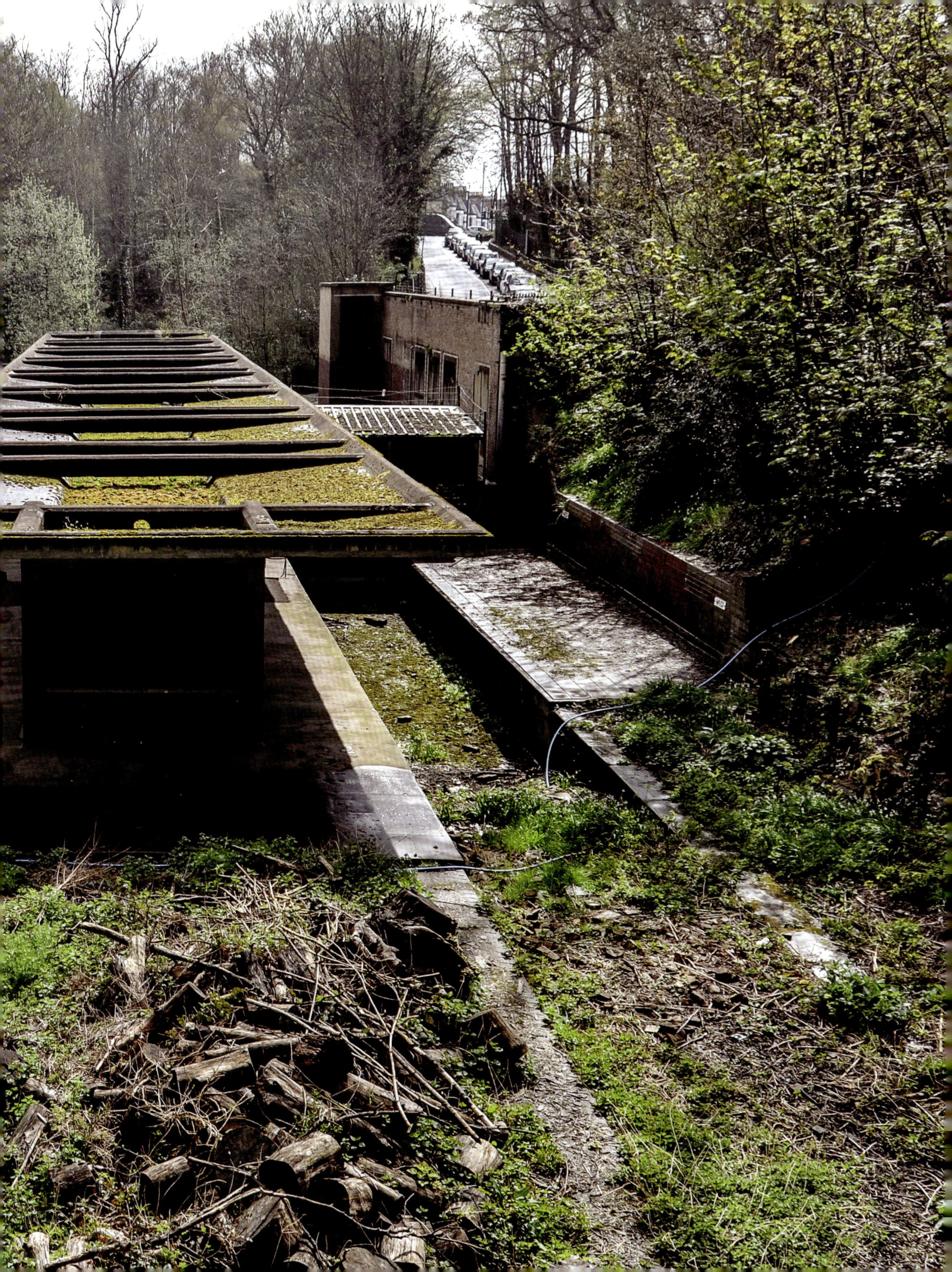

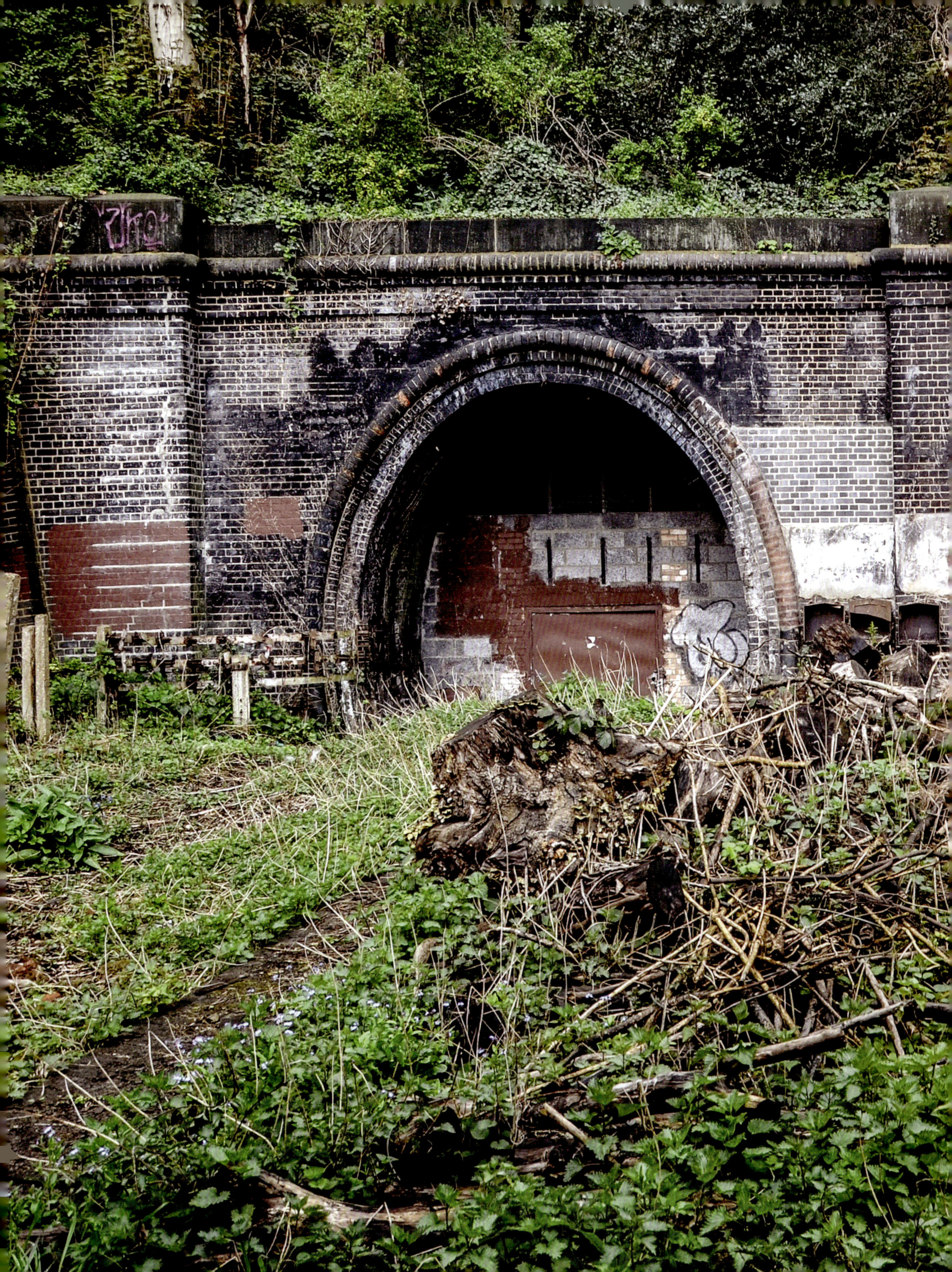

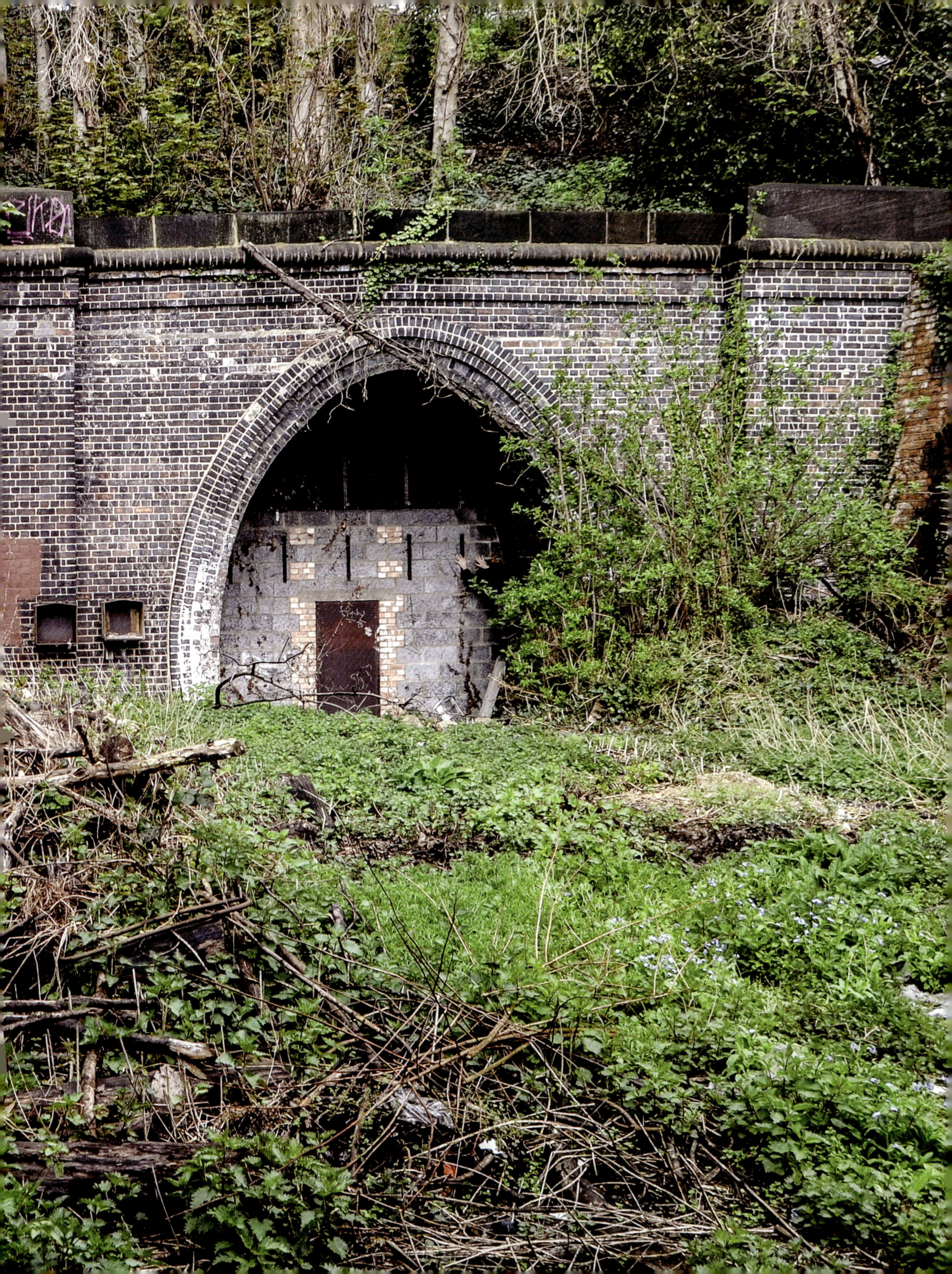

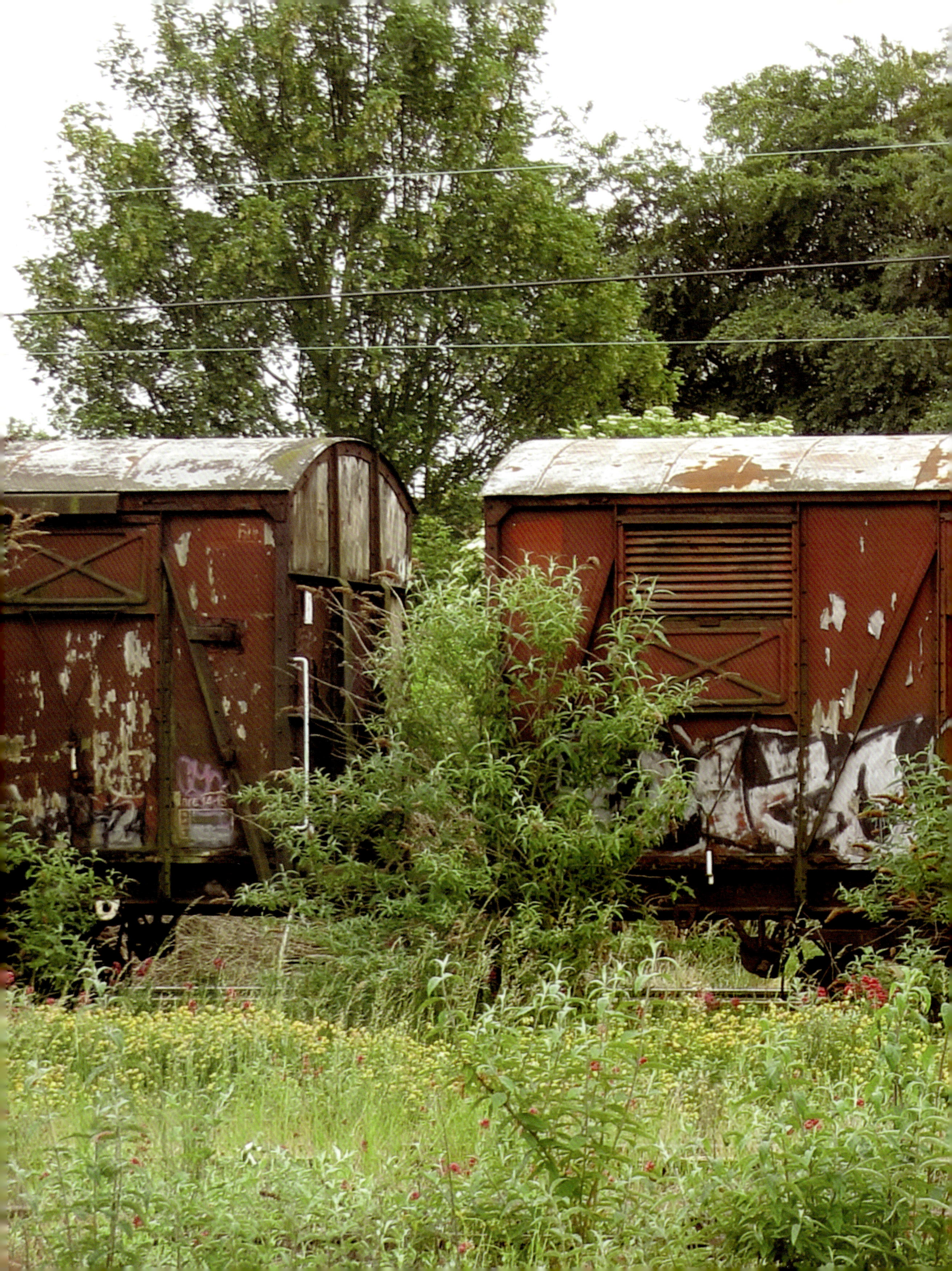

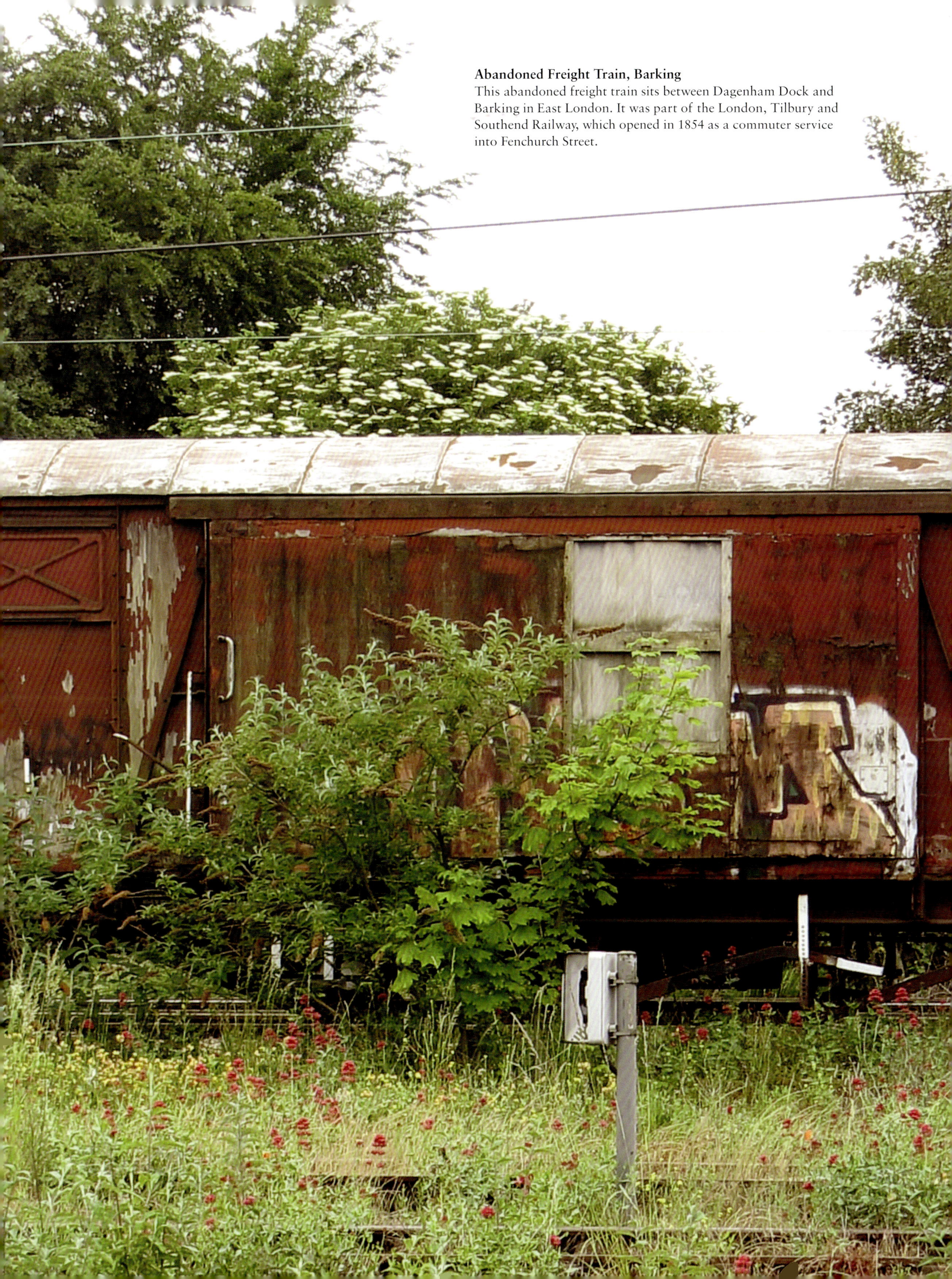

Abandoned Freight Train, Barking

This abandoned freight train sits between Dagenham Dock and Barking in East London. It was part of the London, Tilbury and Southend Railway, which opened in 1854 as a commuter service into Fenchurch Street.

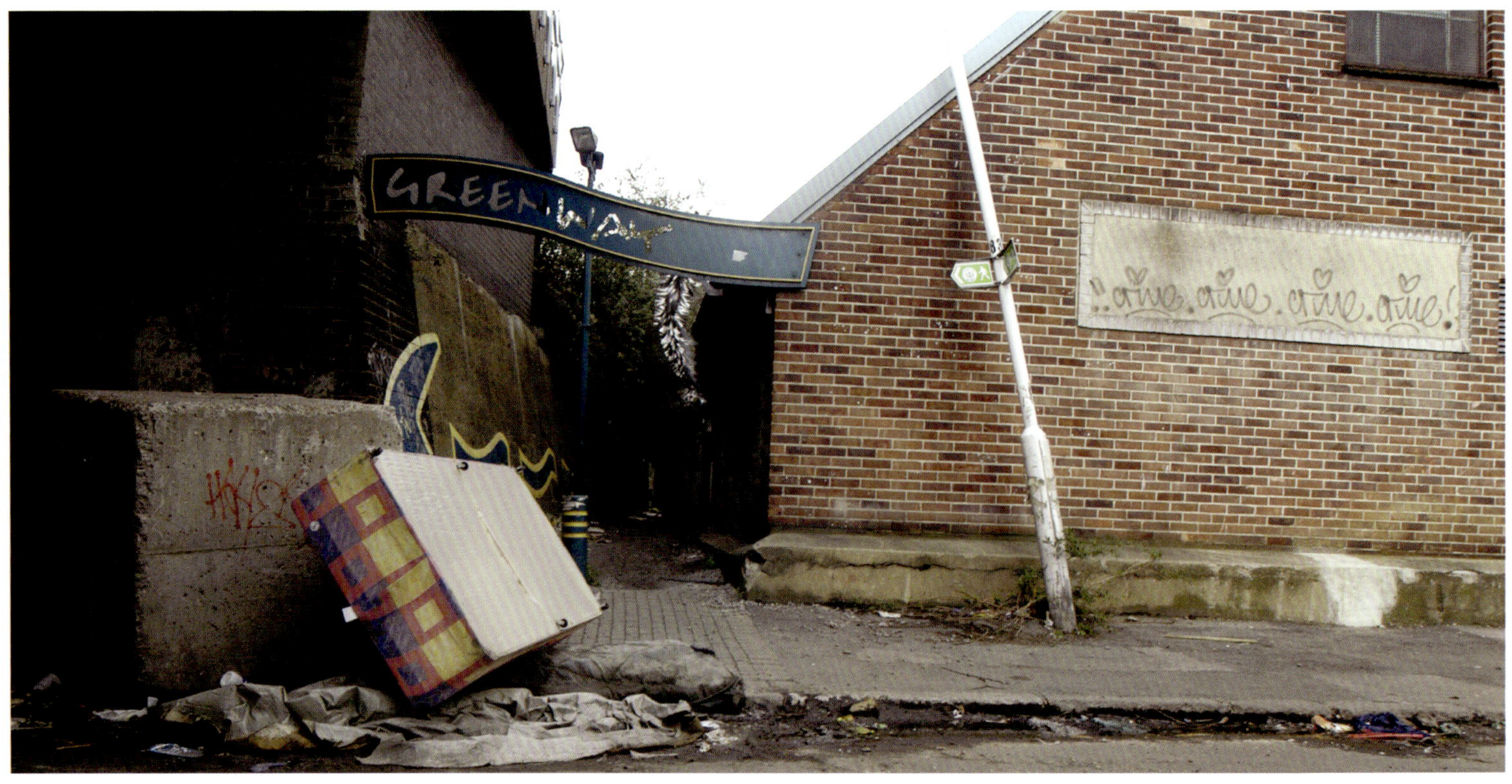

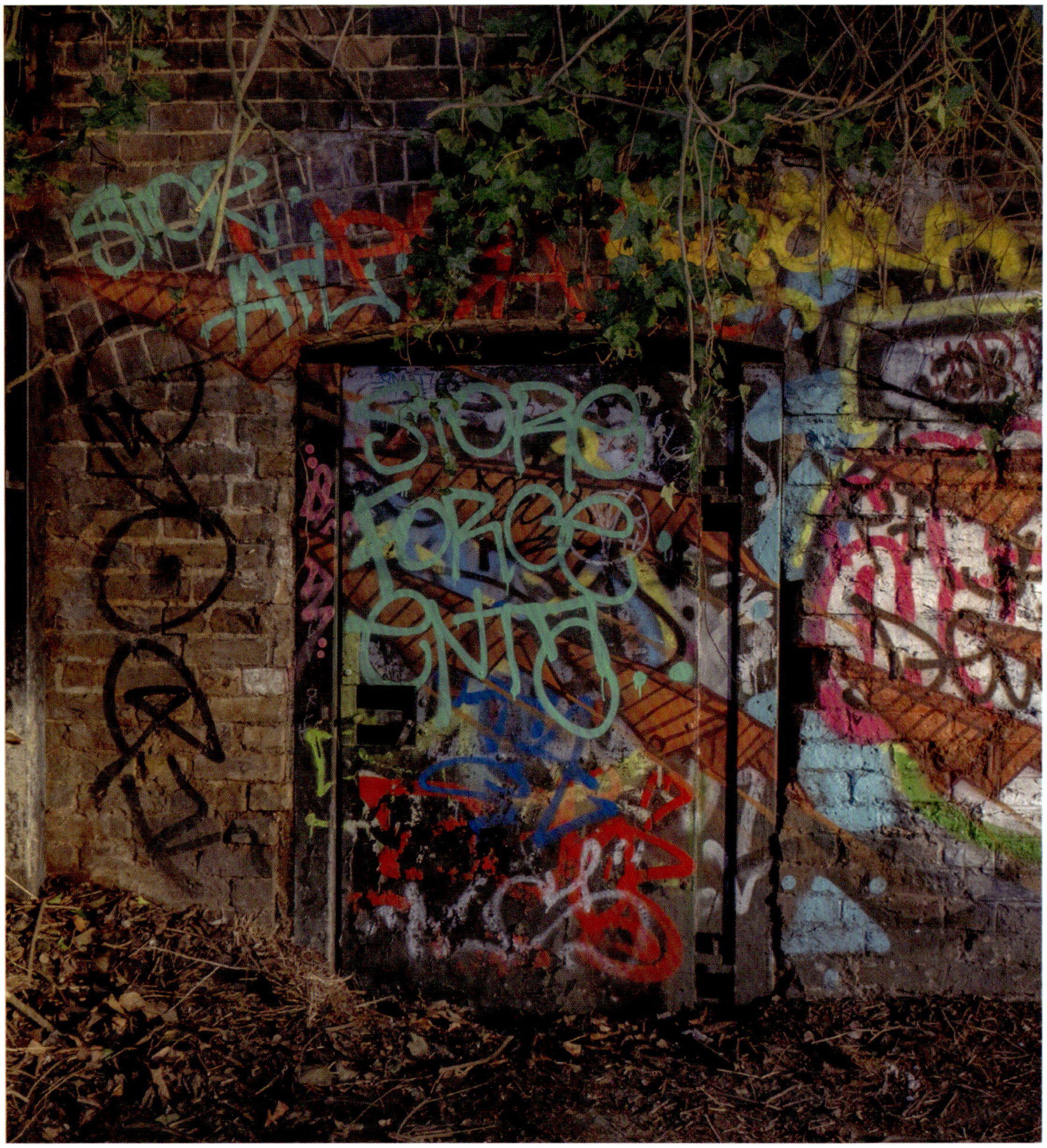

ABOVE:
Greenway Cycle Route, Stratford
Running a distance of seven kilometres (4.3 miles), the Greenway was built in 1991 and originally called the 'Sewerbank'. The unfortunate name came from the fact it was constructed on top of the Northern Outfall Sewer.

LEFT:
Camden Horse Tunnel
The canal system connecting Birmingham to London was built in the 19th century, transforming Camden from a rural village into an industrial hub. Before motor vehicles were widespread, the heavy lifting was done by horses and between 1854 and 1856 the stable blocks were built. To accompany this a network of horse tunnels were constructed below the depot, linking the canal to the railway. Today the abandoned tunnel systems are referred to as the 'Camden Catacombs' and the former stables are part of Camden Market.

OPPOSITE:
Thames Foot Tunnel, Twickenham Road Bridge
With one of these curious little buildings either side of the River Thames in Twickenham, they have often been labelled as entrances to a long-lost foot tunnel. Given their size they might be more likely to house electricity cables or sewage pipes, but they remain something of a London mystery.

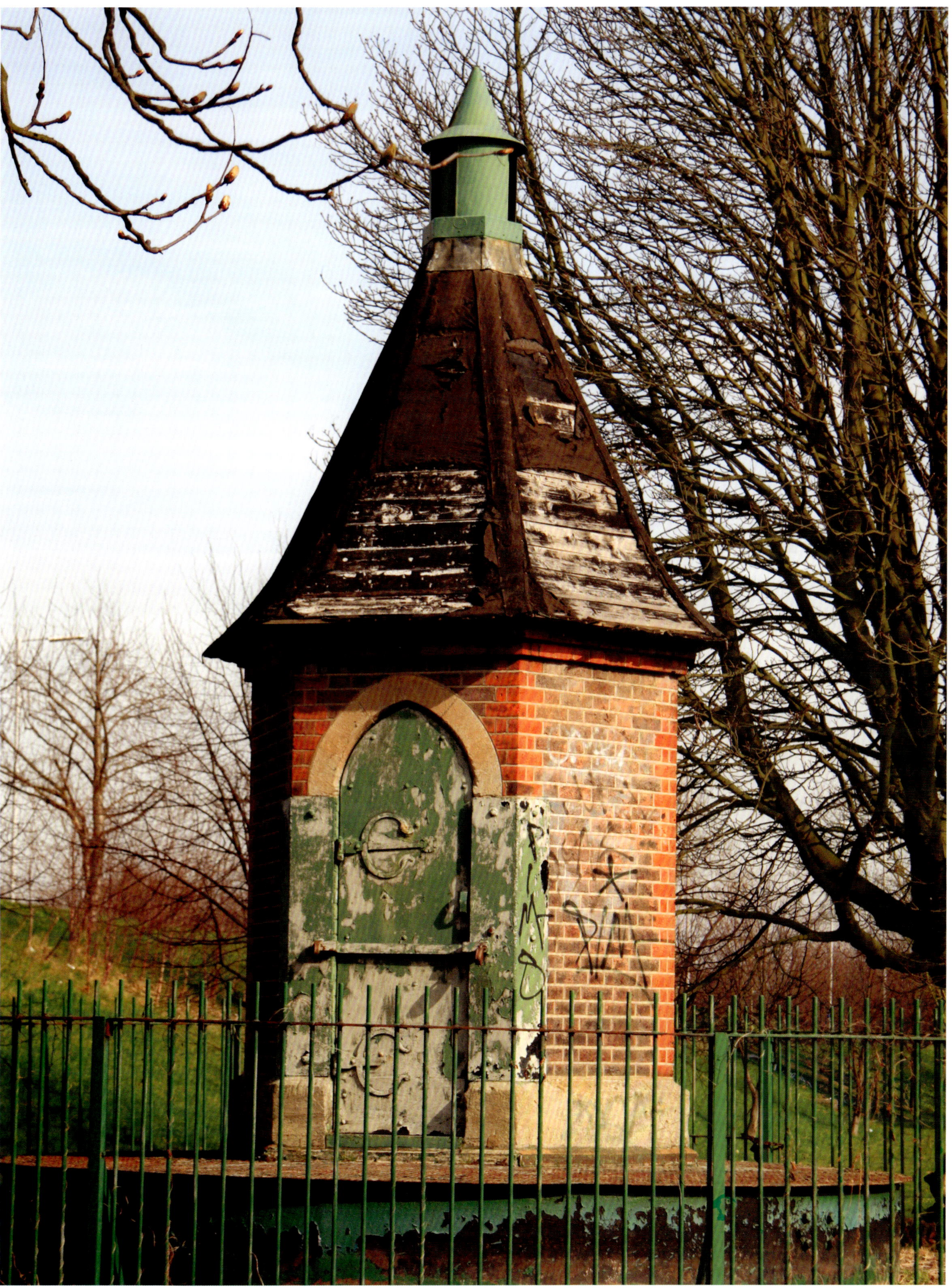

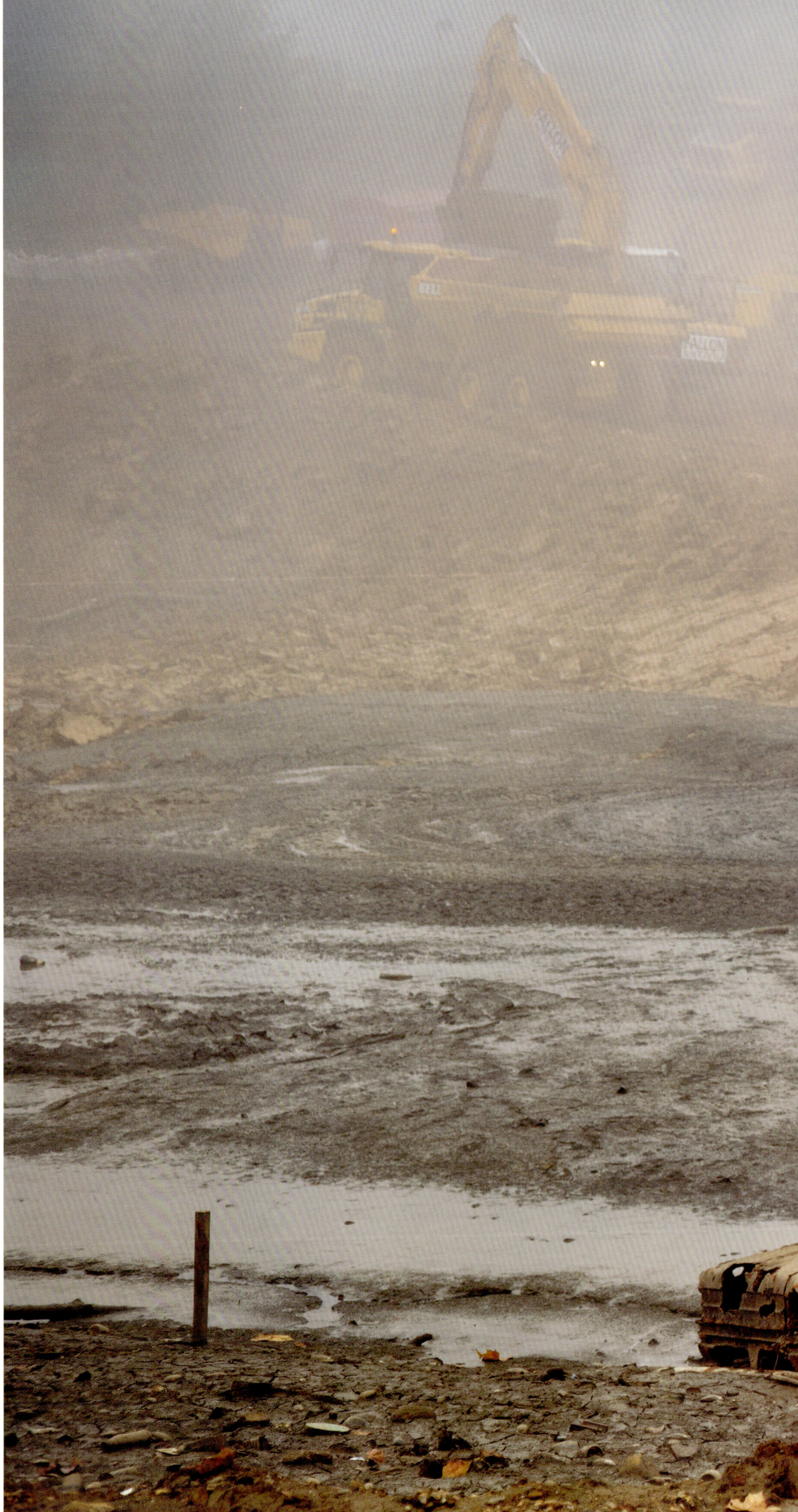

Car Wreck, Hampstead Heath
A dumped 1970s Ford Cortina was recovered from the drained model boating pond on Hampstead Heath in August 2015. Civil engineers began draining the pond as part of the City of London's £23 million dams project, designed to strengthen earth dams and improve wildlife ecology on Hampstead Heath.

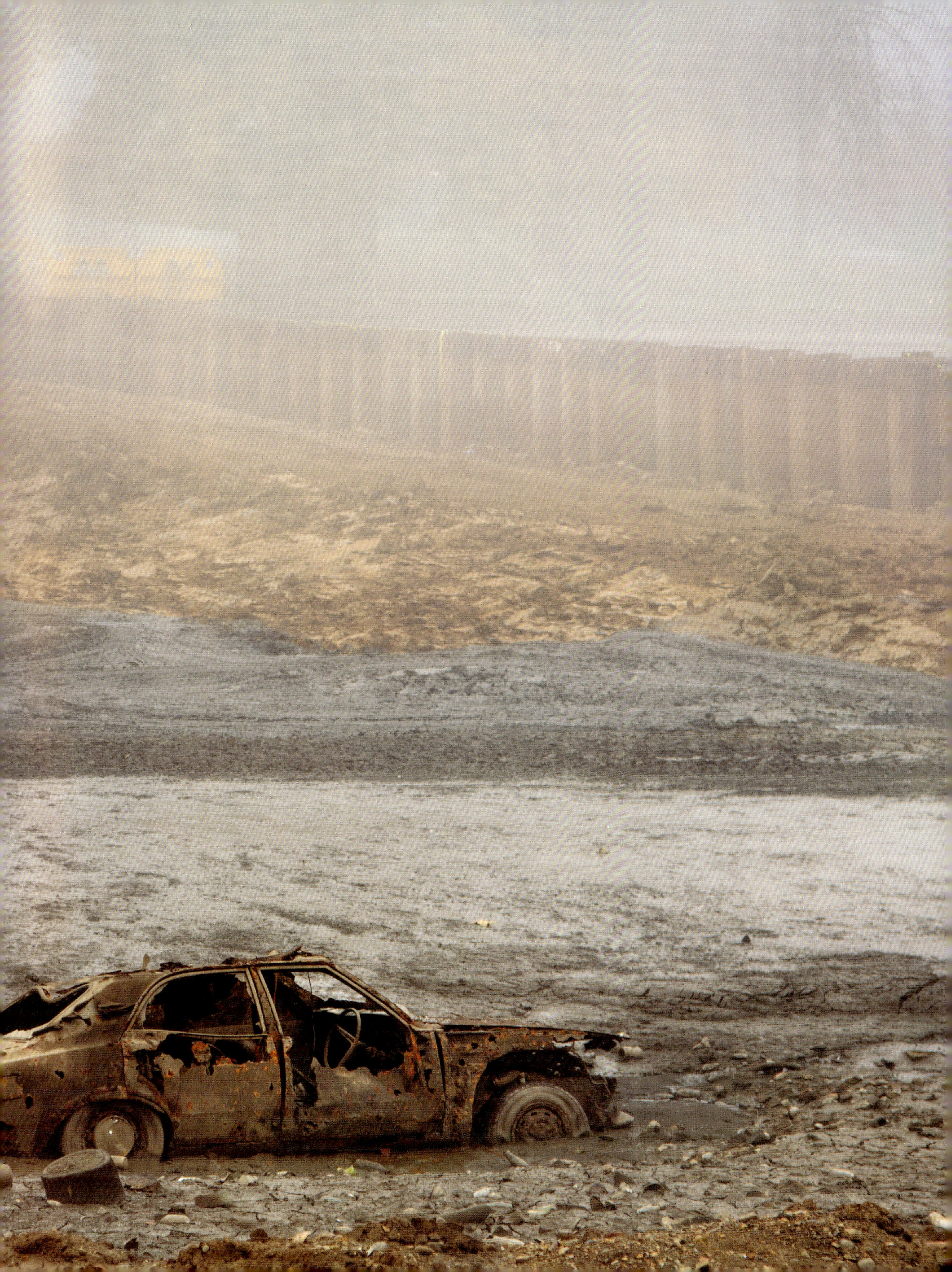

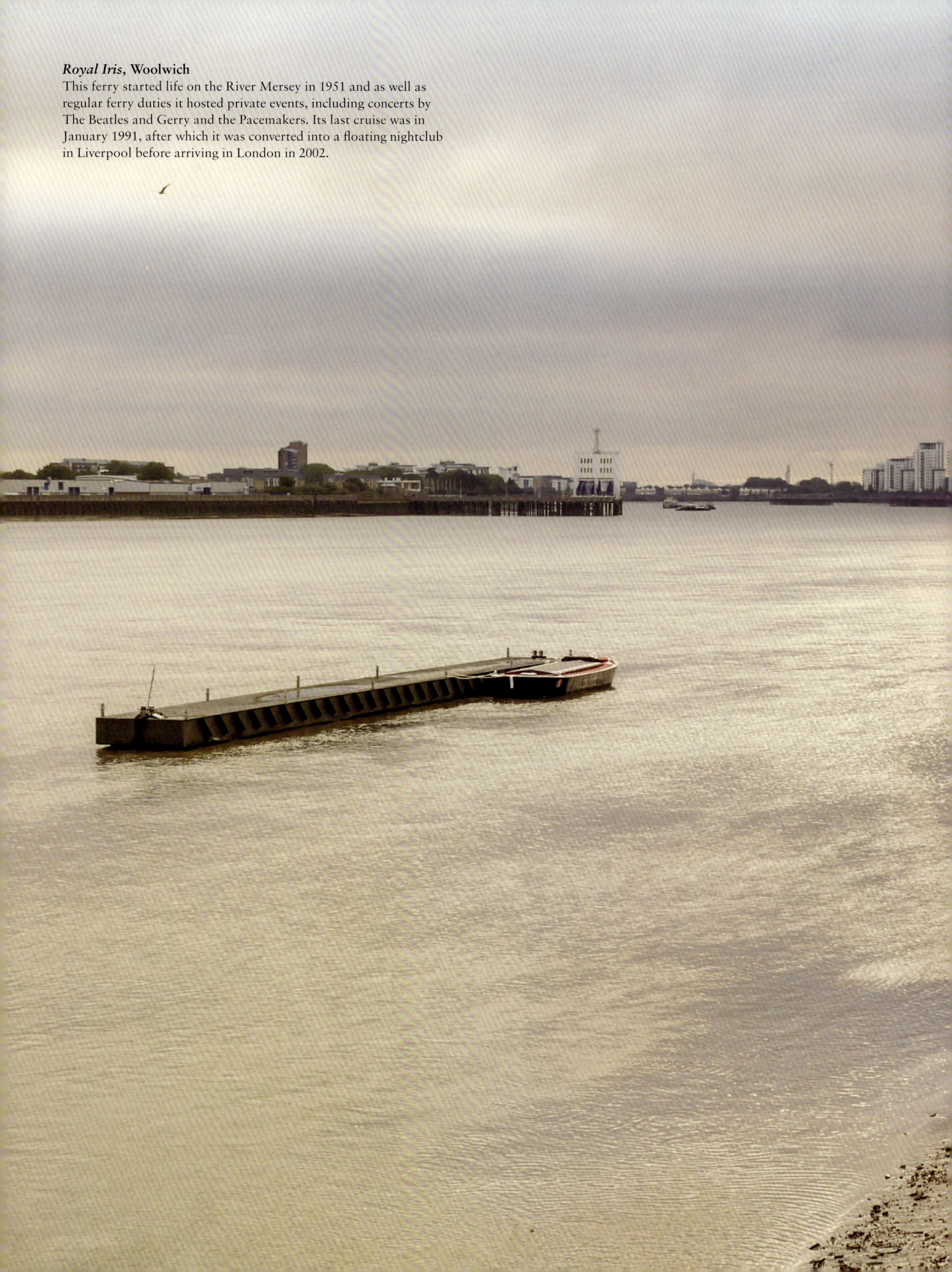

***Royal Iris*, Woolwich**

This ferry started life on the River Mersey in 1951 and as well as regular ferry duties it hosted private events, including concerts by The Beatles and Gerry and the Pacemakers. Its last cruise was in January 1991, after which it was converted into a floating nightclub in Liverpool before arriving in London in 2002.

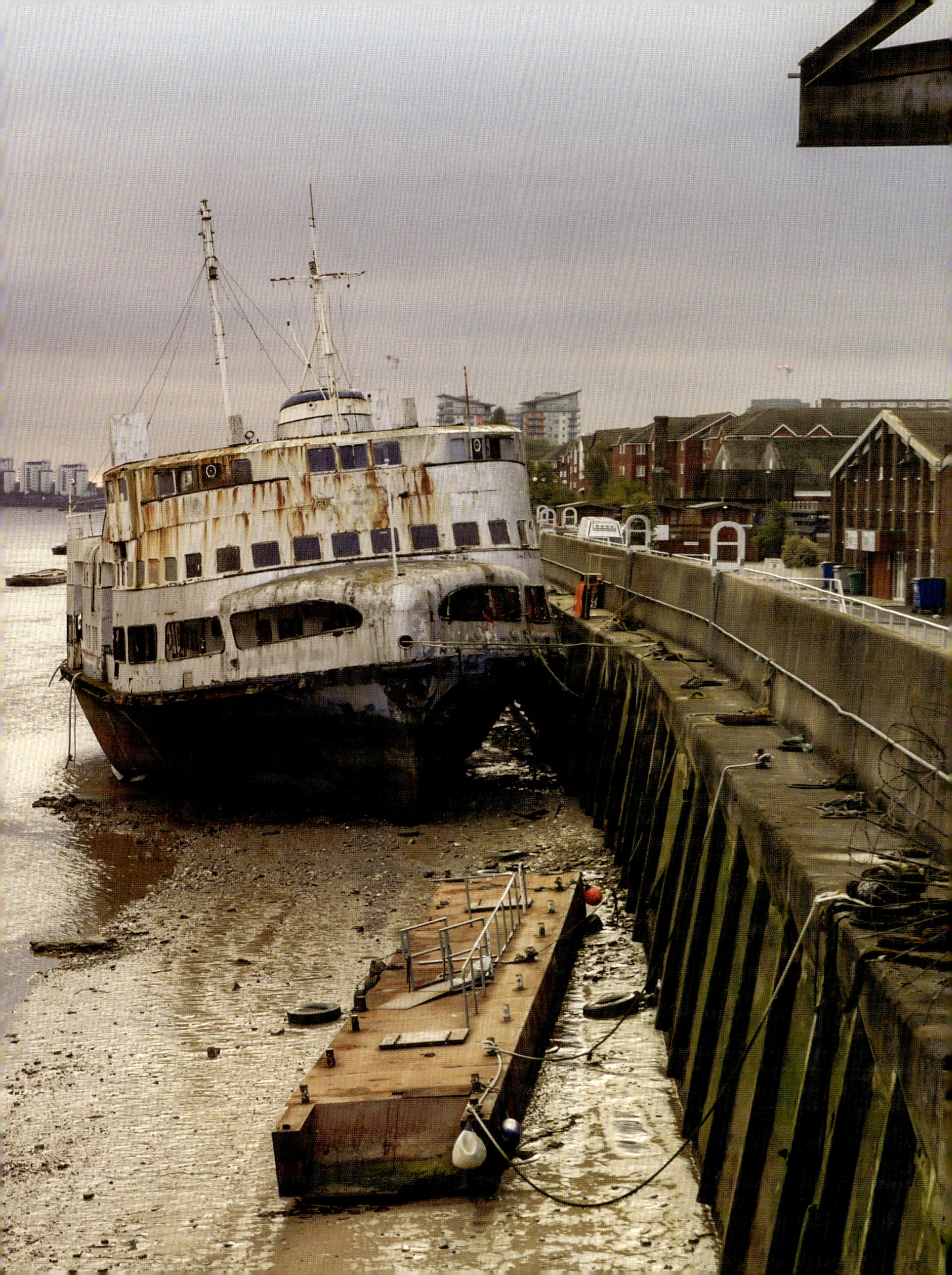

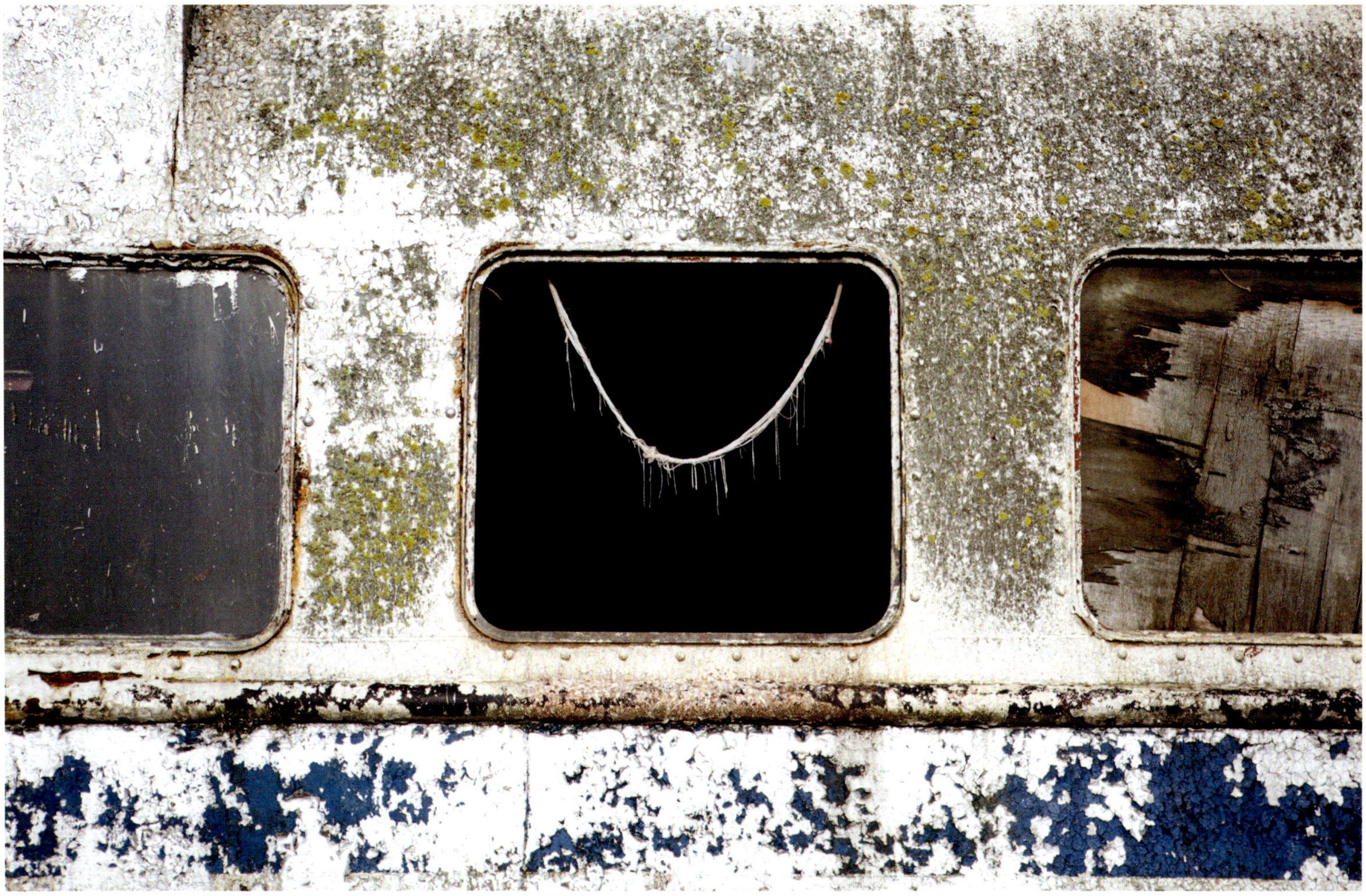

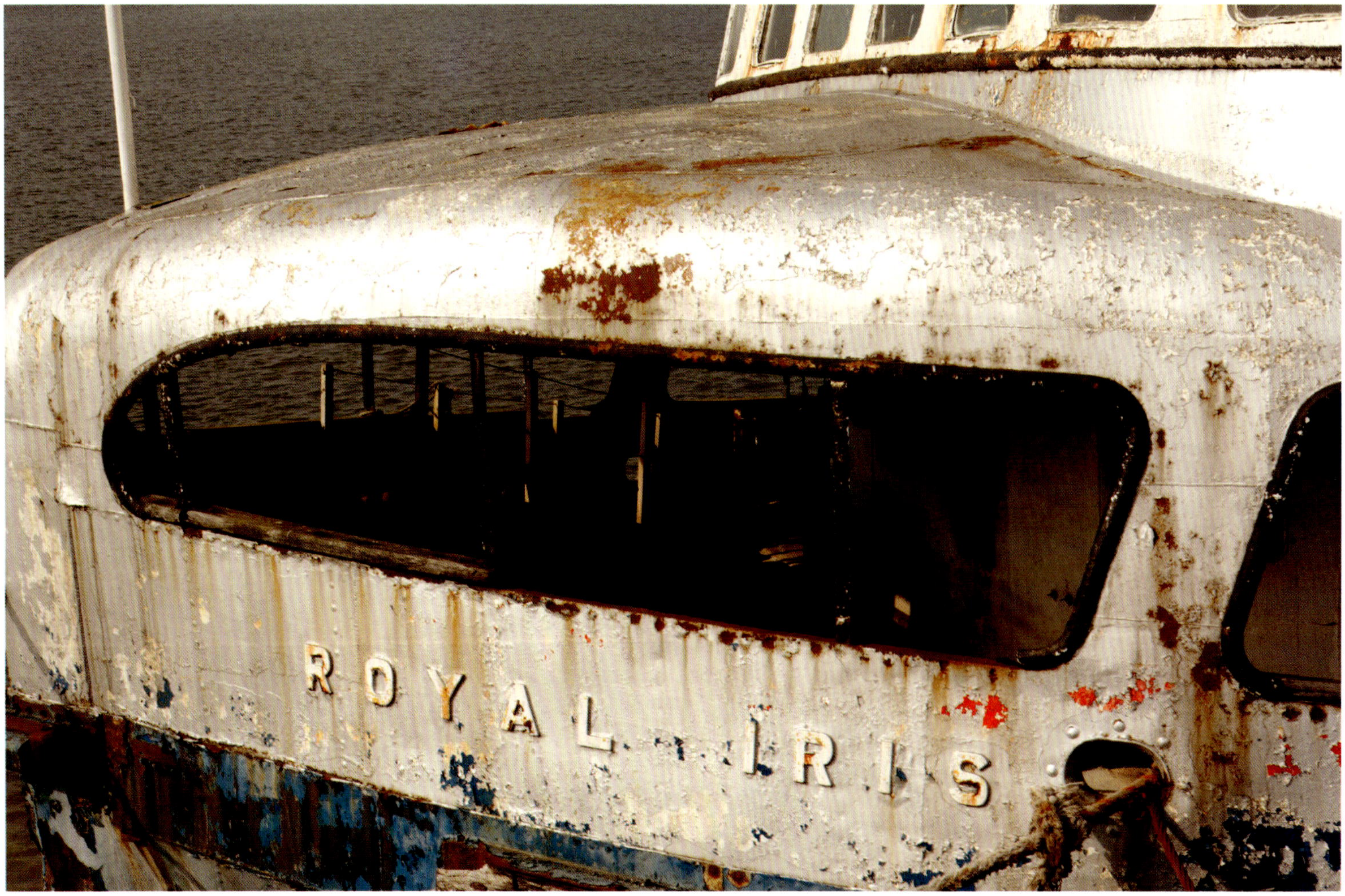

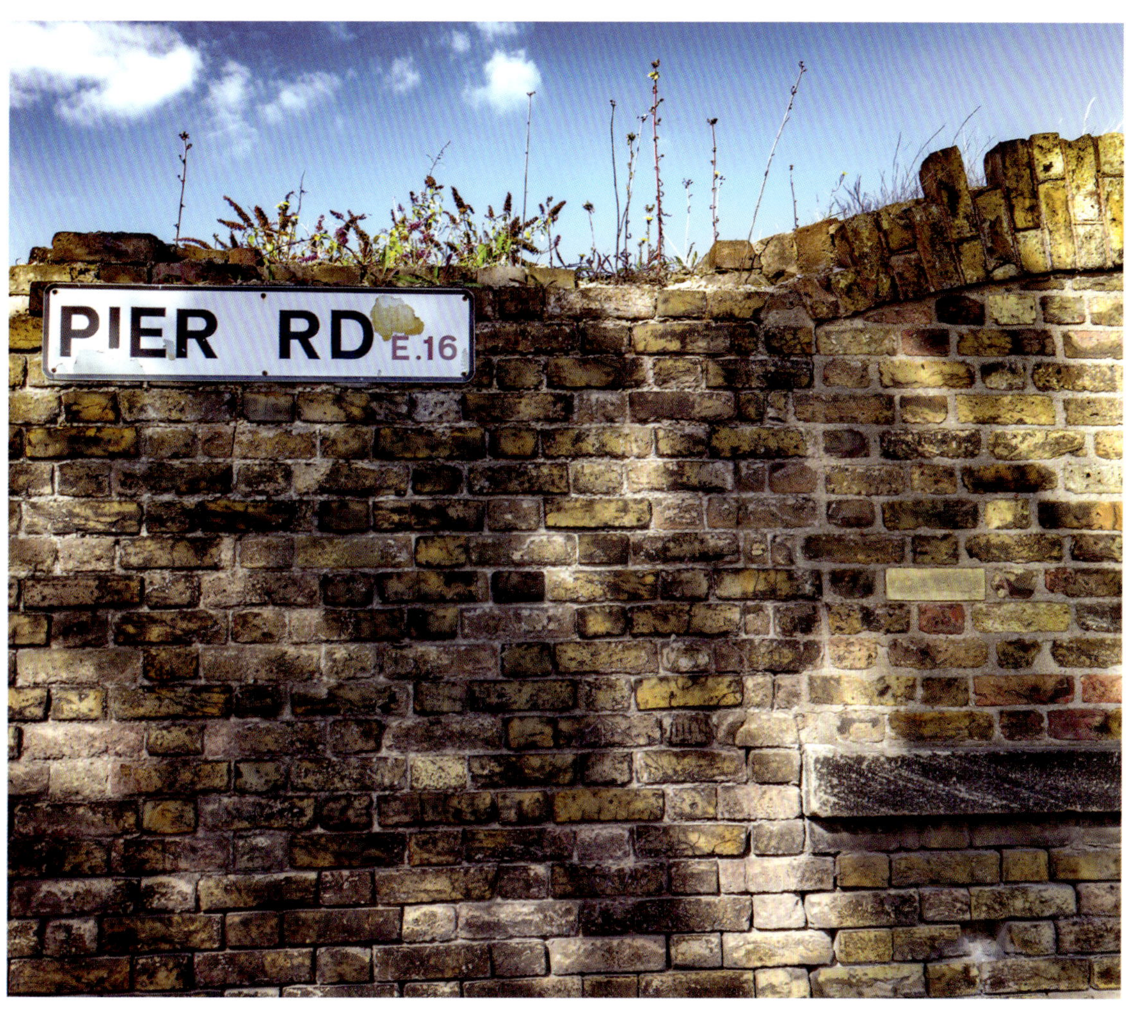

OPPOSITE (BOTH PHOTOGRAPHS):
***Royal Iris*, Woolwich**
Although there have been multiple plans to regenerate the boat – as well as an ongoing campaign to return the *Royal Iris* to Liverpool – the vessel remains in a decaying state at Woolwich.

LEFT AND BELOW:
North Woolwich Pier
North Woolwich Railway Station was opened in 1847, constructed by the Eastern Counties Railway and with a pier built to help connect passengers via boat with central London. The service was unable to compete with the nearby free Woolwich Ferry and by the outbreak of World War II only the North Pier was in occasional use by river steamers.

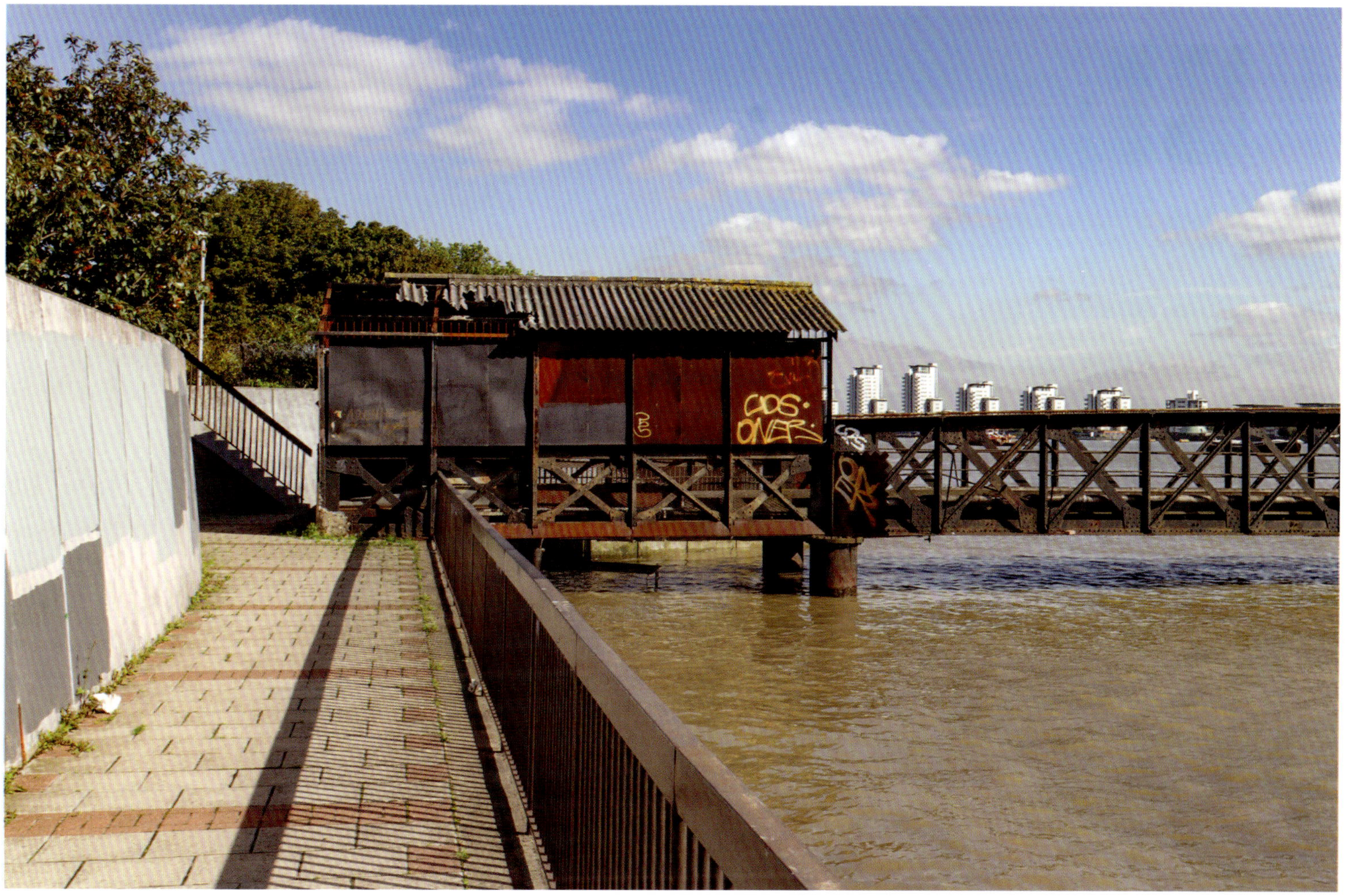

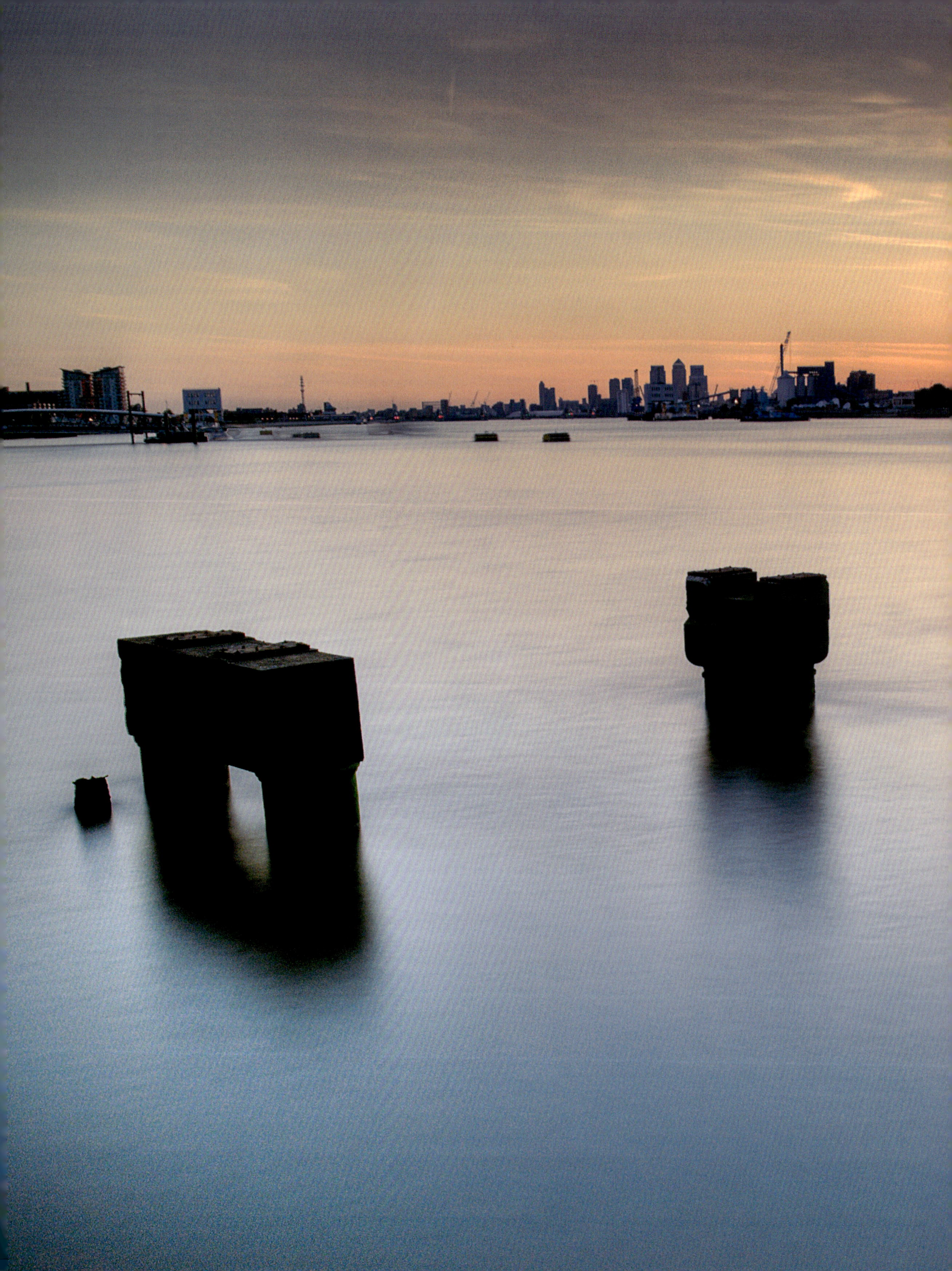

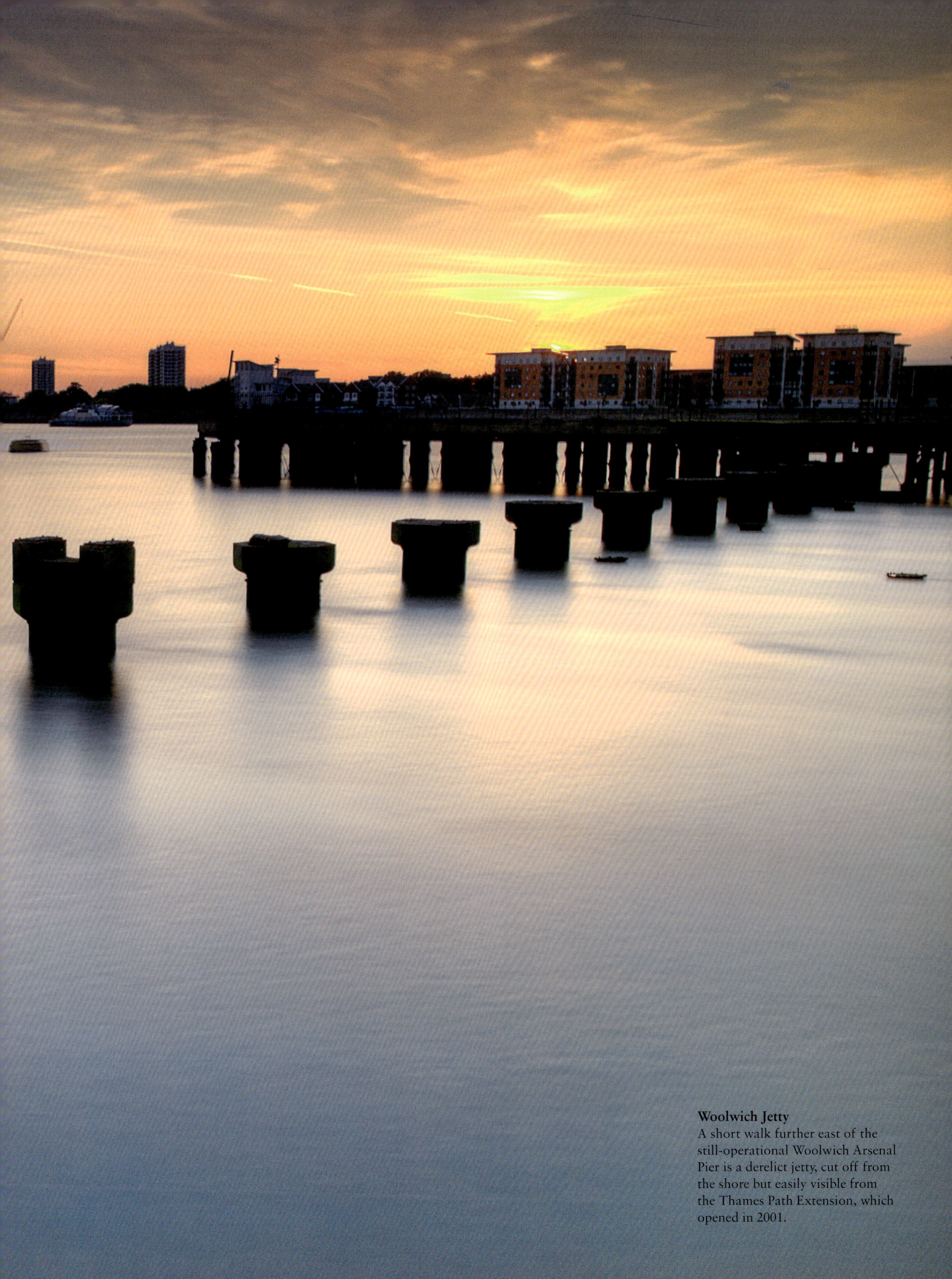

Woolwich Jetty
A short walk further east of the still-operational Woolwich Arsenal Pier is a derelict jetty, cut off from the shore but easily visible from the Thames Path Extension, which opened in 2001.

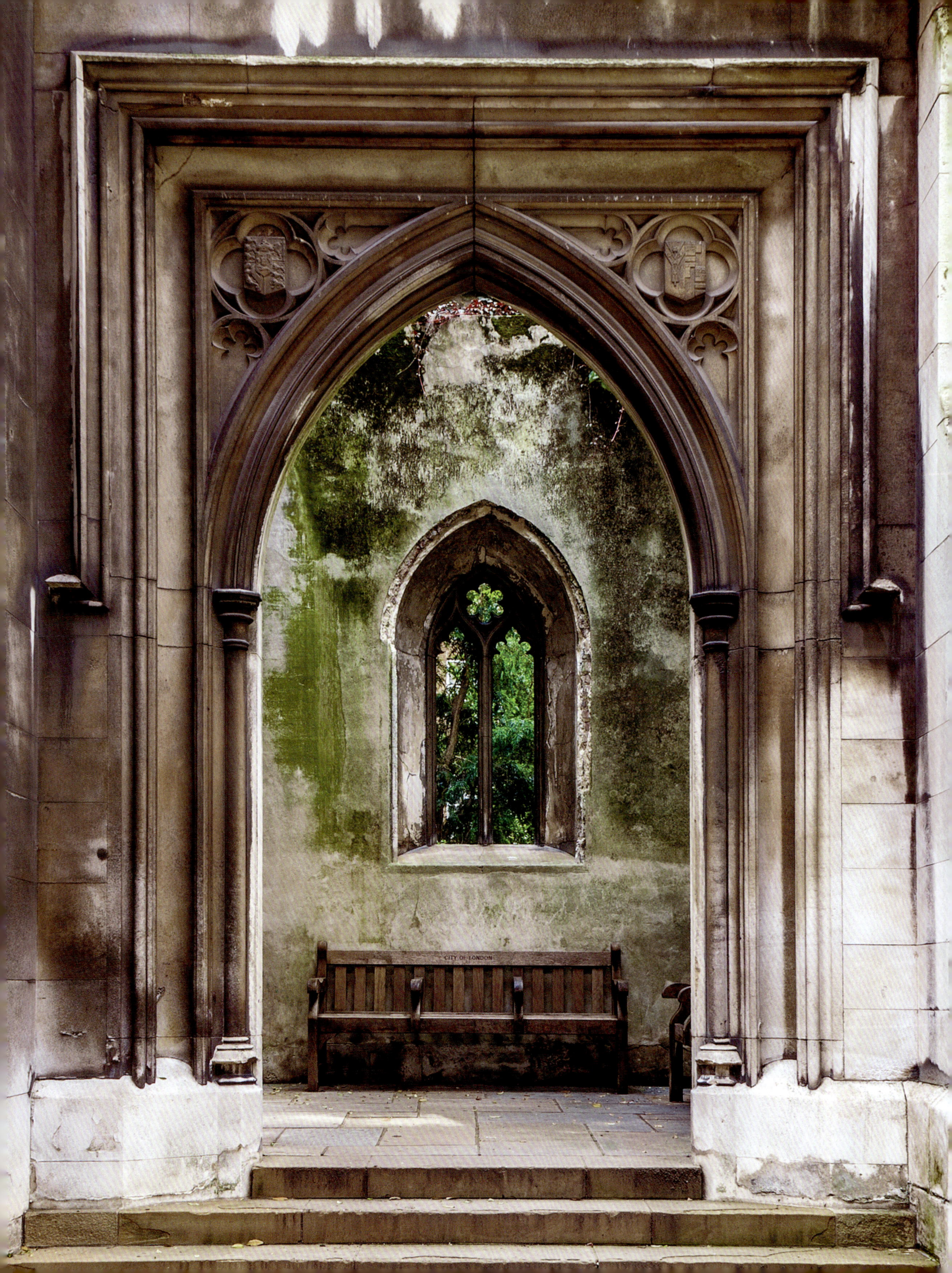
CITY OF LONDON

Public Spaces

What do we expect from London's public spaces? Should they invigorate us? Nurture us? Inspire us? In this chapter we see the neglected remains of hospitals, churches and safe havens. These places were intended to support their community, to ensure the physical, mental or spiritual health of the people who used them. But in the early 21st century they are now abandoned.

However, it's not all negative. Some of the abandoned public spaces in this chapter have been transformed beyond recognition, transcending their previous functions to provide extraordinary – even magical – spaces that are still in use today. These buildings came into being to solve a problem. They were reactions to the poor sanitation of the 19th century, or wartime bombardment in the 20th century, or to cater for the health of an ever-growing city.

Modern life has made redundant the function of many of these places: we can now enjoy indoor plumbing, we don't all go to church as regularly as we used to and now we carry personal phones in our pockets. But seeing the ingenuity of public spaces used to tackle social issues should give us confidence that we can continue to develop London as a modern, vibrant city.

OPPOSITE:
Dunstan-in-the-East Church, City of London
One of London's most charming green spaces, the church was rebuilt by Christopher Wren after the Great Fire of London in 1666. Unfortunately, the church was gutted during the Blitz (1940–41). It was never rebuilt and in 1971 opened as a public garden, a peaceful oasis in London's busy financial district.

OVERLEAF:
Asylum Chapel, Peckham
The misleading name might imply that this was once a hospital for the mentally ill, but it was in fact a retirement home for pub landlords. Built in 1827–33, the building was bombed during the Blitz (1940–41) and left derelict. From 2010 it started to be used as an events space – you can even get married here!

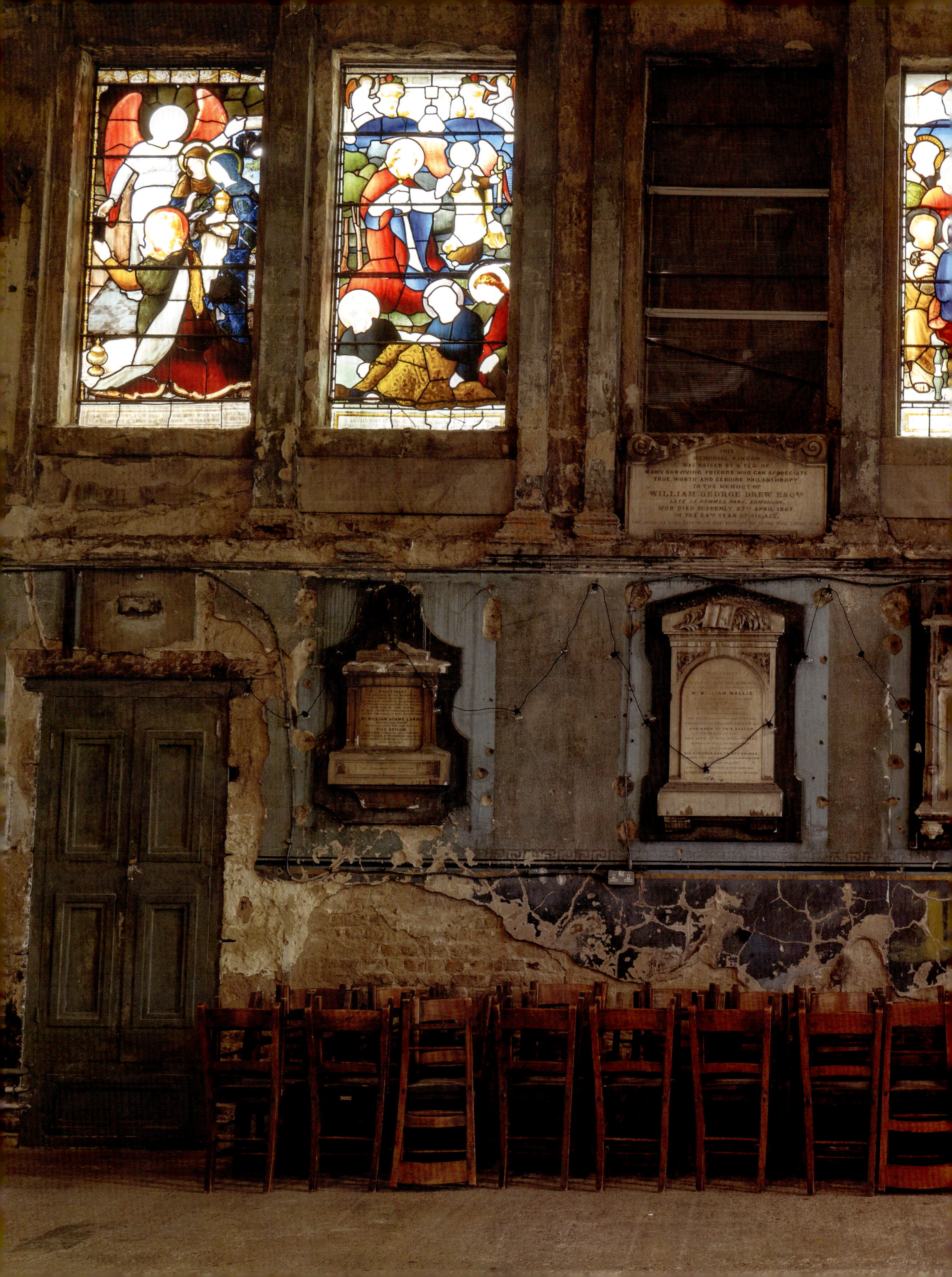
THIS
MEMORIAL WINDOW
WAS RAISED BY A FEW OF
MANY SURVIVING FRIENDS WHO CAN APPRECIATE
TRUE WORTH AND GENUINE PHILANTHROPY
TO THE MEMORY OF
WILLIAM GEORGE DREW ESQRE
LATE OF PYMMES PARK, EDMONTON,
WHO DIED SUDDENLY 27TH APRIL 1867,
IN THE 64TH YEAR OF HIS AGE.

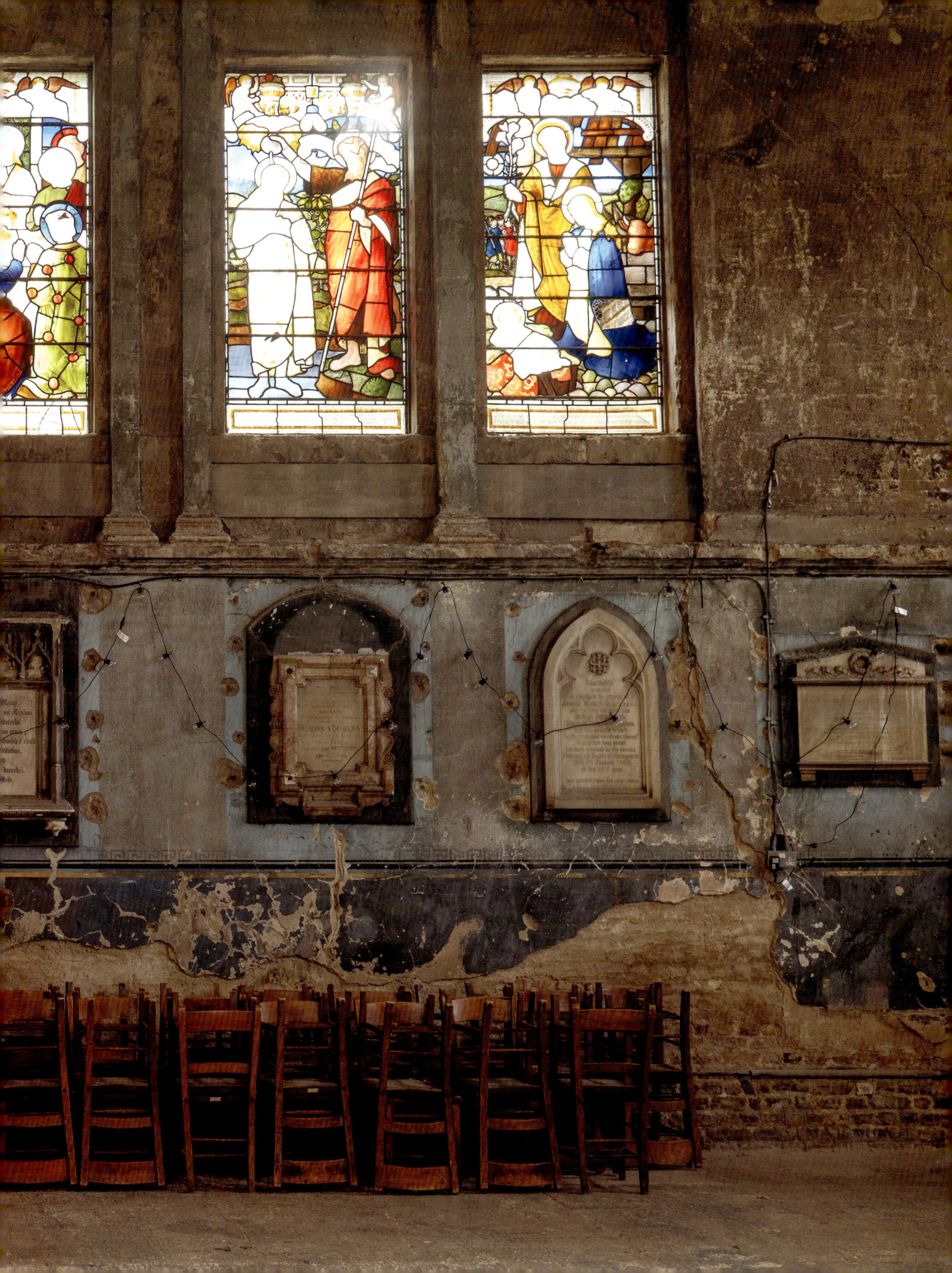

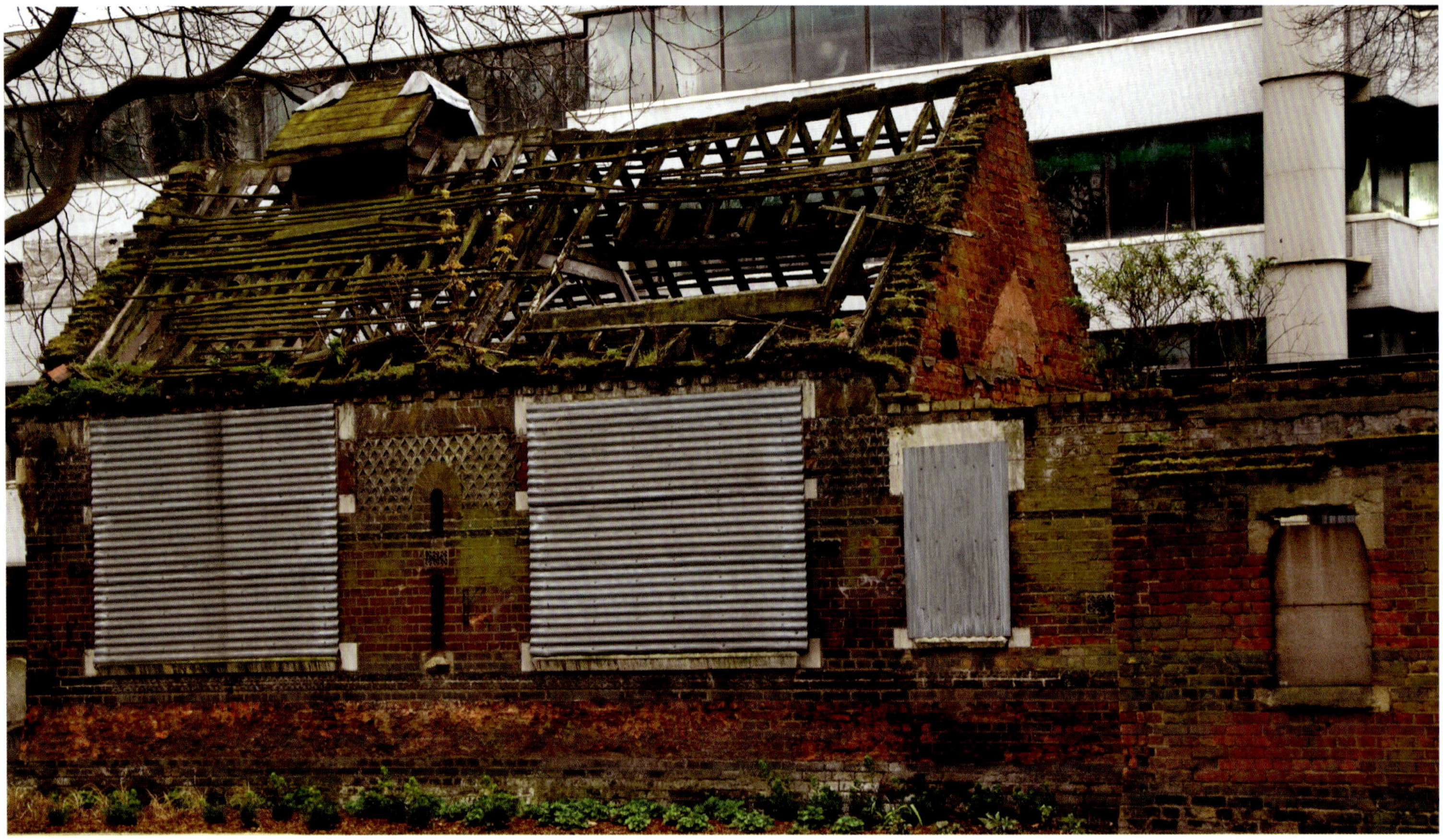

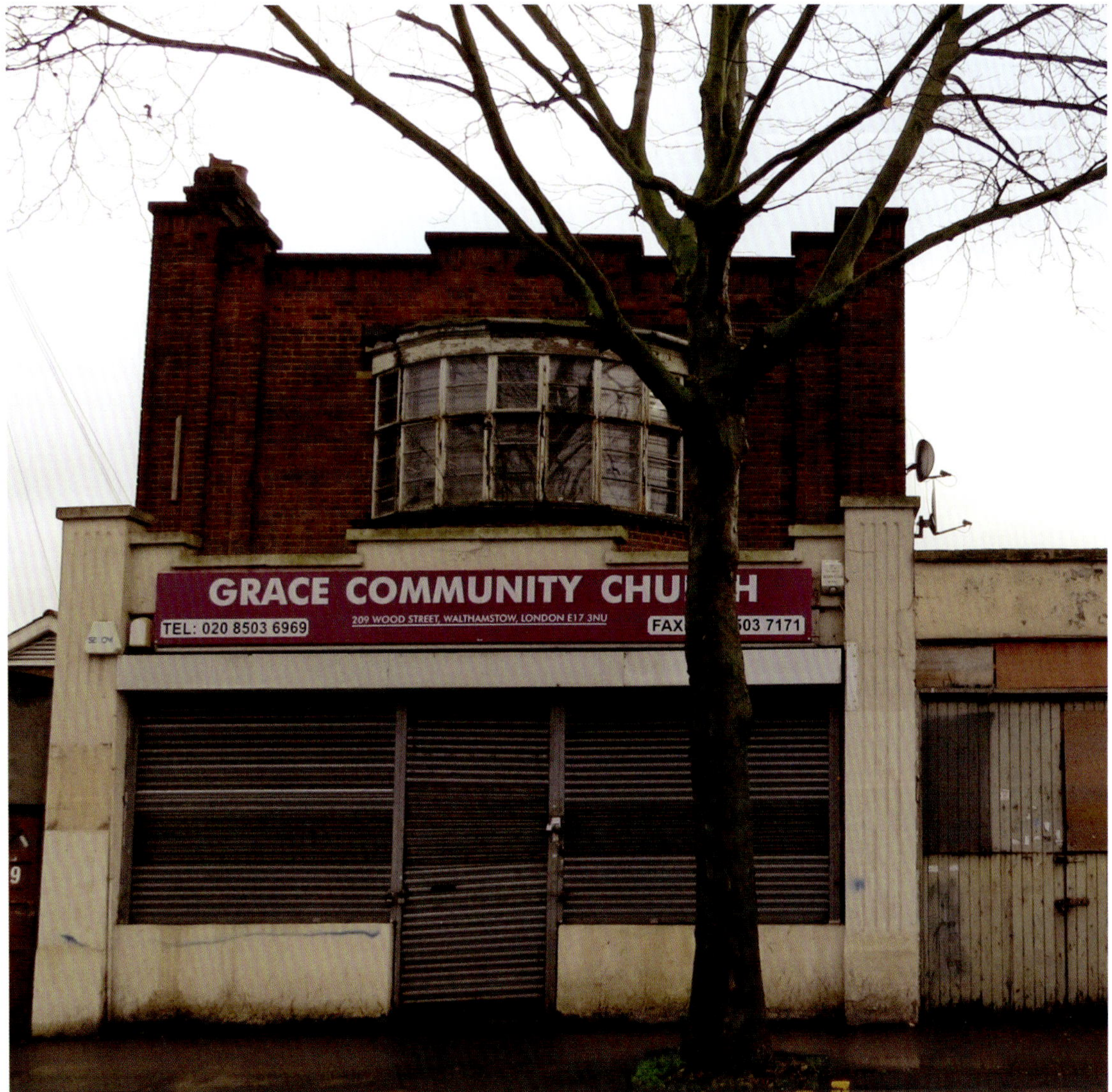

ABOVE:

Nature Study Museum, St George-in-the-East, Shadwell

Built in the 1870s, this brick building was originally part of a mortuary. In 1904 it was converted into the Nature Study Museum, where local children from over-crowded urban environments could get hands-on with nature. It closed in 1939.

LEFT:

Grace Community Church

Between 2005 and 2012, church attendance across Greater London grew by 16 per cent, with around 720,000 people going regularly. This growth, bucking the nationwide trend, is attributed to different immigrant groups; in the 2012 census, 14 per cent of all church services used a language other than English.

OPPOSITE:

Barnes Hospital

Before the foundation of the National Health Service (NHS) in 1948, London had over 500 smaller, specific and specialist hospitals. Barnes Isolation Hospital – established in 1889 – focused on patients with infectious diseases, and was one of many that joined the NHS.

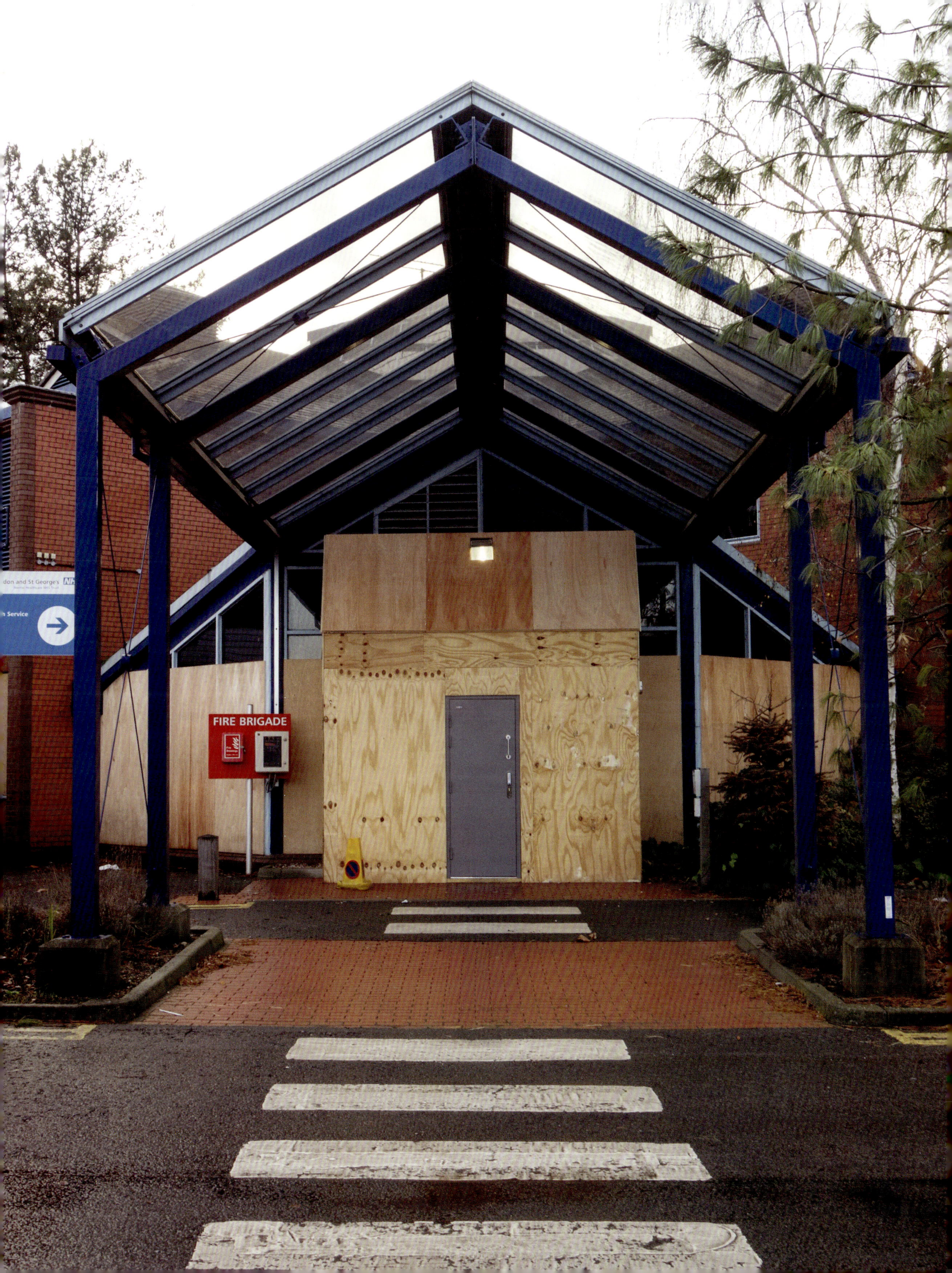
FIRE BRIGADE

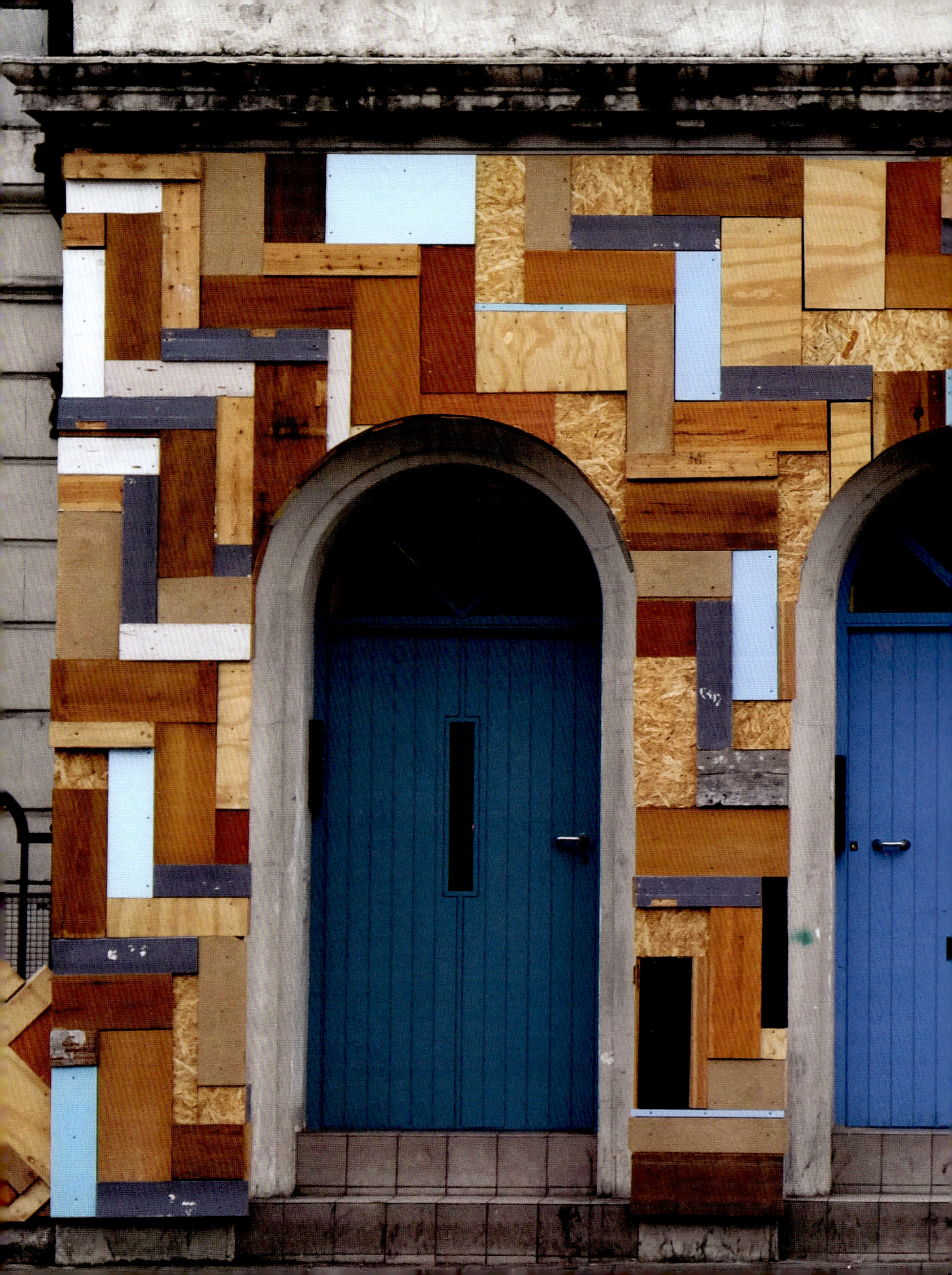

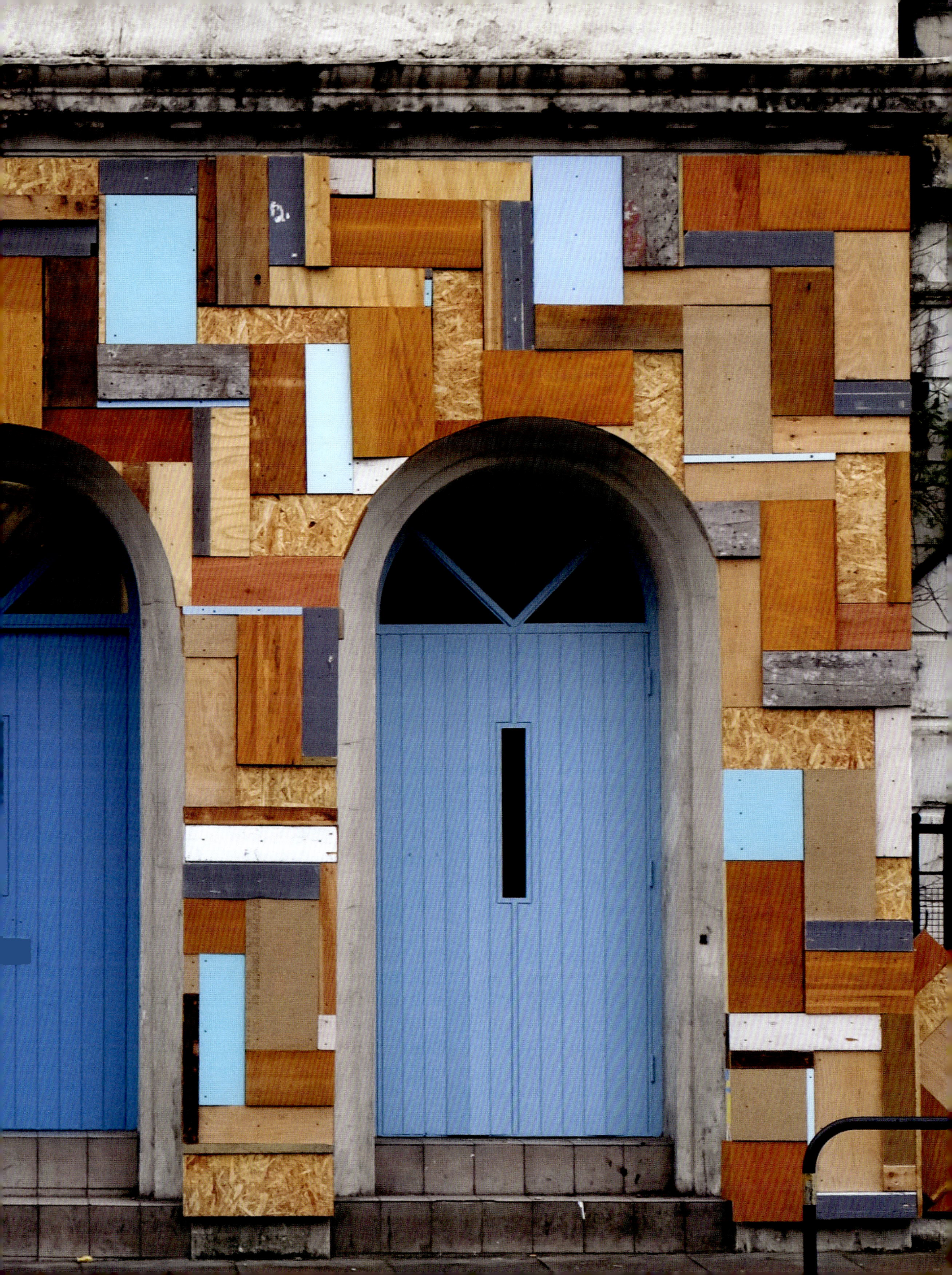

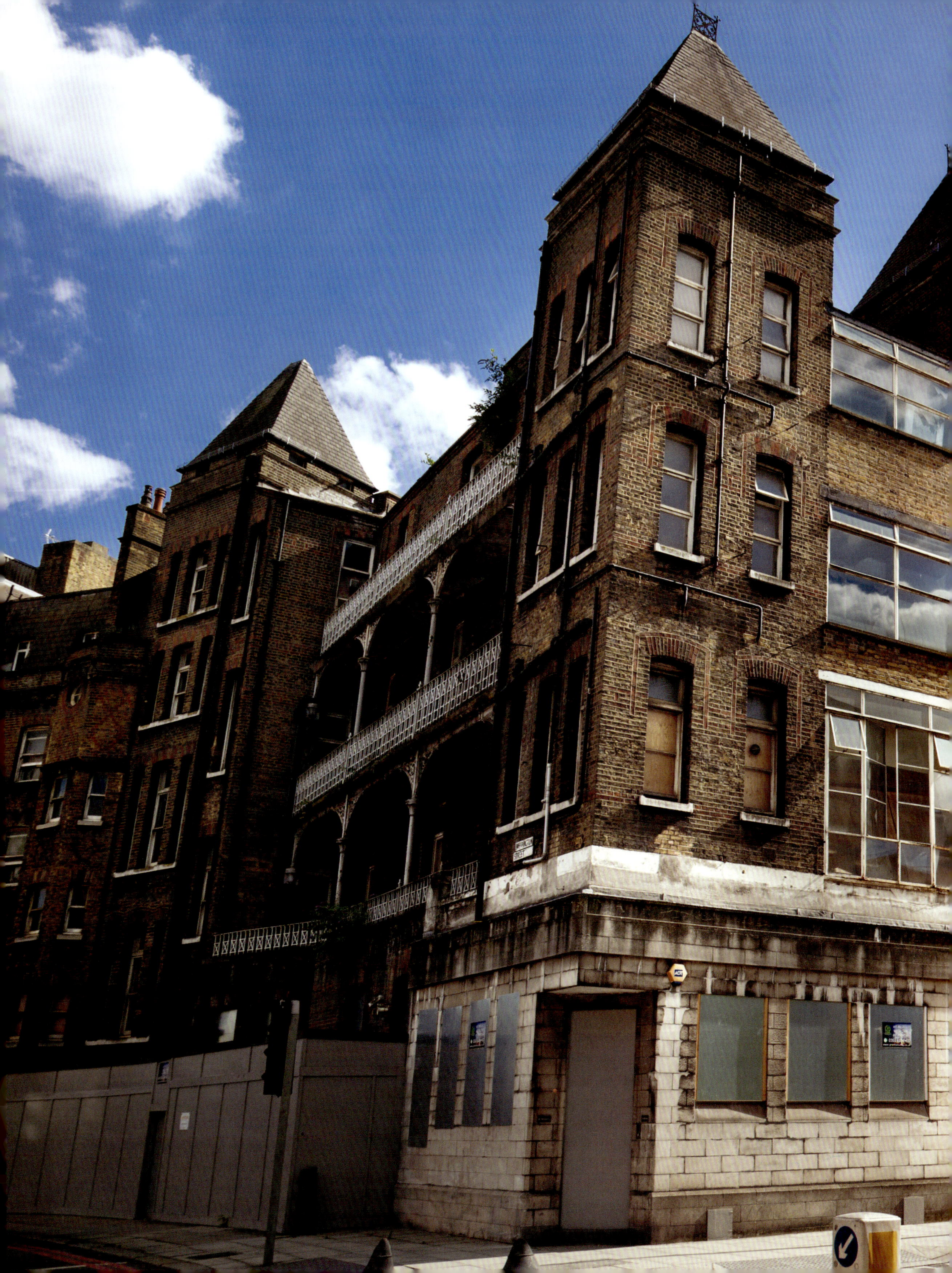

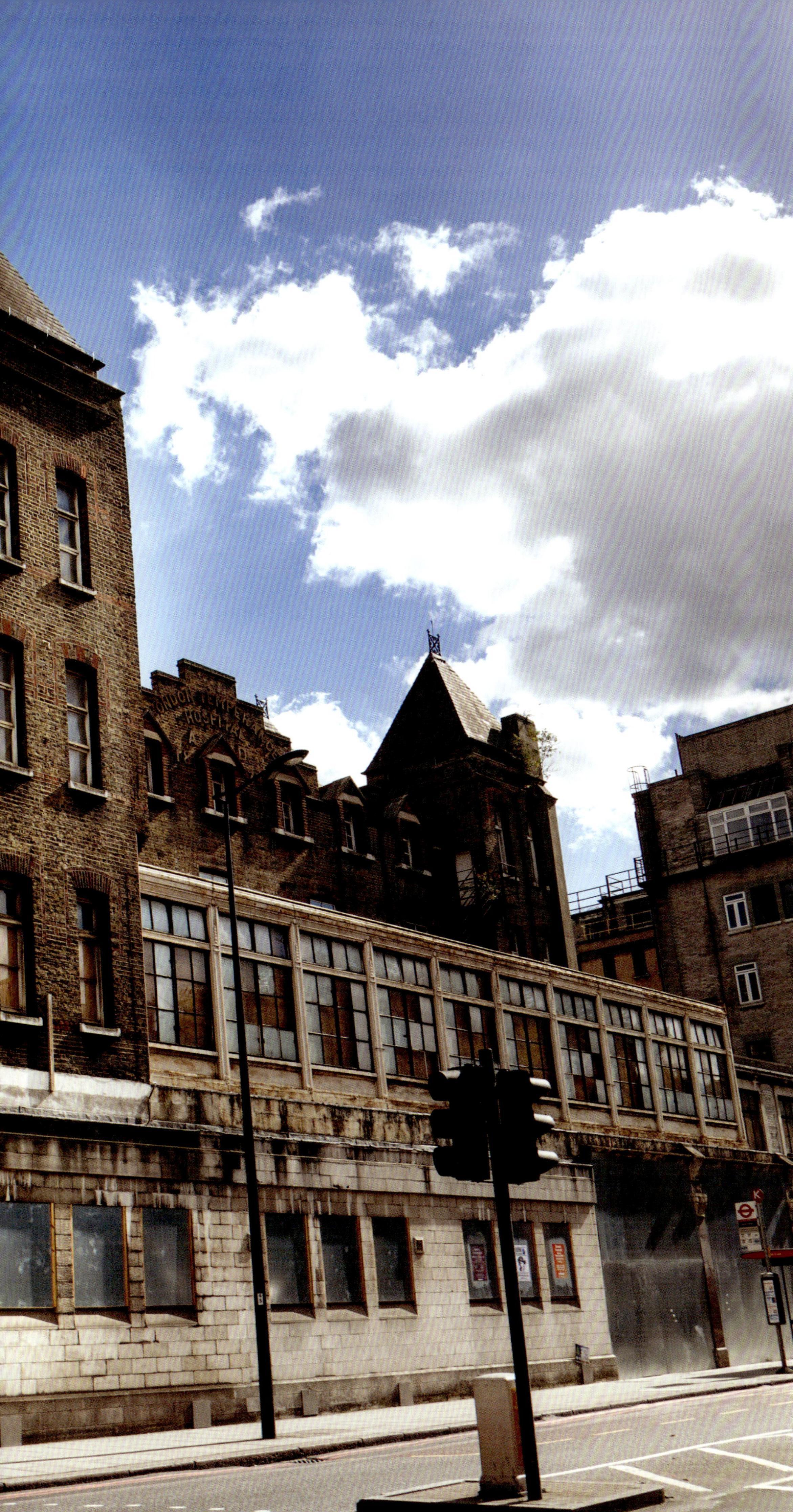

PREVIOUS PAGES AND LEFT:

National Temperance Hospital, Camden

During the 19th century alcohol consumption was widespread, not just socially in pubs, but also prescribed as a medical treatment. The National Temperance Hospital was opened in 1873, managed by a board who discouraged the use of alcohol for medicinal purposes. It closed in 1990.

OVERLEAF (BOTH PHOTOGRAPHS):

St George's Hospital, Hornchurch

Completed just before the outbreak of World War II, this building was taken over by the Ministry of Defence and used as a base by RAF Hornchurch. After the war it became a hospital, mainly for elderly local patients. In 2012 a refurbishment was announced and the majority of patients were transferred; however, a month later, the pathogen Legionella was discovered in the hospital's water system and it was closed immediately. In 2018 the site was sold to developers.

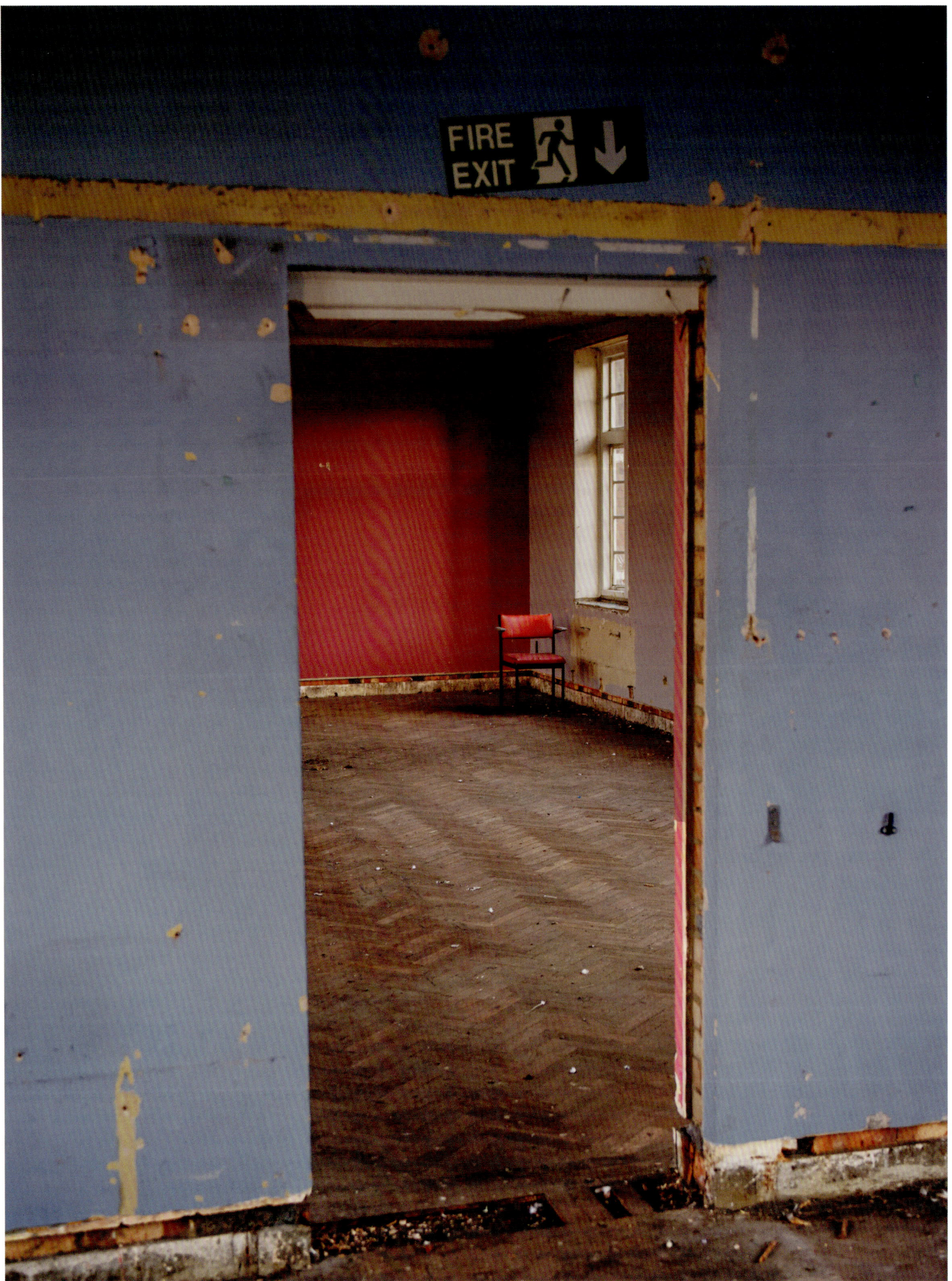
FIRE
EXIT

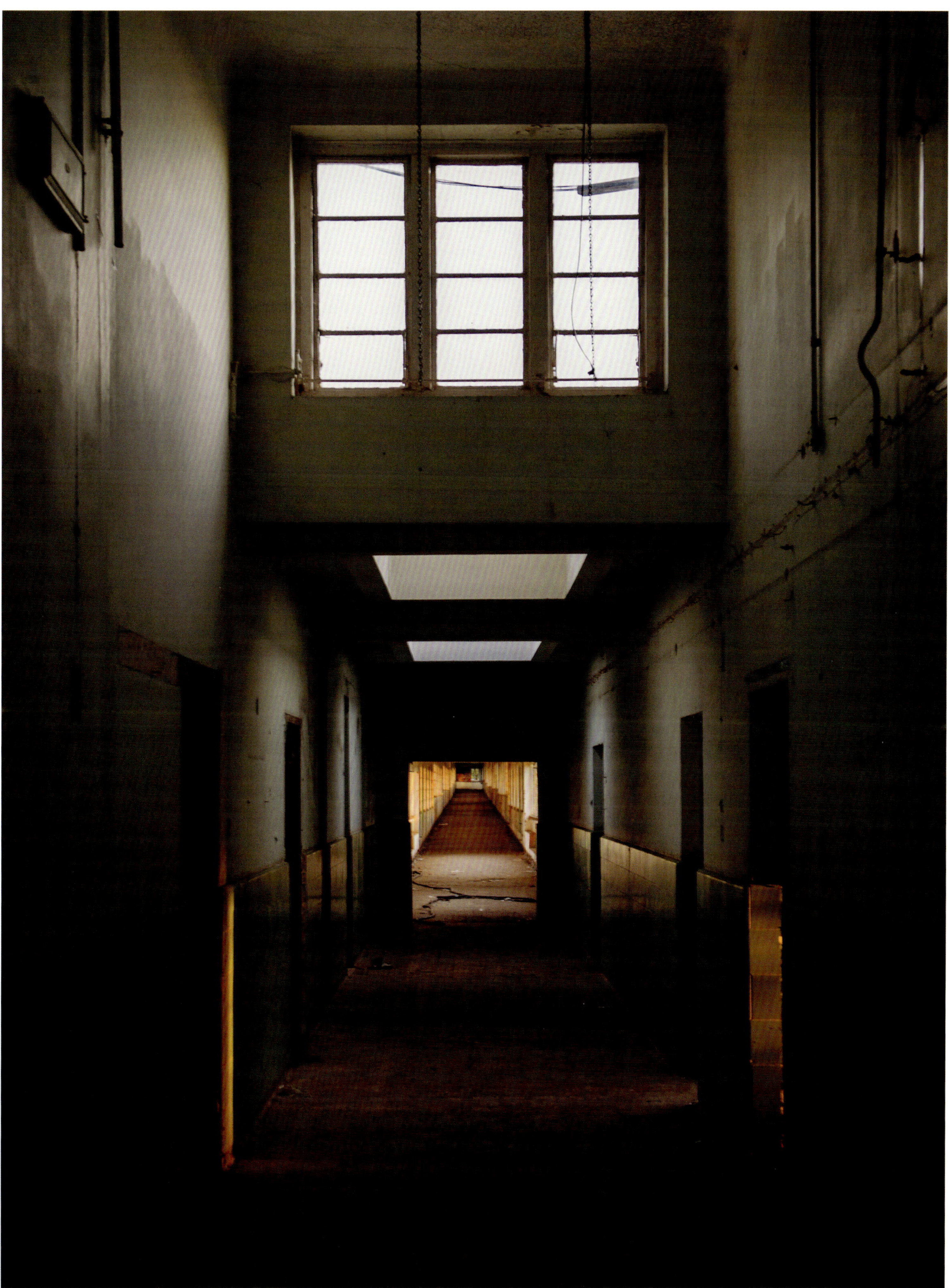

St George's Hospital, Hornchurch
The 29-acre site was sold for £40 million, the largest sale ever by NHS Property. The development by Bellway Homes is called St George's Park.

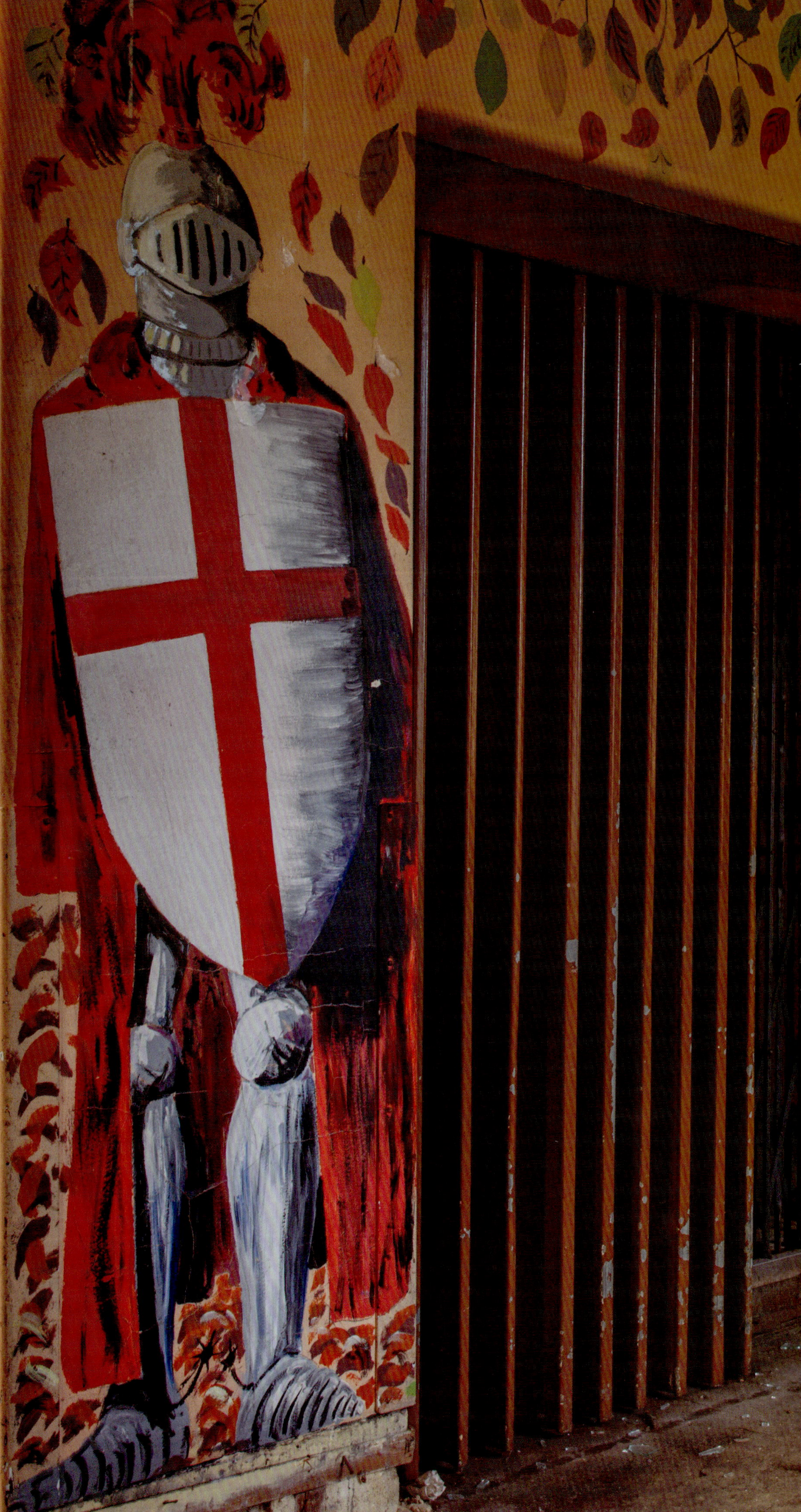

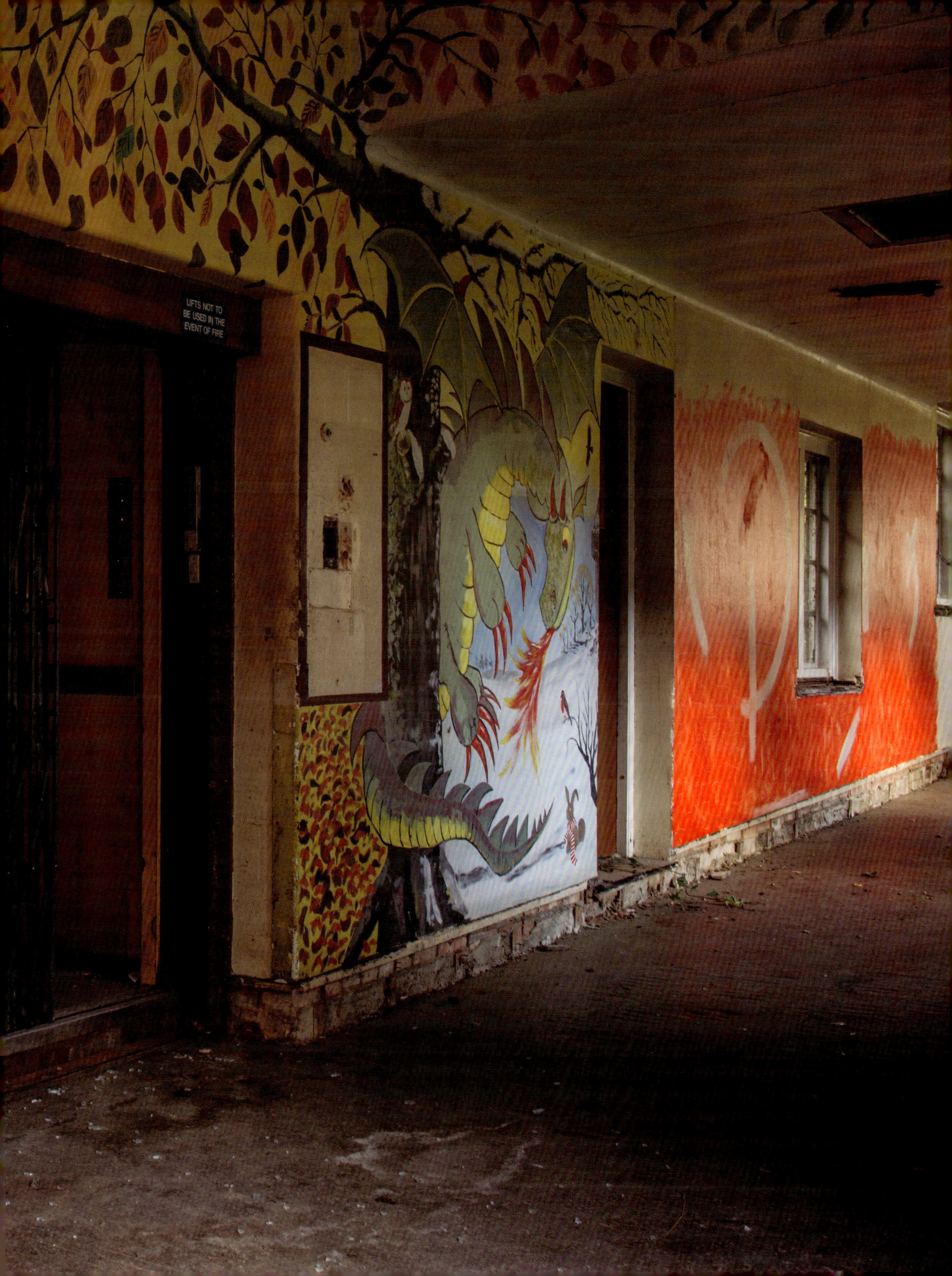
LIFTS NOT TO
BE USED IN THE
EVENT OF FIRE

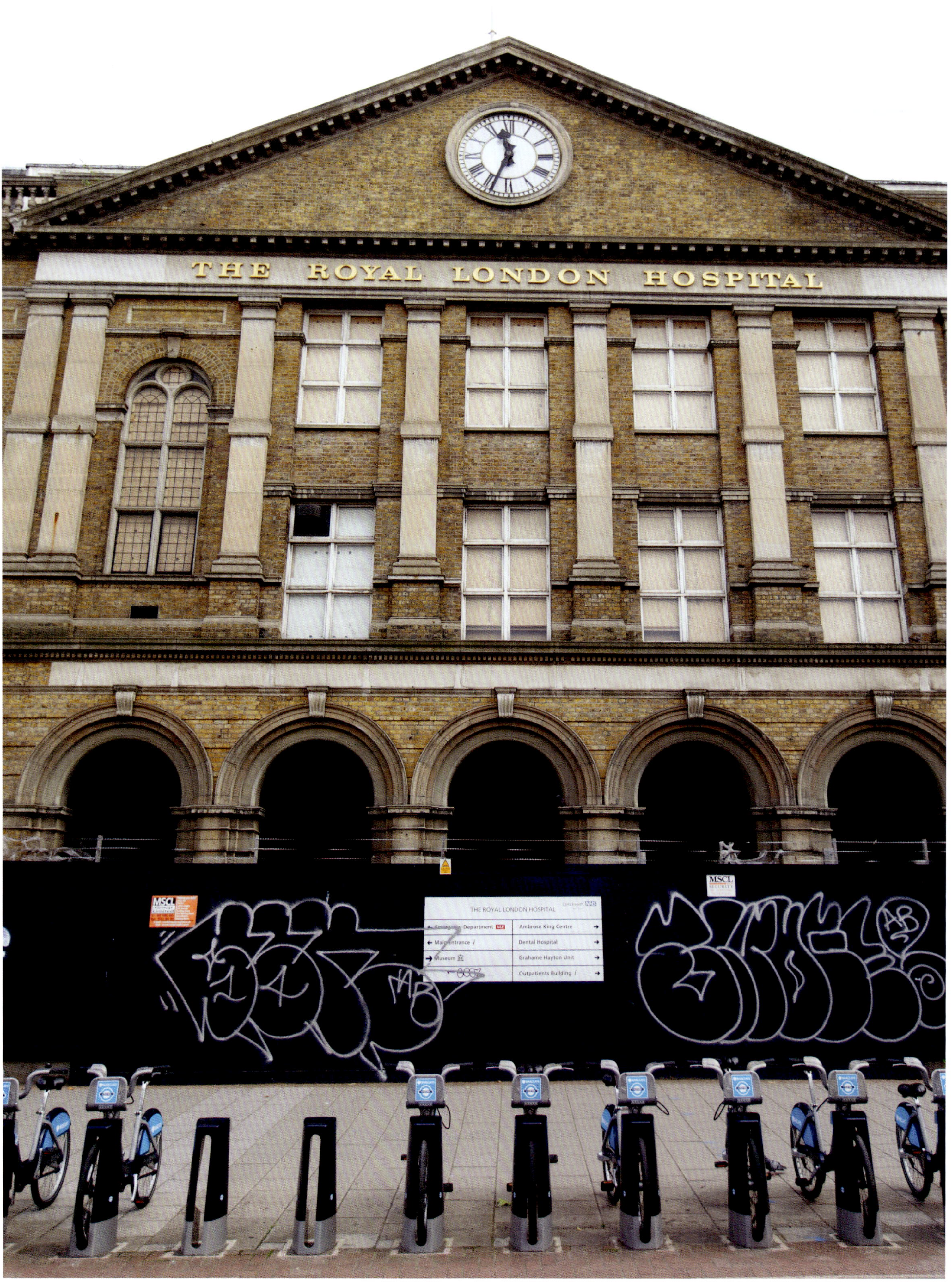
THE ROYAL LONDON HOSPITAL
THE ROYAL LONDON HOSPITAL
Ambrose King Centre
Dental Hospital
Grahame Hayton Unit
Outpatients Building
Museum

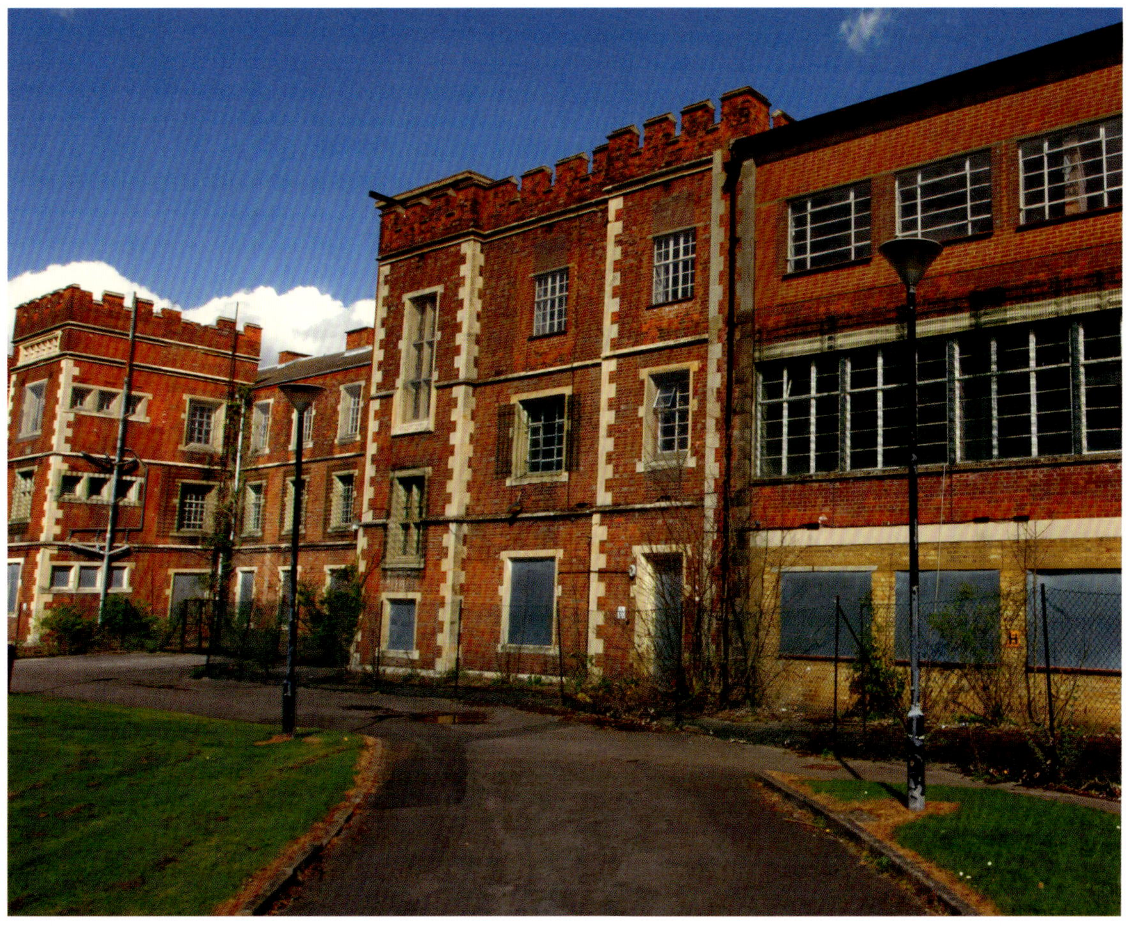

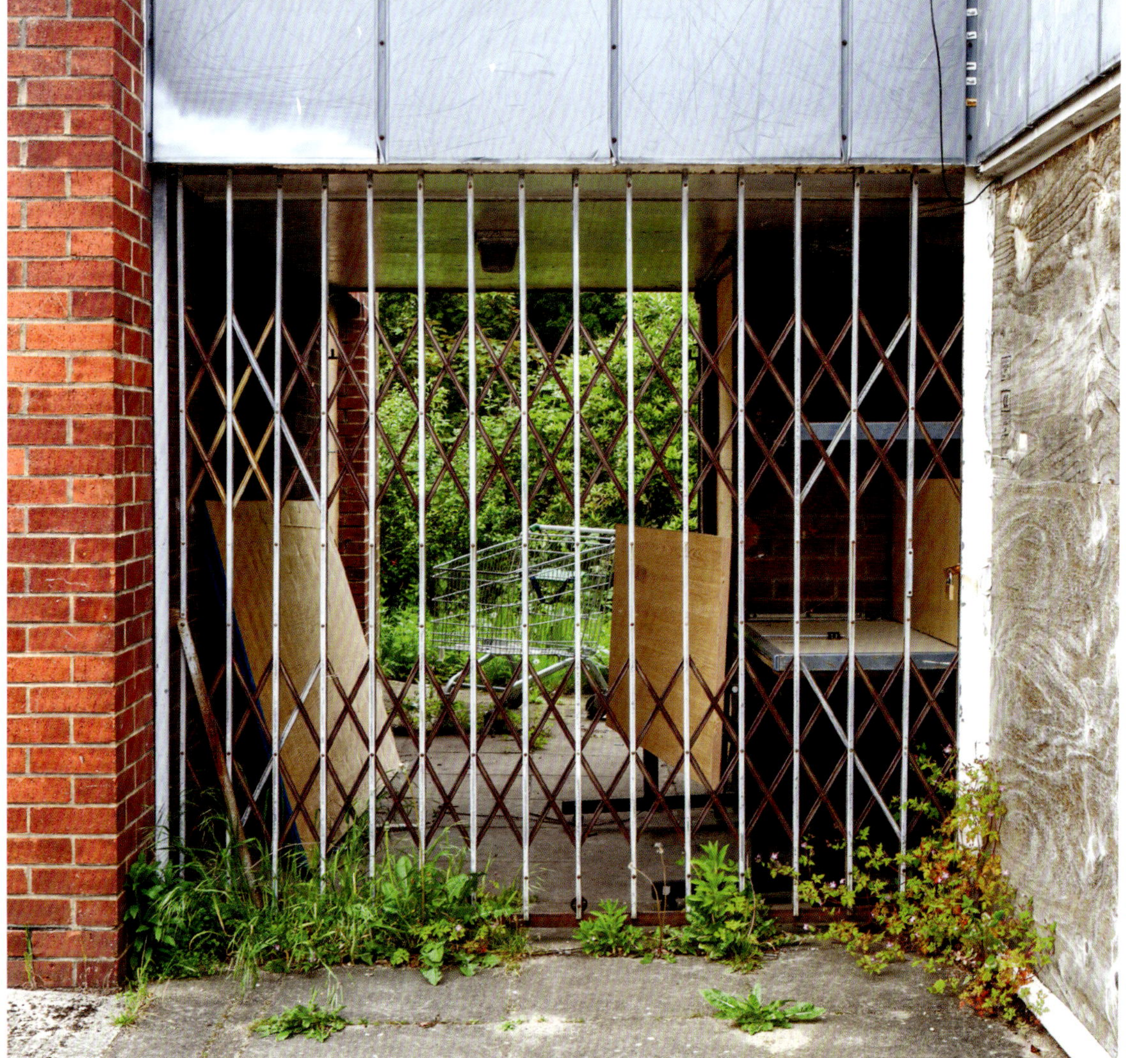

LEFT:

Springfield Psychiatric Hospital, Tooting

Originally Surrey County Pauper Lunatic Asylum, the grand red-brick building was built in a Tudor style and opened in 1840. The site is part of Springfield University Hospital, providing mental health services for Southwest London. The older buildings are in the process of residential redevelopment.

BELOW:

Mereway Day Centre, Twickenham

The centre used to provide social and therapeutic activities as well as hot food and laundry facilities. It closed in 2007 and the council has since approved a residential development.

OPPOSITE:

The Royal London Hospital, Whitechapel

Established by a small group of philanthropists and businessmen in 1740, by the end of the 19th century the Royal London Hospital was the largest in the country. It became famous for its nurse training school, where Elizabeth Garrett Anderson – the first woman to qualify as a doctor – completed her training. Another notable resident in the hospital was Joseph Merrick, known as 'the Elephant Man'. Born in 1862 with severe physical deformities, Merrick was exhibited as part of a 'freak show' in London and Europe, but later lived in the hospital, where he was looked after for the remainder of his life.

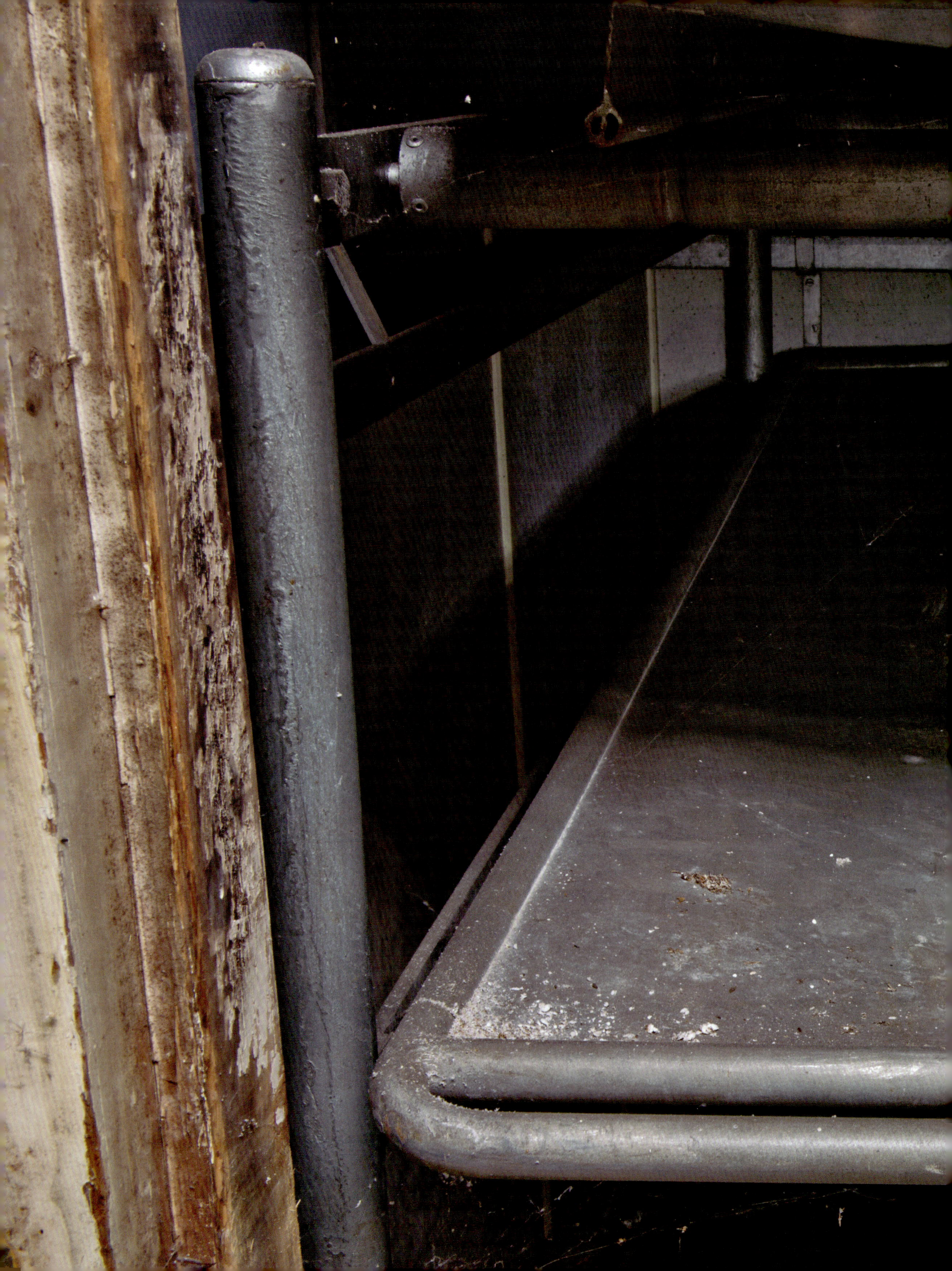

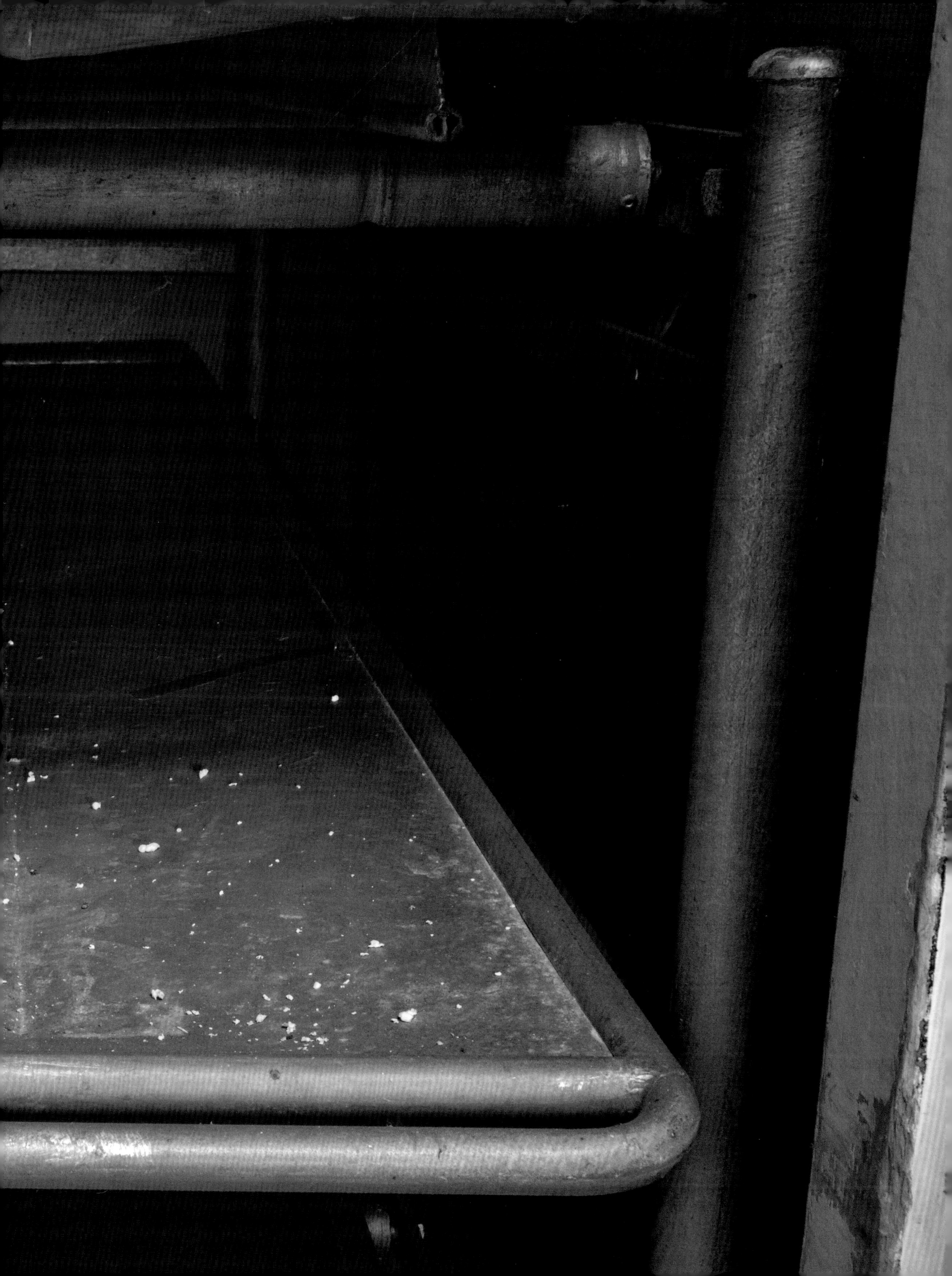

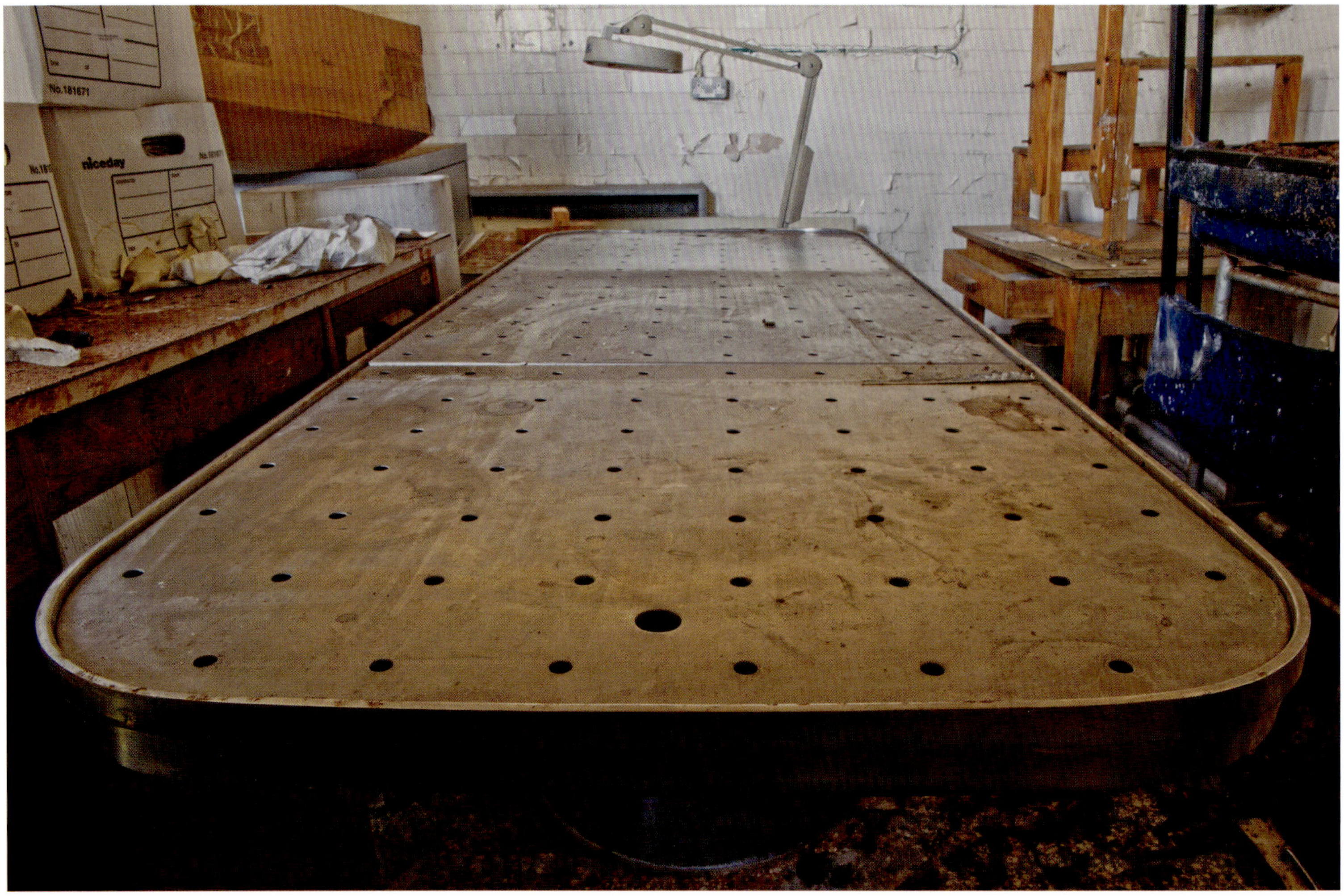

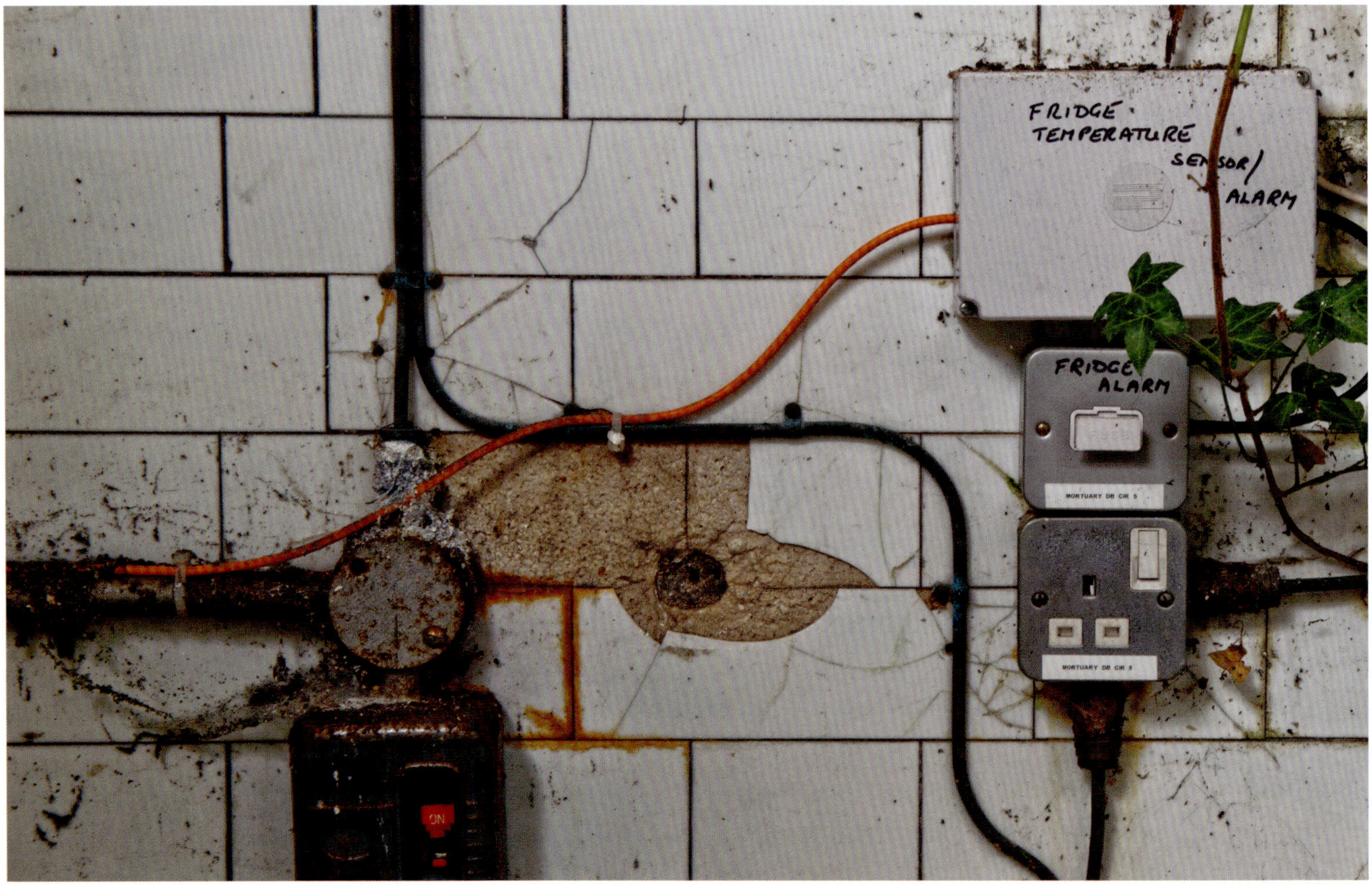

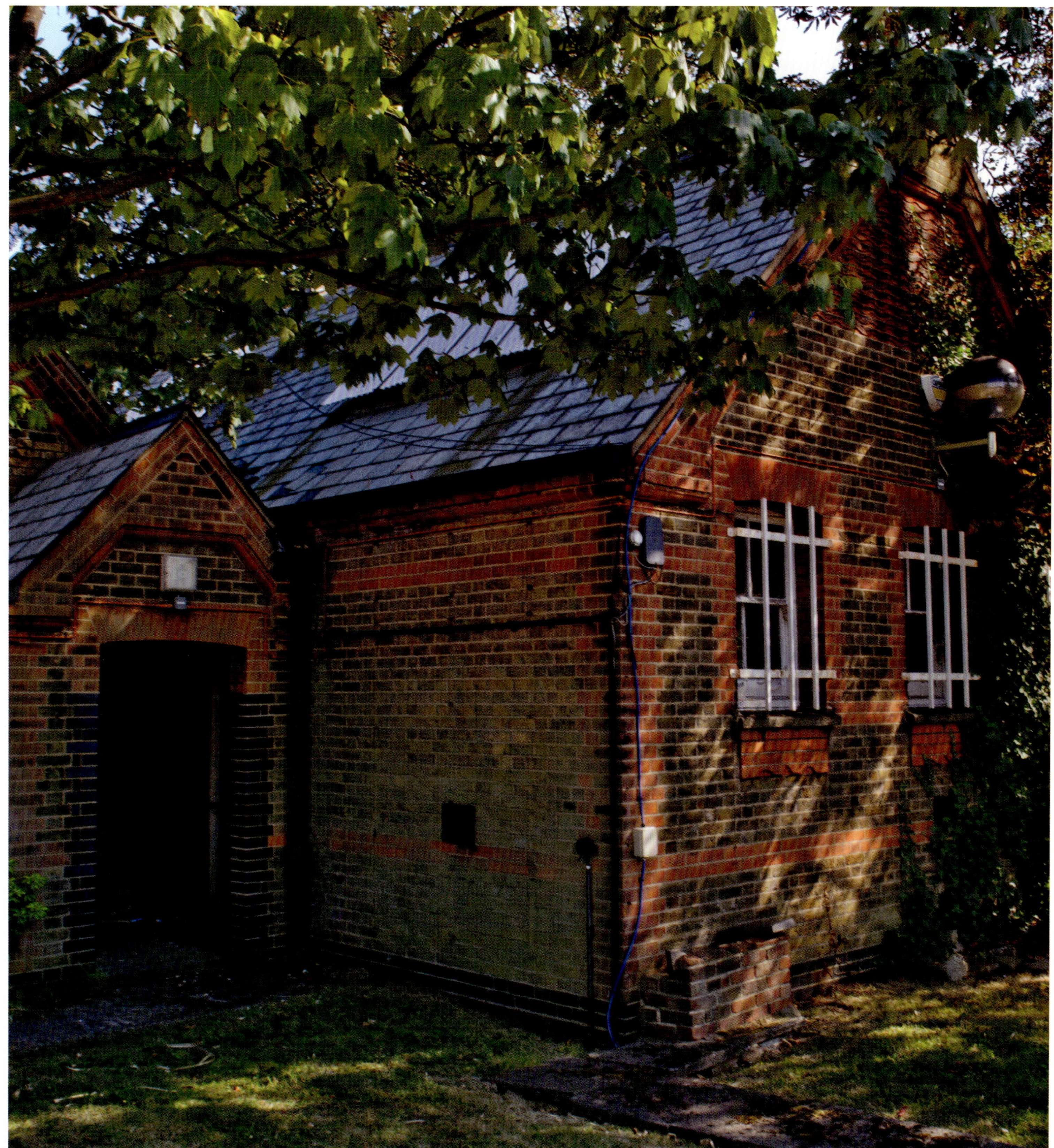

PREVIOUS PAGES AND ALL PHOTOGRAPHS ON THESE PAGES:

St Ann's Hospital Mortuary, Haringey

In 1892 scarlet fever killed 1,169 Londoners, overwhelming hospitals. A 19-acre site for the North Eastern Fever Hospital had been chosen in 1890. However, despite erecting temporary huts in the grounds, patients were still turned away. The name was changed to St Ann's General Hospital in 1951 and it continued to treat acute infectious diseases and patients with chest ailments up until 2012.

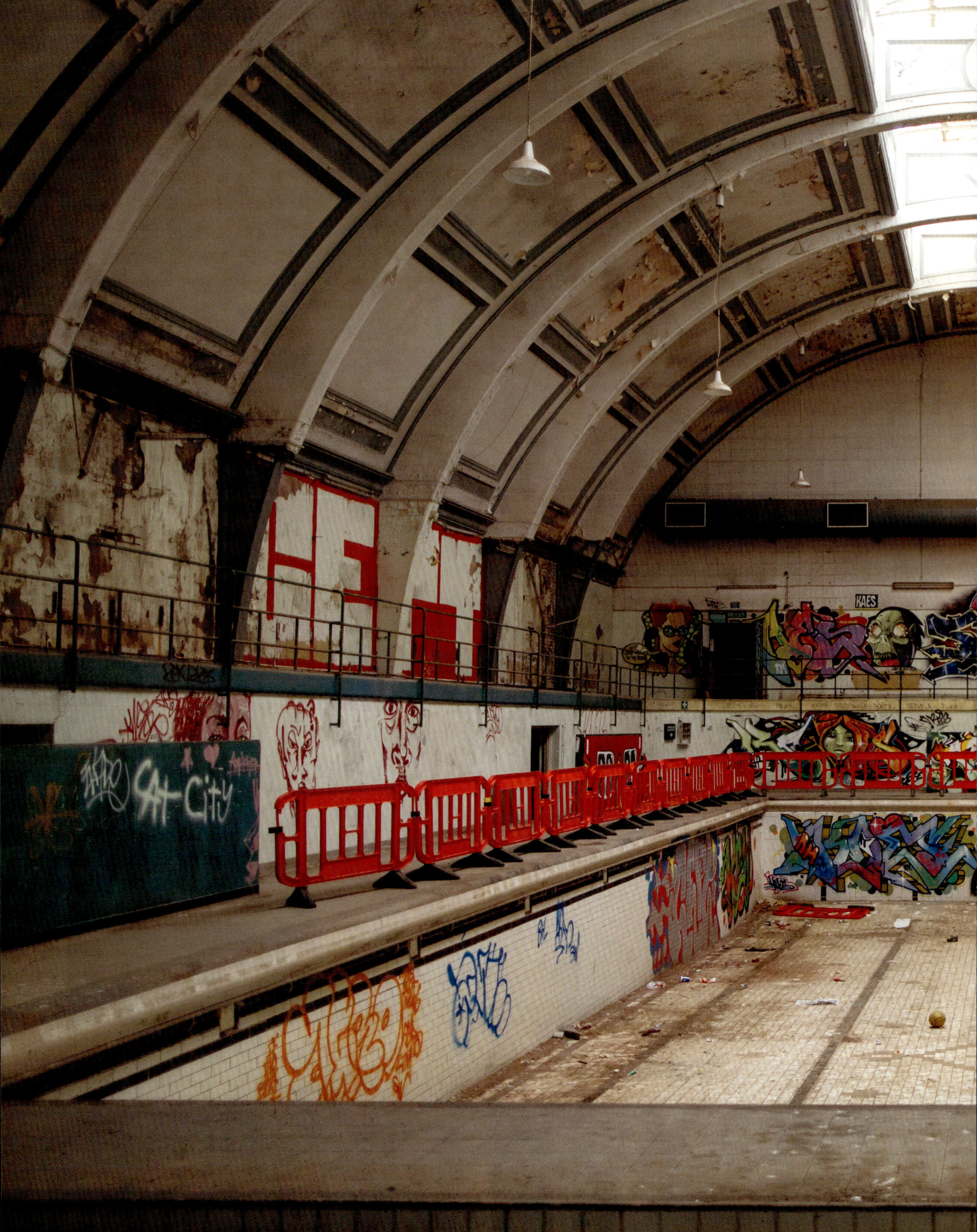
KAES
Cat-City

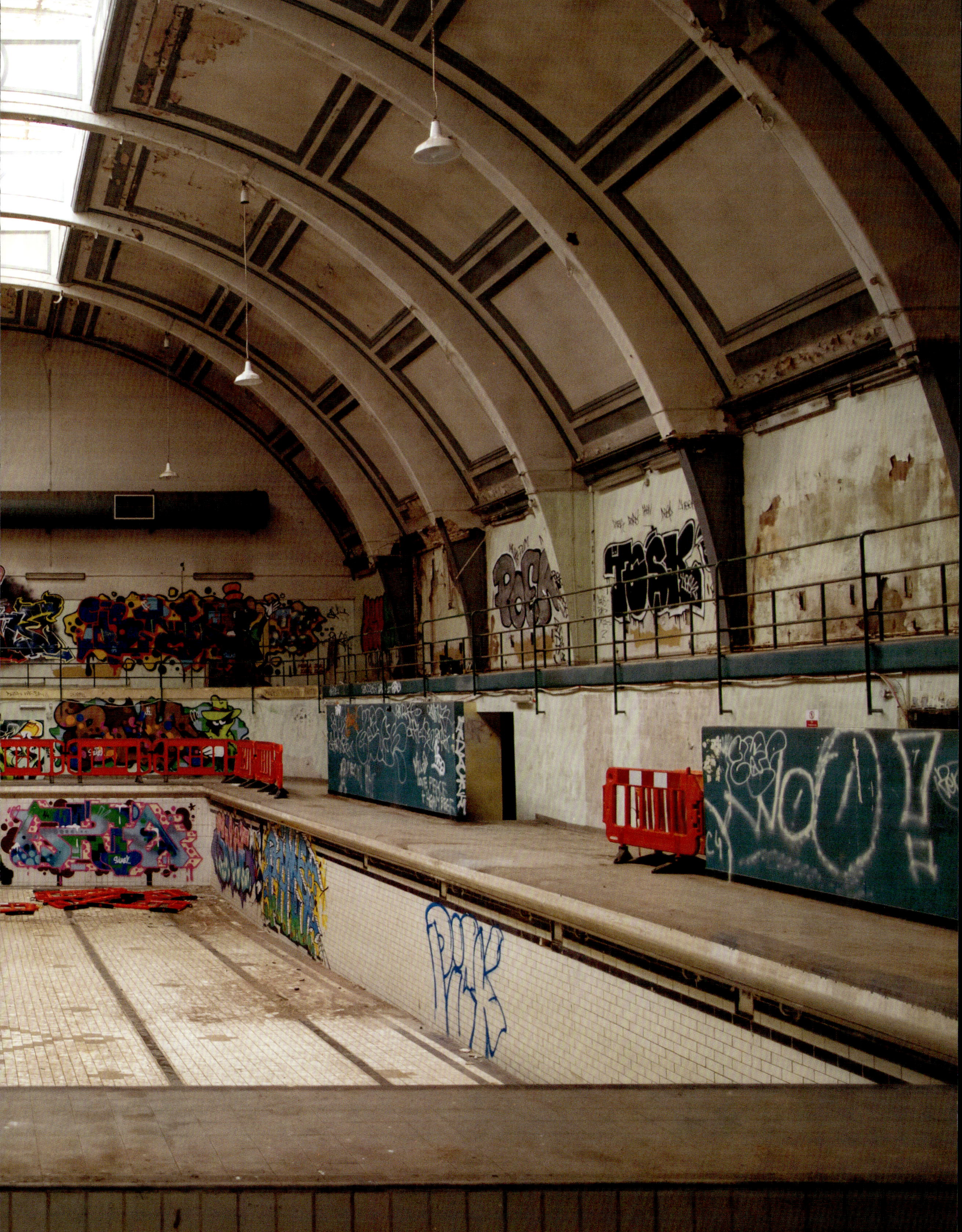

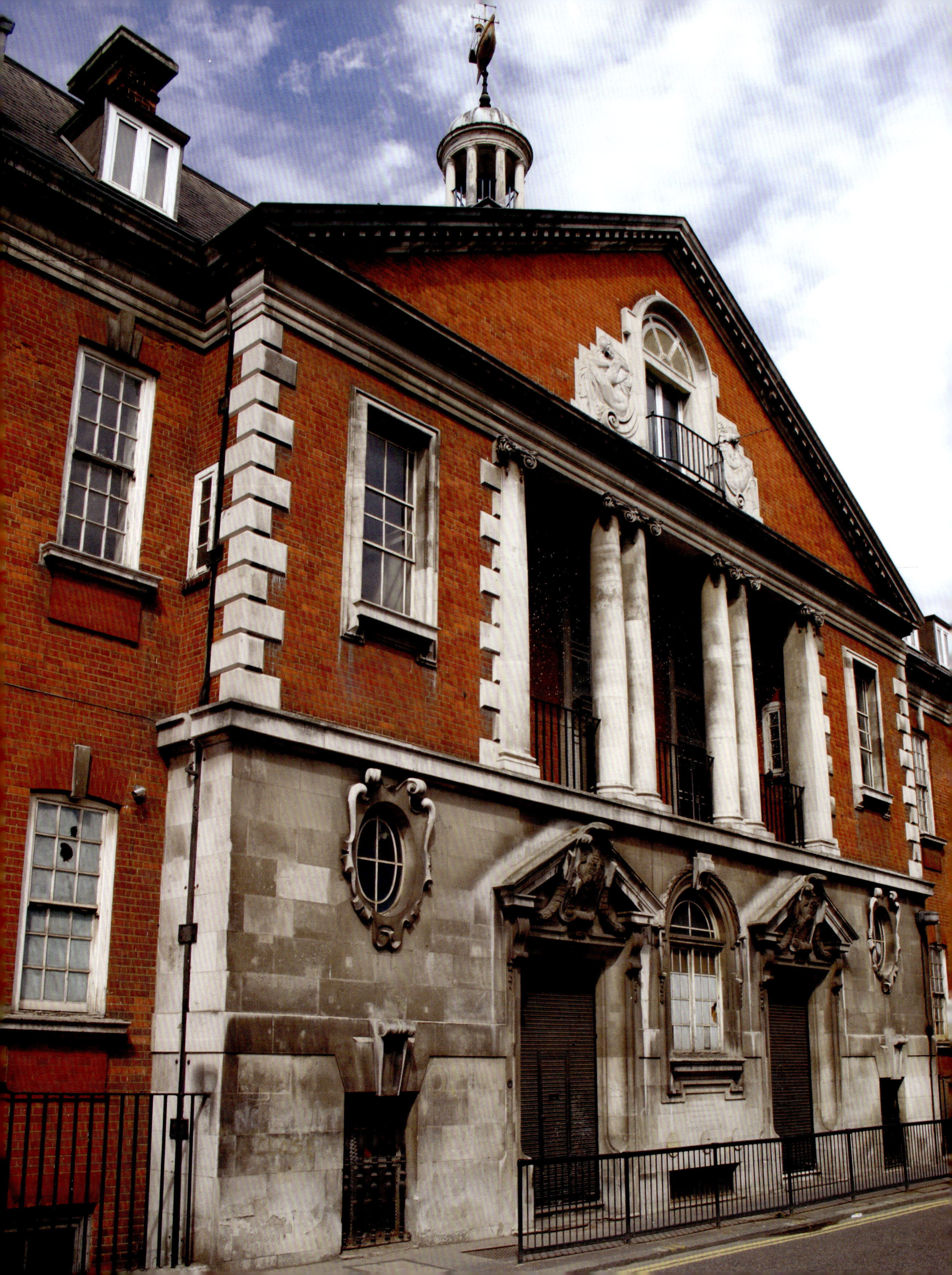

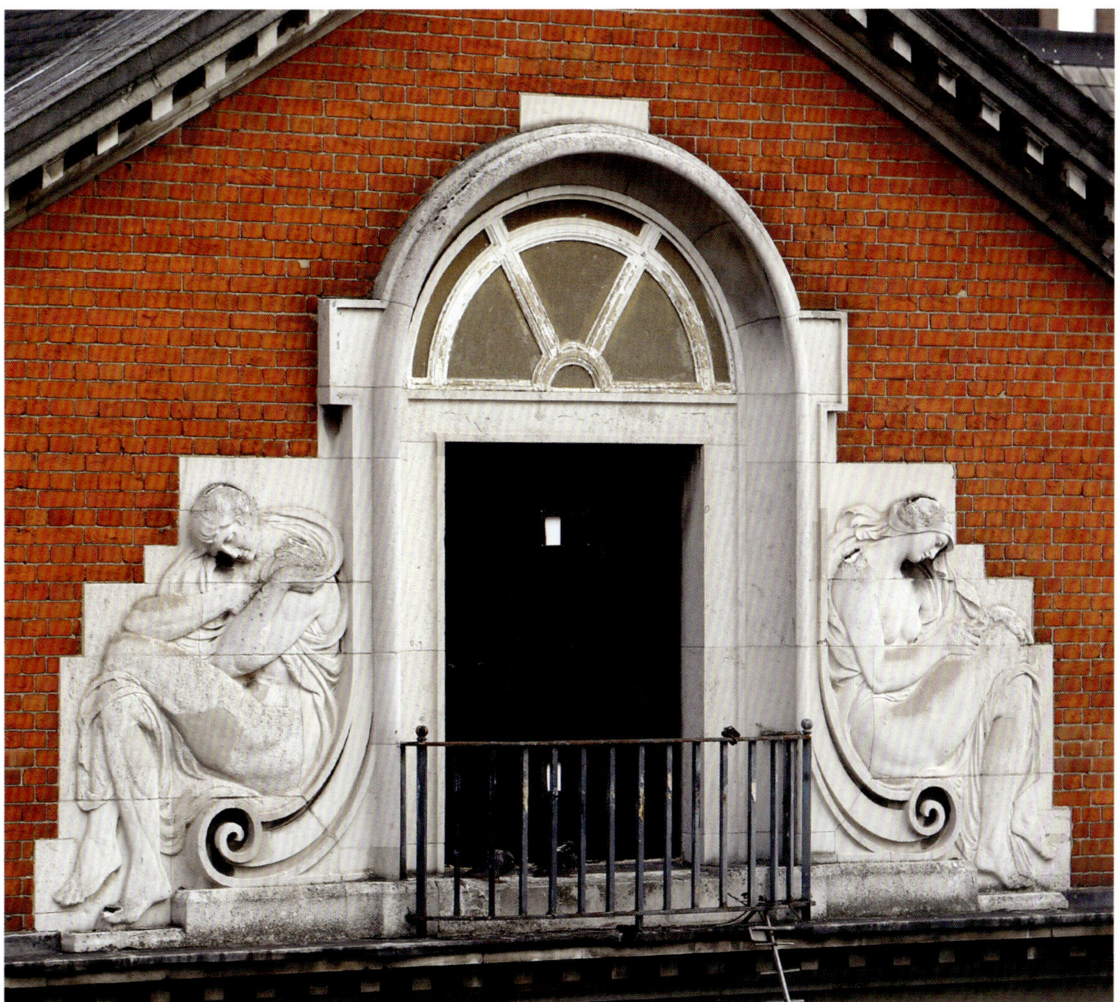

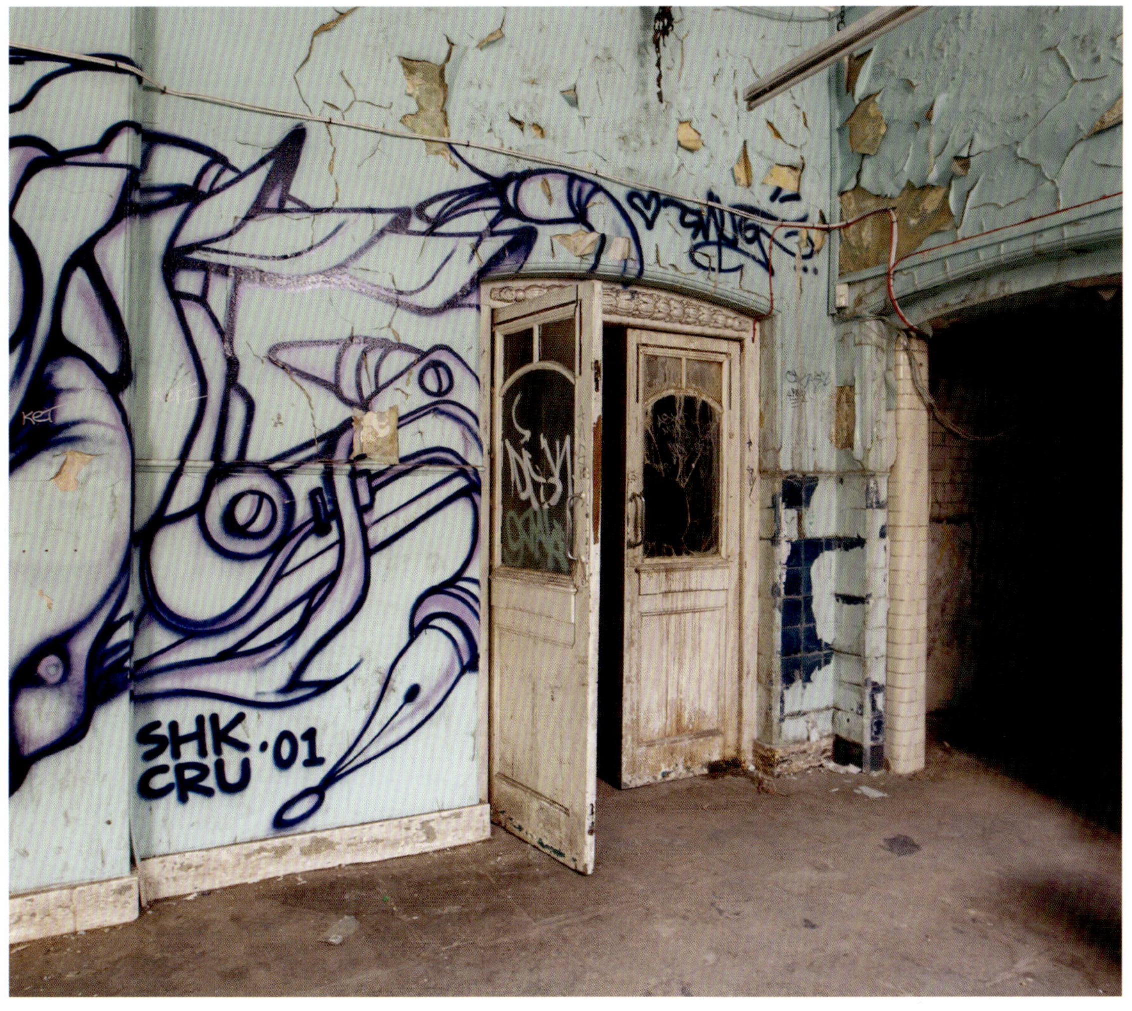

PREVIOUS PAGES AND ALL PHOTOGRAPHS ON THESE PAGES:

Haggerston Public Baths, Hackney

Alfred Cross designed 11 public baths throughout London and this one opened in 1904. At the time, few local residents had indoor plumbing and a local newspaper exclaimed it was needed 'not as a luxury, but as an absolute necessity'. The baths had one central pool as well as 91 slipper baths for individuals and 60 wash houses. They closed in 2000.

The soft red brick has Portland stone details, including two reclining female figures, and the building is topped with a gilded weathervane showing the *Golden Hind*, the ship in which Sir Francis Drake circumnavigated the globe between 1577 and 1580.

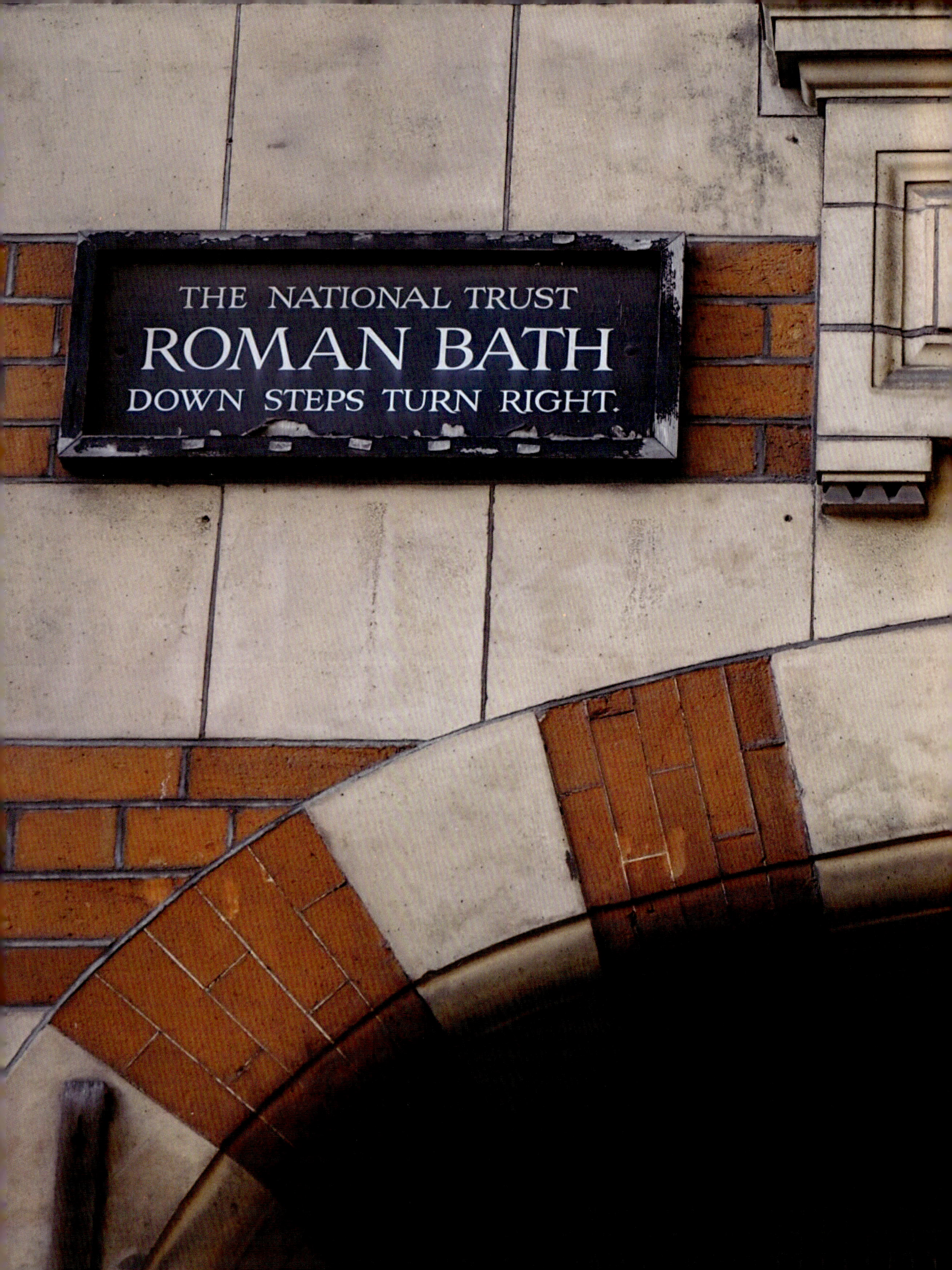
THE NATIONAL TRUST
ROMAN BATH
DOWN STEPS TURN RIGHT.

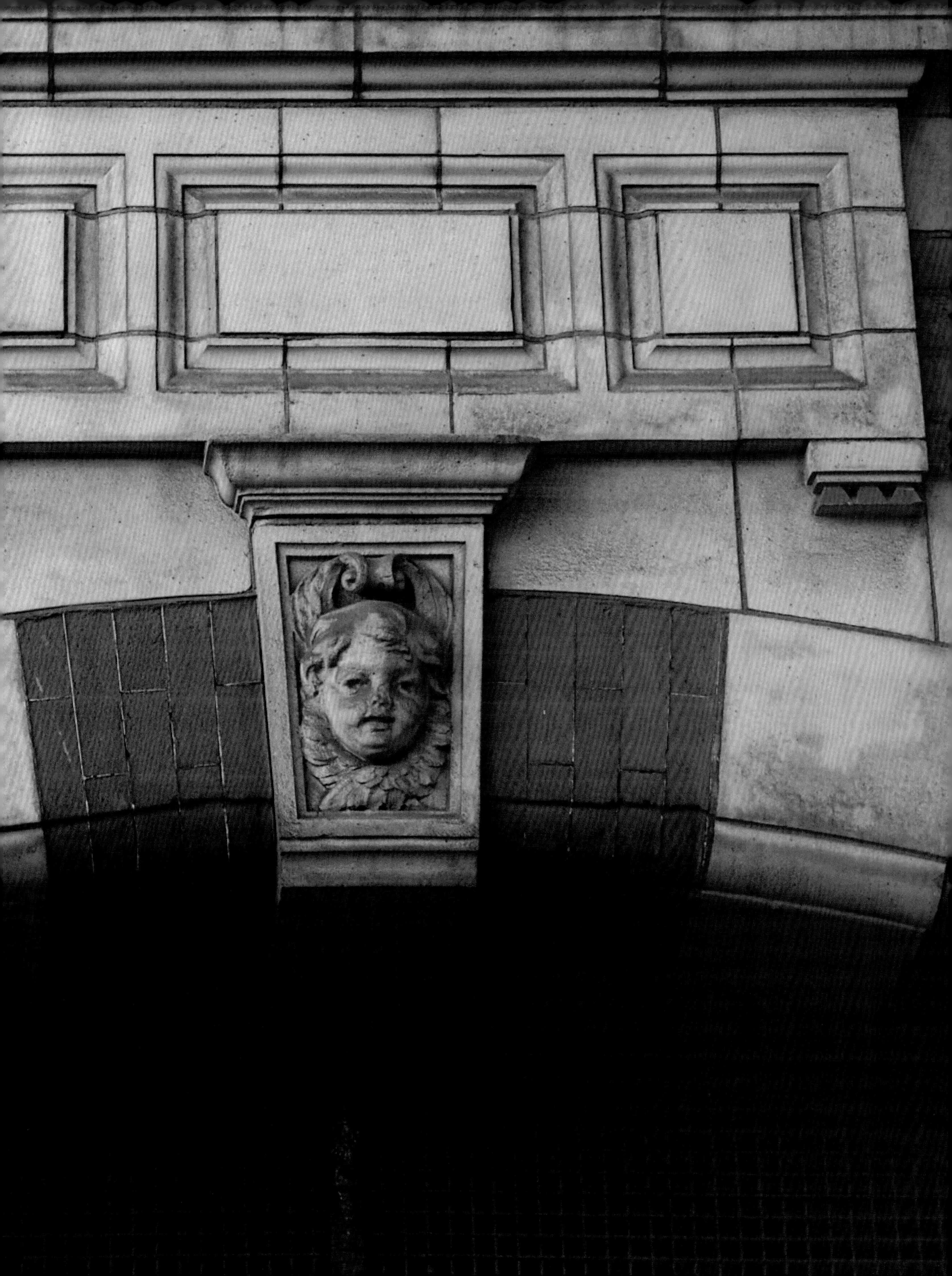

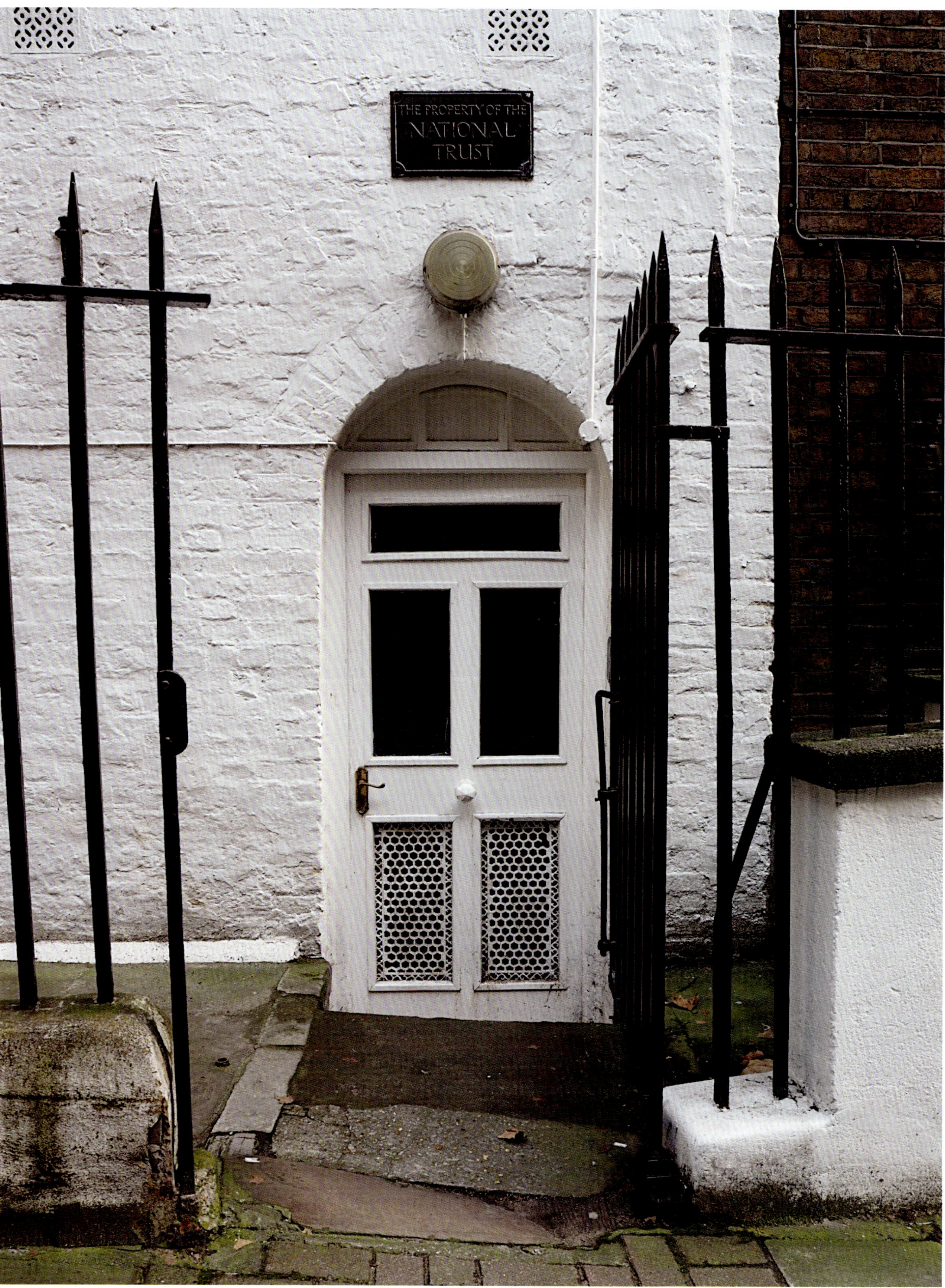
THE PROPERTY OF THE
NATIONAL
TRUST

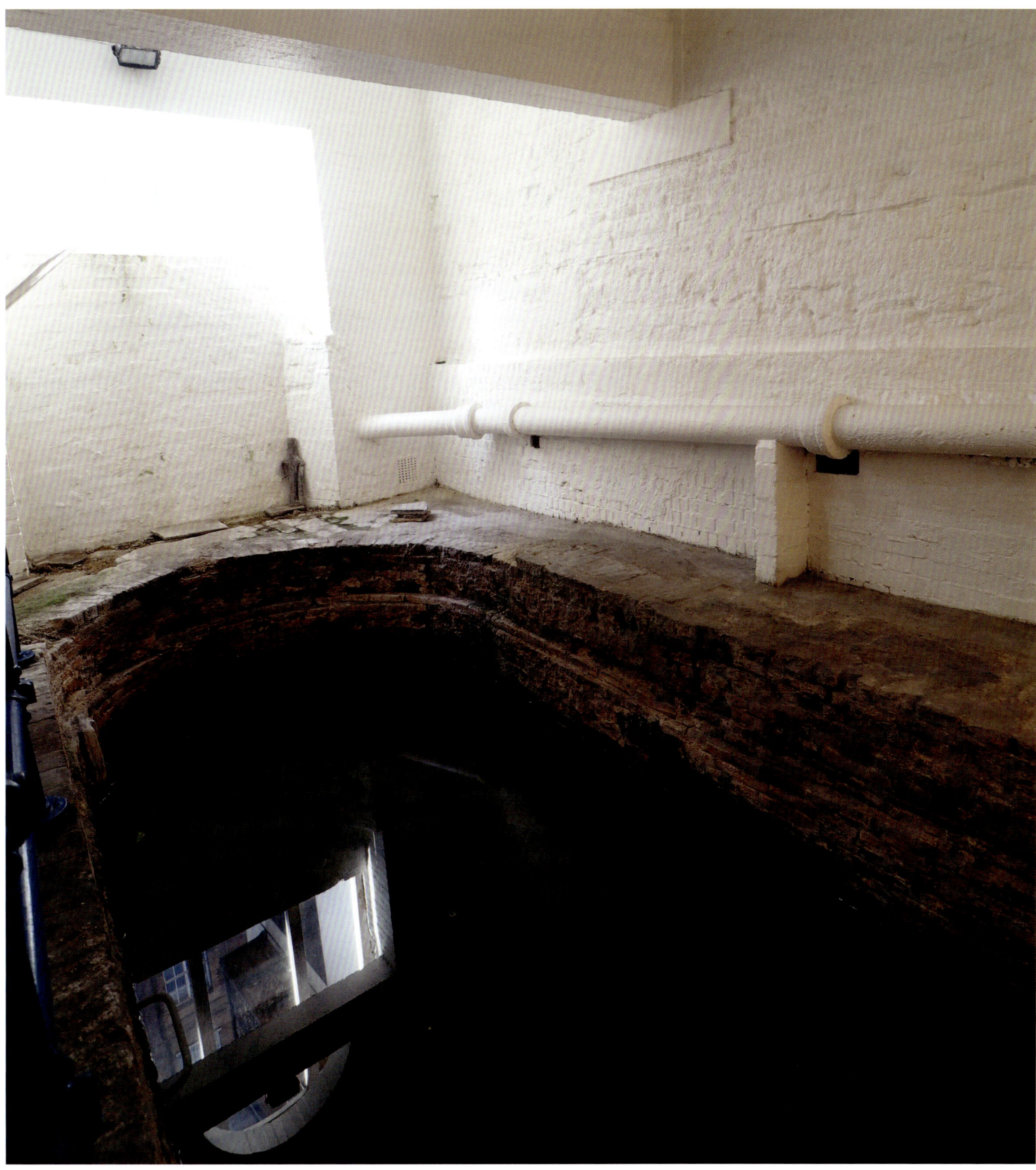

PREVIOUS PAGES AND ALL PHOTOGRAPHS ON THESE PAGES:

National Trust Roman Baths, Strand Lane

The Romans founded London around 43 CE, creating a settlement at the eastern edge of today's City of London. Although there have been Roman bathhouses discovered in London, this is not one of them, despite the authoritative sign above the archway. The baths date from 1612 and were part of a cistern that fed into a fountain complex for the local royal palace, Somerset House. However, a century later this cistern was turned into a working bath for the public, which continued to be popular until the early 1800s. It was during this time that the confusion about their heritage arose, the baths being advertised at the time as 'Old Roman Spring Baths'.

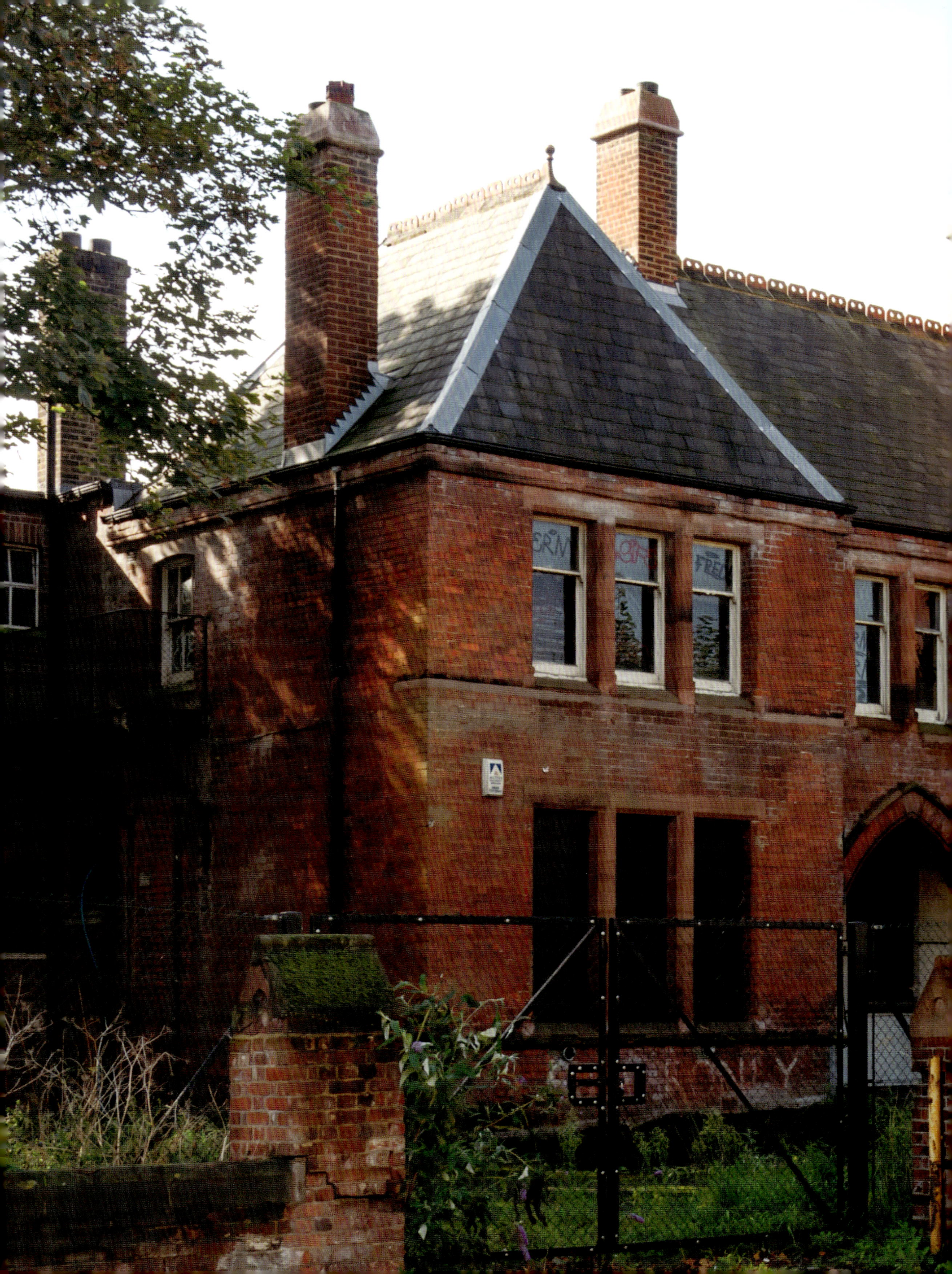

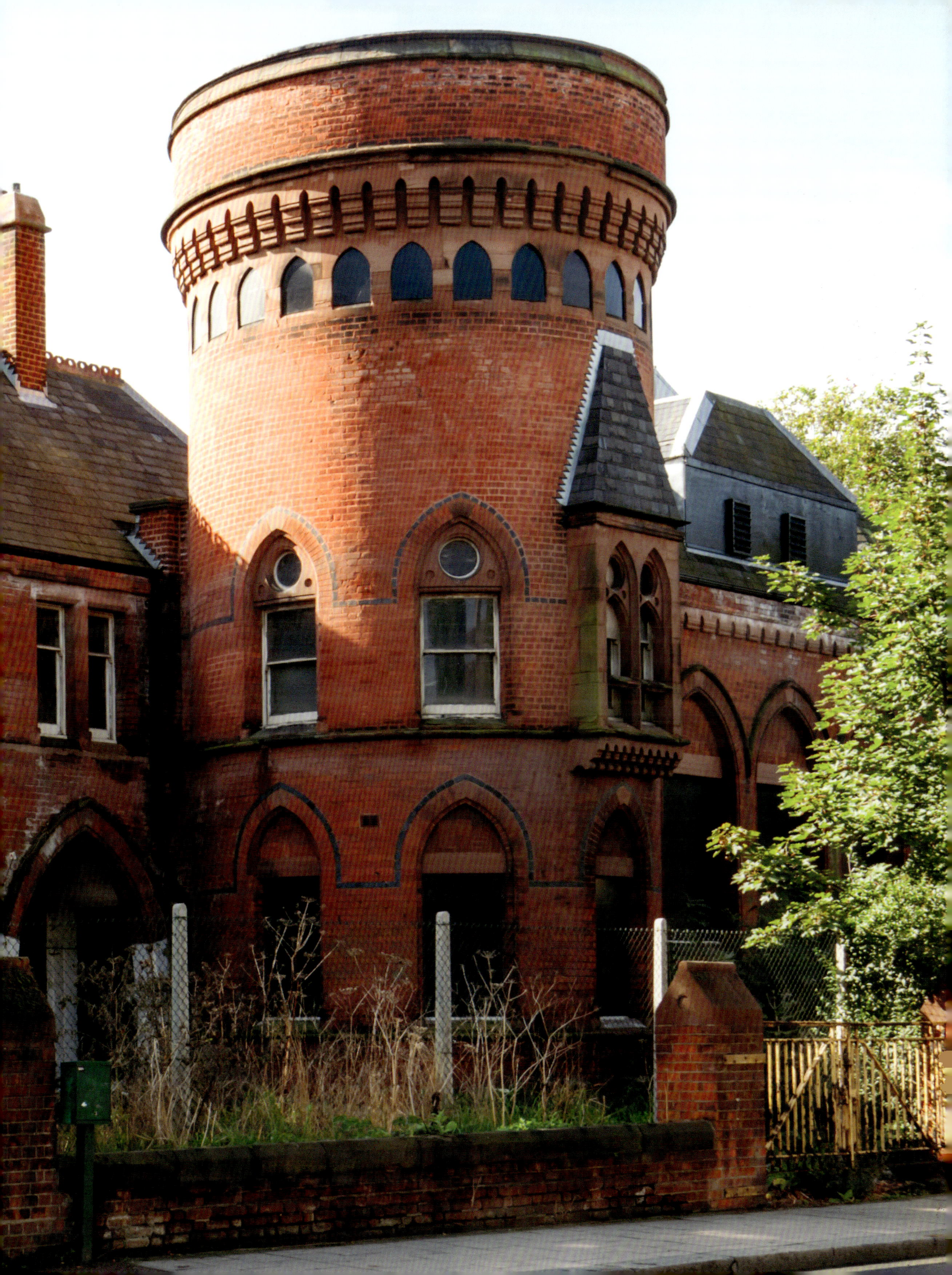

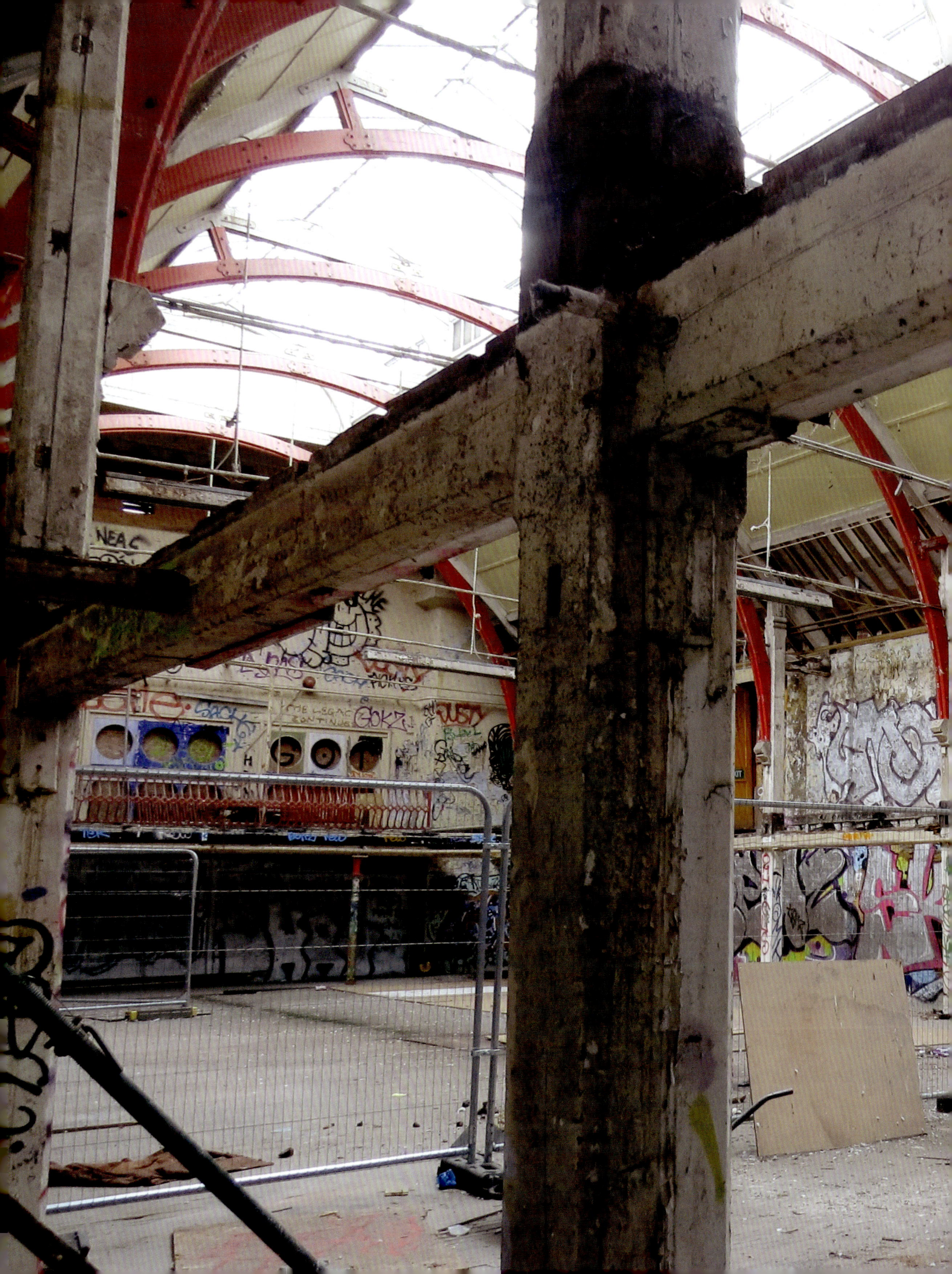
NEAC
GOKZ

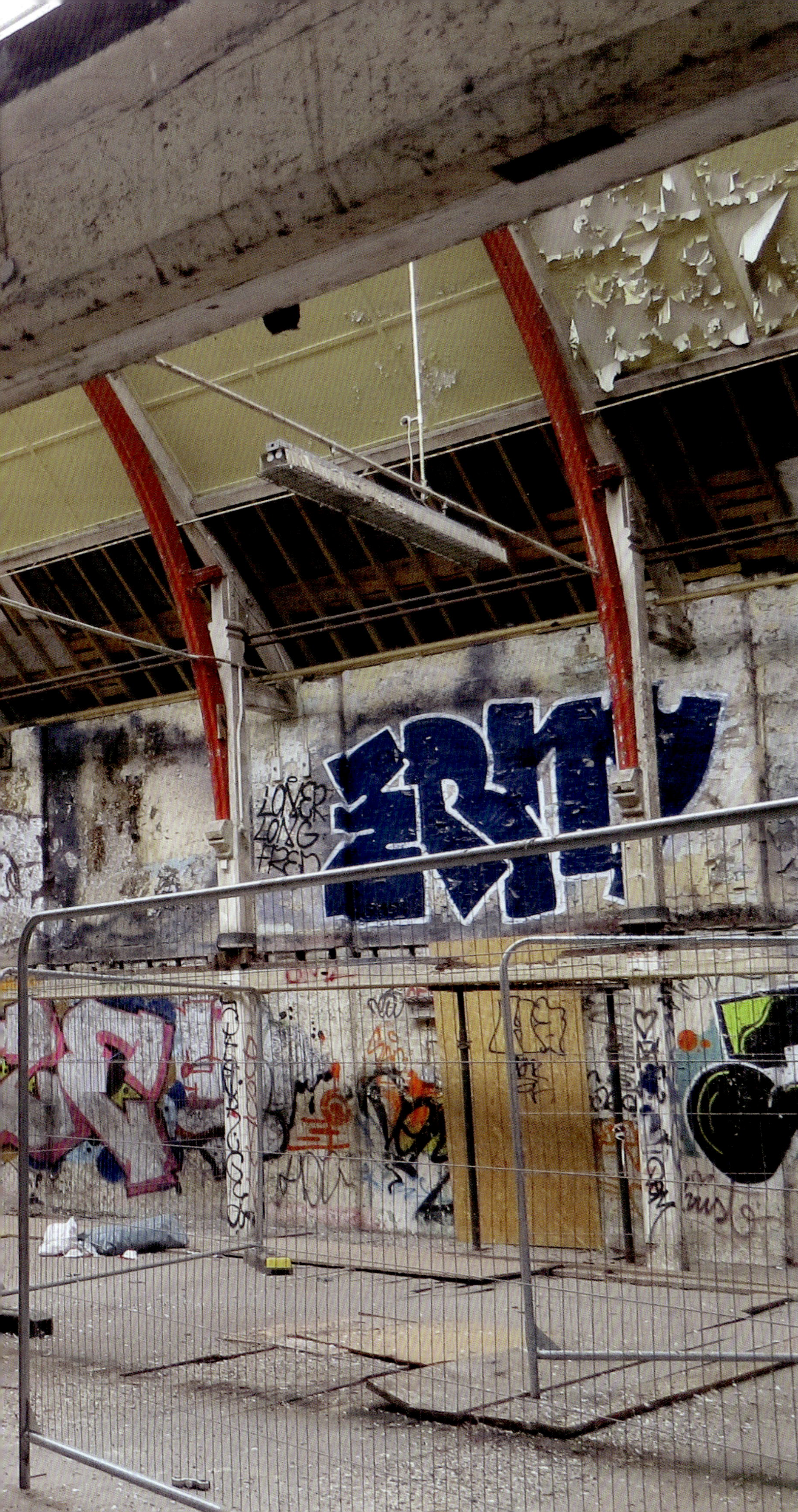

PREVIOUS PAGES AND LEFT:
Ladywell Baths, Lewisham
Appearing on Ladywell Road like a fairytale castle, the former Ladywell Public Baths were built in 1884 in a fanciful Gothic style by Wilson & Son and Thomas Aldwinkle. The location of the baths, opposite St Mary's Church, led to local papers commenting that 'cleanliness was next to Godliness'.

Like all aspects of Victorian society, the bathhouses were organised along class lines. The first-class pool hall was the most impressive, with red iron arches and thin tie beams supporting the roof with huge natural skylights. The whole building is Grade II listed and development plans are being finalised.

OVERLEAF:
Crystal Palace Subway
This underground space in South London is a stunning piece of Victorian engineering. The subway opened in 1865 to provide better access to the Crystal Palace, an entertainment venue originally constructed in Hyde Park for the Great Exhibition in 1851. The 'palace' was sadly destroyed by fire in 1936.

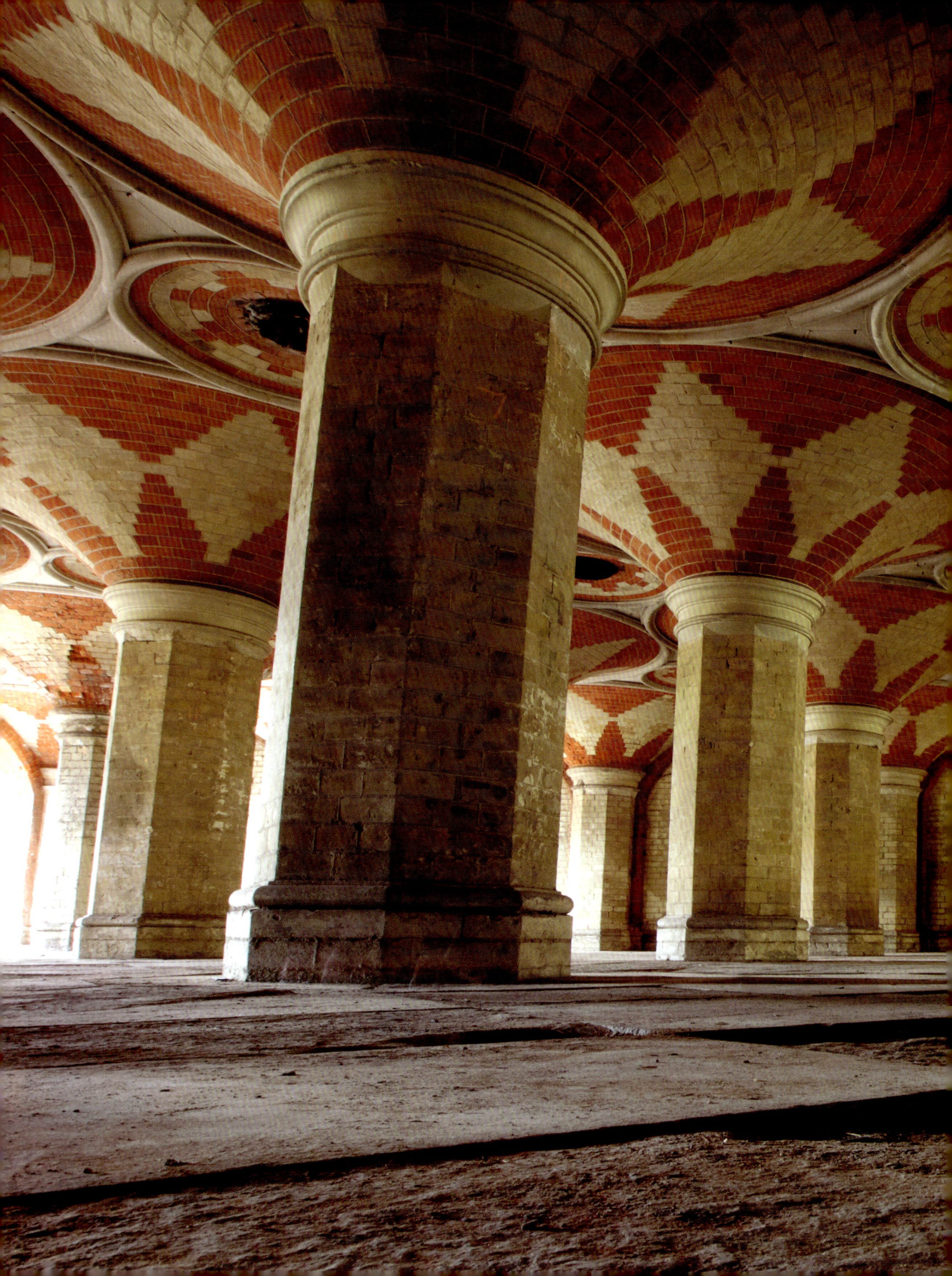

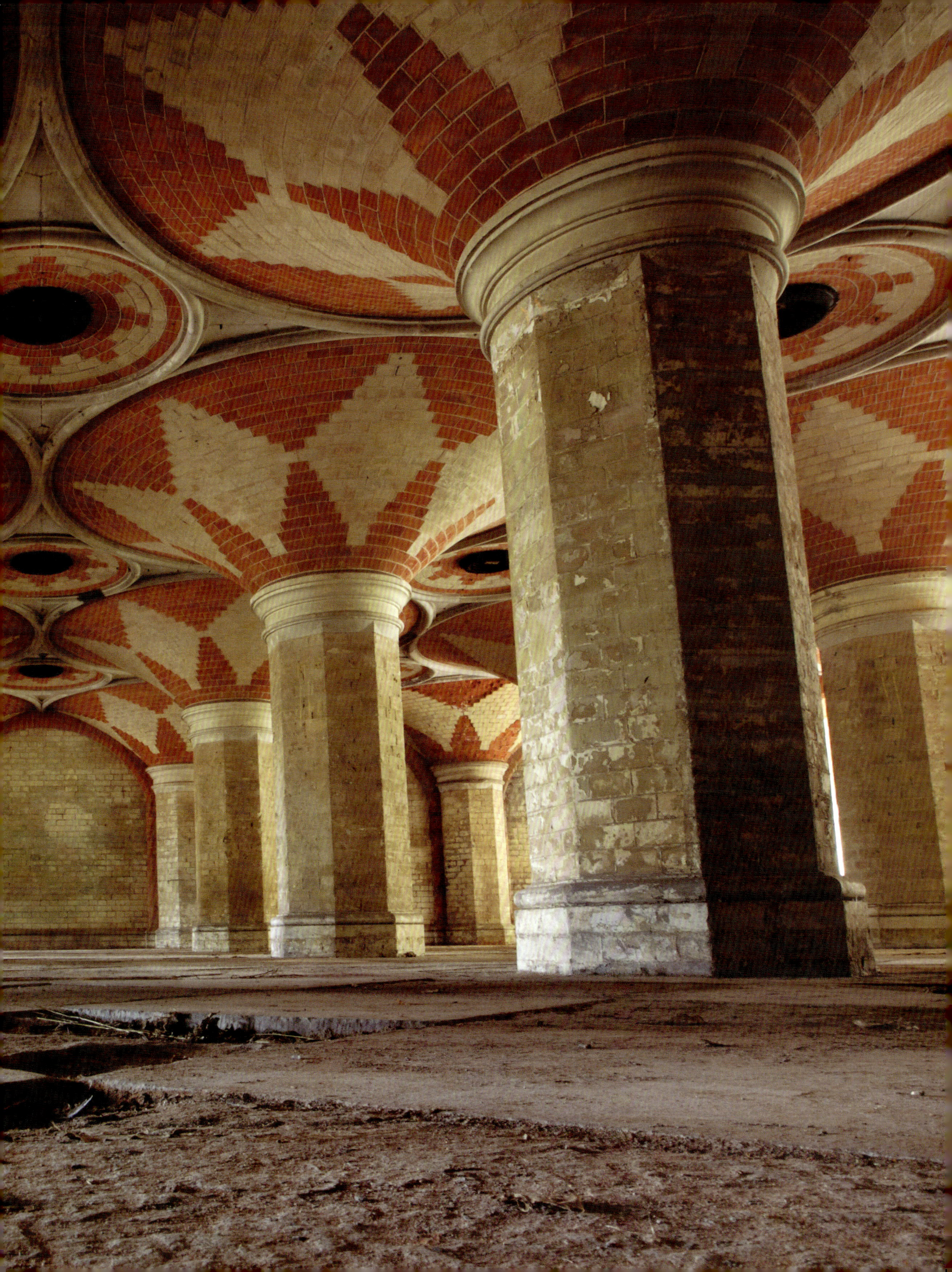

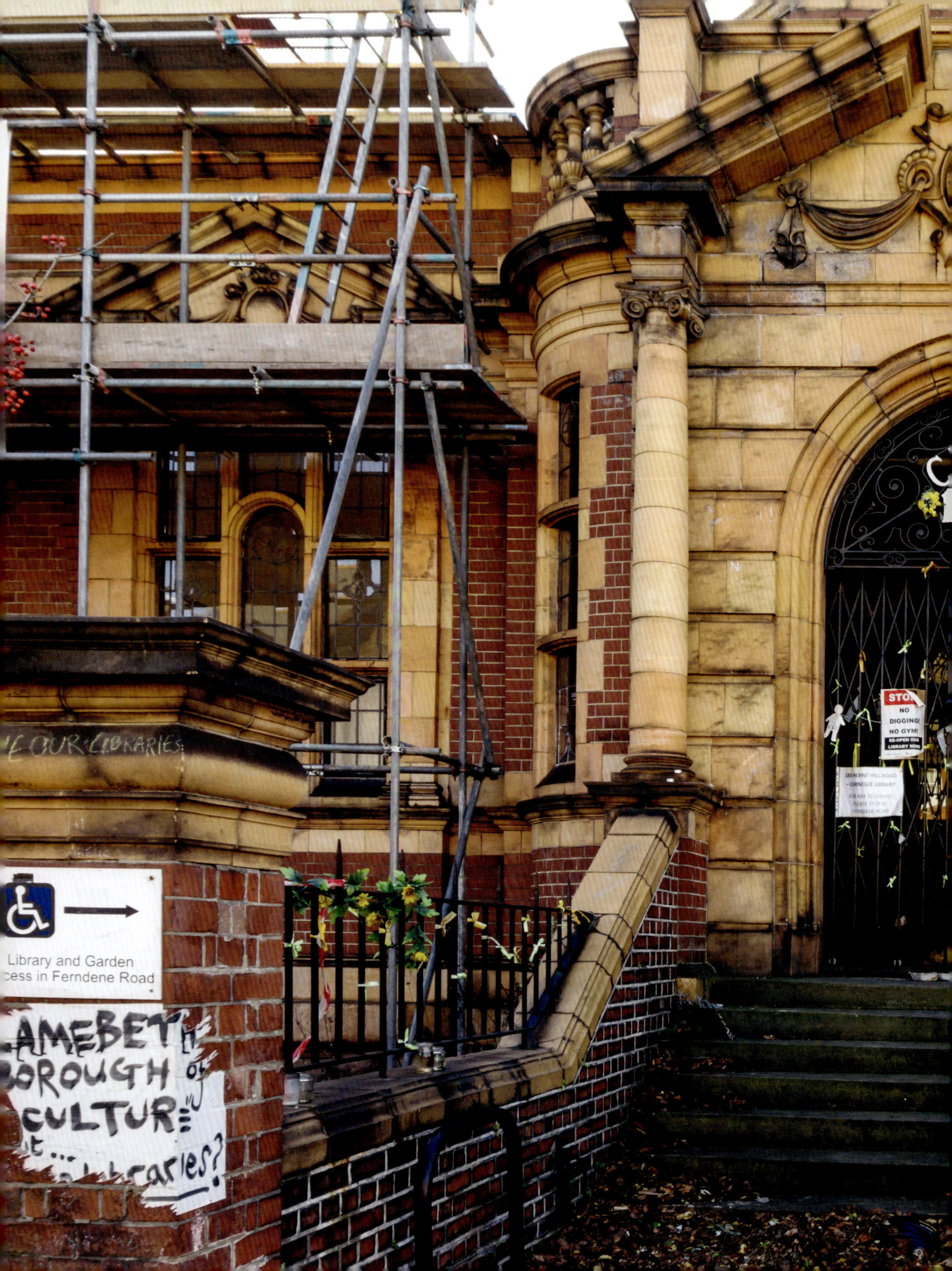
OUR LIBRARIES
Library and Garden
cess in Ferndene Road
LAMEBETH
BOROUGH
CULTURE
NO
DIGGING!
NO GYM!
RE-OPEN OUR
LIBRARY NOW
188 HERNE HILL ROAD
– CARNEGIE LIBRARY
FOR ANY DELIVERIES
PLEASE STOP AT
FERNDENE ROAD

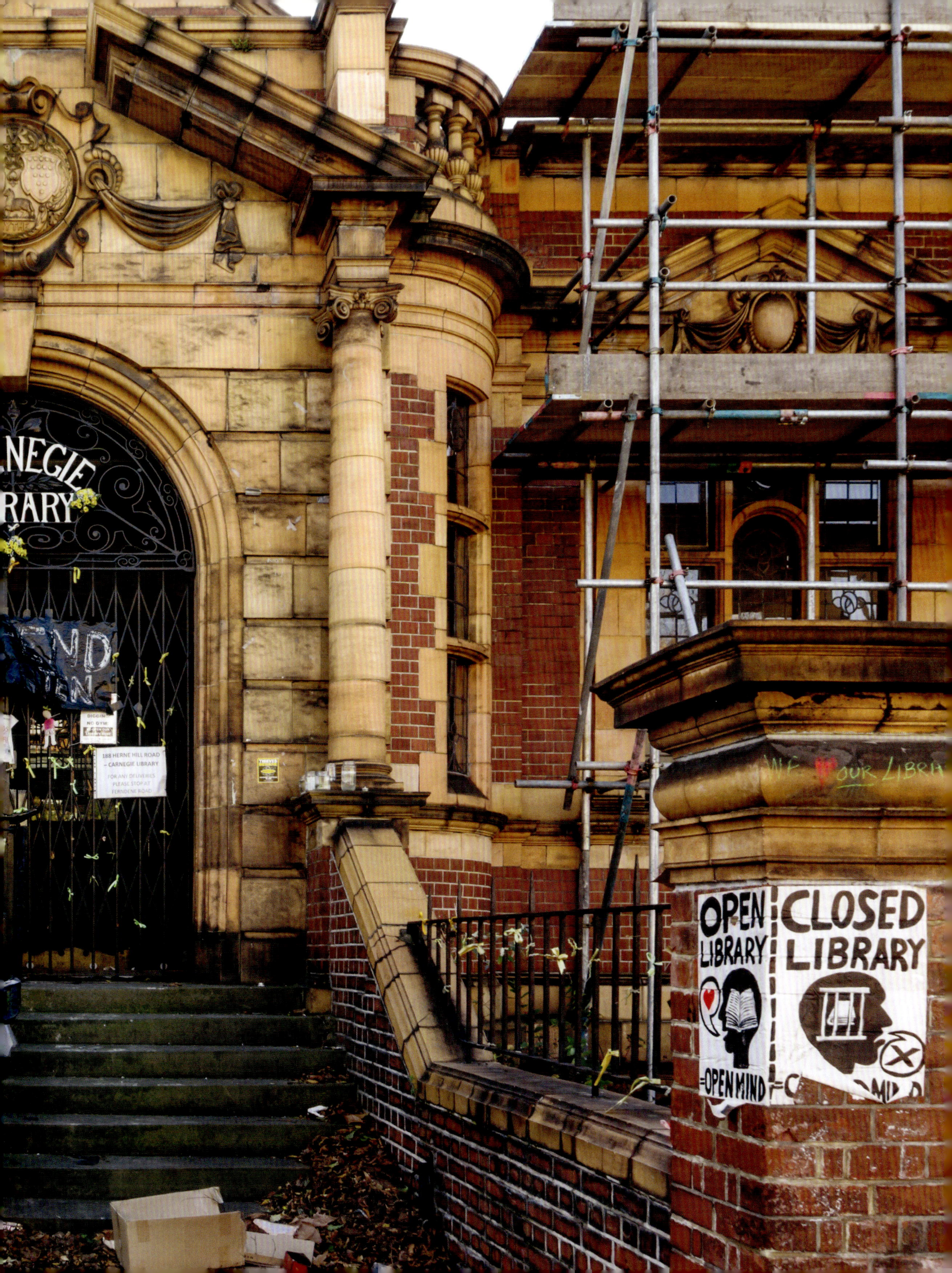
NEGIE
RARY
NO GYM
188 HERNE HILL ROAD
– CARNEGIE LIBRARY
FOR ANY DELIVERIES
PLEASE STOP AT
FERNDENE ROAD
OPEN
LIBRARY
=OPEN MIND
CLOSED
LIBRARY

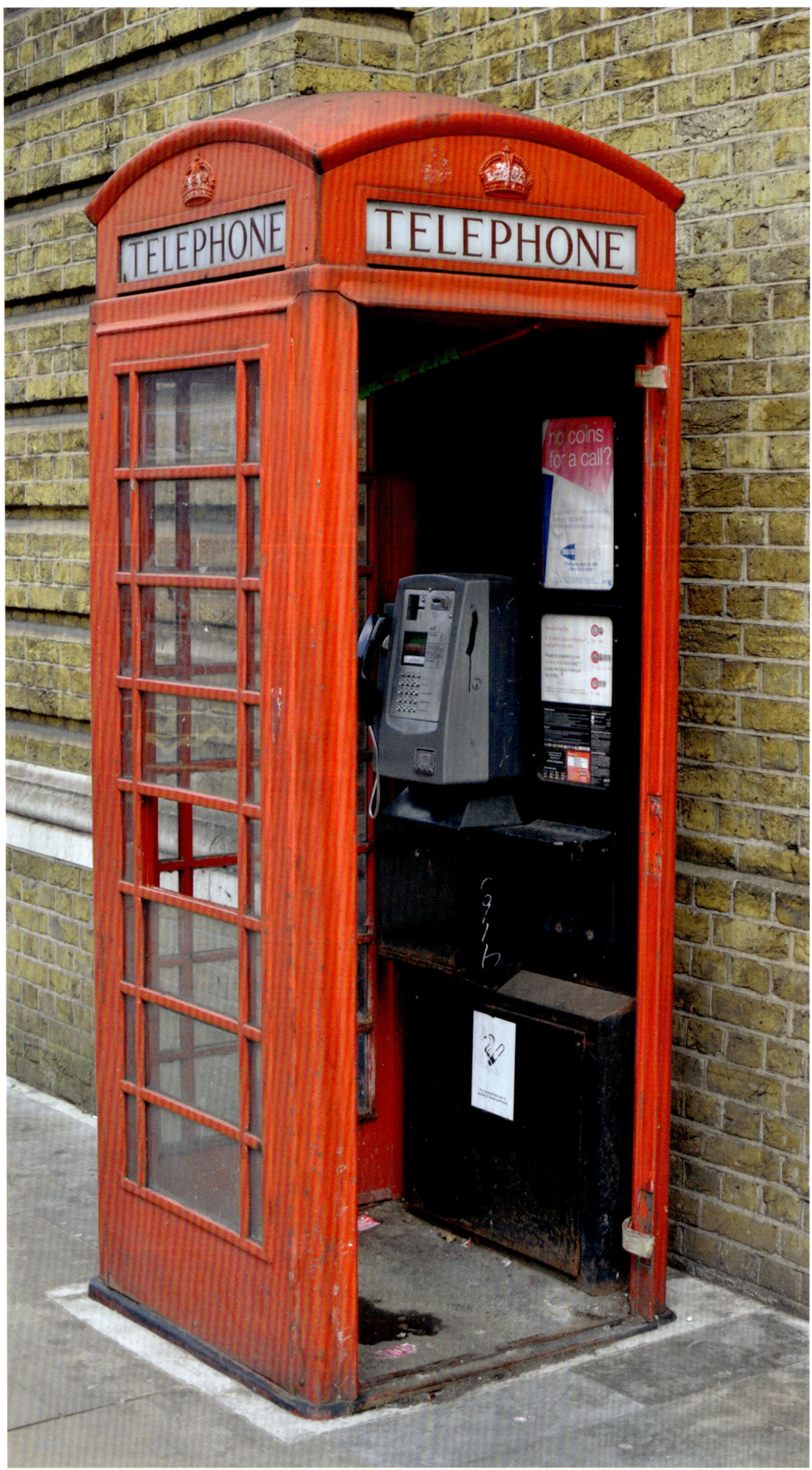

PREVIOUS PAGES:

Carnegie Library, Lambeth

Andrew Carnegie (1835–1919) was a Scottish-born American industrialist, leading the expansion of the steel industry in the late 19th century. He was not only one of the richest Americans in history but also a great philanthropist: 2,509 Carnegie libraries were built across the world, 660 of them in the UK and Ireland. The Lambeth Carnegie Library was completed in 1906 and closed in March 2016. However, it has since been restored and reopened.

LEFT AND OPPOSITE:

Red Telephone Boxes

The red telephone box is one of a handful of British designs that can truly be called iconic. Although there were phone kiosks designed from 1921, the most famous iteration came with Giles Gilbert Scott's competition entry in 1926, known as the K2. The image on the left shows the later K6 design, identified by the wide central glass panel. It was created in 1936 and is the most common type found across the UK.

Following a decline in use as phone boxes, these protected historic structures have found wide-ranging new uses, from tiny libraries to housing defibrillators.

NEW WORLD payphones
TELEPHONE

0123
010
6231
03

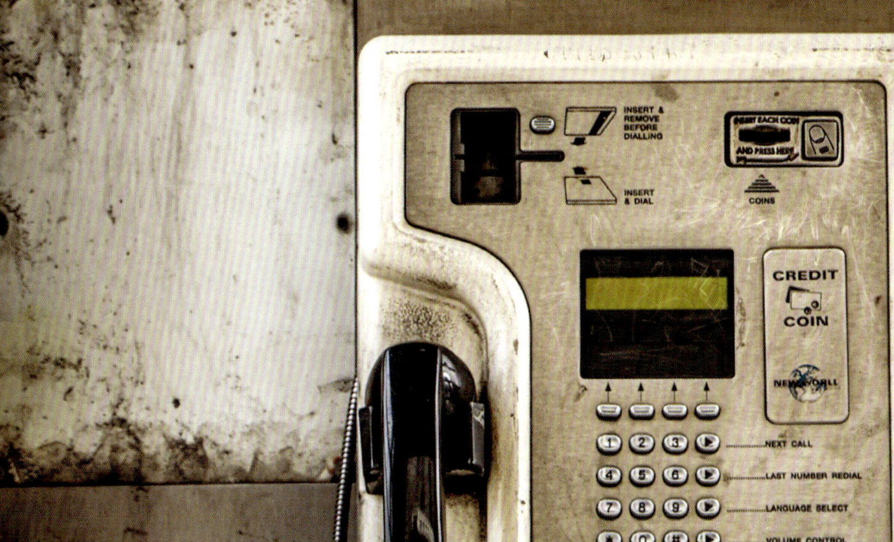
INSERT & REMOVE BEFORE DIALLING
INSERT & DIAL
COINS
CREDIT
COIN
NEXT CALL
LAST NUMBER REDIAL
LANGUAGE SELECT
VOLUME CONTROL

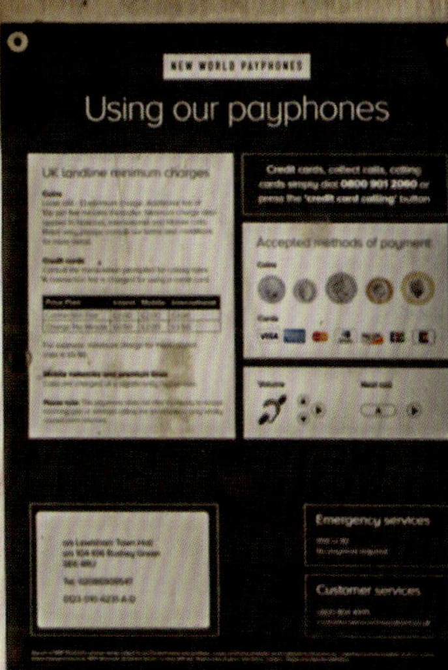
NEW WORLD PAYPHONES
Using our payphones

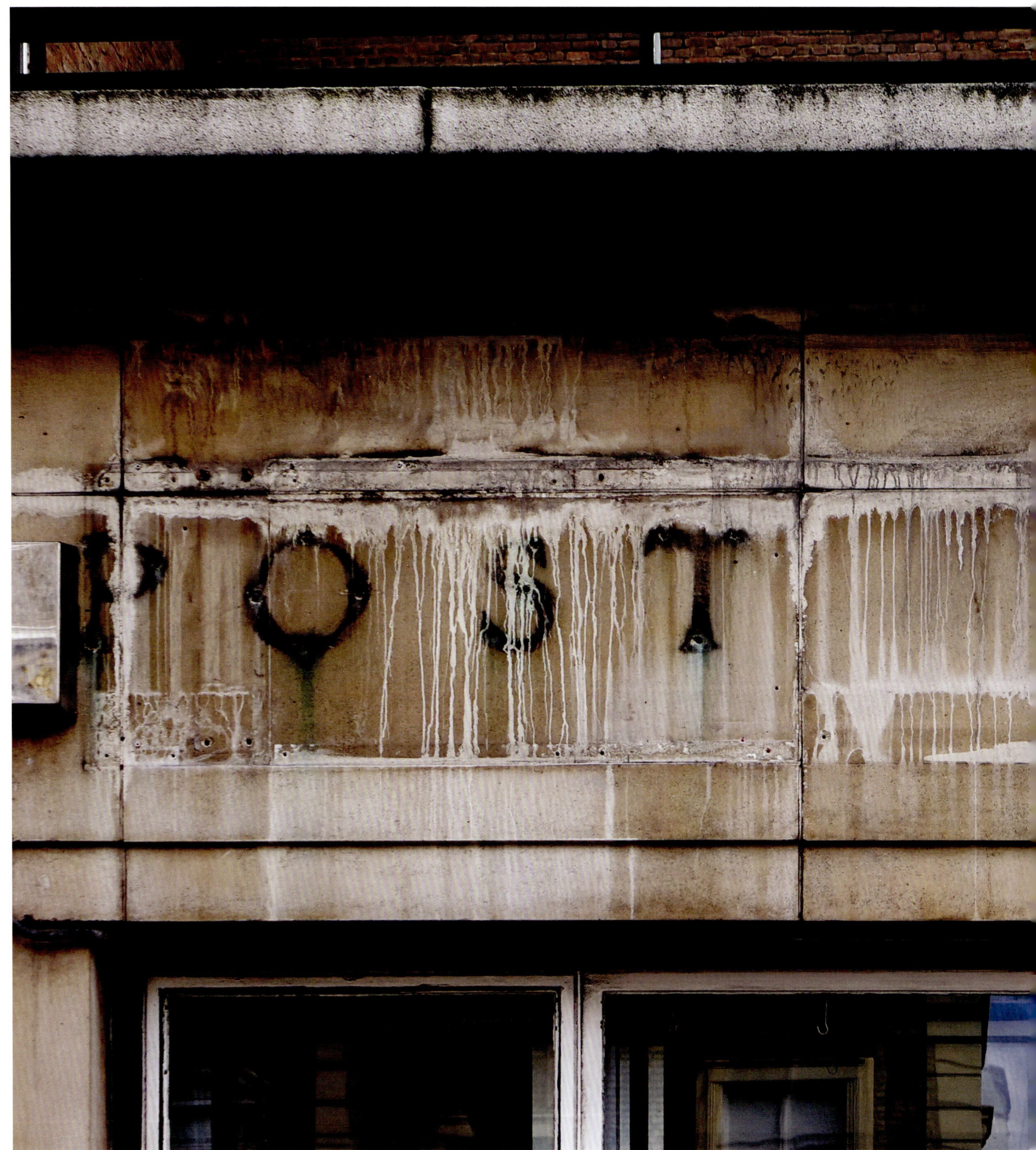

South Kensington Post Office, 41 Old Brompton Road
The Post Office is one of a number of ground floor shops that made up the design of Melton Court, an eight-storey block of flats situated above, first built in the 1930s. The original type pictured here has since been replaced by modern signage and the premises itself closed in July 2019.

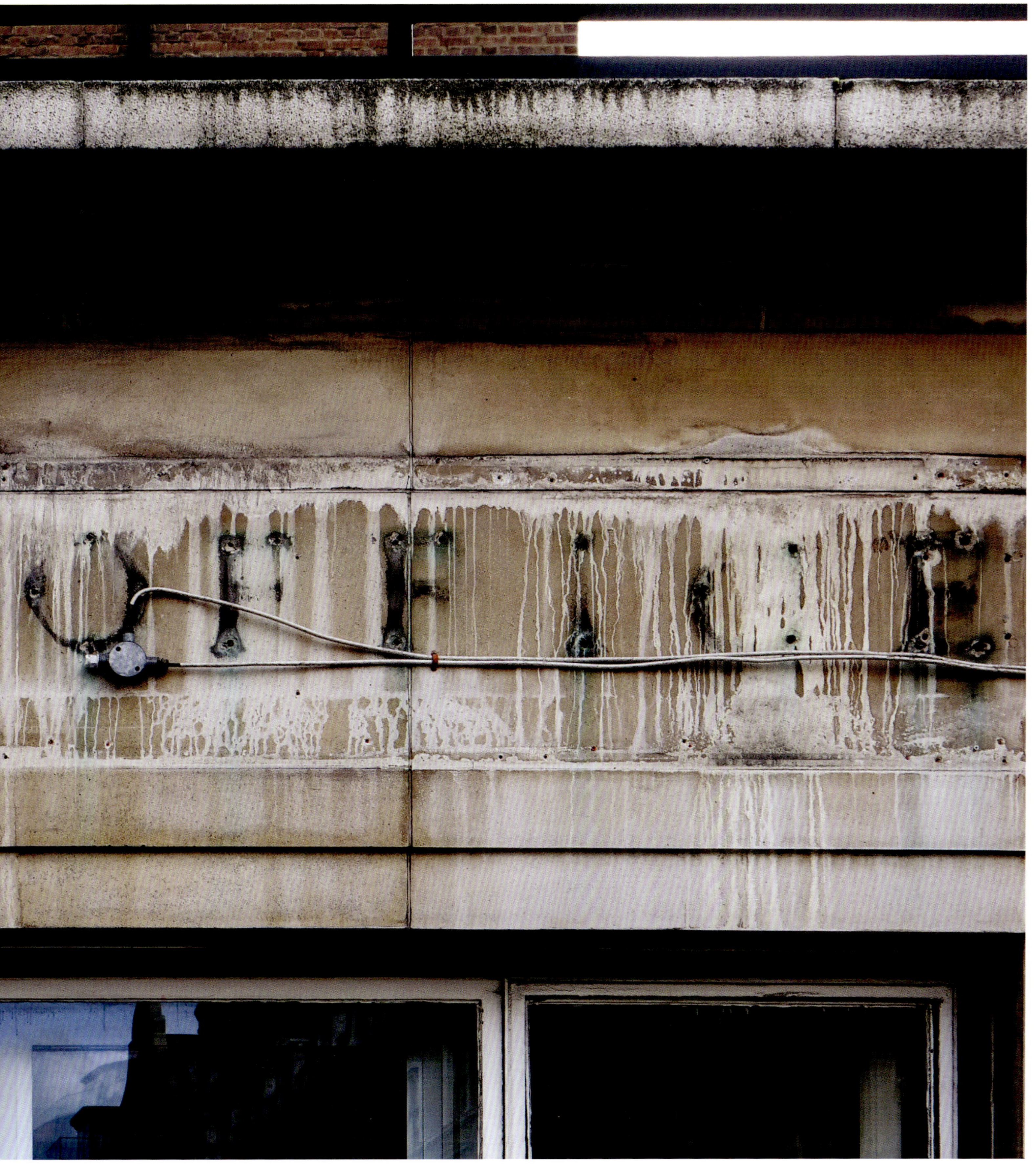

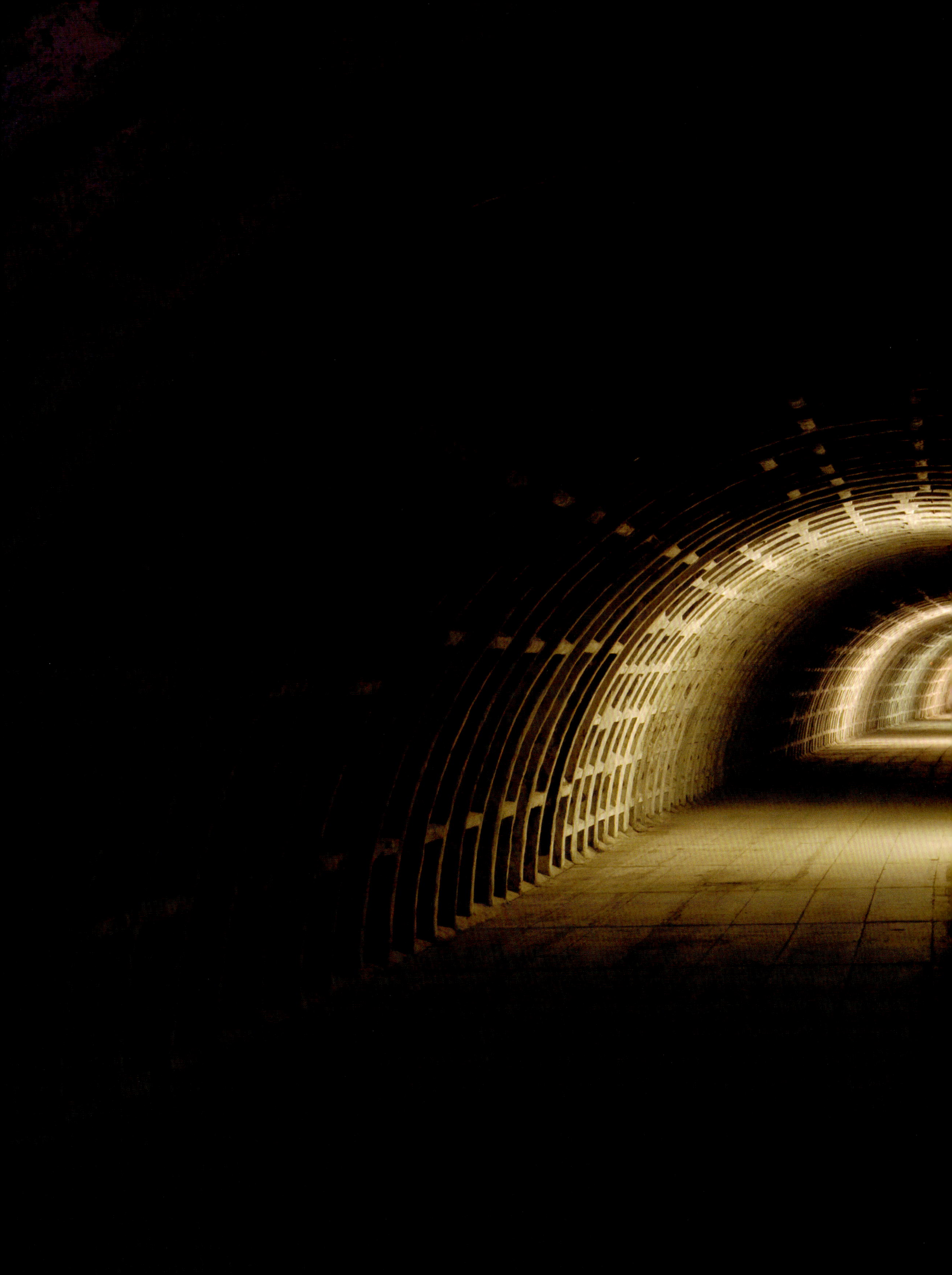

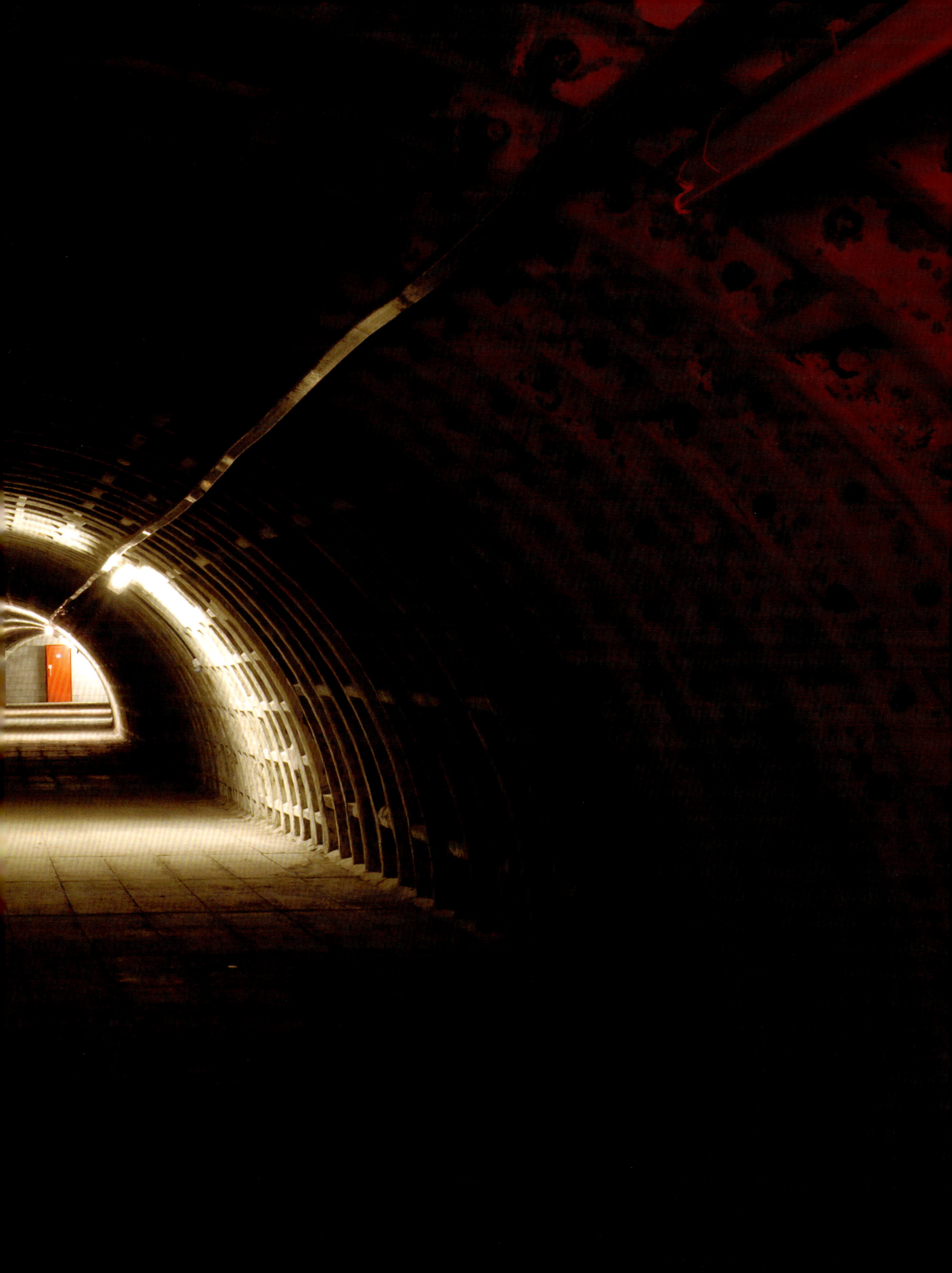

PREVIOUS PAGES AND ALL PHOTOGRAPHS ON THESE PAGES:
Clapham Deep Level World War II Shelters
At the outbreak of World War II, the government ordered London Transport to construct 10 deep-level shelters to provide protection for the public. They were only completed in the summer of 1942, by which time the threat of aerial bombardment from Nazi Germany had largely passed.

However, this didn't mean the shelters weren't useful. The shelters underneath Clapham South tube station were used for medical facilities and temporary housing for homeless Londoners. In 1944 they were also used as air raid shelters against the new V-1 flying bombs launched from mainland Europe by the Luftwaffe, each shelter given the name of a famous British Naval commander. Even after war had ended they were used to house London's new migrant communities that had arrived on the HMS *Windrush*. They were eventually closed to the public in 1956.

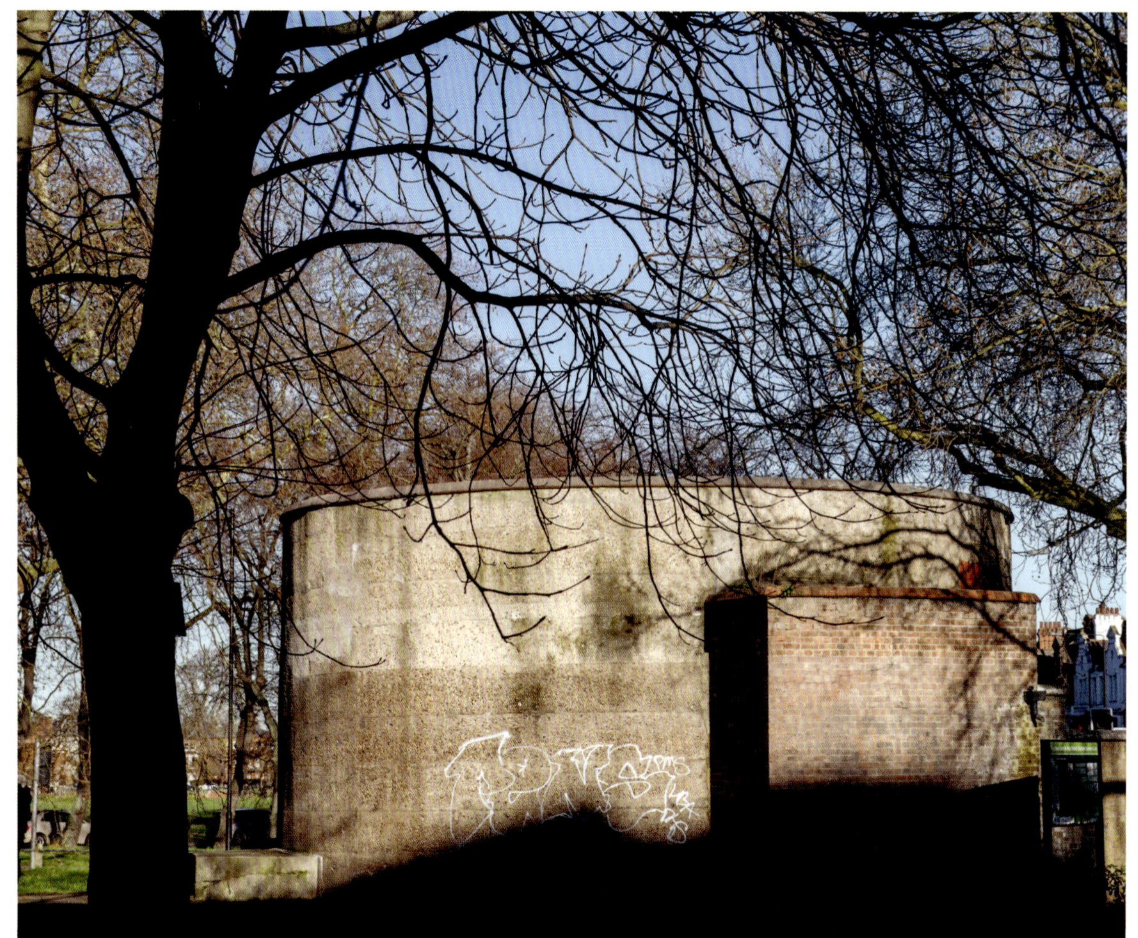

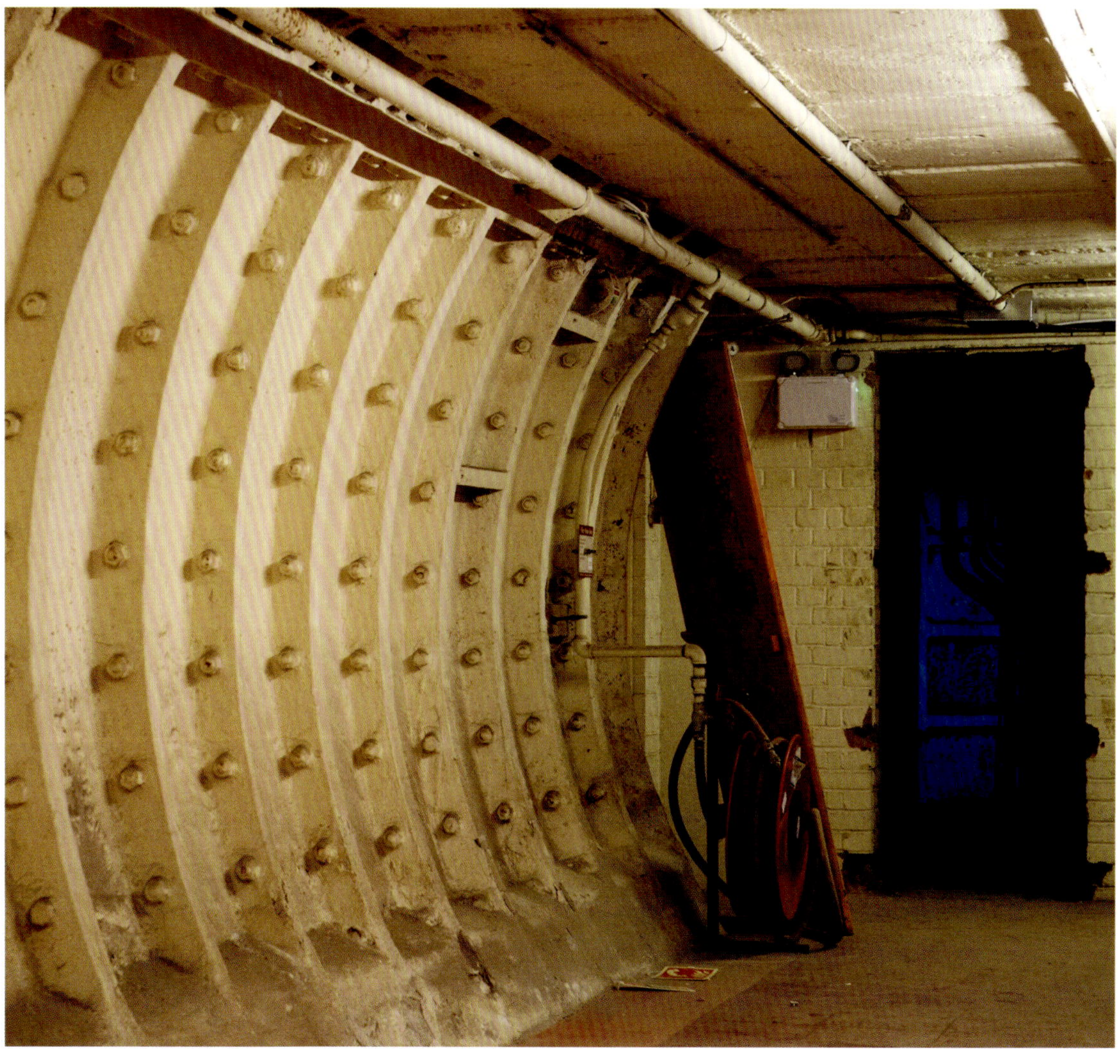

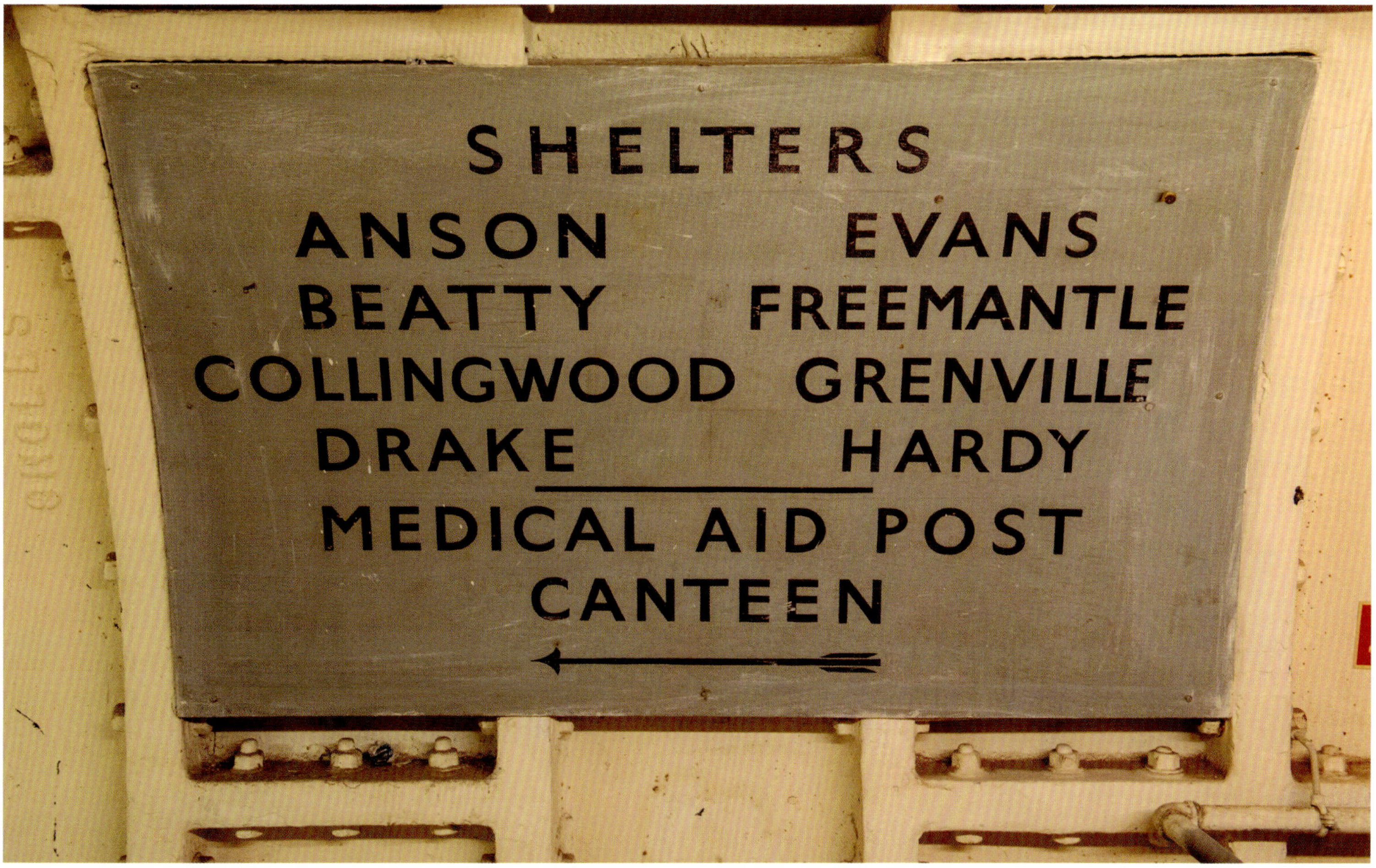
SHELTERS
ANSON EVANS
BEATTY FREEMANTLE
COLLINGWOOD GRENVILLE
DRAKE HARDY
MEDICAL AID POST
CANTEEN

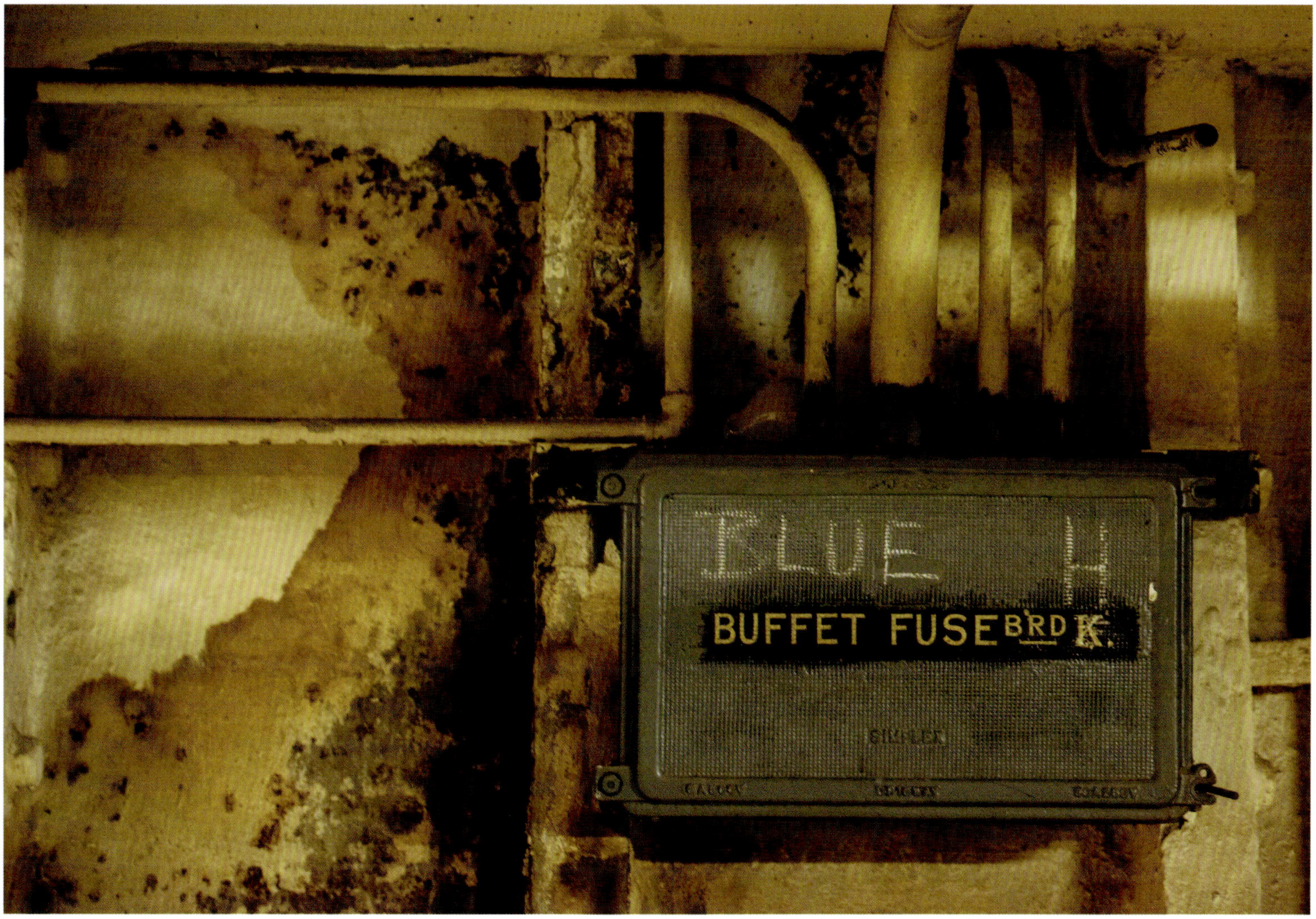
BLUE H
BUFFET FUSE BRD K.

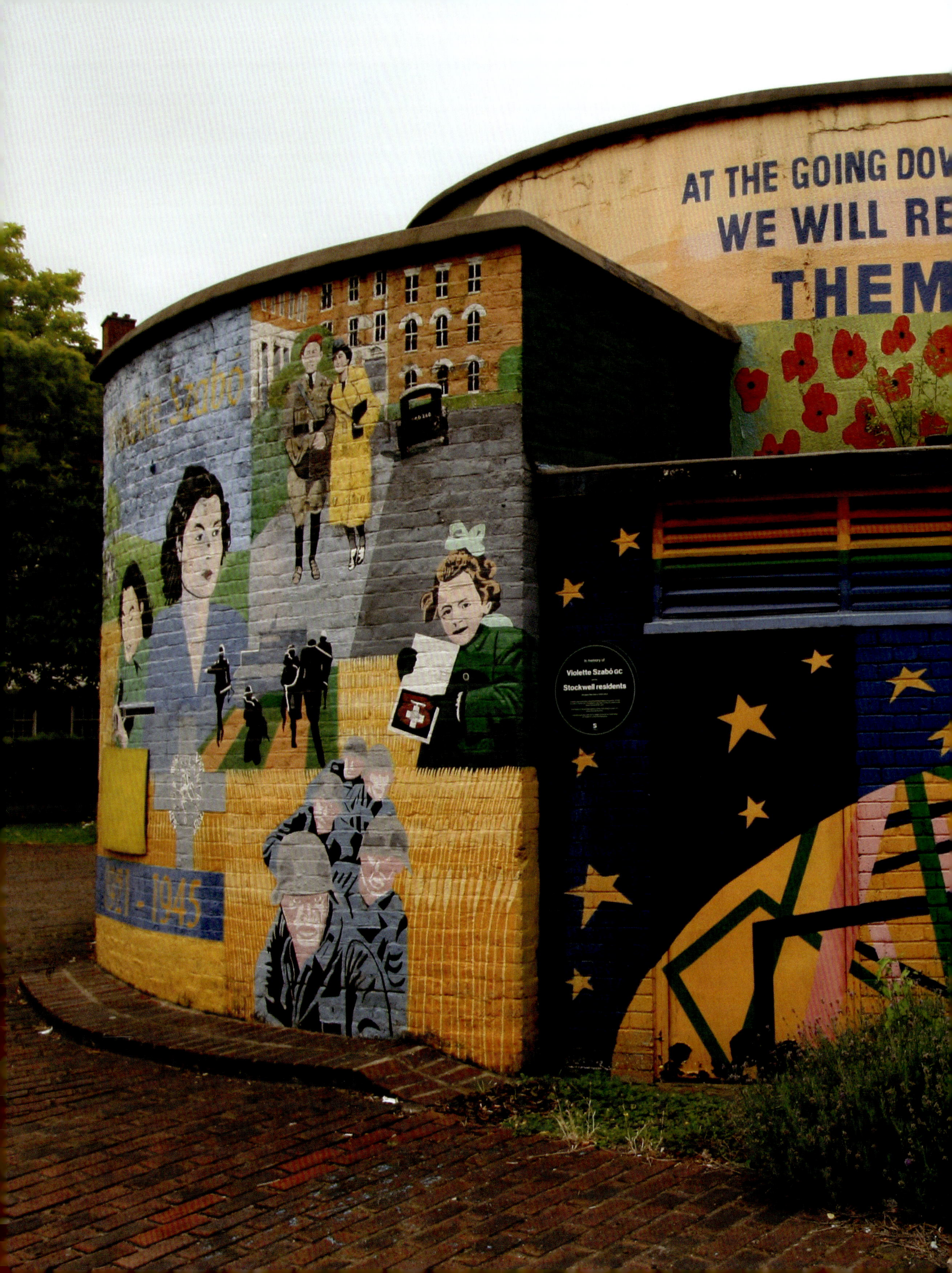
AT THE GOING DOW
WE WILL RE
THEM
Violette Szabó
1945
In memory of
Violette Szabó GC
Stockwell residents

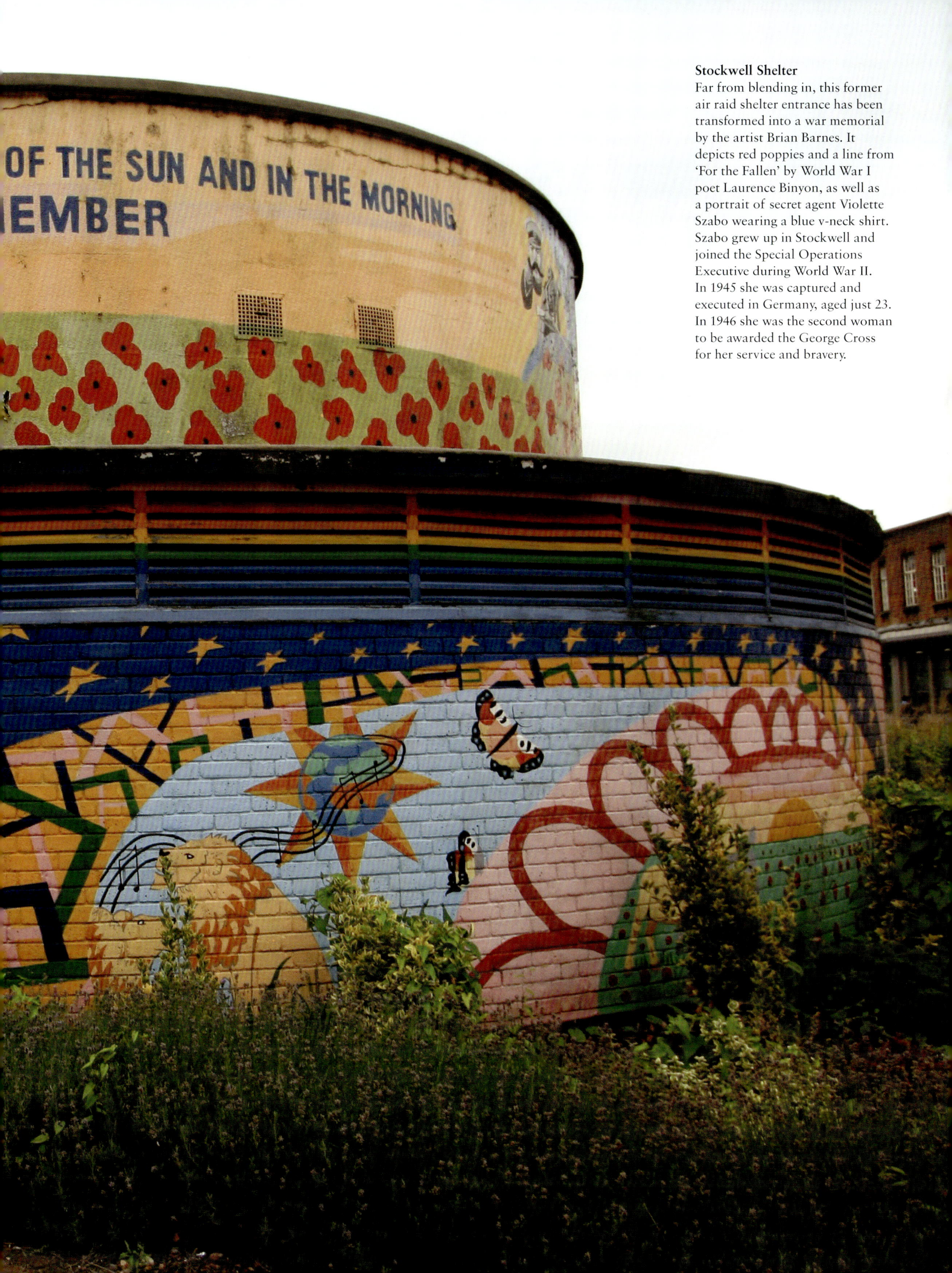

Stockwell Shelter
Far from blending in, this former air raid shelter entrance has been transformed into a war memorial by the artist Brian Barnes. It depicts red poppies and a line from 'For the Fallen' by World War I poet Laurence Binyon, as well as a portrait of secret agent Violette Szabo wearing a blue v-neck shirt. Szabo grew up in Stockwell and joined the Special Operations Executive during World War II. In 1945 she was captured and executed in Germany, aged just 23. In 1946 she was the second woman to be awarded the George Cross for her service and bravery.

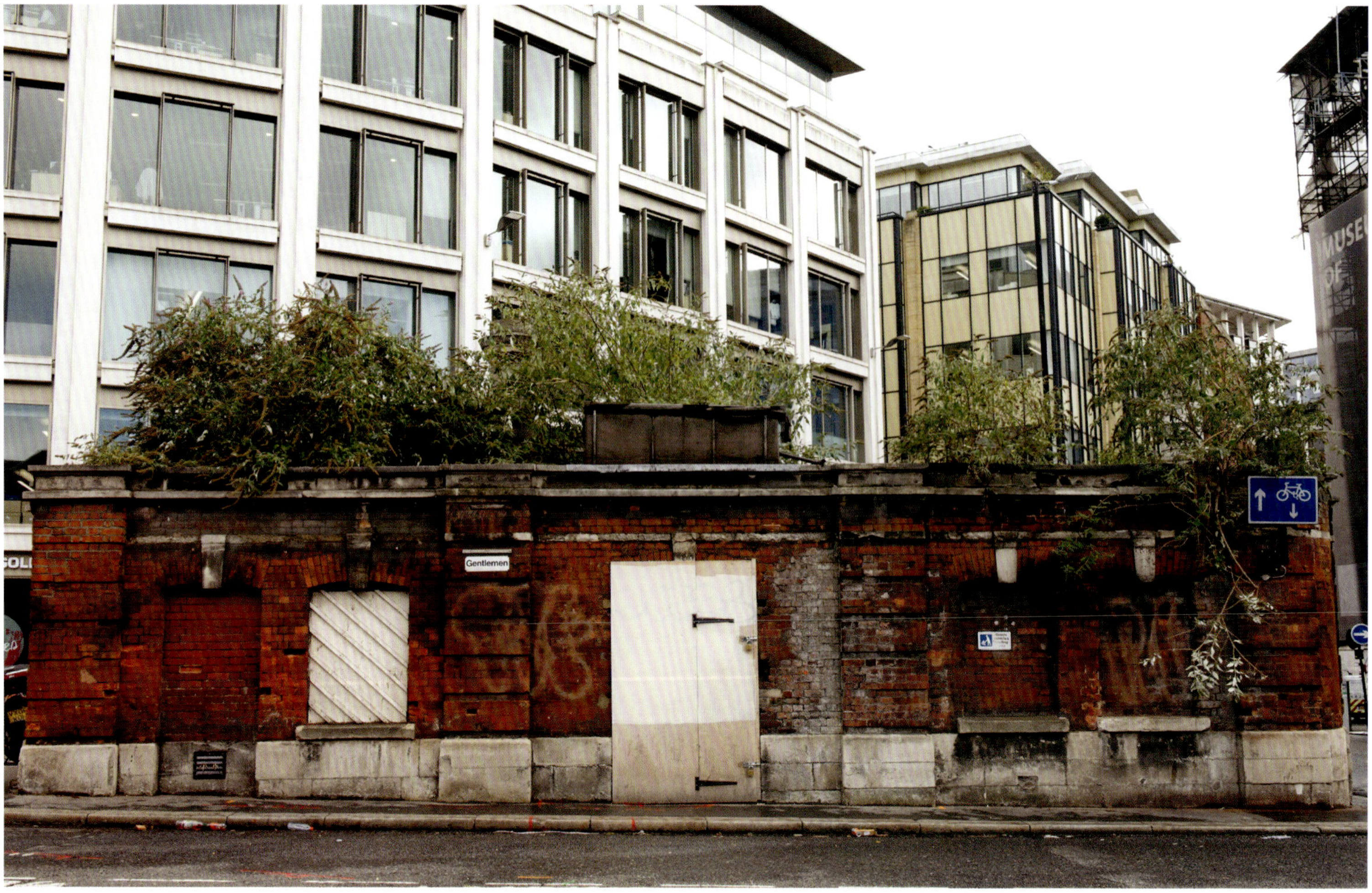
Gentlemen

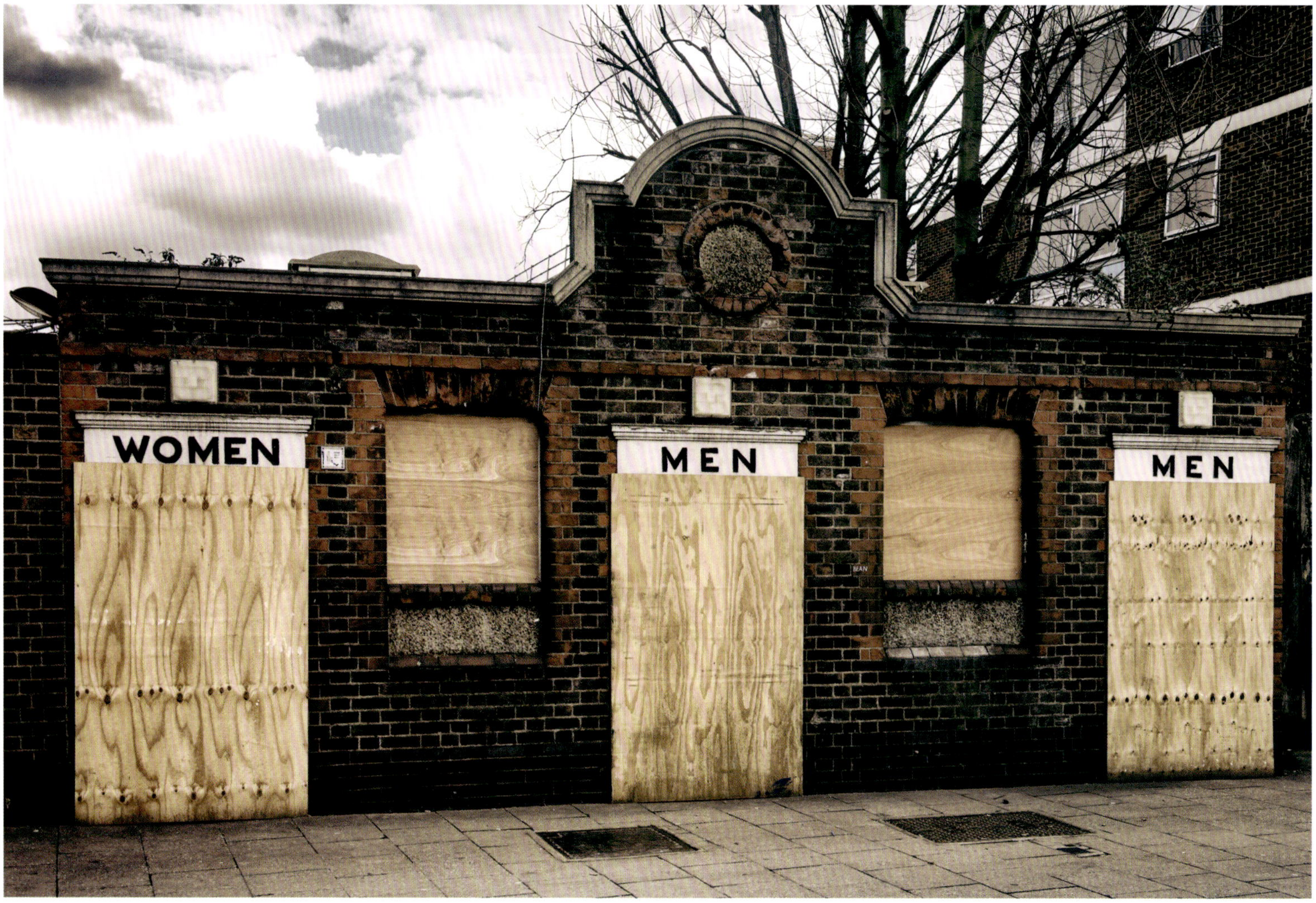
WOMEN
MEN
MEN

OPPOSITE TOP AND BELOW:

Public Toilets, Smithfield

Although they might be a rare sight today, we can thank George Jennings for London's public toilets. In 1851, as part of the Great Exhibition, Jennings had the novel idea of providing flushing lavatories to the public and charging them a penny for use. Flash forward to 2015 and the British Toilet Association estimated that 40 per cent of Britain's public toilets have closed in the last decade.

OPPOSITE BOTTOM:

Public Toilets, Tottenham

In 2017, a UK survey found that 59 per cent of women regularly queue to use the toilet, compared with only 11 per cent of men. Given differences in anatomy and clothing, the British Toilet Association recommends that the ratio of toilet provision should be at least 2:1 in favour of women.

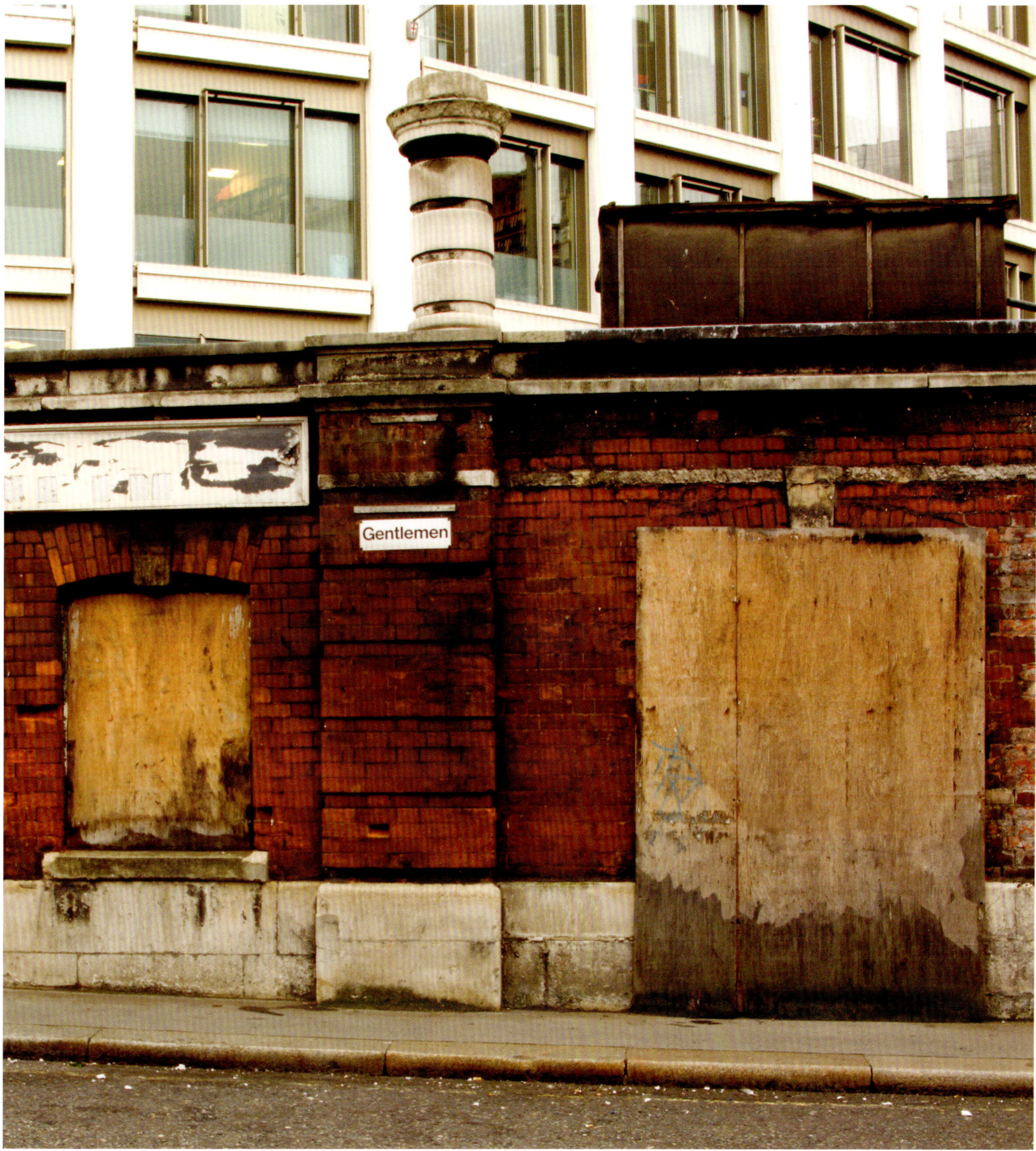

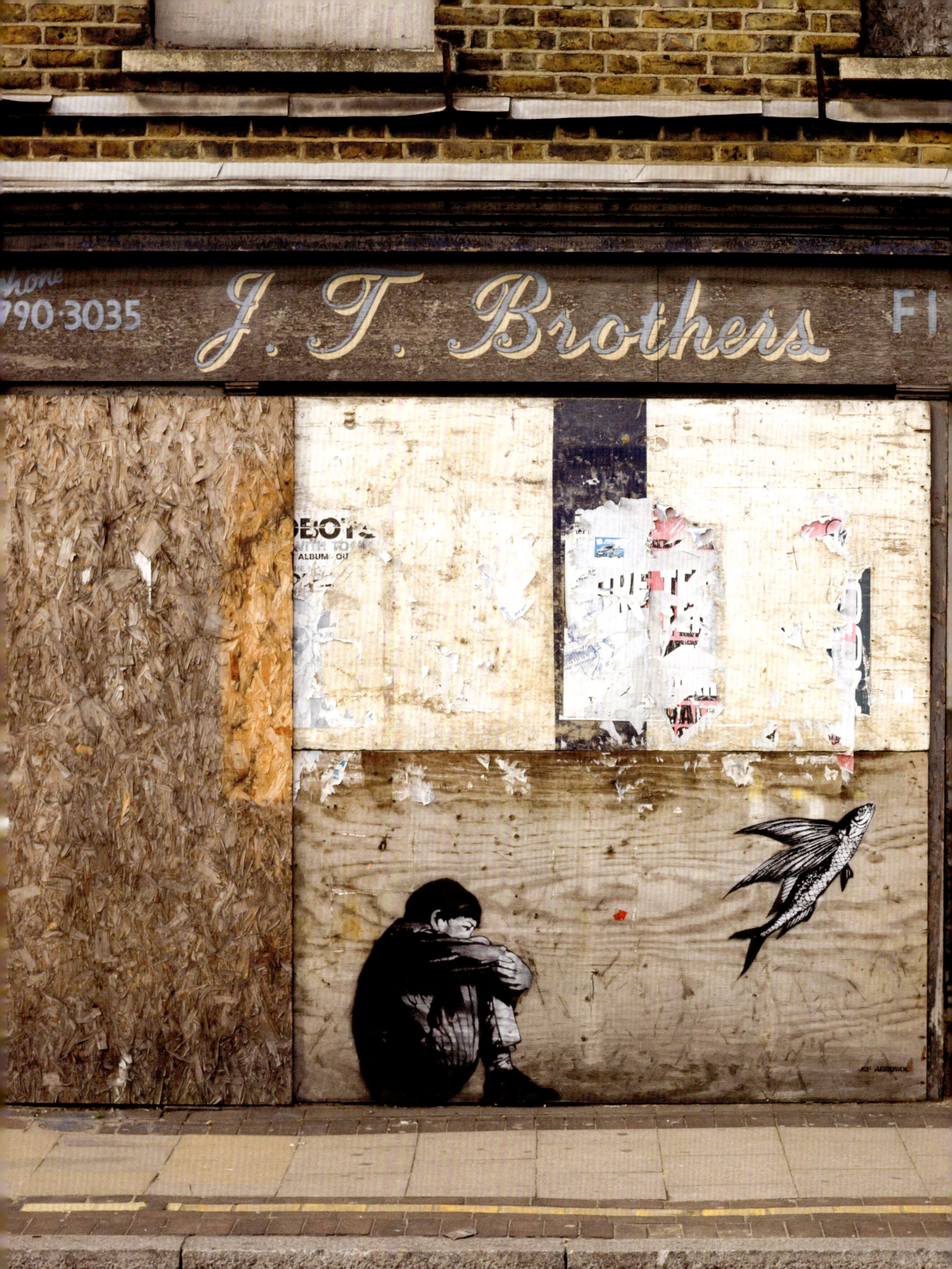
790·3035
J. T. Brothers

Shops and Retail

London is fortunate to have an abundance of 'ghost signs', the faded remnants of businesses that remind us of what came before. Often these are heavily restored, but they provide the curious passer-by with a glimpse into former worlds. It is from these names and the streets themselves that we can piece together the stories of abandoned shop premises.

It has become a truism, not just for London but for the UK as a whole, that the High Street is 'dying'. This can be blamed on the rise in internet shopping, expensive business rates, the failure of shops to adapt or a mixture of all three. Since 2008, when retail chain Woolworths collapsed, more than 30 other household retailers have closed.

In this chapter we turn away from huge chains and mostly focus on the stories of enterprising independents. These are the tales of people who took the plunge to start a family business, who gambled on a dream to set up on their own. Although the title of this book may be somewhat of a spoiler for the fate of these plucky individuals, their entrepreneurial spirit nonetheless deserves celebration.

OPPOSITE:
J.J. Brothers, Commercial Road, Tower Hamlets
As the traffic along the busy Commercial Road rumbles on, not many people notice the stencilled artworks by Jef Aerosol on this former fishmonger. The fish flies away while the small child – an embodiment of the 'East End Street Urchin' trope – watches on, left behind.

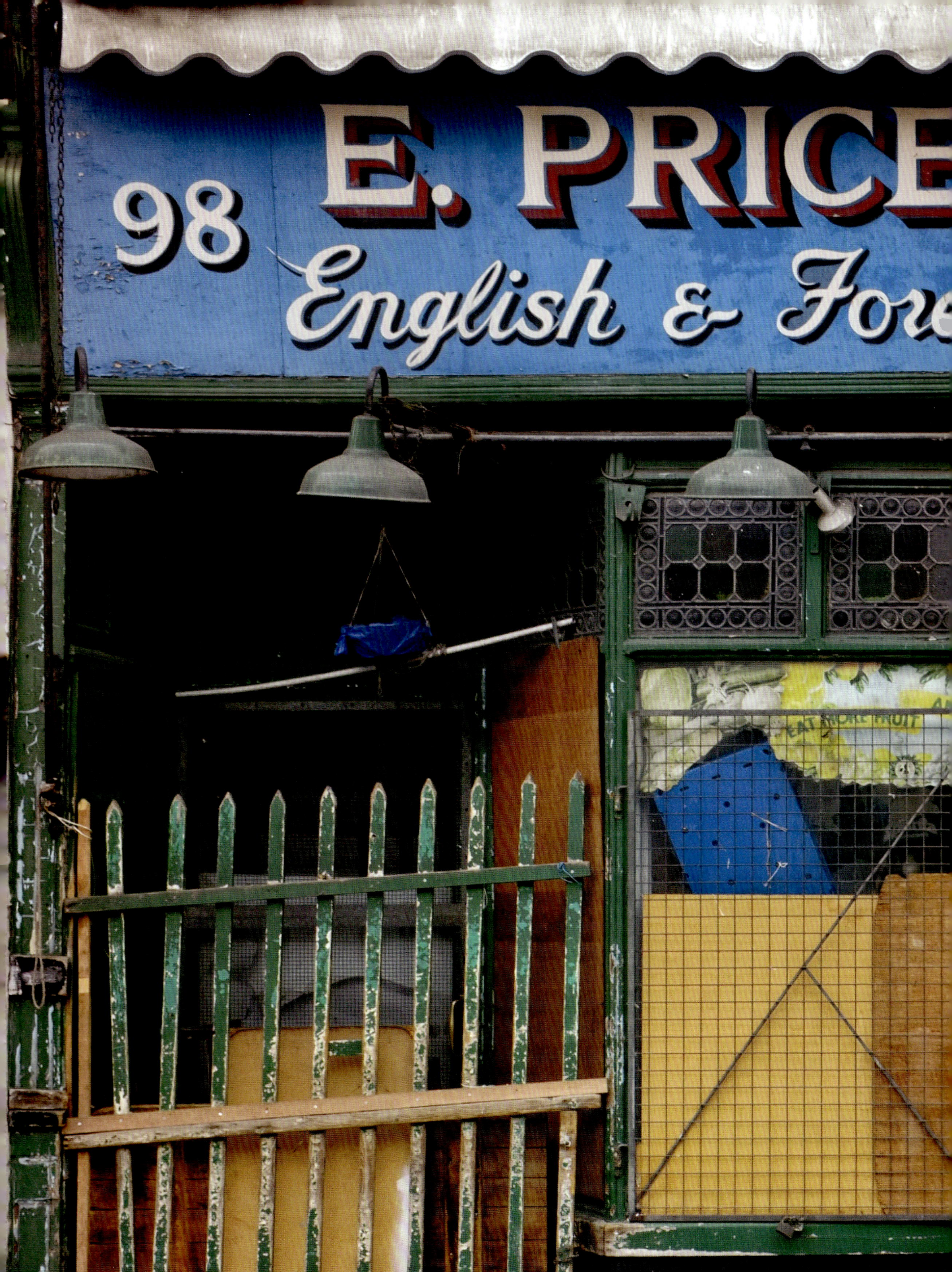
98
E. PRICE
English &
EAT MORE FRUIT

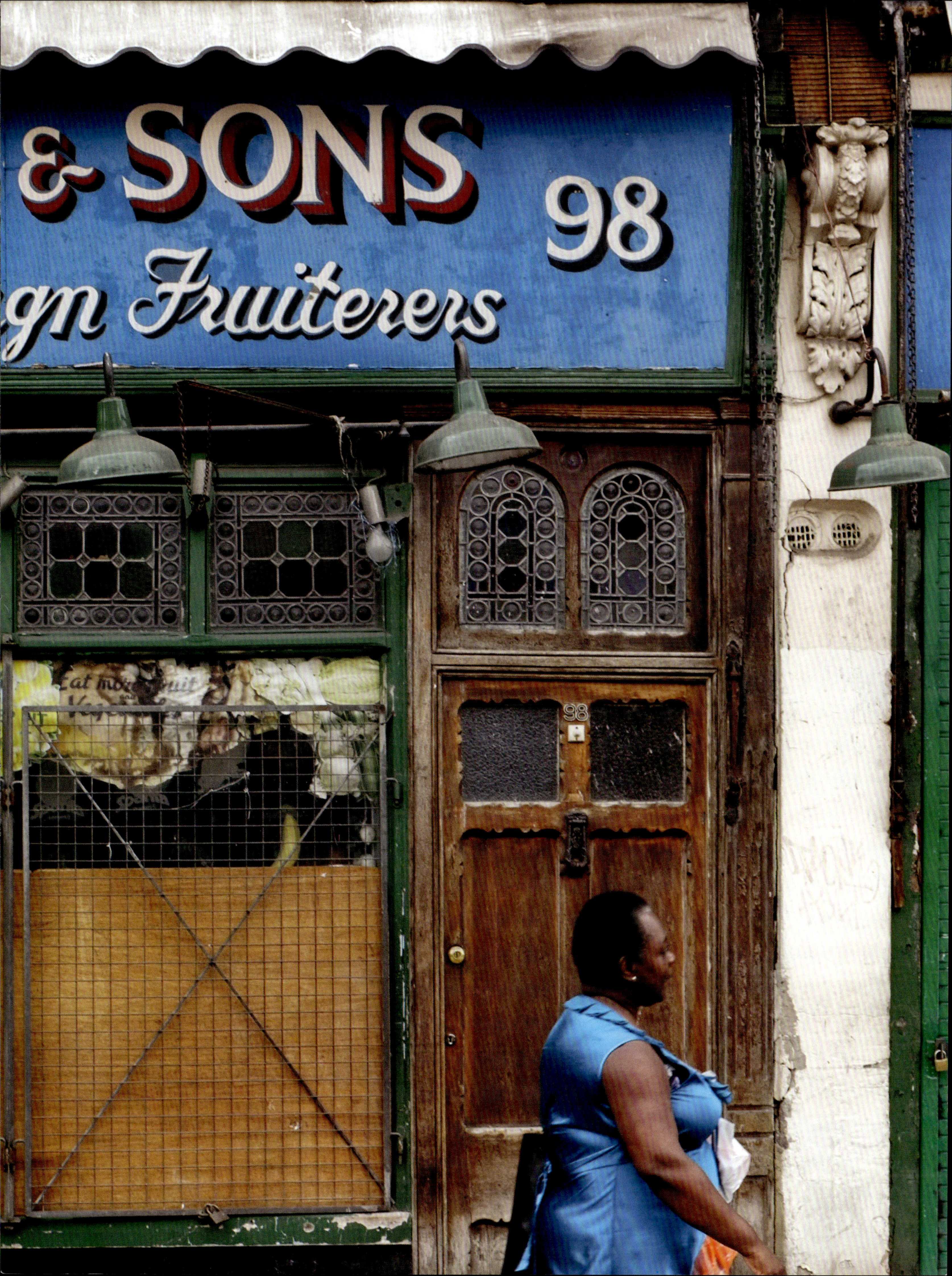
& SONS
98
gn Fruiterers
98

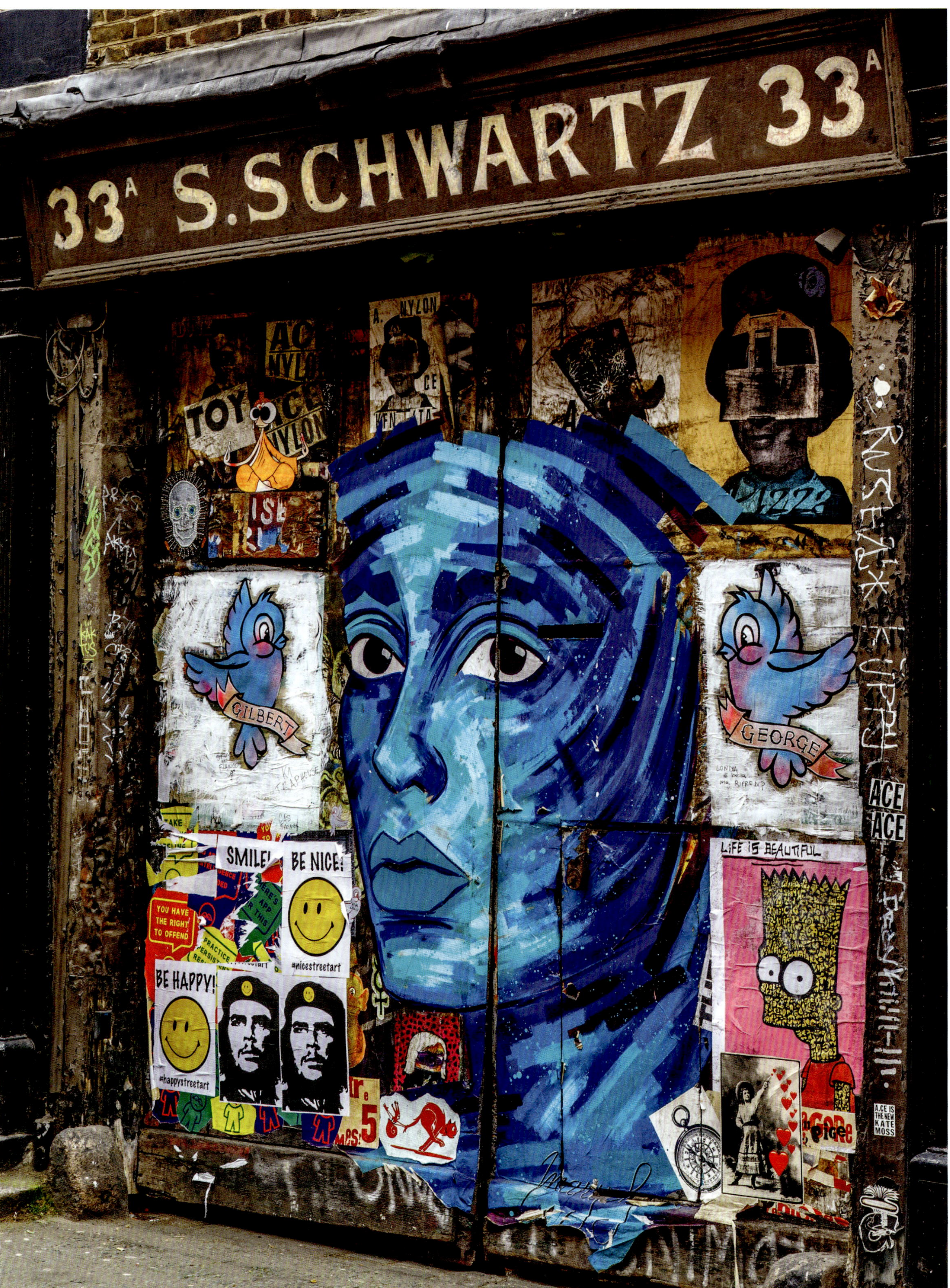
33A S.SCHWARTZ 33A
TOY
GILBERT
GEORGE
SMILE!
BE NICE!
YOU HAVE THE RIGHT TO OFFEND
BE HAPPY!
#happystreetart
#nicestreetart
LIFE IS BEAUTIFUL
ACE
ACE
A.CE IS THE NEW KATE MOSS

PREVIOUS PAGES:
E. Price & Sons, Golborne Road, Kensal Town
The 'E' stands for 'Ephraim', who started trading fruits and vegetables here in 1937. Although the business closed in 2015, Ephraim's great-grandson reopened the shop two years later and it continues to be a community favourite.

OPPOSITE:
S. Schwartz, 33a Fournier Street, Spitalfields
This collection of streets in Spitalfields were laid out in the early 18th century for artisan craftsmen and merchants. They've weathered world wars and slum clearance schemes and are now among some of London's most desirable homes. Walking the streets today offers many layers of history, as well as recent gentrification; Schwartz was a local dairy until the 1950s and the blue figure is by the French street artist Manyoly.

ABOVE RIGHT:
Trade Tyre Services, Bolton Crescent, Kennington
Kennington was developed as a suburb for the middle classes in the early 19th century, but later impoverished areas developed. It was into these slums that one of the most famous movie stars in the world was born in 1899. He is commemorated by the Charlie Chaplin primary school down this road.

BELOW RIGHT:
J.O. Grant & Taylor, Ravey Street, Hackney
In the 1990s, J.O. Grant & Taylor was a subsidiary of Cray Electronics Holdings, specialising in telecoms, software and the electrical industry. The building was demolished after 2014 and is set to be replaced by a 125-bedroom hotel.

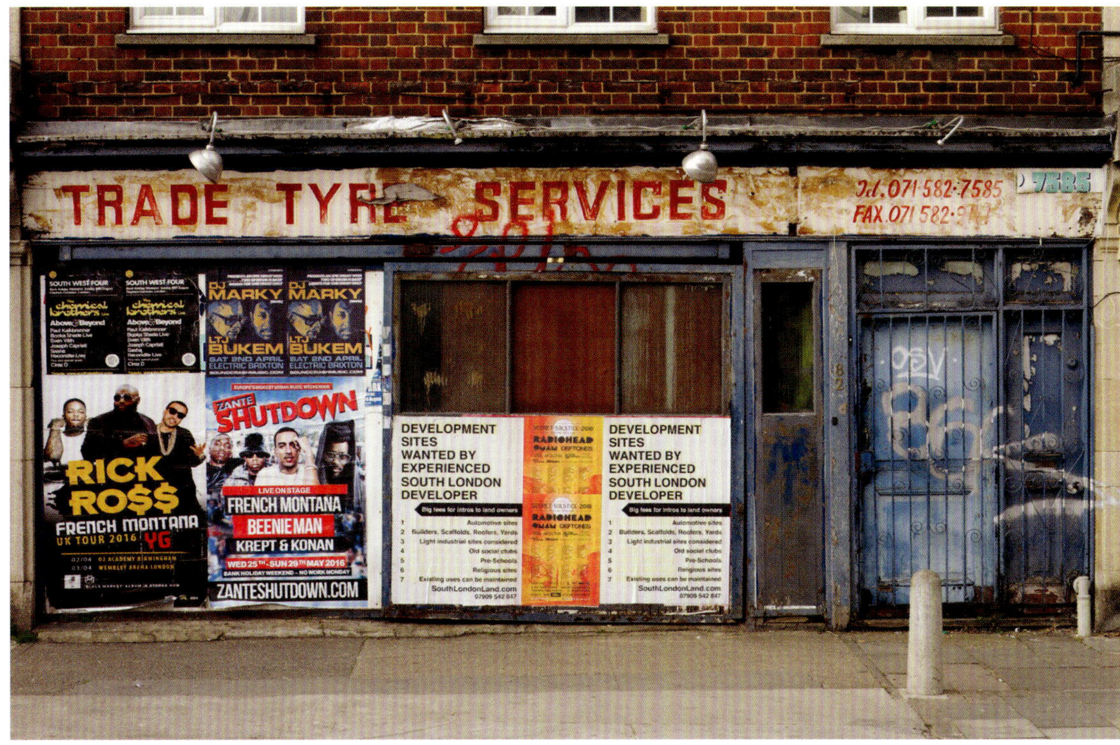

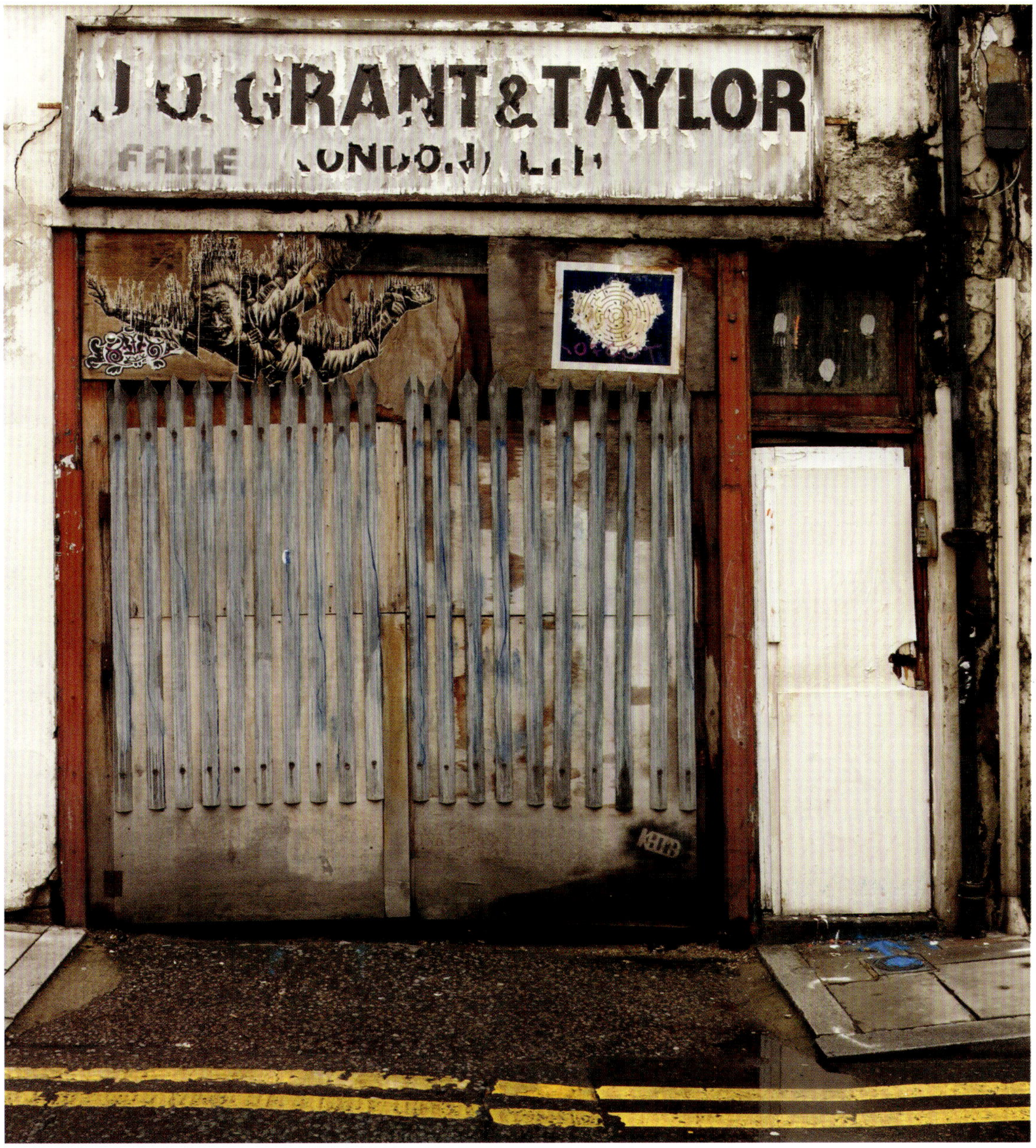

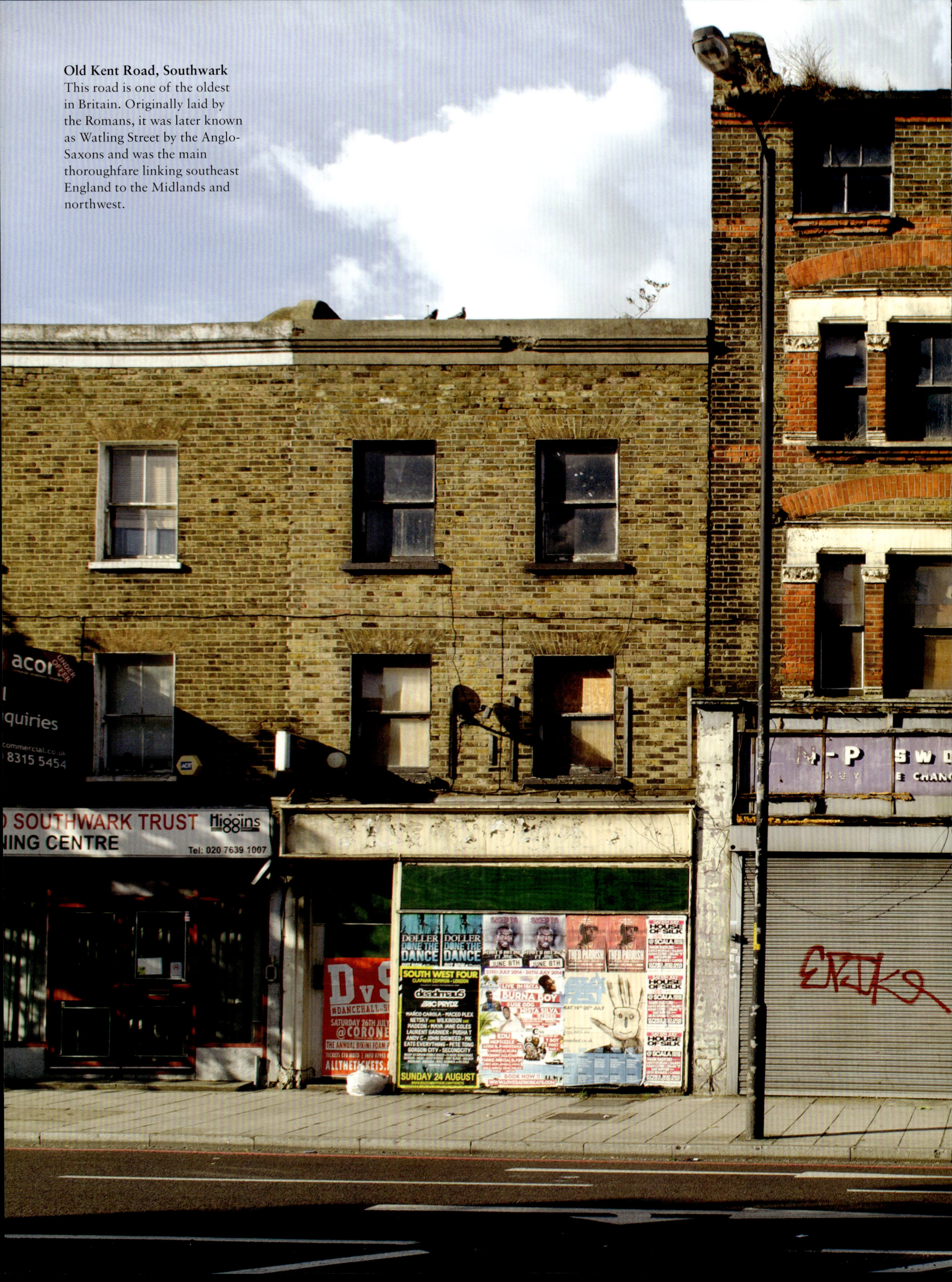

Old Kent Road, Southwark
This road is one of the oldest in Britain. Originally laid by the Romans, it was later known as Watling Street by the Anglo-Saxons and was the main thoroughfare linking southeast England to the Midlands and northwest.

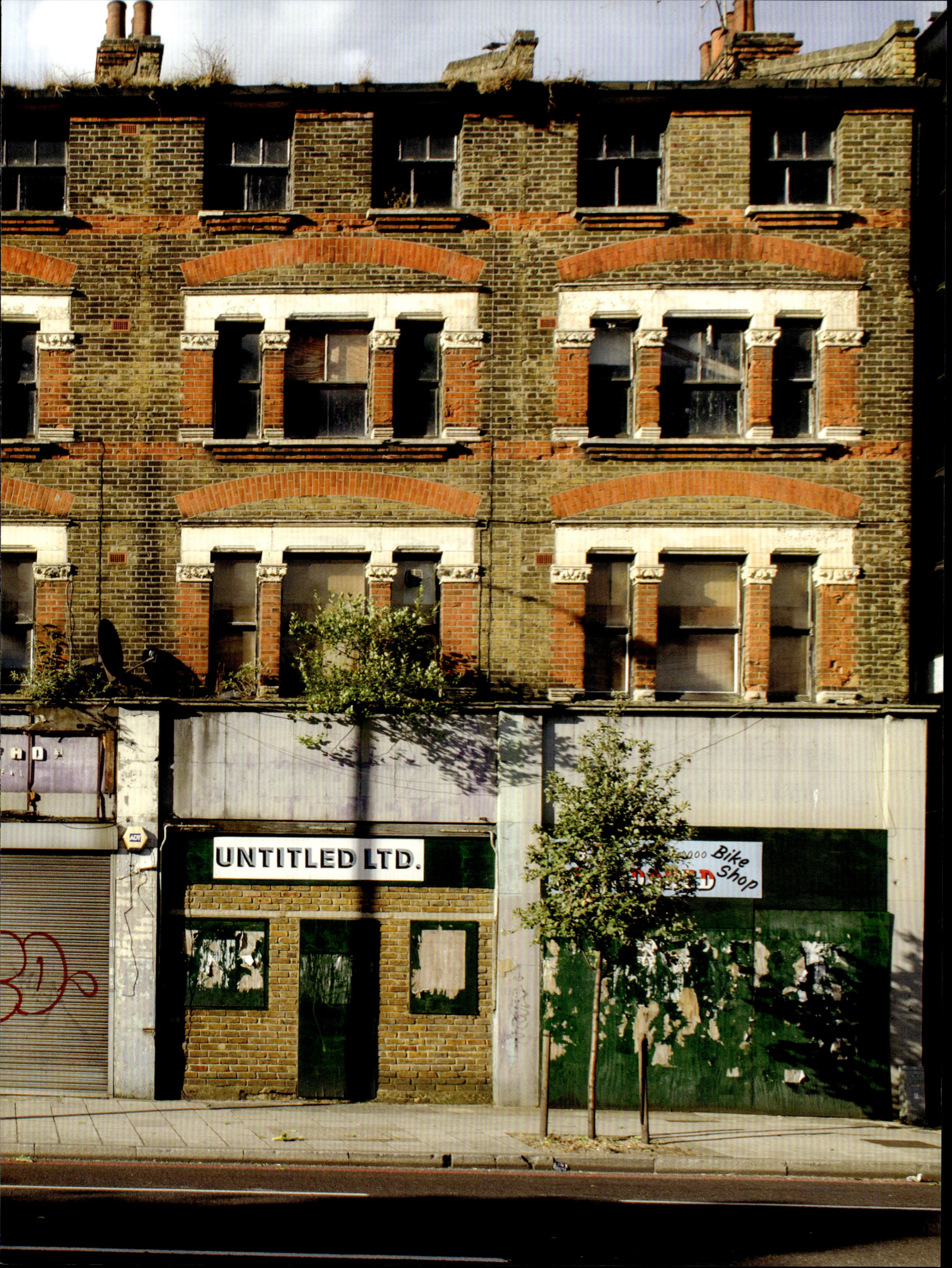
UNTITLED LTD.
Bike Shop

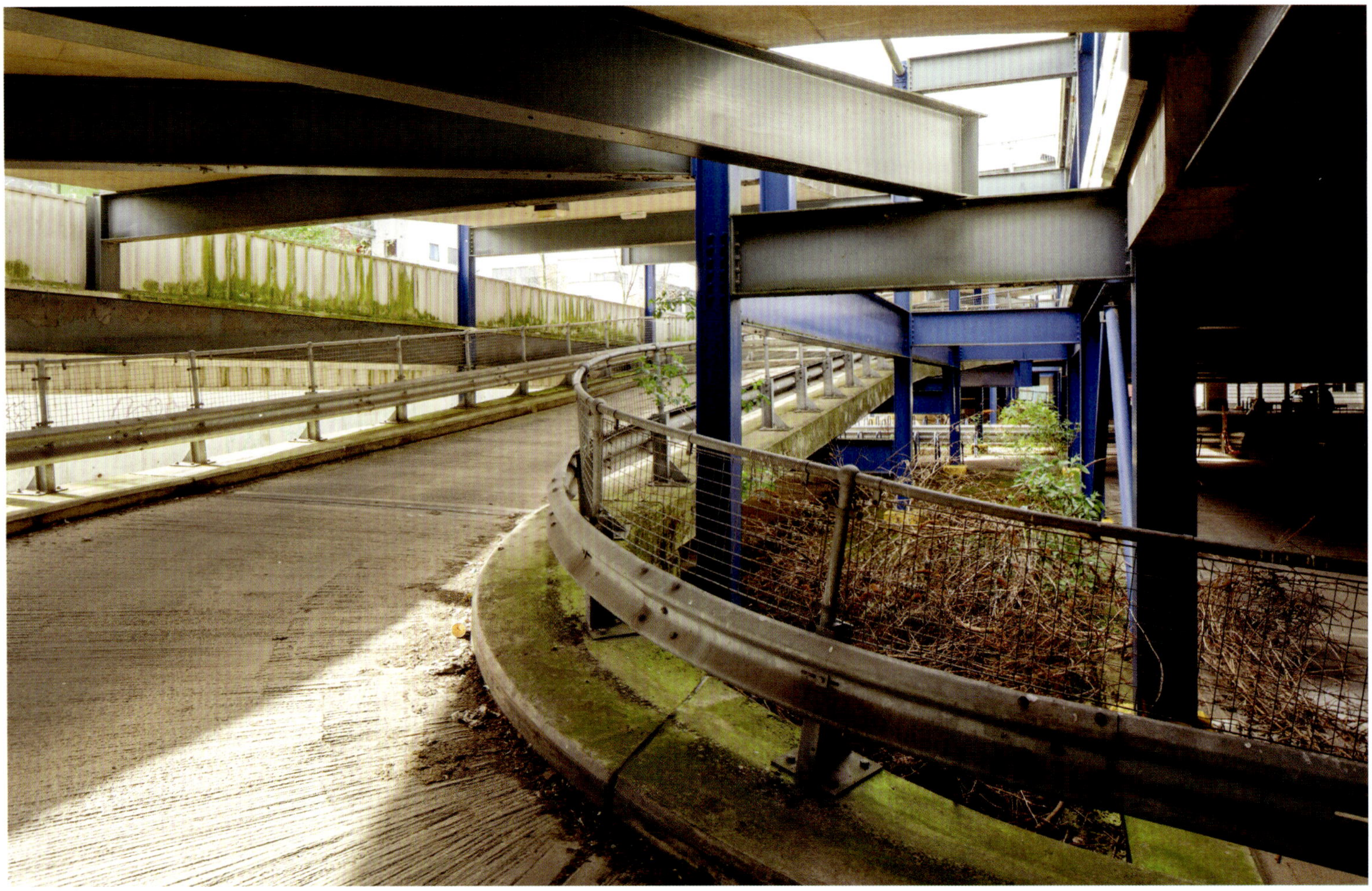

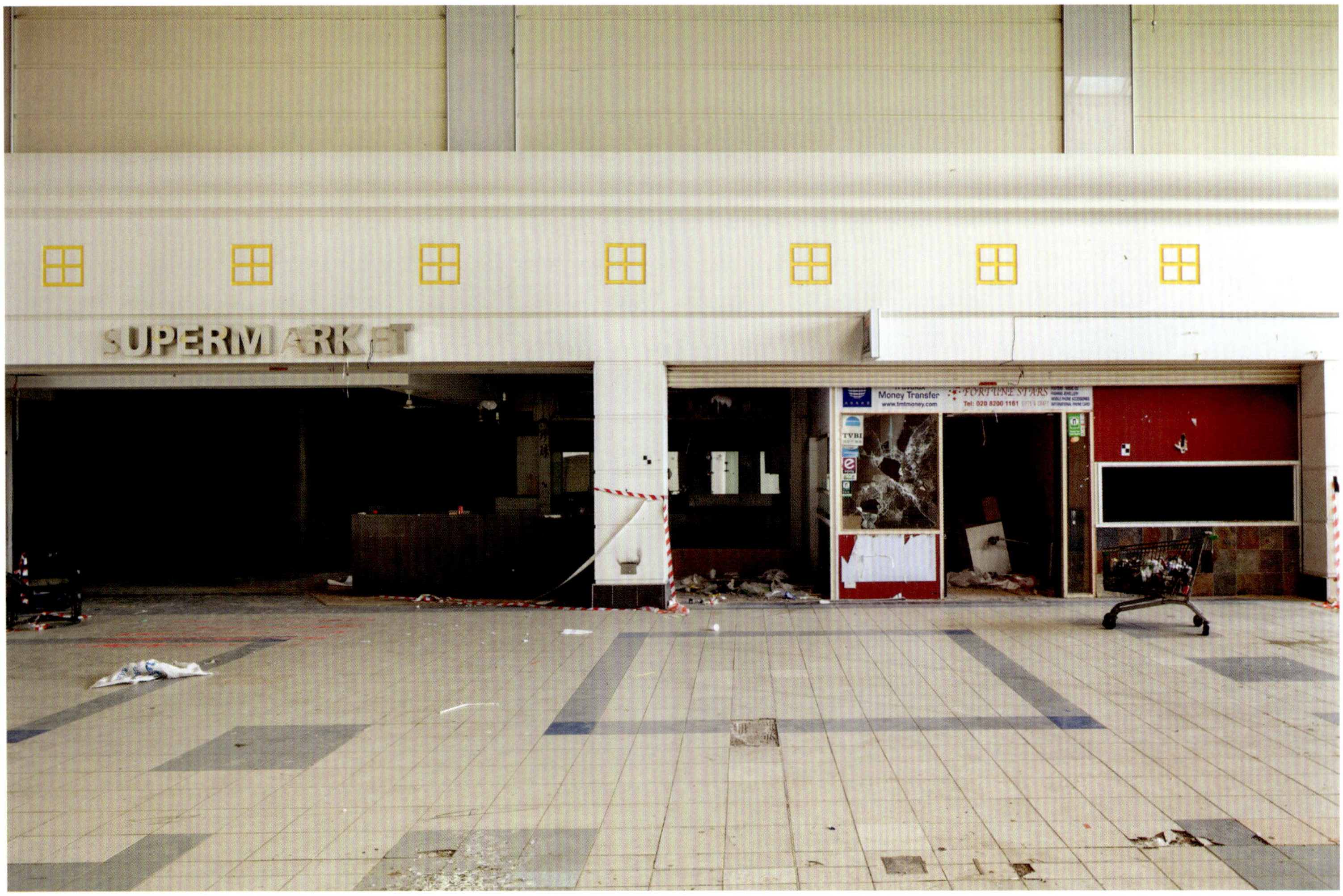
SUPERM ARK ET
Money Transfer
FORTUNE STARS

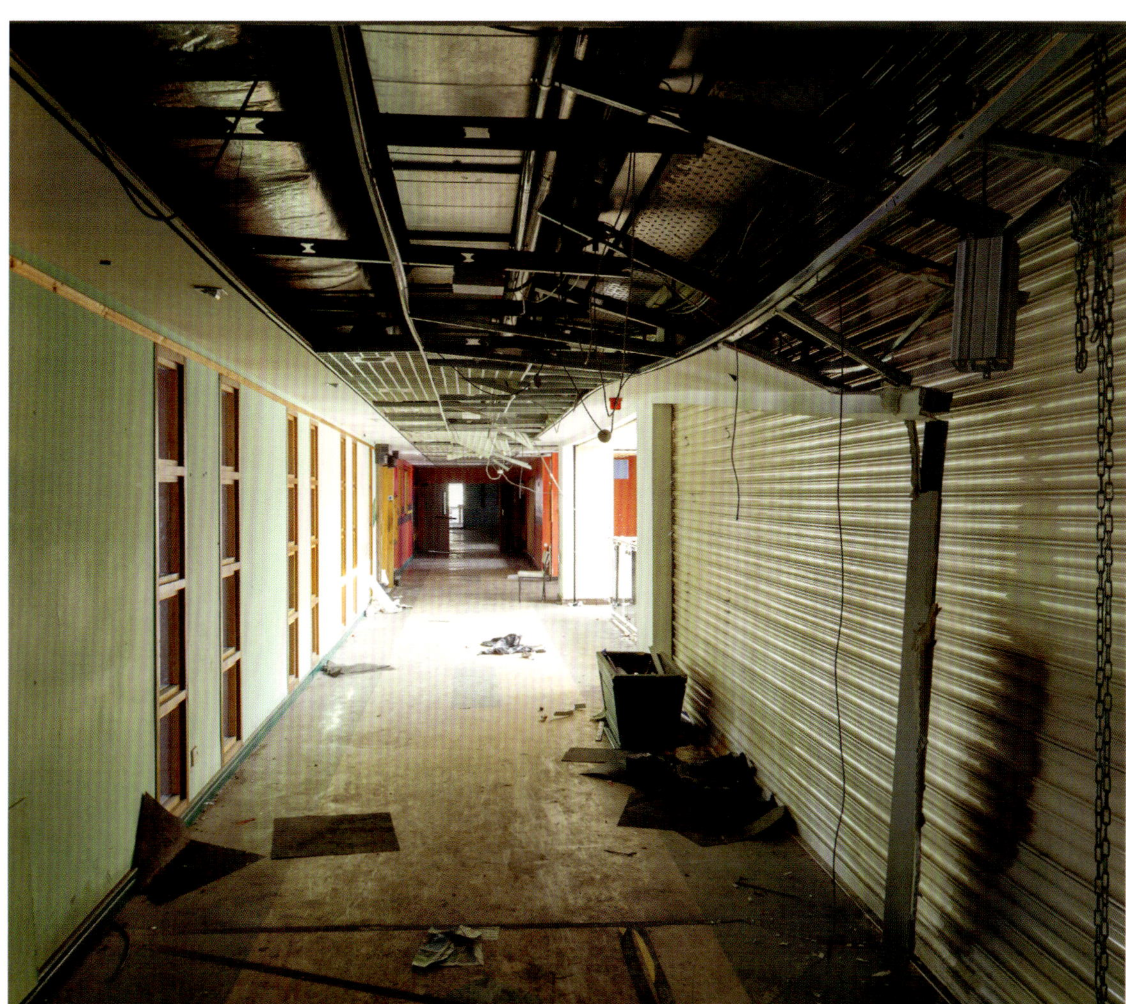

OPPOSITE (BOTH IMAGES) AND LEFT:

Oriental City, Colindale

Yaohan, the Japanese department store, opened Yaohan Plaza in 1993. The 13,100 sq metre (141,000 sq ft) space housed Asian restaurants, speciality shops and a Japanese pub, as well as a beauty parlour and travel agent. The corporation filed for bankruptcy in the late 1990s and the centre was bought by Malaysian owners, becoming famous for its food court. Although it closed in 2008, it reopened in 2017 as Bang Bang Oriental Foodhall, the largest in London. While it was derelict the empty shopping centre was used for filming, featuring in the BBC One series *Luther* and movie *Dredd* (2012).

BELOW:

213 Kentish Town Road, Camden

After 84 years as a family business, Blustons clothes shop was closed down in 2015. Three years later it reopened as the Octavia charity shop, supporting Londoners affected by health issues, unemployment and social isolation. The original sign and interior features have thankfully been preserved.

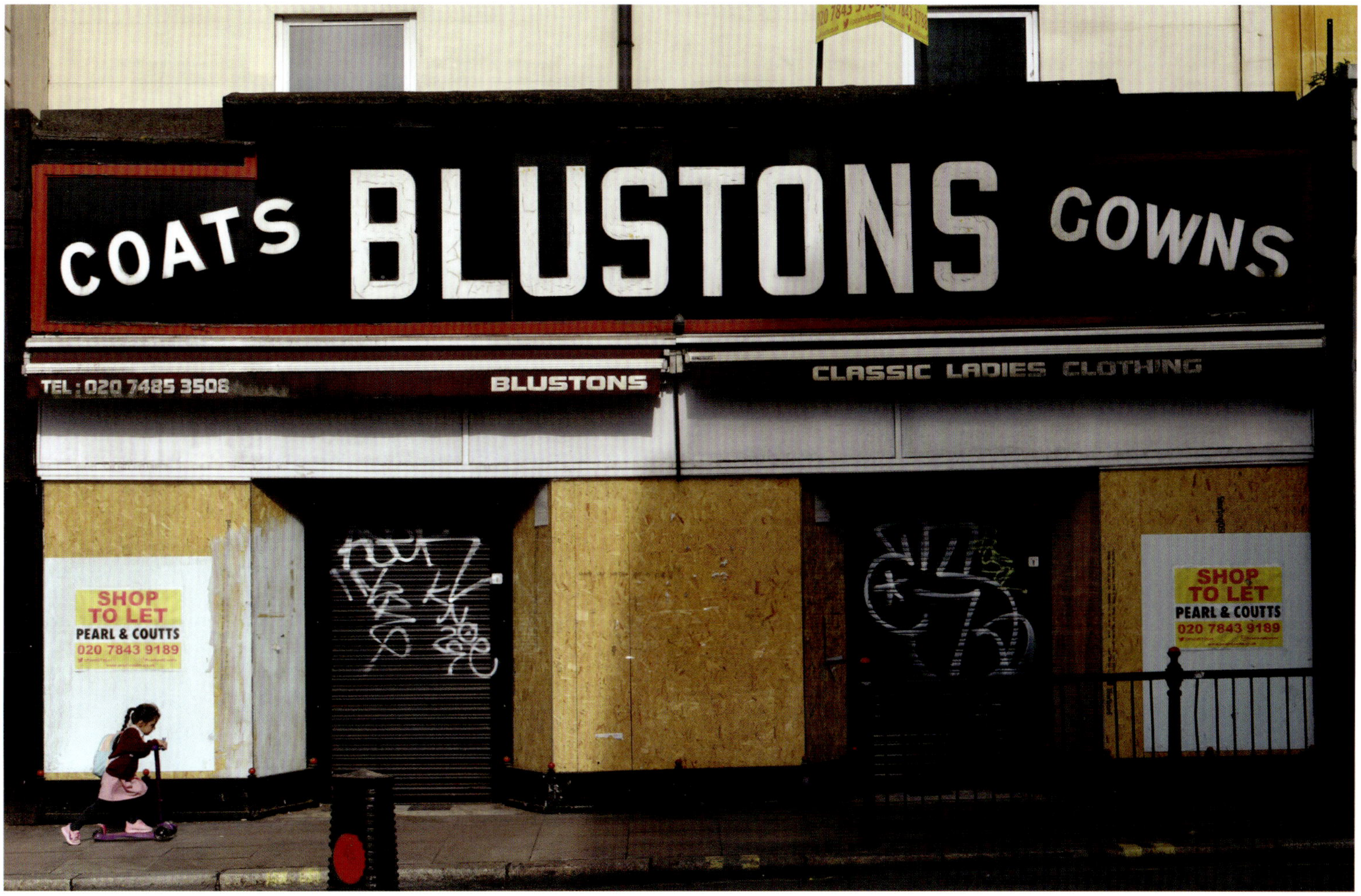

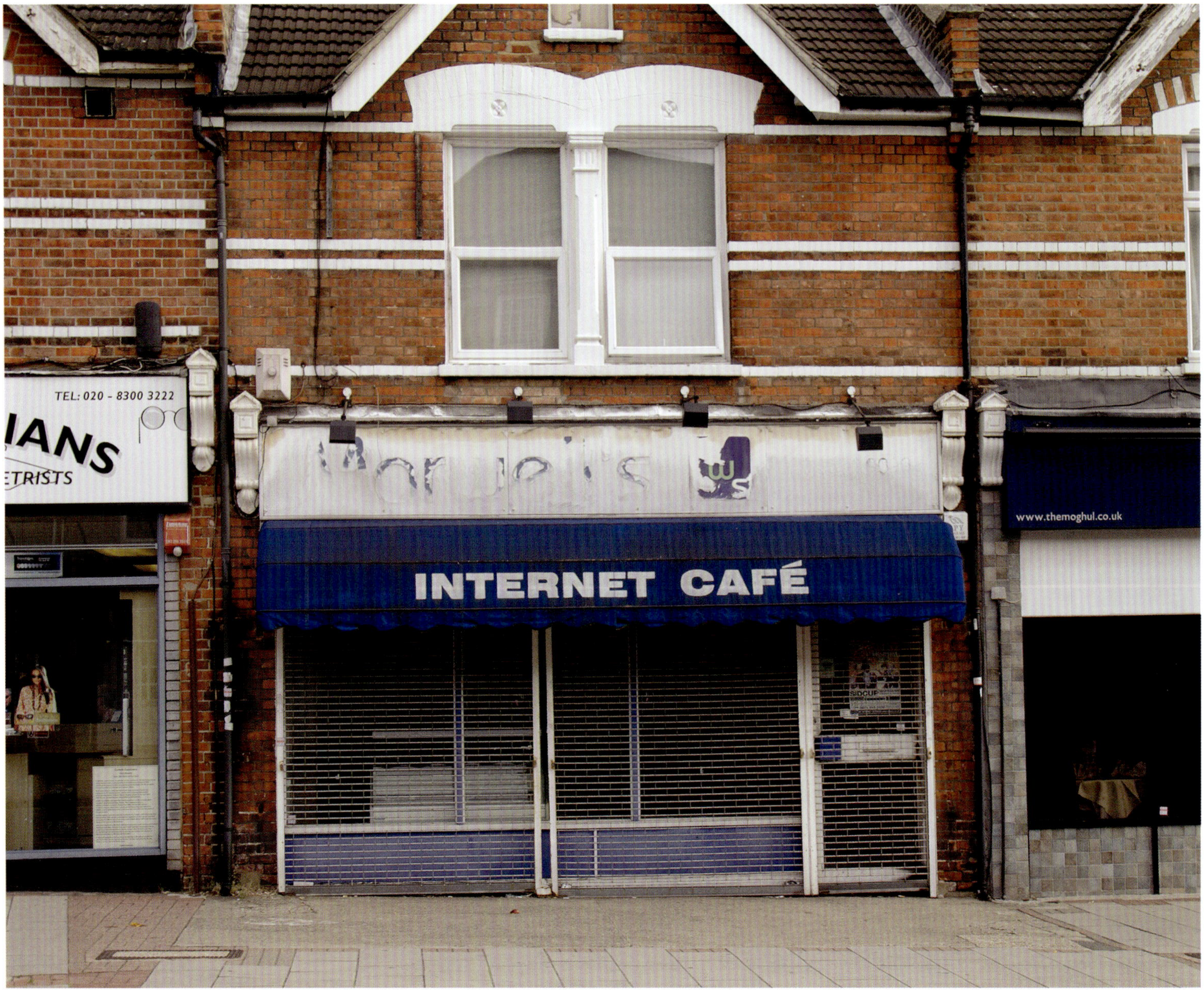

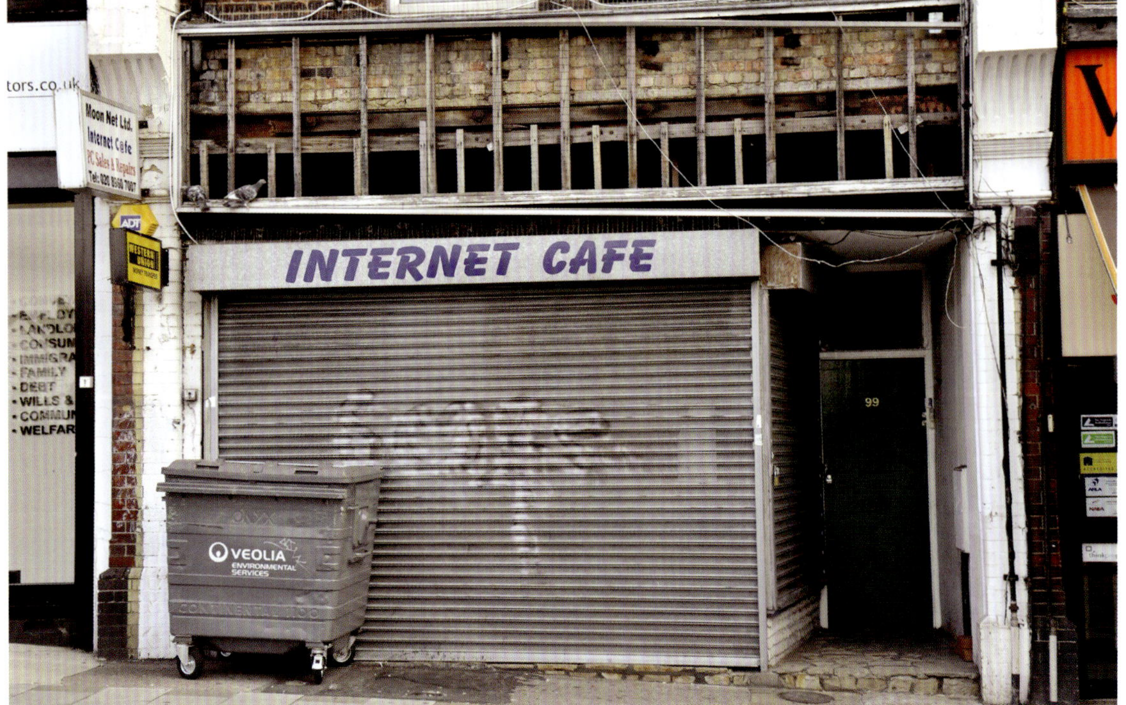

ALL PHOTOGRAPHS:

Internet Cafes

Cyberia, a London first, opened in 1994 and offered something new and exciting. For £3 an hour, while sipping on a cappuccino, you could access the internet. Skip to 2019 and 87 per cent of all adults used the internet daily; in July 2016 the UN issued a statement indicating that access to the internet should be a human right.

Do we still need internet cafes today? There are still hundreds across the capital and for many they provide a community space, workspace and IT training, not to mention the practical need of downloading or printing material.

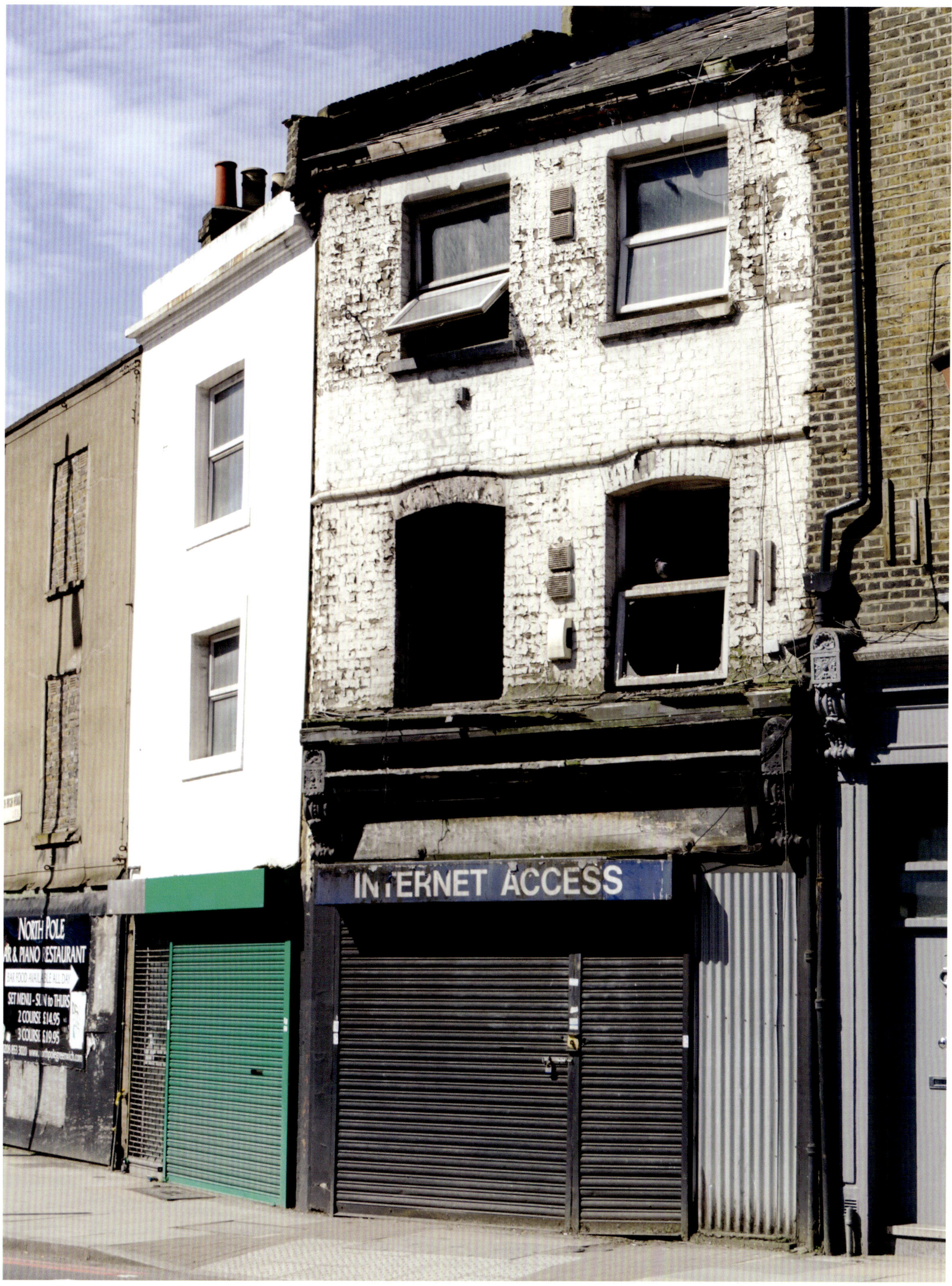
NORTH POLE
AR & PIANO RESTAURANT
BAR FOOD AVAILABLE ALL DAY
SET MENU - SUN to THURS
2 COURSE £14.95
3 COURSE £19.95
INTERNET ACCESS

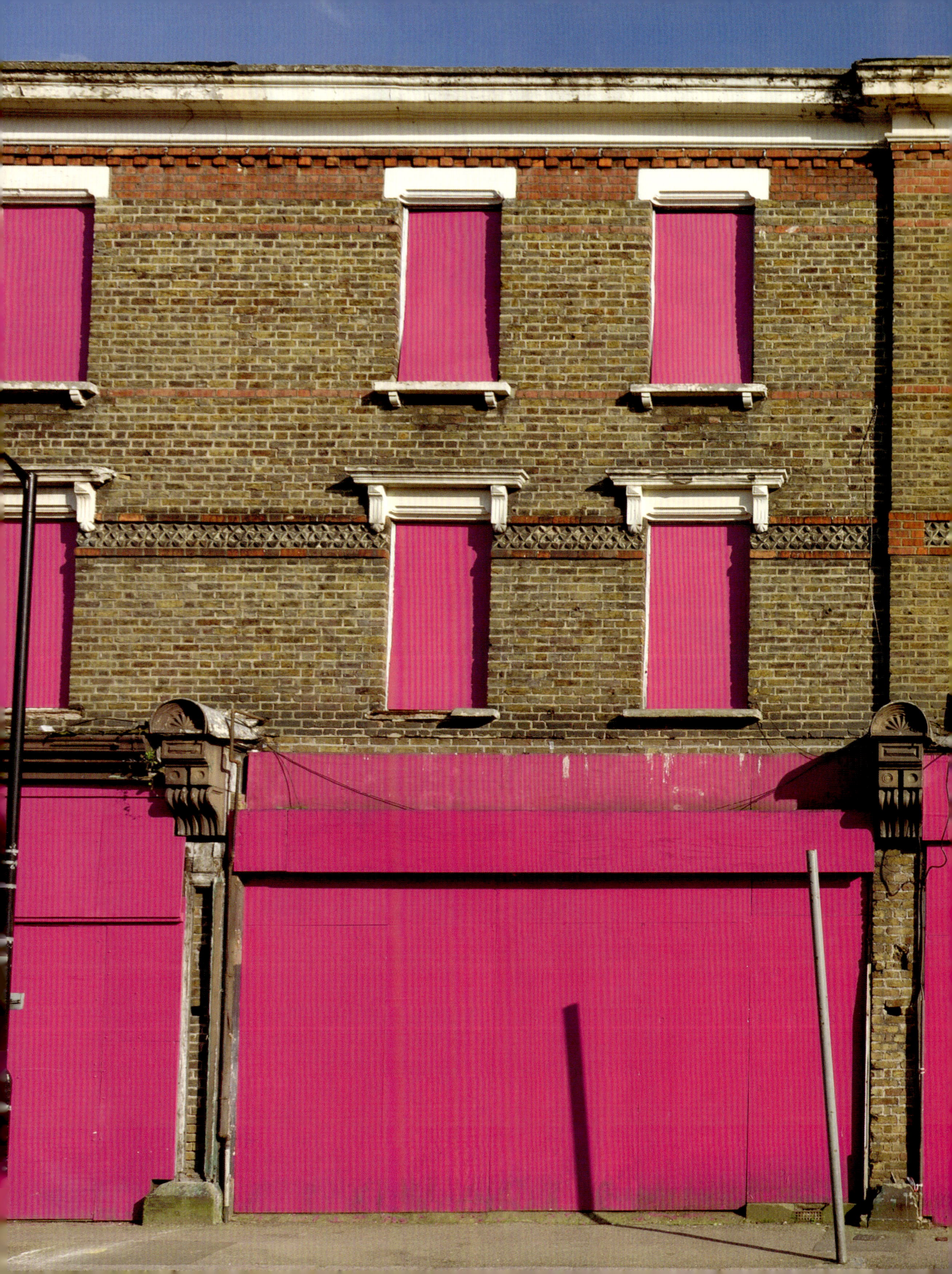

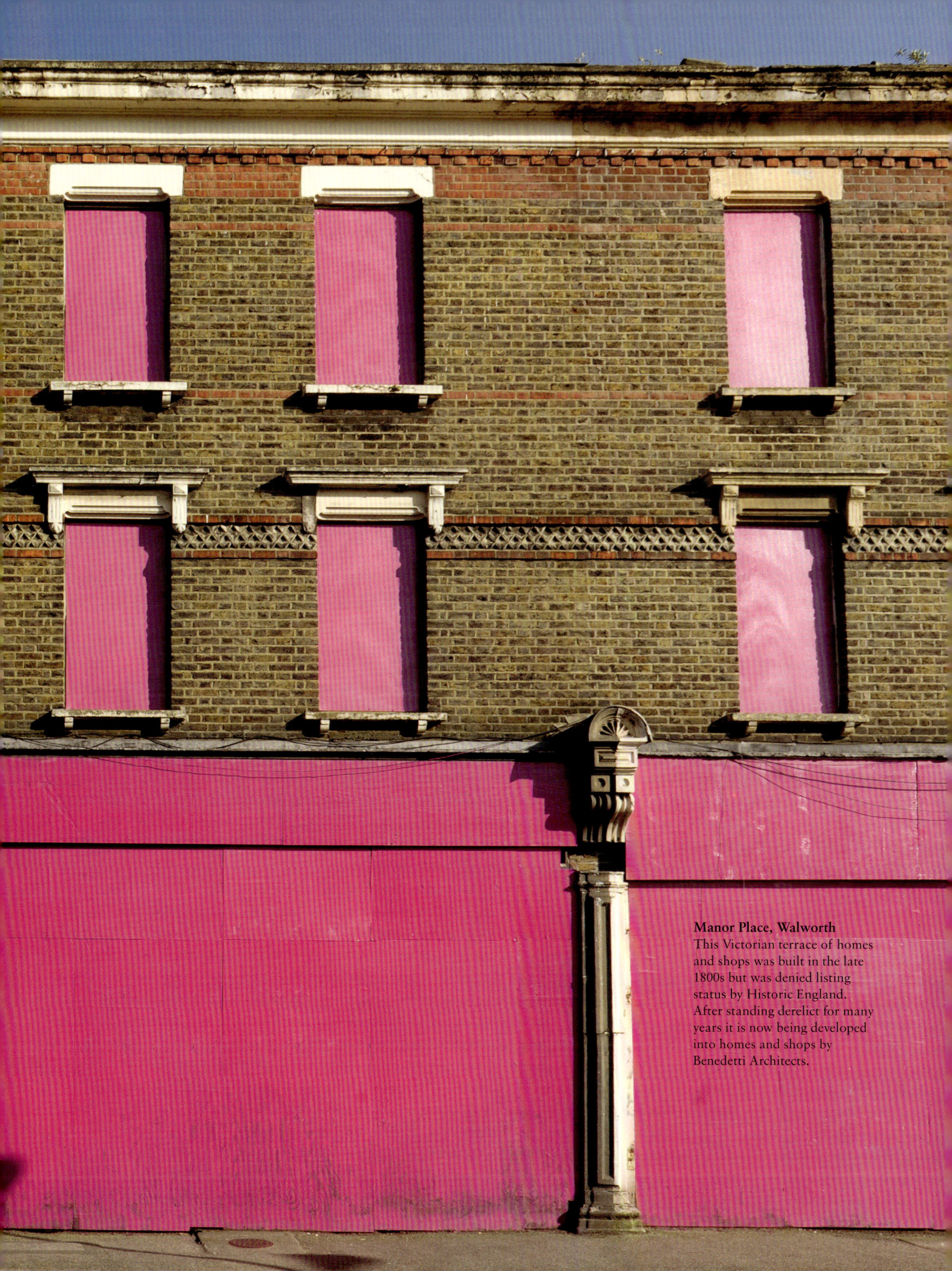

Manor Place, Walworth
This Victorian terrace of homes and shops was built in the late 1800s but was denied listing status by Historic England. After standing derelict for many years it is now being developed into homes and shops by Benedetti Architects.

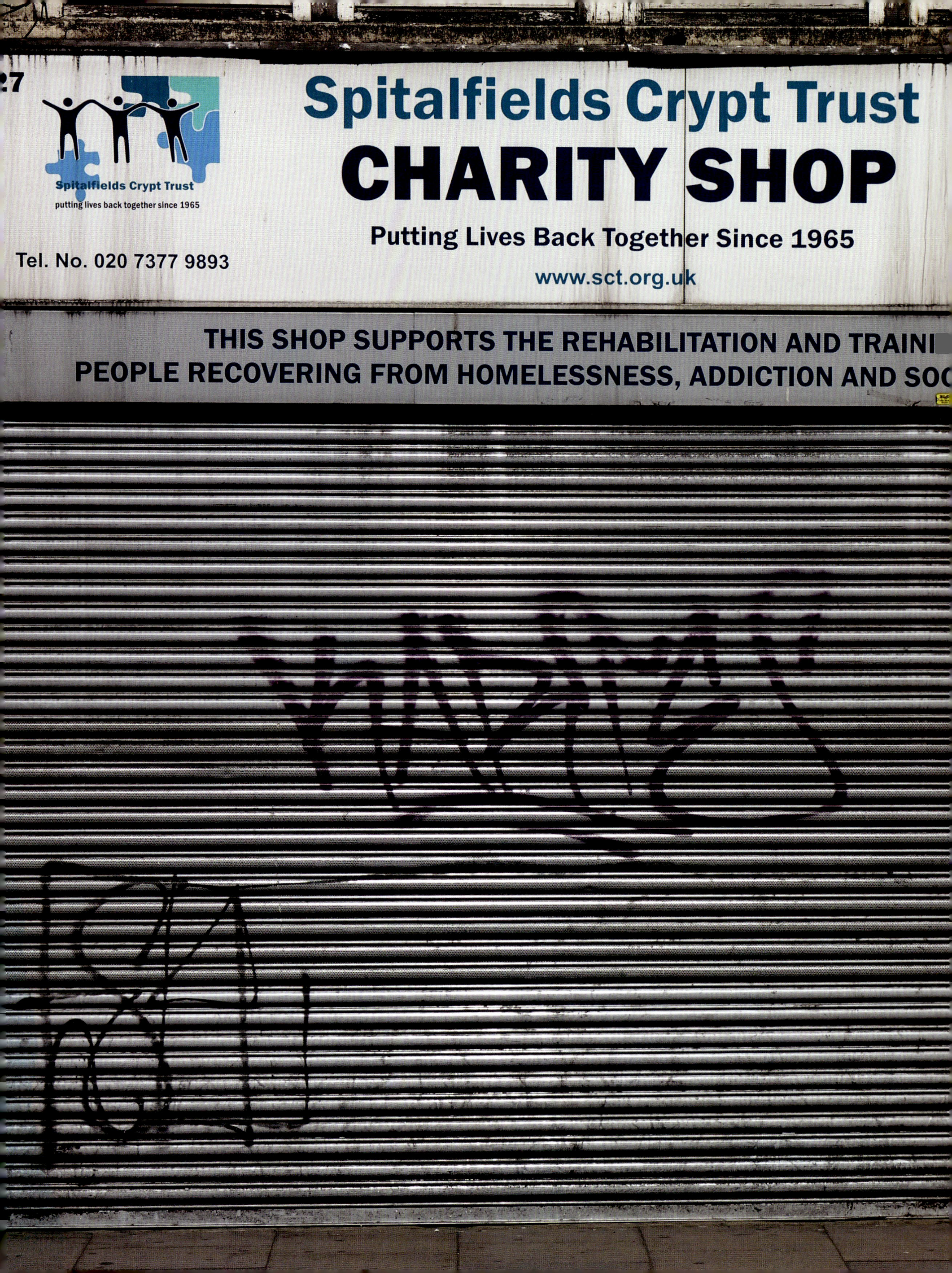

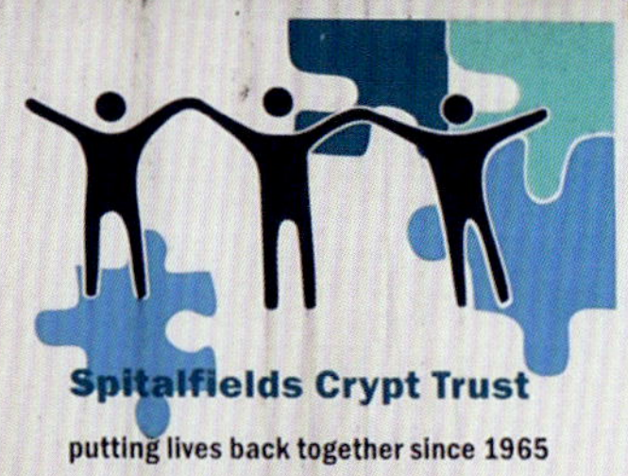
Spitalfields Crypt Trust
putting lives back together since 1965
27
Tel. No. 020 7377 9893
Spitalfields Crypt Trust
CHARITY SHOP
Putting Lives Back Together Since 1965
www.sct.org.uk
THIS SHOP SUPPORTS THE REHABILITATION AND TRAINI
PEOPLE RECOVERING FROM HOMELESSNESS, ADDICTION AND SOC

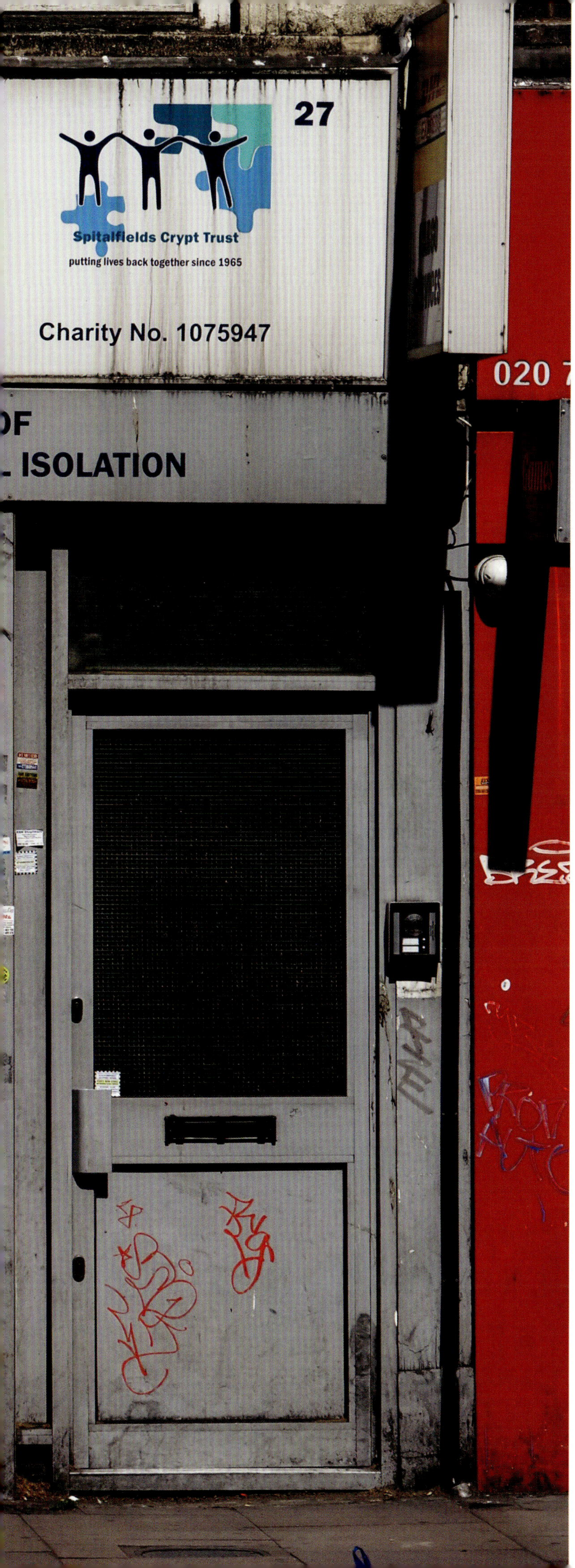

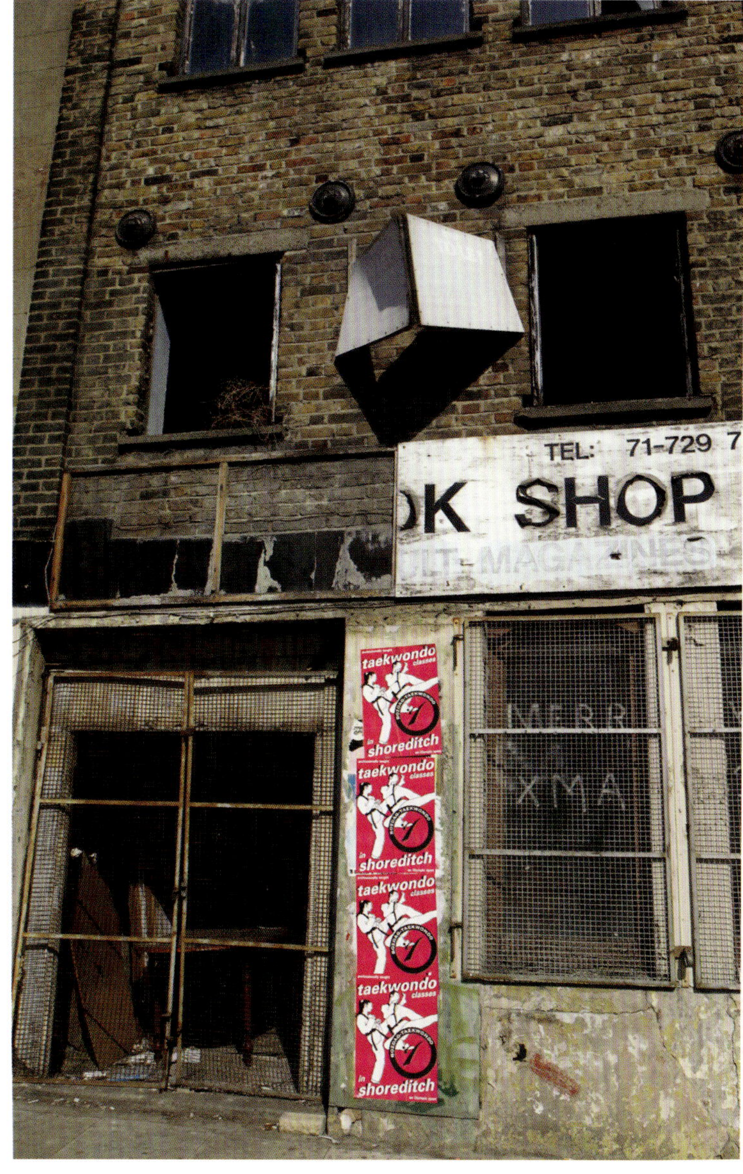

LEFT:
Spitalfields Crypt Trust
The charity began business in 1965, running a soup kitchen and night shelter from the church crypt next door. Christ Church Spitalfields, designed by Nicholas Hawksmoor in the early 18th century, is an East London landmark. It was built thanks to an Act of Parliament in 1711, which had the intention of constructing 50 new churches for the rapidly expanding population. In the end, only 12 churches were actually completed.

ABOVE:
Moorgate
If you look up above the first row of windows you can spot several cast-iron discs. These are commonly found on 18th and 19th century buildings and are known as pattress plates. They are attached to a tie rod running through the building to stop the outer walls spreading.

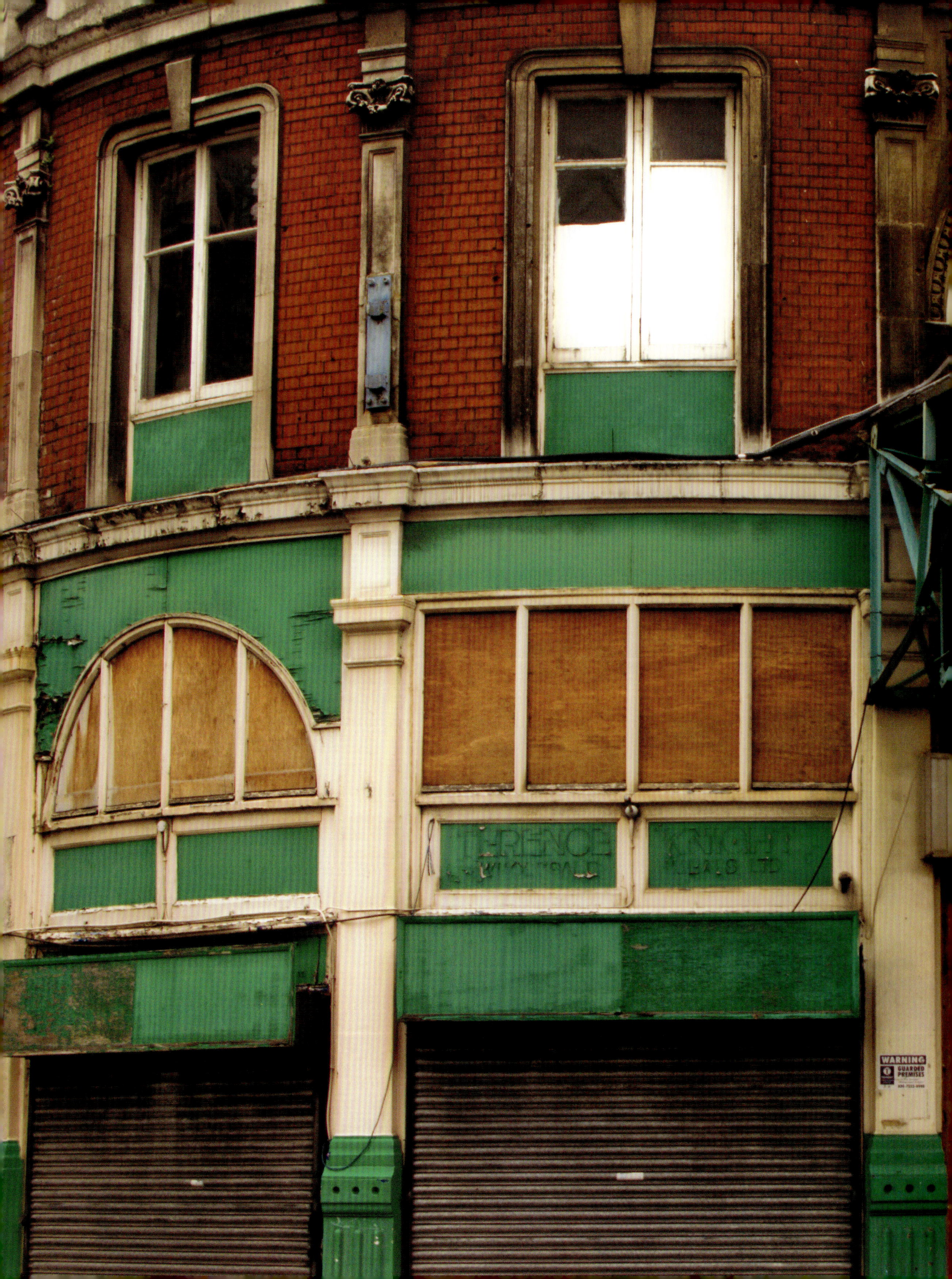
TERENCE
KNIGHT
WARNING
GUARDED PREMISES

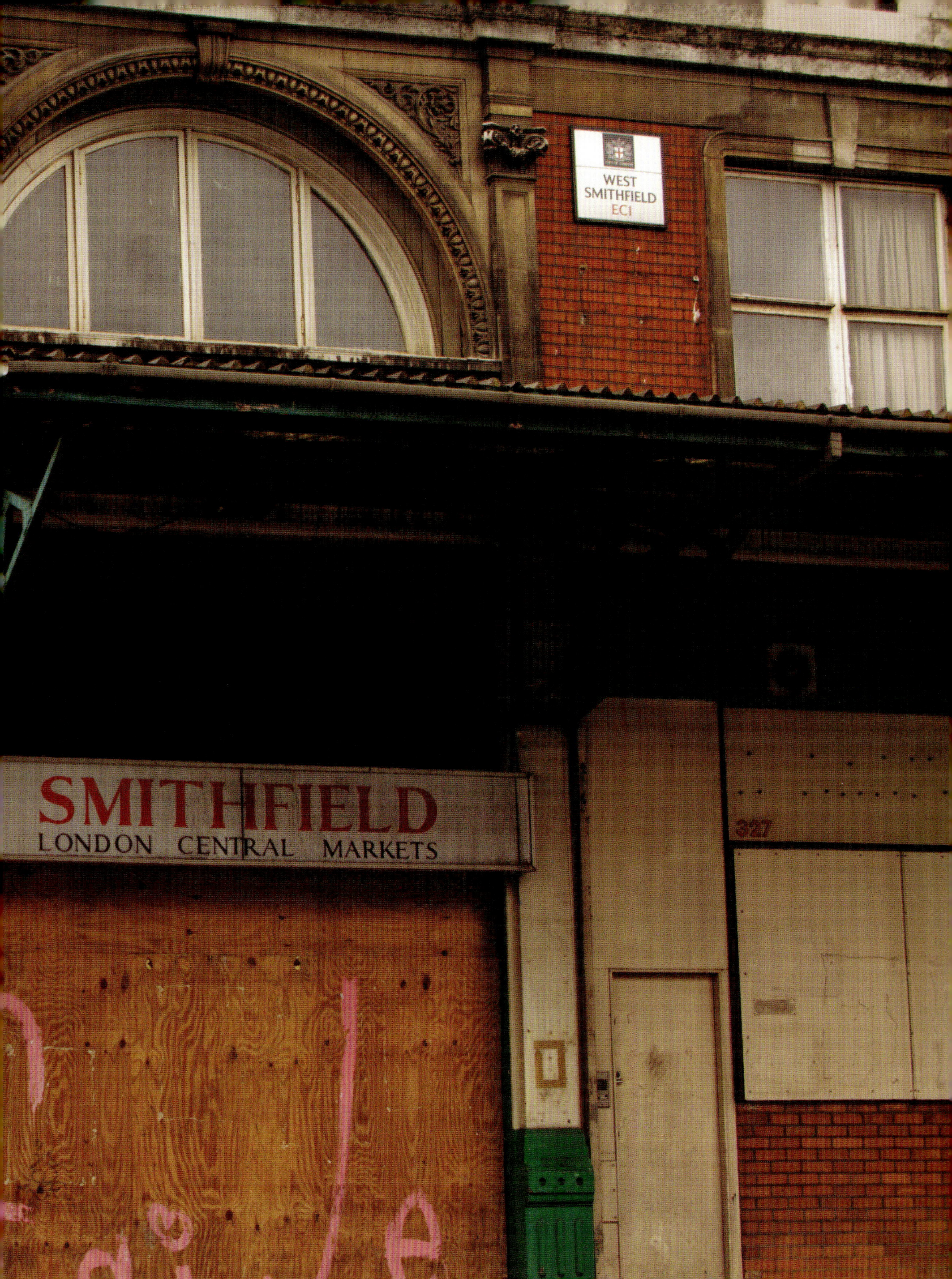
WEST
SMITHFIELD
EC1
SMITHFIELD
LONDON CENTRAL MARKETS
327

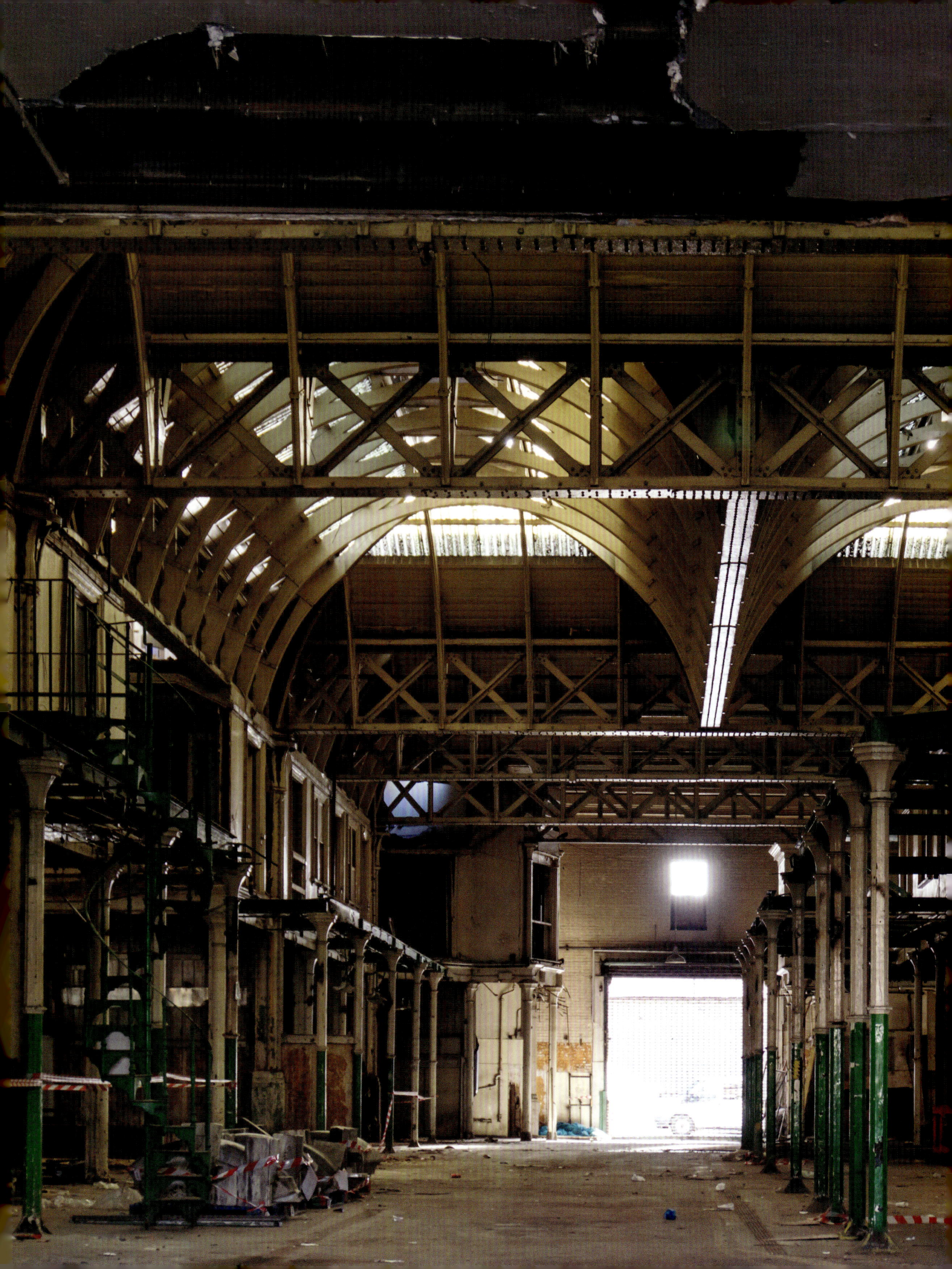

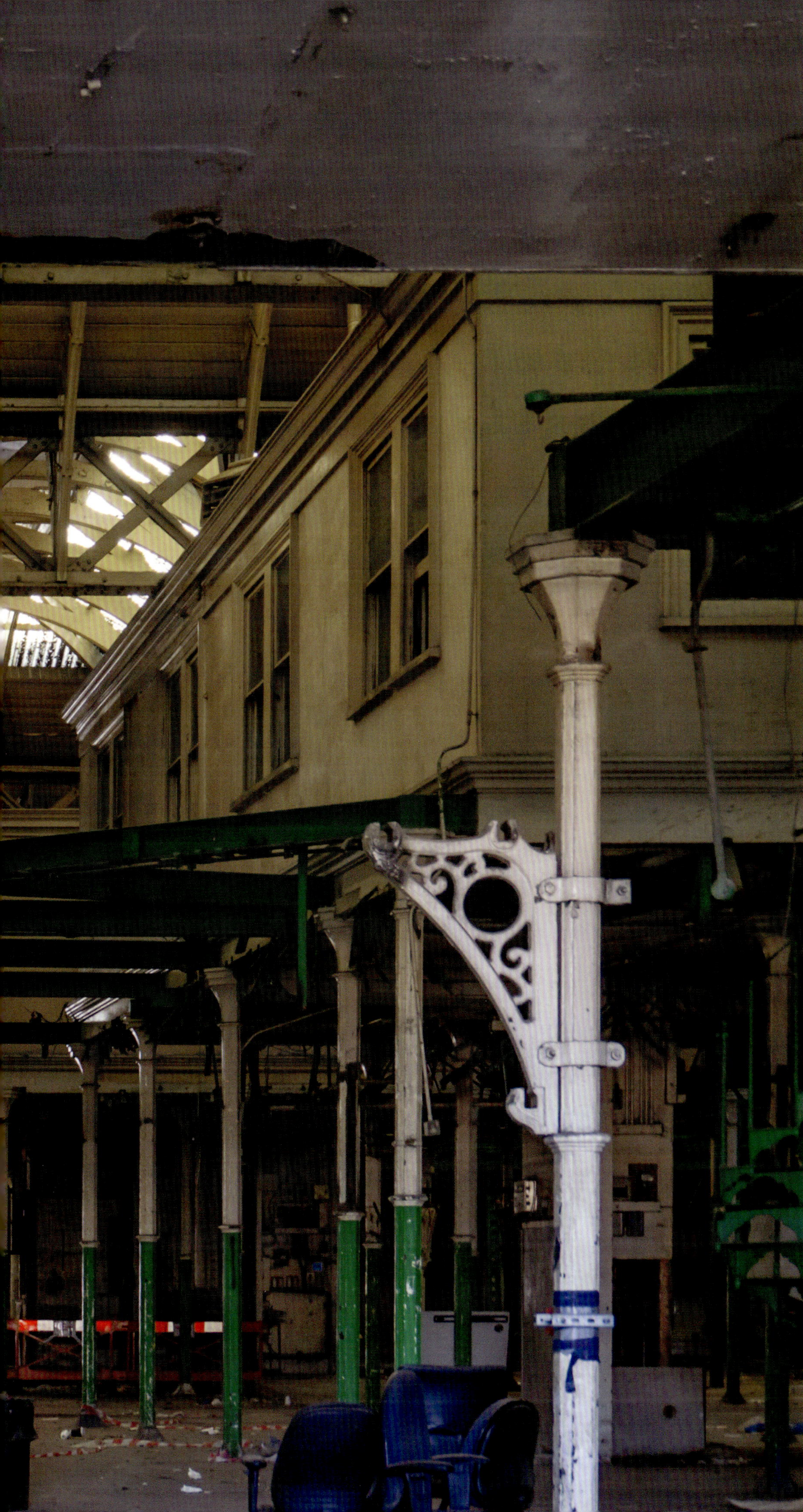

PREVIOUS PAGES AND LEFT:
Smithfield Market
In 1174 an area just north of the City of London was described as 'a smooth field' by the clerk William Fitzstephen. The large, open area was used for celebrations, trading and executions, but is most famous today for its meat market, which has been continuously trading for over 800 years.

The structure of Smithfield General Market was designed by Sir Horace Jones in 1883. He was surveyor to the City of London architect for over 20 years and is most famous for designing Tower Bridge. One cutting-edge technique adopted by Jones was the Phoenix column, named after the Phoenix Iron Company in Pennsylvania, USA. These are made from wrought iron sections riveted together, which makes them able to take far greater weight and withstand vibrations.

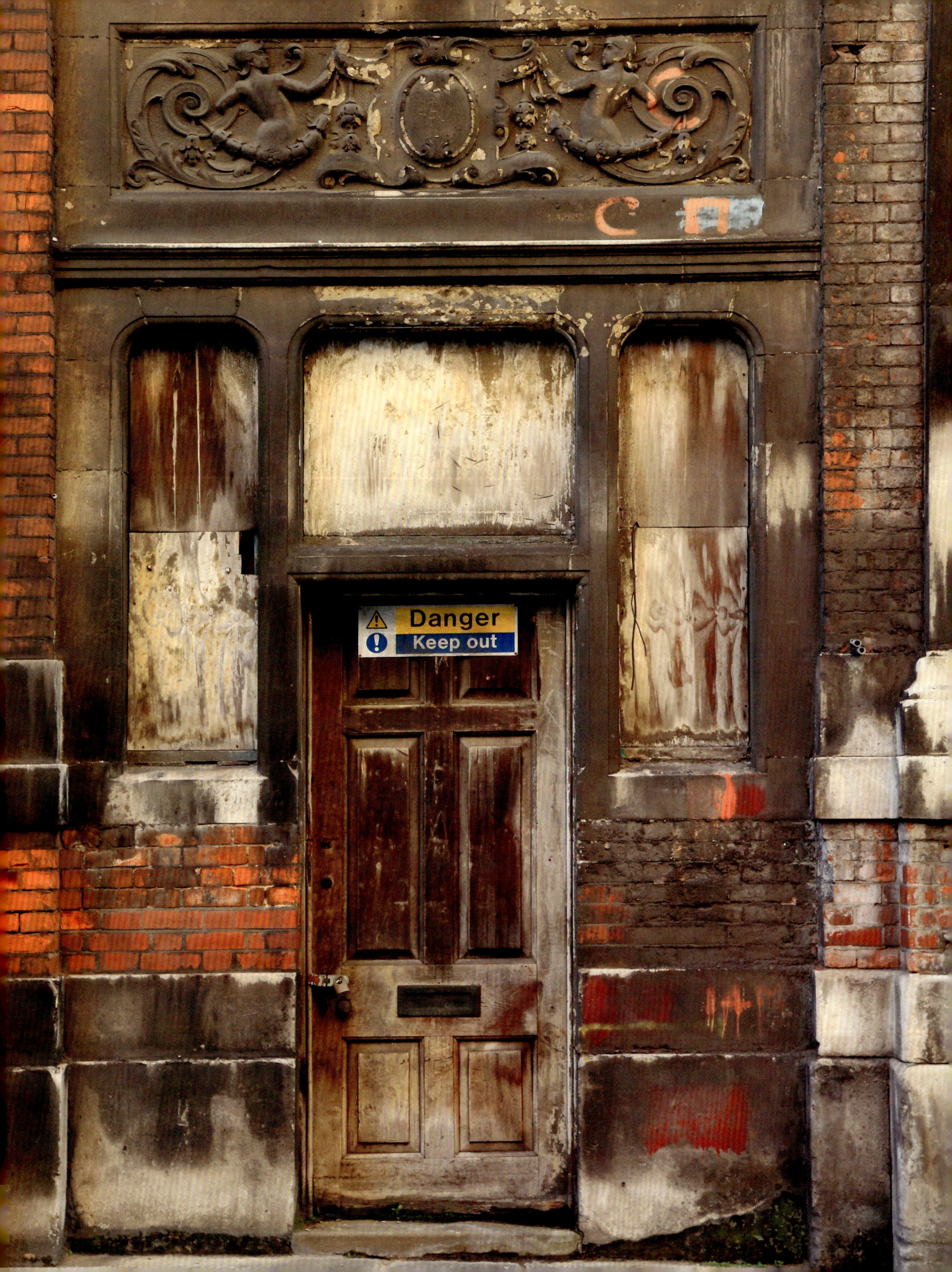
Danger
Keep out

OPPOSITE AND RIGHT:
Smithfield Market
Another innovation of the market building was the Red House, added by architects in 1898. It was one of the country's first refrigerated cold storage units, powered by an engine house that was later transformed into public toilets. The General Market was originally intended as a fruit and vegetable market, but became an extension of the meat market (see right) by 1889. In the 21st century it's set to transform again, becoming the new home for the Museum of London.

BOTTOM RIGHT:
Edmund Martin, Lindsey Street, Smithfield Market
The tiled 1930s frontage of an offal seller opposite the meat market. It was demolished in 2010 and the site is now occupied by the entrance to Farringdon Station on the Elizabeth Line.

OVERLEAF:
West Central Street, Camden
The cluster of narrow streets between Tottenham Court Road and Holborn tube stations give some idea of the Rookery of St Giles. One of the most destitute areas of London in the 19th century, it was a semi-derelict warren of alleys that was overcrowded, unsanitary and impoverished. In the late 19th century the construction of New Oxford Street ploughed straight through the slums in an effort to displace the occupants. All it did was move people into more crowded locations nearby.

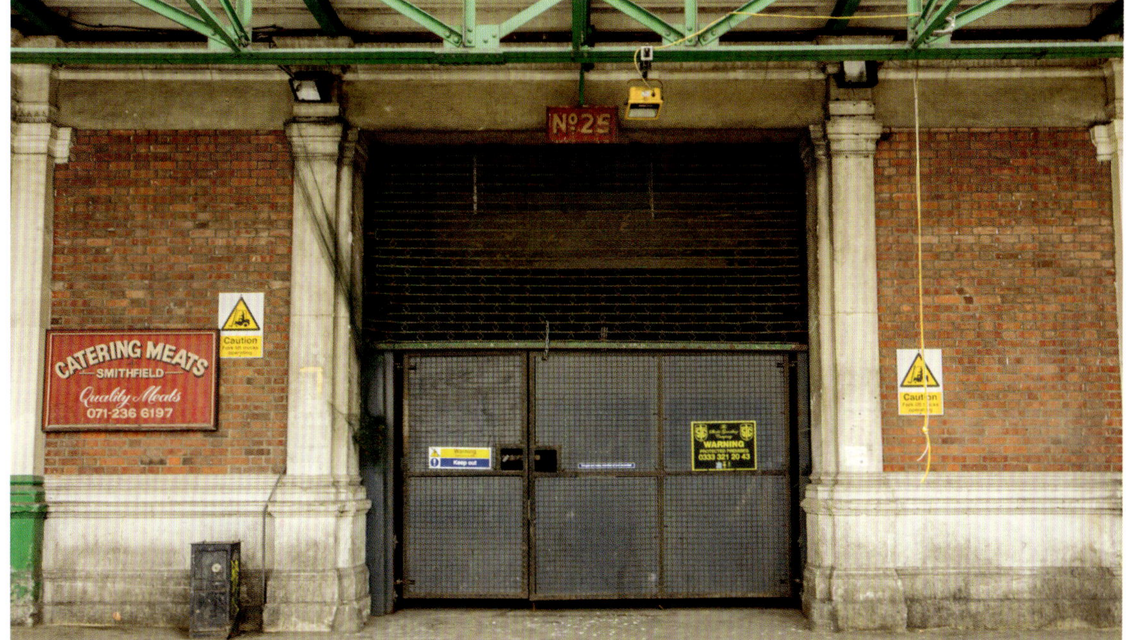

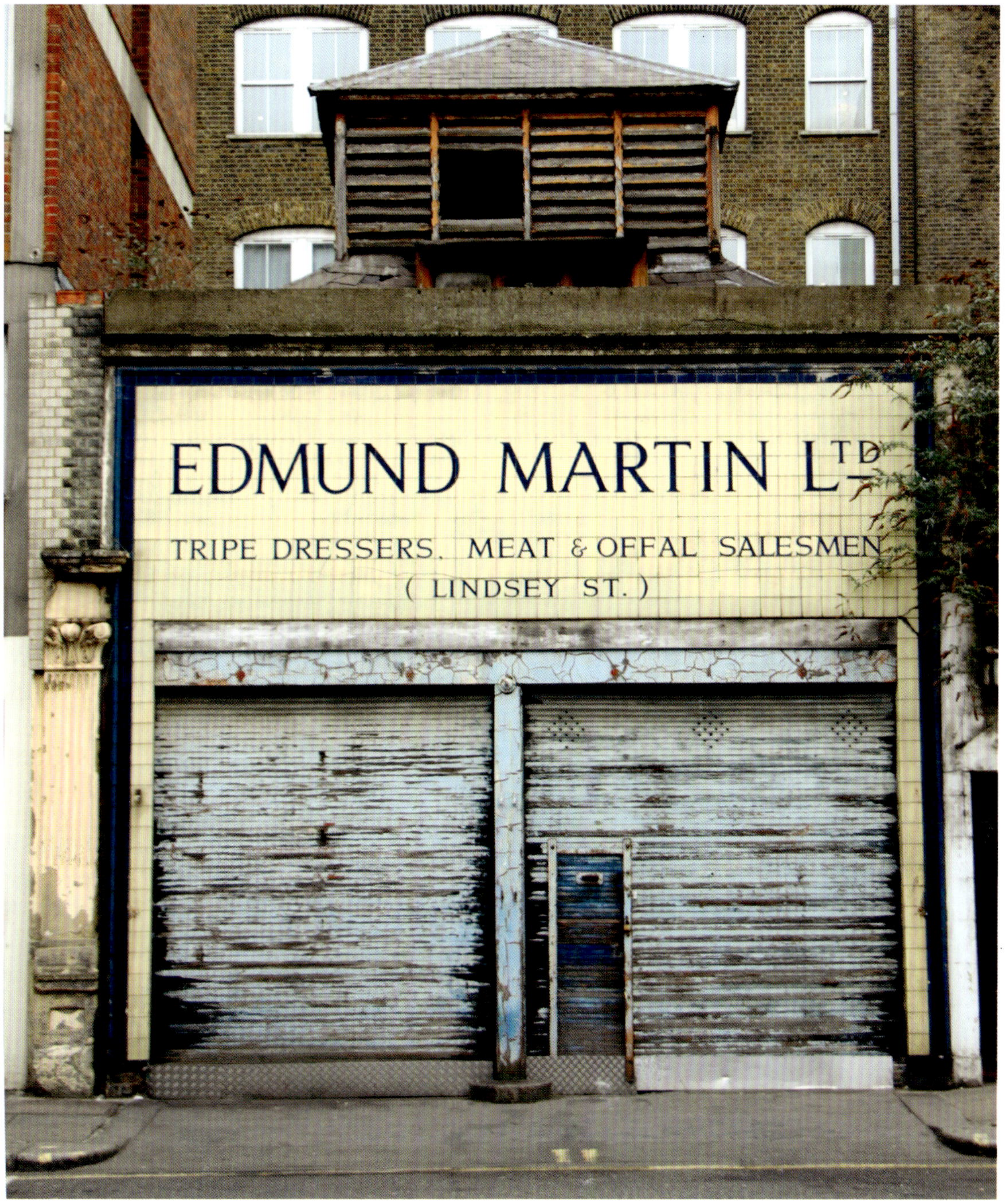

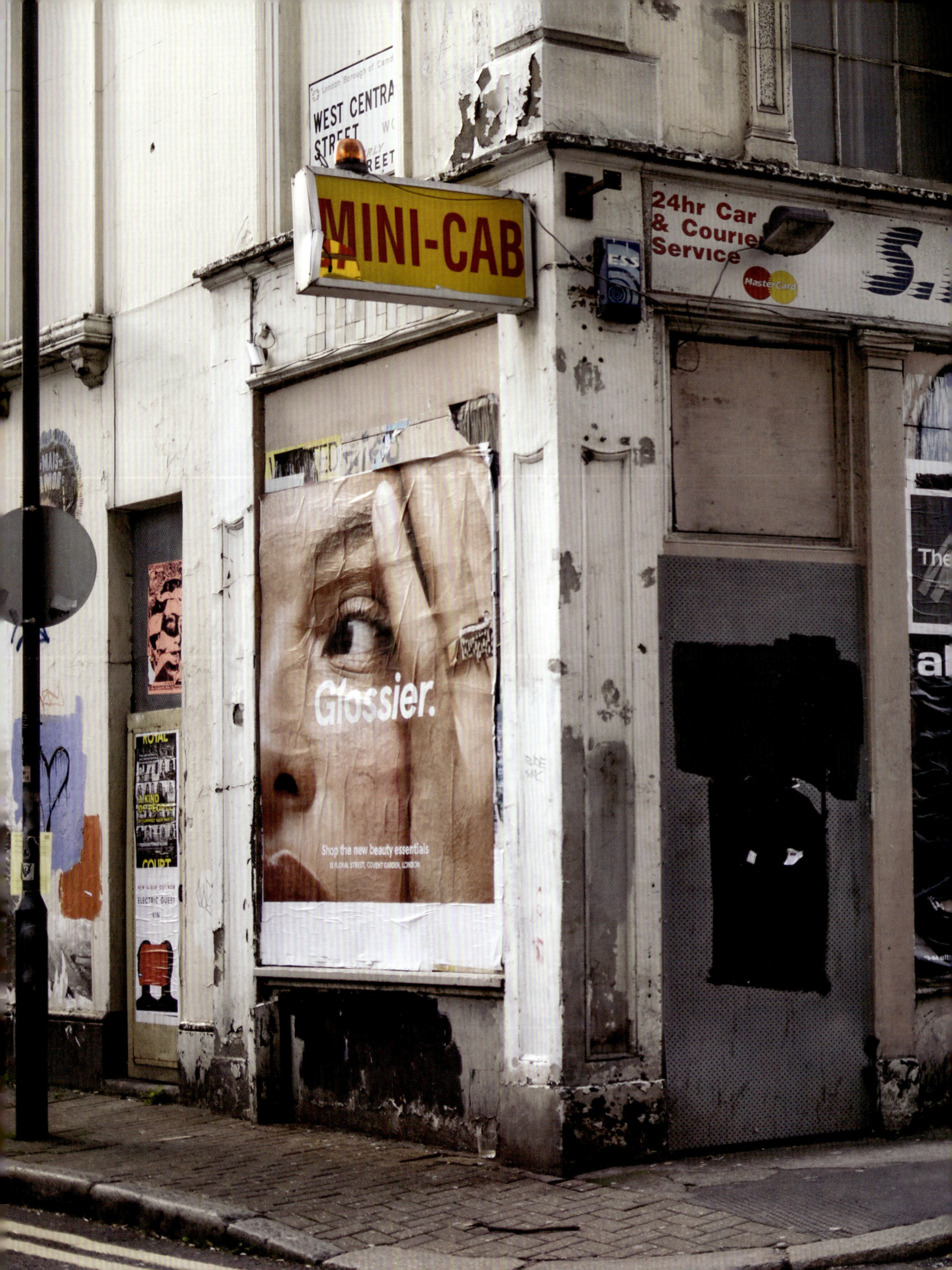
WEST CENTRA
STREET
MINI-CAB
24hr Car
& Courie
Service
MasterCard
Glossier.
Shop the new beauty essentials
ROYAL
COURT

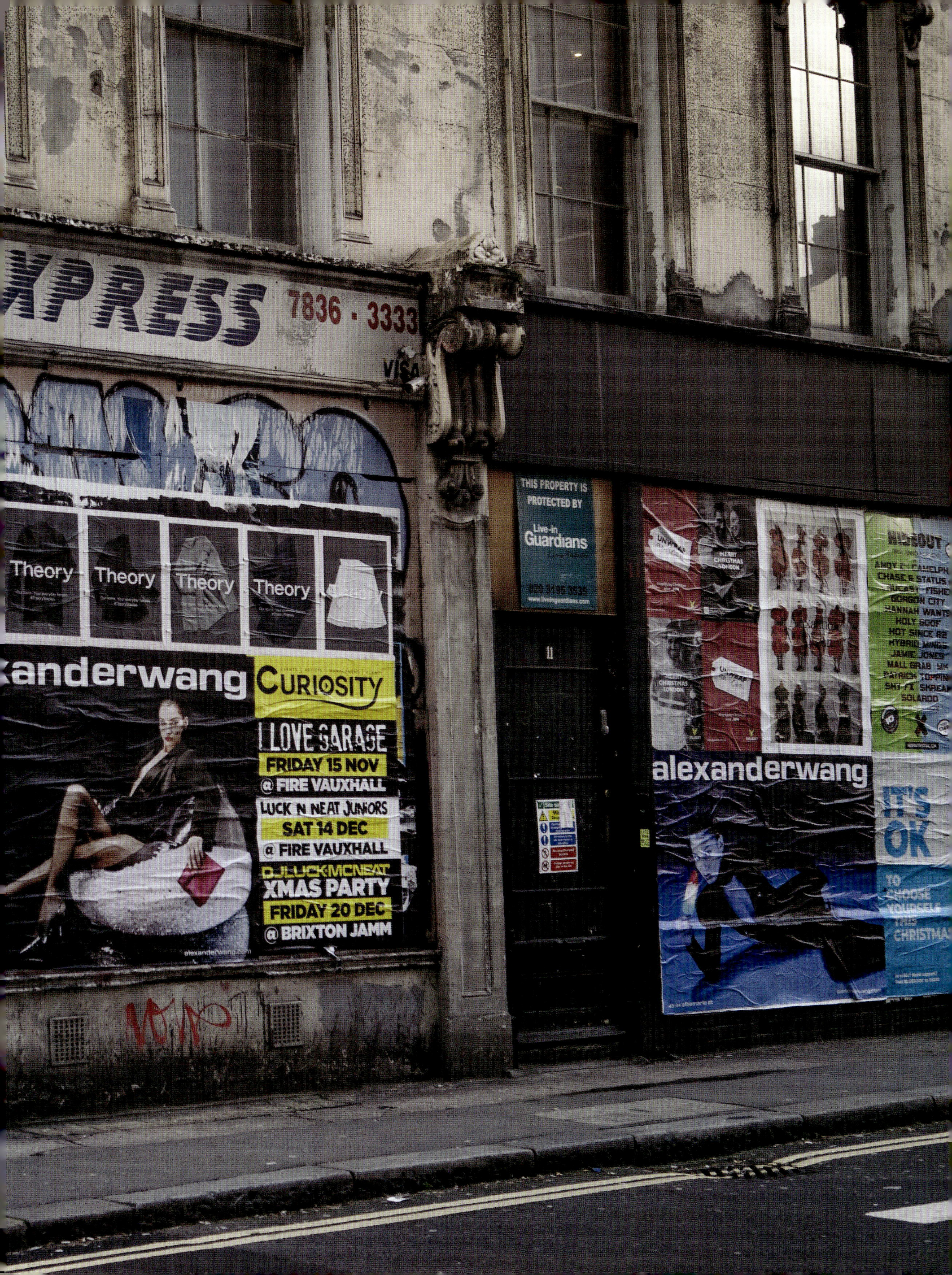
XPRESS
7836 - 3333
VISA
Theory
Theory
Theory
Theory
THIS PROPERTY IS PROTECTED BY
Live-in Guardians
020 3195 3535
www.liveinguardians.com
xanderwang
CURIOSITY
I LOVE GARAGE
FRIDAY 15 NOV
@ FIRE VAUXHALL
LUCK N NEAT JUNIORS
SAT 14 DEC
@ FIRE VAUXHALL
DJ LUCK MC NEAT
XMAS PARTY
FRIDAY 20 DEC
@ BRIXTON JAMM
alexanderwang.com
HIDEOUT
GORGON CITY
HANNAH WANTS
HOLY GOOF
HOT SINCE 82
JAMIE JONES
SOLARDO
alexanderwang
IT'S OK
TO CHOOSE YOURSELF THIS CHRISTMAS

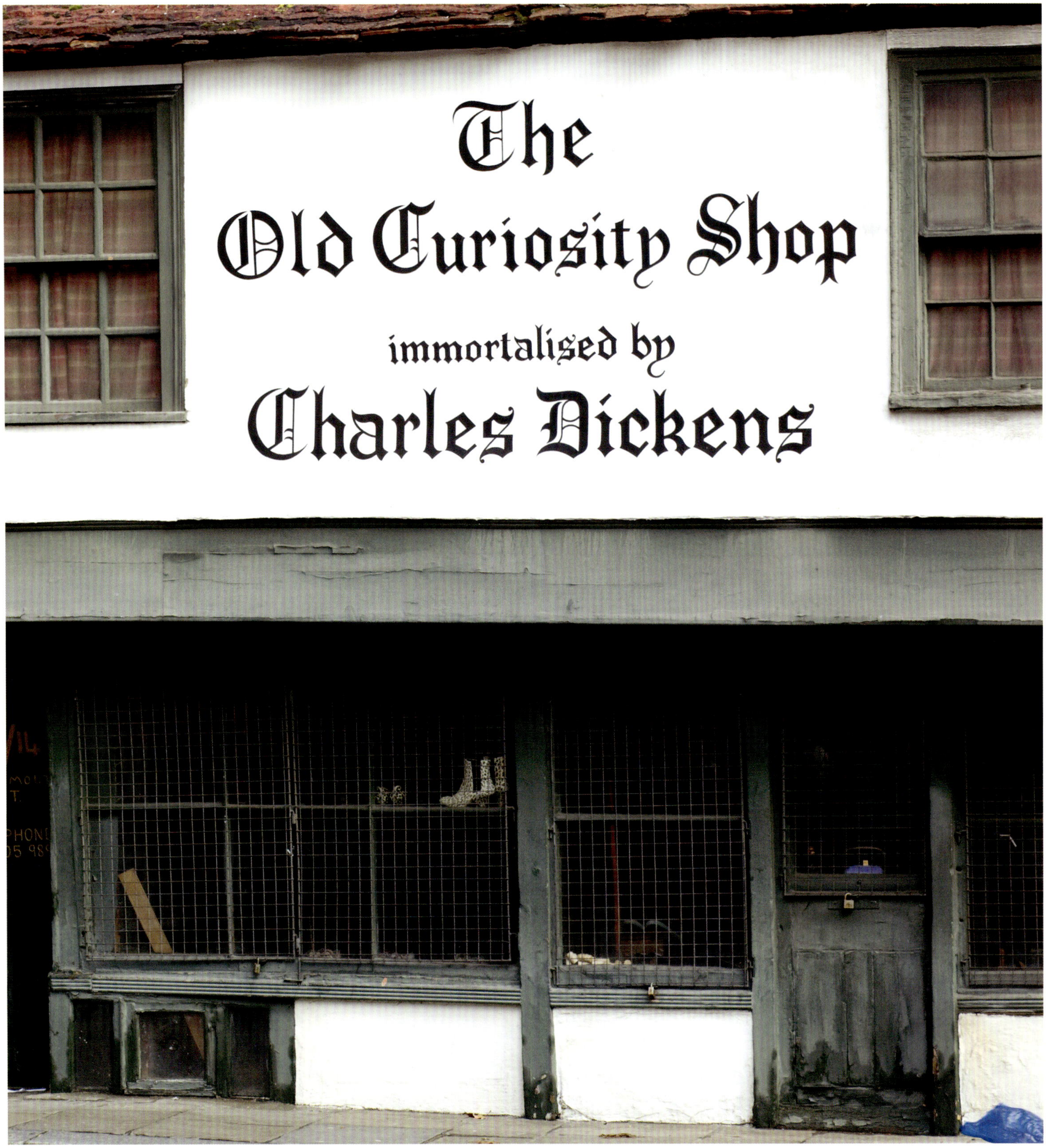

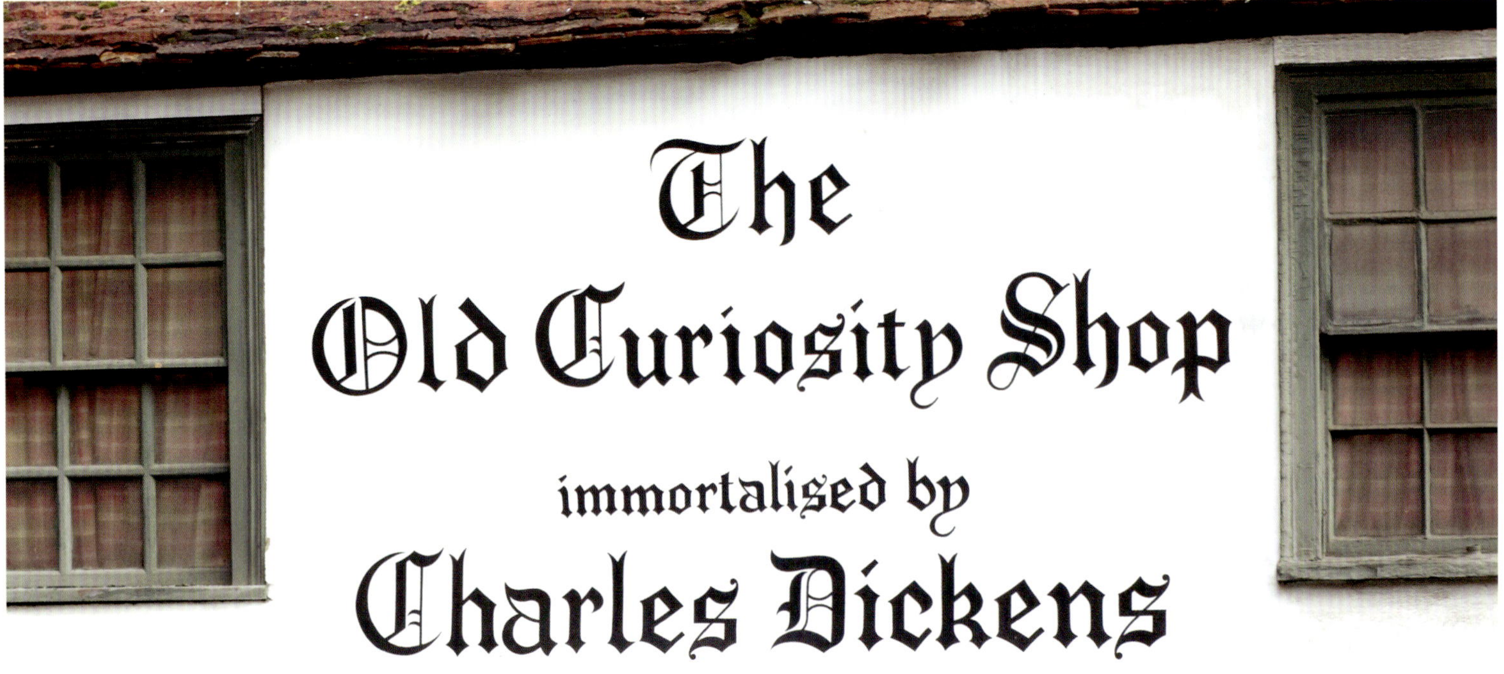

ABOVE:
Old Curiosity Shop
Although it was first built in 1567, the majority of this adorable little shop dates from the early 17th century, with 19th century alterations. The idea that it inspired Dickens' novel *The Old Curiosity Shop* (1841) isn't quite true; the name appeared when a canny bookseller renamed his premises following Dickens' death in 1870. However, it is thanks to this connection that the building was given Grade II listed status. It's had a variety of occupiers through the years, from stationers to tailors and shops selling tacky souvenirs. Currently it is an independent shoe shop.

OPPOSITE TOP:
King's Cross
Pentonville Road was the final section of the New Road built in the 1750s to allow coach traffic to avoid central London. 100 years later it led to another transport hub in the form of Kings Cross Station. The regeneration of the area meant independent costumiers and record shops like these were redeveloped.

OPPOSITE BOTTOM:
Redchurch Street, Shoreditch
The striking green tiles are an original feature of The Dolphin pub, which occupied this spot from 1808 until it closed in 2002. Since then it's been home to Labour and Wait, a shop selling household objects. Over the past few years Redchurch Street has become a hub of small independent British designers.

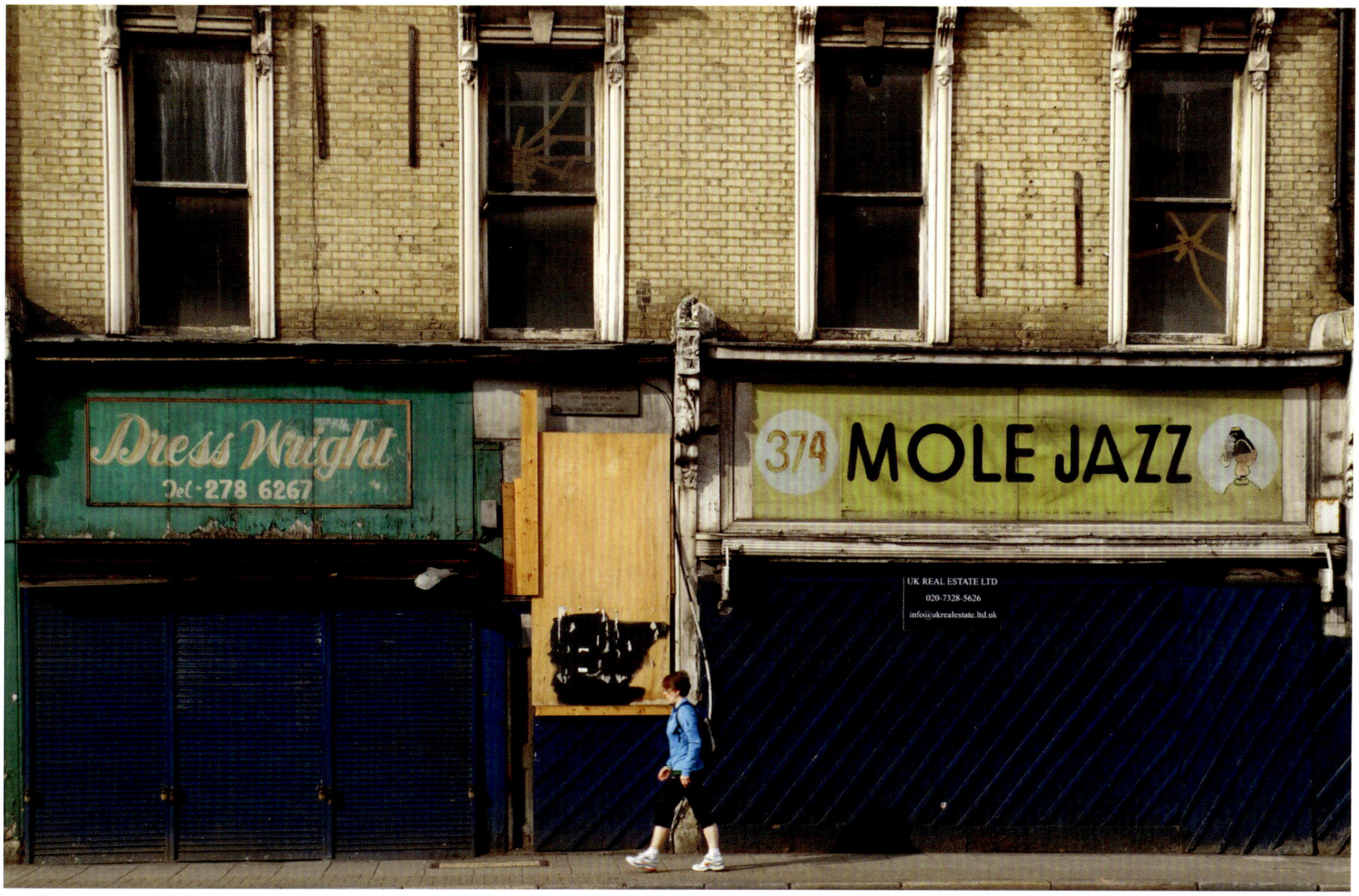
Dress Wright
Tel-278 6267
374 MOLE JAZZ
UK REAL ESTATE LTD
020-7328-5626
info@ukrealestate.ltd.uk

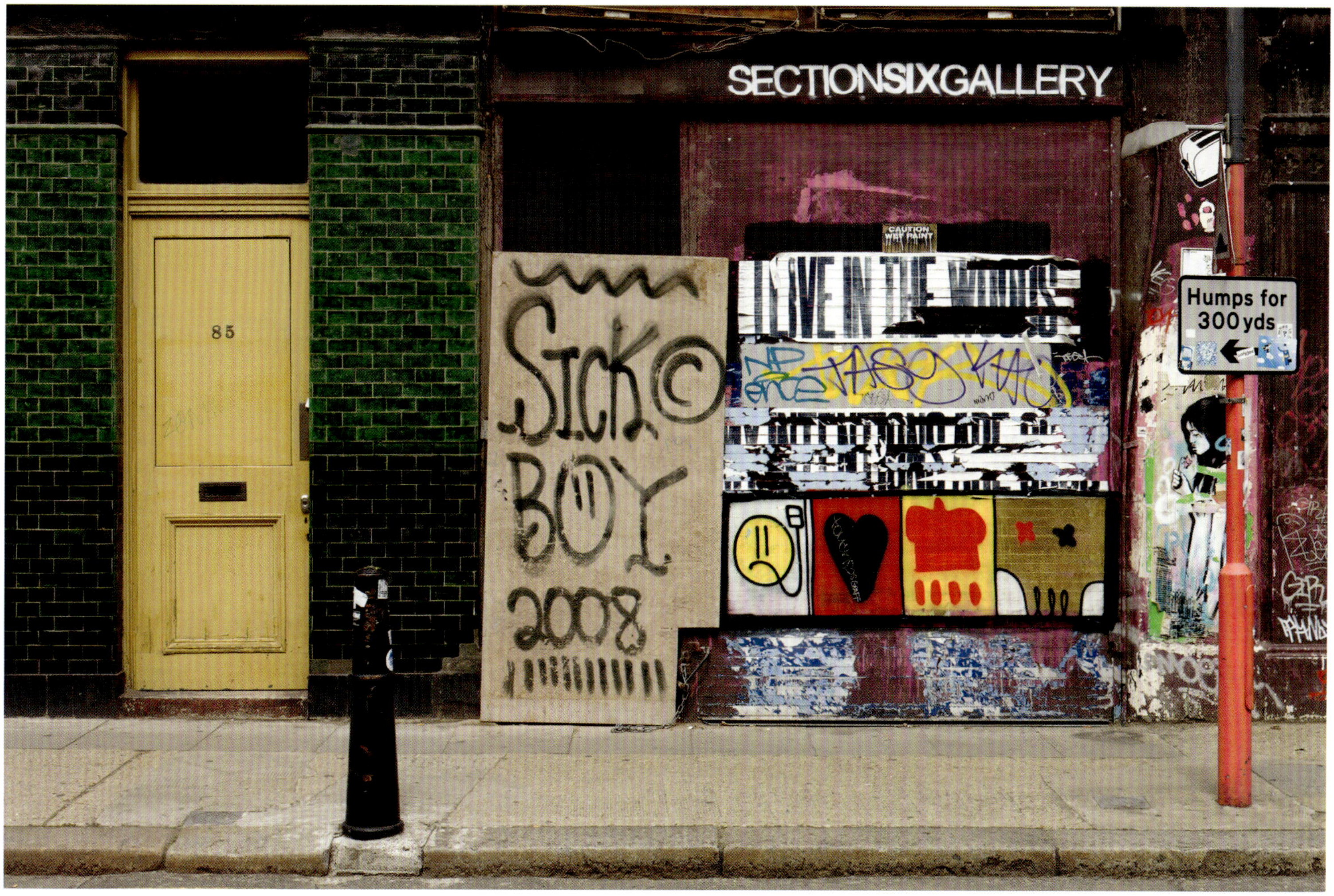
SECTIONSIXGALLERY
85
SICK© BOY 2008
Humps for 300 yds

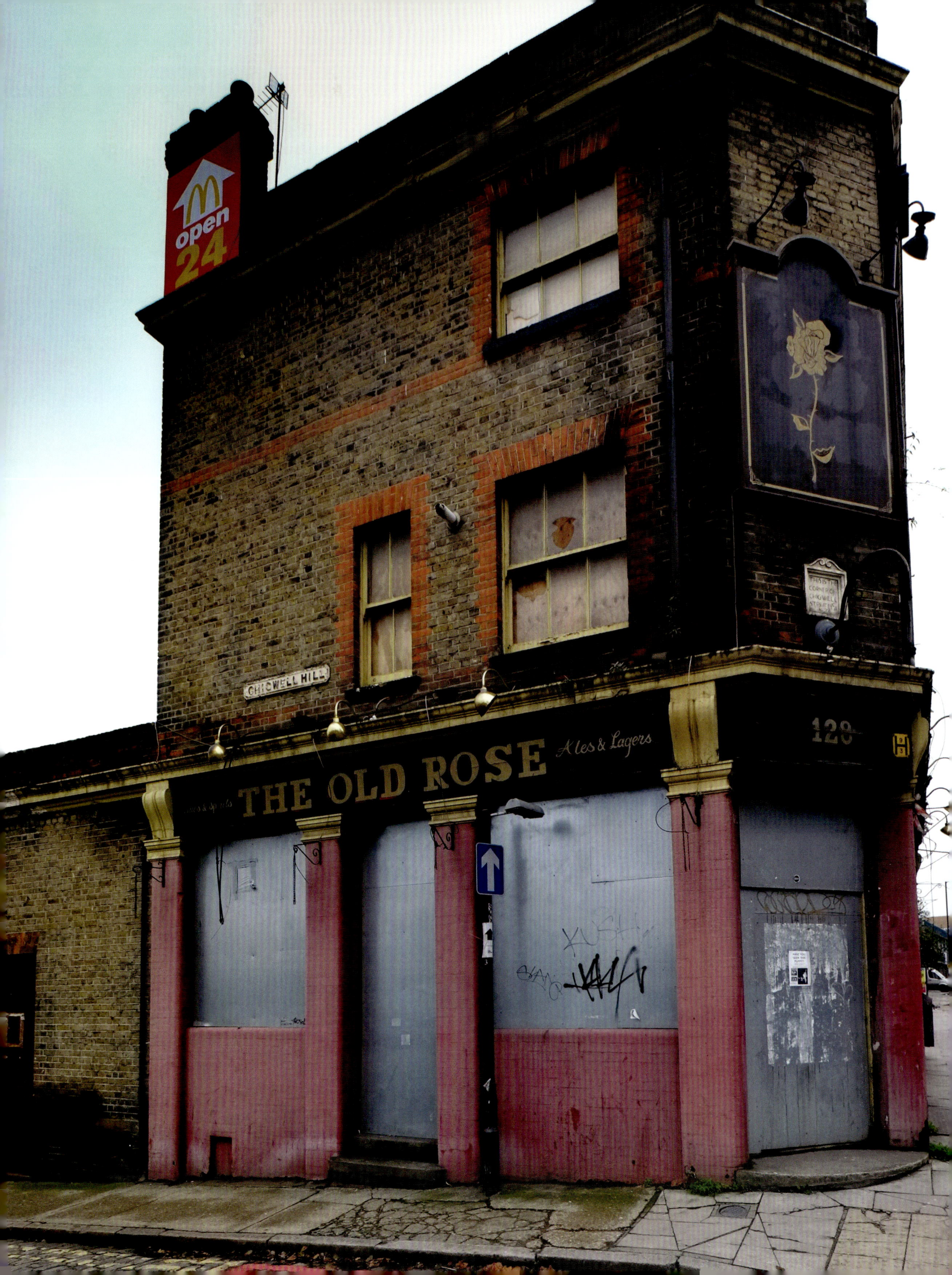
open
24
CHIGWELL HILL
THE OLD ROSE
Ales & Lagers
128

Pubs, Cafes and Restaurants

Pubs are entwined with our history and culture. They were first established with the Romans as *tabernae* (wine shops), later corrupted into 'taverns', and by the late 16th century there were thousands of alehouses, inns and taverns licensed across the UK. They are the heart of communities, a place for social gatherings and where we mark important life events and national moments. But the situation for local pubs has changed as they face rising rents and taxes. Between 2001 and 2016 the number of London pubs fell by a quarter. High costs naturally affect cafes and restaurants, too.

The images here may present a bleak picture for businesses across London, but it's worth remembering that plenty of new pubs, cafes and restaurants have also opened in the past few years. Some London boroughs have actually reported a rise in the number of new pubs since 2001 and – where relevant – the stories of refurbishment and reopenings have been shared in the text.

OPPOSITE:
The Old Rose, Wapping
The Highway has seen a lot of change in the past 50 years. Originally it was known as The Ratcliffe Highway, notorious for crime in the 19th century. But since London's docks closed in the late 1960s, this area east of the City of London has been redeveloped, first with the newspapers and media companies moving in, then with residential blocks. The Old Rose pub closed in 2011.

OVERLEAF:
The Black Horse, Camden
Built in the mid-19th century, the pub has since been converted into the Black Horse Apartments. The name is one of the most common pub names in the UK and is sometimes a reference to Black Bess, the horse of notorious highwayman Dick Turpin, who supposedly rode from York to London (300 km/200 miles) overnight. The story is, of course, fictional and appears in the 1834 bestselling novel, *Rockwood*.

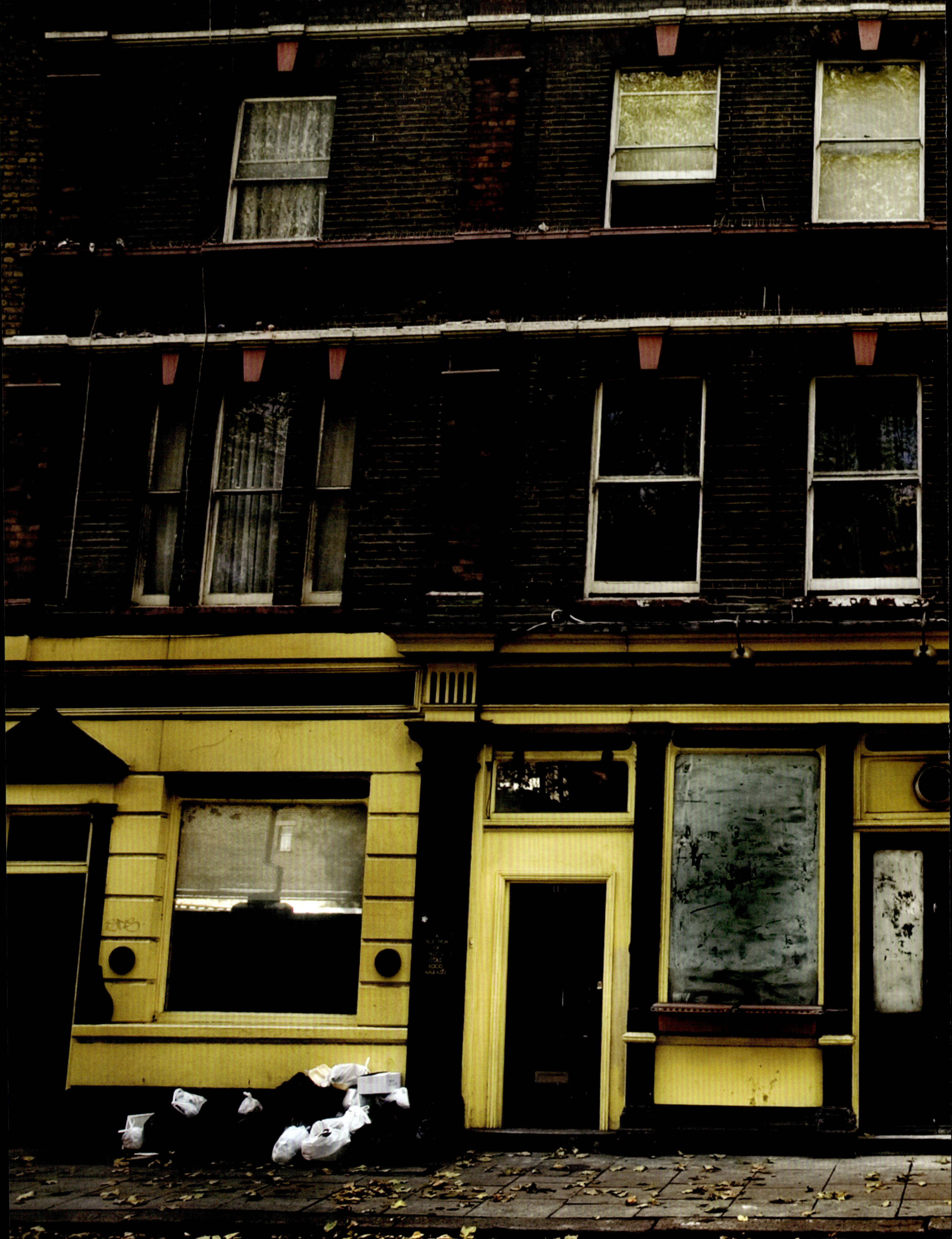

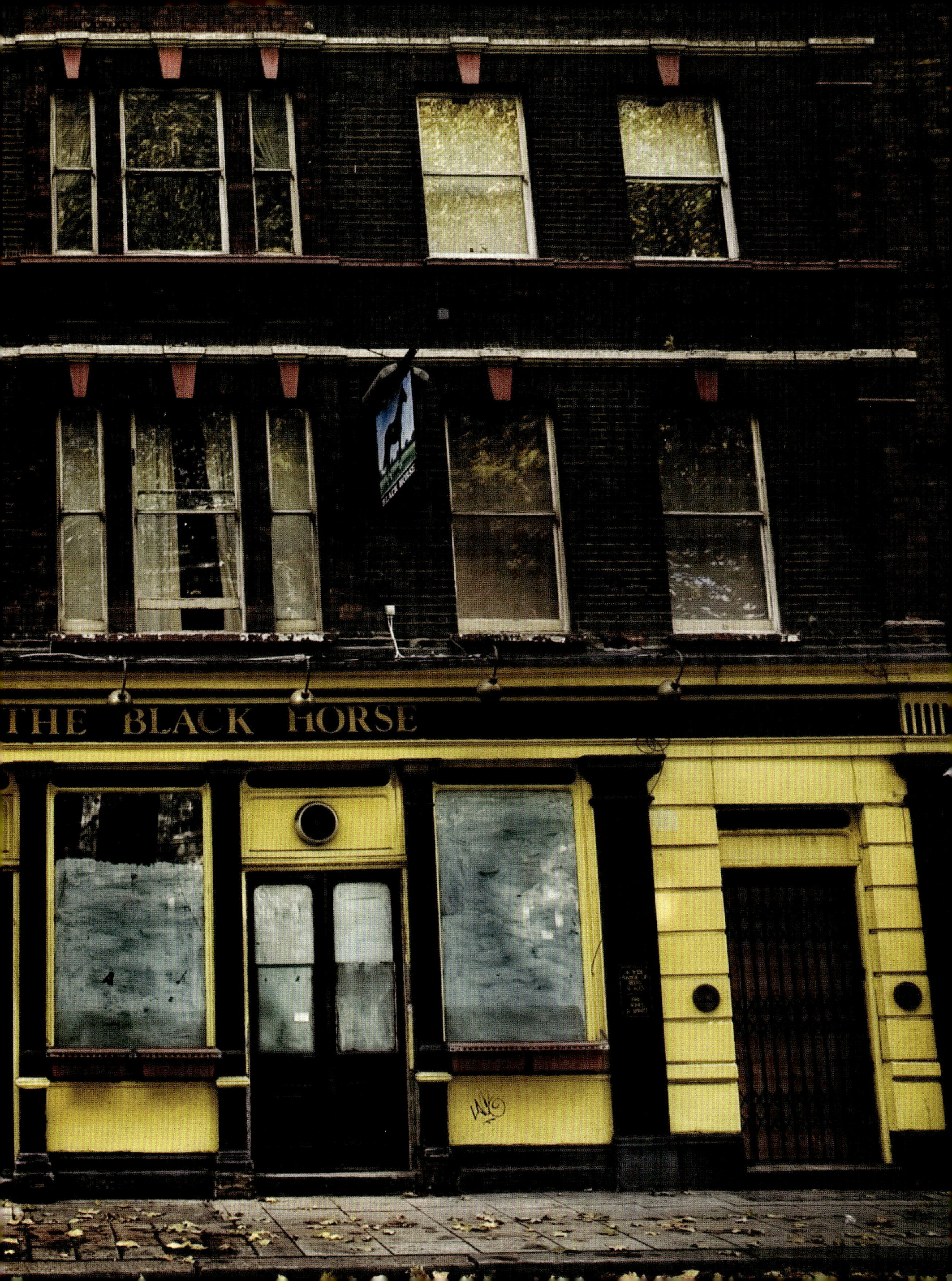
THE BLACK HORSE

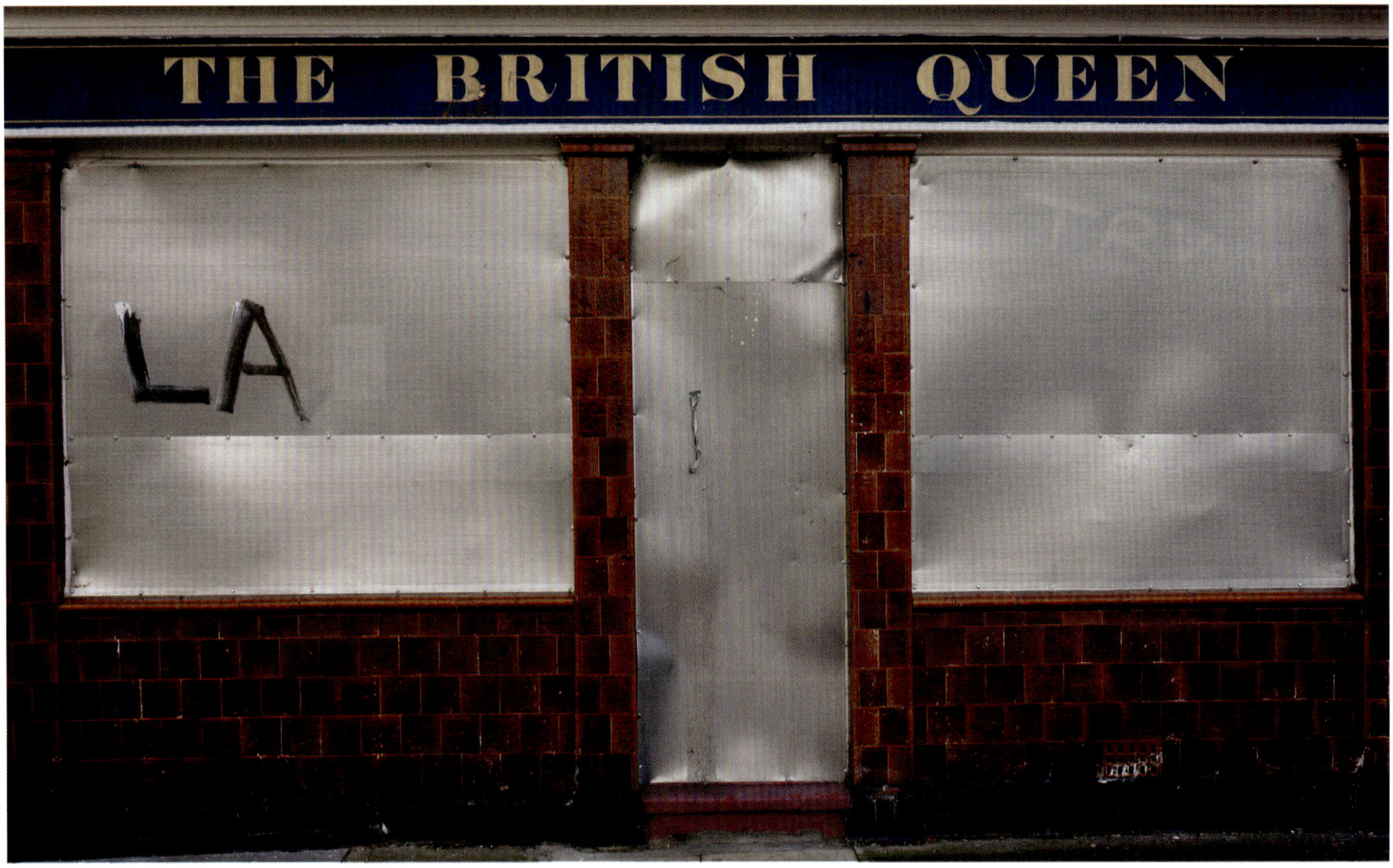
THE BRITISH QUEEN
LA

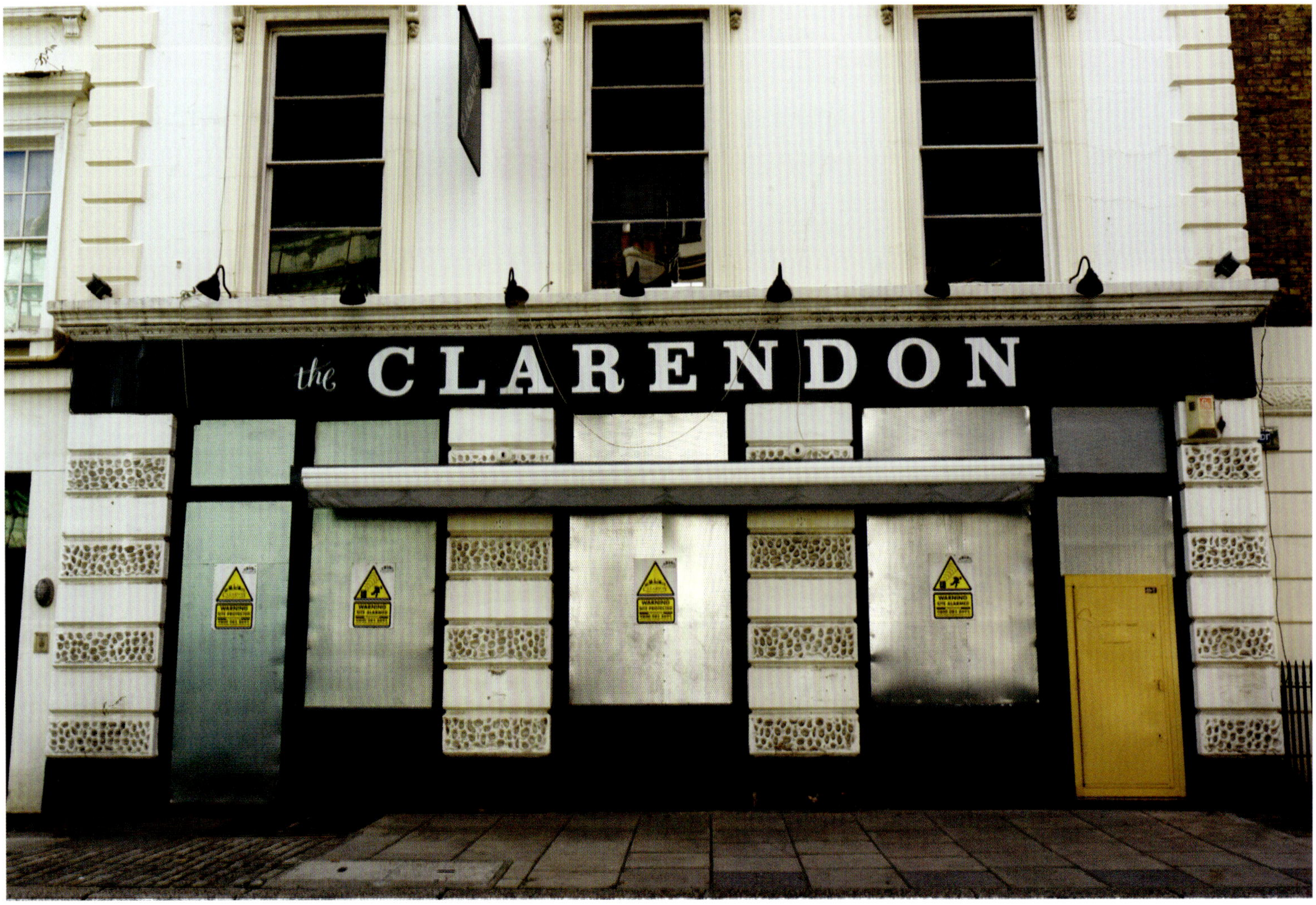
the CLARENDON

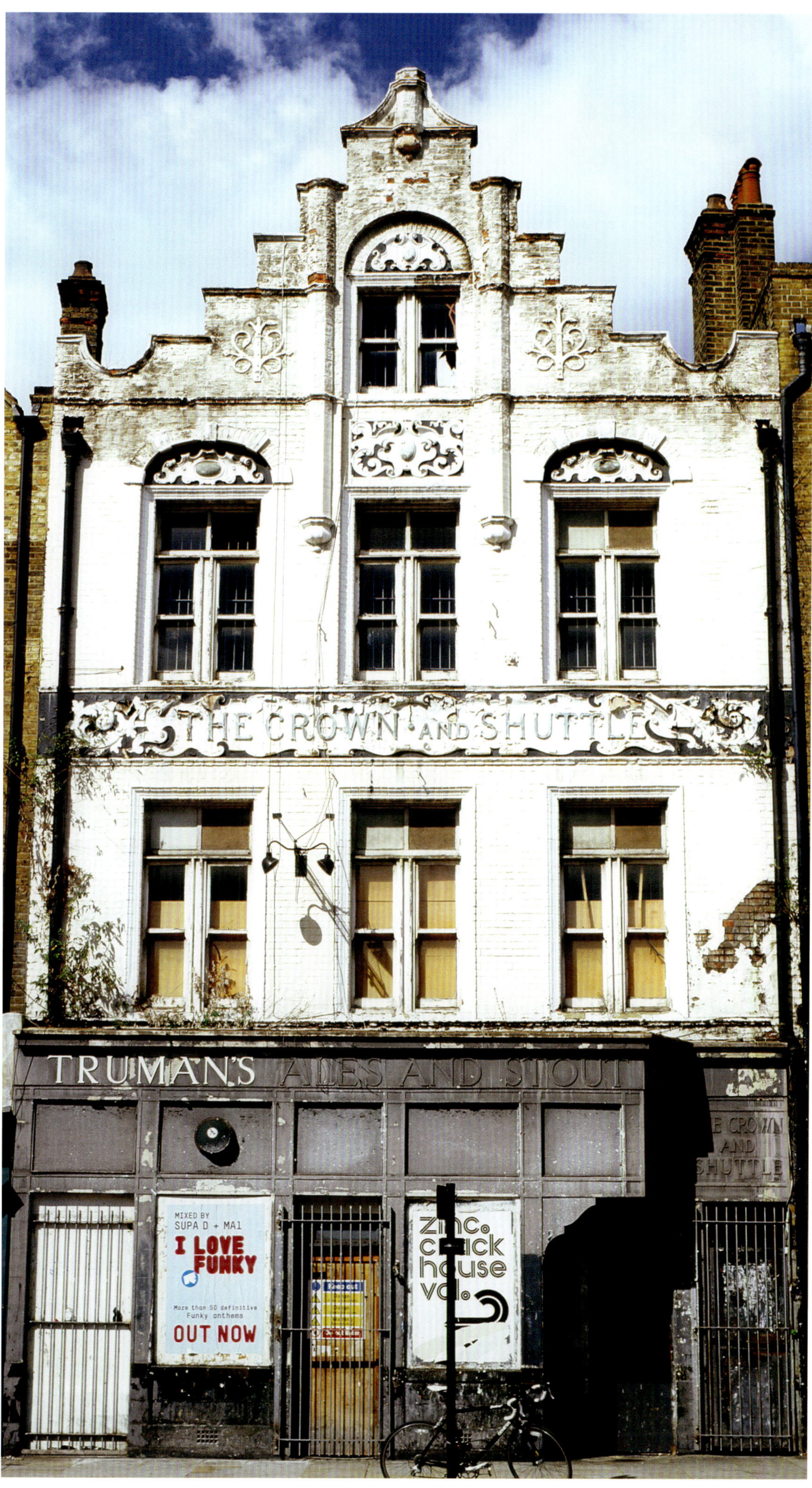

OPPOSITE TOP:

The British Queen, Camberwell

This Victorian pub stood on the corner of a residential street until it was demolished in 2017. Pubs are often found on corners throughout the UK and this is usually because of the way streets were built. The landowners let the land to a developer, who in turn organised the construction. The pubs kept the builders happy and later became a focus for the residential community.

OPPOSITE BOTTOM:

The Clarendon, Pimlico

In 1825 Robert Grosvenor, 1st Marquess of Westminster, enlisted Thomas Cubitt to develop Pimlico as a suburb for the wealthy. It never quite matched Belgravia and Mayfair for well-heeled residents, but it was described in 1877 as 'genteel, sacred to professional men'. It was laid out in a grid form, with lines of terraced houses in white stucco to replicate stone. The pub closed in 2012.

LEFT:

The Crown and Shuttle, Shoreditch High Street

Built in 1885, this pub stands within the Liberty of Norton Folgate. Liberties were areas detached from certain royal and parish responsibilities. This didn't mean they were totally lawless places, but it did mean that the authorities tended to turn a blind eye to much of what went on there. In the 17th century Norton Folgate was a haunt of thespians, including playwrights William Shakespeare and Christopher Marlowe.

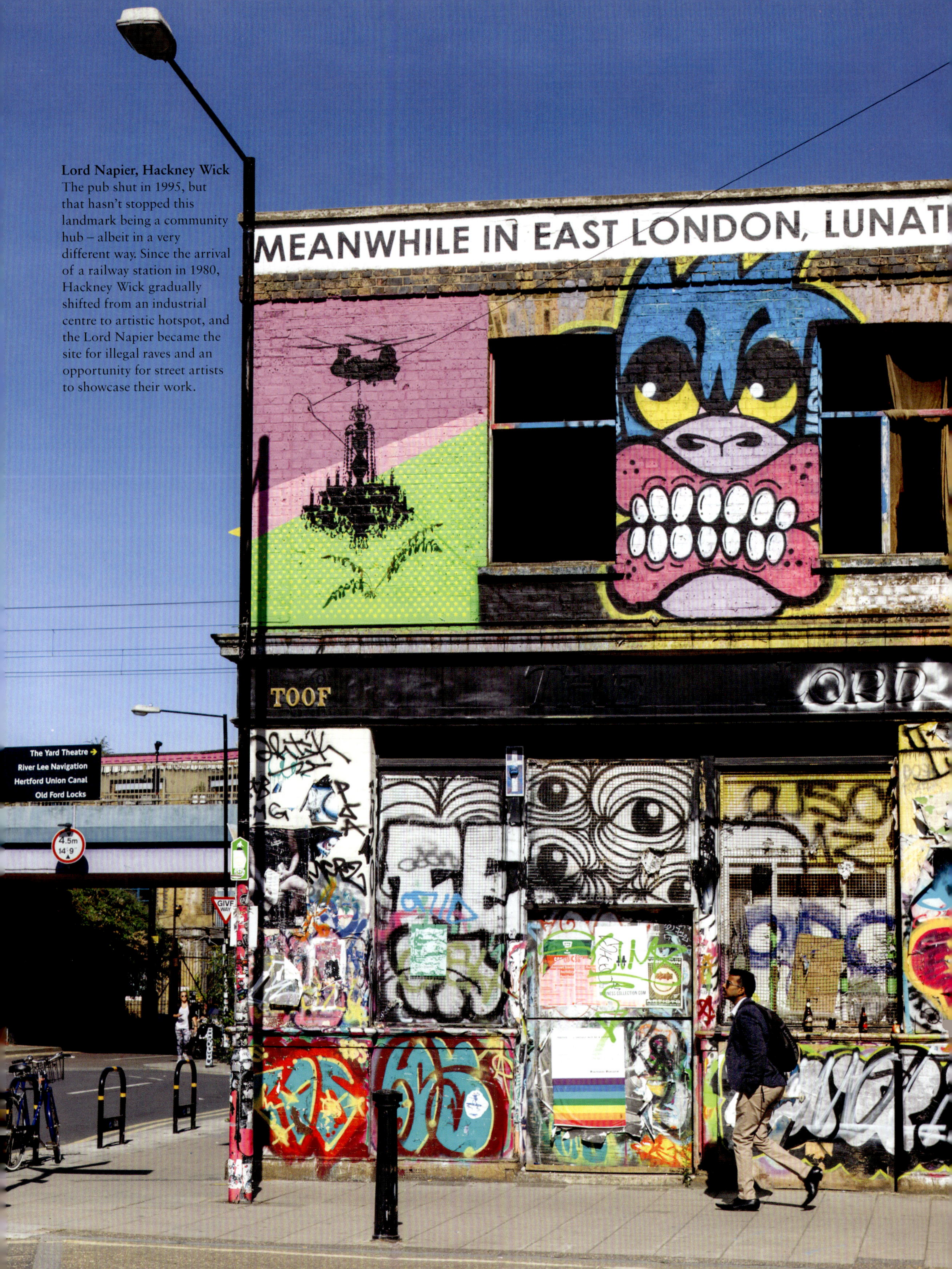

Lord Napier, Hackney Wick
The pub shut in 1995, but that hasn't stopped this landmark being a community hub – albeit in a very different way. Since the arrival of a railway station in 1980, Hackney Wick gradually shifted from an industrial centre to artistic hotspot, and the Lord Napier became the site for illegal raves and an opportunity for street artists to showcase their work.

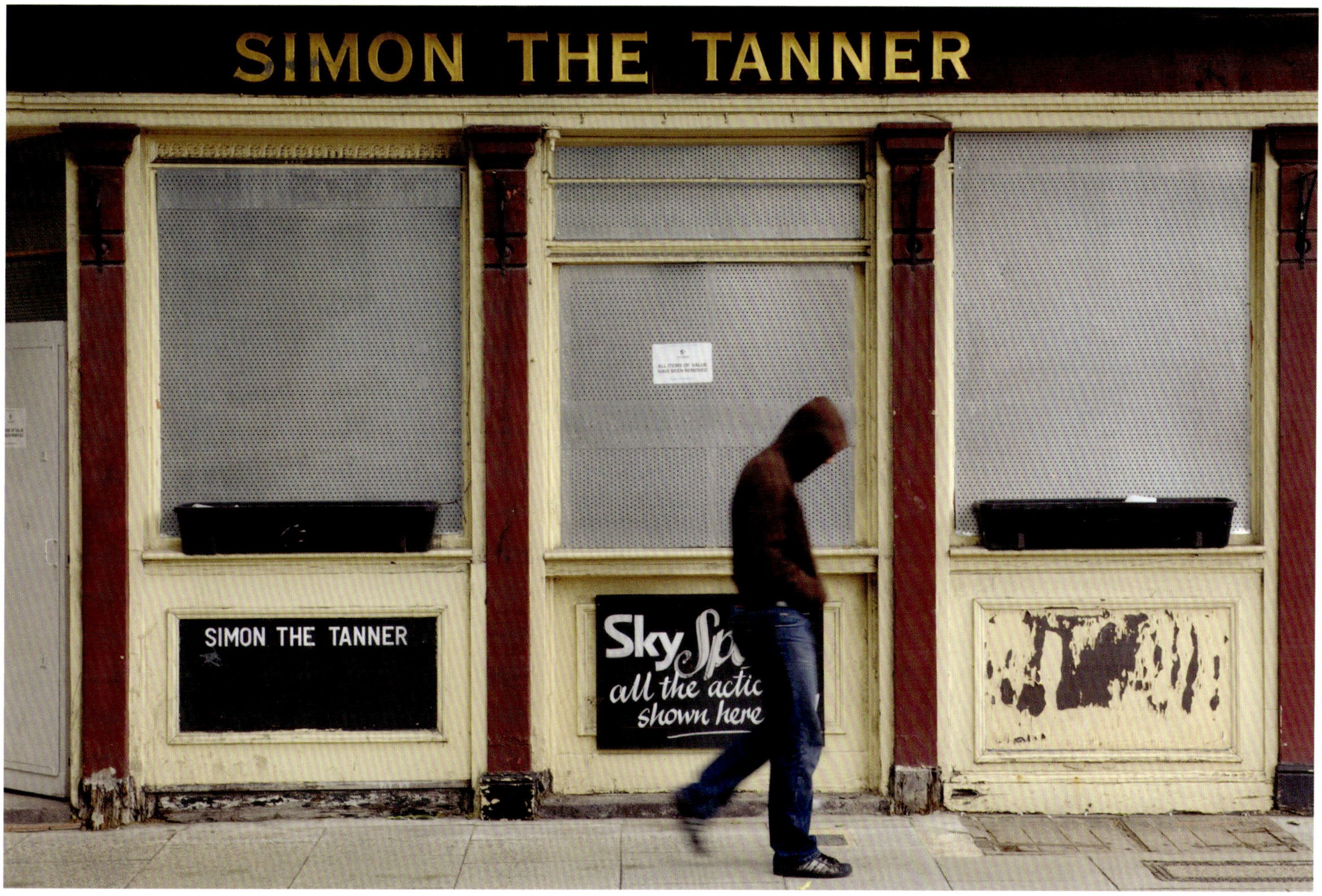

ABOVE:

Simon the Tanner, London Bridge

You wouldn't want to live beside a tannery. The trade required copious amounts of urine and dog excrement to soften the leather. That didn't seem to bother Simon, the 10th century Egyptian Saint and namesake of this pub. The last working tannery in Bermondsey shut in 1997 and this pub was refurbished and reopened in 2011.

RIGHT:

The Tournament, Old Brompton Road, Earls Court

In February 2016 Kensington and Chelsea Council issued an 'untidy land' notice for The Tournament pub and it was demolished. The pub had closed in 2011 and stood opposite the Grade II listed Brompton Cemetery.

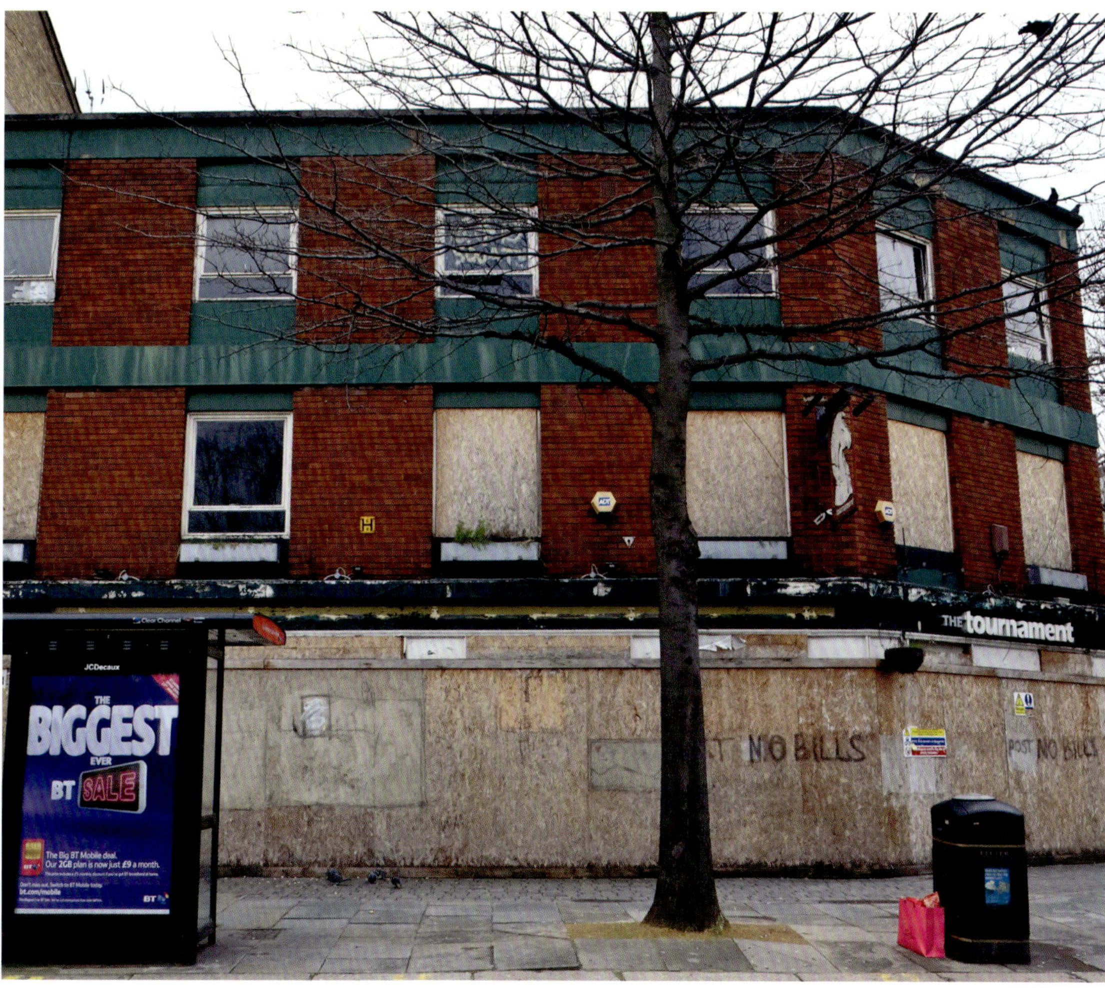

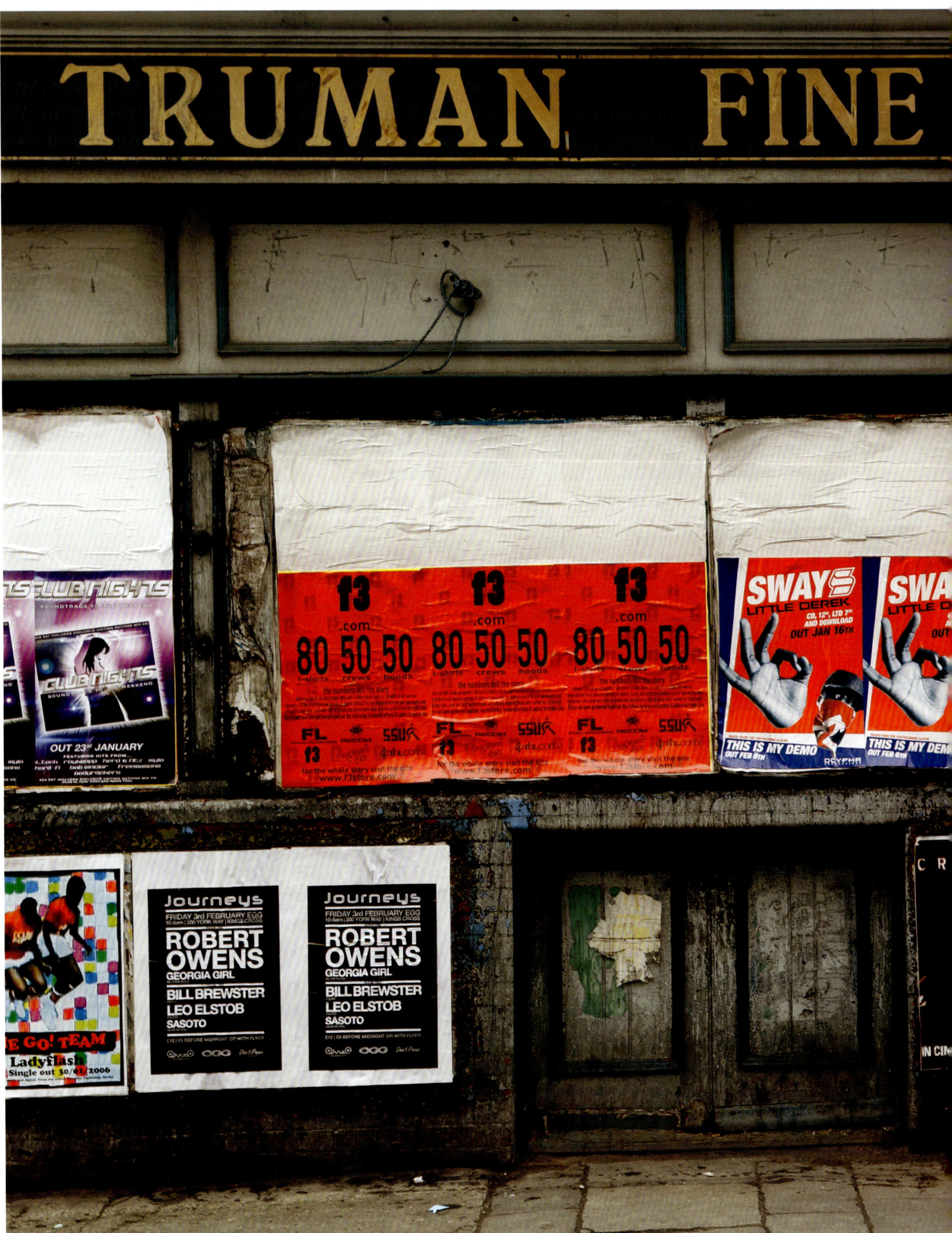
TRUMAN FINE
CLUB NIGHTS
SOUNDTRACK TO THE WEEKEND
OUT 23rd JANUARY
f3
.com
80 50 50
t-shirts crews hoods
the numbers tell the story
for the whole story visit the site
www.f3store.com
SWAY
LITTLE DEREK
CD, 12", LTD 7" AND DOWNLOAD
OUT JAN 16TH
THIS IS MY DEMO
OUT FEB 6TH
Journeys
FRIDAY 3rd FEBRUARY EGG
10-6am | 200 YORK WAY | KINGS CROSS
ROBERT OWENS
GEORGIA GIRL
BILL BREWSTER
LEO ELSTOB
SASOTO
E GO! TEAM
Ladyflash
Single out 30/01/2006

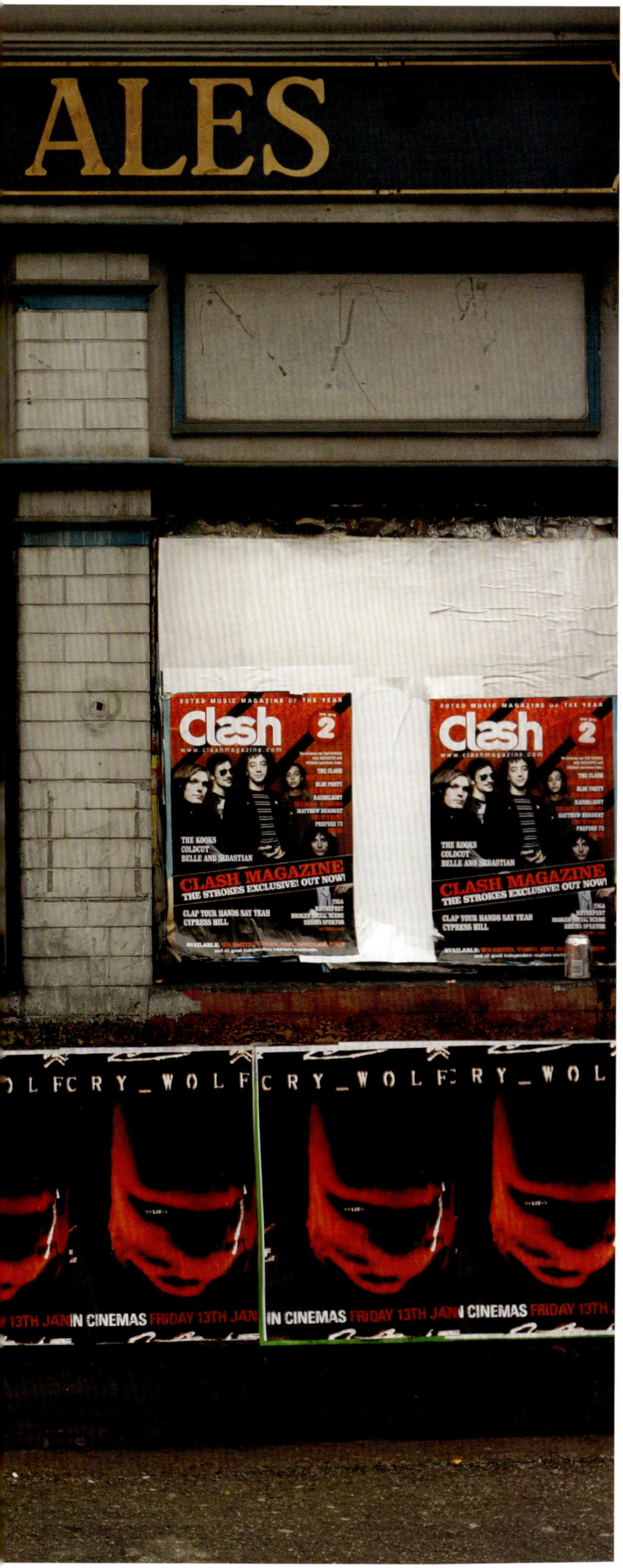

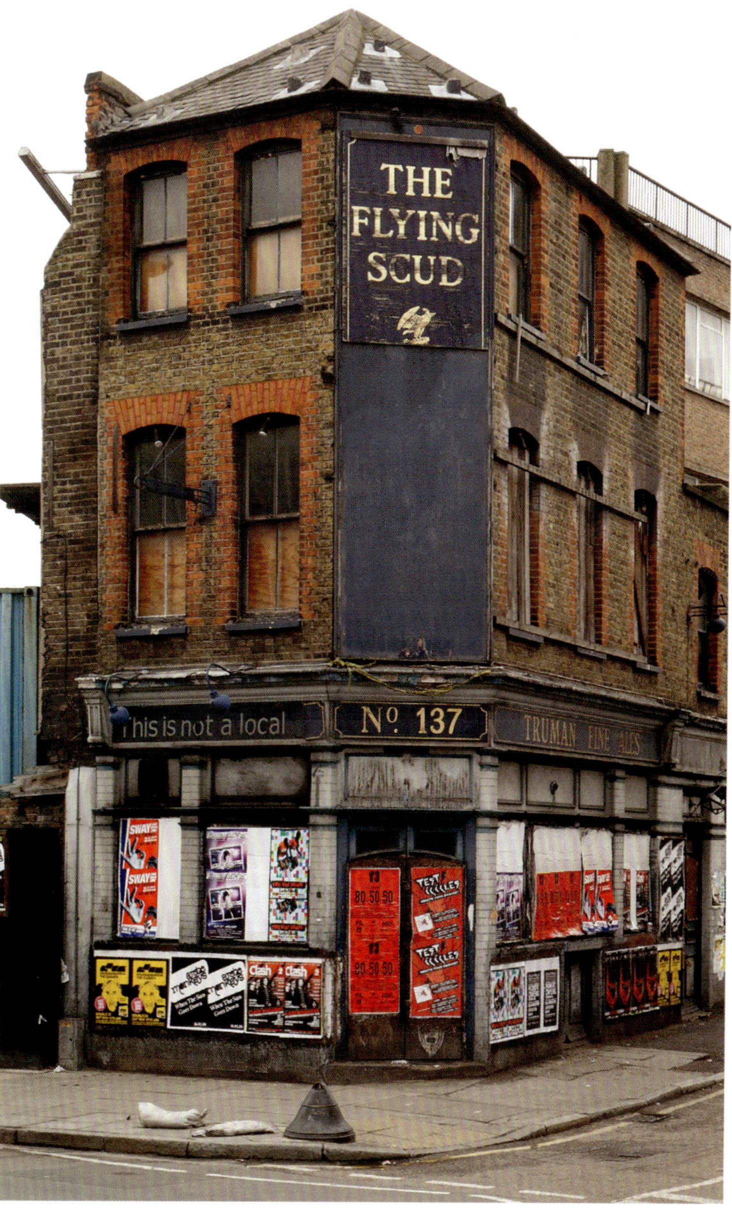

ALL PHOTOGRAPHS:

The Flying Scud, 137 Hackney Green Road, Shoreditch

Built in 1872, the curious name could be a reference to aviation, 'scud' being a reference to clouds or mists. A few years prior to the pub closing in 1994, there was an extraordinary case of a bungled surveillance operation by the Metropolitan Police. The pub licensee – while out for a jog with a friend – was shot at. Neither men were injured, but both policemen involved lost their jobs. The pub was demolished in 2009.

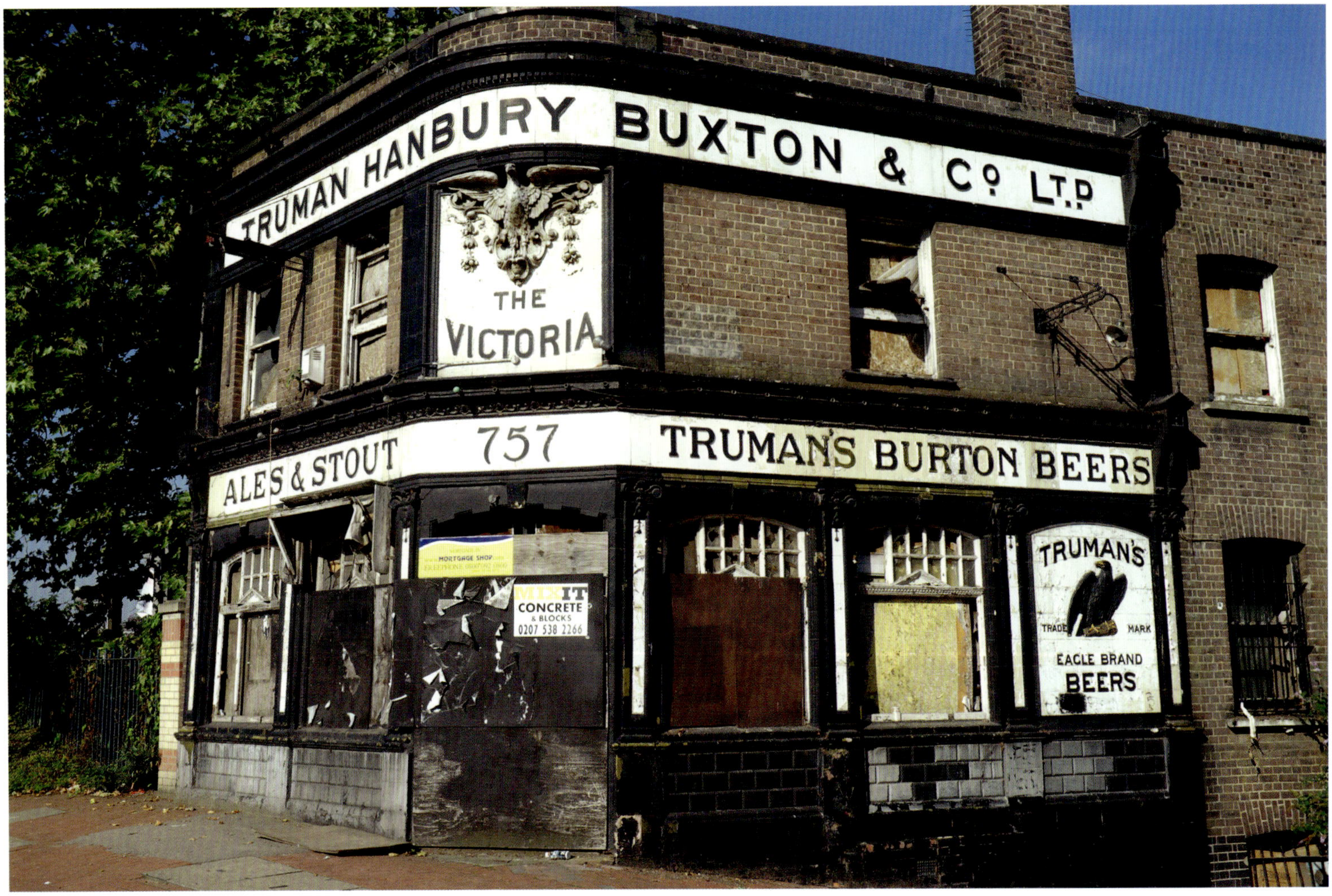

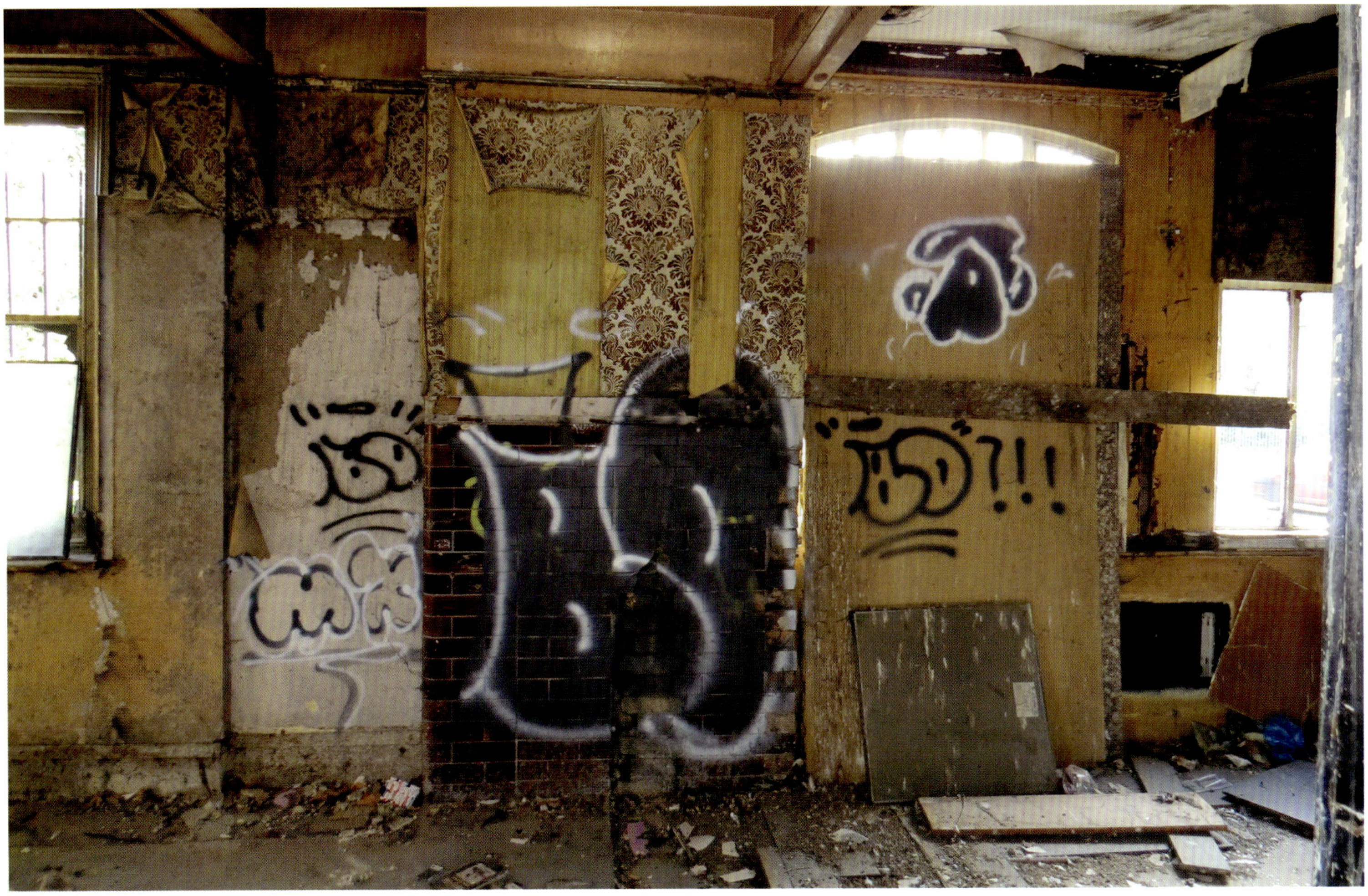

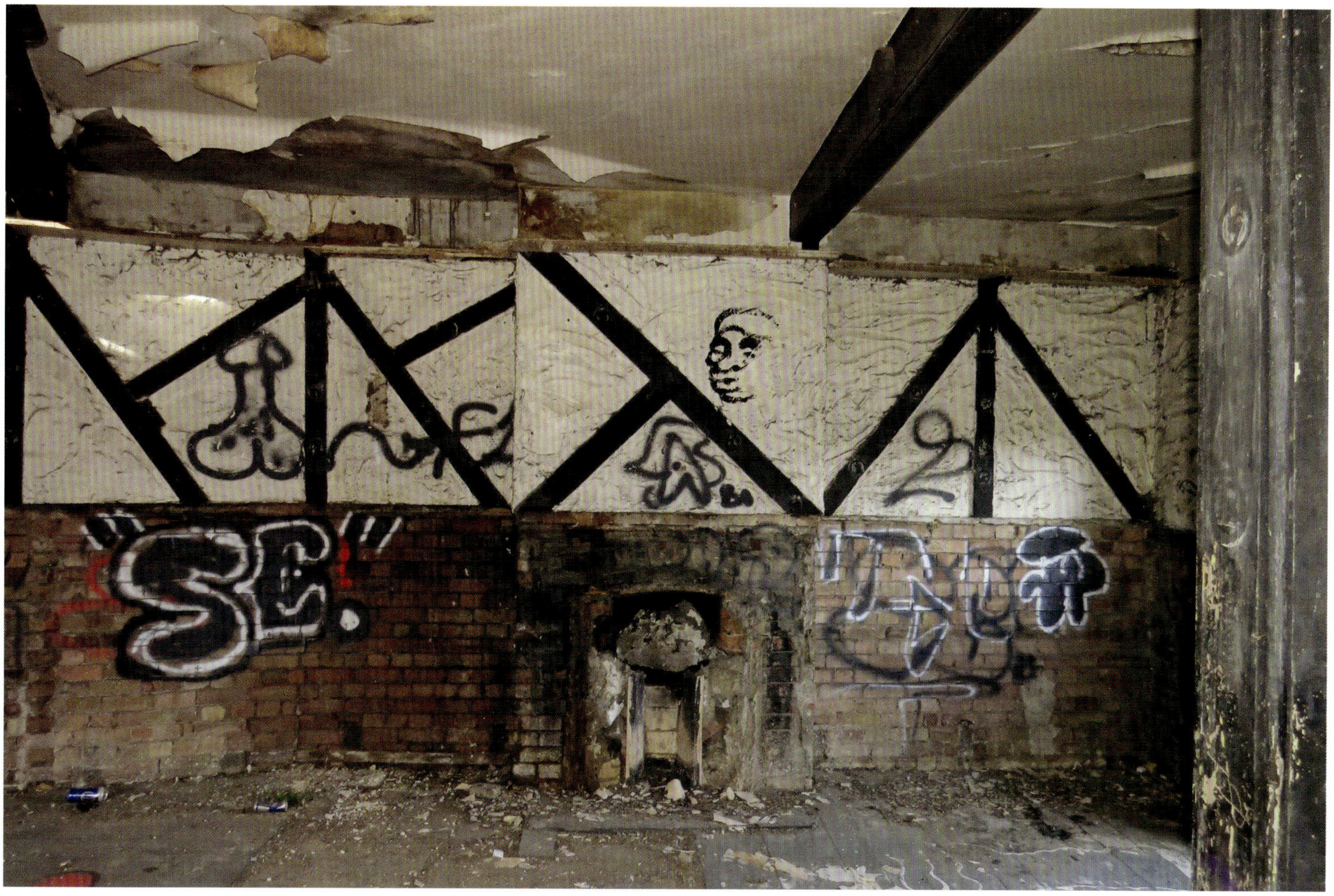

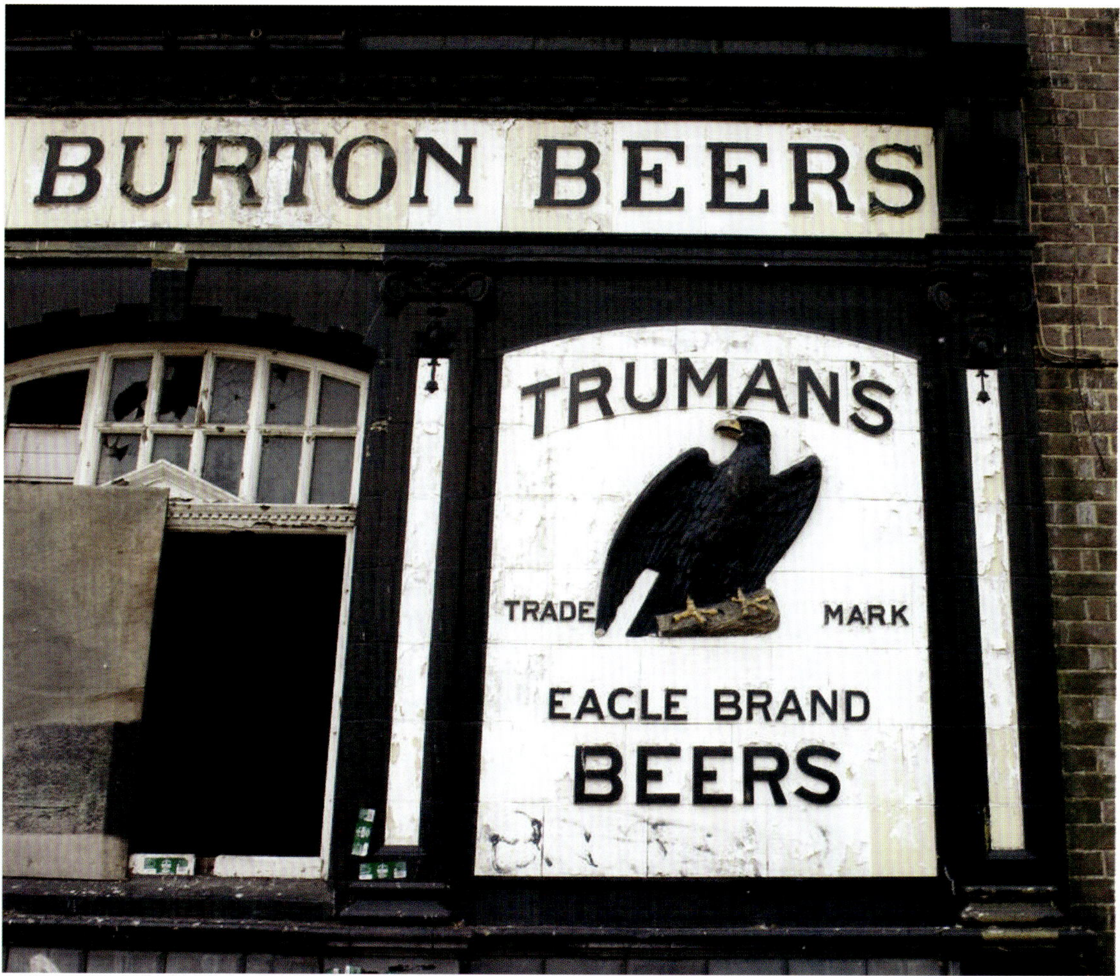

ALL PHOTOGRAPHS ON THESE PAGES:
The Victoria, Woolwich Road
Truman's Brewery was established on Brick Lane in 1666 at the Black Eagle Brewery, which became their trademark. In the early 1800s Truman's was the biggest brewery in the world, sending beers to the Imperial Russian Court and British Raj in India. In 1989 the brewery and its pubs were sold, but in 2010 two Londoners – James Morgan and Michael-George Hemus – re-established the brand. In 2013, they opened a new brewery in Hackney Wick.

OVERLEAF:
Cafe, Isle of Dogs
Heinz Baked Beans first appeared in London in 1886 when a young entrepreneur called Henry Heinz presented his patented tinned goods at Fortnum & Masons. The famous shop on Piccadilly was established in 1707 and is grocer and provision merchant to Her Majesty the Queen.

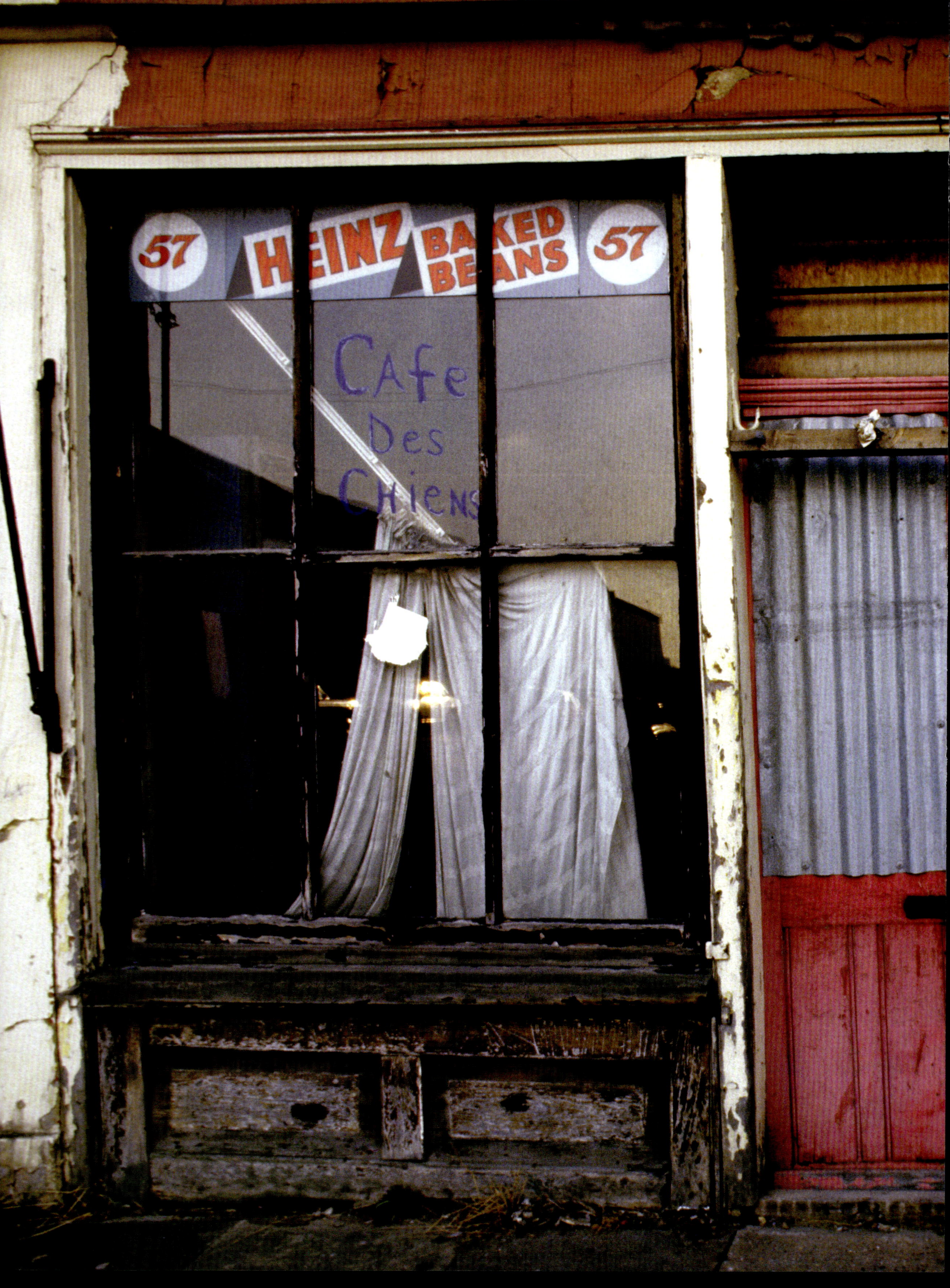
57
HEINZ
BAKED BEANS
57
Cafe
Des
CHiens

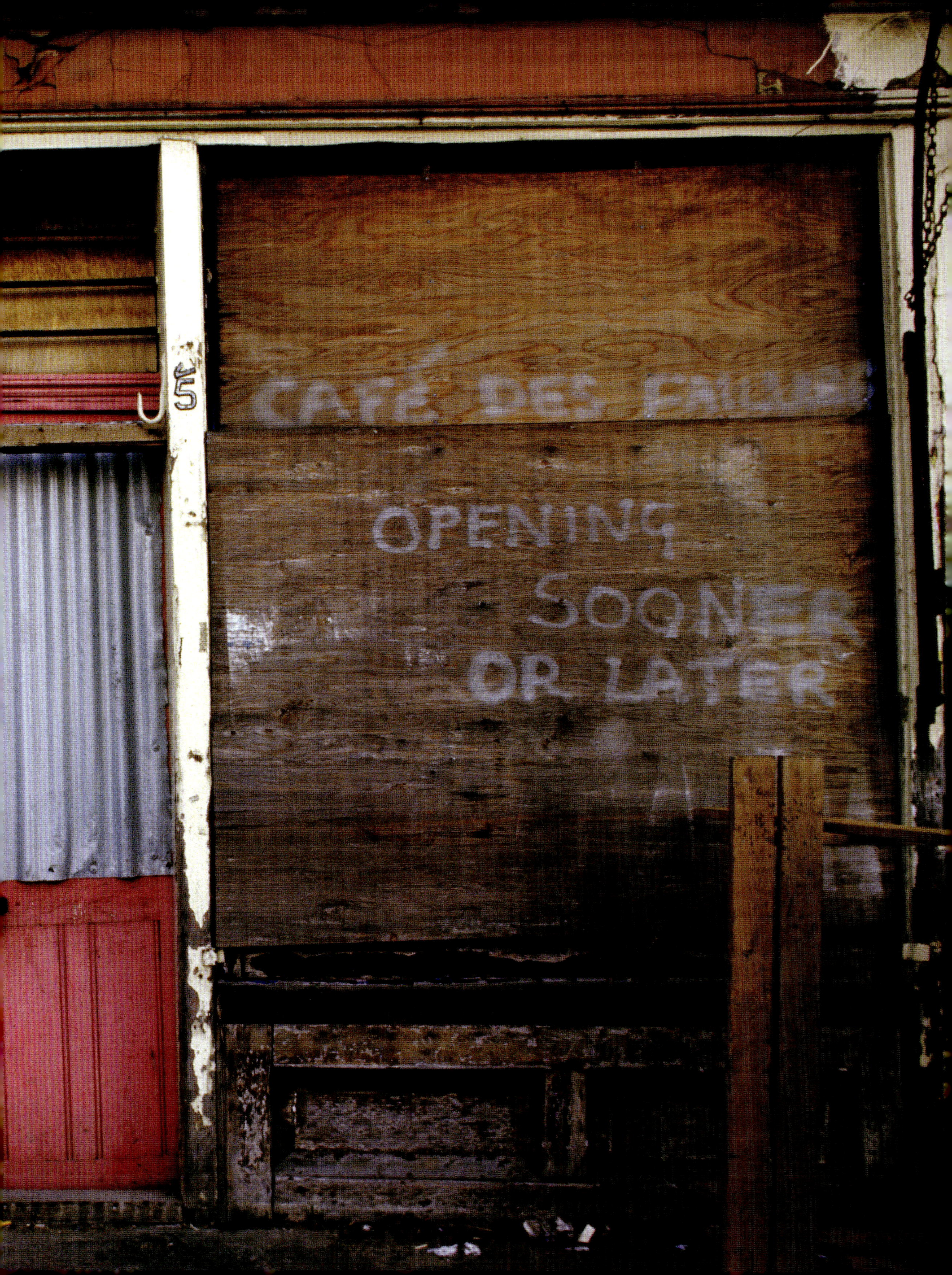
5
CAFÉ DES
OPENING
SOONER
OR LATER

BELOW:
Gay Hussar, Soho
Soho, first laid out for aristocrats in the 17th century, later became a hotbed of industry, bohemians and illicit activities. The Gay Hussar was a local institution, established in 1953, serving goulash and political gossip. It closed in 2018.

OPPOSITE:
China Man, Dalston Lane, Hackney
Until the 19th century, Dalston Lane was the only road between the villages of Kingsland and Hackney. This row of homes with shops on the ground floor are Victorian. Until they were demolished in 2017, they represented an eclectic mix of an East London neighbourhood that had fallen into disrepair over the previous few decades.

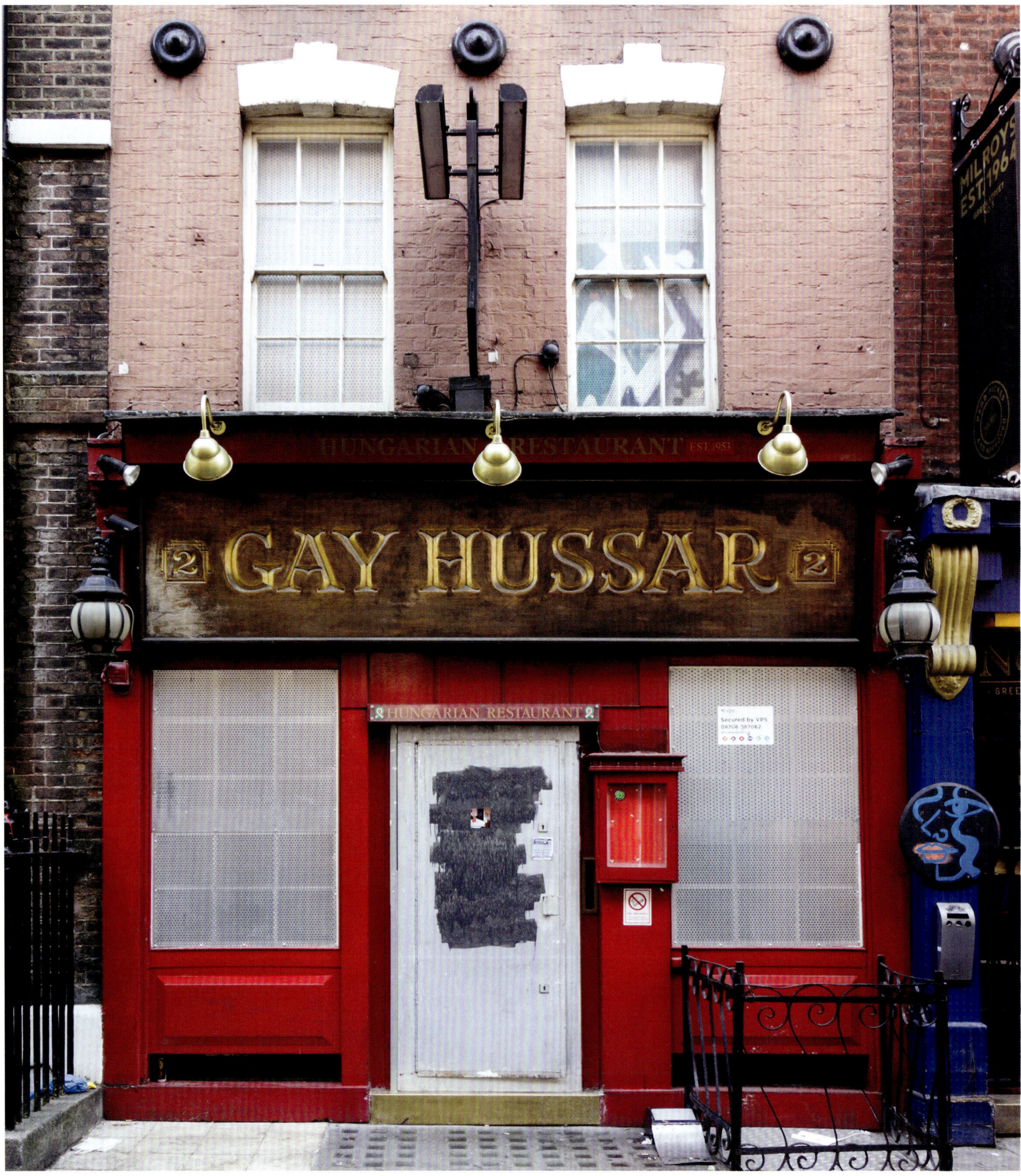

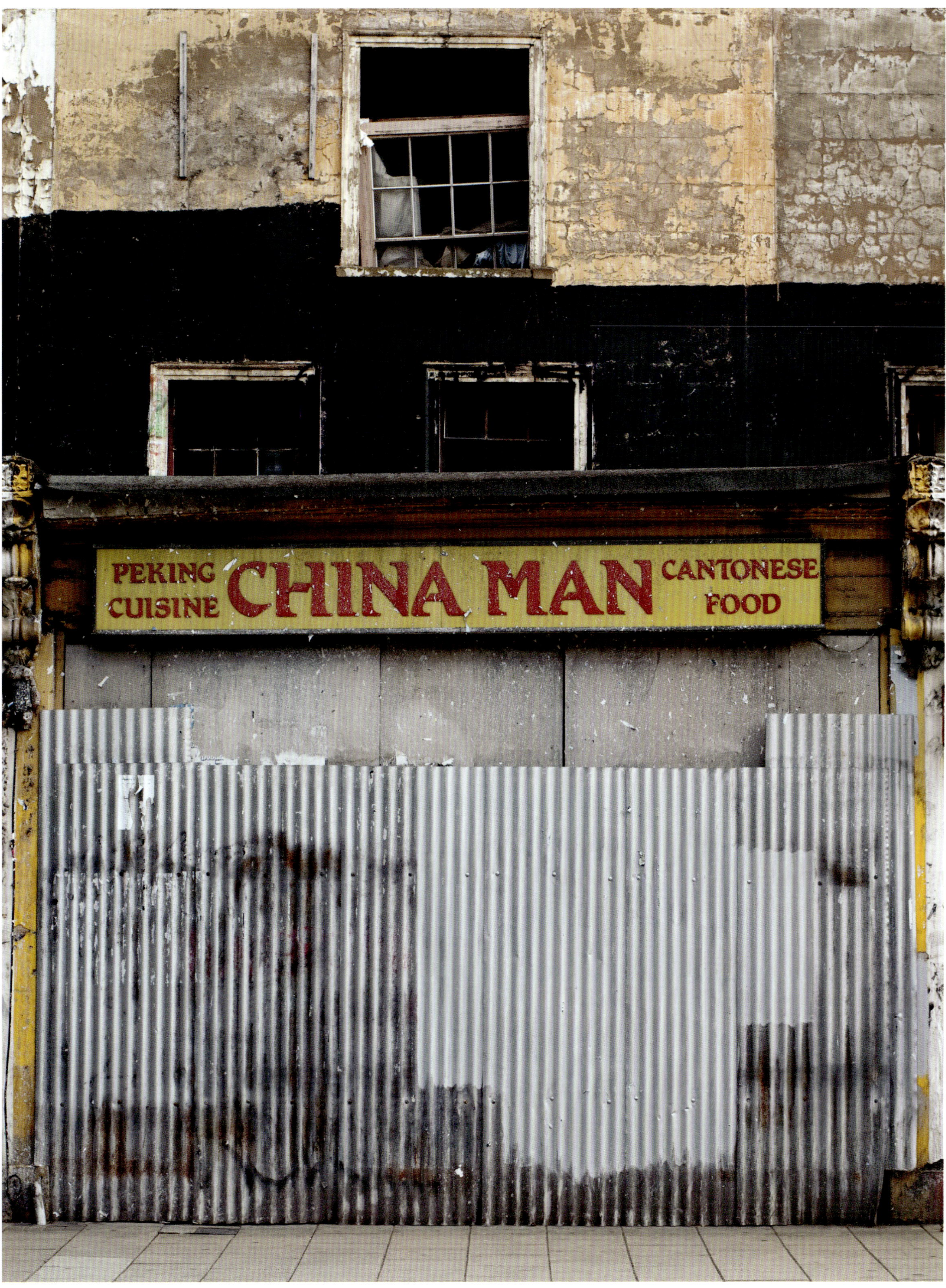
PEKING
CUISINE
CHINA MAN
CANTONESE
FOOD

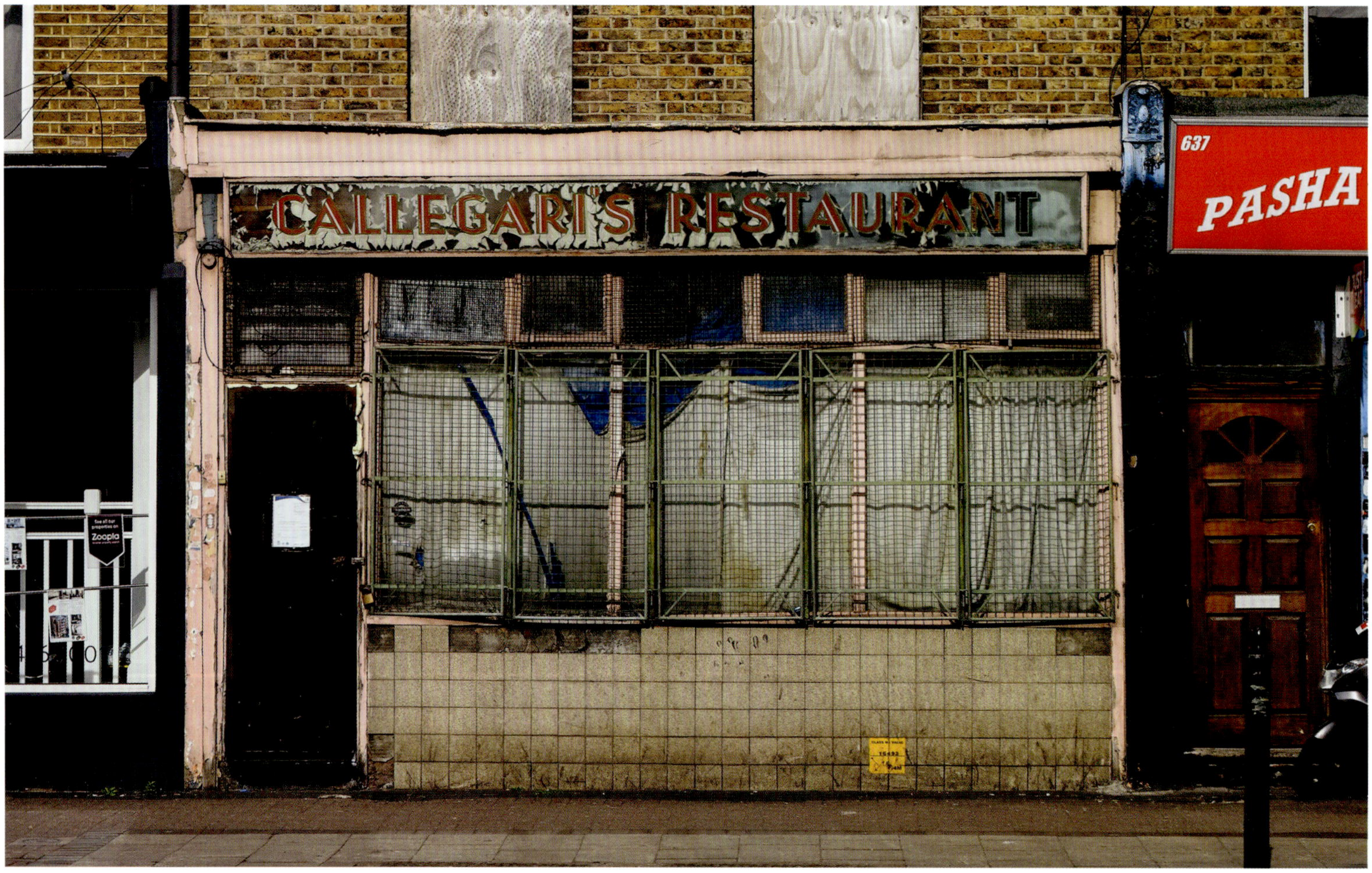
CALLEGARI'S RESTAURANT
637
PASHA

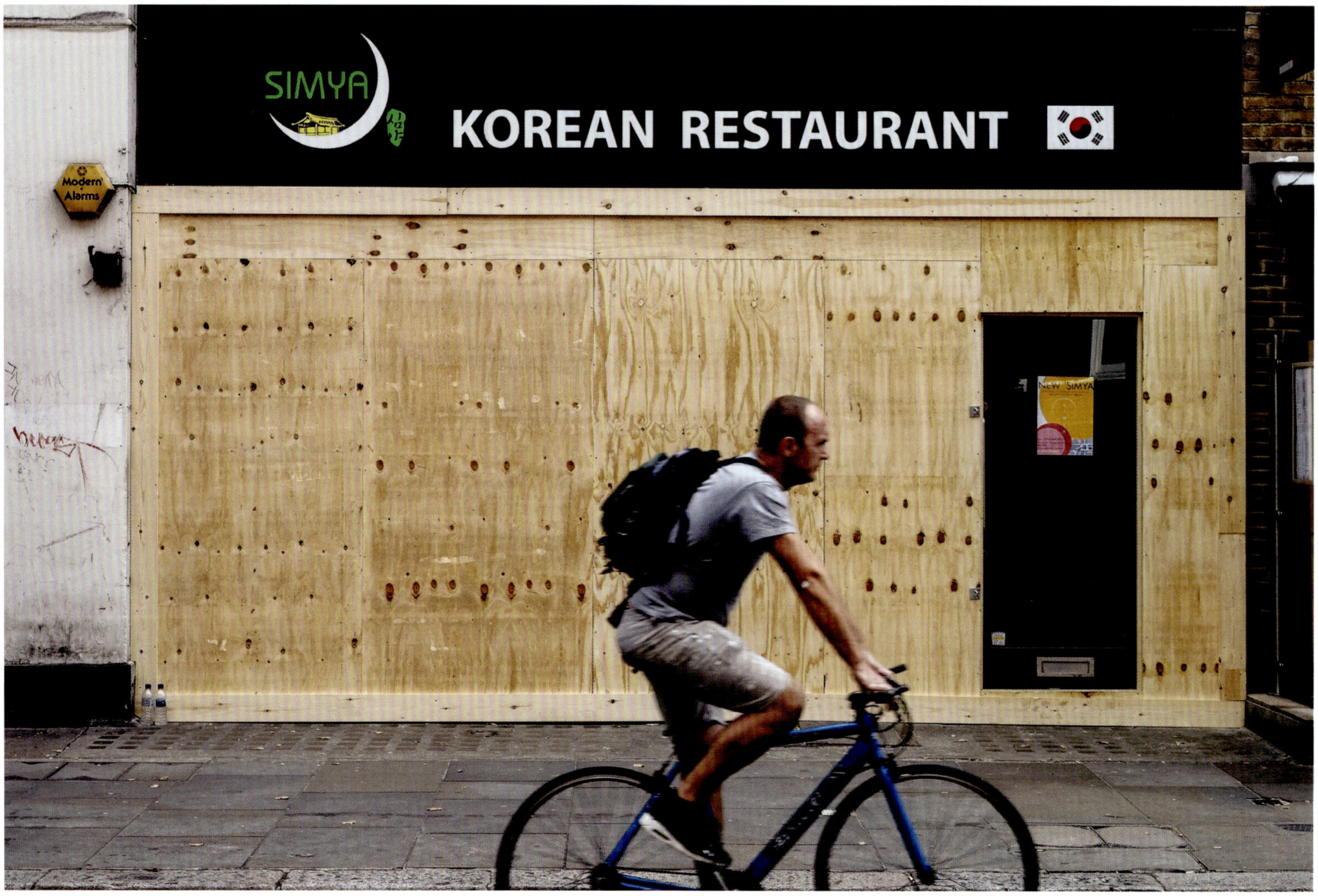
SIMYA
KOREAN RESTAURANT
Modern Alarms
NEW SIMYA

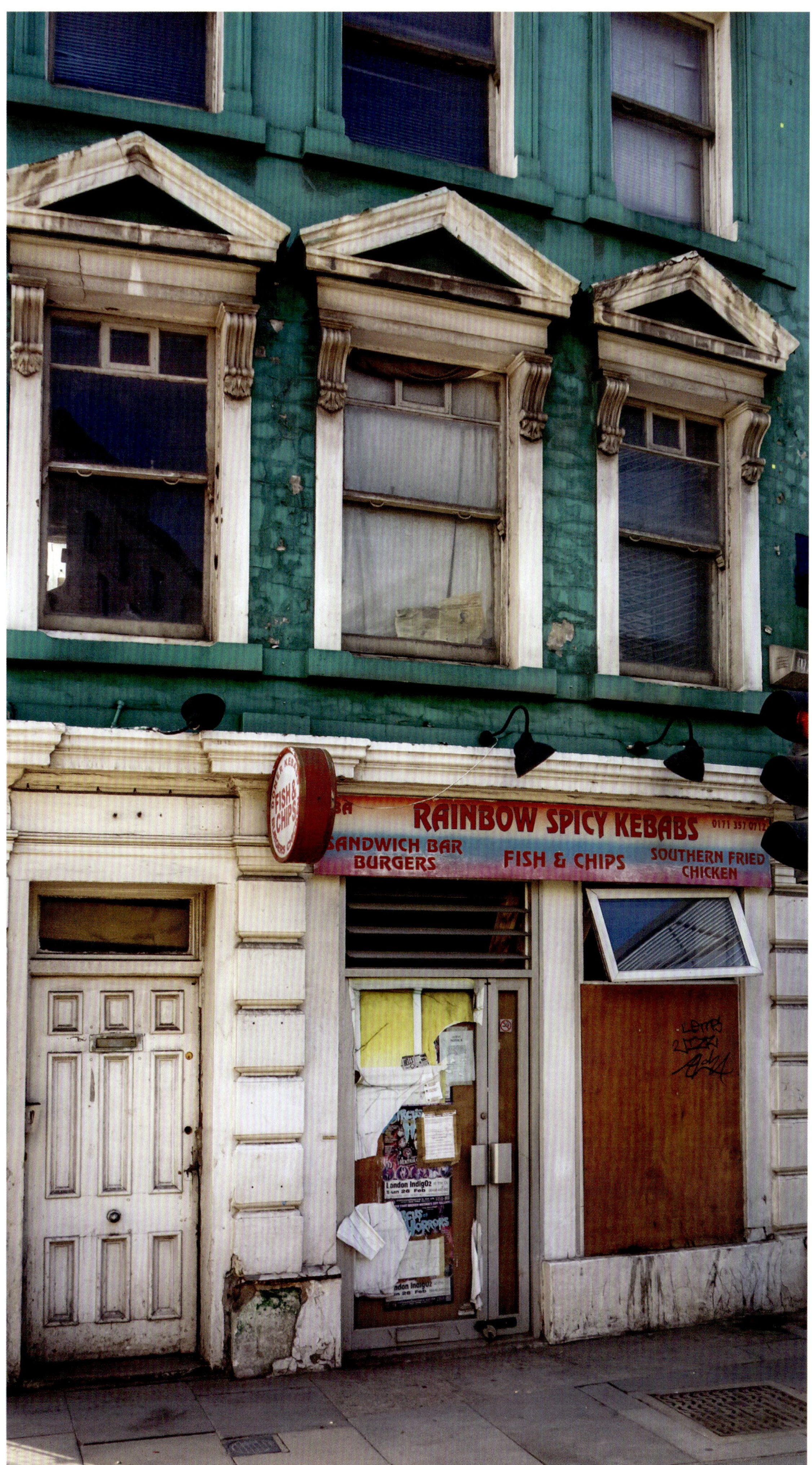

OPPOSITE ABOVE:

Callegari's Restaurant, 635 Commercial Road

Derelict for over a decade, this little row of shops sits underneath a railway bridge connected to Limehouse Station. The railway station opened in 1840 but in 1987 it became part of the Docklands Light Railway (DLR). The DLR was built to connect the City of London with the new financial centre of Canary Wharf in the former Docklands, just as the road had done in the early 19th century.

OPPOSITE BELOW:

Simya, Old Brompton Road

Since 2008 this retail space has been used by two different Japanese restaurants and this Korean restaurant, which closed in 2019.

LEFT:

Rainbow Spicy Kebabs, Tooley Street, Bermondsey

Running parallel to the River Thames, Tooley Street can be seen on the earliest London maps. This Victorian shop building stands in front of London Bridge Station, the first central London railway terminus, which opened in 1836.

OVERLEAF:

Tea Rooms, Museum Street, Soho

The Street is named for its proximity to the British Museum, established in 1753 after the physician Sir Hans Sloane donated his collection of antiquities and natural history curiosities to the nation in his will. Sloane spent 15 months in Jamaica as doctor to the new governor, and while there he was introduced to cocao. Not liking it at first, Sloane made it more palatable by mixing it with milk and brought his treat back to England. Although his was not the first chocolate recipe, many manufacturers used Sloane's name to sell their product, most notably Messrs Cadbury in the 19th century.

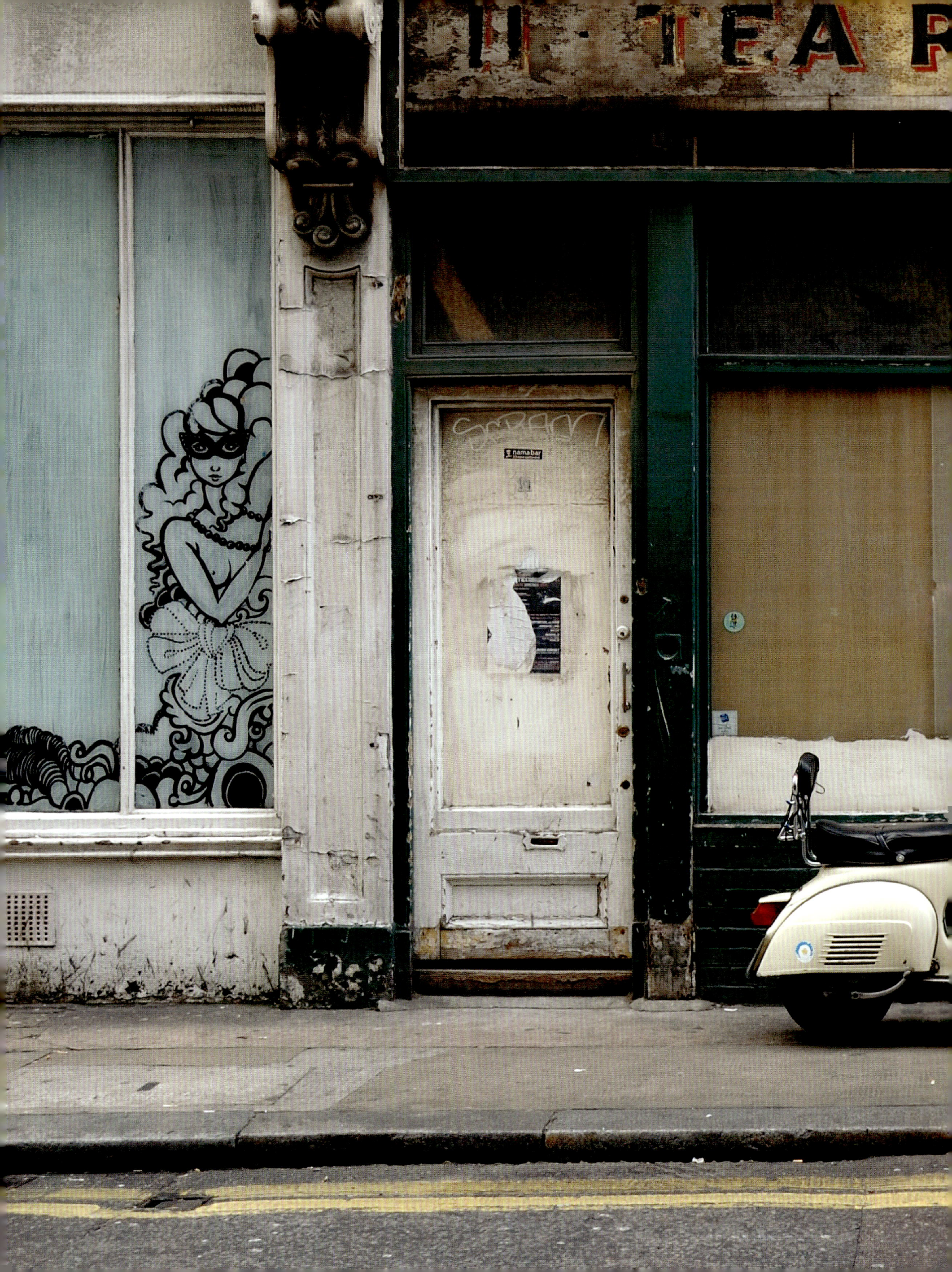
TEA

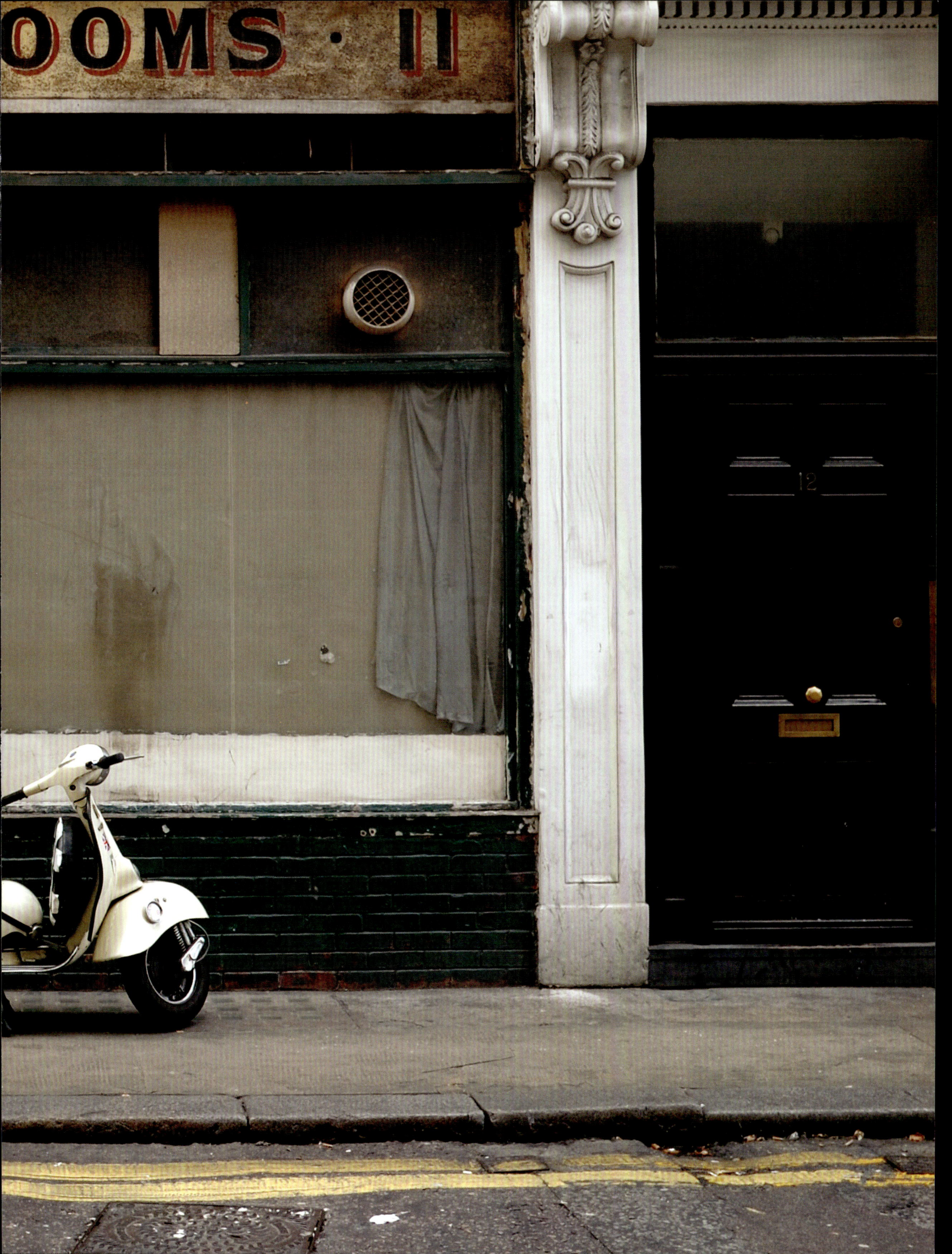
OOMS · 11
12

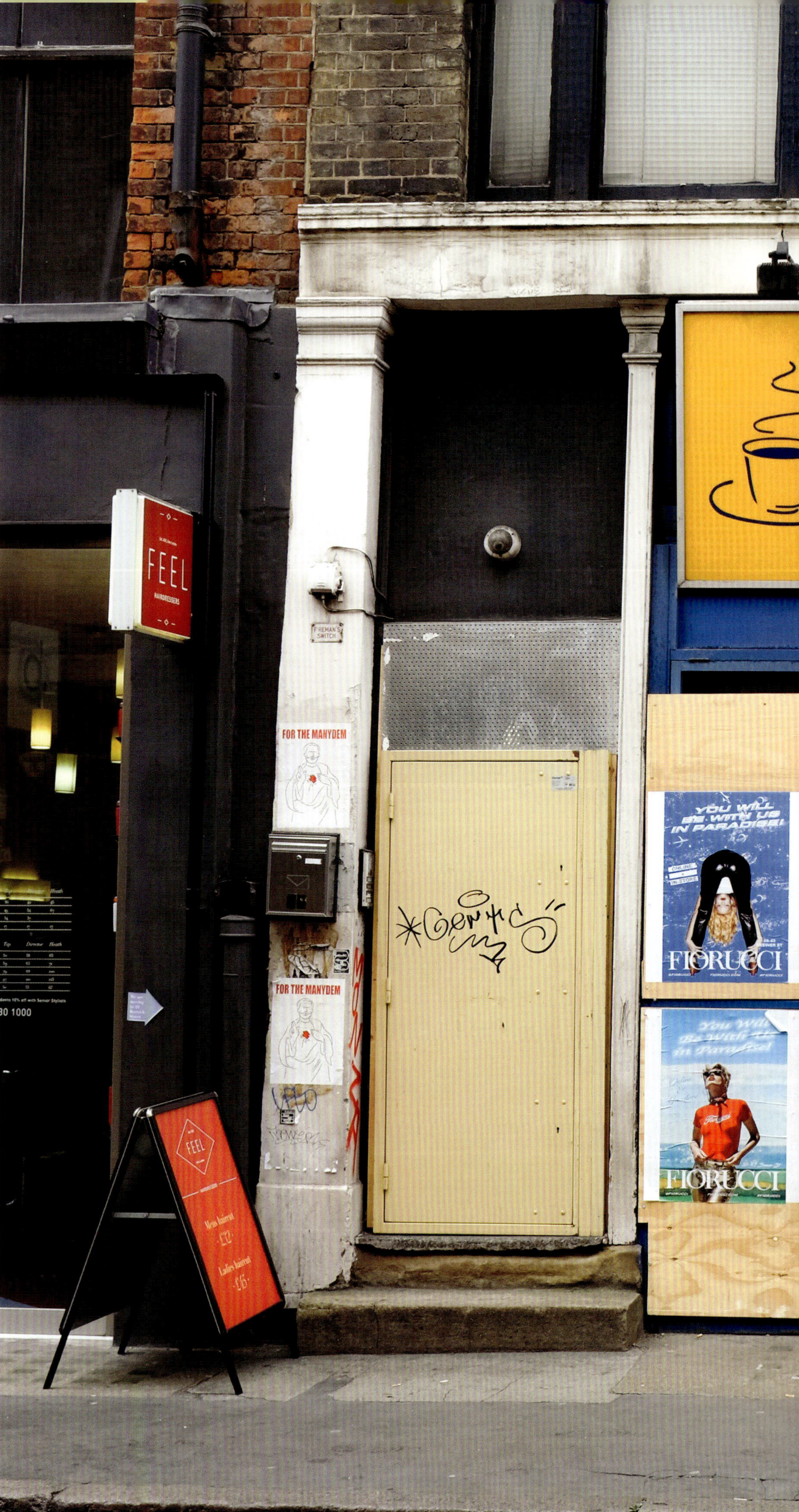

Cotton Cafe, Berwick Street, Soho

Laid out in the 17th century, Berwick Street in Soho was popular with French immigrants, the Protestant Huguenots who had fled persecution in Catholic France following the Wars of Religion (1562–98). It is most famous for its street market, a little further to the south from here, which was first recorded in 1778.

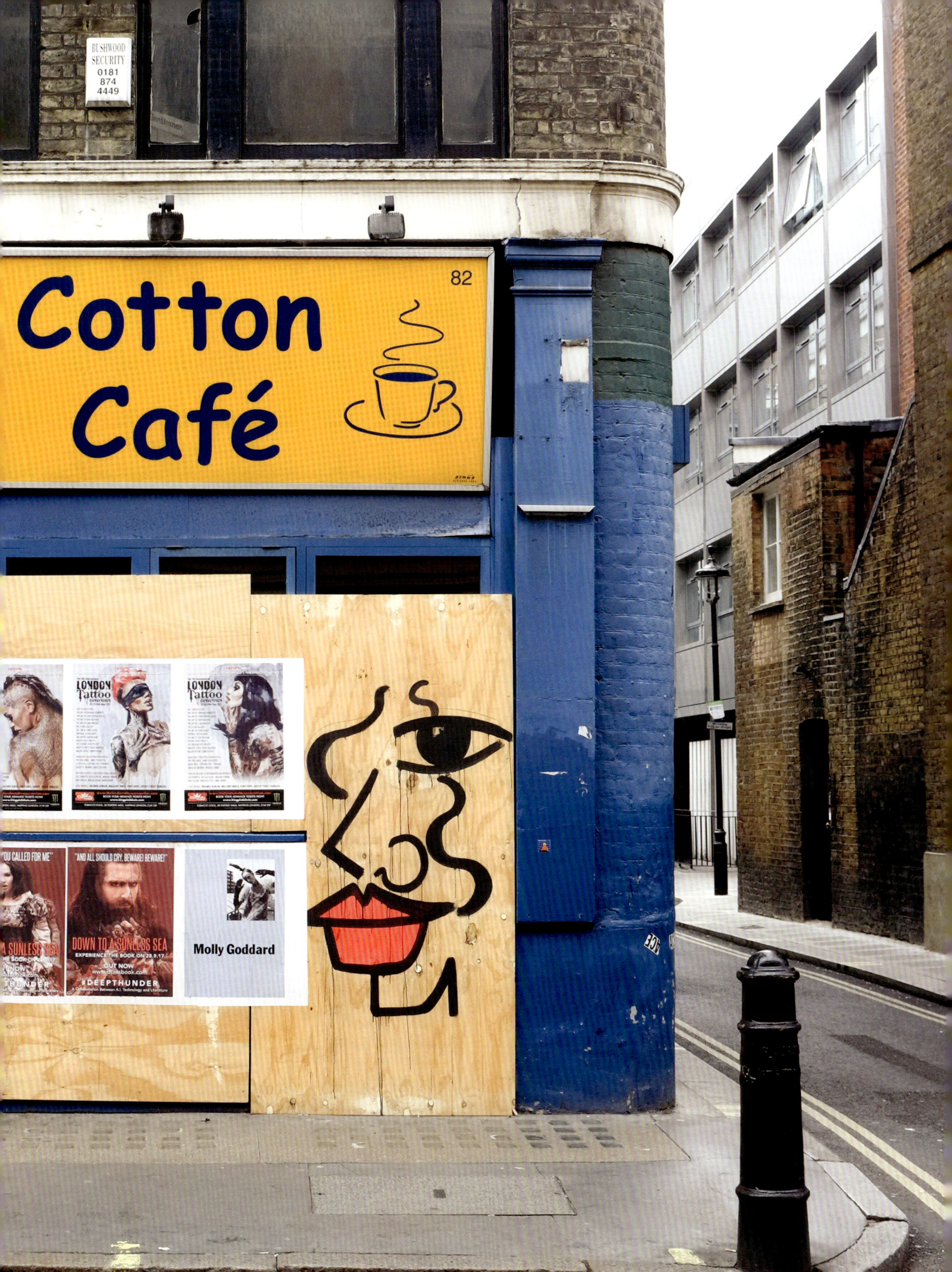
BUSHWOOD SECURITY 0181 874 4449
Cotton Café
82
LONDON Tattoo
DOWN TO A SUNLESS SEA
Molly Goddard

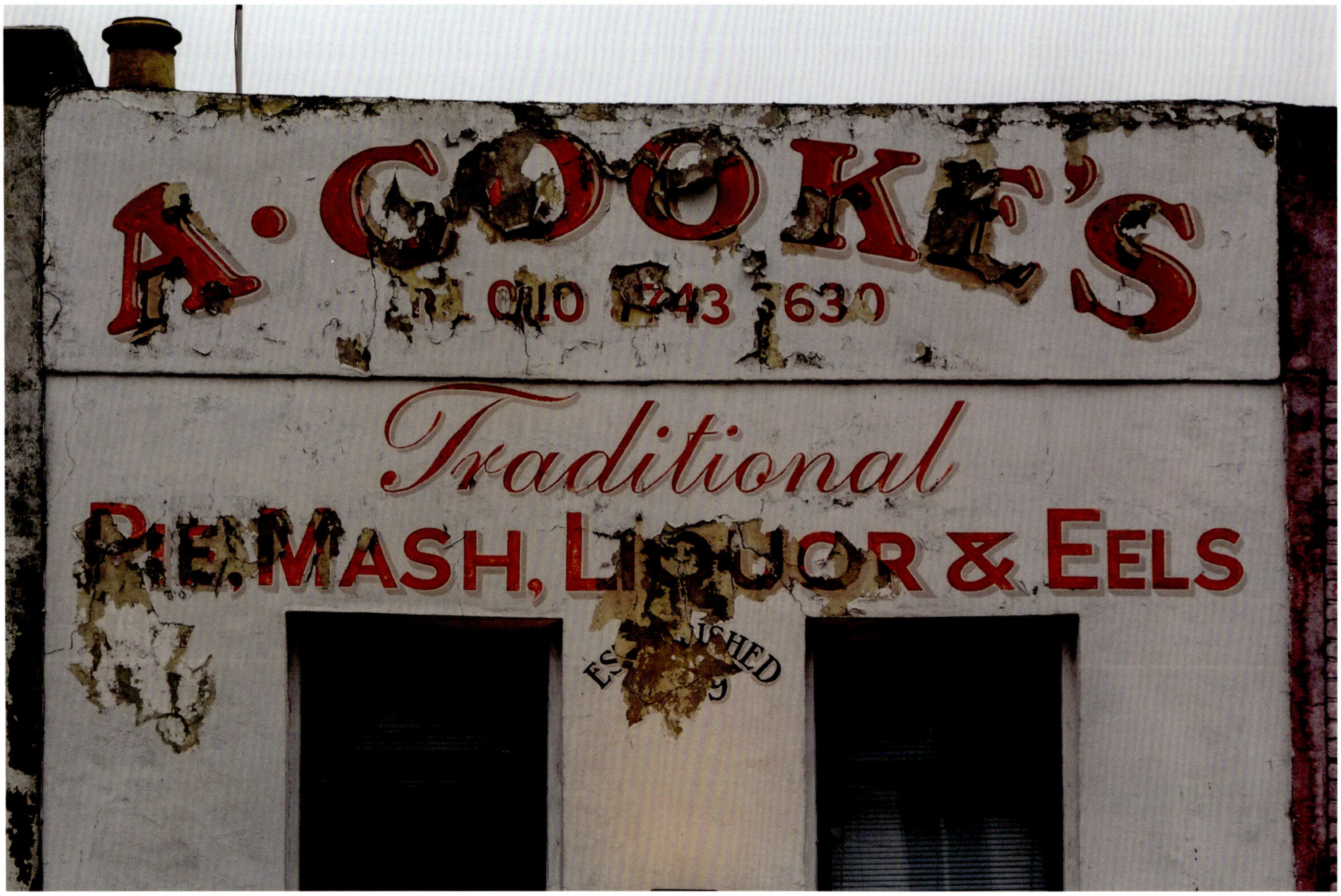

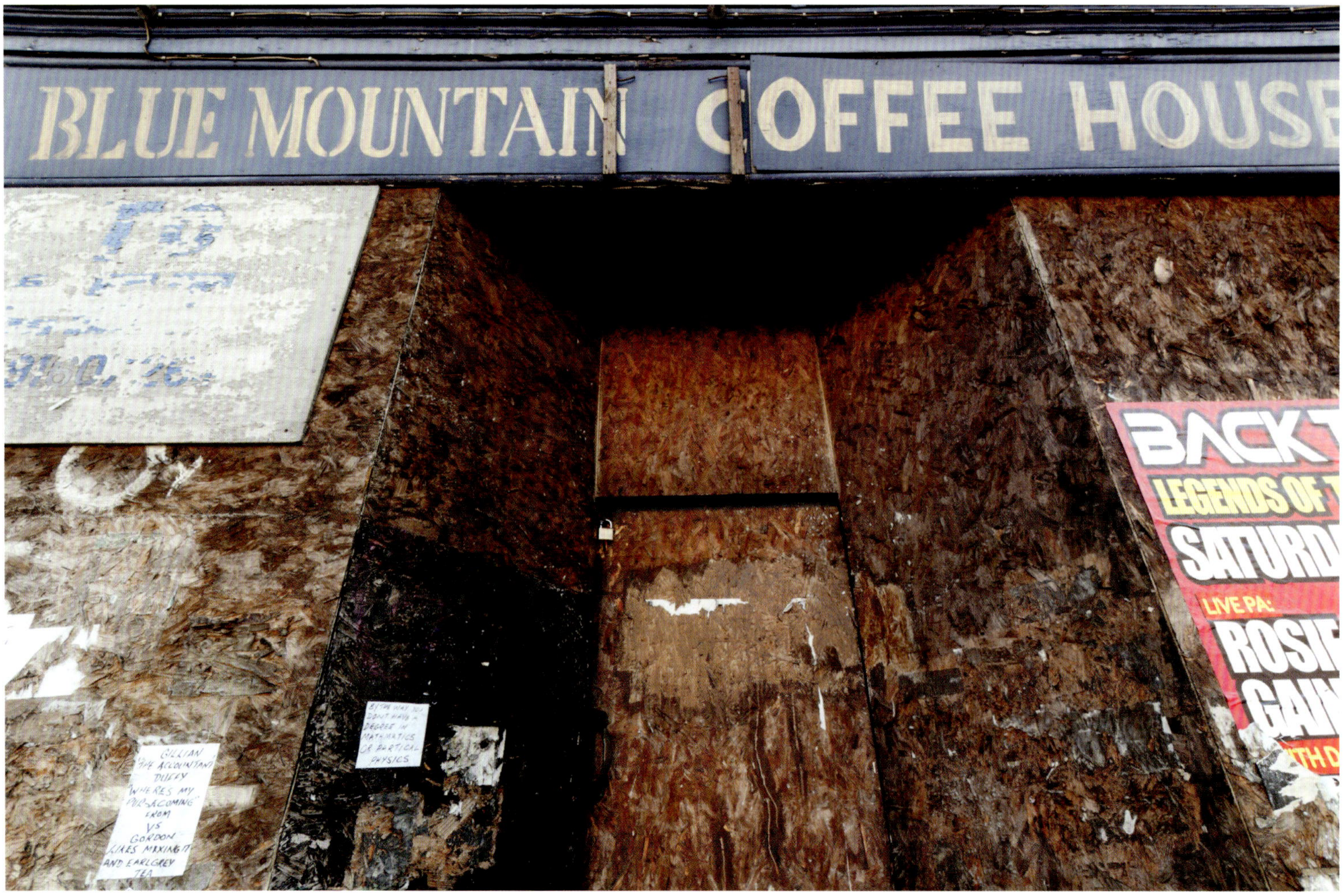

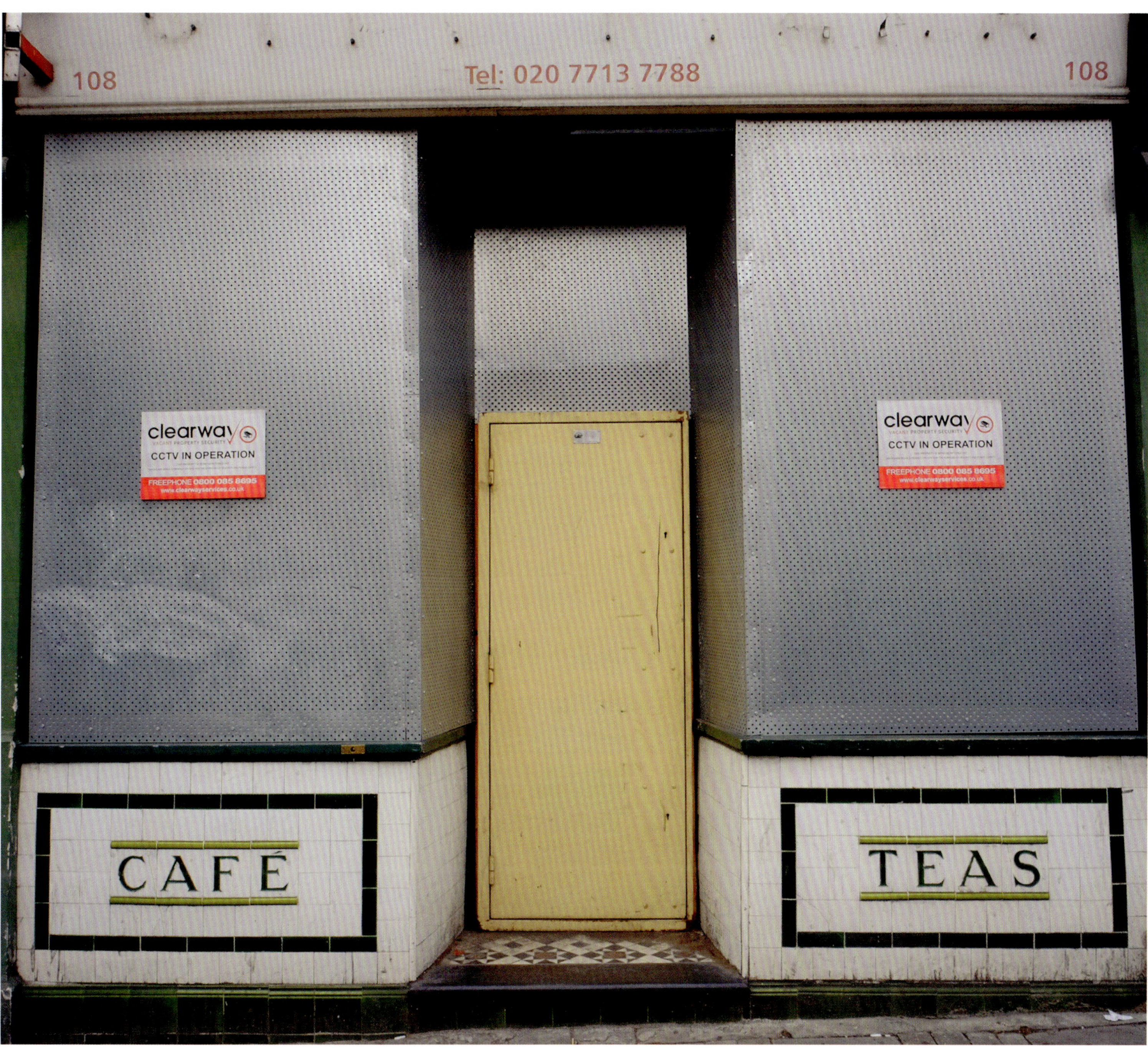

OPPOSITE TOP:
A. Cooke's Pie and Mash, 48 Goldhawk Road, Shepherd's Bush
Alfred Cooke established his pie and mash shop in 1899 and moved to 48 Goldhawk Road in 1934. Although the shop closed its doors in 2015, they still supply their customers with an online frozen delivery service.

OPPOSITE BELOW:
Blue Mountain, Forest Hill
Coffee was first introduced to Londoners in 1652 by Pasqua Rosée, who opened a stall in the churchyard of St Michael's Cornhill in the City of London. In 2020 there are almost 30,000 coffee shops across the UK.

ABOVE:
Cafe, Islington
Islington gets its name from a corruption of 'Gisla's Hill', a Saxon landowner who lived here in 1000 CE. Over the following centuries it became a thoroughfare for cattle and sheep on their way to Smithfield Market, then in the 18th century developed into an elegant suburb for the London middle classes.

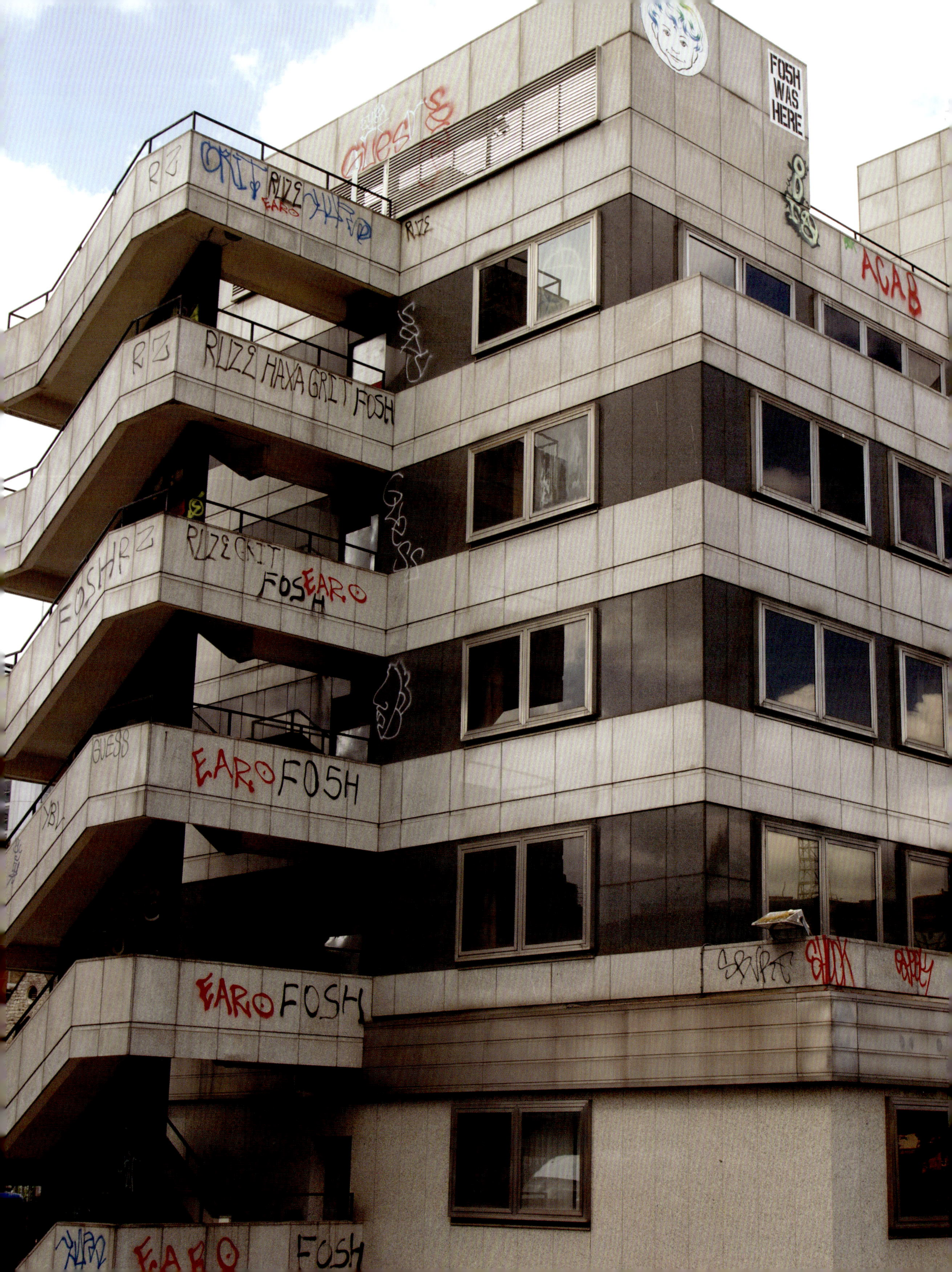
FOSH
WAS
HERE
ACAB
RUZE HAXA GRIT FOSH
EARO FOSH
EARO FOSH

Residential Property

London's population is growing relentlessly and the city itself is sprawling outwards. The question of how to house all of its residents is political and emotive: after all, one cannot stay disinterested when thinking about a place to call home.

This is thrown starkly into focus with cases of communities forced out of homes on estates in Hackney and Southwark, the residents finding themselves not 'fitting' into the new vision for London. As an endless appetite for London property has created a price surge, living in the centre of the metropolis has become unrealistic for most people.

The other subject we examine in this chapter is extraordinary homes: listed properties in the midst of renovation and buildings that were once industrial and have become residential. Another change we shall observe with London's housing stock is historic buildings that have been transformed from rags to riches – and one row of residences where the exact opposite has happened.

OPPOSITE:
Old Street, Shoreditch
Built in the 1950s as warehouses and workshops for a local printing firm, parts of Development House were taken over by the Ethical Property Company for residential use. As the prices in the South Shoreditch area have risen drastically, the building is currently scheduled for demolition and awaiting a final decision.

OVERLEAF:
Clarges Mews, Mayfair
Mews were historically rows of stables found behind grander terraces of housing. Often they would have rooms above them to accommodate the servants. Today most London mews have been renovated into boutique homes. They are small, but perfectly formed little homes that can be found in the most expensive neighbourhoods.

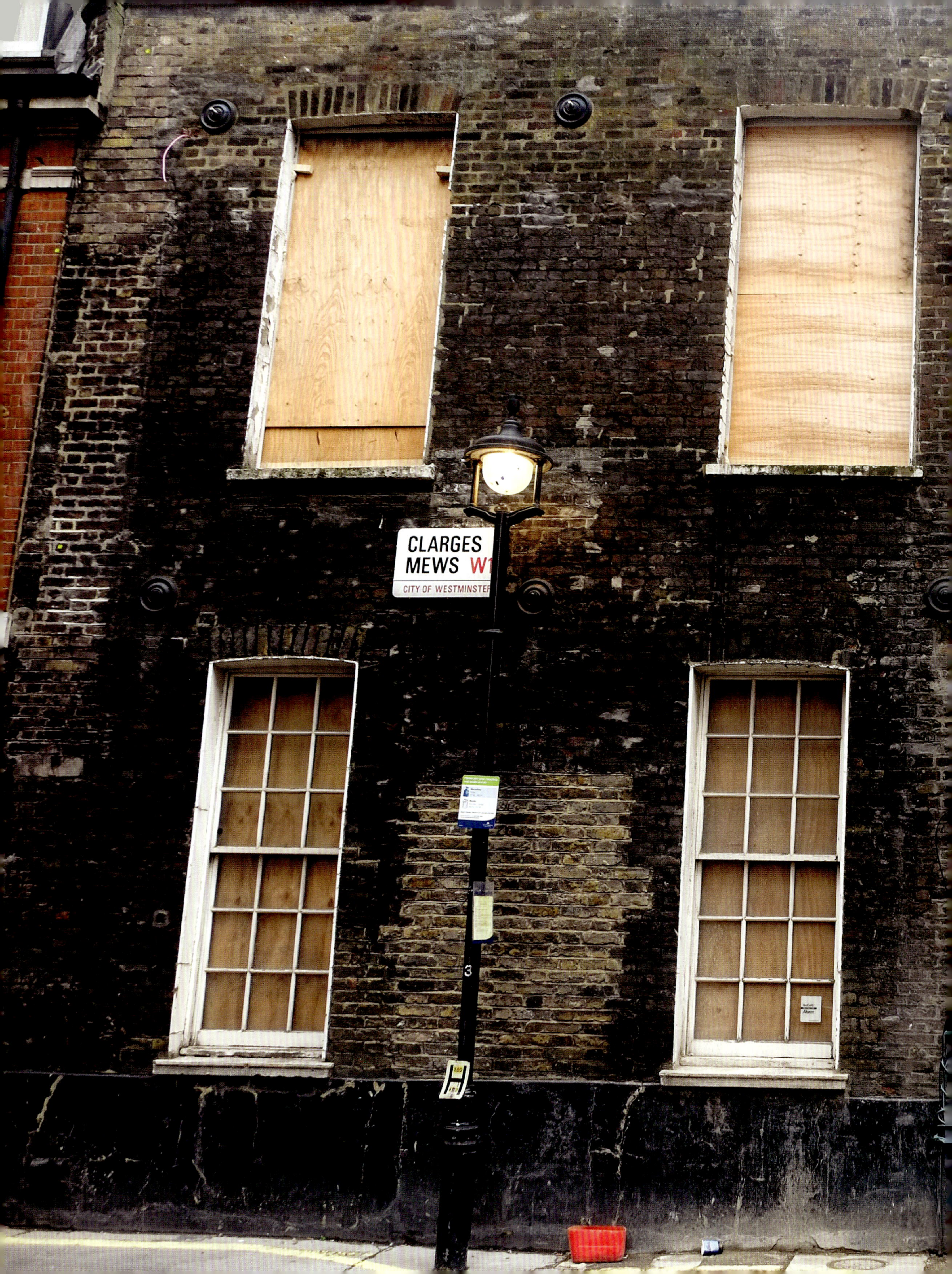
CLARGES
MEWS W1
CITY OF WESTMINSTER

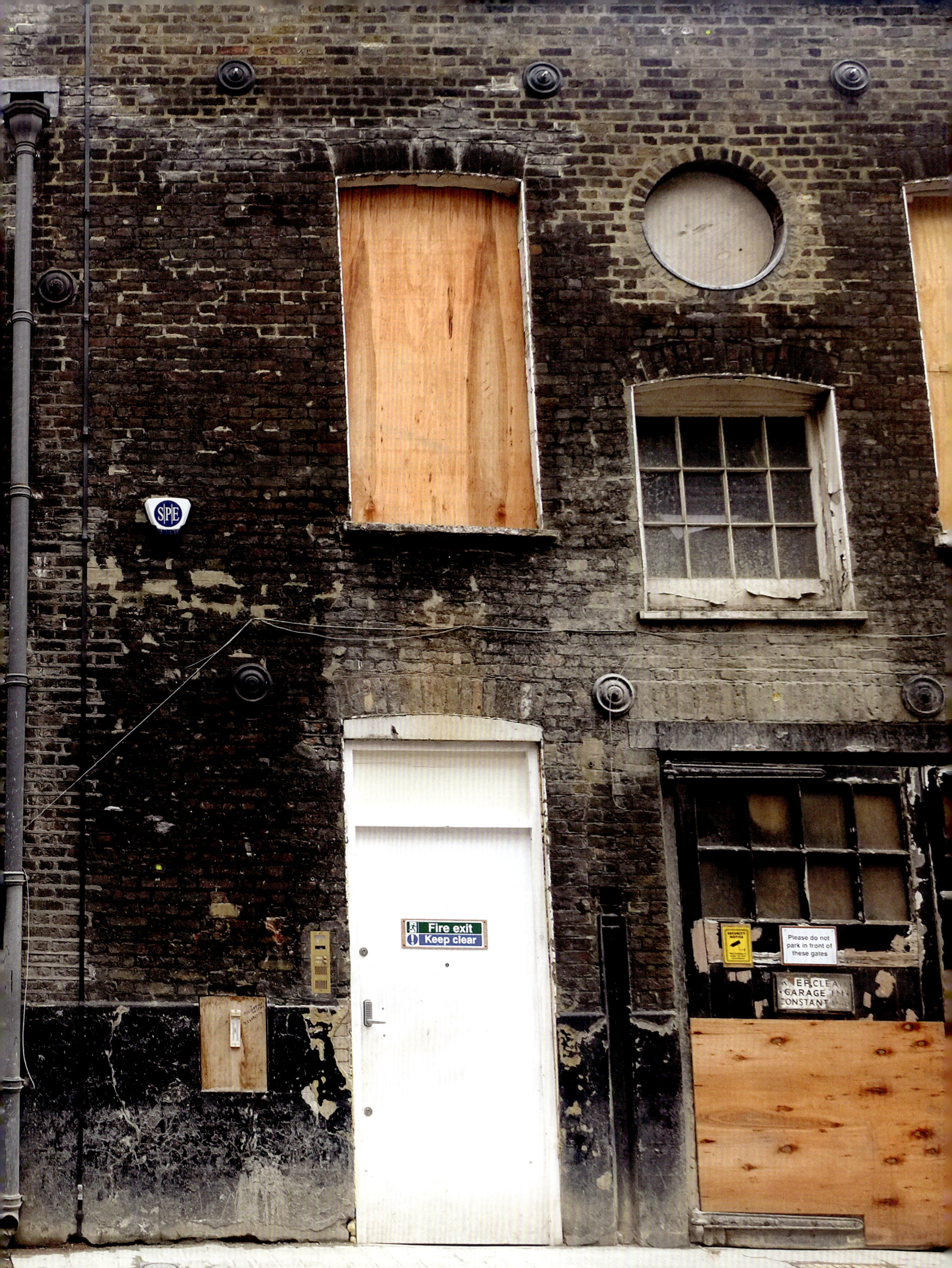
SPE
Fire exit
Keep clear
SECURITY NOTICE
Please do not park in front of these gates
GARAGE

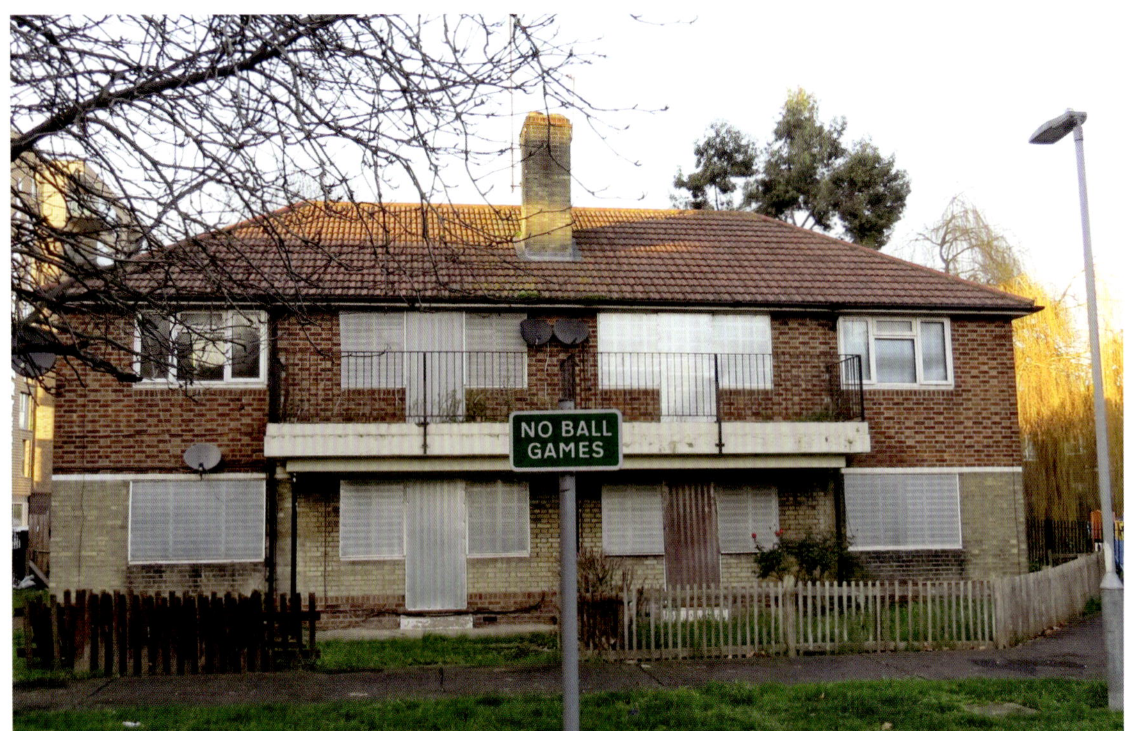

LEFT:
Abbey Street, Barking
Abbey Street runs along the remains of Barking Abbey, founded in the seventh century by the Bishop of London, Saint Erkenwald. It was run by his sister, Saint Ethelburga, but the only surviving part of the building still visible today is the Curfew Tower, which dates from 1460.

BELOW:
Robin Hood Gardens, Poplar
Designed by Alison and Peter Smithson and completed in 1972, this housing estate is in the New Brutalist style. In 2009 an attempt for listed status was rejected and a redevelopment scheme, Blackball Reach, is in progress. In 2017 a section of the building was acquired by the Victoria and Albert Museum.

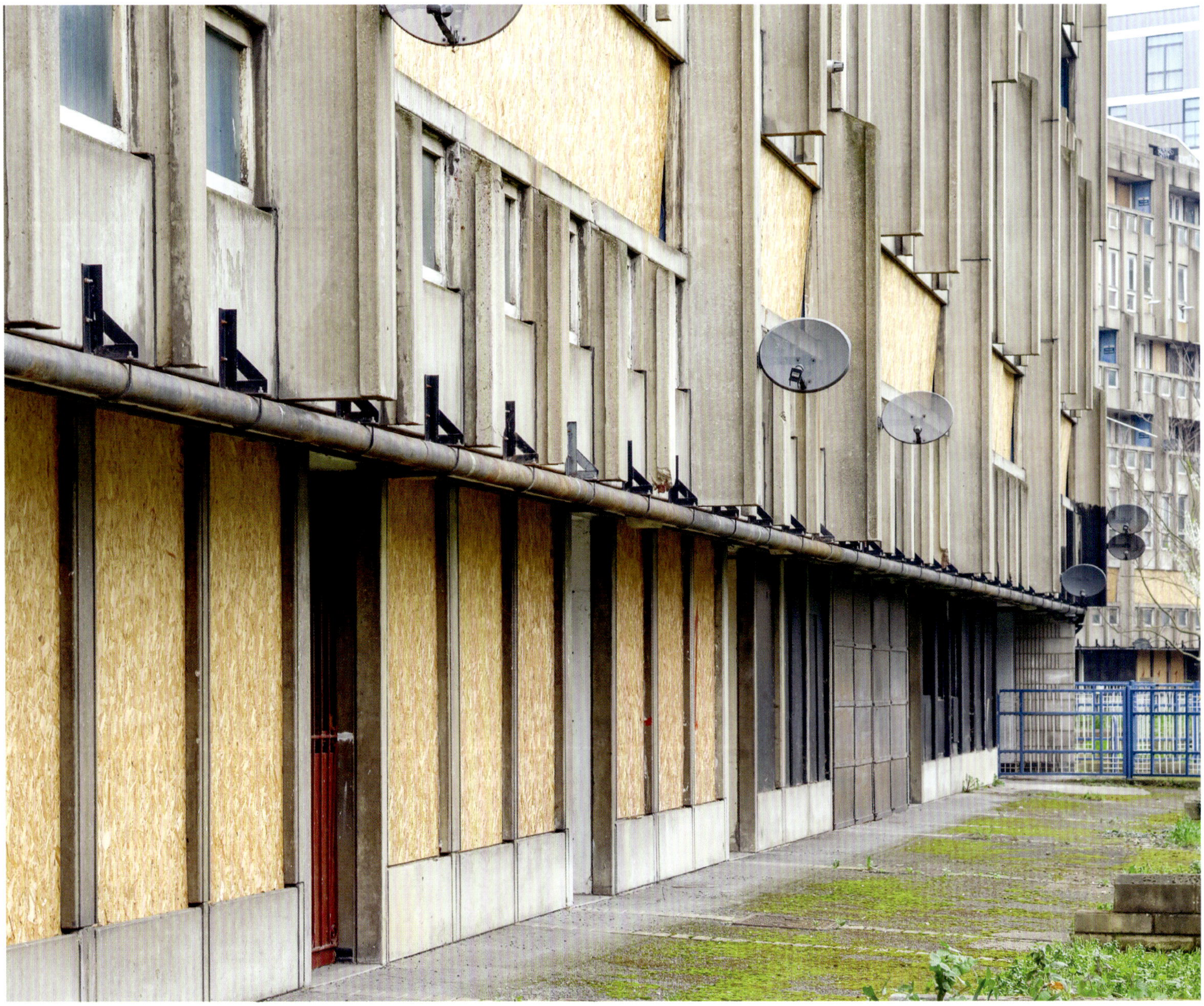

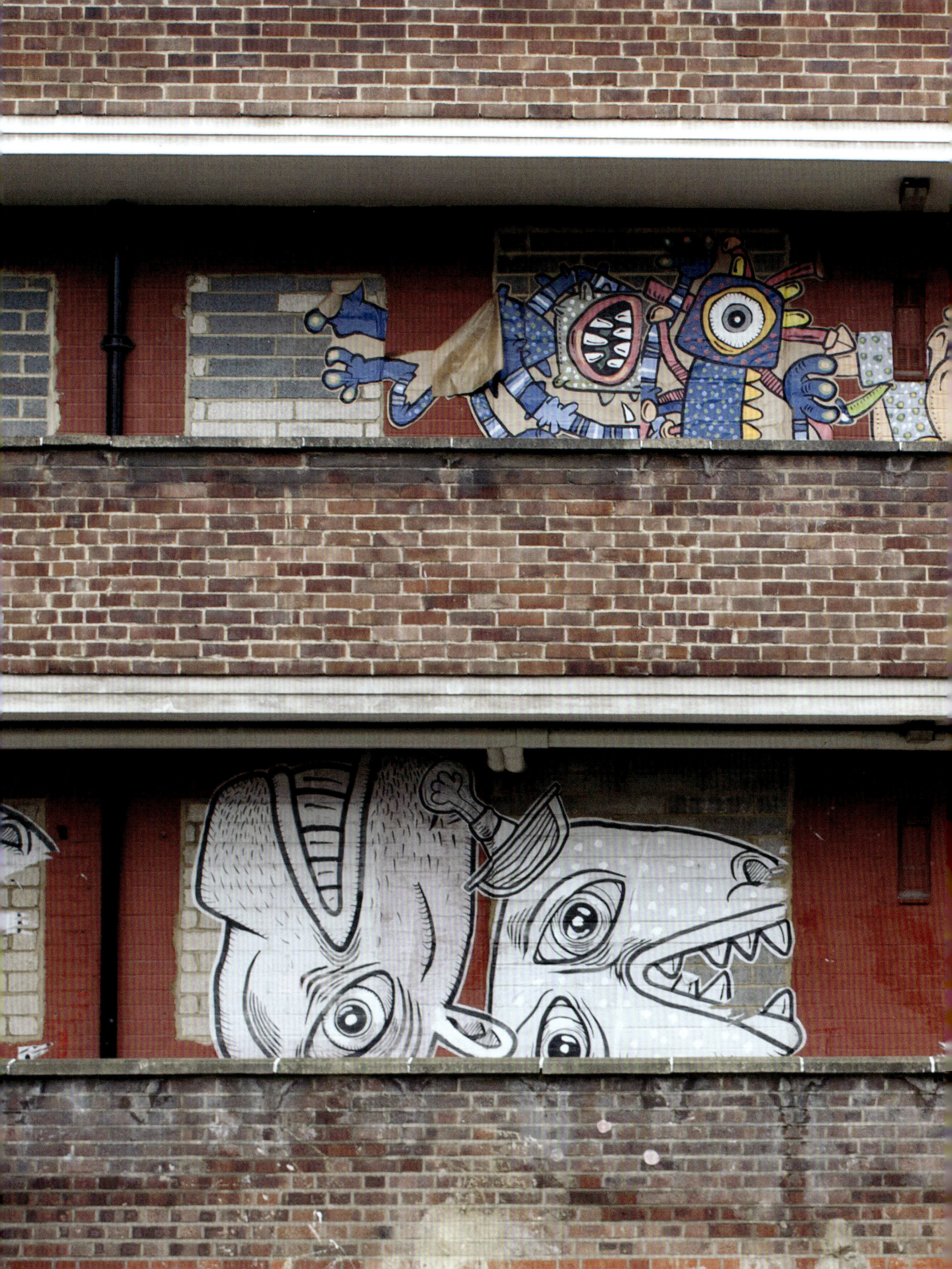

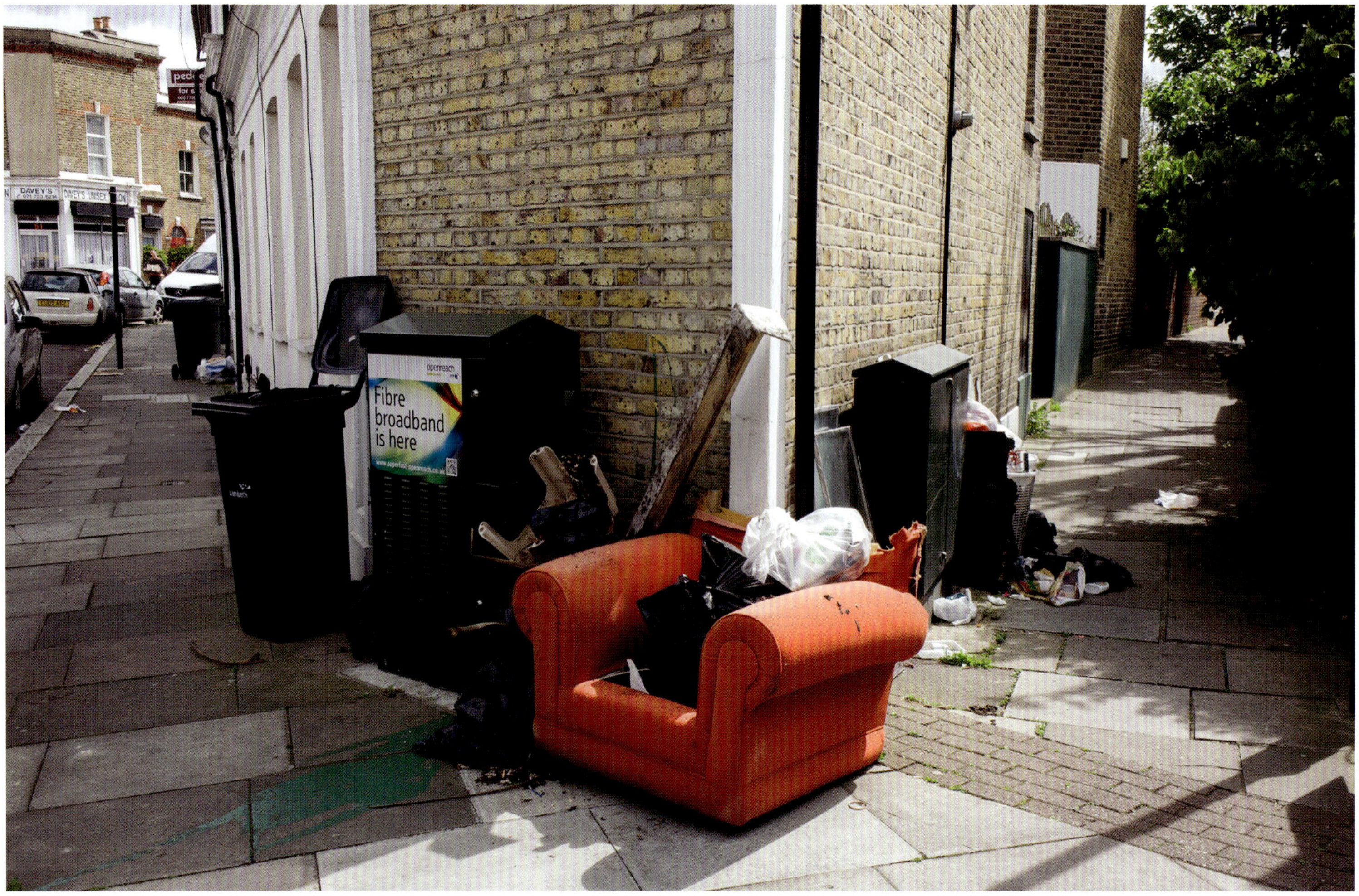

PREVIOUS PAGE:

Haggerston Estate, Hackney

Although most street art is associated with aerosol cans, many artists choose to use paste-ups. These are prepared in advance and then stuck in place quickly using wheat glue. It allows the artist to create multiple, impressive graphics quickly.

ALL PHOTOGRAPHS ON THESE PAGES:

Fly-tipping

Over a thousand incidents of fly-tipping were reported in London every day throughout 2016–17. With the growth of London's population, fly-tipping has increased by 58 per cent over the past four years. The habit is a blight on the landscape and a drain on local councils, which have to clear up the refuse. These photos show fly-tipping in Lambeth (above), Lewisham (right) and Drayton Park Station (opposite).

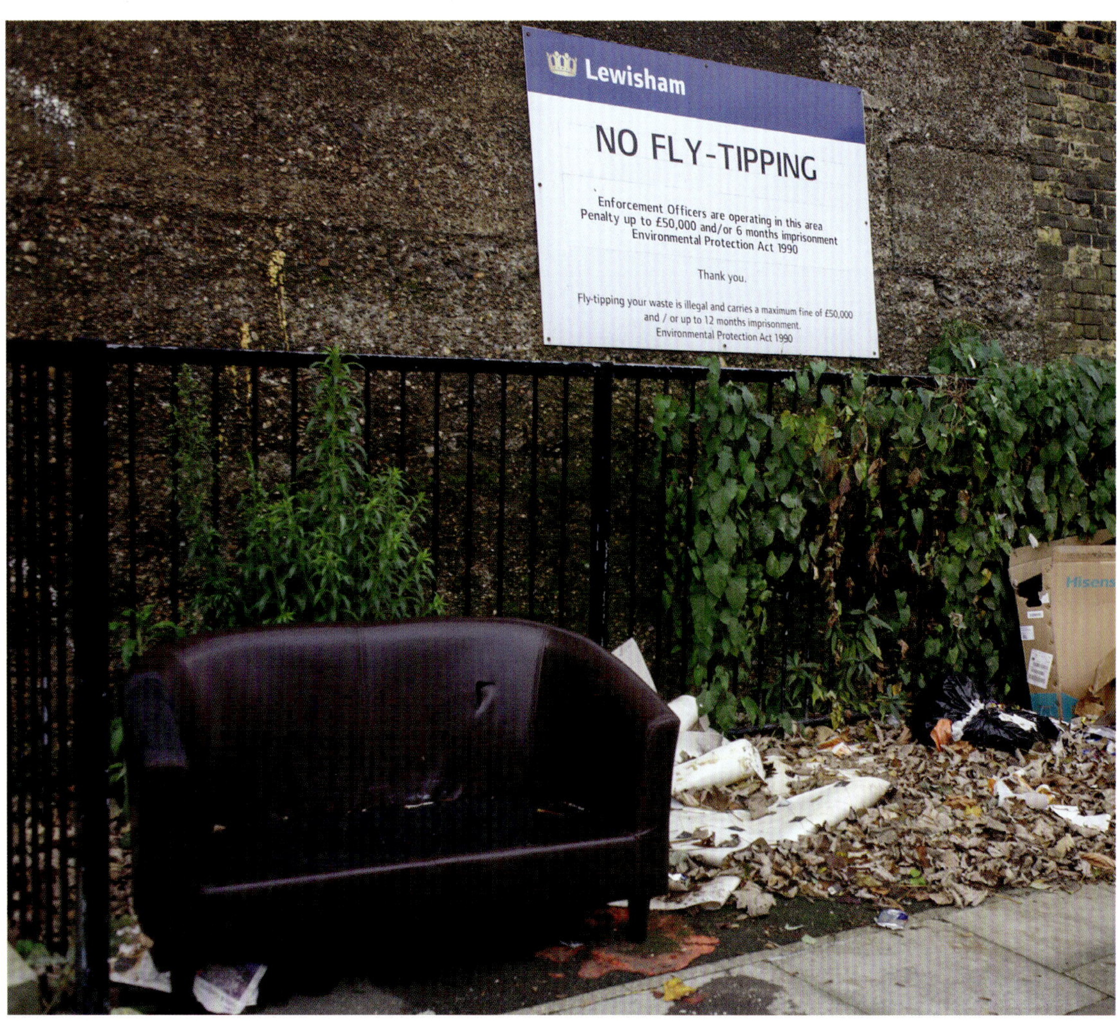

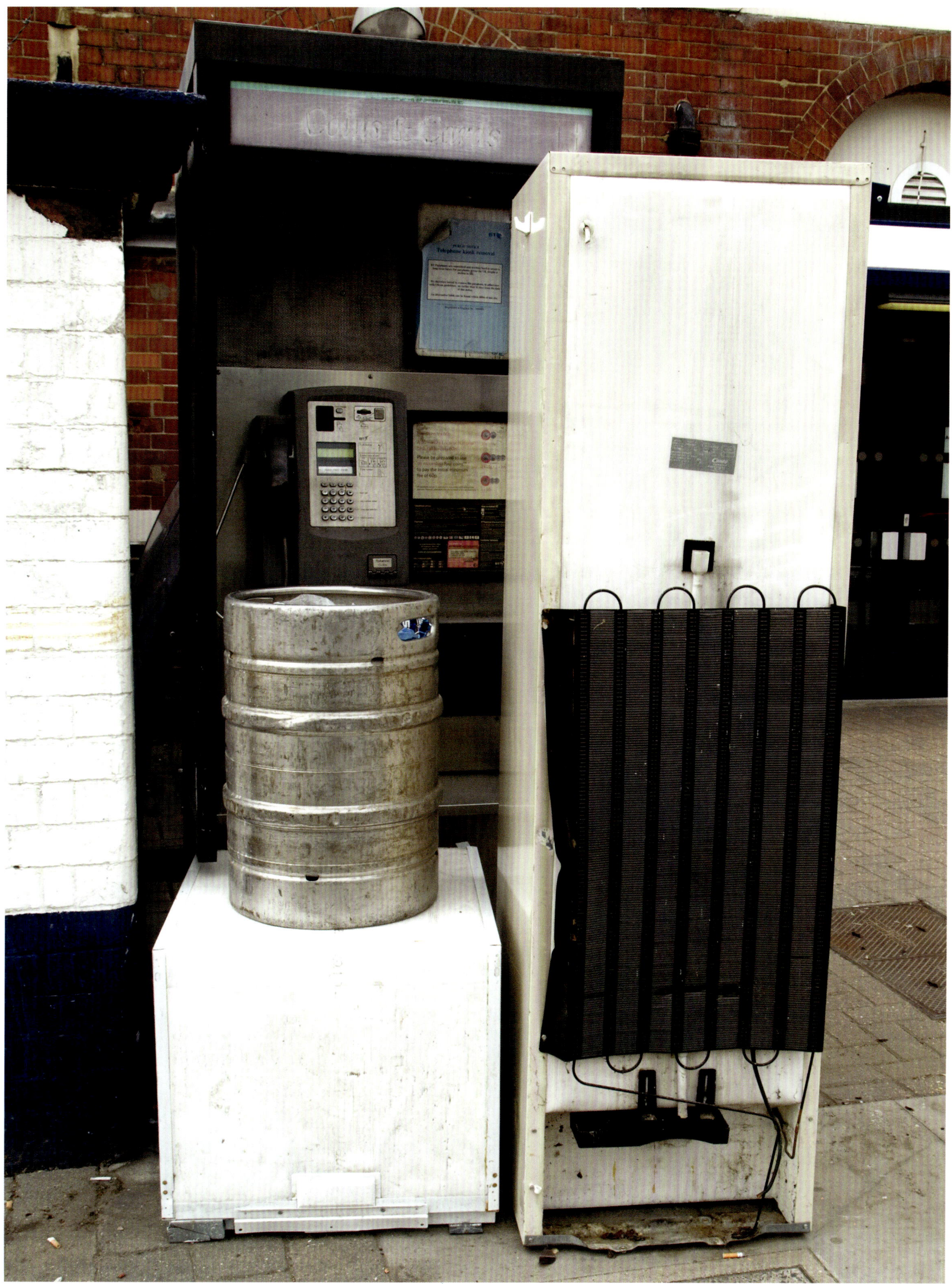
PUBLIC NOTICE
Telephone kiosk removal
to pay the initial minimum
fee of 60p

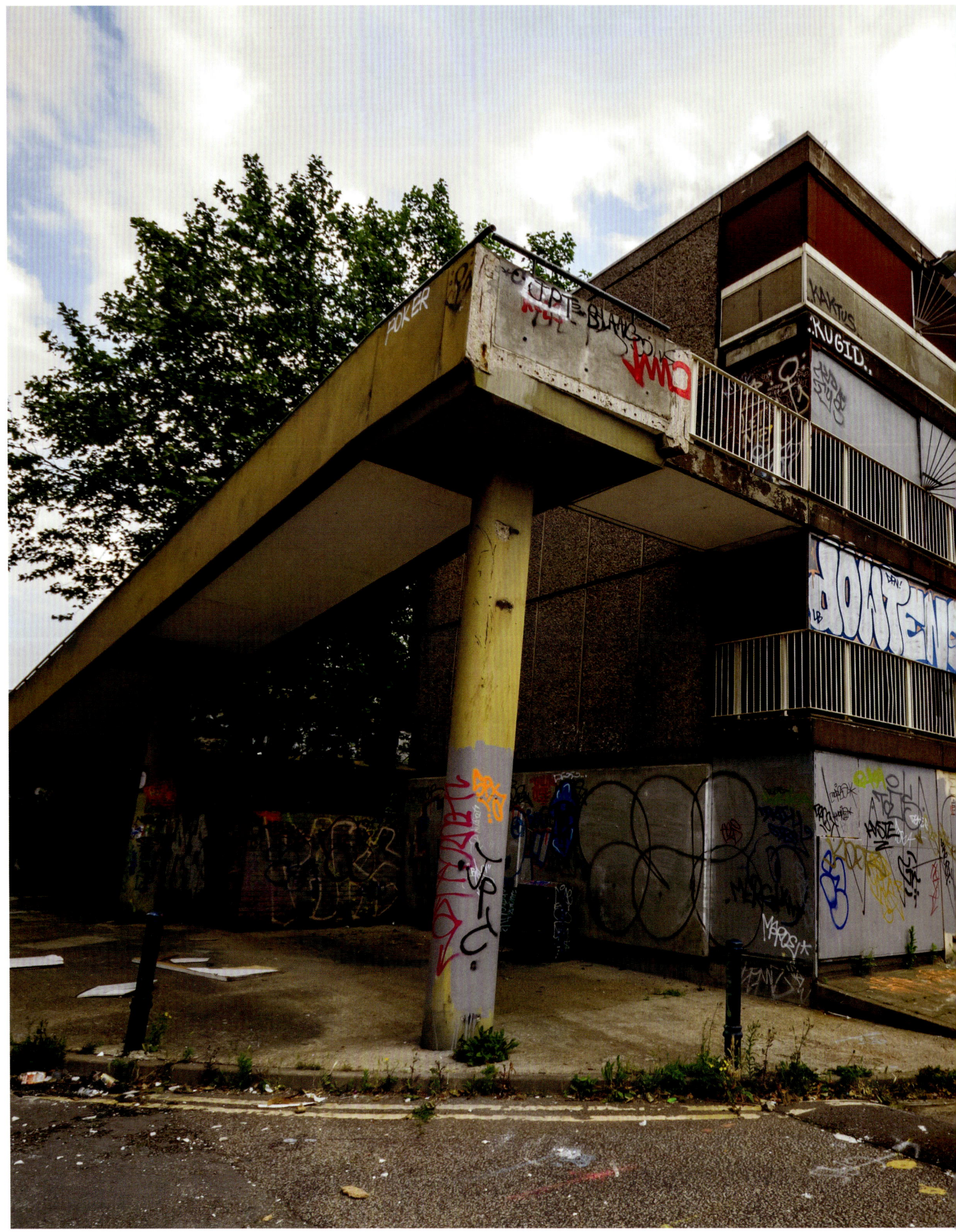

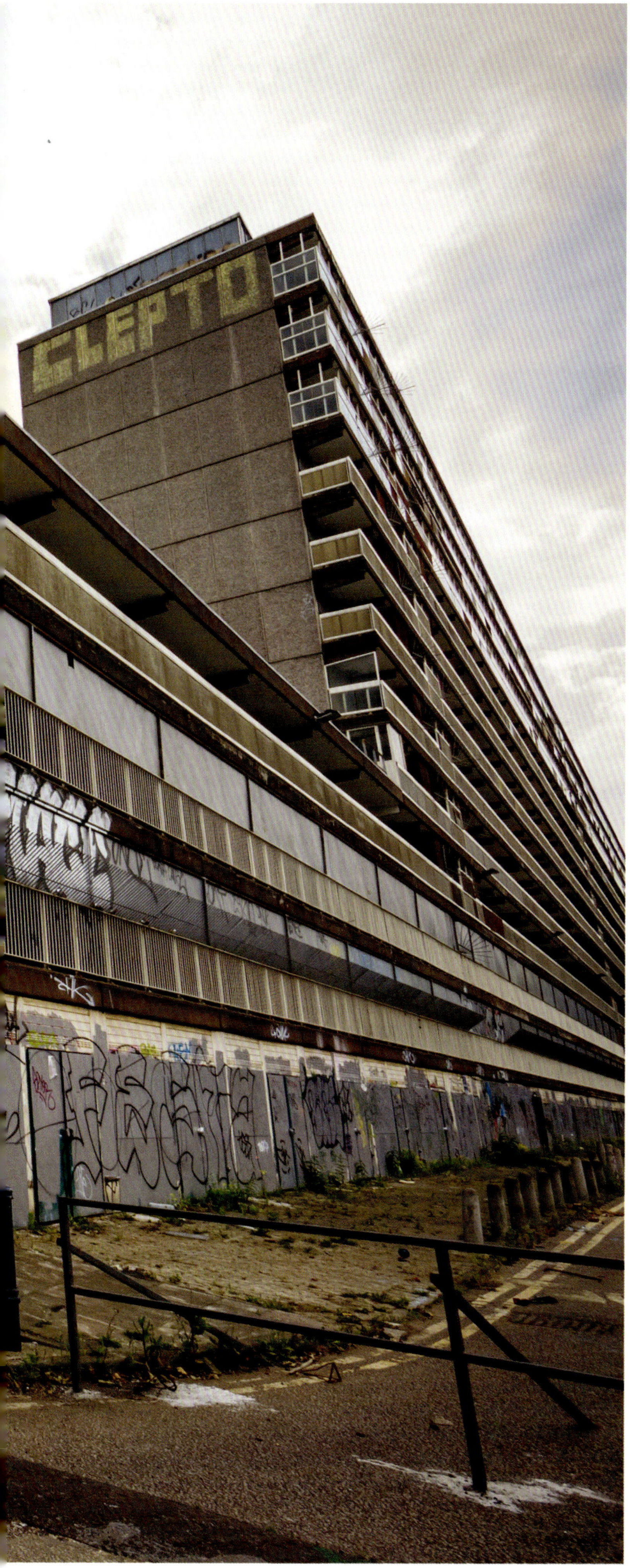

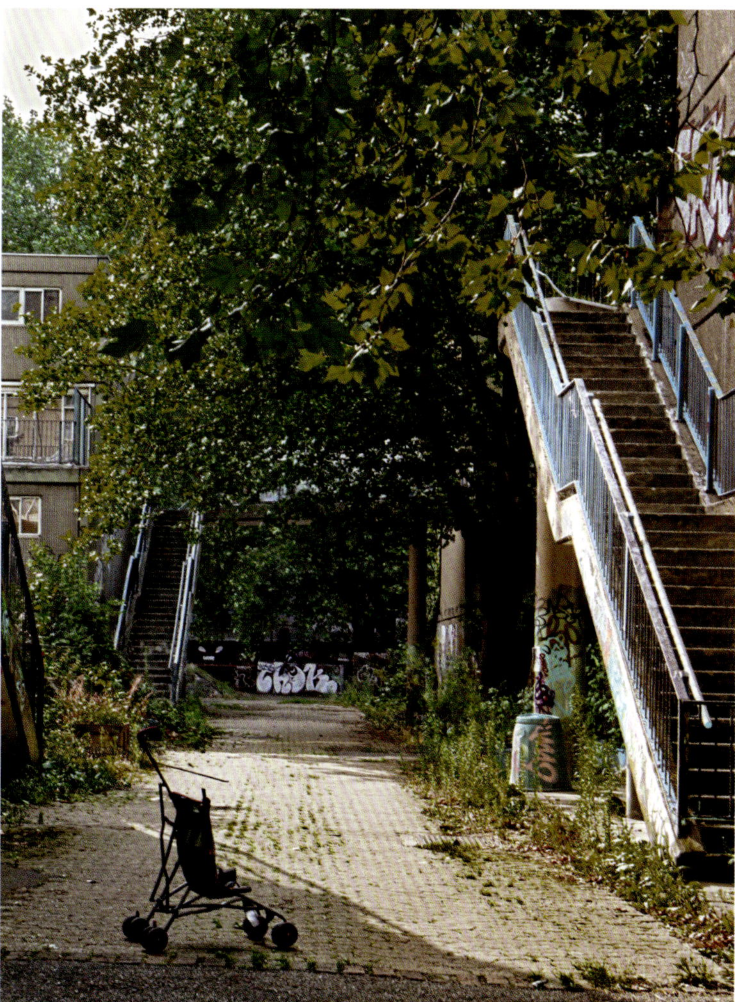

ALL PHOTOGRAPHS ON THESE PAGES AND OVERLEAF:

Heygate Estate, Walworth

In 1974, the Heygate Estate in Elephant and Castle housed around 3,000 people inside its 1,214 flats. When it opened the blocks offered spacious, well-lit homes with modern conveniences.

The land was bought by Lendlease property developers in 2010 and the estate was demolished between 2011 and 2014. There were 284 'affordable homes' (priced between £350,000 and £1.1 million) made available, but for many of the existing tenants these were too expensive. The estate has come to exemplify 'social cleansing' in London. Only one in five residents remains in the local area.

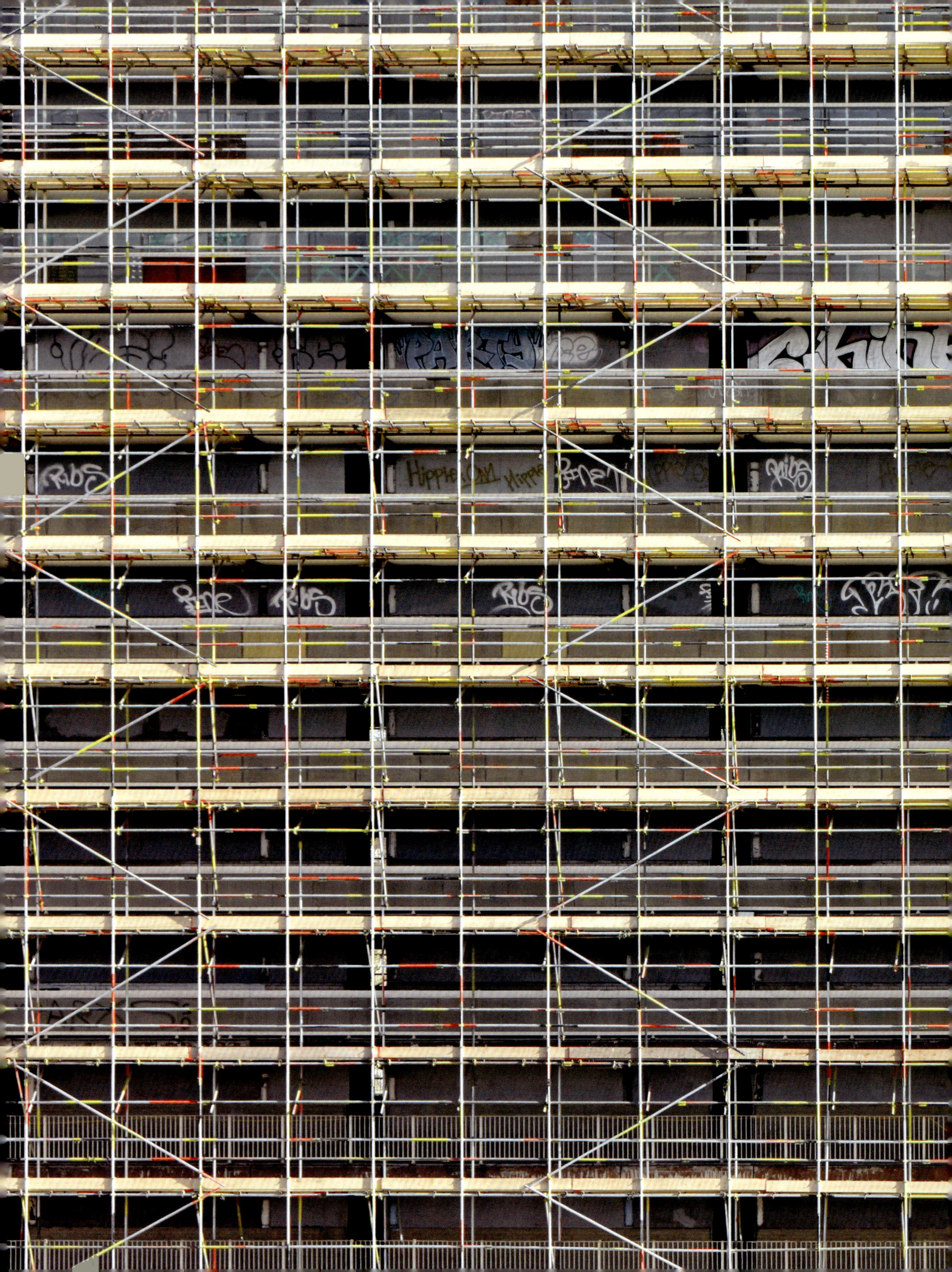

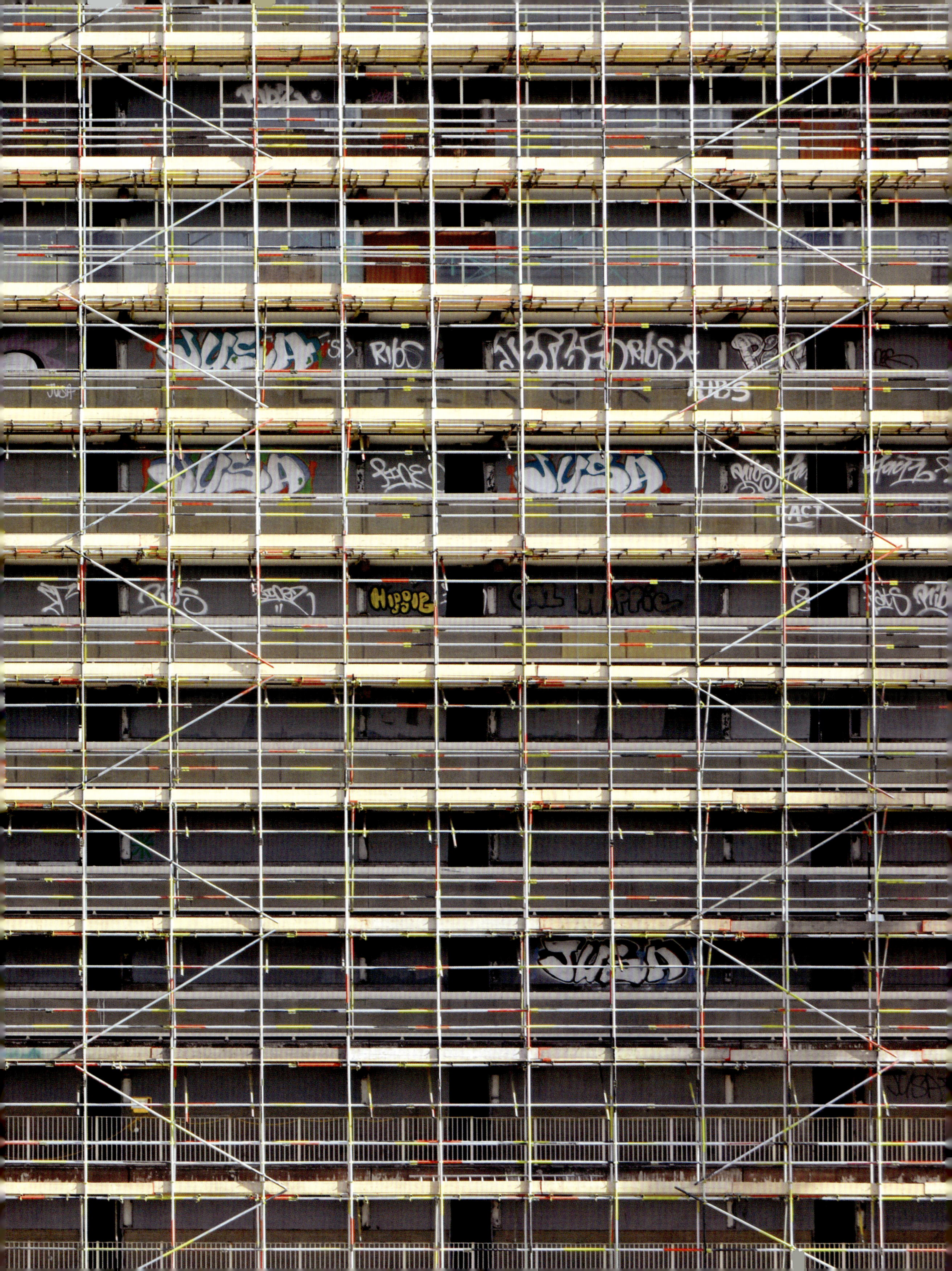

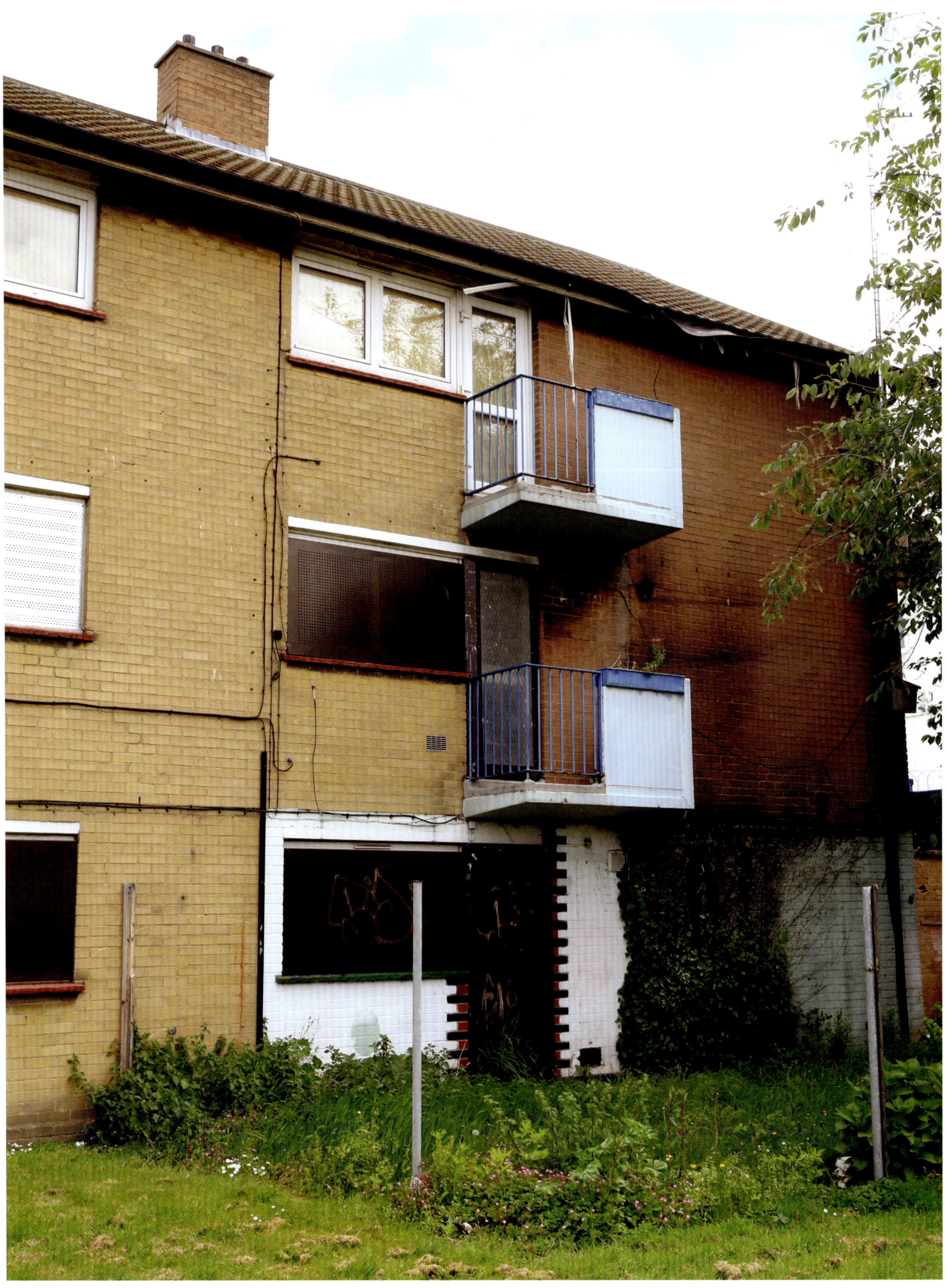

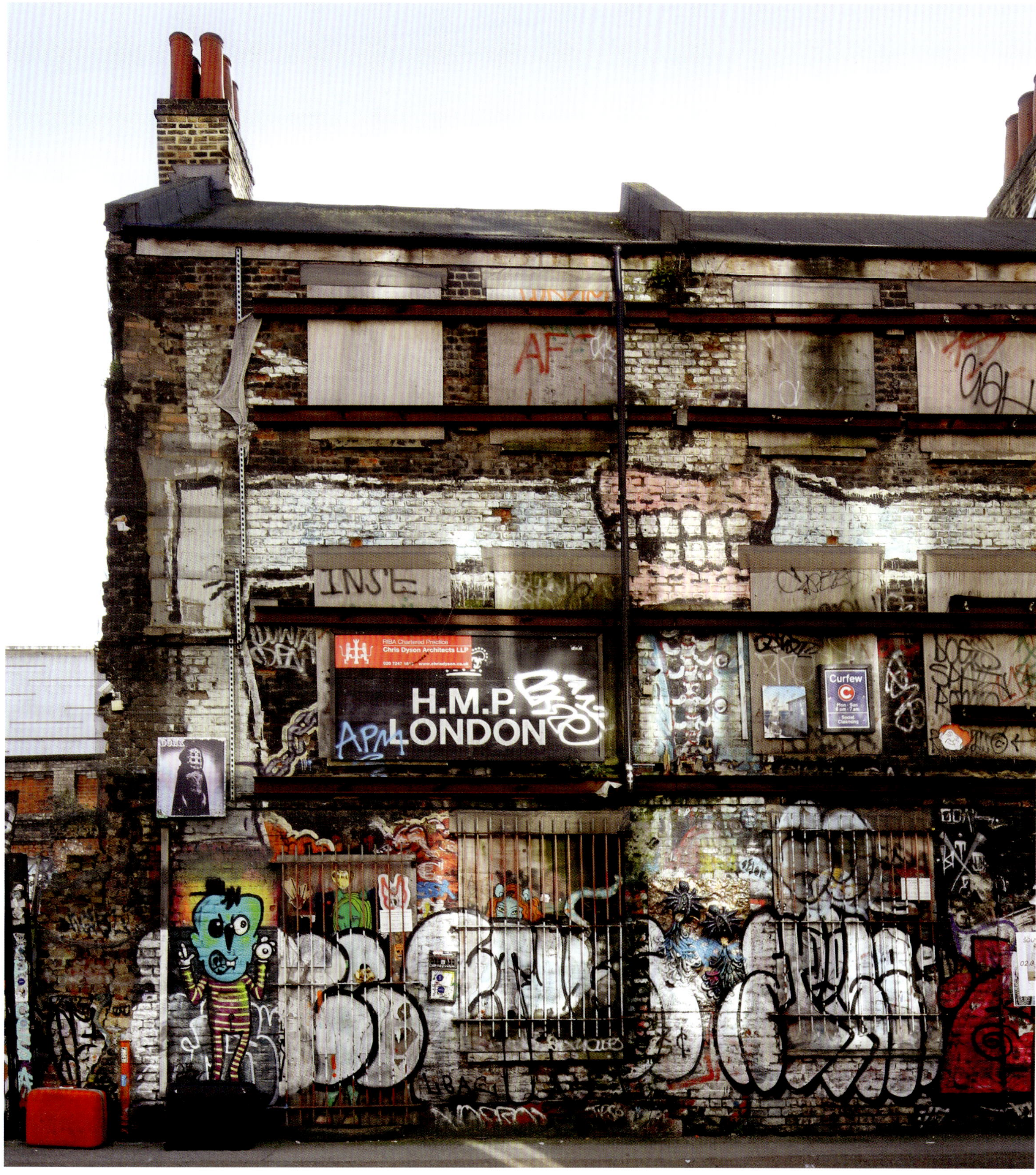

OPPOSITE:
Newham
The London Borough of Newham was created in 1965 and was one of the six host boroughs for the 2012 Olympics. However, some locals feel that the London Legacy Development Corporation has not delivered on its promise of positive development for the area.

ABOVE:
Shoreditch
The street art figure with the turquoise face is Mikglor, based on Mickey Mouse and a creation of the artist Mauricio Glor. Glor describes the character as a curious explorer of our messy, chaotic world – you can find him all over London.

OVERLEAF:
Old Street, Shoreditch
This late Victorian warehouse building can be seen from Clere Place in south Shoreditch.
The whole area was a thriving manufacturing hub from the 18th century, mainly for the furniture trade. Clues to its industrial past are still visible in the winch and loophole doors on the far righthand side. The building is now used as office space.

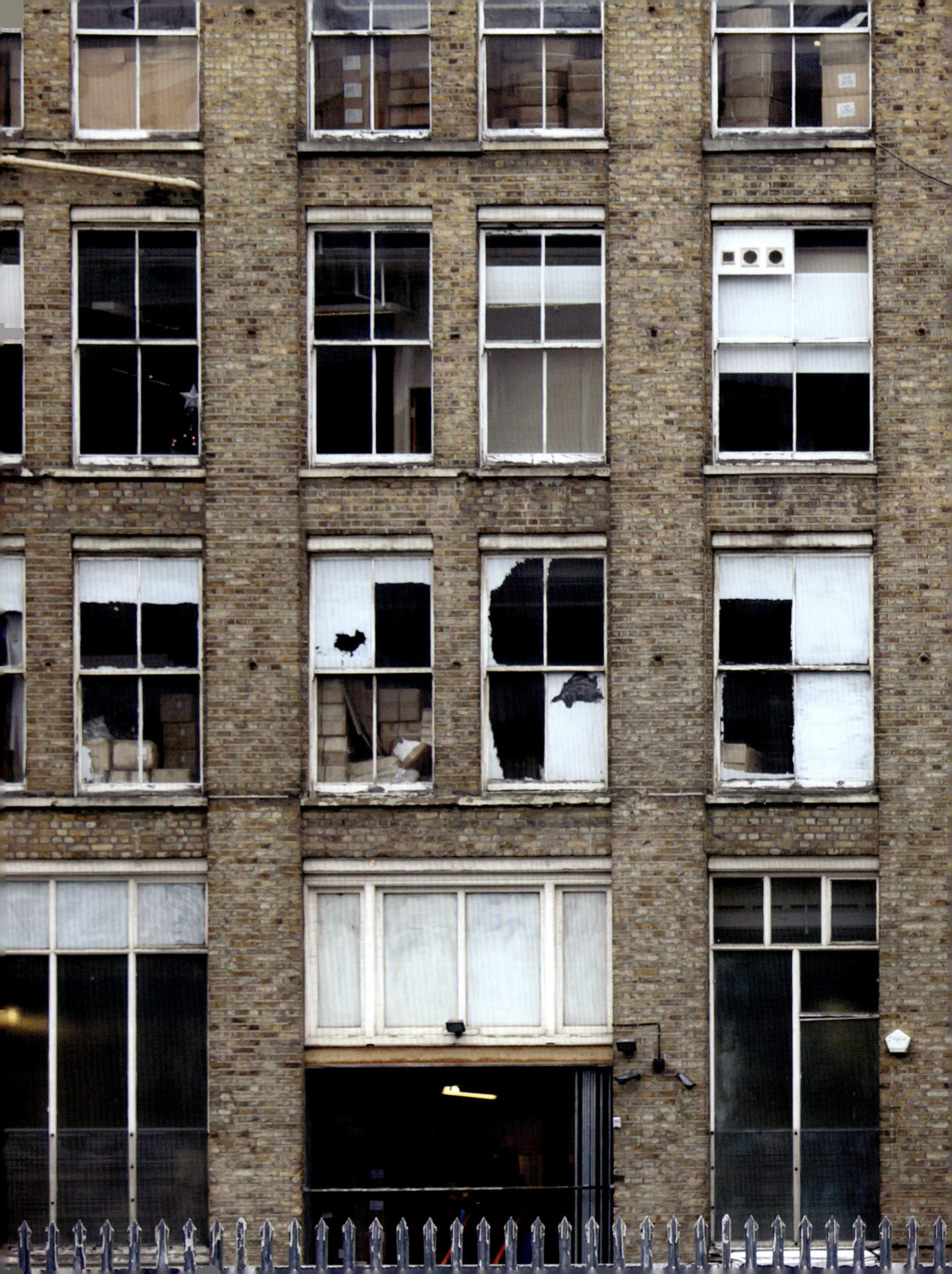

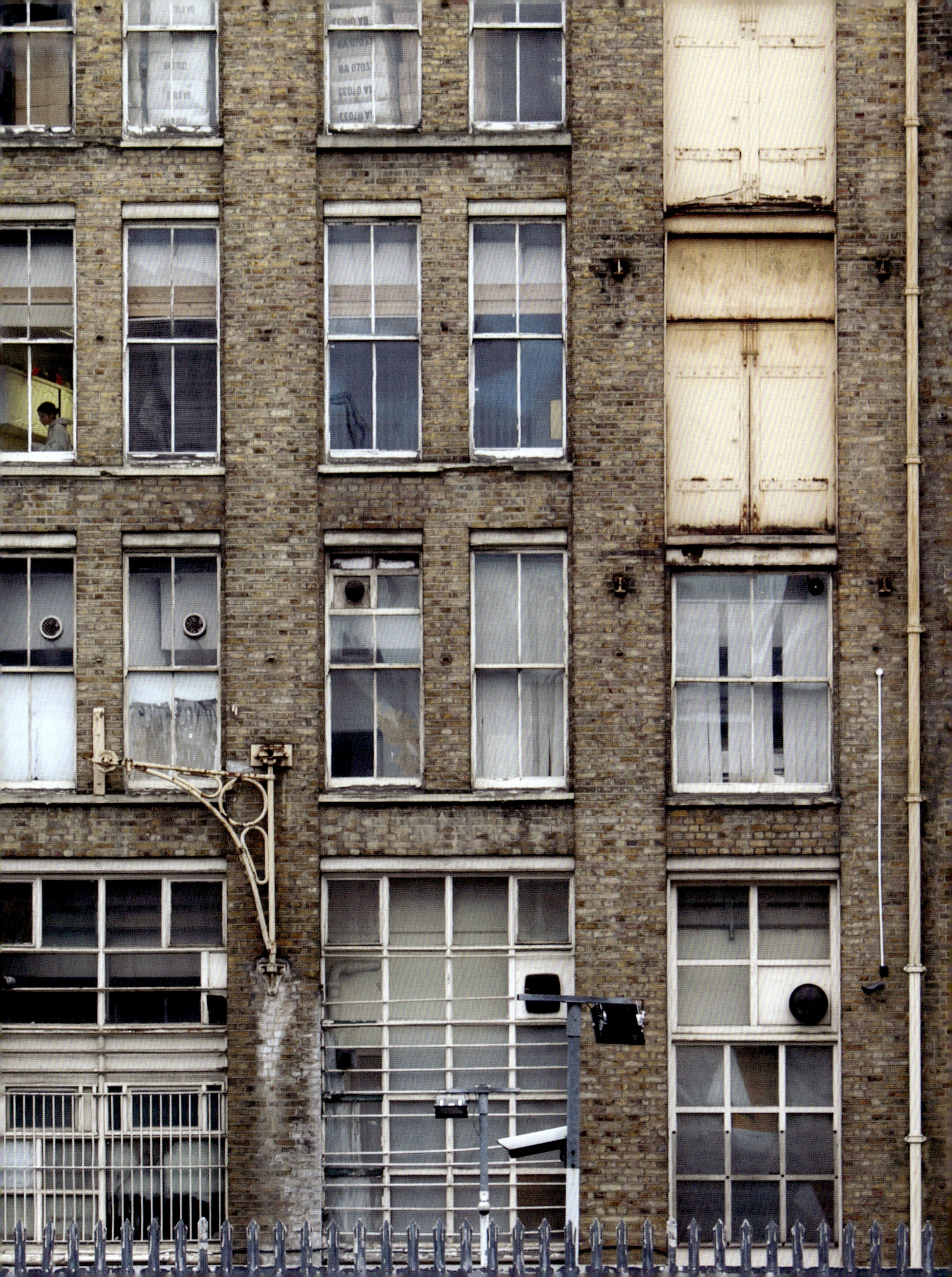

**Wingate House,
51 Warton Road, Stratford**

Abandoned since 2000, this former warehouse building in Stratford has become a regular haunt for urban explorers and sits in the shadow of the Queen Elizabeth Olympic Park. There are repeated calls from local residents for its demolition.

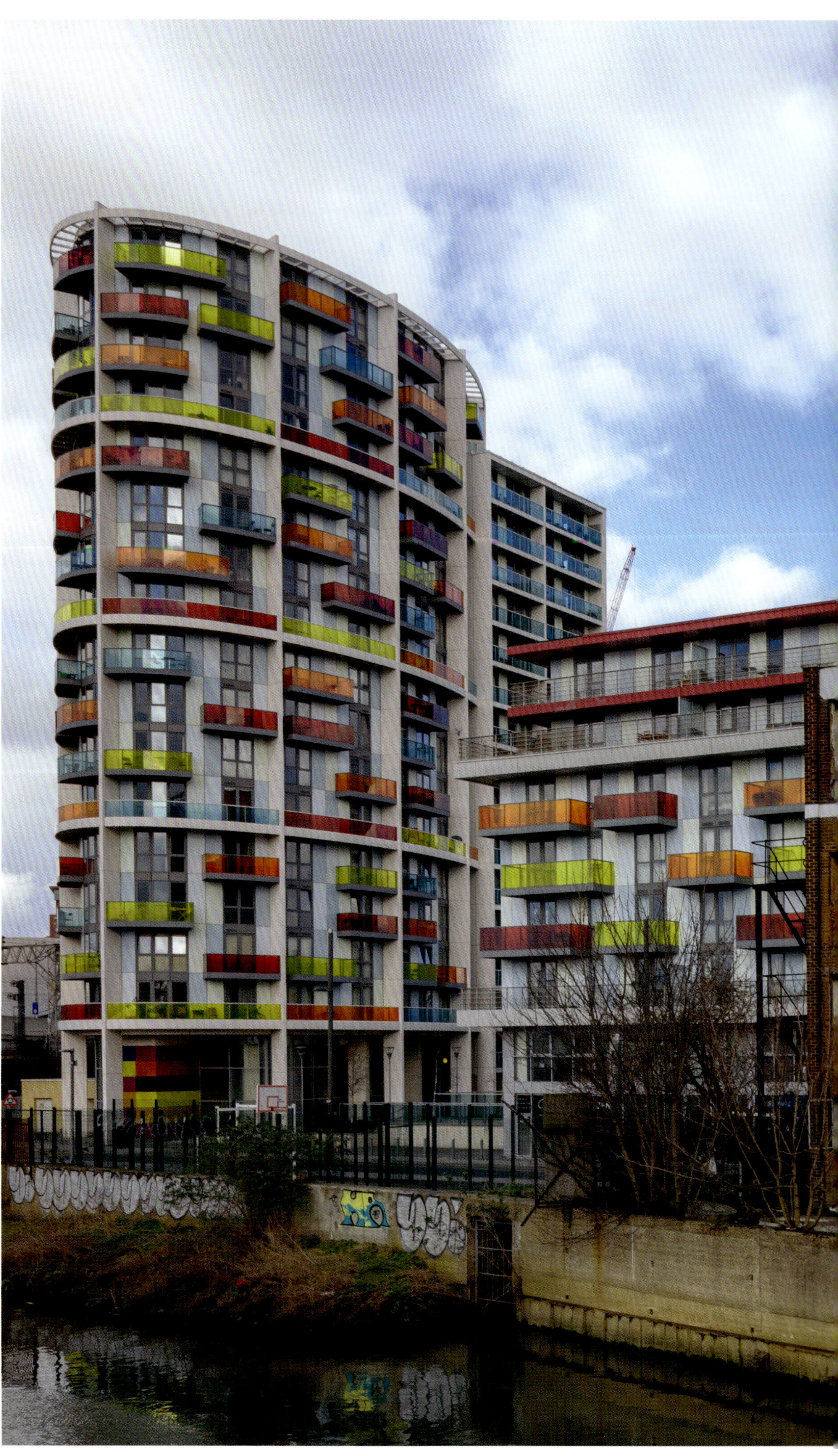

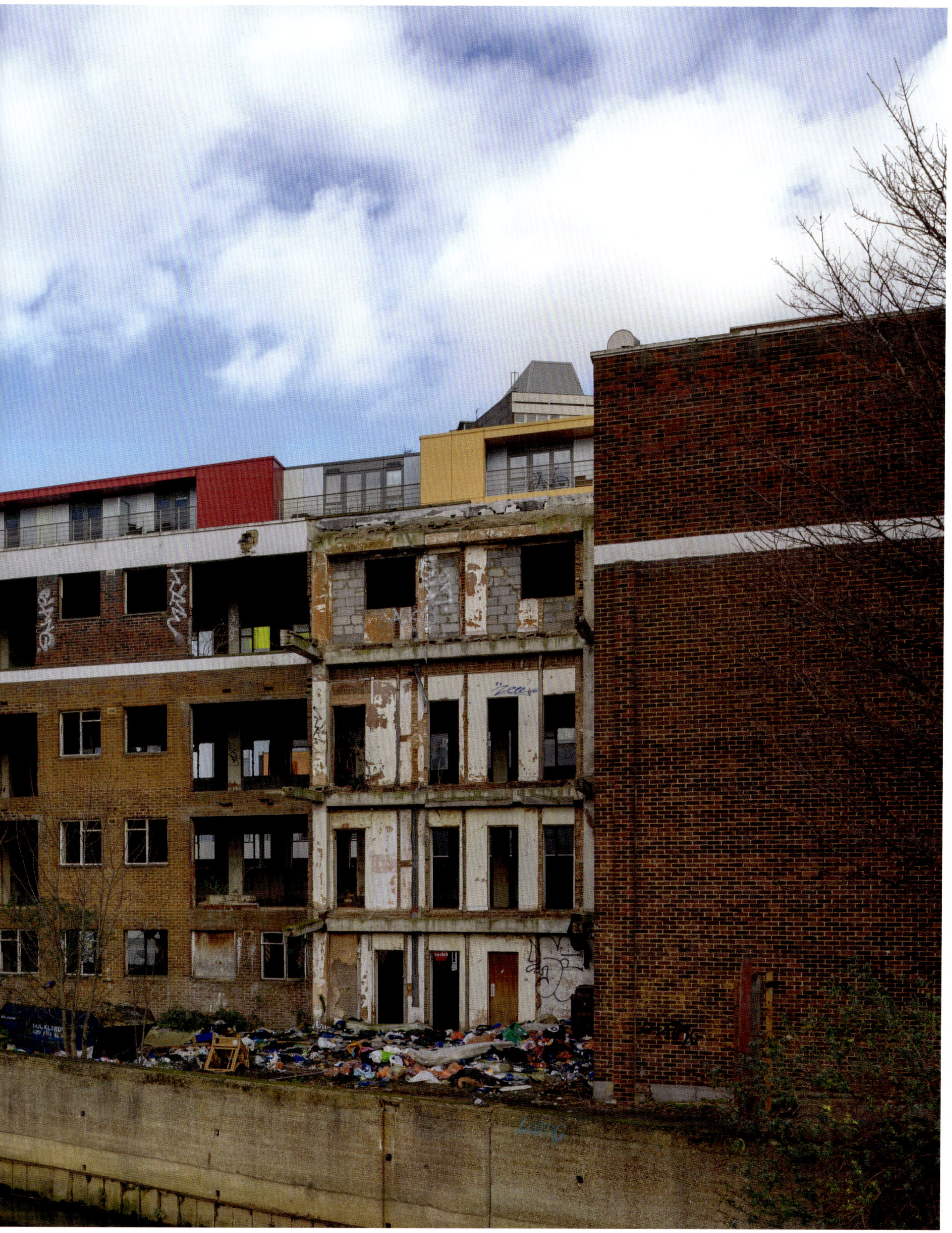

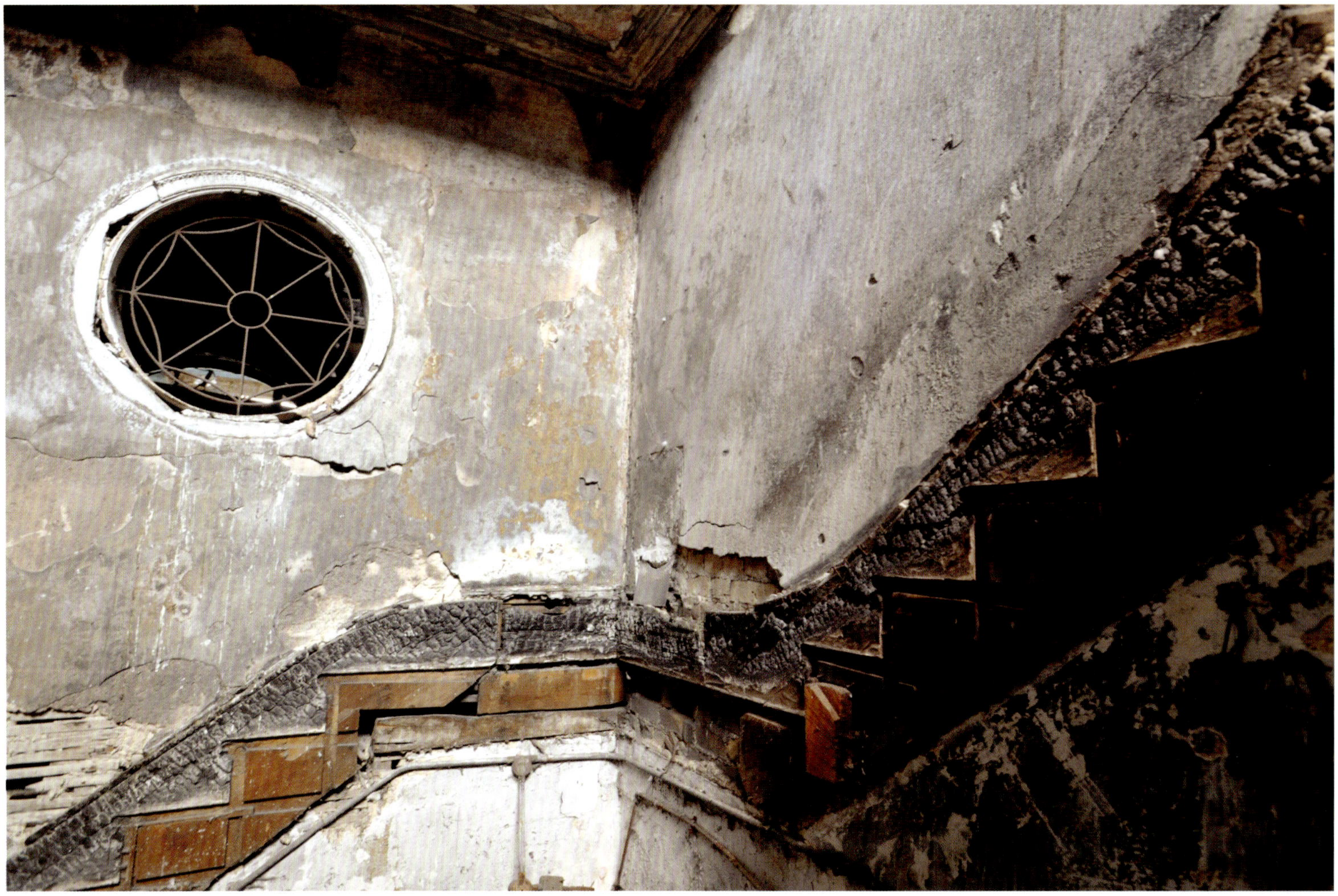

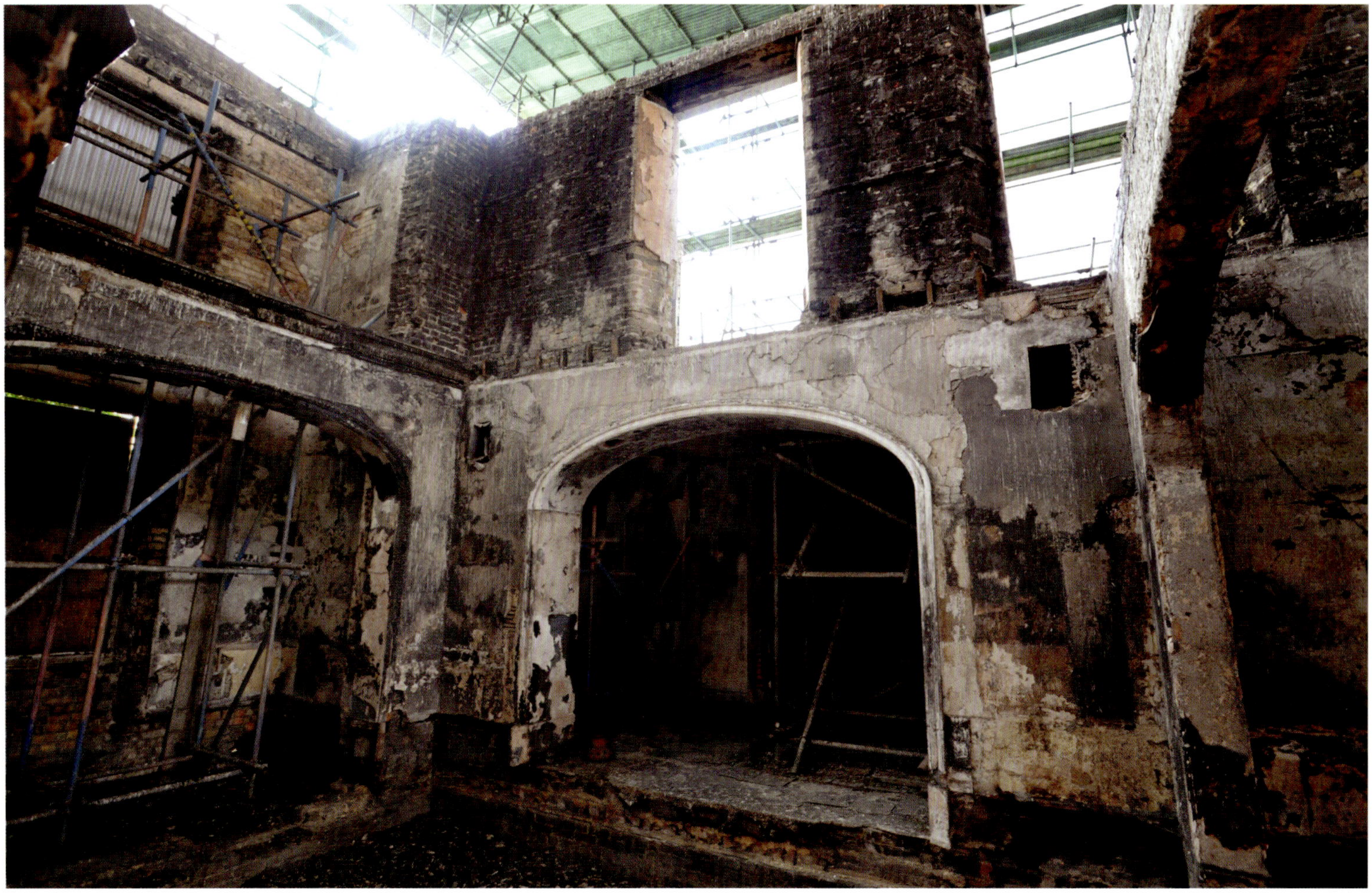

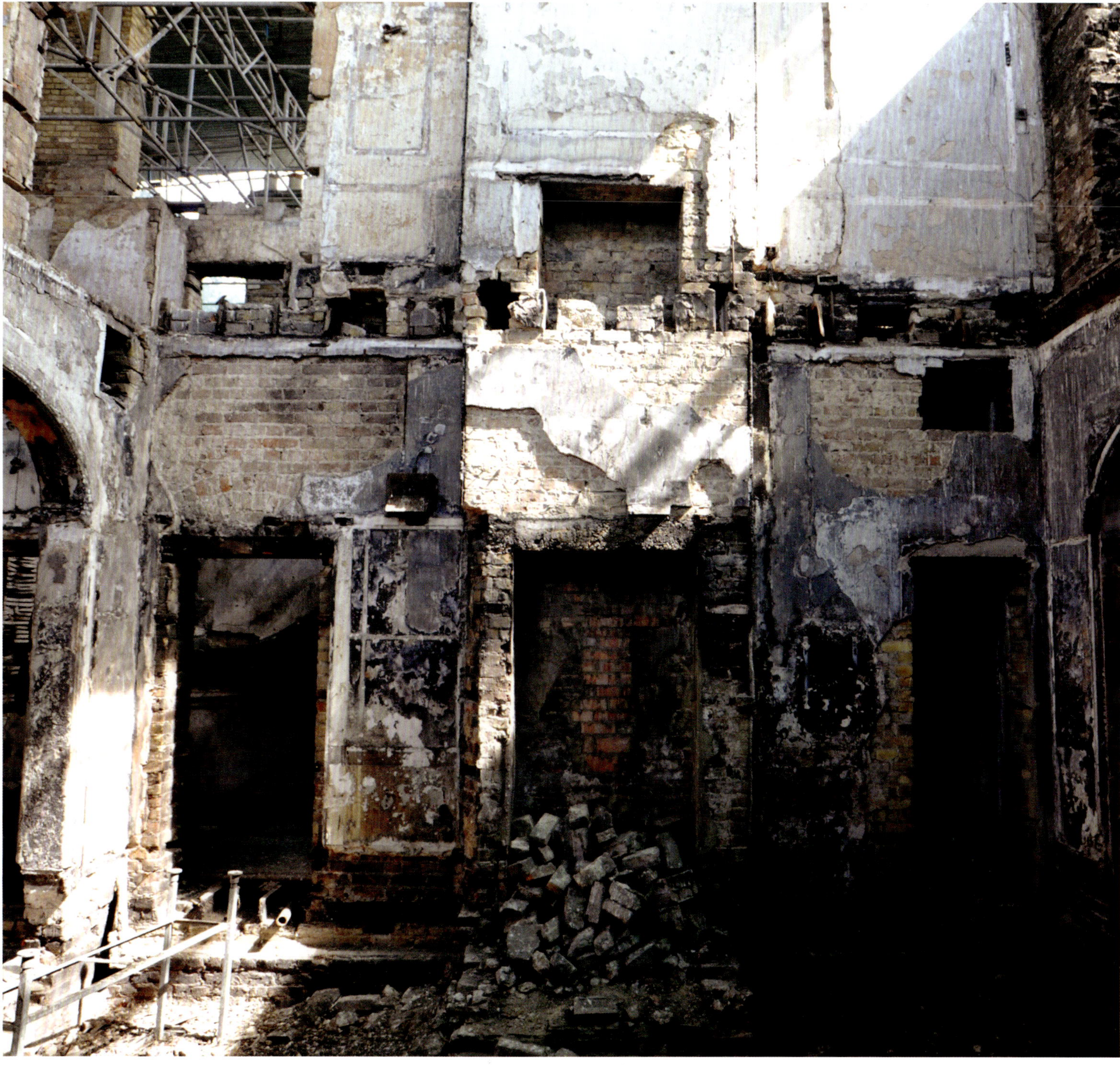

ALL PHOTOGRAPHS:

Dollis Hill House

Right on the edge of Gladstone Park, Dollis Hill House was built in 1825 by one of the most wealthy local families, the Finch family. By the late 19th century it was home to Lord Tweedmouth, who entertained many distinguished guests here, including the four-time Prime Minister William Ewart Gladstone.

After a prolonged battle by local residents to save the house, it was finally demolished in 2012 when funds from the Mayor of London were withdrawn. On the site today Brent Council have erected brickwork showing the floor plan of the building.

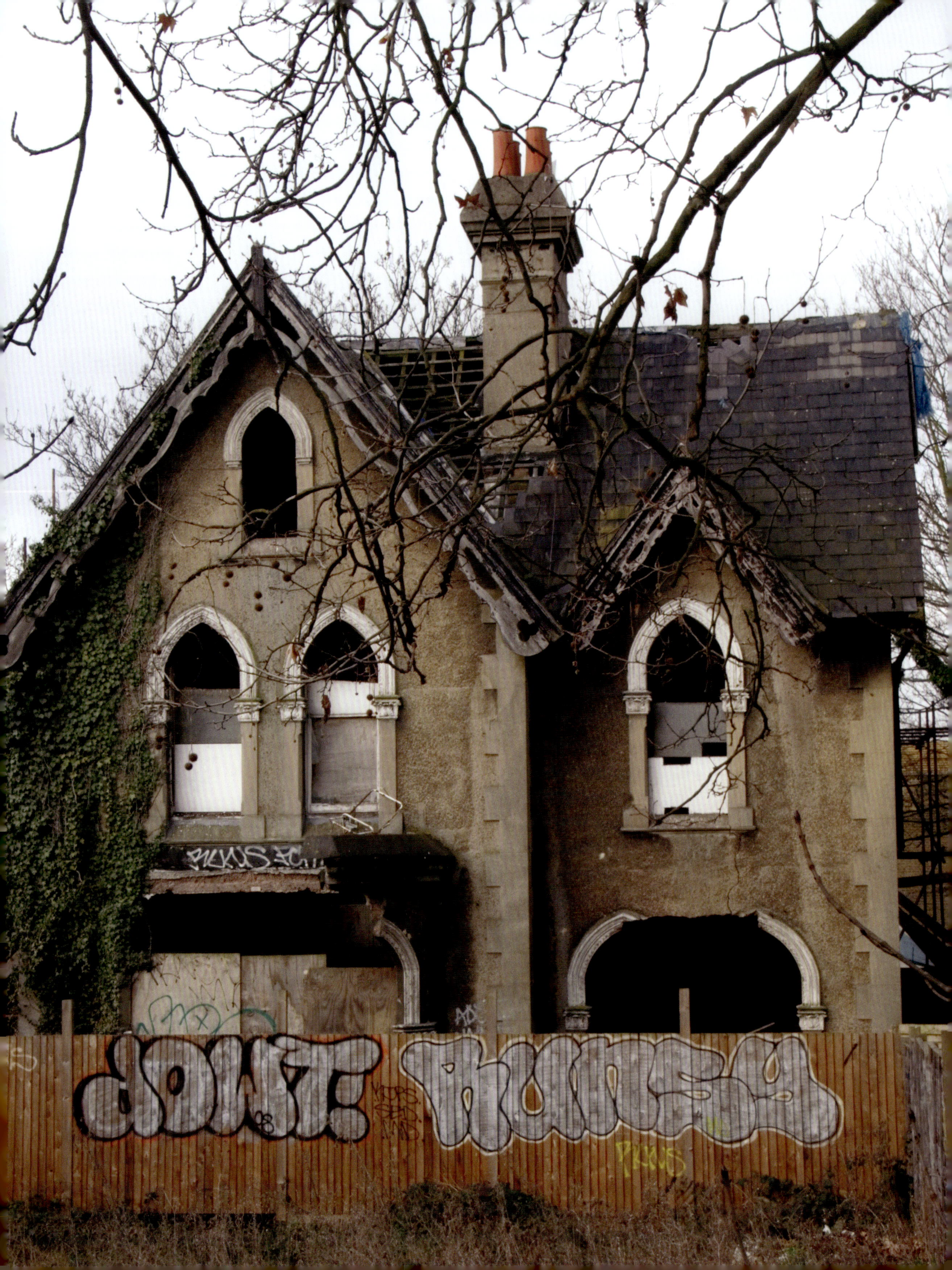

OPPOSITE:

Concrete House, Lordship Lane

What at first seems like a typical Victorian home deserves a closer look. Built in 1873, the former home is made entirely of concrete. It was constructed in 1873 by Charles Drake, founder of the Patent Concrete Building Company, and was given Grade II listed status in 1994. The house was acquired by Southwark Council in 2009 and was converted into five flats in 2013.

BELOW:

Enderby House, Greenwich

This house was owned by Samuel Enderby, a firm that pioneered Antarctic exploration and was the largest whaler and sealer in Britain in the mid-19th century. The decline in the whaling trade meant the company abandoned Enderby Wharf, but their legacy is remembered in Herman Melville's classic novel *Moby Dick*, which describes their crew and flagship. The building has recently been bought by Young's Brewery, who have planning permission to open a pub.

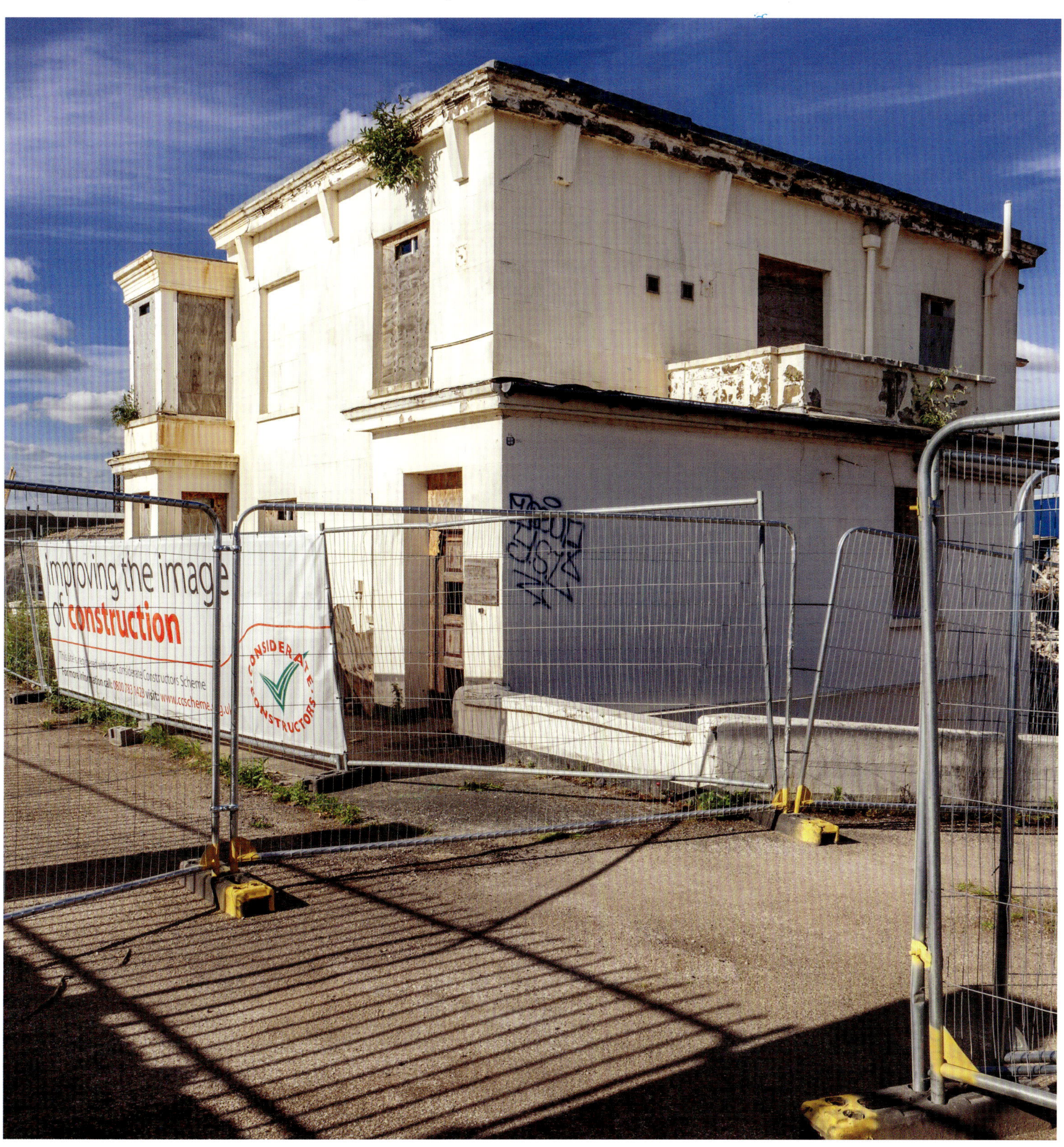

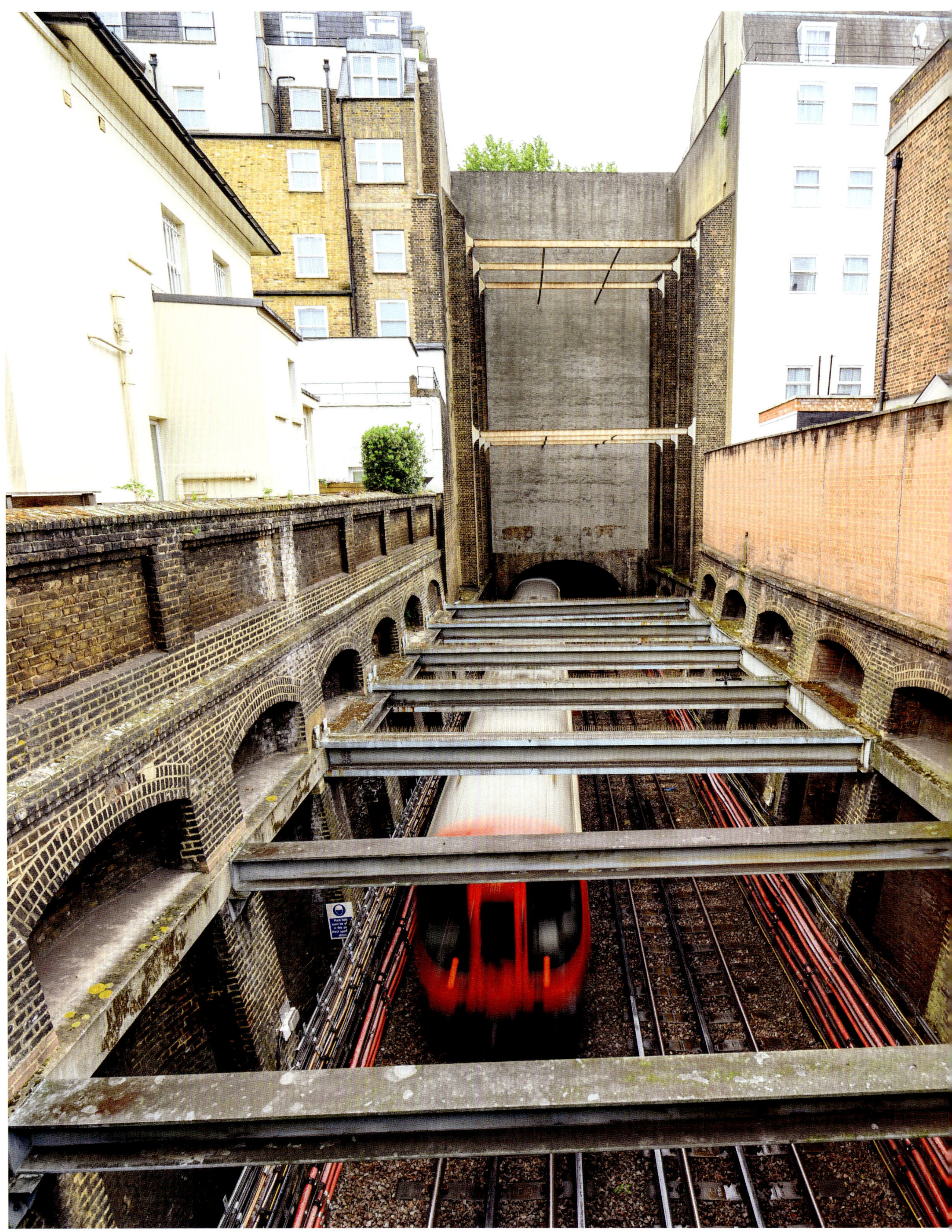

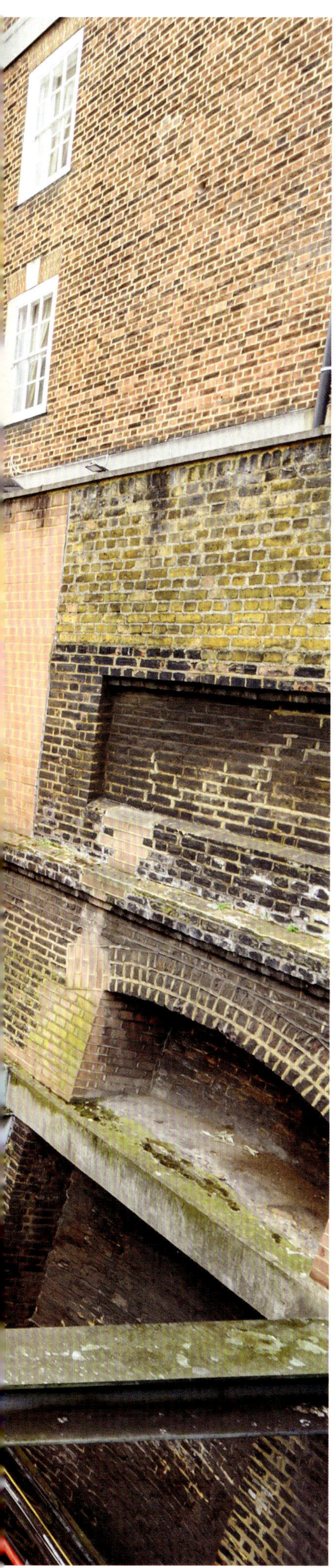

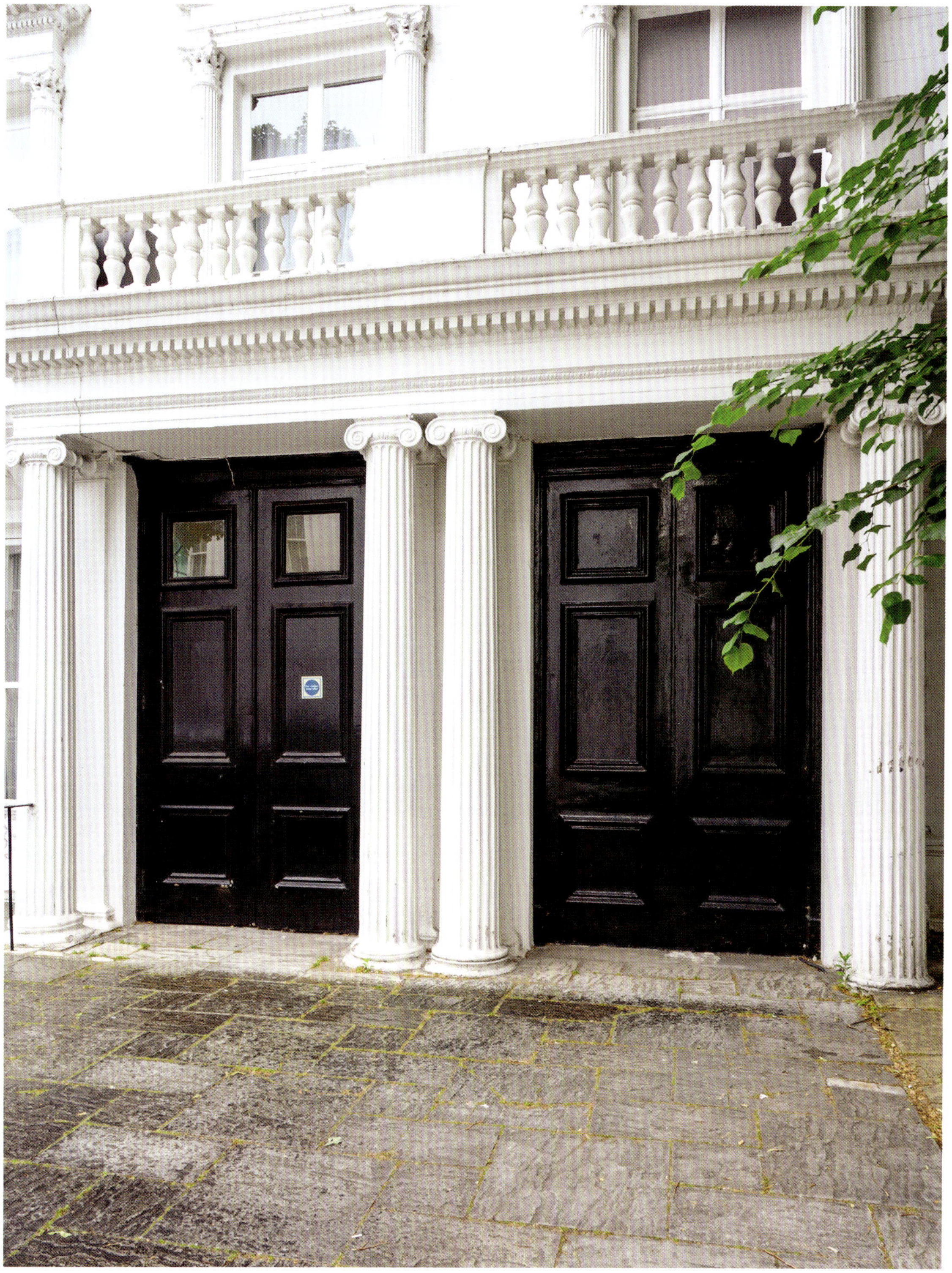

ALL PHOTOGRAPHS:
Leinster Gardens, Bayswater
One of London's many fun oddities, the so-called 'fake' houses at nos. 23 and 24 Leinster Gardens are just a façade. The rest of the terrace was built in the 1850s, but look a little closer and you'll find no door knockers or letter boxes at these houses.

The houses were demolished to make way for the railway line between Paddington and Bayswater, operational from 1868. Today they are merely false fronts of a 1.5m (5ft) thick wall that hides the tracks behind!

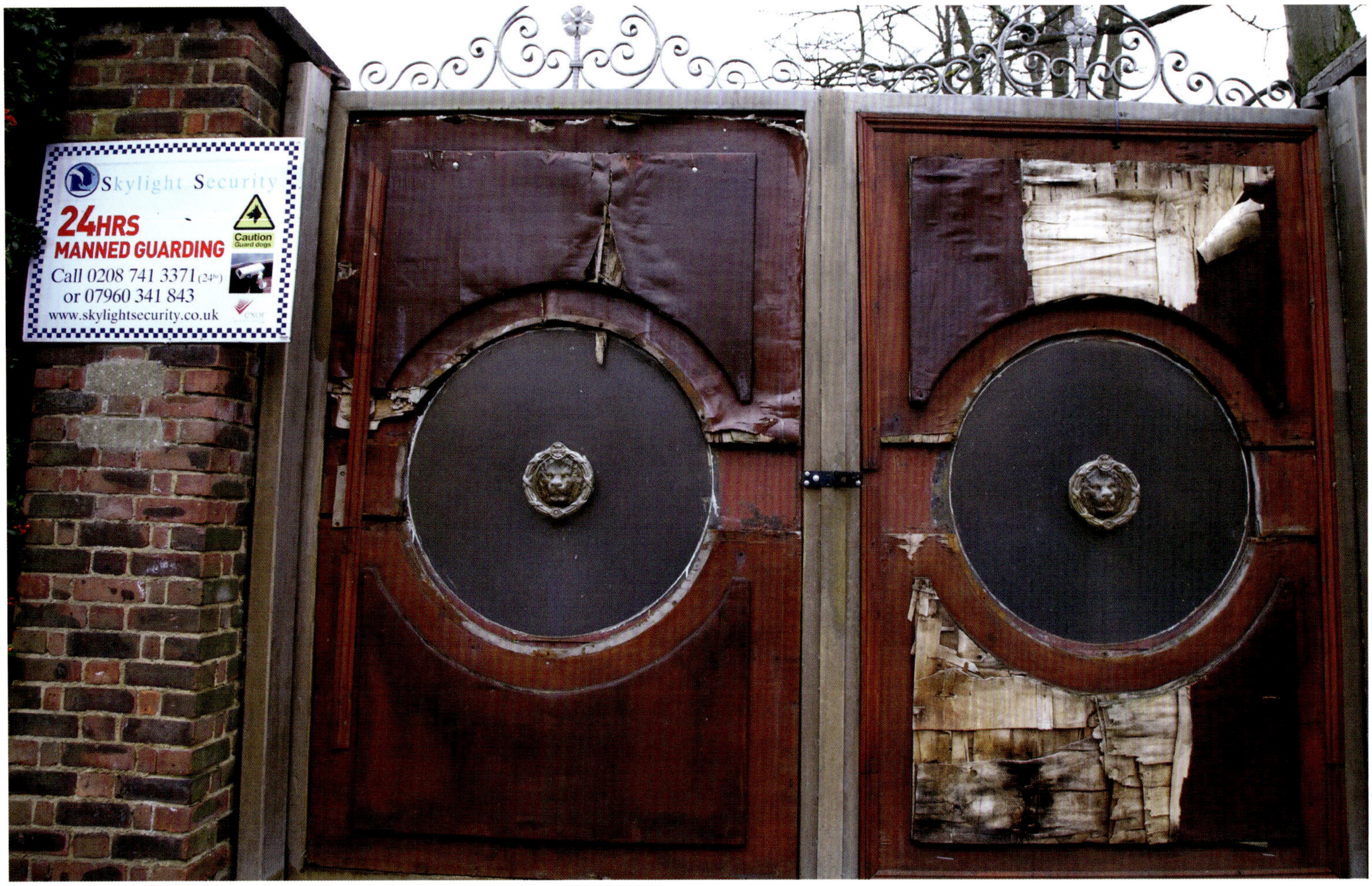
Skylight Security
24HRS
MANNED GUARDING
Caution
Guard dogs
Call 0208 741 3371 (24hr)
or 07960 341 843
www.skylightsecurity.co.uk

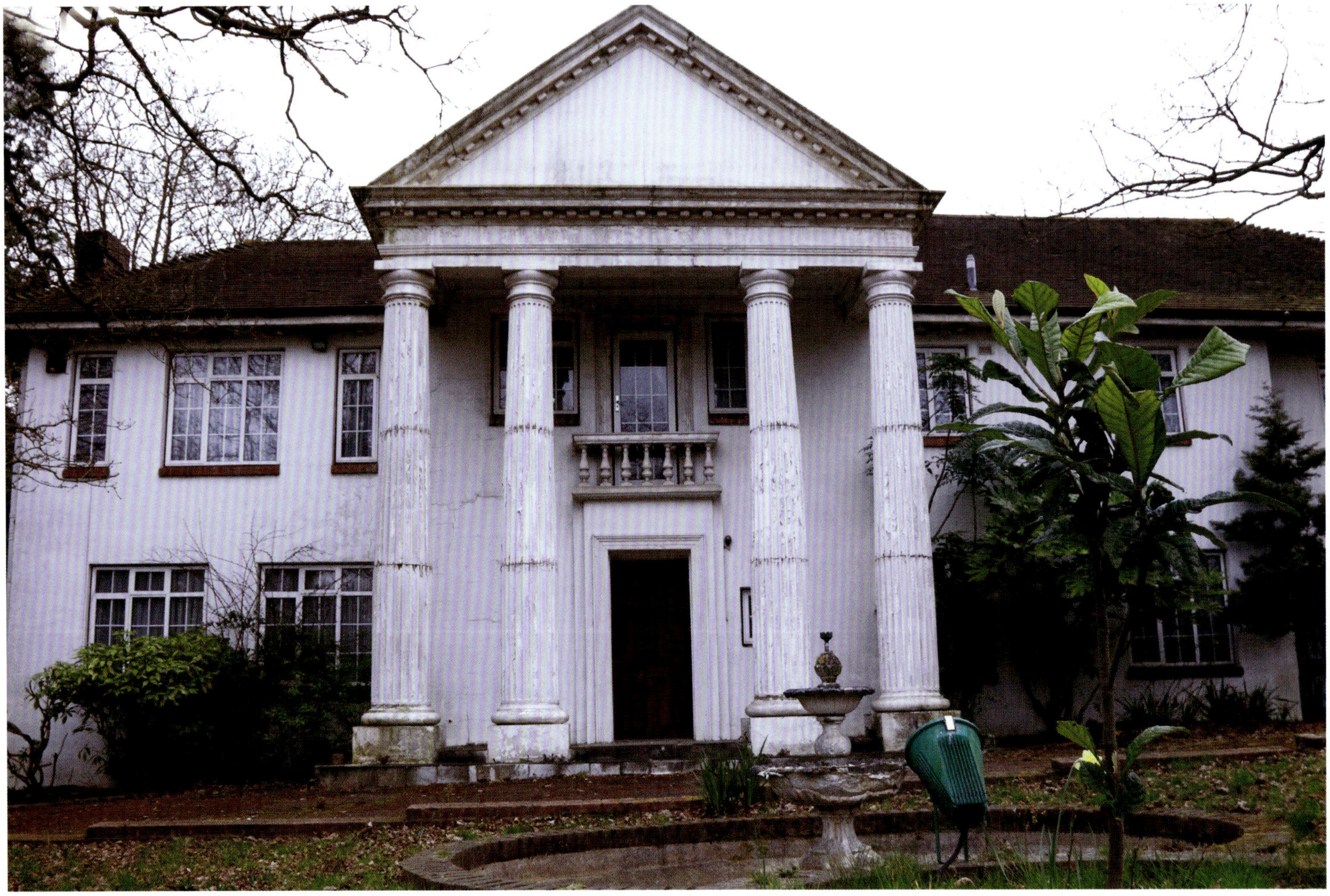

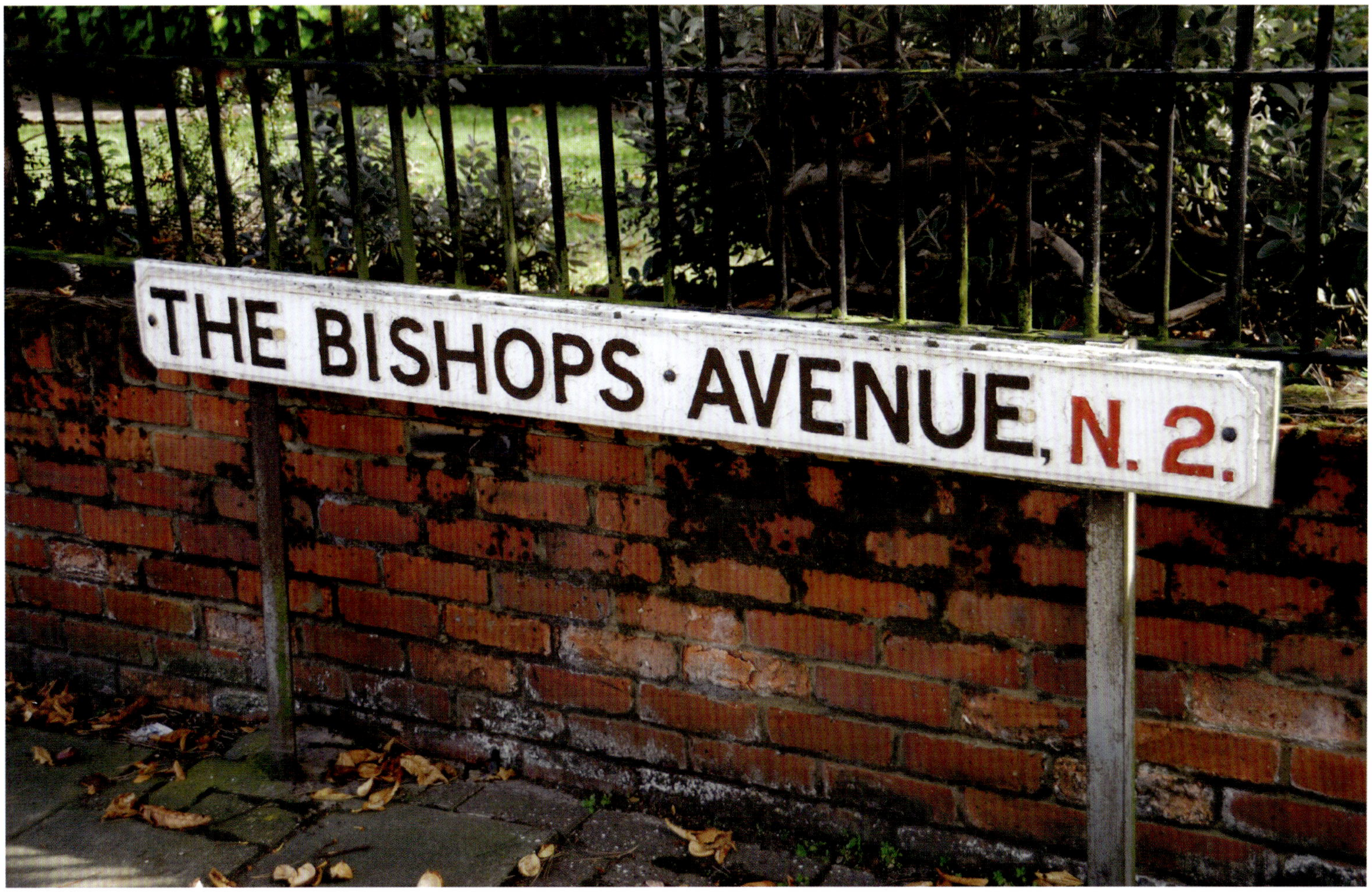

ALL PHOTOGRAPHS:

The Bishops Avenue, East Finchley

Known as 'Billionaires' Row', the houses along this North London street were bought by, among others, the Saudi Royal family in the 1990s. Newspaper investigations revealed in 2014 that 16 of the properties (worth an estimated £350 million) are derelict and have not been lived in for several decades. The homes have since been sold and have been left to return to nature, damp and decay taking over.

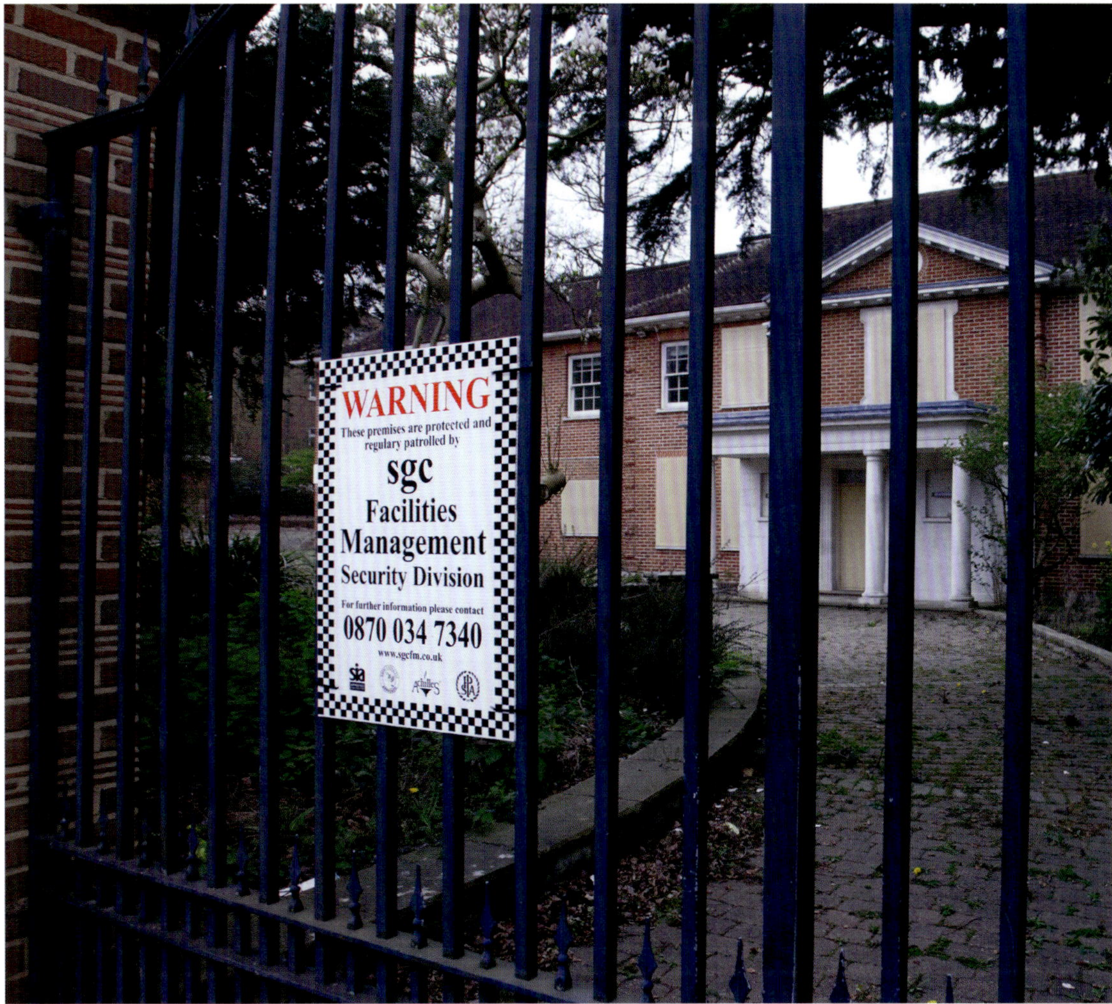

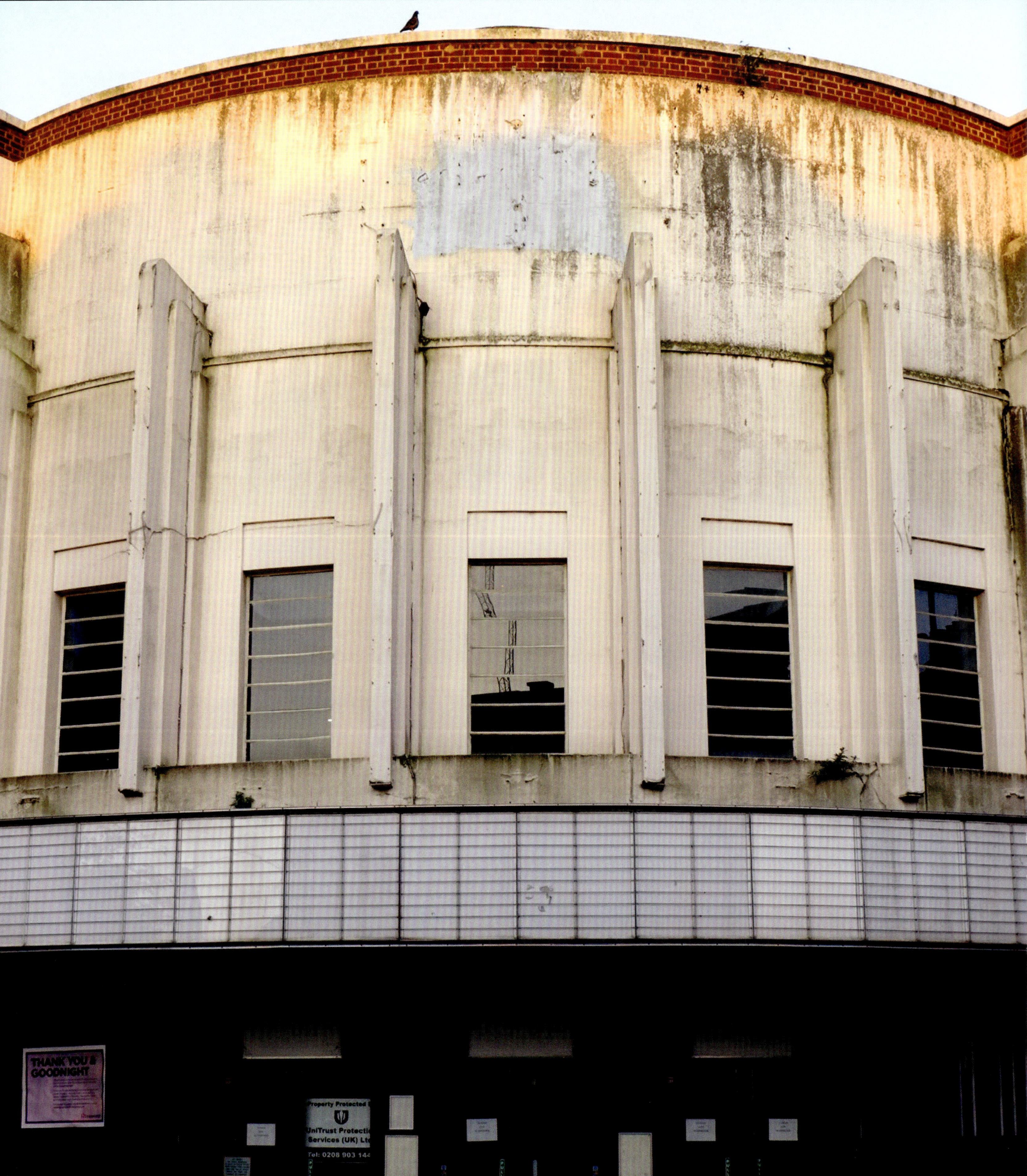
THANK YOU &
GOODNIGHT
Property Protected

Sport and Leisure

London has never been short of entertainment venues. The first theatrical experiences were religious – priests performing biblical stories in the open air. Later, London was a hub for theatres, bawdy places where people congregated for the overall experience as much as what was performed on stage.

This chapter explores more contemporary leisure spaces, mainly built in the 20th century. In the early 1900s cinema was at its height of popularity and the venues that housed them were opulent spaces that reflected their prestige. As their glamour waned with the rise of television, their use may have changed, but their immediately recognisable Art Deco facades can be spotted all over the city. Thankfully, the majority of them have been protected in some way.

In a densely populated city we all need a bit of space to stretch and move, and later in the chapter we also see the fate of some open spaces in London. These are the sporting venues that have been underfunded and under-appreciated and whose future today is sadly uncertain.

OPPOSITE:
Cineworld, Hammersmith
On the corner plot at 207 King Street stood this Art Deco cinema, designed by William R. Glen, the in-house architect for Associated British Cinemas. It was known as the Regal Cinema and opened in 1936. The cinema later became a Cineworld and eventually closed in 2016. It was demolished in March 2017.

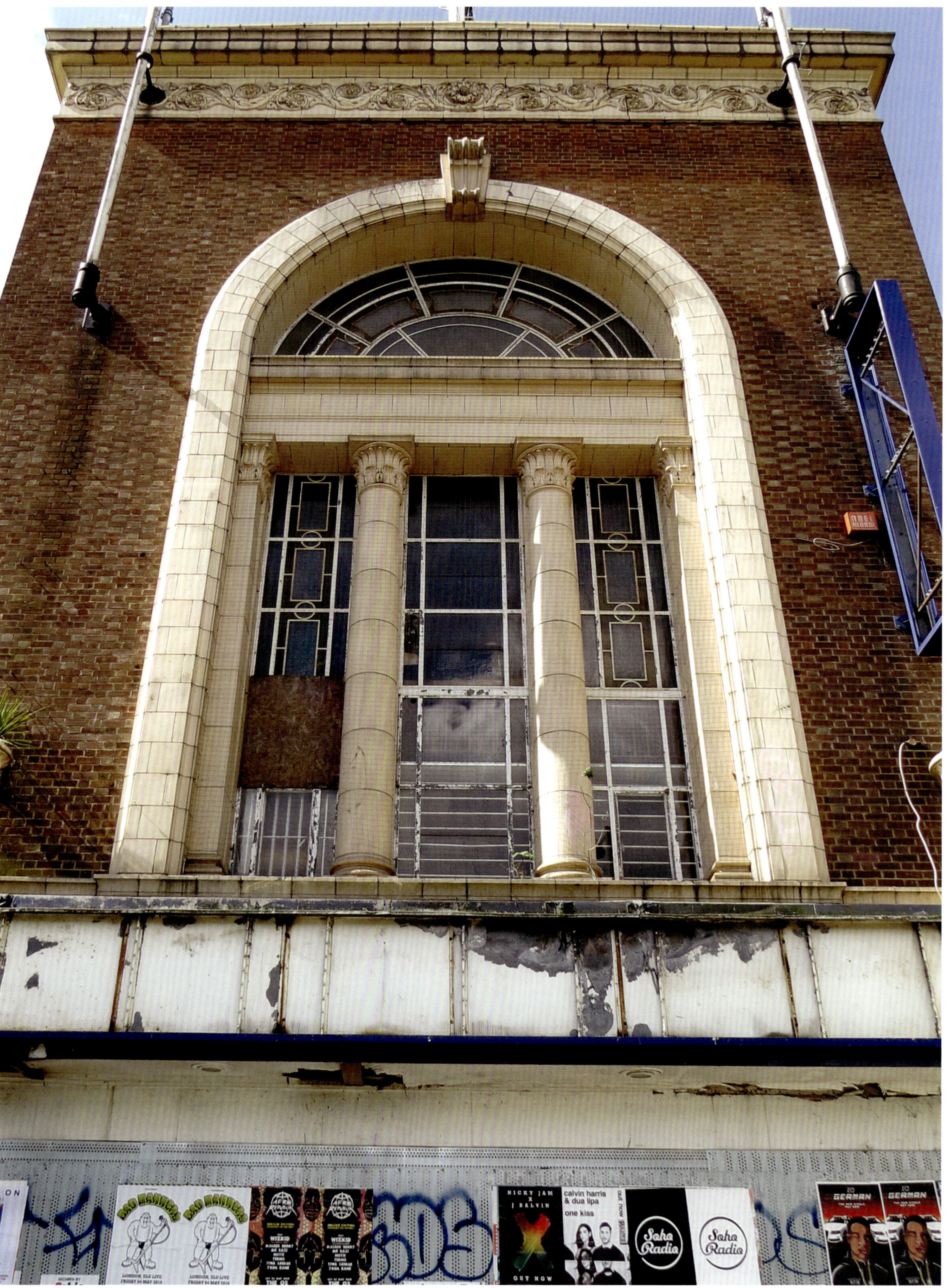
BAD MANNERS
LONDON, O2 LIVE
WIZKID
NICKY JAM
X
J BALVIN
OUT NOW
calvin harris
& dua lipa
one kiss
out now
Soho Radio
GERMAN

OPPOSITE:

Savoy Cinema, Burnt Oak

Designed by George Cole, the building in Edgware was one of many cinemas to be built in the 1930s. Following the rise of television and the number of larger cinemas, the site became a bingo hall in 1961. Although it is now closed, the building's elegant design and internal modern fittings secured Grade II listed status from Historic England.

BELOW:

Regal Cinema, Highams Park

Originally Highams Park Electric Theatre, the cinema first opened in 1911. Designed by W.A. Lewis, the building is locally listed thanks to its Art Deco features, such as the brick detailing and slim, vertical windows. Although it closed as a cinema in the 1970s, it is currently part of a regeneration project in which the integrity of the original design is being preserved.

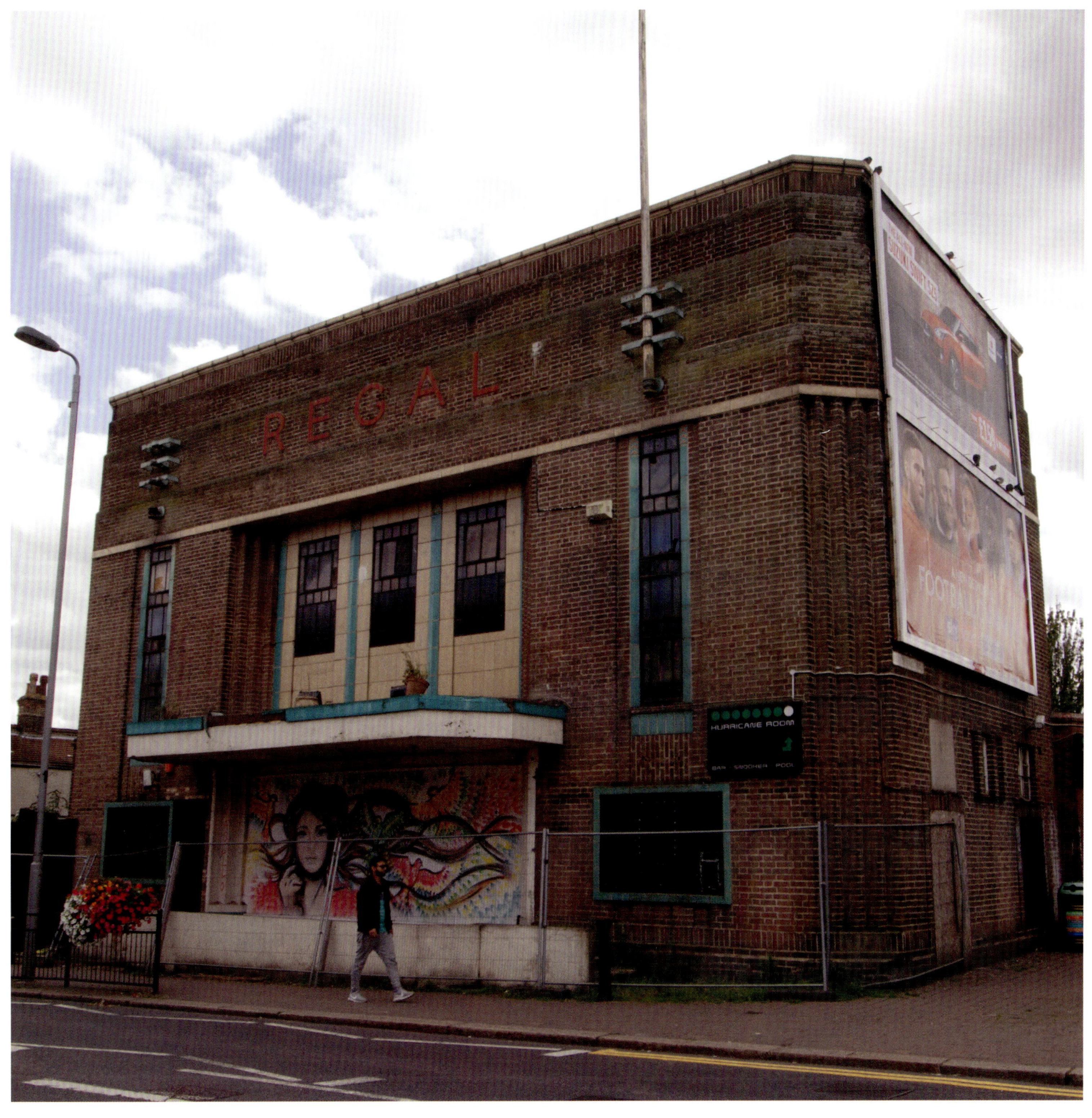

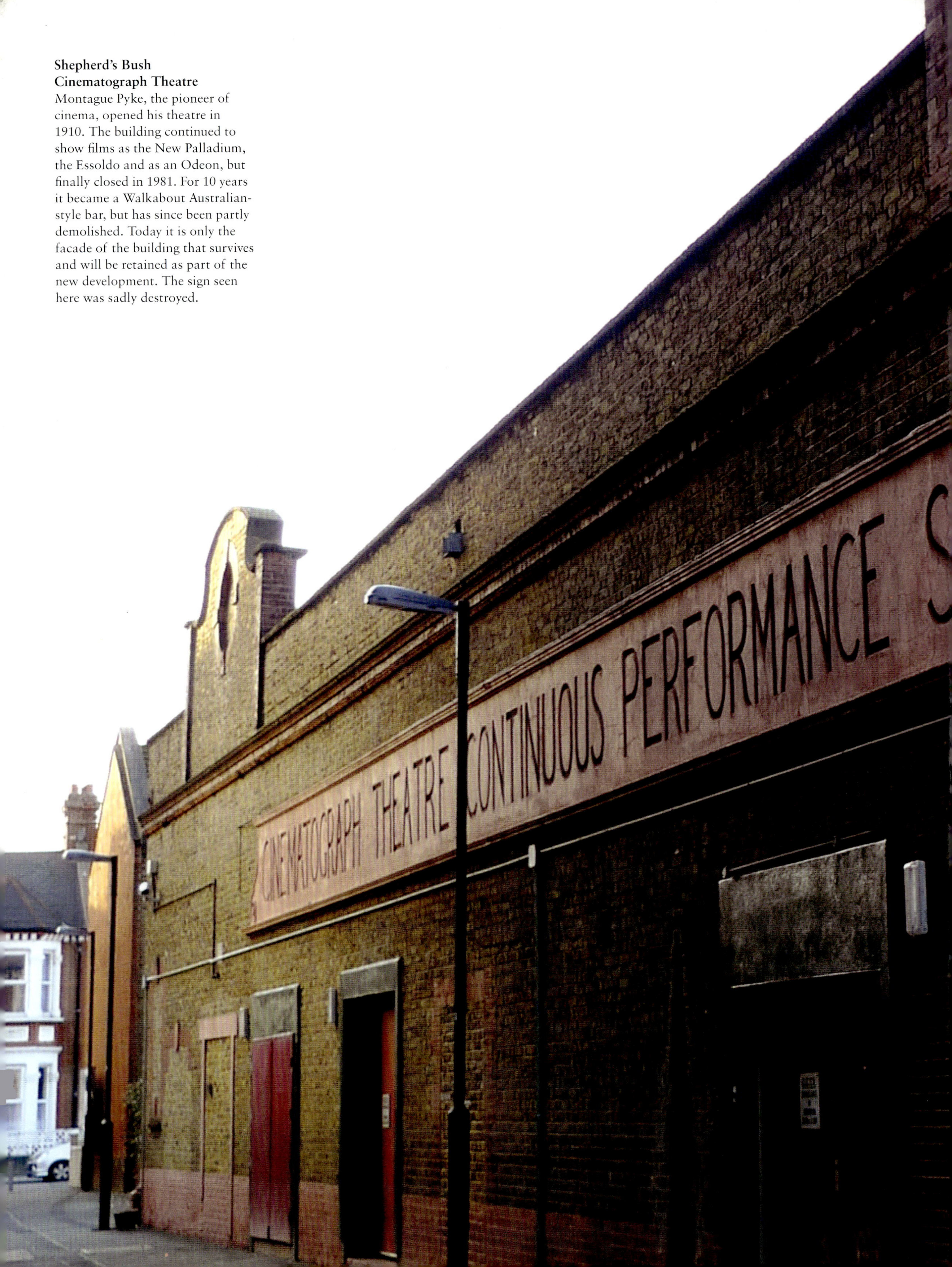

Shepherd's Bush Cinematograph Theatre
Montague Pyke, the pioneer of cinema, opened his theatre in 1910. The building continued to show films as the New Palladium, the Essoldo and as an Odeon, but finally closed in 1981. For 10 years it became a Walkabout Australian-style bar, but has since been partly demolished. Today it is only the facade of the building that survives and will be retained as part of the new development. The sign seen here was sadly destroyed.

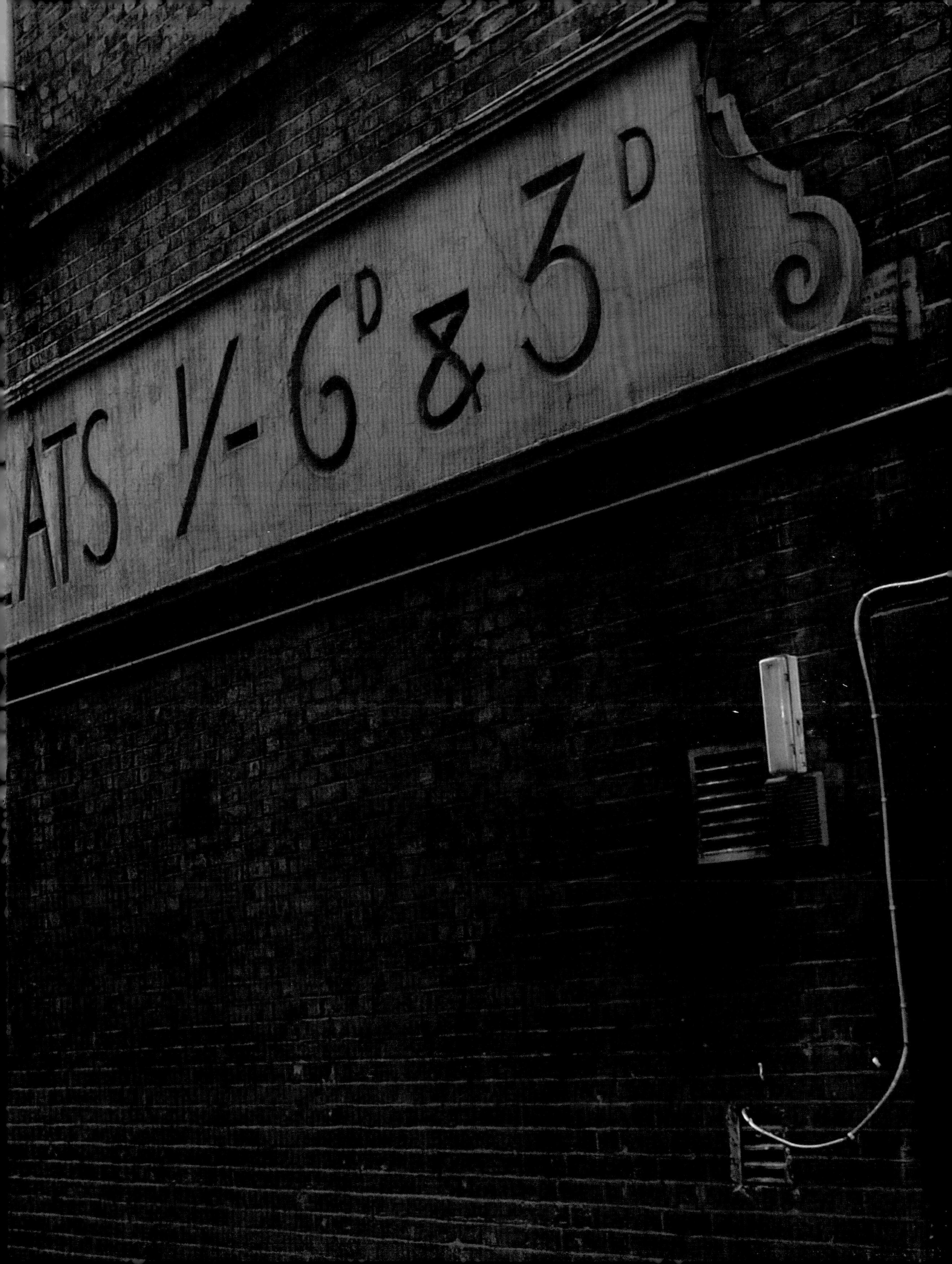
ATS 1/- 6D & 3D

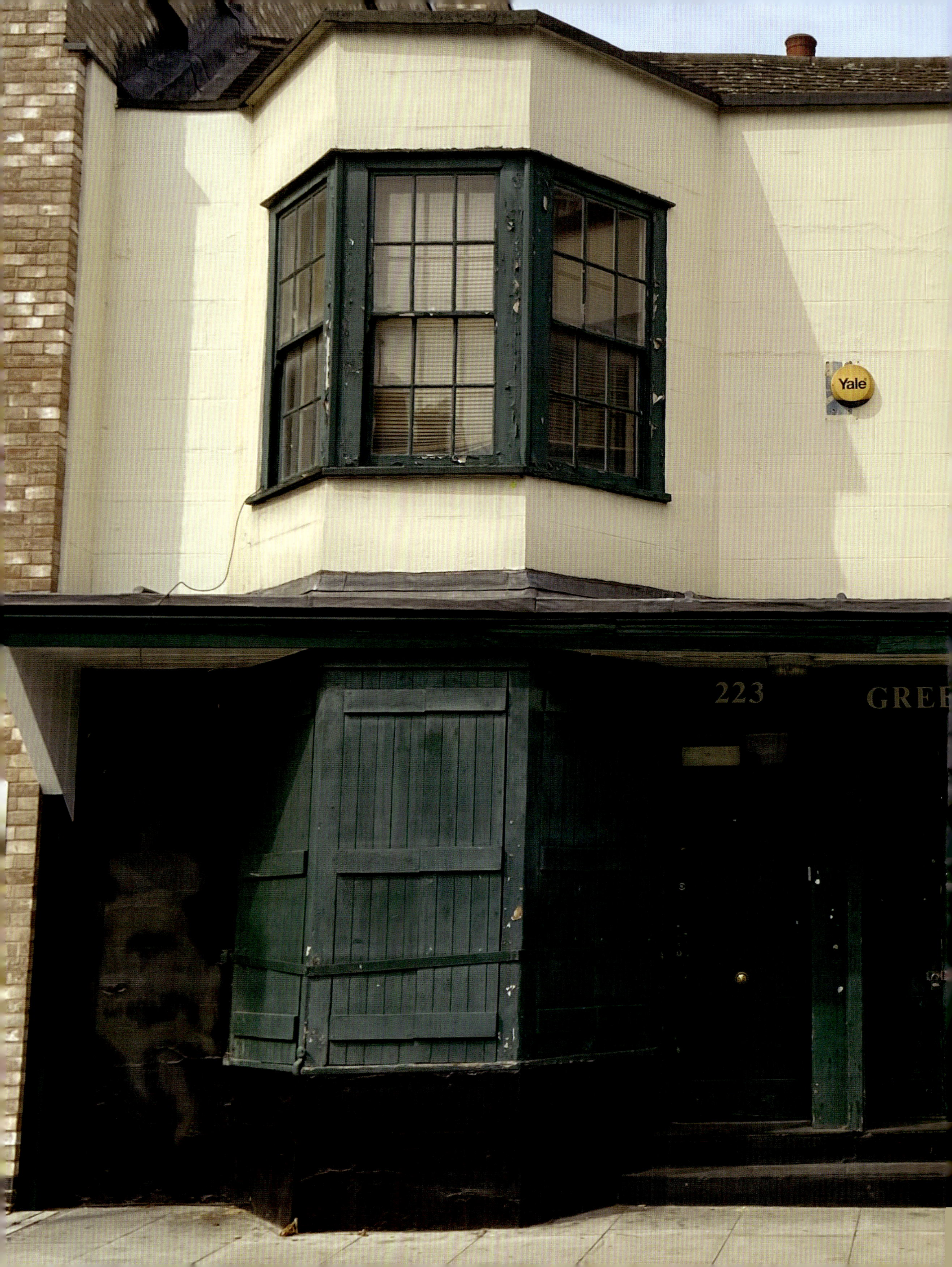
Yale
223

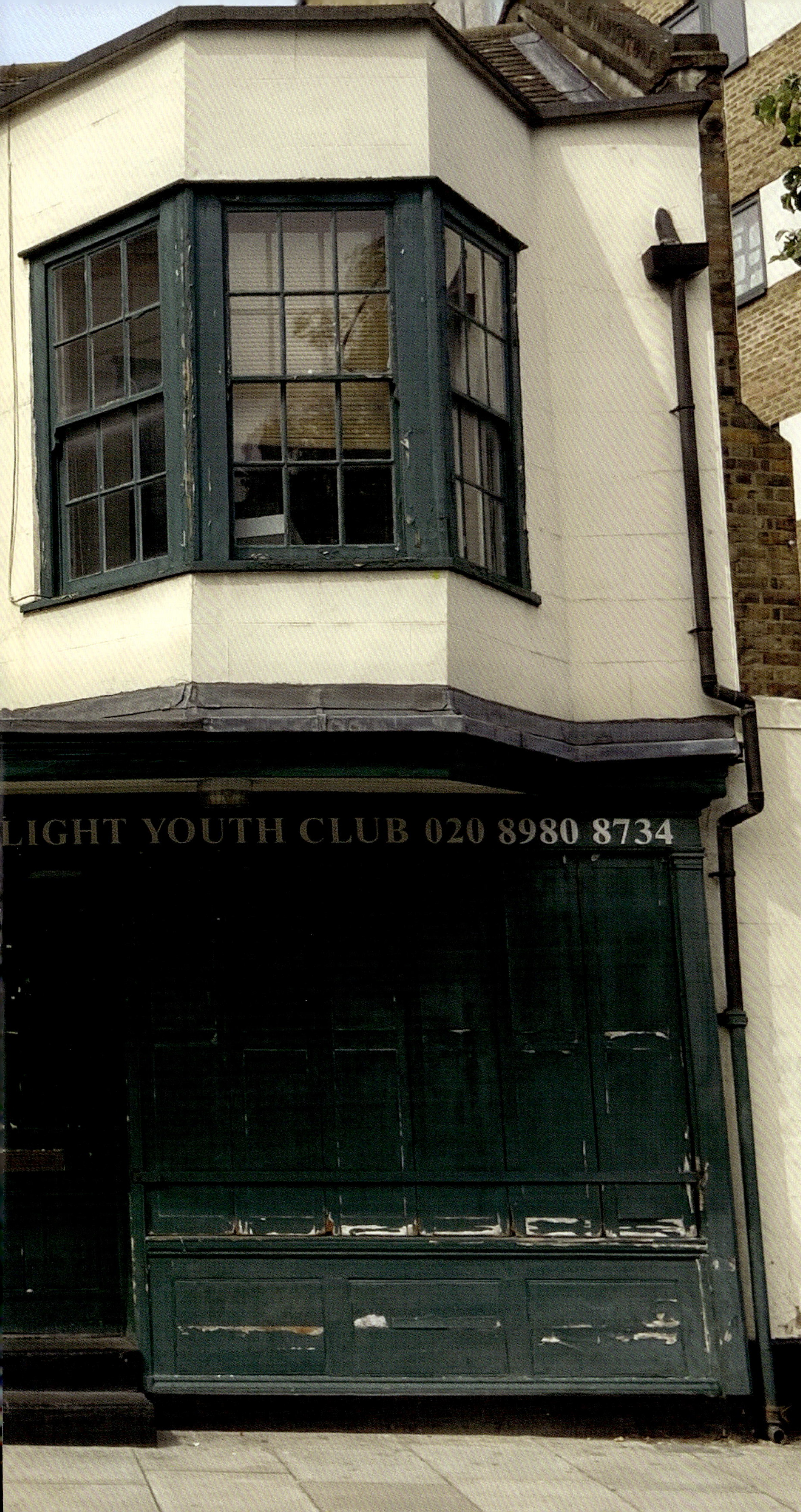

Greenlight Youth Club, Bow
Along a busy stretch of Bow Road is an incredible survivor – a Grade II listed shop. Strictly speaking, the ground-floor shop front is actually a 19th century addition, but the rest of the fabric of no. 223 dates from the late 17th century. It has functioned as a grocers and sweetshop, and today is still listed as the premises for Greenlight Youth Club, a registered charity.

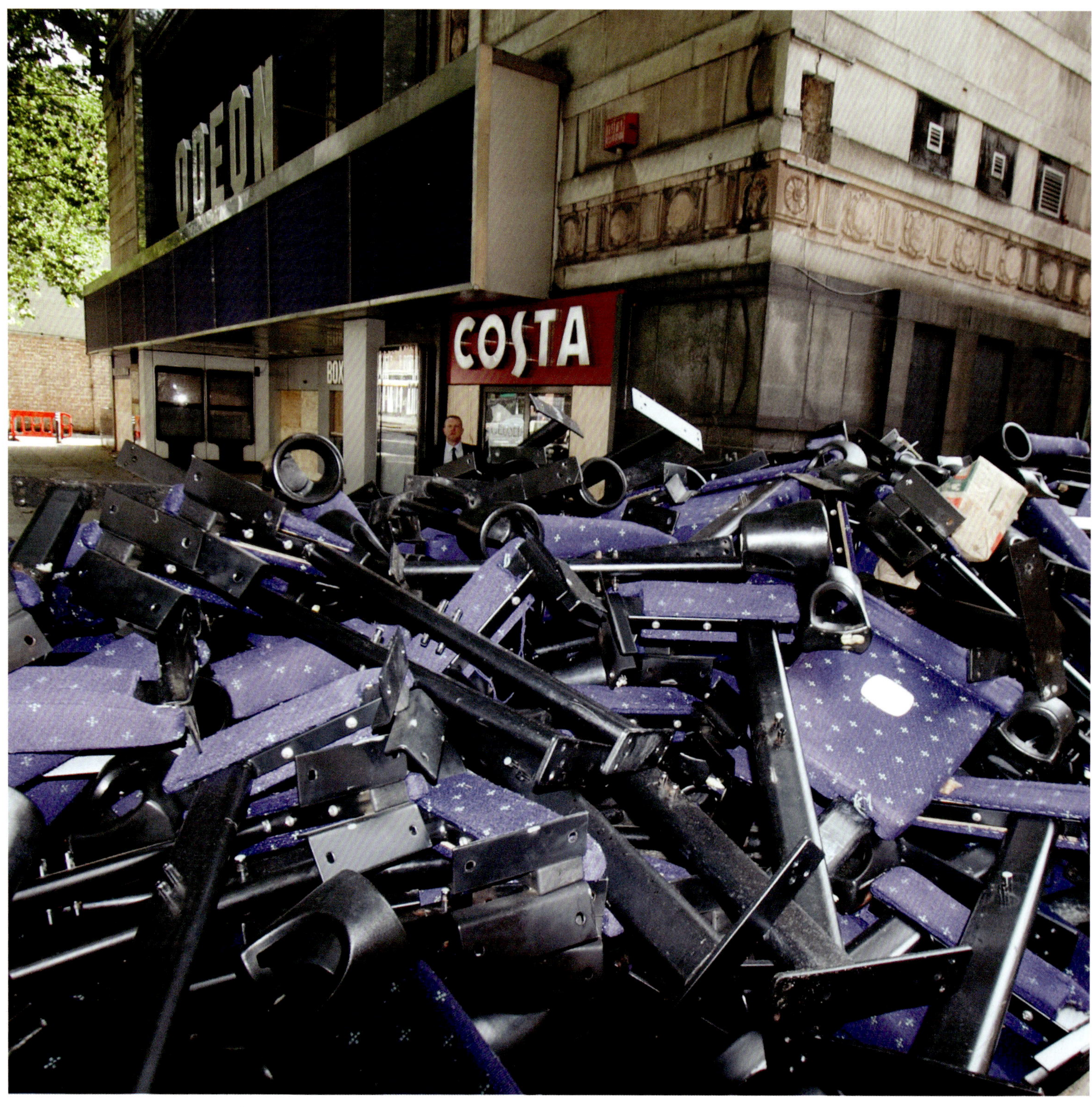

PREVIOUS PAGES AND ALL PHOTOGRAPHS ON THESE PAGES:

Kensington Odeon

This huge cinema opened as 'Kensington Kinema' in 1926, with a capacity for almost 3,000 people. It was one of the earliest buildings in the UK to be constructed with a steel frame and the Neo-Classical frontage has elaborate details around the recessed entrance. Odeon Theatres Ltd took over the site in 1944 and the building underwent a total refurbishment in 1998, retaining the original facade.

Since the early 2000s there has been fierce debate over the site and the fate of the building, exacerbated by the discovery of a damaged but ornate 1920s interior during the demolition process in 2017. The site is currently set to become private apartments.

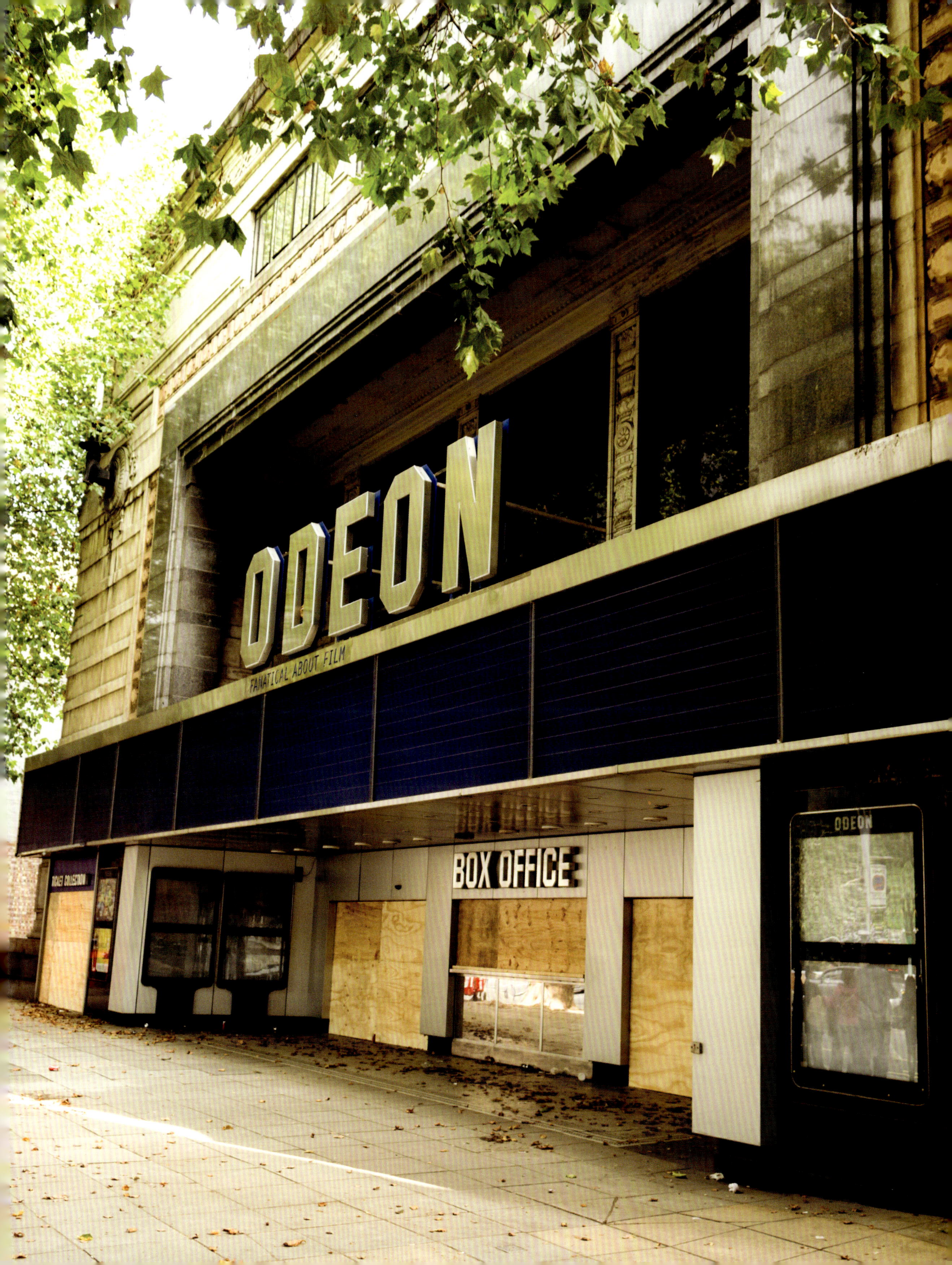
ODEON
FANATICAL ABOUT FILM
BOX OFFICE
ODEON

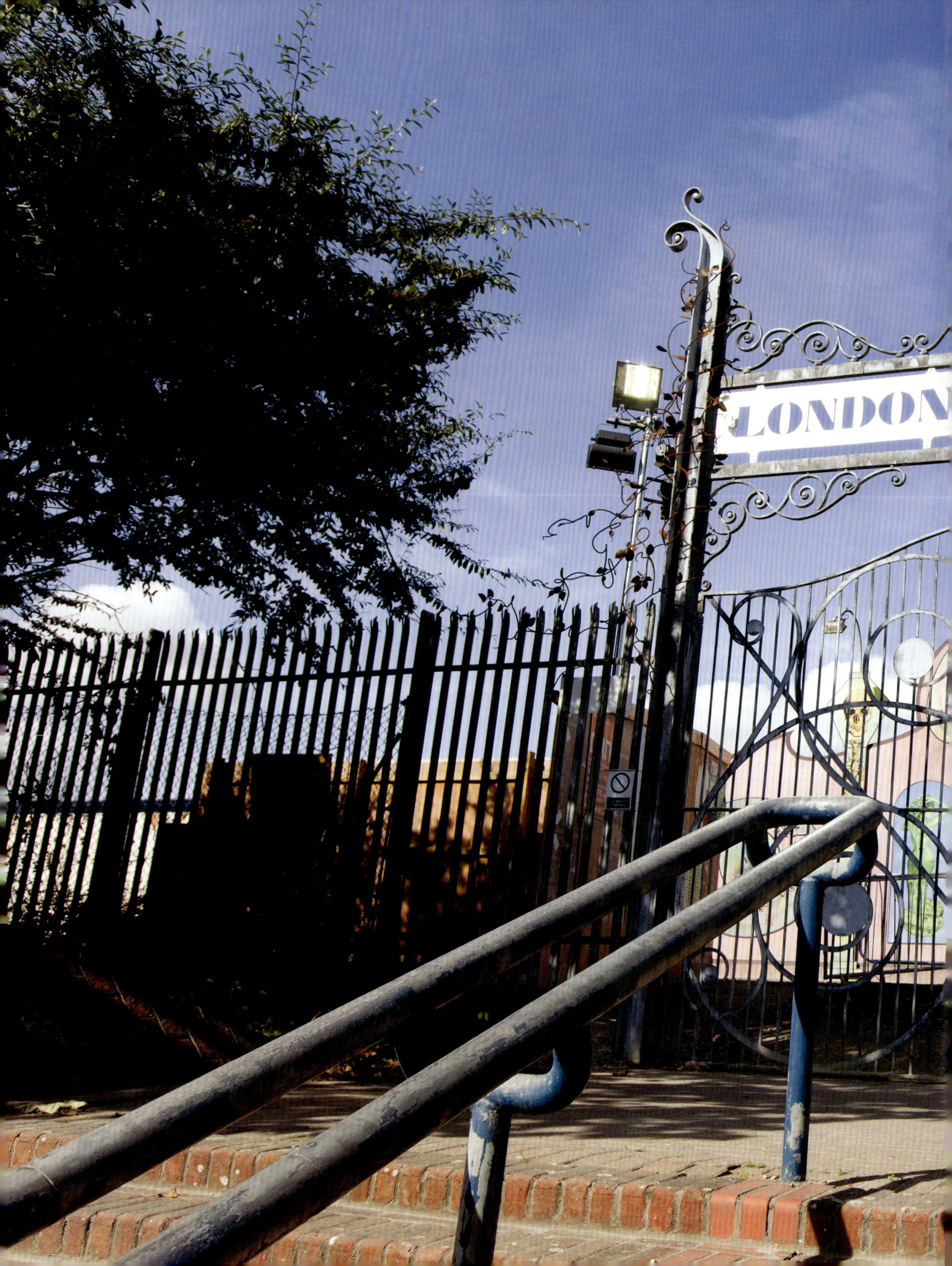
LONDON

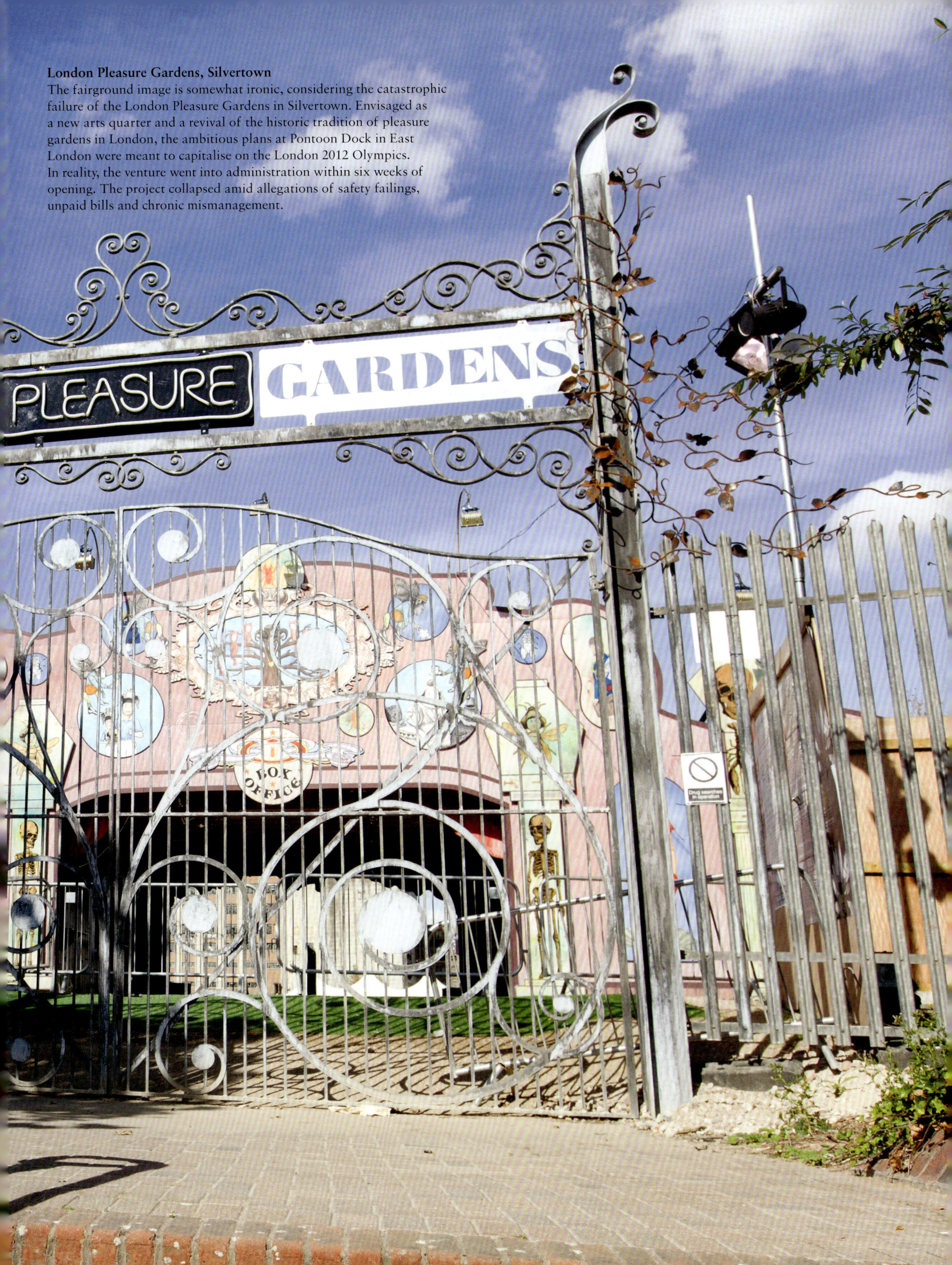

London Pleasure Gardens, Silvertown
The fairground image is somewhat ironic, considering the catastrophic failure of the London Pleasure Gardens in Silvertown. Envisaged as a new arts quarter and a revival of the historic tradition of pleasure gardens in London, the ambitious plans at Pontoon Dock in East London were meant to capitalise on the London 2012 Olympics. In reality, the venture went into administration within six weeks of opening. The project collapsed amid allegations of safety failings, unpaid bills and chronic mismanagement.

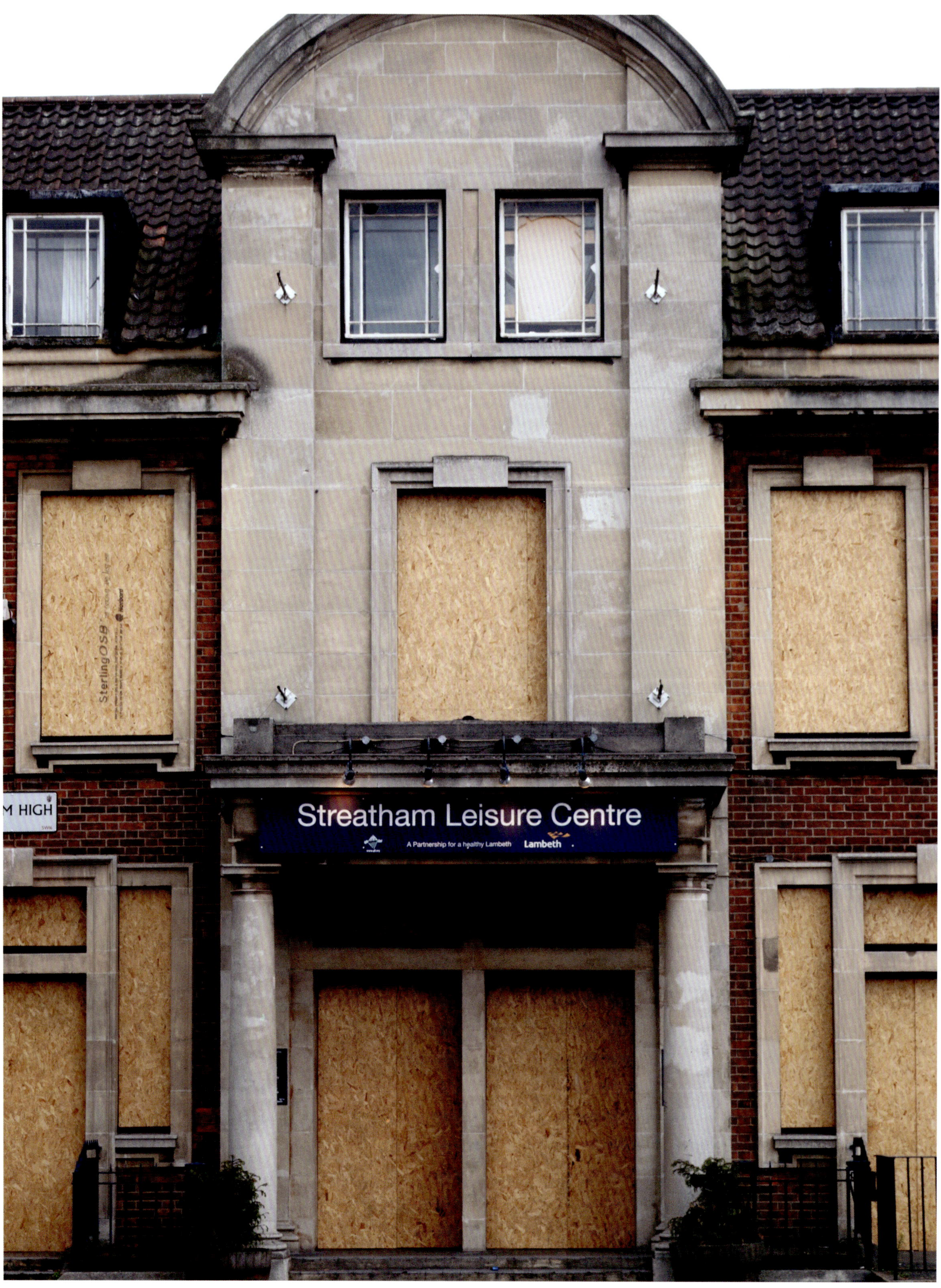
Streatham Leisure Centre
A Partnership for a healthy Lambeth
Lambeth
M HIGH

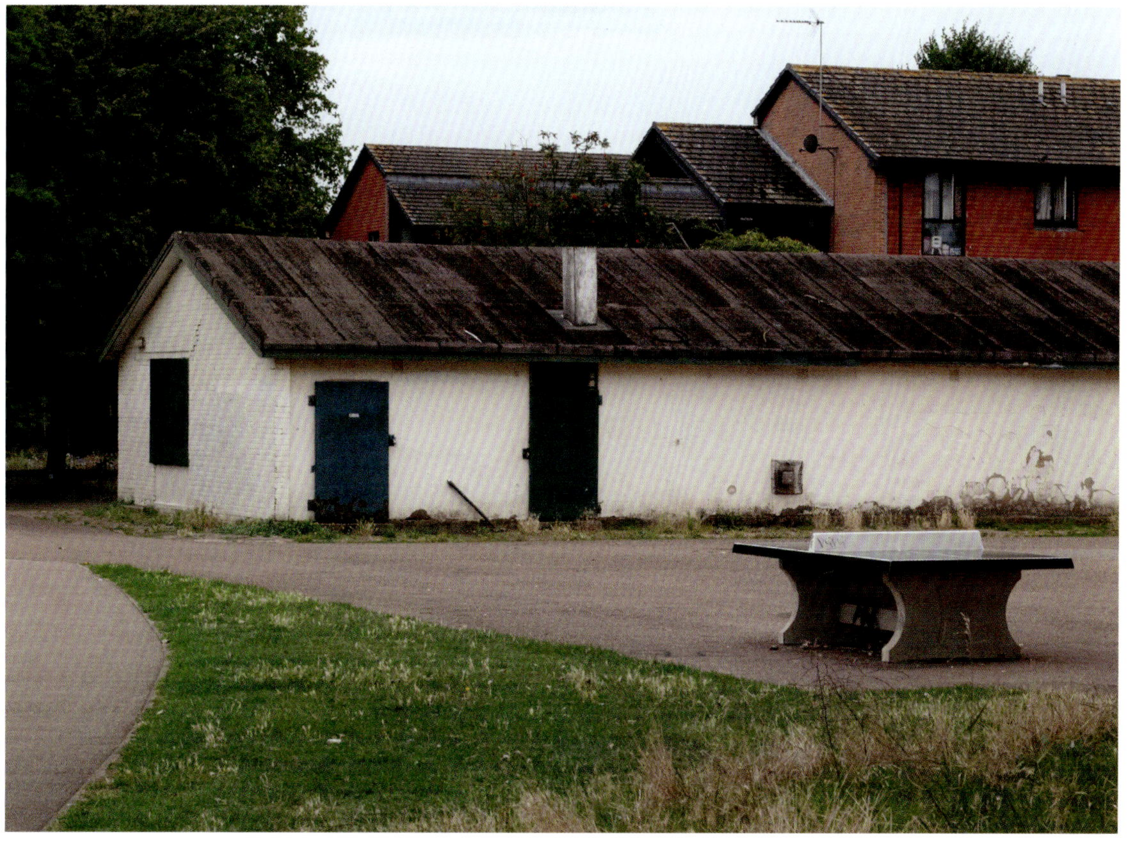

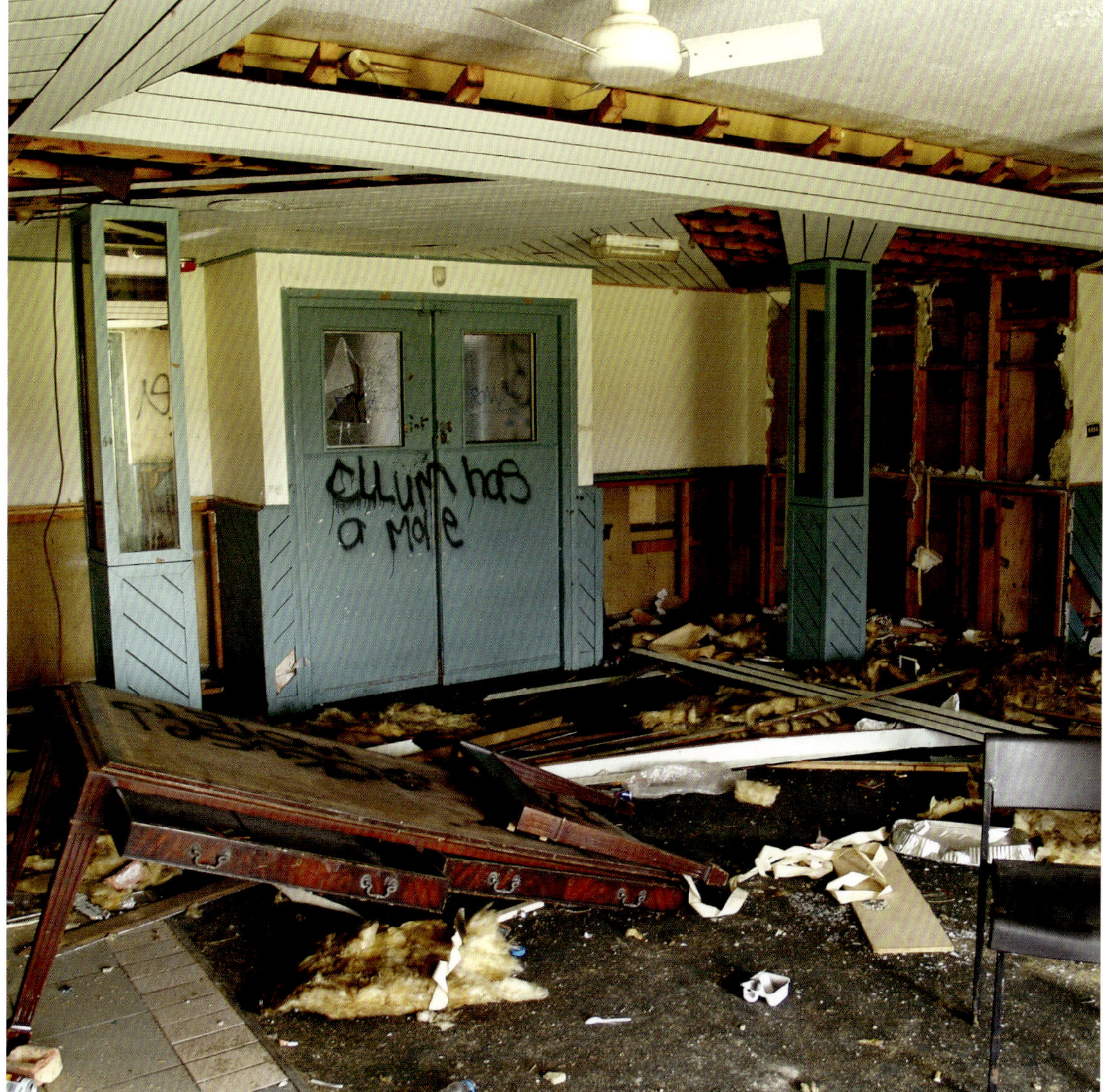

OPPOSITE:

Streatham Leisure Centre

With the structure crumbling and concerns over safety, Streatham baths closed in 2009. It's a stark difference from when the baths opened in 1927, celebrated as an example of the most advanced in swimming pool design. The building was demolished in 2012 and the site is now occupied by a Tesco Extra.

LEFT:

Southfield Park Pavilion, Southfields Recreational Ground, East Acton

In 1908 Ealing Council bought four fields from the Wilkinson Sword Company, which once operated a factory near this site. During World War II they produced over two million bayonets and a nearby street, Wilkinson Way, recalls their presence.

BELOW:

White Lodge Ground, Osterley

Here is the derelict remains of the former clubhouse of Harrow Hill Rovers, a short-lived local football club founded in 1987 and disbanded in 2007.

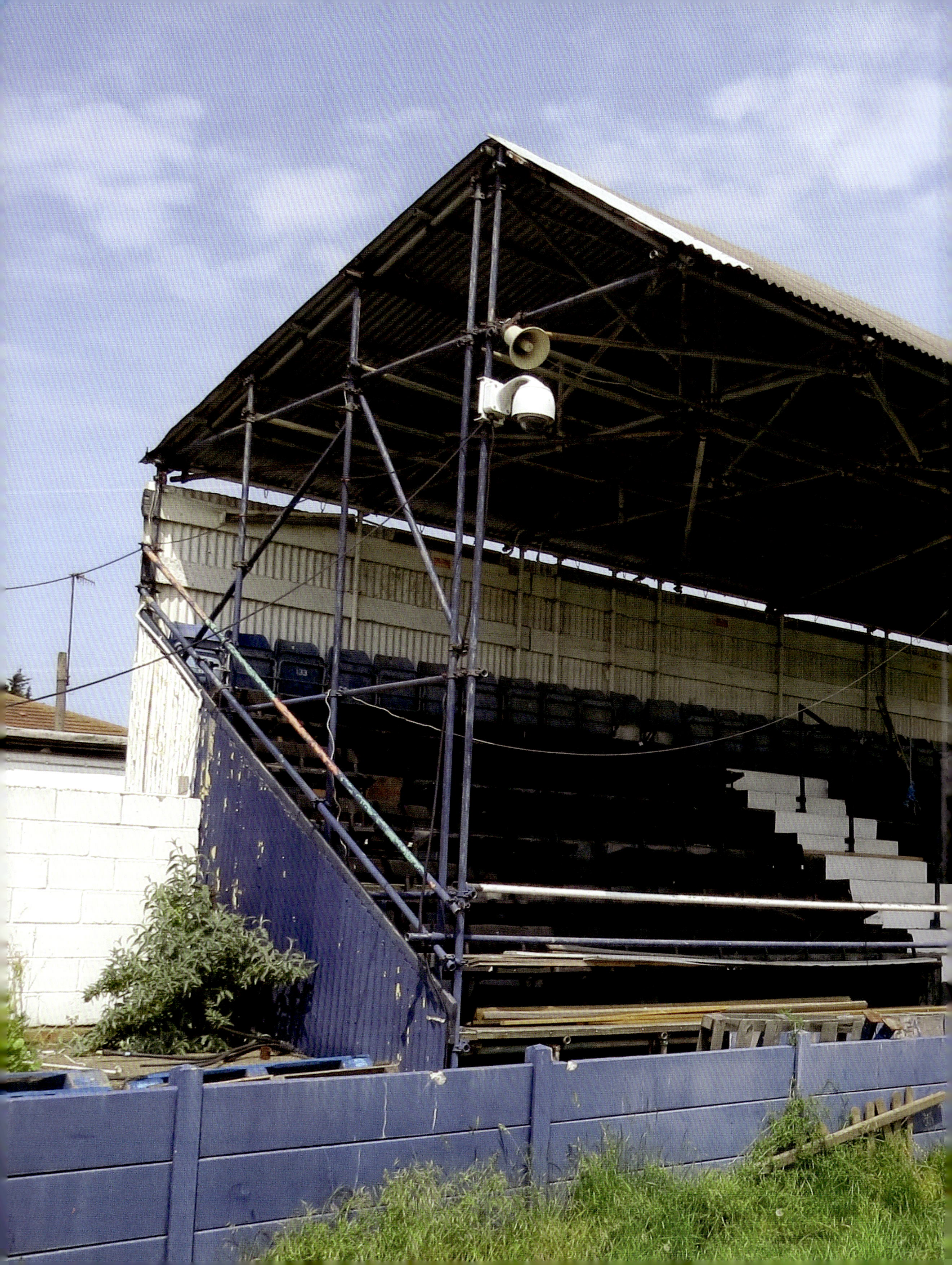

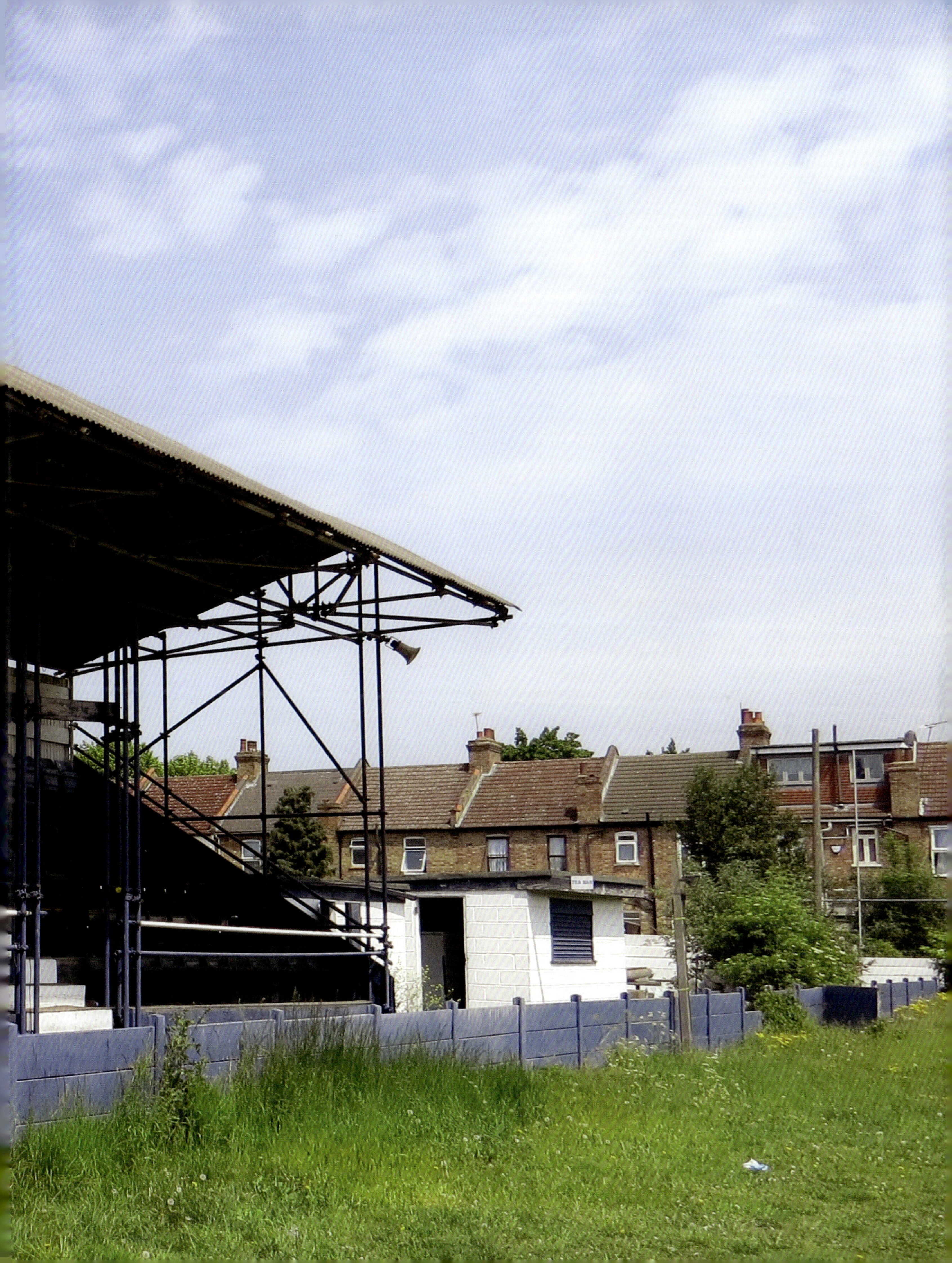

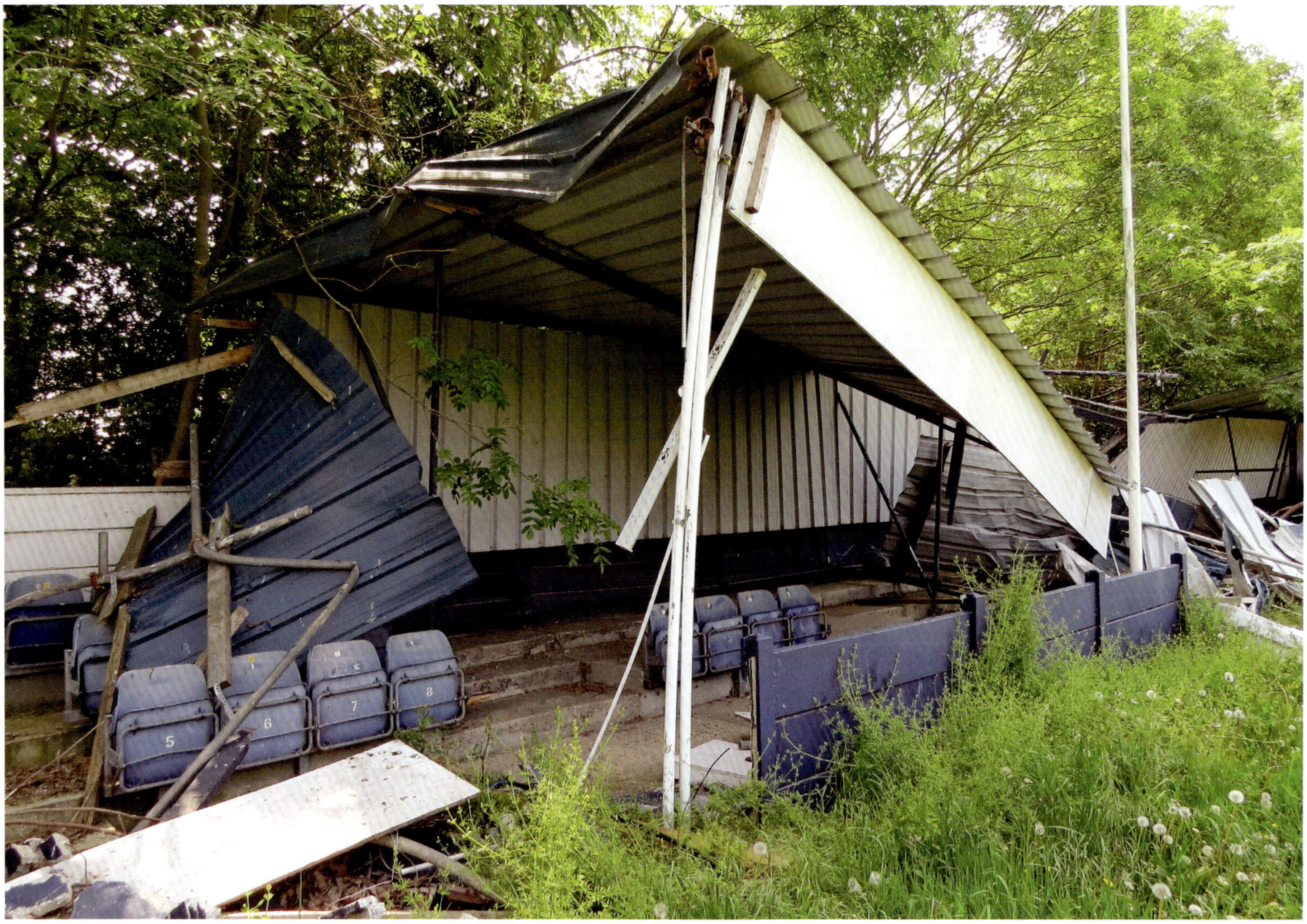

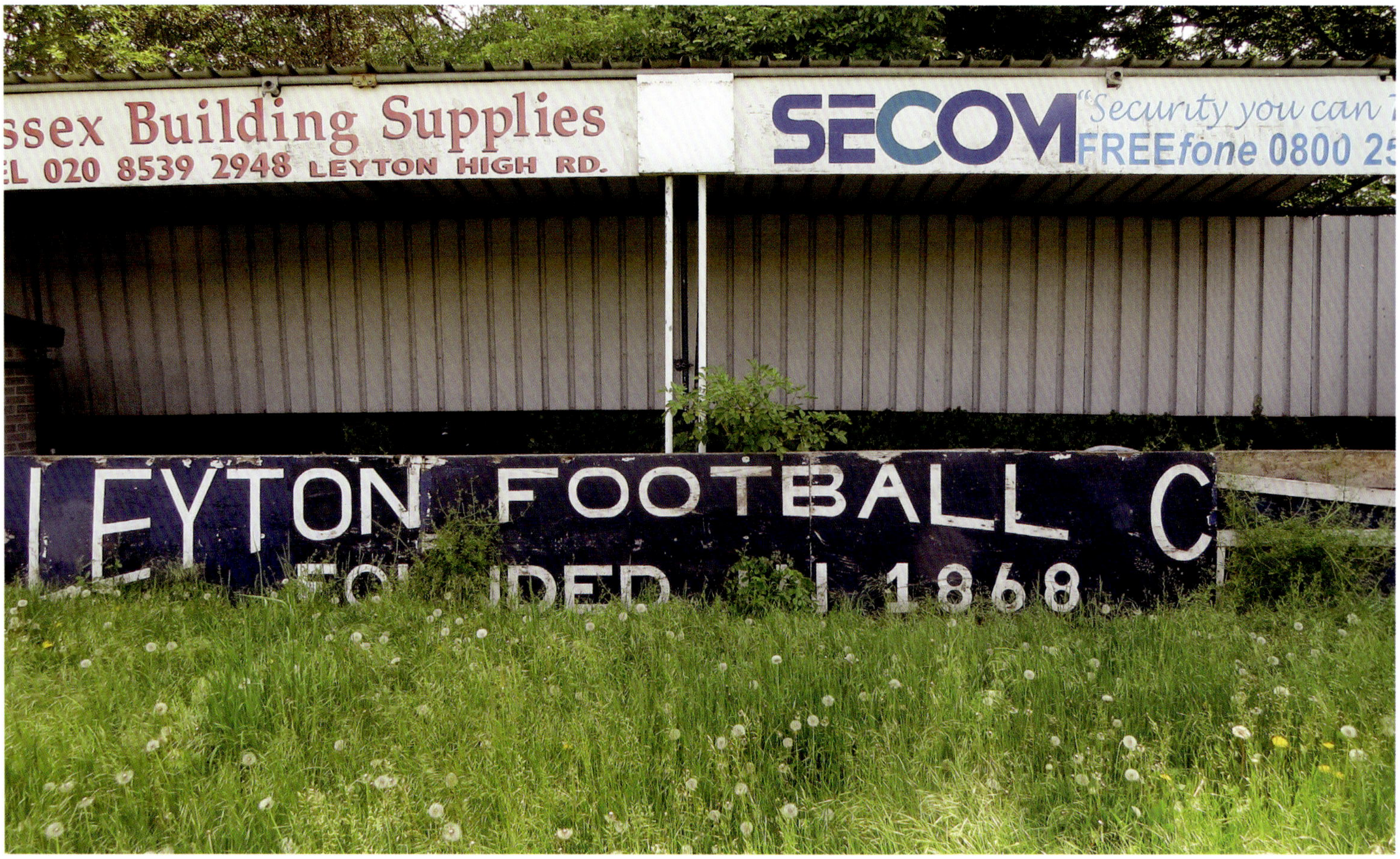

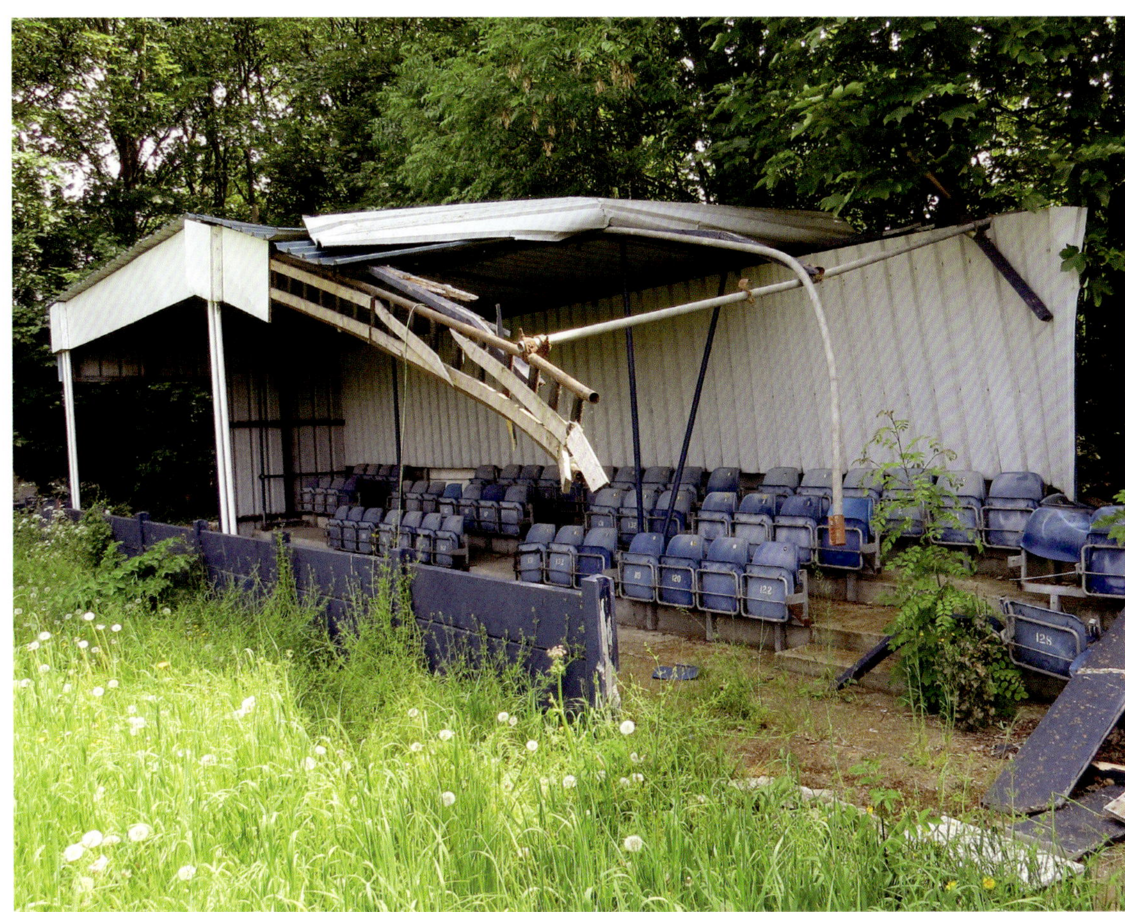

PREVIOUS PAGES AND ALL PHOTOGRAPHS ON THESE PAGES:

Leyton Stadium (Hare and Hounds Ground)

Although the current Leyton Football Club only started playing in 1997, a high court action in 2002 allowed the club to continue using the original club identity, which was founded in 1868. It makes it the second-oldest existing club in London. The stadium could hold up to 4,000 spectators.

In 2011 the indebted club was forced to abandon the league and its stadium – named after the local Hare and Hounds pub – was left derelict. In 2016 the Leyton FC Ground was declared an 'Asset of Community Value' by Waltham Forest Council, which meant it was protected against development.

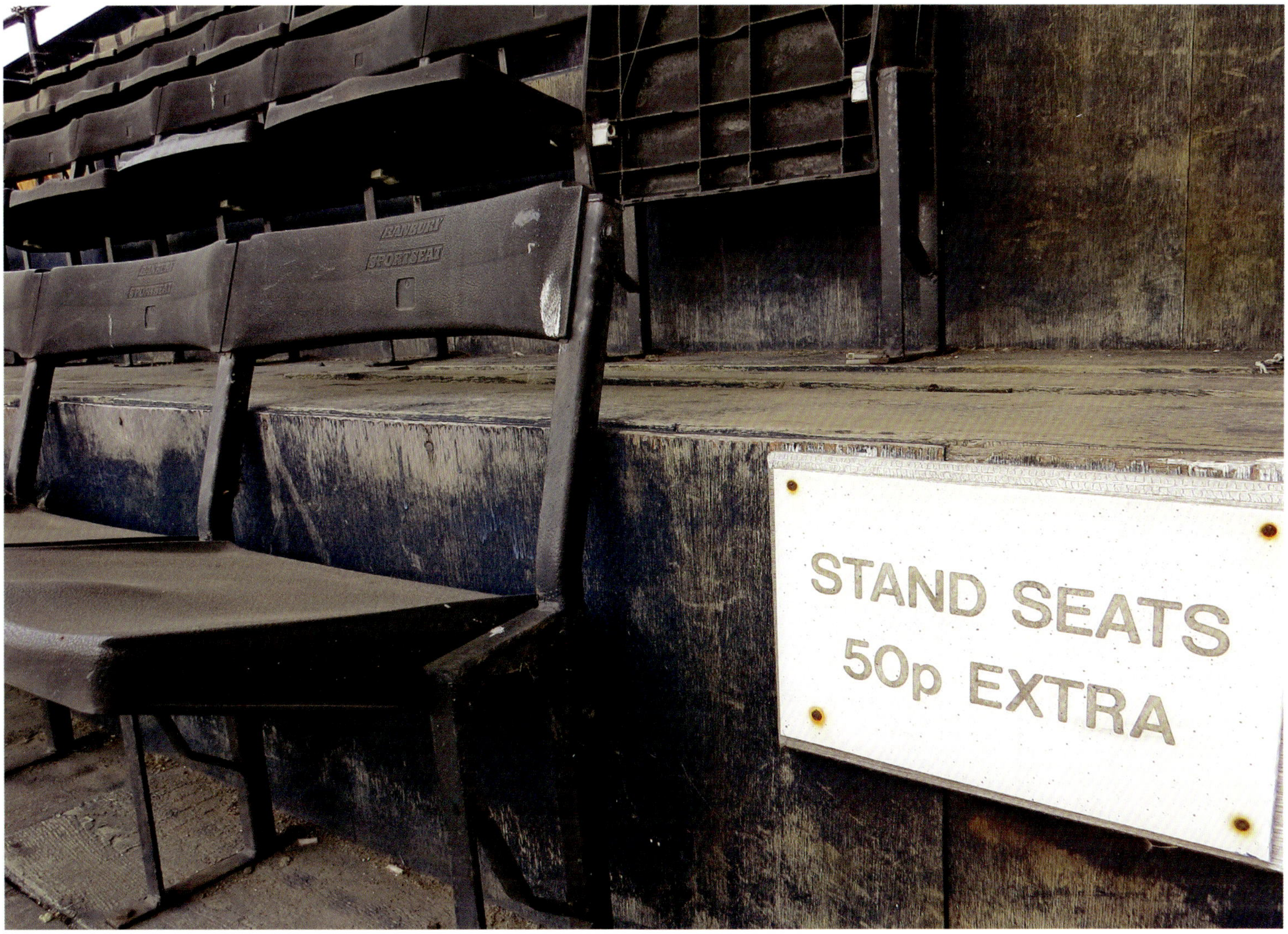

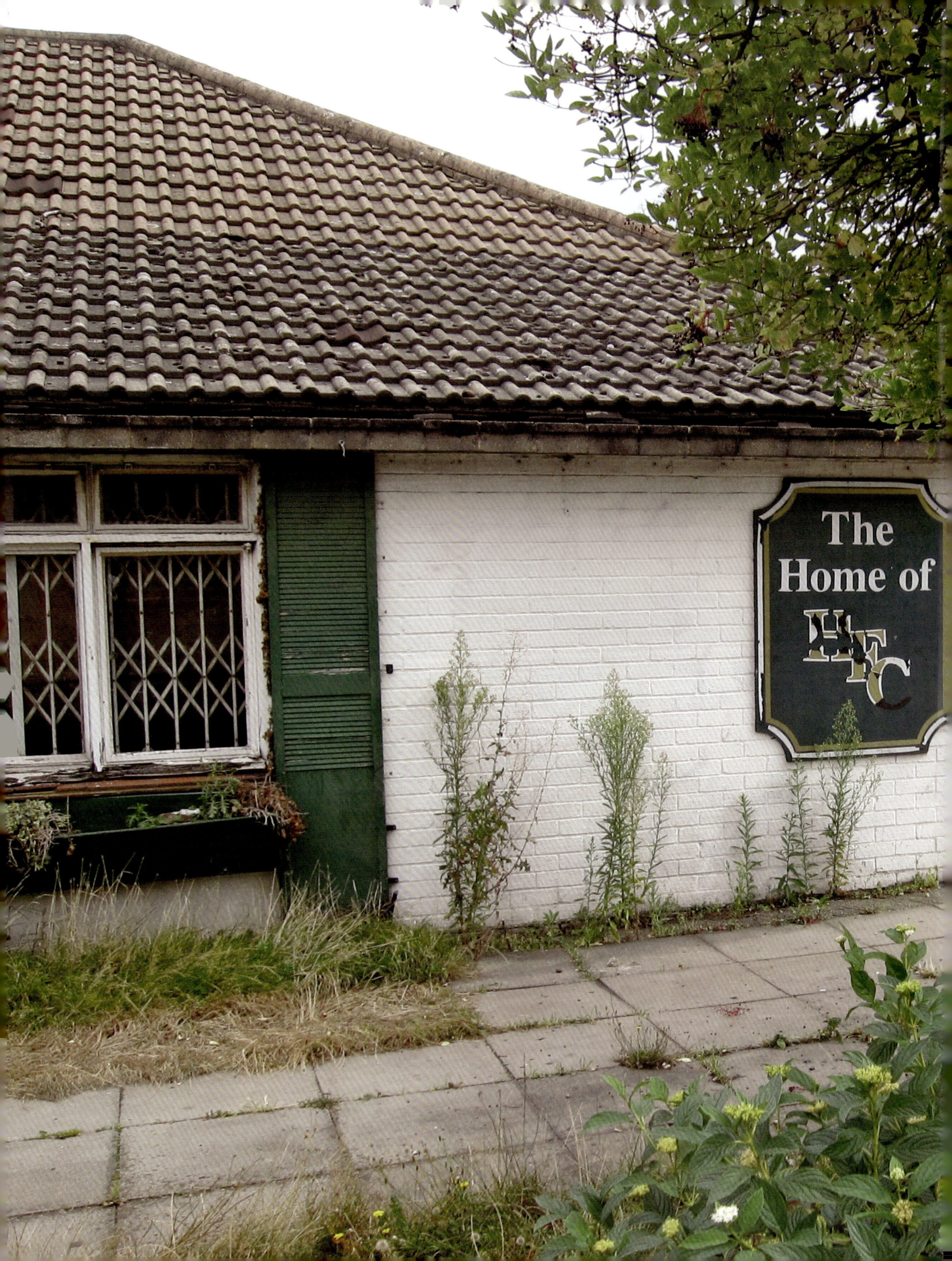
The
Home of
HFC

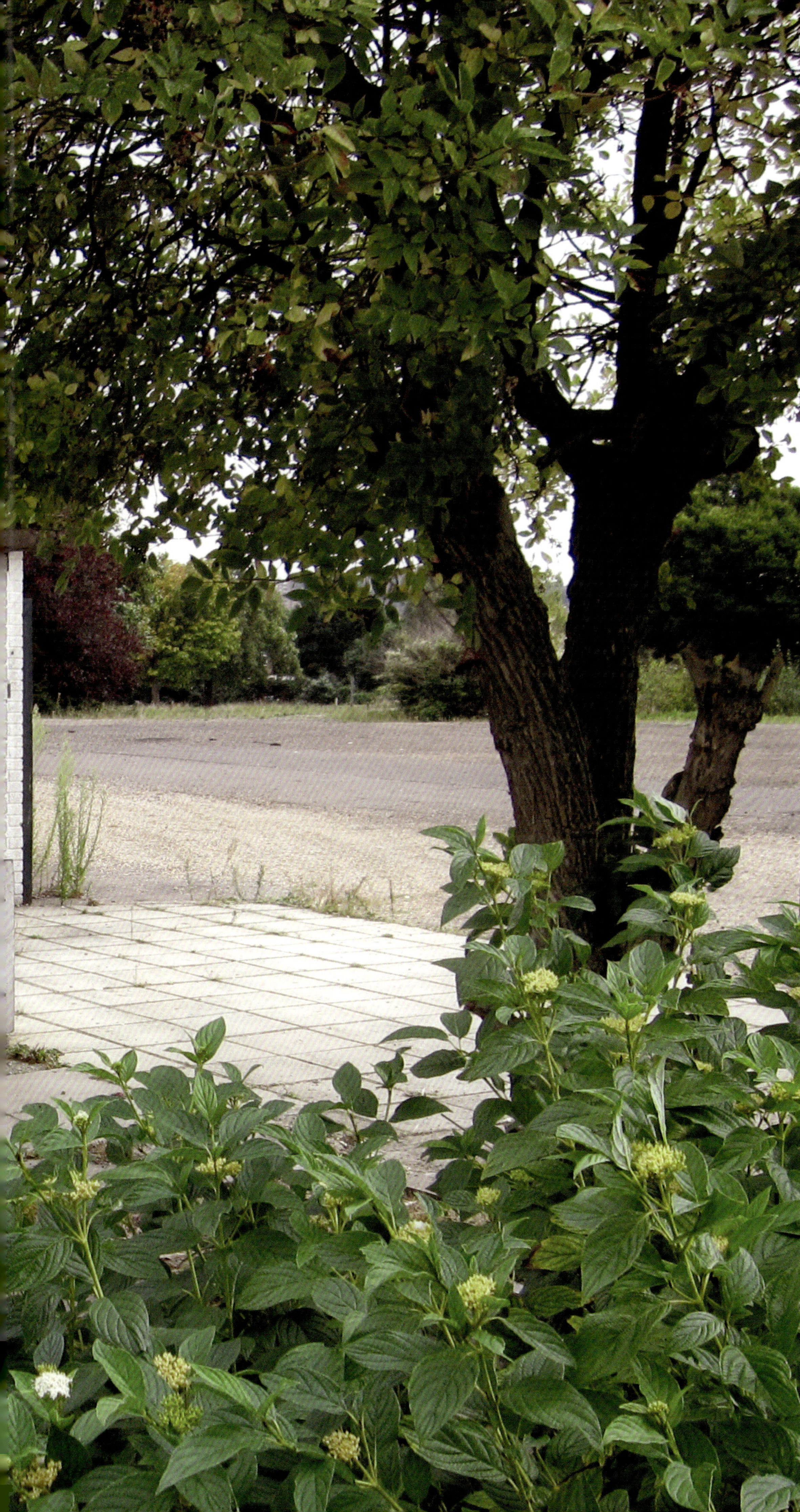

LEFT AND OVERLEAF:

Loot Stadium, Hendon

Hendon Football Club began life as Christchurch Hampstead in 1908. The club moved to Claremont Road, known as Loot Stadium, in 1926, with a capacity of just under 2,000. The site was sold to a developer in 2006, and the club was forced to vacate two years later. In 2014 Barnet Council submitted plans to redevelop the site for housing, but thus far the application has been challenged and failed to materialise.

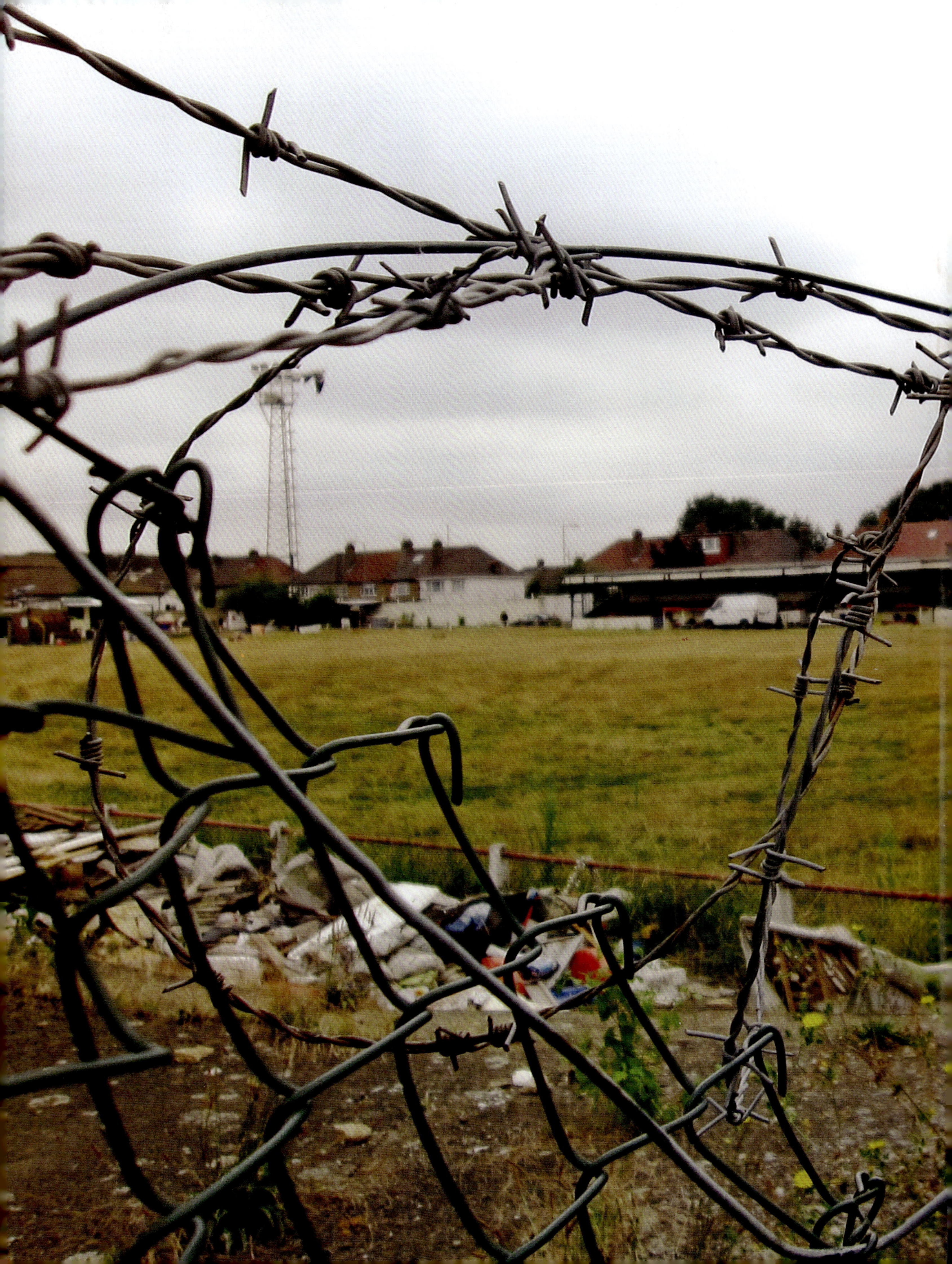

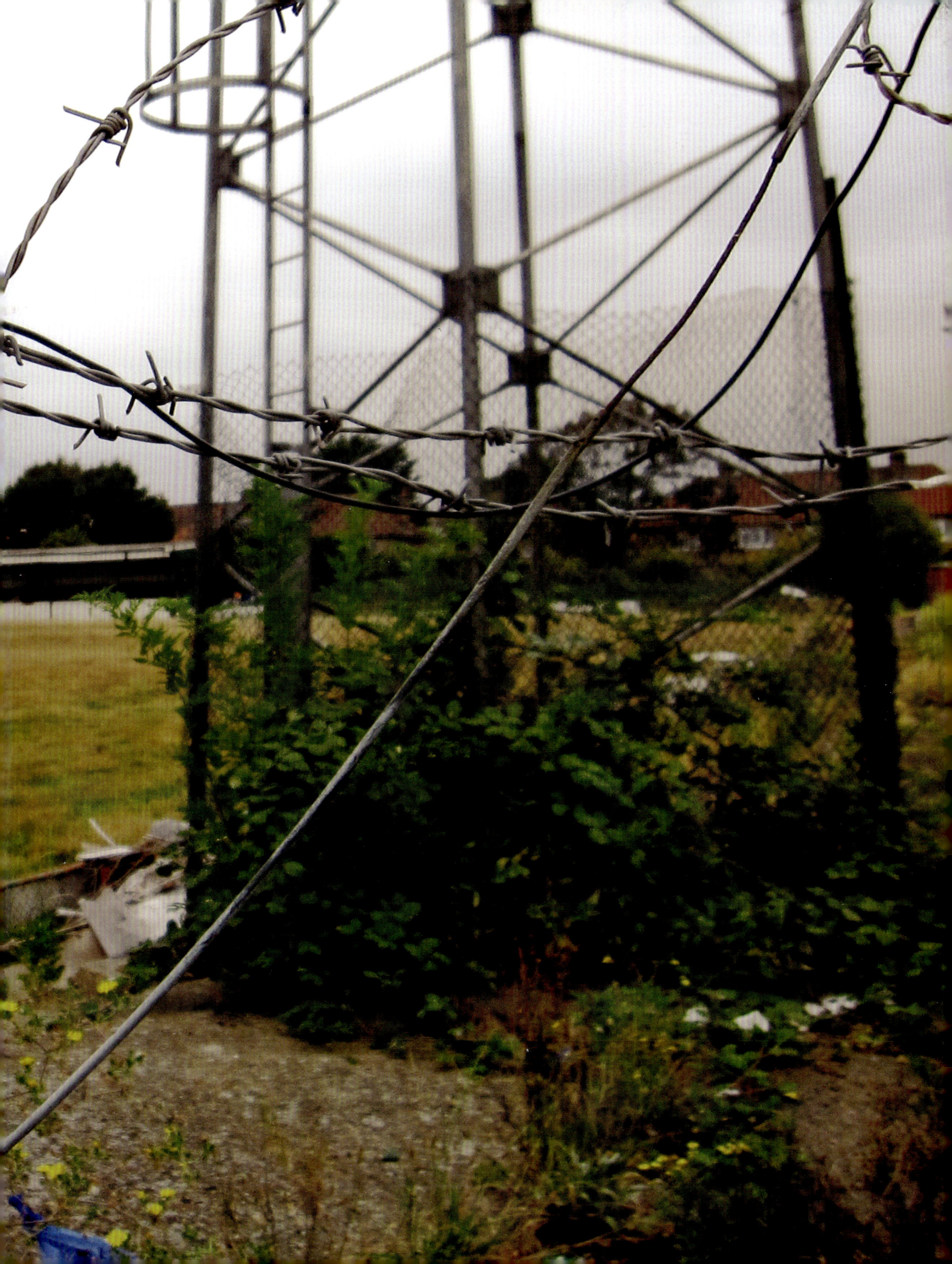

Picture Credits

Alamy: 6 (Benjamin John), 7 (Kathy deWitt), 10 bottom (Martin Beddall), 12/13 (Simon Webster), 16 bottom (Brian Harris), 18/19 (Joe Dunckley), 20 (D J Rogers), 21 top (Nigel Stollery), 26 (Charlotte Steeples Photography), 30/31 (Richard Arthur), 32 top (Tim Cordell), 32 bottom (Marion Bull), 33 (CAR PubImage), 35 bottom (Richard Harvey), 36 top (Joe Dunckley), 37 top (Stockimo/Imars), 37 bottom (A C Manley), 38 bottom (HIP/Damian Grady), 40 (Louis Berk), 41 (Joe Dunckley), 42/43 (Alex McNaughton), 48 (Dan Highton), 50/51 (HIP/Derek Kendall), 53 bottom (Joe Dunckley), 54/55 (Steve Speller), 56–57 all (Nick Harrison), 58 top (Media Drum World), 58 bottom & 59 (Nick Harrison), 61 (Monica Wells), 62/63 & 64/65 (Media Drum World), 68 bottom (Louis Berk), 69 (Maurice Savage), 74 top (PGP), 74 bottom (Jon Wilson), 75 both (Richard Donovan), 82 top (Douglas Lander), 83 (Jansos), 86/87 (Nathaniel Noir), 88–91 all (Simon Webster), 92 (Simon Balson), 93 top (London Snapper), 93 bottom (Eden Breitz), 94–97 all (Simon Webster), 100 (Mark Dunn), 110/111 (Richard Gray), 114 (Roberto Herrett), 118/119 (Robert Stainforth), 122/123 (Ratislav Kolesar), 124 top (Pat Tuson), 125 (Chris Poole), 126 (Anthony Palmer), 128/129 (Jonathan Katzenellenbogen), 130 (pbvision), 131 both (Alex MacNaughton), 132 (Joe Dunckley), 134 both & 135 top (Arcaid Images/Diane Auckland), 135 bottom (Troika), 136 top (Yon Marsh), 137 (James D Evans), 138/139 (Alex MacNaughton), 141 (Avalon/Construction Photography), 142/143 (Chris Poole), 146 (Beata Moore), 147 top (Benjamin John), 147 bottom (Maurice Savage), 150 (Mim Friday), 151 top (Robert Morris), 151 bottom (Alex MacNaughton), 154/155 (Jonny Cochrane), 157 (Kathy deWitt), 158 (Julian Castle), 159 top (Nathan King), 160 & 161 (Alex MacNaughton), 162 top (Phil Wills), 163 bottom (Stan Kujawa), 164/165 (Brian Harris), 166 (Jansos), 167 (Diana Pappas), 168 (John Edwards), 170/171 (Gareth Dobson), 172/173 (Trevor Mogg), 175 (Panorama), 181 (Tall Dwarf), 183 (Nature Picture Library/Pat Tuson), 184 (Guy Curbishley), 185 (Simon Webster), 186/187 (Justin Kase), 188 (Monica Wells), 189 (Simon Turner), 192/193 (James D Evans – Architectural Photography), 194–195 all (Stuart Emmerson), 197 (Eden Breitz), 198 & 199 (Nick Harrison), 200 both & 201 bottom (Jeffrey Blackler), 201 top (Roberto Herrett), 205 (Chris Batson), 206/207 (Benjamin John), 210 (Amer Ghazzal), 211 (Benjamin John), 215 top (Laurence Mackman)

Alamy/Stephen Burrows: 39, 84/85, 116/117, 140, 152, 159 bottom, 169 both, 174 top, 178/179, 202

Alamy/UrbanImages: 106/107, 112/113, 144/145, 156 bottom, 174 bottom, 196, 214

Dreamstime: 14/15 (Basphoto), 78 (I Wei Huang)

Getty Images: 28/29 (Photofusion/Peter Marshall), 52 both (AFP/Nicolas Asfouri), 70/71 (Barry Lewis), 76/77 (Andy Linden), 80/81 (InPictures/Sam Mellish), 98/99 & 101 both (Dan Kitwood), 120–121 all & 124 bottom (Chris J Ratcliffe), 156 top (Richard Baker), 176 (In Pictures/Mike Kemp), 182 both (In Pictures/Richard Baker), 212/213 (Photofusion/Sam Appleby)

Andy Kay, BCD Urbex: 24/25

Ewan Munro: 204/205 (Creative commons attribution-share alike 2.0 generic licence)

Shutterstock: 11 (Kiev.Victor), 21 bottom (Roberto La Rosa), 22/23 (Joe Dunckley), 60 (Myer Liebman), 72/73 (Jordi Prats), 115, 148/149 (Travers Lewis), 178 bottom (I Wei Huang), 190/191 (Elena Rostunova)

Shutterstock Editorial: 53 top (Time Out/Andy Parsons), 68 top (Photofusion), 136 bottom (Ray Tang)

Paul Talling (derelictlondon.com): 16 top, 17, 34, 35 top, 38 top, 44–47 all, 66/67, 82 bottom, 108/109, 162 bottom, 163 top, 180 top, 204, 215 bottom, 216–223 all

Katie Wignall: 8, 10 top, 27, 36 bottom, 102–105 all, 208/209